The German Polity

The German Polity

Tenth Edition

David P. Conradt and Eric Langenbacher

ROWMAN & LITTLEFIELD PUBLISHERS, INC.
Lanham • Boulder • New York • Toronto • Plymouth, UK

Published by Rowman & Littlefield Publishers, Inc.
A wholly owned subsidiary of The Rowman & Littlefield Publishing Group, Inc.
4501 Forbes Boulevard, Suite 200, Lanham, Maryland 20706
www.rowman.com

10 Thornbury Road, Plymouth PL6 7PP, United Kingdom

British Library Cataloguing in Publication Information Available

Library of Congress Cataloging-in-Publication Data

Conradt, David P.
The German polity / David P. Conradt and Eric Langenbacher.—Tenth edition.
    pages   cm
  Previous edition published by Houghton Mifflin.
  Includes bibliographical references and index.
  ISBN 978-1-4422-1644-0 (cloth : alk. paper)
  ISBN 978-1-4422-1645-7 (pbk. : alk. paper)
  ISBN 978-1-4422-1646-4 (electronic)
  1. Germany—Politics and government—1990–   I. Langenbacher, Eric.   II. Title.
JN3971.A58C66   2013
320.943—dc23

                                                          2012048483

∞ ™ The paper used in this publication meets the minimum requirements of American National Standard for Information Sciences—Permanence of Paper for Printed Library Materials, ANSI/NISO Z39.48-1992.

Printed in the United States of America

Contents

Preface to the Tenth Edition xi

Introduction to the Tenth Edition 1
 The Study of German Politics 2
 The Plan of This Book 3

1 The Historical Setting 5
 The First Reich 5
 The Rise of Prussia 6
 The Empire, 1871–1918 8
 World War I and the Collapse of the Second Reich 9
 The Weimar Republic, 1919–1933 10
 The Nazi Seizure of Power 12
 The Third Reich and World War II 14
 Foreign Occupation and National Division 18
 The Formation of the Federal Republic 20

2 Eastern Germany before and after Reunification 25
 Building Socialism, 1949–1961 26
  The Stasi 26
  The June 1953 Uprising 27
 After the Wall—Stability and Consolidation, 1961–1970 28
 The Honecker Era, 1971–1985 29
 Perestroika and the Crisis of the Regime, 1985–1989 30
 The Collapse of Communism 31
 The Unification Process 33
  The West German Response 33
  The East German Opposition 34
  The Soviet Factor 36
  Legal and Constitutional Dimensions of the Unification
   Process 37

Unification: A Brief Analysis   38
The Aftermath of Unification   39
   The Economy   40
   The Environment   45
   The "Wall in People's Heads"   47

3 The Social and Economic Setting   55
  Area and Population   55
  Urbanization and Industrialization   57
  An Export-Oriented Economy   58
   The Rural Sector   59
  Regionalism   60
  Occupational and Class Structure   61
  The Economy   62
   From Economic Basket Case to Savior of the Euro   65
   The Economy's Hidden Champions: The Mittelstand   66
   Continued Challenges   67
  Income Structure   67
   Capital Resources   69
  Religious Composition   71
  Age and Family Structure   74
   Family Structure   77
  The Educational System   78
   Basic Structure   78
  Mass Media   80
   The Press   81
   Television and Radio   83
  Summary and Conclusion   85

4 Political Culture, Participation, and Civil Liberties   91
  Political Values   92
   National Identity   92
   Legitimacy   96
   Democratic Support in East Germany   99
  Political Interest and Involvement   103
   The General Pattern   103
   Social Capital   104
   New Forms of Political Participation: Citizen Groups and
     Movements   105
  Civil Liberties and Human Rights   106
   Civil Liberties Controversies   108
  The Status and Role of Key Social Groups   114
   Residents with a Migration Background   114
   Women   119
   Women in Eastern Germany   121
   Youth   122

      Refugees and Resettlers   124
      Political Radicals and Extremists   125
    Summary and Conclusion   128

5   The Party System and the Representation of Interests   135
    The Party State   135
    The Party System   138
      The Christian Democrats   138
      The Social Democrats   146
      The Free Democrats   154
      The Greens   158
      The Left Party   162
      Other Parties   164
    The Representation of Interests   166
      Extent of Interest Groups   166
      Major Interest Alignments   168
    Summary and Conclusion   179

6   Elections and Voting Behavior   183
    Electoral Mechanics   184
    The Electoral System   185
    Nomination and Candidate Selection   189
      Criteria for Selection   191
    Electoral Politics and Campaign Styles   191
      Media   192
      Campaign and Party Finance   194
    The Pattern of Federal Elections   195
      Elections after Reunification   197
      The 2005 and 2009 Elections: The End of Two-Party
        Dominance?   199
    Basic Orientations of the Electorate   202
      Ideology   202
      Party Preference   203
    Determinants of Voting Behavior   203
      Sociodemographic Factors   203
      Voter Dynamics   206
    Summary and Conclusion   212

7   Policy-Making Institutions I: Parliament and Executive   217
    Legislative Institutions   218
      The Bundestag: The Main Political Battleground   218
      The Bundesrat: The "Quiet" Second Chamber   228
    Executive Institutions: Chancellor and Cabinet   233
      Chancellor Democracy   233
      The Chancellors of the Federal Republic   241
    The Federal President   253

Summary of the Formal Lawmaking Process   257
   Preparliamentary Stage   257
   Parliamentary Stage   258

8 Policy-Making Institutions II: Administration, Semipublic
Institutions, and Courts   263
  Development of the German Administrative and Judicial System   264
  State Administration   265
   Structure   265
   Personnel   268
   Pressures for Reform   271
  Semipublic Institutions   272
   The Social Security and Health Systems   273
   The Federal Labor Agency   278
   The Bundesbank   279
  The Judiciary and the Court System   282
   The Character of German Law   282
   The Judiciary   284
   Court Structure   285
   Judicial Review and the Federal Constitutional Court   287
  Summary and Conclusion   293

9 Subnational Units: Federalism and Local Government   299
  The Development of German Federalism   299
  State-Level Politics   301
   Unity and Diversity among German States   301
   The Constitutional Structure of the States   306
   State-Level Party Systems   309
   Electoral Politics in the States   310
   Leaders and Policies   312
   Federal-State Integration: Revenue Sharing   314
   Vertical Equalization and Tax Sharing   316
   The Future of Federalism   317
  Federalism Reform   319
  Local Government   320
   Structures and Functions   321
   Challenges to Local Government   323
  Summary and Conclusion   327

10 The Return of German Power: The Federal Republic's Foreign and
European Policy   331
  The German Question   332
  Postwar Transformation   333
   Institutions and Socialization   334
   Reconciliation   335
   Soft Power   335
   Multilateralism   336

The Postunification Period: A New Version of the German
    Question   337
    From the 1991 Gulf War to Kosovo   340
Into the Twenty-First Century   341
The European Union   344
    The Impact of European Integration on Germany   348
The Euro   352
    The Never-Ending Euro Crisis?   355
    The Euro Stops Here   357
Summary and Conclusion   358

11   Conclusion: Germany's Rise and Future Challenges   363
The Past and Future of German Exceptionalism   363
Reforming the Gridlocked Republic?   365
The Future of the Welfare State and the New Poverty   368
Germany after Merkel   371
Looking Back and Looking Forward: The German Experience of
    Political Development and the Future of German Power   373

Bibliography   379

Index   407

About the Authors   421

Preface to the Tenth Edition

The previous edition of *The German Polity* focused on the important concerns typical of a relatively stable political situation—the change in power after the Bundestag election of 2005, slowly evolving sociopolitical and economic problems, and specific public policy challenges such as revising the European Union's treaties or the reform of the federal system. The years since the publication of the ninth edition, by contrast, have witnessed the most momentous changes in German and European politics since the end of the Cold War over twenty years ago. Indeed, from one perspective, the events of the last few years are even more important than the 1989–1990 period. The financial, economic, and Euro crises have produced the most precarious economic situation since the Great Depression (or the aftermath of World War II) and have necessitated almost constant crisis policy responses in the context of extreme uncertainty. Moreover, other long-simmering trends—the ineffectiveness of an overly stretched European Union and the decline of British, French, Russian, and U.S. influence on the continent—have become obvious. Finally, after a decade of malaise, the German economic and social model regained its luster. Accounting for these epochal changes and the reasons behind Germany's newfound strength makes a new edition of this book timely and necessary.

About two hundred years ago, German idealist philosopher Hegel wrote about the "cunning of reason in history" to describe unintended, even ironic outcomes. Rarely has this been as true as with the Euro. Most authors state that agreeing to the common European currency was the price that Germany had to pay to receive French support for unification and neutralize British and Soviet/Russian opposition. Germany would have to give up the solid deutsche mark and be bound forever economically to its European partners. Through giving up this last bastion of sovereignty, a common currency would irrevocably anchor the Federal Republic of Germany to a larger European entity and thus preclude a repetition of the disastrous first half of the twentieth century. Indeed, Helmut Kohl, the chancellor who presided over unification and the negotiations surrounding the establishment of the Euro, repeatedly framed the Euro as a question of war and peace—that without the common currency, Germany and Europe would return to the bad old days of violence and strife before 1945. In short, the

Euro was supposed to truncate German sovereignty and forever contain German power. The common currency was the means whereby Germany would perpetuate its comfortable (to all) postwar persona, remaining a political dwarf or a large Switzerland.

At first, this is exactly how things played out. Germany had a lackluster decade after the effects of the immediate postunification economic boom weakened. Disappointing economic growth, persistently high unemployment, a seemingly permanent depression in eastern Germany, weak public finances, an aging and eventually shrinking population, an inability to construct a functioning multicultural society, and political paralysis contributed to the widespread perception that the country had become a permanently weakened "sick man of Europe." Moreover, the early years of the Euro (after its physical introduction in 2002) produced exactly the wrong monetary policy for the needs of the anemic German economy.[1] Emblematic of this malaise, from 2003 to 2006, the country breached the 3 percent budget deficit threshold and the 60 percent debt limit of the Stability and Growth Pact, which it had advocated in the 1990s as part of the European Monetary Union, and was threatened with punitive fines by the European Commission. Economic and labor market reforms pushed through by the Gerhard Schröder government between 1998 and 2005 (Agenda 2010, Hartz IV) were bitterly opposed by the trade unions and segments of the Social Democratic Party and were widely considered to be insufficient and ineffective.

Under such circumstances, there was little capacity to exert more influence and power. Internationally, German foreign policy was seen as inconsistent—nonintervention in Bosnia, partial cooperation with allies in Kosovo and Afghanistan, staunch opposition to the U.S.-led invasion of Saddam Hussein's Iraq, souring of relations with the United States and enhanced cooperation with an increasingly authoritarian Russia. The situation was perhaps best captured by Condoleezza Rice, secretary of state under President George W. Bush, in 2003 with her policy prescription to "ignore Germany," although this was probably better than the "punishment" that the French reportedly received for opposing the Iraq war.[2]

Beginning with the Grand Coalition government led by Chancellor Angela Merkel (2005–2009), this situation changed. Merkel has rebuilt international relationships, especially with the United States and Israel, and took on a leadership role in furthering European integration, resulting in the Treaty of Lisbon, or the Reform Treaty, that came into force in 2009. Partially as a delayed effect of Schröder's reforms, the economy regained momentum in 2006, especially as exports surged and companies achieved historic profit levels. Public finances improved due to ongoing trimming of public spending and to the 2007 increase in the value-added tax. Long-neglected policy areas such as the integration of people with a migration background, family policy, the status of women, and education were tackled. As the successful hosting of soccer's World Cup in 2006 exemplified, the country's mood and reputation became quite positive.

This altered environment has had two noteworthy effects. On the one hand, there has been a marked increase in goodwill and respect toward Germany. Continuing a multiyear trend, with a score of 62 percent in 2011, Germany was once again the most positively assessed country in a BBC poll of twenty-seven states.[3]

Instead of the myriad weaknesses and flaws emphasized previously, numerous accomplishments have been highlighted—export champion of high value-added products, defender of an equitable social market economy, purveyor of fiscal prudence, environmental policy pioneer, cultural leader, exemplary political institutions, a model of contrition and coming to terms with the past, and civilian power with normative influence internationally. Indeed, an older notion, Modell Deutschland, is back in vogue, and there are numerous examples of countries emulating German practices, policies, and institutional structures.

Thus Germany was ideally positioned to make a quick recovery from the 2008–2009 worldwide economic crisis and to assume a leadership role when the current Euro crisis began in late 2009. It is currently without question the most powerful actor in Europe. The European Union has proven to be ineffectual during the Euro crisis. Germany rarely defers anymore to France and does not allow Paris to take the spotlight. The other major European countries do not have the resources or, in the case of the United Kingdom, the will to aspire to a major leadership role. The United States with its own troubled economy has been on the sidelines cheering for the Europeans and their central bank to mirror the policies of the American Fed.

Thus, contrary to the intentions of its creators, the Euro has enabled Germany to regain the leading position that it had on the European continent prior to World War II. This is not to say that Germans intended or planned for this to happen. Nor are those on whom power is being exercised ecstatic, as demonstrated by protesters in Greece with their placards depicting Merkel as Hitler and by pundits in the UK with their invocations of a new Fourth Reich.[4] In fact, Germany has been behaving like a "reluctant hegemon," as William Paterson has aptly put it.[5] But, even these inhibitions are rapidly falling away. Simply put, the Euro—in a classic, "cunning" case of unintended consequences—has facilitated the restoration and caused the augmentation of German power. The rise (or better, return) of German power is one of the most important global developments of the last decade. And this fact makes the study of Germany and German politics more important than ever.

What this means for the present and future will take some time and effort to work out. But, for the purposes of this edition of *The German Polity*, it means that interest in Germany has increased dramatically, and so too has the need for a thorough and deep analytical understanding of the German political system. This is what we hope to provide in this book.

There are many individuals and organizations that have been instrumental in the writing of this book. The Department of Government and BMW Center for German and European Studies at Georgetown University in Washington, D.C., provided much-needed research support. Special thanks go to Jeffrey Anderson, BMW Center director and editor of *German Politics and Society* and to research assistants Mouchka Darmon, Svitlana Orekhova, and especially Michael Grasso. In Germany, we are indebted to the Wissenschaftszentrum Berlin für Sozialforschung and Brent Goff. From his perch in Bonn, Gerd Langguth has been a source of countless insights into German politics in general and the CDU/CSU in particular. We must also acknowledge the valuable assistance provided by the outside reviewers who meticulously read through the ninth edition of this book and provided useful feedback.

In writing this book, which attempts to synthesize a large body of scholarly research and journalistic reporting on the Federal Republic, we enjoyed an embarrassment of riches. The scope and breadth of information and analysis of modern German politics is equal to or surpasses that of any country in the world. Much of the data, of course, is generated by the Germans themselves. Simply put, they count just about everything.

We recognize that the reader is exposed to a large array of statistical material in this text. This is simply because the Germans produce so much of it.

NOTES

1. "Germany's Euro Test," *Economist*, June 12, 2003.
2. http://www.nytimes.com/2004/11/17/politics/17rice.html.
3. http://www.worldpublicopinion.org/pipa/articles/views_on_countriesregions_bt/680.php?lb = brglm&pnt = 680&nid = &id = .
4. http://www.dailymail.co.uk/news/article-2026840/European-debt-summit-Germany-using-financial-crisis-conquer-Europe.html.
5. William E. Paterson, "The Reluctant Hegemon? Germany Moves Centre Stage in the European Union," in *Annual Review of the European Union in 2010*, special issue of *Journal of Common Market Studies* 49, suppl. no. 1 (September 2011): 57–75.

Introduction to the Tenth Edition

This book is intended as an introduction to the contemporary German political system that will enable students of comparative and European politics to acquire detailed knowledge of this case and to compare it meaningfully with others.

For many years, the key question structuring the study of the German polity was how democratic and stable it was. Sometimes the question was framed in terms of how much Germany had learned from its past and to what extent that past had been overcome—that is, how different Germany was from its terrible incarnation of the early twentieth century. Such concerns even characterized analyses of unification and its aftermath. Nevertheless, the united Germany of the second decade of the twenty-first century is almost seventy years beyond the caesura of 1945 and over twenty years beyond unification. Virtually all of the individuals who personally experienced the Nazi period and were socialized by that regime have left the historical stage. Even the heroic student rebel generation—so influential since the 1960s—is rapidly retiring. Today, almost 20 percent of the population has some sort of "migration background," creating a much more multicultural society. Moreover, unlike the bad old days, Germany is embedded in a deep web of alliances and transnational institutions and is surrounded by friends. Despite the images of jackbooted Nazis that so many students in the English-speaking world still associate with the country, Germany has been utterly transformed. The previously dominant concerns about the stability of the political system and the internalization of liberal democratic values no longer have much analytical value.

This is not to say that the German past is irrelevant. There are few, if any, countries where the impact of the past and memories based on those historical events have been so influential. As Josef Joffe has pointed out, the intensive and extensive examination of Germany's tragic past and, of course, above all the responsibility of Germans for the Holocaust, has been and continues to be a vital part of the Federal Republic's identity and a major reason for Germany's half century of peaceful and positive relationships with its neighbors in Europe and the larger world community.[1] The capacity of postwar Germans to undertake this painful confrontation with their past is an important factor in the Republic's international status. And, as we show in many of the chapters of this book, this confrontation with the past has had a massive impact on numerous public policy decisions—especially in foreign and European policy—and has helped to catalyze and sustain the general public's transformation of values.

Recent years, however, have witnessed a shift in the impact of the past. Instead of being an ever-present concern, historical consciousness and collective memories have declined in salience. They are still an important part of socialization and education, but they are now more in the background, conditioning more fundamental values, rather than affecting present-day policy concerns.[2]

THE STUDY OF GERMAN POLITICS

To the student of comparative politics, understanding the contemporary German polity is important for several reasons. First, Germany offers an excellent example of the complexities, difficulties, and tragedies of political development. In contrast to the experiences of the United States or the United Kingdom, political stability—much less democratic political stability—was a rarity in the German political experience before 1949. Throughout its history, Germany frequently faced the same basic problem confronting many less-developed countries today: establishing a political order that achieves a balance of conflict and consensus, liberty and order, individualism and community, and unity and diversity. Economic development and increasing wealth were supposed to provide stability and facilitate the emergence and perfection of liberal democracy—not the worst totalitarian regime in human history. Understanding this terrible outcome led to new research on the role of culture, national identity, civil society, and institutional design. Moreover, various responses to the tragedy of Nazism—above all, the process of European integration—have generated a burgeoning literature on supranational and regional integration. The study of modern Germany has been exceptionally important for concept and theory building in the comparative politics subfield, and in political science more generally.

Second, German politics offers the student a laboratory in which to study political change. Since 1871, not only specific governments but also the entire regime or form of government have been subject to frequent and abrupt change. The empire proclaimed in 1871 collapsed with Germany's defeat in World War I and was followed by the formation of a democratic republic in 1919. This first attempt at political democracy lasted only fourteen years and was replaced in 1933 by the Nazi dictatorship. The Nazis' Thousand-Year Reich lasted twelve years, with catastrophic consequences for Germany and the world. The destruction of the Nazi regime in 1945 brought a system of military occupation to Germany, which was followed in 1949 by the creation of two German states: a democratic (if semisovereign) Federal Republic of Germany, composed of the western American, British, and French zones of occupation, and a communist state, the German Democratic Republic (GDR) in the eastern Soviet zone. In 1989, the communist regime in the GDR collapsed. In East Germany's first free election in 1990, voters left little doubt that they wanted unification with West Germany as soon as possible, and on October 3, 1990, East Germany ceased to exist as an independent state and joined the Federal Republic. Europe once again has a single German state. Thus, in less than a century, Germany has had two republics, one empire, one fascist dictatorship, one period of foreign military occupation, and one communist dictatorship. Few countries present the student with a better opportunity to examine the causes and consequences of such a diverse array of governmental and regime types.

Third, German politics illustrates the effects of the international political system on domestic politics. As discussed in chapters 1 and 2, the current political organization of the German people is a by-product of the Cold War standoff between East and West and the end of that struggle in the early 1990s—just as the Westphalian system of competitive nation-states had such an impact in previous centuries. The basic decisions from 1945 to 1949 that established the two German states and ceded large portions of the prewar *Reich* (literally, "empire") to Poland and the Soviet Union were not made by German political leaders. Similarly, the breaching of the Berlin Wall in 1989, the end of the East German state, and formal unification in 1990 were in part the consequences of Soviet president Mikhail Gorbachev's reform policies and upheaval especially in Poland and Hungary. Finally, governments have willingly ceded sovereignty to the supranational institutions of the European Union. The postwar politics of Germany, more than of any other Western European country, have been affected by decisions made in Washington, Moscow, London, Brussels, and elsewhere.

Fourth, the study of German politics gives the student an opportunity to examine one of the most important capitalist economies in the world today, and particularly the relationship between the policies of government and this economic system. The postwar "social market economy" has been lauded for effectively combining capitalist freedom with social protections. Indeed, for most of the past half century, Germany has dealt with the problems of inflation, unemployment, and economic growth more successfully than most of her neighbors and economic competitors. Economic performance has been cited as a prime factor in the postwar growth of popular support for the values and institutions of liberal democracy. After a decade of malaise ending around 2005, the country regained exemplary performance. But, have the problems of the recent past truly been overcome? Are the much-lauded social market economy and fiscal prudence sustainable in the future?

Finally, Germany is an important country in the international political system. It is the strongest member of the twenty-seven-nation European Union (EU), accounting for over 30 percent of its total economic output. Recent years have witnessed an unprecedented increase of German power in the EU and especially in the seventeen countries (as of January 1, 2012) that use the Euro. Germany is playing a key role in the development of postcommunist societies in Eastern Europe and the former Soviet Union. Globally, it has been involved in various peacekeeping missions (primarily Afghanistan where is has had approximately 5,000 troops since 2001) and is one of the most important providers of development aid. Indeed, knowledge and understanding of German politics offer the student insights into a key actor in the future of Europe and the global system.

THE PLAN OF THIS BOOK

Knowledge of the major historical developments preceding the establishment of the Federal Republic is essential background for the later chapters. This information is provided in chapter 1. Chapter 2 examines the communist regime in East

Germany from 1949 to 1989, the unification process that culminated in October 1990 with the accession of the former East German territories into the Federal Republic, and the difficult challenges of integrating the two regions. The social and economic structure of the Federal Republic is surveyed in chapter 3. Emphasis in this chapter is placed on postwar changes and their impact on political attitudes and behavior. German political culture and participation, as well as the role and status of minority groups and women, are discussed in chapter 4. The postwar party system; the key role of the three established parties (Social Democrats, Christian Democrats, and Free Democrats); and the emergence of the Greens and Left Party, along with the activity of the major interest groups, are the topics of chapter 5. Postwar elections and electoral politics are analyzed in chapter 6. The major national policy-making institutions—parliament, the executive, the bureaucracy, the courts, and an array of semipublic institutions—are the subjects of chapters 7 and 8. Germany's subnational governmental units—the states and local communities—are examined in chapter 9. Chapter 10 looks at Germany's foreign and European policy with emphasis placed on the rehabilitation of the country in the postwar decades and the return of German power in recent years. The work concludes with an examination of several ongoing challenges confronting the Federal Republic.

Throughout these chapters, we attempt to develop three major themes. First, since 1949, the Federal Republic has achieved a degree of legitimacy and consensus unmatched by any other German regime in the modern era; Germany and the Germans have changed. In fact, the high-functioning German political system (Modell Deutschland) in many respects has even influenced institutional reform in many other countries. Second, since unification, this system has had to deal with a variety of policy problems that could not be addressed earlier because of the country's division and the importance of first achieving a consensus on political democracy. Moreover, a decade-long economic malaise after the mid-1990s necessitated a variety of policy and institutional changes. How effective, comprehensive, and sustainable have these efforts been? Third, the Merkel governments have been forced to respond to a constant series of crises, which have had the unexpected consequence of greatly expanding German power in Europe and beyond. How has this newfound power been exercised and with what effects? What will the future look like?

The postwar development of the Federal Republic, examined in this book, has for the most part been a remarkable success story, and recent years have seen a marked increase in German power. But whether this past success and current power is a help or hindrance in dealing with the challenges of the future remains an open question.

NOTES

1. Josef Joffe, "Erinnerung als Staatsräson," *Süddeutsche Zeitung*, December 12, 1998 (Internet edition).
2. See "Wann vergeht Vergangenheit," *Die Zeit*, August 30, 2012, 36.

The Historical Setting

Established in 1949, the Federal Republic of Germany is one of Europe's younger political systems. Yet the people within its borders belong to one of Europe's oldest linguistic, ethnic, and cultural units—the German nation. This nation dates back at least to AD 843, when Charlemagne's empire was partitioned following his death into the West Frankish (much of modern France); Central Frankish (the modern Netherlands, Belgium, Alsace, and Lorraine); and East Frankish (modern Germany) empires. The East Frankish empire under Otto the Great (936–973) was later proclaimed the Holy Roman Empire. But neither this first empire, or *Reich*, nor any of its successors has ever united all of Europe's German-speaking peoples into a single state with a strong central government.

THE FIRST REICH

The medieval Reich was, in fact, a loose-knit collection of many different regions, each with distinct dialects and varying degrees of economic and military strength. Some principalities like Schaumburg-Lippe were miniscule, but others like Bavaria, Saxony, and Württemberg were medium-size powers in the medieval and early modern eras. Although this empire held together formally and was not finally abolished until the time of Napoleon, it had in fact ceased to exist as a viable political entity by the end of the seventeenth century and the rise of the western nation-states. The first German Reich then became little more than a fragmented collection of hundreds of principalities, Church-owned lands, and free cities.[1] While the process of building a unified nation-state continued in the United Kingdom and France, the German peoples of central Europe were deeply divided. This decentralization of political authority, characteristic of feudalism, meant that many separate political institutions and processes took root within the German nation.

Through Luther's translation of the Bible into High German, the Reformation of the sixteenth century brought a uniform style of written German, but it did little else to facilitate unity and integration. Indeed, it divided central Europe still further into Protestant and Catholic territories. The Thirty Years War (1618–1648) that followed the Reformation was fought largely on German soil, with

5

the different German states allied with various foreign powers and fighting one another. The war severely weakened the states, both individually and collectively, and reduced the Germanies' population by approximately one-third. Some areas needed a century to recover, and the war permanently shifted power away from previously prosperous places like Nuremberg and Augsburg in the south and Lübeck and Danzig in the north. On the eve of Europe's transformation from an agrarian-feudal to a capitalist-urban society, much of Germany—unlike the UK or France—remained backward and divided, lacking many of the elements needed for a smooth transition to modernity:

1. a strong central state with established administrative, legislative, and legal institutions;
2. a middle class growing in political importance; and
3. an emerging national culture.

THE RISE OF PRUSSIA

The second major effort at unifying Germany began in a distant eastern territory: the province of Brandenburg.[2] Ruled by the Protestant Hohenzollern dynasty, the Kingdom of Prussia, as it was known after 1701, undertook territorial expansion at the expense of its Polish, Austrian, and Saxon neighbors, while other German states served as the helpless pawns of the far stronger nation-states of France, Sweden, and England. Although it was a relatively poor and backward area, Prussia did have a series of skillful monarchs, from Frederick Wilhelm, the Great Elector (1640–1688), through Frederick William I (the Soldier King) and Frederick II, the Great (1740–1786), who through wars, diplomatic coups, and a strong and efficient administration transformed Prussia into one of Europe's Great Powers. Lacking wealth or natural resources, the Hohenzollerns demanded discipline, hard work, and sacrifice from their subjects. Prussia was the first German state with a bureaucracy and an army comparable to those of the major powers of Western Europe. Indeed, from the mid-eighteenth century onward, Prussia was part of most major wars and was already clashing with Habsburg-ruled Austria over supremacy in Germany and Central Europe, especially during the Seven Year's War (1756–1763).

This style of statist, even authoritarian politics worked, but there was little room in the Prussian system for the values of political liberalism, which together with nationalism had begun to sweep Western Europe in the wake of the French Revolution. Moreover, the Prussian approach to politics was also disliked and feared by many smaller German states and free cities, which admired Prussian successes but were less enthusiastic about the emphasis on militaristic discipline and territorial expansion through military conquest.

The misgivings of the various German states regarding Prussia soon gave way, however, to a far greater concern with revolutionary France under Napoleon. Beginning in 1806, Napoleon invaded and dissolved most of the small German principalities and the Holy Roman Empire itself, consolidating them into larger units and, in effect, preparing the way for a major modern effort at unification.

By invading Germany, the French also introduced the ideologies of nationalism and liberalism, finding considerable support among the small but growing urban middle classes, especially in the western German states.

Following Napoleon's defeat, under the settlement reached at the Congress of Vienna in 1815, the number of German political units was reduced to thirty-nine. Only two of them—Prussia and Austria—had the size and resources needed to create a single unified German nation-state. Between 1815 and 1866, these states formed a confederation within which the struggle for supremacy between Prussia and Austria took place. Perhaps as significant as the German Confederation was the creation of the Zollverein, a customs union founded in 1818 under Prussian auspices (excluding all Habsburg-ruled lands) that paved the way economically for eventual political unification. Prussia also benefited immensely from gaining much of the Rhineland and the resource-rich Ruhr region in 1815 because these areas became the locus of the German industrial revolution later in the century. With its own multinational empire spreading over central, eastern, and southeastern Europe, Austria felt far less enthusiastic about German nationalism and unity than did Prussia or the liberals in the other states. The Habsburgs preferred a weak confederation and defended the autonomy of the constituent units. Most liberals, although still distrustful of Prussia, were also committed to national unity.

In 1848 liberal uprisings in Berlin, Vienna, Frankfurt am Main, and elsewhere culminated in the establishment of a national parliament in Frankfurt to draft a liberal constitution for a unified state that was to include a constitutional monarch. However, the German liberals of 1848, predominantly middle-class intellectuals and professionals, were at least a generation behind their British counterparts in political finesse and expertise. They were unable to agree whether a Prussian or an Austrian should become emperor, and their own disunity allowed the various rulers in the constituent states to regain power. When the parliament finally offered the crown to the Prussian king almost a year after it was convened, he scornfully rejected it, and the Revolution of 1848 was soon crushed by Prussian and Austrian troops loyal to the monarchs. If Germany were to have a second Reich, it would not be acquired through political liberalism.

After 1848 the Prussian and Austrian rivalry continued within the confederation, but the combination of Prussian military superiority and the skillful diplomacy and leadership of the Prussian prime minister, Otto von Bismarck, overwhelmed the larger but internally divided Austria. Prussia under Bismarck fought successfully against Denmark (1864), Austria (1866), and France (1870), thereby establishing its hegemony in most of northern Germany and permanently excluding Austria from an eventual nation-state—the *kleindeutsch* (small German) solution, as opposed to the *grossdeutsch* (large German) alternative. These military successes dazzled the political liberals and won most of them over to the rather illiberal Prussian imperial vision. In 1871, after some last-minute bargaining with the reluctant southern Germans, Bismarck was able to inform the Prussian king that all the German princes and free cities such as Hamburg, Bremen, and Lübeck wanted him to accept the imperial crown. Thus at Versailles, the temporary headquarters of the army after the victorious war against France, Wilhelm I became the kaiser (emperor) of the Second Reich.

THE EMPIRE, 1871–1918

Although the empire consisted of twenty-seven constituent states, it was dominated in every way by Prussia, which accounted for approximately 60 percent of
the population and land area. Moreover, the Second Reich was largely Bismarck's
creation, and he dominated German and European politics for the next two decades. His constitution for the empire, a complex structure, ensured Prussian
hegemony behind a liberal and federal facade. The emperor, who was also the
Prussian king, appointed the chancellor (head of government), who was responsible to him and not to the parliament. The chancellor then appointed his cabinet
ministers. Moreover, the key policy areas of defense and foreign affairs were
largely the domains of the emperor and chancellor. Parliament had only indirect
control over these matters through its power of appropriations. But in the event
of a deadlock between chancellor and parliament, the constitution gave sweeping
emergency powers to the emperor.

The imperial parliament was bicameral. A lower house (*Reichstag*) was
directly elected on the basis of universal male suffrage (one of the most progressive franchises at that time), but important legislation also required approval by
the upper house (*Bundesrat*, or Federal Council), which was dominated by
Prussia. This upper house was composed of delegates sent by the governments of
the constituent states; its members were thus not directly elected by the people.
Prussia, as the largest state, controlled seventeen of the chamber's fifty-eight
votes and could, in fact, veto most legislation. The Prussian government, which
sent and instructed these delegates, was led by the omnipresent Bismarck, who
was both premier of Prussia and chancellor of the Reich. To complete the picture,
Bismarck headed the Prussian delegation to the Bundesrat and, as leader of the
largest state, served as president of the upper house. Bismarck's power within
Prussia was based not only on his relationship to the king, but also on a voting
system for elections to the Prussian parliament that was heavily weighted in
favor of conservative, nationalist, and upper-status groups. Thus Bismarck, who
brought the empire into being, also dominated its politics.

Although it was strongly biased in favor of Prussian executive power, this
complex system was nonetheless far from being a totalitarian or even a dictatorial
state. The lower house was directly elected and did exercise considerable
authority over appropriations. There were also some genuine federal elements in
the system. The states had major responsibilities for education, domestic order
and security (police), and cultural affairs.

Bismarck's success in creating this empire, his resultant prestige, and his
unquestioned political skill enabled him largely to control both parliament and
the states. Bismarck was able to maintain a broad coalition of support—the
famous "alliance of iron and rye" between the rising class of industrialists
(Krupp, Thyssen, and Siemens) and the traditional landholding Prussian nobility,
the Junkers. In addition to the conservatives, the middle-class liberals were
beholden to his foreign policy successes. Finally, the burgeoning industrial
working classes were simultaneously repressed through the infamous Anti-
Socialist Laws in force from 1878 to 1888 and co-opted through the implementation of the first modern welfare programs in the 1880s. Prussian Catholics were

also discriminated against during the so-called *Kulturkampf* (cultural struggle) of the 1870s, as were Poles—mainly in the eastern territories of Prussia—throughout this period. In retrospect, the middle class should have known better and worked to increase the power of parliament instead of supporting the continued dominance of traditional Prussian elites—the nationalistic nobility and military.

WORLD WAR I AND THE COLLAPSE OF THE SECOND REICH

As long as Bismarck led the Prussian and Reich governments, the complex system survived and, indeed, prospered. After 1871 the new Reich was unquestionably the strongest military power in continental Europe and was rivaled in the world only by the United Kingdom with its still superior fleet. Moreover, a period of rapid industrialization and urbanization after 1871, as well as a flourishing scientific and cultural scene, brought relative economic prosperity. Yet, by forging the Second Reich, Bismarck and the Prussians made many enemies in Europe—chiefly France, humiliated in the 1870 Franco-Prussian War and deprived of the regions of Alsace and Lorraine. Russia and increasingly the UK were also fearful of further German expansion. Bismarck was able to prevent a Franco-Russian alliance, although his rather hapless successors such as von Caprivi were not.

As the political power of the middle classes in the UK and France grew and generally exerted a moderating influence on policy, in the Prussian-dominated Second Reich the old feudal classes—the nobility, military, and large landowners—maintained and expanded their domestic hegemony, while pursuing defense and foreign policies designed to unify a divided society and maintain their own position of power. Growing imperialist sentiment and romantic nationalism was epitomized by the ruler Kaiser Wilhelm II (1888–1918) and was manifested in the effort at the turn of the century to expand its fleet in order to match or exceed that of the UK and to acquire, like the UK and France, an extensive overseas empire. The empire did succeed in gaining several colonies—present-day Cameroon, Namibia, and Tanzania—but at the high price of rising international tensions, especially with the UK.

Moreover, the extremely rapid pace of industrialization created a large working class and a strong Social Democratic Party. The middle class, also expanding in size because of modernization, did not assume and—for the most part—did not seek political power and influence commensurate with its socioeconomic importance. In fact, the middle classes felt threatened by the rising urban proletariat and thus supported the conservative status quo.[3]

In sum, between 1871 and 1914 Germany was a society that was rapidly modernizing, yet it was still ruled by traditional elites. A creeping liberalization in many political, social, and economic areas was apparent, so that the overall system was much less authoritarian than it had been in 1871. However, the stagnant political system could not deal effectively with the rising socioeconomic tensions and increasingly looked to international distractions to divert attention away from problems at home.[4] This strategy—in combination with the Great Power alliances; tensions in other countries, for example Austria in the Balkans;

and the nationalistic enmities of the era—led to the outbreak of continent-wide hostilities in 1914 for the first time since the Napoleonic era.

Germany's unstable social and political order could not survive a lengthy war. Indeed, World War I exposed its fatal weaknesses. After the failure of the initial German offensive in the West, designed to produce a quick victory, the prospect of a protracted conflict on several fronts, with eventually two million battlefield casualties, began to make manifest the latent tensions and contradictions in the social and political structure of the Second Reich. The Liberal, Socialist, and Catholic political parties in the parliament became less enthusiastic about supporting a war against countries such as the United Kingdom and the United States, whose level of constitutional democracy they hoped some day to achieve in Germany. Indeed, victory would strengthen the authoritarian regime. Food and raw materials became ever scarcer as imports, which had accounted for one-third of prewar supplies, dwindled under the pressure of the Allied (mainly British) blockade. Officially forbidden, strikes broke out in various industries as workers reacted to mounting casualty lists and severe wartime rationing. A virtual military dictatorship emerged by 1917 as the army, intent on achieving maximum production and mobilization, began to make key political, social, and economic decisions. However, when the army could not deliver victory in the West—the empire did defeat tsarist Russia by 1917—the generals, chief among them Paul von Hindenburg, advised the kaiser to call for a cease-fire and abdicate. The parliamentary leadership then proclaimed a republic and attempted to negotiate a peace with the Western powers.

THE WEIMAR REPUBLIC, 1919–1933

The departure of the kaiser, and the proclamation of a republic in the wake of Germany's surrender, took place in an atmosphere of increasing revolutionary fervor. Mindful of the Bolshevik success in Russia, several German Marxists split from the moderate Social Democratic Party (SPD) and formed the Spartakus League, which later became the Communist Party (KPD). Workers' and soldiers' councils based on the Bolshevik model were formed in major cities. In Bavaria, a short-lived Soviet socialist republic was proclaimed. Germany seemed for a time to be on the verge of a communist revolution.

Conservatives and middle-class liberals combined with the Social Democrats to crush the communist uprising with military and paramilitary units. Many conservatives and nationalists, shocked at the prospect of a communist revolution, were willing to accept, at least in the short run, a parliamentary republic. In the small town of Weimar, in 1919, a constitution was prepared and later ratified by a constituent assembly. Germany's first attempt at liberal democracy had begun.

The Weimar Constitution, drafted by learned constitutional and legal scholars such as Max Weber, was widely acclaimed as one of the most democratic in the world. It featured universal adult suffrage; proportional representation; extensive provisions for popular referenda, petitions, and recalls; and an extensive catalog of civil liberties. The constitution created a dual executive: a chancellor as head of government appointed by the president but enjoying the confidence of the lower house, and a directly elected president as chief of state. Under Article 48 the president also had the power to issue decrees in lieu of legislation in case of a state of emergency. Many historians and political scientists cite this latter provision as a major defect of the document.

The Weimar Republic could hardly have been started under less favorable circumstances. Defeat and national humiliation following the world war, widespread political violence, severe economic and social dislocation, and a political leadership with no real executive policy-making experience were major challenges that the new state never entirely surmounted. The World War I peace settlement saddled Germany with a huge war debt; deprived it of 15 percent of its arable land and 10 percent of its population; and ensured the loss of all its foreign colonies and investments, much of its military and merchant fleet, and its railway stock. Finally the Versailles Treaty in the controversial "war guilt" clause forced Germany to accept sole responsibility for the outbreak of the war. The dismantling of the Austro-Hungarian Empire also reopened questions regarding the German-speaking populations of the Austrian Republic and Czechoslovakia. Conservatives and nationalists, soon forgetting the help of liberals and socialists in defeating the communists, openly opposed the new system. The still-powerful military, whose antirepublican officer corps was never purged, fostered the myth that Germany in World War I had been "stabbed in the back" by liberal, socialist, Jewish, and Marxist civilian politicians. For some, the entire Weimar Republic was a conspiracy—a system devised by criminals. The bureaucracy and especially the judiciary harbored many avowed opponents of democracy who were never removed from their positions. Likewise, on the left, communists and some socialists viewed Weimar as simply a brief prelude to the socialist revolution that, in their view, had only been delayed by the failure of the radical revolutionaries in 1918.

Shortly after its inauspicious beginning, the Republic had to confront an attempted military coup (the Kapp *putsch* of 1920), a disastrous wave of inflation (1922–1923) that virtually wiped out the savings of the middle class, an attempted communist revolution in the state of Saxony (1923), Hitler's unsuccessful *putsch* in Munich (1923), and the French occupation of the Rhineland due to the Weimar government's inability to pay the huge war reparations imposed by the victorious powers at Versailles.

For an all too brief period in the mid-1920s, Weimar nonetheless appeared to have stabilized itself. Long-term loans from the United States and less stringent payment plans eased the debt and reparations problem and aided the state's economic recovery. Conservatives appeared to be slowly accepting the system as legitimate, and the 1925 election of the World War I hero Paul von Hindenburg as president brought still more conservatives and nationalists into a position of at least tacit acceptance of the Weimar Republic.[5]

But the worldwide depression sparked by the collapse of the U.S. stock market in 1929 dealt a new blow from which Weimar never rallied. By 1931 roughly half of all German families were directly affected by unemployment. Voters began to desert the republican parties. Between 1919 and 1932 the proportion of the electorate supporting the Social Democrats, the Liberals, and the

Catholic centrists declined from 64 percent to only 30 percent. The big beneficiaries were the Nazis on the right and the communists on the left. Between 1930
and 1933 no government could secure majority support in the lower house of
parliament (the Reichstag). Indeed, by 1932 the two antisystem parties, the Nazis
and communists—who both in their own way were determined to overthrow the
institution to which they belonged—had a majority of seats. They were able to
bring the regular lawmaking process to a halt. In 1932 parliament met for only
thirteen days and could pass only five laws. President Hindenburg, always ambivalent toward parliamentary democracy, had to govern by the decree-granting
powers given to him in Article 48 of the constitution. After issuing only five such
decrees in 1930, by 1932 he made use of this authority sixty-six times.

THE NAZI SEIZURE OF POWER

By 1932 the Nazis had legally become the strongest party in the Reichstag,
although never a majority. Traditional authoritarian conservatives and nationalists wanted them in a right-wing, national-unity government but refused to
accept the demand of their leader, Adolf Hitler, that he head such a government.
Caught between extremes of right and left and plagued by internal divisions, the
weak democratic middle was unable to act decisively to save the Republic. Convinced that the Nazis could be handled, Hindenburg eventually overcame his
contempt for the "Austrian corporal," and on January 30, 1933, Hitler became
chancellor. By March 1933, Hitler had eliminated all significant opposition in
parliament after the Nazis pushed through an Enabling Act that essentially
granted him dictatorial powers. The Third Reich, which was to have lasted a
thousand years, had begun.

   Why did the Weimar Republic fail? What happened to make a highly developed modern society turn to the primitive racist and nationalist appeals of the
Nazis? Certainly there is no more important question confronting the student of
modern German history. Some historians view Hitler's triumph as an abnormal,
unique event unrelated to previous German historical and political development.
They emphasize (1) the specific set of circumstances facing interwar Germany
and Europe, coupled with (2) the relative youth and catchall appeal of the
National Socialist German Workers Party, which deemphasized considerably its
anti-Semitism during the period of its greatest electoral success; (3) defects in the
Weimar Constitution, especially proportional representation, which worked to
the benefit of small splinter parties and increased the difficulty of forming stable
majorities in parliament. Thus with at times only 3 percent of the vote, the Nazis
were still represented in the Reichstag as a very noisy minority. The dual executive of the Weimar system, which created a strong president independent of parliament, has also been cited by numerous analysts. The disappointing leadership
of the democratic parties, the absence of any strong commitment to the system
among many of its supporters, the behavior of key personalities such as Hindenburg, and the effects of the foreign policies of the victorious Western powers are
cited as other factors that contributed to the Nazi dictatorship.[6] Had one or more
of these factors been lacking, the Nazi seizure of power could have been avoided.

According to this view, there was nothing inevitable about Nazism; it represented a clear break from Germany's course of political development.

Many non-German historians, especially those from the United States and the UK, have taken a different approach to the origins of the Third Reich. They see Nazism more as the logical, if not predictable, outcome of German historical development and political culture. They point to the absence of a liberal middle-class revolution, such as those that took place in France and the UK, and the later unification of the Reich, which occurred not on the basis of constitutional procedures but through the "blood and iron" policies of Bismarck. The cultural emphasis on authoritarian values—deference and obedience to superiors, reverence for order and discipline—and the hierarchical character of child rearing in the family and school are also cited. In addition, the German tradition of political philosophy (with its particular stress on *statism*, or the treatment of the state as an organization superior to other social organizations), collectivism, intolerance toward minorities (especially Jews), and the absence of a strong tradition of liberal individualism in political theory have also been singled out as precursors of Nazism. Racialized anti-Semitism certainly motivated many Germans to support the Nazis.[8]

Other scholars emphasize the disunity and internal contradictions within the German middle class as major factors in the collapse of the Weimar system. According to this perspective, the capitalist class was divided among heavy industry, export industry, and the *Mittelstand* (the lower middle class of shopkeepers, artisans, and some salaried employees). Each of these groups had a somewhat different view of what kind of Republic it wanted and, above all, the extent to which it was willing to cooperate with Germany's manual workers and their major political party, the Social Democrats. Internal disunity plagued the capitalist camp throughout the Republic and left it with no viable alternative to the Nazis after 1930, when further cooperation with the Social Democrats became impossible for all capitalist groups; that is, when none was willing to support or finance the social welfare programs that were an indispensable condition of any continuation of a coalition with the Social Democrats. According to this view, Nazism or fascism was not the inevitable result of the capitalist system but rather the consequence of the German middle class's inability to develop an alternative solution (e.g., a presidential dictatorship or a corporatist system) to the post-1930 economic and political crisis.[9]

A fourth category of explanation stresses the relationship between socioeconomic structure and National Socialism. Specifically, the success of the Nazis is explained by the support of the German upper and middle classes who, fearing a socialist revolution and their loss of status more than incipient fascism, gave Hitler and the Nazis key political and financial support. Other analysts have argued that fascism is a phase in the development of late capitalist societies and the Nazis simply exploited this conservative aversion to the democratization of German political, social, and economic life, something the Weimar Republic might eventually have achieved had it not been for the conservative counterrevolution. As we discuss in chapter 3, some critics of the Federal Republic have argued that it represents a restoration, following the Nazi defeat, of the same capitalist institutions and processes that produced fascism in 1933.

THE THIRD REICH AND WORLD WAR II

The Nazi or National Socialist German Workers Party (NSDAP) was only one of numerous radical nationalist and *völkisch* (racialist) parties and movements that sprang up in the chaotic atmosphere of postwar Germany. Founded in 1919 in Munich, the party probably would have remained insignificant and eventually disappeared had it not been for the extraordinary leadership ability of Adolf Hitler. The son of a low-level Austrian civil servant, Hitler had fought in World War I as a volunteer for the German army. Before the war he was a sometime art student in Vienna, where he absorbed the pan-German nationalism, anti-Semitism, and anti-Marxism characteristic of right-wing circles in the Austrian capital.[10] A powerful orator, Hitler quickly assumed leadership of the National Socialists, and by the early 1920s the party had become the most prominent of the radical right-wing groups in Munich. In 1923 the Nazis, allied with other nationalist groups including one led by World War I hero Ludendorff, made an amateurish attempt to overthrow the Bavarian government in Munich and trigger a revolution throughout Germany. The *putsch* (coup) failed, and Hitler was arrested and tried for treason. Although he was convicted, he was treated very leniently by sympathetic Bavarian authorities.

Imprisoned—or, rather, detained—for just over a year, Hitler used the time to outline his future political plans in his book *Mein Kampf* (My Struggle), which appeared in 1925 and 1926 and became the oft-cited but seldom read "bible" of the Nazi movement. The Munich fiasco convinced Hitler that in order to succeed, the party would have to come to power legally. A legal seizure of power would ensure the Nazis the support of most of the bureaucracy, the judiciary, and the army. Thus with a program that promised a national renewal, rearmament, revision of the hated Versailles Treaty, and social and economic reform for the working classes, the Nazis attempted to appeal to all members of the racial community (*Volksgemeinschaft*). The party was particularly attractive for the marginal groups in German society: the small shopkeepers and artisans caught between big labor and big business, the small farmers losing out to larger enterprises and middlemen, and the unemployed university graduates or university dropouts blaming the system for their condition. Yet in spite of its program and well-developed propaganda apparatus, the party remained a negligible factor until the Great Depression. Not until the economic crisis of 1929 could the Nazis break through and become the strongest force in the antirepublican camp.

After the appointment of Hitler as chancellor and the March 1933 Enabling Act, which suspended the parliament and constitution and essentially gave the Nazis *carte blanche*, the process of consolidating totalitarian one-party rule began in earnest. What Hitler and the Nazis sought was the *Gleichschaltung*, or coordination, of all areas of German life to the Nazi pattern. By the end of 1934 this objective was largely accomplished; all major social, economic, and political institutions were brought under the control of the party and were subjected to reorganizations corresponding to the party's hierarchical, centralized structure. The leadership principle—unquestioning obedience and acceptance of the *Führer's* (leader's) will as the highest law and authority—became the overriding organizational criterion.

Most Nazi coordination efforts took place under the pretext of legality. The burning of the Reichstag in February 1933 was used to secure a presidential emergency decree outlawing the Communist Party and simultaneously allowing the Nazis to destroy the independence of the Reich's constituent states. Even the murder of hundreds of counterrevolutionary SA (storm troop) leaders and other "enemies" in June 1934 was later legalized by the puppet parliament. This pattern of lawlessness or flagrant manipulation of the law lasted until the collapse of the regime through military defeat in 1945. Despite important differences in motivation and context, there was a common thread among the June 1934 murders, the elimination of other political and racial enemies in the concentration camps, and the later extermination of six million Jews.

Rule by a racially "superior" "Aryan" elite, manipulation of the racially acceptable but "stupid" masses, and the extermination of Jews and other "inferior" peoples was, according to one authority, "the only genuine kernel of Hitler's ideology."[11] The socialist aspect of National Socialism and Hitler's professed opposition to plutocracy were designed to generate mass support for the leader. Indeed, the Nazis implemented a variety of popular measures for the masses—including holidays through the Kraft durch Freude (Strength through Joy) program, goods such as cheap radios and the "people's car" (Volkswagen), and numerous free-time activities such as the annual Nazi Party Rally in Nuremburg and the Hitler Youth. Of course, all of these measures were used for propaganda and indoctrination purposes. Moreover, the Nazis did reduce unemployment through public works schemes (the Autobahn), rearmament, and remilitarization—although many authors have pointed out that the economy would have improved under any regime.

Regardless of the party's rhetoric or the views of its "left" wing, whose leaders were liquidated or had fled by 1934, "a strong state and the leadership principle, not economic and social reform, were the ideas guiding Hitler's policies on capitalism and socialism, organizations and group interests, reform and revolution."[12] Such a vision was buttressed by intensive coercion. The concentration camp system proliferated rapidly after the first camp was established at Dachau near Munich in March 1933. By 1945, over three million Germans had spent some time in such a camp, with the first internees being political opponents. A dense system of domestic surveillance—the secret police (Gestapo), criminal police, and SS (elite guard)—monitored the population and punished all forms of deviance and opposition. Finally, many of the most prominent members of the intellectual and political elite such as Bertolt Brecht and Thomas Mann fled the country during the war years or retired into a form of "inner emigration." As Hitler had promised in *Mein Kampf*, the elimination of the Jews as the greatest threat to the German *Volk* (people or race) began shortly after the seizure of power. On April 1, 1933, the Nazis initiated a boycott of Jewish shops in Berlin. Over succeeding months, Jews were dismissed from political positions and limited in their economic activities. In 1935 the Nuremberg Race Laws deprived Germany's half million Jews of all political and civil liberties. Terror and violence were used on a mass scale beginning in November 1938 when the Nazis used the assassination of a German diplomat in Paris by a young Jew as an excuse to loot and burn Jewish shops and synagogues throughout the Reich—the so-called

Night of Broken Glass (Kristallnacht). Moreover, the remaining Jews were forced to pay for the damages caused by the Nazi mobs. By 1939 about 400,000 German and Austrian Jews had emigrated, including major figures such as Albert Einstein, Max Born, and Henry Kissinger. Most of the remaining 300,000 were eventually to suffer the same fate as the rest of European Jewry, namely mass extermination.

There can be little doubt that the Nazi regime, at least until the onset of World War II, enjoyed considerable mass support. Even in 1951, 42 percent of adult West Germans and 53 percent of those over thirty-five still stated that the prewar years of the Third Reich (1933–1939) were the "best" that Germany had experienced in the twentieth century. Those were years of economic growth and at least a superficial prosperity. Unemployment was virtually eliminated; inflation was checked; and the economy, fueled by public expenditures, boomed. The fact that during these "good years" thousands of Germans were imprisoned, tortured, and murdered in concentration camps, and hundreds of thousands of German Jews were systematically persecuted, was apparently of minor importance to most citizens in comparison with the economic and policy successes of the regime. In fact, the suppression of civil liberties and all political opposition— along with the *Gleichschaltung* of the churches, schools, universities, the press, and trade unions—was accepted with little overt opposition. In a sense most Germans (at least between 1933 and 1939) were willing to give up the democratic political order and liberal society and accept the regime's racism and persecution of political opponents in exchange for economic prosperity, social stability, and a resurgence of national pride due to Hitler's many early foreign policy successes.

Yet sizable segments of German society remained relatively immune to the Nazis even after Hitler became chancellor in January 1933. For example, the Nazis never received an absolute majority of votes in any free election during the Weimar Republic. Even in the last election in March 1933 (approximately five weeks after Hitler took power), which was less free than preceding polls because of Nazi agitation and terror tactics against opposing parties, the party received only 44 percent of the vote; in some electoral districts its support was as low as 10 or 20 percent. Catholics and socialists with strong ties to the highly developed secondary organizations of the church and party, such as youth, labor, and women's groups, were especially resistant to Nazi appeals.

From the beginning, the Nazi system was directed at the total mobilization of Germany for the purpose of conducting an aggressive war. Military expansion was intended not only to secure *Lebensraum* (living space) for the superior German race but also to justify one-party dictatorship and unify the racial community. Capitalizing on the internal weaknesses and division among the major European democracies (the UK and France), the isolationist United States, and a suspicious Soviet Union, Hitler marched from success to success, beginning with the remilitarization of the Rhineland and the Berlin Olympic Games in 1936, the 1938 annexation of Austria, later the Sudetenland (the German-speaking area of Czechoslovakia) and then the rest of Czechoslovakia, and World War II itself, from the rapid defeat of Poland in 1939, the fall of France in 1940, and the invasion of the Soviet Union (Operation Barbarossa) from June 1941 until late 1942 when Soviet troops finally turned the tide at Stalingrad.

Each military and foreign political success strengthened the Nazi system at home, while at the same time rendering the small and scattered opposition groups unable to mount any serious challenge to the regime. Although there were numerous attempts on Hitler's life, it was not until July 1944, less than a year before the end of the war, that a group of military officers and civilian opponents made a desperate attempt at a coup d'état. But the key element in the plan, the assassination of Hitler, failed—with the result that the entire opposition movement was soon crushed by large-scale arrests and executions.

In territories conquered by the German armies, the full horror of Nazism was experienced. To establish Hitler's "New Order," millions of European civilians and prisoners of war—men, women, and children—were systematically murdered by special Nazi extermination units and regular German army personnel. "Useless human material"—the mentally handicapped in hospitals and asylums and Europe's gypsies—were murdered. Also marked for extermination were actual or potential political opponents—the Polish intelligentsia, the political commissars in the Soviet army, and resistance fighters. Finally, military conquest meant the "final solution" of the "Jewish problem." After a period of deportation from all over occupied Europe and forced ghettoization, as well as the mass shooting of over two million Jews, large extermination camps such as Auschwitz-Birkenau, Treblinka, and Majdanek, serviced by special railway lines and selected Nazi personnel, killed millions more. By 1945, six million European Jews had been murdered.

Although the SS mobile killing squads and extermination camps were officially top secret, there is little doubt that millions of ordinary Germans knew something of the Jews' fate and that very few made any effort to find out more about what the Nazis and the German army were doing in the occupied territories, much less to try and stop it.[13] Caught up in the increasingly horrifying demands of war, subjected to incessant propaganda, and fearful of the regime's extensive domestic terror apparatus, most Germans remained passive until the end.

But many ordinary Germans also remained docile because they profited from the Holocaust by acquiring the stolen assets of murdered Jews. In Hamburg alone between March 1942 and July 1943 at least 100,000 households were the recipients of property (furniture, clothing, jewelry) stolen primarily from Dutch and French Jews.[14] The bank accounts, stocks, real estate, insurance policies, and social security contributions of murdered Jews enriched the Reich's treasury. From these stolen Jewish assets Germany bought "iron ore from Sweden, butter and machines from Switzerland, grain, cooking oil and aluminum from Hungary. In the final analysis every German had something on his or her table that came from the assets of murdered Jews."[15] Indeed, recent scholarship has emphasized the degree to which the Nazis and their genocidal policies were motivated and sustained by plunder.[16] Many Germans benefited from the positions vacated by their Jewish compatriots. Finally, there is convincing evidence that many Germans embraced the Nazis' anti-Semitic message—that is, they supported the elimination of the Jews from German society, if not necessarily their physical extermination.[17]

The years 1943 to 1945 saw the total war come home. There were between 5.5 and 7 million dead (about 10 percent of the prewar population), including 4.5 to 5 million battlefield casualties. The Allied strategic bombing campaign decimated every major and many minor German cities. Fifty percent of the built-up areas of the largest cities was destroyed—20 percent of the country's housing was gone. Berlin, Hamburg, Cologne, Frankfurt, and Dresden were in ruins; in the east, there was nothing left in cities like Breslau and Königsberg. Between 300,000 and 600,000 people died in the air raids. As the Red Army advanced westward, millions of civilians fled and many women were raped—estimates range between 600,000 and two million.[18] The Third Reich finally collapsed in May 1945 as American, Soviet, British, French, and their Allied forces defeated the German armies and occupied the Reich. Unlike 1918, there could be no stab-in-the-back legend following this total defeat. The destruction of the Nazi system brought military occupation and massive uncertainty about the future of Germany as a national community, much less a political system. The decimated country and the tens of millions of victims killed by the war that Nazi Germany unleashed brought Germany to what at the time was called "Zero Hour" (*Stunde Null*). The absolute bottom had been reached.

FOREIGN OCCUPATION AND NATIONAL DIVISION

Between 1945 and 1949, Germany's conquerors reduced the size of its territory, divided the remainder into four zones of military occupation, and established two new states out of these zones: the Federal Republic of Germany (British, French, and American zones) and the German Democratic Republic (Soviet zone). All territories annexed by the Nazis between 1938 and 1941 were returned to their former Austrian, Czechoslovakian (the Sudetenland), Yugoslavian (Slovenia), or French (Alsace-Lorraine) owners. Consistent with the Allied agreements at Yalta, those German provinces east of the Oder and Neisse rivers (the Oder-Neisse line), including East Prussia, Silesia, and most of Pomerania—which totaled approximately 25 percent of Germany's prewar territory—were put under "temporary" Soviet or Polish administration. The ultimate fate of these eastern territories was to be decided by a final peace treaty between Germany and the wartime Allies. However, such a treaty was never signed because of the Cold War. In 1970 provisionally and in 1990 unequivocally, following the accession of East Germany into the Federal Republic, treaties with the Soviet Union and Poland recognized these losses as permanent (see figure 1.1).[19]

The vast majority of the Germans living in these regions, as well as Germans in Czechoslovakia, Hungary, Yugoslavia, and elsewhere had fled from or been expelled by Soviet and Polish forces after 1945 and resettled in the remaining German territory or Austria. All in all, 12 to 14 million people were affected—one of the largest movements of people in modern history.[20] Many expellees died or were murdered en route to the west. Deprived of their property without compensation, the surviving expellees had to build new lives in what remained of a war-ravaged country. The integration of millions of refugees into postwar German society was but one major task confronting the new Federal Republic and the

Figure 1.1.   Territorial changes after World War II.

Source: Der Spiegel.

communist state in the Russian zone in 1949. Finally there were millions of captured German soldiers who had to try and rebuild their shattered lives. It was not until 1956 that the Soviet Union released the last of its German prisoners.

The rest of the prewar Reich was divided into British, French, American, and Soviet zones of occupation. The former capital, Berlin, lying within the Soviet zone, was given special status and was also divided into four sectors. Each military commander exercised authority in his respective zone, and an Allied Control Council, composed of the four commanders, was jointly and unanimously to make decisions affecting Germany as a whole. During the war the Allies had determined the general lines of postwar policy toward Germany:

1. Germany was to be *denazified;* all vestiges of the Nazi system were to be removed, its top Nazi and government officials tried as war criminals, and lesser party activists punished by fines and imprisonment.
2. The country was to be *demilitarized,* with its capability to wage aggressive war permanently removed.
3. Postwar Germany was to become a *democratic* society. To this end, extensive programs of political education were to be designed and implemented in the postwar period. A complete reform of the educational system was included under this democratization program.
4. The former Reich was to be *decentralized,* with important political responsibilities delegated to states (*Länder*) and local governments under a system of constitutional federalism.

THE FORMATION OF THE FEDERAL REPUBLIC

The wartime consensus that produced these policy plans quickly disintegrated after 1945, as differences between the three Western powers and the Soviet Union made any common occupation policy impossible. In the Soviet occupation zone, local governments controlled by Communist Party officials or pro-Soviet elements were quickly established. Entire plants were dismantled and shipped to the Soviet Union; the remaining industry was eventually nationalized and agriculture collectivized.

These actions, basically designed to turn the Soviet zone into a communist state and society, were politically and ideologically unacceptable to the Western powers already alarmed by similar Soviet moves in Poland and Hungary. By 1948 it was apparent that no all-German political or economic cooperation was possible. In the face of what was perceived by Western policy makers to be a growing Soviet threat, the Western Allies began to envision a postwar German state excluding the Soviet zone of occupation—a West German entity composed of the American, British, and French zones. The French were reluctant at first to agree to the establishment of even a centralized West German state, which might become a power rivaling France on the European continent. By 1948, however, French fear of the Soviet Union exceeded its fear of Germany, enabling the three Western Allies to announce a common economic policy and issue a common currency in their zones. The Soviet Union responded with an attempt to deny the Western powers access to Berlin (the Berlin Blockade from June 1948 to May 1949) and undertook the construction of another separate German state in its zone, the German Democratic Republic (GDR) with its capital in East Berlin (see figure 1.2).

By the late 1940s it was clear that neither the United States nor the Soviet Union were prepared to allow "their" Germans to pursue policies that they could not control and that could possibly be directed against their interests. Each superpower wanted a single German state only on its own terms: a liberal, pluralistic democratic state for the United States; a communist, worker-and-peasant state for the Soviet Union. Unable to achieve such a unified state without military conflict, the two superpowers settled for two states, each having the social, economic, and political characteristics of its respective protector. Ironically, the division of Germany enabled both states within a relatively short time to achieve a status within their respective power blocs that a single German state could never have attained.

These fateful developments, which sealed the division and dismemberment of the prewar Reich, took place with little direct German participation, even though German governments had existed at the local and state levels since 1946. The initial intent of Western and especially American occupiers was to democratize Germany in stages, beginning at the local level, where a stronger tradition of democratic self-government existed. Thus the establishment of local and state institutions *preceded* the creation of central institutions for West Germany.

Most Germans were neither concerned with the future of their nation nor with their own responsibility or guilt relative to Nazism, much less with politics. Their immediate problem was physical survival: obtaining food, clothing, and

Figure 1.2.   The Federal Republic of Germany today.

shelter. According to surveys, six out of every ten Germans stated that they "suffered greatly" from hunger in the postwar years. The average caloric intake during the period 1945–1947 was less than 70 percent of that deemed adequate.[21] Almost half of all families suffered partial or total loss of their households through bombing raids. After physical survival came the problem of putting their personal lives back together again: returning to school, resuming a career, reopening their business, finding a job, or raising a fatherless family. Thus the events and decisions between 1945 and 1949 so crucial to the birth of the Federal Republic were made within a context of mass indifference to politics. Germans in the immediate postwar years had reduced their sphere of social concern to the most basic level: the self and the immediate family.

On July 1, 1948, the three Western Allied military governors met in Frankfurt with the *Ministerpräsidenten*, or premiers, of the various states and "recommended" (i.e., ordered) the calling of a constituent assembly by September 1, 1948, which was to draft a constitution for the three Western zones. This constitution was then to be placed before the electorate for approval. None of the state premiers was enthusiastic about establishing a separate West German state, fearing that the constituent assembly and the resultant constitution would seal the division of Germany. Meeting before the assembly with the leaders of the two major political parties, the state executives decided to term the document they were to draft a "Basic Law" rather than a constitution and to stress in it the provisional character of the new state. After a long delay, the states finally convened an assembly to draft the document. Nine months later, in May 1949, their work was completed. Again, wanting to avoid the appearance of permanence, they asked for ratification through the state parliaments rather than through a popular referendum. This proved acceptable to the Allied authorities. Thus the citizens of West Germany never directly approved the constitution.

The declaration of ratification hardly evoked any celebration. One influential news magazine termed the document a "bastard of a constitution," produced in nine months through pressure by the military occupation.[22] In one national survey conducted at the time, 40 percent of the adult population stated that they were indifferent to the constitution, 33 percent were "moderately interested," and only 21 percent were "very interested." Only 51 percent, in another 1949 survey, favored the creation of the Federal Republic; the remainder of the sample were either against it (23 percent), indifferent (13 percent), or undecided (13 percent).[23] Like it or not, however, Germans in the Western-occupied zones of the former Reich had a new constitution and political system that took effect on May 23, 1949.[24] As we discuss throughout the remainder of this book, according to standards used to judge political systems and especially in comparison to past regimes, the institutions of the Federal Republic have performed well. The reluctant drafters of the constitution produced a document that, unlike the constitution of the Weimar Republic, has survived to structure meaningfully the behavior of Germans and their political decision makers. Moreover, the success of the West German political order served as a powerful model and magnet for East Germans living under a one-party communist system.

On October 7, 1949, the thirty-second anniversary of the communist revolution in Russia, a second postwar German state, the German Democratic

Republic, was proclaimed in East Berlin. The boundaries of this state corresponded to the Soviet zone of military occupation. The evolution of the GDR, the chain of events that rapidly led to the unification of Germany in October 1990, and the difficult postunification period that has followed are the subjects of chapter 2.

NOTES

1. Donald S. Detweiler, *Germany: A Short History* (Carbondale: Southern Illinois University Press, 1976), 46ff.

2. See Thomas Ertman, *Birth of the Leviathan: Building States and Regimes in Medieval and Early Modern Europe* (Cambridge: Cambridge University Press, 1997); Christopher Clark, *Iron Kingdom: The Rise and Downfall of Prussia, 1600–1947* (Cambridge: Belknap Press of Harvard University, 2006).

3. Ruth Berins Collier, *Paths toward Democracy: The Working Class and Elites in Western Europe and South America* (Cambridge: Cambridge University Press, 1999).

4. On Germany's war aims and the tensions in the late imperial system, see Fritz Fischer, *Germany's Aims in the First World War* (New York: Norton, 1968); Hans-Ulrich Wehler, *The German Empire, 1871–1918*, translated from the German by Kim Traynor (Leamington Spa: Berg Publishers, 1985).

5. See Charles S. Maier, *Recasting Bourgeois Europe: Stabilization in France, Germany and Italy in the Decade after World War I* (Princeton, NJ: Princeton University Press, 1975); Anna von der Goltz, *Hindenburg: Power, Myth and the Rise of the Nazis* (Oxford: Oxford University Press, 2009).

6. Karl Dietrich Bracher, *The German Dictatorship* (New York: Praeger, 1970).

7. Bertram Schaffner, *Fatherland: A Study of Authoritarianism in the German Family* (New York: Columbia University Press, 1948); Leonard Krieger, *The German Idea of Freedom* (Chicago: University of Chicago Press, 1957).

8. For an excellent critique of this approach, see Richard Hamilton, "Some Difficulties with Cultural Explanations of National Socialism," in *Politics, Society and Democracy*, ed. H. E. Chehabi and Alfred Stephan (Boulder, CO: Westview Press, 1995), 197–216.

9. David Abraham, *The Collapse of the Weimar Republic: Political Economy and Crisis* (Princeton, NJ: Princeton University Press, 1981).

10. Brigitte Hamann, *Hitler's Vienna: A Dictator's Apprenticeship*, translated from the German by Thomas Thornton (New York: Oxford University Press, 1999).

11. Bracher, *The German Dictatorship*, 181.

12. Bracher, *The German Dictatorship*, 183.

13. Daniel Jonah Goldhagen, *Hitler's Willing Executioners: Ordinary Germans and the Holocaust* (New York: Knopf, 1996). See also David Bankier, *The Germans and the Final Solution: Public Opinion under Nazism* (Oxford, UK: Blackwell, 1992).

14. Frank Bajohr, *Arisierung in Hamburg*, cited in Götz Aly, "Der Holocaust," *Der Spiegel*, September 6, 1999, 76ff.

15. Götz Aly, "Der Holocaust."

16. Richard J. Evans, *The Third Reich in Power, 1933–1939* (New York: Penguin, 2006).

17. Bankier, *The Germans and the Final Solution*.

18. See Jörg Friedrich, *The Fire: The Bombing of Germany, 1940–1945*, trans. Allison Brown (New York: Columbia University Press, 2008); Anonymous, *A Woman in Berlin: Eight Weeks in the Conquered City*, trans. Philip Boehm (New York: Metropolitan Books, 2005).

19. East Germany had recognized the "peace border" with Poland already in 1950.

20. Alfred-Maurice de Zayas, *A Terrible Revenge: The Ethnic Cleansing of the East European Germans* (New York: Palgrave Macmillan, 2006).

21. In some urban areas in the Rhine-Ruhr region, daily food rations in the winter of 1946–1947 dropped to eight hundred calories per person. By the end of 1946, per capita industrial production had declined to the level of 1865. Günter J. Trittle, "Die westlichen Besatzungsmächte und der Kampf gegen den Mangel, 1945–1949," *Aus Politik und Zeitgeschichte*, May 31, 1986, 20–21.

22. *Der Spiegel* commentary cited in Karl-Heinz Janßen, "Das dauerhafte Provisorium," *Die Zeit*, May 24, 1974, 10.

23. Institut für Demoskopie, *Jahrbuch der öffentlichen Meinung*, 1947–1955, vol. 1 (Allensbach: Verlag für Demoskopie), 161.

24. An excellent overview of this period can be found in Michael H. Bernhard, *Institutions and the Fate of Democracy: Germany and Poland in the Twentieth Century* (Pittsburgh: University of Pittsburgh Press, 2005).

2

Eastern Germany before
and after Reunification

Neither of the two German states founded on the ruins of the Third Reich in 1949 was the result of an indigenous, grassroots movement.[1] As we discussed in chapter 1, the two postwar superpowers, the United States and the Soviet Union, installed models of their own political systems in their respective parts of Germany: a liberal democratic republic in the west and a communist dictatorship in the east. However, in the east, there was substantial opposition to communism. Millions of East Germans fled the country between 1949 and the building of the Berlin Wall in 1961; the remainder accommodated themselves to the regime in a variety of ways. A combination of internal police state repression, the presence of twenty-one Red Army divisions, and modest but steady improvements in the standard of living encouraged this accommodation. Thus, until 1989 there had never been a successful, much less peaceful, democratic revolution on German soil. Such an extraordinary development is the subject of this chapter. But before we examine the revolution and its aftermath, the unification process, we offer a brief review of the German Democratic Republic's forty-year history to provide the necessary background.

The German Democratic Republic (GDR) was from the time of its birth smaller and poorer than its cousin in the west. Its area of 41,700 square miles was less than half that of West Germany, and its population, which stabilized only after the construction of the Berlin Wall in 1961, was about one-fourth that of the Federal Republic. Bounded loosely by the Elbe River on the west, the Oder and Neisse rivers on the east, the Baltic Sea on the north, and the Czech Republic on the south, the GDR was also less urbanized and industrialized than the Federal Republic. Its northern regions were largely agricultural, and the south, although industrialized, could not match the prosperous and productive Rhine-Main and Ruhr regions in the west, especially since many of the most successful prewar eastern businesses relocated there after 1945.

Unlike the Federal Republic, East Germany did not benefit from the postwar Marshall Plan, which served as an important catalyst to economic reconstruction in Western Europe. Indeed, the Soviet occupiers dismantled substantial portions of East Germany's industrial base (factories, machines, and power plants) and shipped them to the Soviet Union as reparations for the destruction caused by Hitler's armies. Following the lead of the Soviet Union, the GDR, like other satellite states in Eastern Europe, sought to greatly reduce or eliminate the private economic sector. Much property and many businesses were seized or put under the "people's"—in actuality, the state's—control. Farmers were forced to put their land into large collective farms, which became dependent on the state for equipment and markets.

BUILDING SOCIALISM, 1949–1961

East Germany's forty-year history can be divided into four fairly distinct periods. During the first period, from 1949 until the construction of the Berlin Wall in 1961, the regime attempted to construct a socialist state and society modeled after the Soviet Union. By 1950 most opposition had been suppressed. Any independent noncommunists had either fled to the west, accepted communist control, or found themselves in prison. In 1950 alone the GDR courts, staffed with politically reliable judges and prosecutors, meted out more than 78,000 prison sentences in political trials. In some cases recalcitrant citizens were terrorized. In January 1950, Communist Party "shock troops" stormed the offices of the Christian Democrats in Saxony and forced the independent-minded party chairman to resign. The country was ostensibly governed by a "National Front" composed of the communists, officially the Socialist Unity Party, or SED, the product of a forced merger in 1946 between the communists and the Social Democrats, several "bloc" or satellite parties (the Christian Democrats, Liberals, National Democrats, and Democratic Farmers' Party), and the "mass organizations" (trade unions, youth, and women's groups).

Apart from the communists, none of these parties and organizations exercised any independent power. Their leaders and functionaries received special privileges—housing, automobiles, and luxury goods—in exchange for their cooperation. All worked in some form with either the East German (*Stasi*) or Soviet (KGB) secret police. The budgets of the bloc parties were heavily subsidized by the state. With these funds the parties maintained extensive staffs, newspapers, and even recreational facilities and hotels.

The Stasi

During this period, a crucial institution for the maintenance of the regime—the Ministry for State Security, or "*Stasi*"—was founded. Like its counterpart in the Soviet Union, the KGB, the Stasi considered itself the "sword and shield" of the party. With 90,000 full-time employees and up to 500,000 unofficial coworkers or "officers with special duties" (i.e., spies and informers), the Stasi sought to observe and control all areas of life. The Nazi *Gestapo*, by contrast, had 65,000 full-time employees in a much larger population. The central office in Berlin alone had a staff of 33,000; in the fifteen district offices the number of full-time employees ranged from 1,700 to almost 4,000. In addition, the Stasi had auxiliary units in most factories, military bases, universities, and even hospitals.[2]

The Stasi's operative principles, as summed up by one East German dissident group, presumed that (1) everyone is a potential security risk, (2) therefore everything possible must be known, and (3) security always takes precedence over the law.[3] Largely through information supplied by informants and through mail intercepts, wiretaps, and other electronic surveillance methods, the Stasi assembled files on more than six million citizens—almost two-thirds of the adult population. Even children as young as nine years of age were observed for the Stasi by their teachers and school principal if they expressed views critical of the communist system or favorable to the west. In addition, the agency was very active in West Germany and West Berlin. Following the collapse of the regime, almost two million dossiers on West Germans were discovered in Stasi offices. Other Stasi activities included the brutal interrogation and torture of prisoners, special internment camps for regime opponents, the attempted sabotage of West German nuclear power plants, the training of West German communists for paramilitary activities, and the support of international terrorists including West Germany's Red Army faction (see chapter 4). After the Soviet army, the Stasi was probably the most important instrument for the maintenance of the party dictatorship.[4]

The June 1953 Uprising

Following Stalin's death in 1953 the East German regime began its "New Course" program. The coercive activities of the secret police were somewhat reduced, more consumer goods were made available, and prices were stabilized. In June 1953 the hard-liners in the party leadership sought to push through an increase in work norms (quotas) for manual workers. The increases sparked demonstrations throughout the country, with the largest taking place in East Berlin. This was the first attempted revolt in the Soviet Union's postwar Eastern European empire; it would be followed by more extensive protests in Poland (1955), Hungary (1956), and Czechoslovakia (1968). Soviet tanks and troops quickly put down the uprising in the GDR. Without this intervention the regime very likely would have collapsed. Deploying its full arsenal of propaganda, the party denounced the revolt as a "fascist plot." Fourteen hundred people were arrested and sentenced to long prison terms.[5] In the aftermath of the affair, the regime dropped the increase in work norms. The Soviets also stopped the reparations program—that is, the systematic looting of the country.

Two years earlier, in 1951, the GDR embarked on its first Soviet-style five-year plan. Its goal was to double the 1936 level of production by 1955. Despite these efforts, the country's economy still lagged far behind West Germany. Well into the 1950s, meat, sugar, butter, and cooking oil were rationed. The second five-year plan (1956–1960) saw some improvement in living standards and a decrease in overt police coercion. Over 20,000 political prisoners were released. Rationing was eliminated in 1958, but the forced collectivization of agriculture, completed in 1960, produced severe shortages of meat, butter, and milk.

During this period, East Germans continued to flee the country. Between 1949 and 1961 over three million residents left, usually via West Berlin, which although located within the GDR's borders remained under Western (American, British, and French) control. A subway ride from East Berlin was all that was necessary. As a consequence of this drastic loss of people, the East German authorities, with the consent of the Soviet Union, did the unthinkable. In August 1961 they sealed off the borders between the two parts of Berlin, first with barbed wire and later with a large wall consisting of heavily reinforced concrete. In addition, the 850-mile border between East and West Germany was fortified with minefields and automatic firing devices. Border guards were ordered to shoot to kill any East Germans seeking to escape—and hundreds were killed between 1961 and 1989. Apart from diplomatic protests, the Western powers made no attempt to stop the building of the Wall or the fortification of the border. To the dismay of many Germans, none of Bonn's Western allies were willing to risk a possible nuclear conflict with the Soviet Union over Berlin. As long as the communists did not threaten West Berlin directly, the west would take no action.[6]

AFTER THE WALL—STABILITY AND CONSOLIDATION, 1961–1970

Shortly after the sealing of the borders, the party sought to make it easier for the East German population to reconcile itself with the system. A "New Economic System"—promising more consumer goods, greater independence for individual firms, and salaries and wages more related to performance—was announced. The system did lead to some improvements in living standards, such as better-quality goods and improved housing, but the GDR continued to fall further behind prosperous West Germany. "The Republic needs everybody and everybody needs the Republic," summarized the new line. In 1968 a new constitution and legal code with ostensibly greater protection for civil liberties and rights was also approved. The GDR's fabled sports program, which would lead to many Olympic medals in the 1970s and 1980s, was initiated during this period.

Most East Germans who remained behind after the Wall was erected made their own private peace with the system. Many accepted the terms of the regime's social contract: (1) a generally free, personal, private sphere; (2) a tolerable standard of living and consumption, especially when compared to that of other communist societies; (3) social security (a guaranteed job, cheap housing, free health care, and pensions); and (4) some social mobility. The regime, in turn, asked for (1) a readiness to work more or less diligently and (2) formal acceptance of party and state authority, with the tacit understanding that one could talk, in private, about the system more critically than in public. Authors called this the "niche society." As elsewhere in communist Eastern Europe, jokes against the regime proliferated in private: "We pretend to work and they pretend to pay us," or "What would happen if a desert became a socialist country? Nothing for a while, and then there would be a sand shortage."

After the building of the Wall, West German efforts to normalize relations with Eastern Europe and the Soviet Union put the GDR in a difficult position. The Federal Republic concluded a treaty in 1970 with the Soviet Union, the GDR's protector. In the pact the two countries pledged to respect each other's territory and to improve their economic, cultural, and political relations. But before the treaty could take force, West Germany, supported by its Western allies, insisted that Moscow and the three occupying powers conclude an agreement over West Berlin. West Germany wanted the city's independence and Bonn's access rights guaranteed by the Soviet Union. In 1971 the Berlin Quadripartite Agreement was completed; this in fact guaranteed western access to the city through the GDR and undercut East Germany's claim that it had to be involved in any decision affecting the city's future. The GDR leader at the time, Walter Ulbricht, had attempted to sabotage the entire process but thereby provoked Moscow's wrath. He was forced to resign as party and state chief in May 1971.

THE HONECKER ERA, 1971–1985

Erich Honecker had been the longtime head of the party's youth organization, the Free German Youth, and chief of the security apparatus. In 1961 he had assumed primary responsibility for the building of the Berlin Wall. Improved supplies of consumer goods, the development of an extensive welfare state, and increased contacts with the west characterized this period of GDR history. Honecker stressed that economic policy and social policy should be linked. That is, increases in industrial production should lead directly to improvements in living standards, especially wages, pensions, consumer goods, and housing. To finance many of these programs the GDR began to borrow heavily from Western Europe and, above all, from the Federal Republic. Honecker quickly discovered that in exchange for liberalizing his regime and allowing more of his citizens to visit the west, the Federal Republic would respond with increased economic and humanitarian aid.[7]

In 1972 a Treaty of Basic Relations was concluded between the two states, which constituted the de facto recognition of the GDR by West Germany. Prior to this treaty Bonn had insisted that it was the only legitimate German state and had refused to recognize East Germany or any other state that recognized it. The Basic Treaty abandoned this policy. Soon afterward, both German states were admitted to the United Nations, and East Germany assumed diplomatic relations with more than 150 states.

In 1975 the GDR participated in the Helsinki Conference on Peace and Security in Europe and became a signatory to the Helsinki Agreement on Human Rights. Over the next several years many GDR citizens, citing this document, submitted formal applications to leave the country. In certain cases involving personal or medical problems, these petitions were approved.

During the Honecker era the party achieved a *modus vivendi* (workable compromise) with the Protestant Church, the only major social institution not under the complete control of the party. Under the slogan "Not the Church against, nor the Church next to, but the Church in Socialism," the regime agreed to certain concessions, including increased support for the training of pastors and the maintenance of church property. The Protestants, in turn, agreed not to challenge the fundamental assumptions of the regime: one-party rule and a planned economy. Several small dissident groups were somewhat protected by the Church, but discrimination against Christians continued. Their employment prospects and access to higher education remained limited. Communist discrimination against religion has had a long-term impact on East German society, which today is one of the most secular in the world.

Honecker's efforts to improve the living conditions of East Germans sharply increased the country's foreign debt. But the GDR had a rich cousin, and throughout the early 1980s the GDR's dependence on West German aid increased. Several multibillion-dollar credit lines were negotiated, and Bonn secured favorable terms for East German exports to Western Europe. In 1984 a record 35,000 GDR residents were allowed to emigrate to the west. Visits by West Germans to the GDR also increased. The country's small opposition movement, consisting largely of Church-oriented peace and ecology activists, was closely watched by the secret police, and some of its leaders were arrested and deported to the west, but the movement was not eliminated. Nevertheless, over its entire history, the East German regime used coercion or the threat of coercion to maintain social control. The Stasi remained omnipresent. The arrest and imprisonment of alleged political opponents was a constant feature of the regime.

PERESTROIKA AND THE CRISIS OF THE REGIME, 1985–1989

During this period no Eastern European state feared the Soviet leader Mikhail Gorbachev's reform policies more than the German Democratic Republic. "Socialism" as practiced in the GDR—a one-party dictatorship with control of the economy and society—is what gave this state its identity and its reason for existence. If the GDR were to abandon this system, there could be no realistic alternative to unification with West Germany. The regime's attempts to create a separate "East" German identity had failed.[8] East Germans watched western television daily, wore western-style clothes if they could afford them, listened to western music, and from the 1980s onward traveled to the west in increasing numbers on short trips.

At first the party elite denied that Gorbachev's reforms had any relevance for the GDR: "Just because your neighbor puts up new wallpaper does not mean that you have to do so too" was the oft-quoted response of one GDR leader. However, the obstinacy of what reformers called the "cement heads" in the East German leadership was based on a very rational and realistic calculation of their interests. Without socialism, without the Wall and the sealed borders, there would be no GDR. They were correct.

Honecker attempted to deflect criticism of his opposition to *perestroika* (restructuring) by further improving economic conditions (again largely with West German aid), increasing cultural ties with the Federal Republic, and allowing more and more East Germans to visit the west. In 1987, just two years before the collapse of his state, Honecker himself became the first GDR leader to step onto West German soil.[9] The visit, which the Kohl government after 1989 regretted, represented at the time the culmination of fifteen years of improved relations. In 1987 a million East Germans under the pension age were allowed to visit the Federal Republic—up from only 50,000 in 1985. The regime also announced a general amnesty for thousands of political and other prisoners, and

East Germany became the first communist state to abolish the death penalty. In 1988 the GDR for the first time acknowledged its responsibility to Jewish victims of the Holocaust and announced a special program of reparations, as well as the partial reconstruction of the prominent Oranienburger Strasse Synagogue in East Berlin.

Encouraged by changes in the Soviet Union, the GDR's fledgling human rights, environmental, and peace groups increased their activity. The regime reacted at times with mass arrests, but on other occasions such dissident activity was tolerated. In January 1988, demonstrators at the celebration of the seventieth anniversary of the death of the founders of the German Communist Party, Rosa Luxemburg and Karl Liebknecht, were arrested, jailed, or expelled to West Germany. A few months later in a meeting with the leader of the Protestant Church, Honecker apologized for the incident, claiming that he had not been properly informed. The regime's policy of allowing its citizens to visit the Federal Republic continued, and by 1988 East Germans had made more than five million trips to the west. Yet the shoot-to-kill order remained in effect for citizens attempting to flee. In February 1989 a young East German was shot and killed at the Wall. He was the last victim of the communist system.[10]

In spite of various forms of West German aid, the economy and the supply of consumer goods continued to worsen. But the party leadership rejected any dialogue with the growing opposition. Honecker defiantly declared that the Wall would stand for another fifty or one hundred years. Meanwhile, church leaders and some officials of the satellite parties began to criticize the regime publicly and call for change.

THE COLLAPSE OF COMMUNISM

Although developments in the Soviet Union—specifically the reforms undertaken by Soviet president Gorbachev—were fundamental to the collapse of communist regimes in Eastern Europe, the chain of immediate events that led to East Germany's revolution in 1989 started in May when Hungary began to dismantle its fortified border with Austria. By midsummer some East Germans ostensibly vacationing in Hungary discovered that they could cross unhindered into Austria and then, of course, on into West Germany. When in August the Hungarian authorities stopped GDR citizens from crossing, several hundred East Germans took refuge in West Germany's embassy in Budapest. A few days later they were transported to the west under the auspices of the International Red Cross.

At a pan-European festival celebrating the opening of the Austro-Hungarian border on August 19, 1989, almost seven hundred GDR residents crashed the party and raced over the boundary. The Great Escape had begun. By the end of the month, more than 4,000 had fled through Hungary and an additional 2,000 East Germans still in the country were seeking permission to leave for the west.

Czechoslovakia became the next escape hatch. In early September approximately one hundred East Germans "vacationing" there were allowed to leave. Then on September 10, 1989, in a critical decision, the government of Hungary suspended a 1969 treaty with the GDR under which it had agreed not to allow

East Germans to cross its borders. Hungary declared its western borders open to all.[11] By the end of the month almost 25,000 East Germans had left via this route. The GDR now attempted to close this exit by suspending the issuance of travel permits to Hungary. The action prompted a renewed stream of refugees into Czechoslovakia and also Poland.

With its fortieth anniversary celebration and a visit by Gorbachev just a week away, the Honecker regime on September 30, 1989, announced that the 6,000 GDR refugees camped around West Germany's embassies in Prague and Warsaw could leave for the west after they were "expelled" from the GDR. Meanwhile, the wave of refugees from Hungary continued, and by the end of October an additional 24,000 had found their way to the west.

Then, just five days after 6,000 refugees left Prague, an additional 7,600 appeared at the West German embassy in the city. They, too, were allowed to leave after traveling by train briefly through East Germany so that they could be "expelled." At train stations in Leipzig and Dresden, police and secret police agents used clubs and tear gas to stop other East Germans from jumping on the "freedom trains." In the first few days following the opening of the Czech border, more than 10,000 additional East Germans fled.

Emboldened by the regime's inability to stop the mass exodus, dissident groups began to organize in the GDR. In mid-September the "New Forum" became the first formal opposition group to apply to the government for official recognition; it had already set up organizations in eleven of the GDR's fifteen government districts. Soon thereafter the government declared the group to be "antistate" and rejected its application. Ignoring the ban, the New Forum held its first congress in Leipzig on September 24.[12] It proclaimed itself the umbrella organization for all dissident groups in the country. Numerous other opposition groups and parties, including an East German version of the Social Democrats, were also founded throughout September and October.

The growing opposition movement and the Protestant Church urged East Germans to take to the streets in peaceful demonstrations. The largest center of opposition was in Leipzig, where the weekly Monday-evening "peace prayer vigil" at the Nicholas Church was followed by marches around the center of the city. The Monday demonstrations spread to other cities, and by early October hundreds of thousands of East Germans throughout the country filled the streets chanting "Wir sind das Volk!" (We are the people!) and "Wir bleiben hier!" (We're staying here!). For the first time in German history a peaceful, grassroots democratic revolution was under way.

On October 7, 1989, the regime's fortieth anniversary celebrations were overshadowed by massive opposition demonstrations in East Berlin and other major cities. Denounced as "rowdies" by the party and official media, demonstrators met with violence from police and security forces who attempted to suppress the protests. Gorbachev told Honecker that the time for reform had come, citing a Russian proverb: "Life punishes those who arrive too late." His warning fell on deaf ears.

Ten days after the anniversary, Honecker resigned under heavy criticism from all sides, including his own party, the SED. His successor, Egon Krenz, was forced by the pressure of the demonstrations to retreat quickly from prior positions and grant increasing concessions to the opposition. On November 1, Krenz continued to defend some of the policies of the Honecker regime. One week later he placed all the blame for the upheaval on the ailing former leader. Upon taking office, Krenz emphasized that the Socialist Unity Party would not under any circumstances give up its leading role, enshrined in Article 1 of the constitution. A few weeks later, he conceded that the party would have to give up its privileged constitutional position. The SED's policy on the participation of the new opposition groups (for example, the New Forum and Democratic Breakthrough) also changed from rejection to acceptance. Opposition within the Communist Party to its own leadership further weakened the regime. Many party members supported the new opposition groups; between October and December 1989, more than one million members left the SED. Given this division within the party and Gorbachev's refusal to allow Soviet troops to intervene, it was impossible for party diehards to make any last stand against the revolution. Clearly on the defensive, the party leadership began seeking some credibility among the mass of the population.

The dictatorship that could only exist by walling in its citizens collapsed when its wall went down. On November 9, 1989, in a desperate attempt to save the regime, the country's borders with the west, including the Berlin Wall, were opened.[13] As the world watched, millions of East Germans flooded into West Berlin and West Germany. But it was too little, too late for the communists. The more the regime conceded, the more East Germans demanded. They wanted freedom and prosperity as soon as possible. Both appeared to be available through unification with West Germany. The demonstrators' chant of "We are the people!" began to be replaced by the slogan, "We are *one* people!"

THE UNIFICATION PROCESS

The West German Response

Bonn was ill prepared for the collapse of the East German regime. Prior to the opening of the Wall, there was no committee or department of the government working on any plans for unification. Few believed that unification would take place quickly, especially in view of East Germany's ties to the Soviet Union. Clearly, the key to unification lay in Moscow. German leaders were also aware that the country's western neighbors were somewhat anxious about what unification would mean for the European Community and for its neighbors in Eastern Europe. Finally, there was the (largely unspoken) fear that a unified Germany might once again seek to dominate Europe.

While not denying these problems, West Germany had to move quickly. By the end of 1989 the East German state was on the verge of collapse. Noncommunist and opposition groups were brought into the government, but the flow of Germans from East to West did not abate with the opening of the borders or with the liberalization of the regime. Clearly, the continuation of these trends would have been a demographic and economic disaster for both states.

In late November the government of Chancellor Helmut Kohl (1982–1998) attempted to gain control over the process (see chapter 7). In parliament, Kohl announced a ten-point program that envisaged a package of treaties between the two states, leading in four or five years to "confederal structures," then to a confederation (*Staatenbund*), and, finally, to a federation (*Bundesstaat*) between them. The entire process would take approximately ten years, and the two states would remain equal partners throughout the process. The proposal drew widespread support, including from the political opposition in the west; but some of the Federal Republic's allies thought the chancellor was moving too fast and had failed to adequately consult them before announcing the plan.

The East German Opposition

The small, marginal groups of political activists who sparked the revolution and brought down the communist regime did not want rapid unification with West Germany. In spite of differences over policies and ideologies, this indigenous GDR opposition shared some common characteristics. First, they held a strong belief in *nonviolence;* the tactics of nonviolence as developed in the West European peace movement and the civil rights movement in the United States had strongly influenced their thinking. Second, they were largely antipolitical or apolitical in their thinking. According to one authority, "These groups were oriented to issues of *Kultur* (culture) and society rather than of power."[14] They had little experience in the give-and-take of democratic politics and were hence ill equipped to assume political responsibility when the communist regime collapsed. Third, the opposition *lacked leadership.* There was no East German Lech Walesa as in Poland or Vaclav Havel in Czechoslovakia. The communist regime's practice of isolating dissidents through imprisonment or deportation had hindered the development of any significant leadership. Fourth, the opposition was fragmented by *conflicting goals and personalities.* Some groups wanted to emphasize a renewal of socialism, while others concentrated on environmental problems. Fifth, most opposition figures belonged to what East Germans termed the *intelligentsia,* the relatively large number of artists, writers, dramatists, academics, and pastors whom the regime subsidized. Many of these intellectuals had built their own "self-contained" counterculture. Few if any of their ideas had ever been tested in public debate.

Despite differing characteristics, the opposition groups did have a general agenda.

1. They wanted a humane, socialist East Germany. For the opposition, socialism as an ideal had not failed because it had not been given a chance. The opposition also argued that there were aspects of East Germany worth preserving: low rents, full employment, free health care, cheap public transportation, and extensive day-care programs. The opposition thus sought a third way between capitalism and socialism, a goal other intellectuals in Eastern Europe—especially in Poland and Hungary—had sought but not found during the 1960s and 1970s.
2. The opposition agreed that the new East Germany would have to be a democratic system with direct citizen participation, a multiparty system, abolition of the secret police, the rule of law, and drastic reductions in

military spending. The GDR opposition also wanted democratically controlled economic structures, although its leaders never made clear what they meant by this term. As Daniel Hamilton has pointed out, "A feature common to all groups was a lack of economists, businessmen, or people with economic experience in government, which proved to be a severe handicap to the opposition once the Communist-dominated government collapsed."[15]

3. The opposition agreed on the necessity of maintaining a separate East German state as an alternative to the Federal Republic. Some actually proposed that the Wall be kept up a while longer to enable the new state to mobilize some popular support.

The great majority of East Germans, however, were not impressed by this idealistic vision of the opposition. With the breaching of the Wall and the opening of the borders, the "common people" of the GDR could see for themselves how they had been deceived by their own media, schools, and intellectuals. The decay of East German cities; the life-threatening water, air, and ground pollution; the low productivity of most businesses; the inadequate health care system; the impoverished state of many elderly people; and the cynical disregard for human rights exhibited by the hated Stasi and party *Bonzen* (bosses) convinced most East Germans that little if anything about the GDR was worth preserving. For better or worse, the average East German in early 1990 finally wanted his or her share of the good life, West German style, as soon as possible: bananas year round, a western automobile, a VCR, CD players, trips to Paris and London and Rome, and western clothes and appliances. One worker in Leipzig said to great applause, "I have worked hard for 40 years, paid the rent on time, am still with my wife, I haven't seen the world, and my city is decaying. I won't allow myself to become a guinea pig again."[16]

In spite of their courage and idealism, the native East German revolutionaries had little to offer this population beyond their hopes for some vaguely defined "third way" between capitalism and socialism. This was difficult to maintain in the face of West Germany's "social market economy" with its extensive, redistributive welfare state. These opposition groups were unable to fill the vacuum that was created once the communist regime fell. Revolutionaries who had lived on the margins of East German society now had to become campaign managers and political operatives within weeks. They were not up to the task. So the vacuum was ultimately filled by the West German parties, with their well-organized campaign staffs, media-savvy elites, and promises of prosperity and integration with the west. Their success, however, was based on solid support among East Germans. By early 1990 over 90 percent of the adult population in the GDR supported unification.[17] East Germany's indigenous revolutionaries were once again a small minority.

In a variety of polls conducted between November 1989 and September 1990, the great majority of West Germans (75 to 80 percent) also supported unification. Opposition was centered among those West Germans who were wary of the costs involved, or who felt that the whole process was going too fast and disregarded the interests and feelings of East Germans. But this high level of West German support was conditional upon the Federal Republic's remaining in the European Community and NATO. In a June 1990 survey, the proportion of Germans favoring unification dropped from 77 percent to only 21 percent when the respondents were asked if they would support unity "if it meant leaving NATO and the European Community."[18]

The Soviet Factor

Following the opening of the Berlin Wall, the Soviet Union steadily backed down from its opposition to a united Germany within the Atlantic Alliance. Less than a week after the opening of the Wall, Gorbachev declared that German unification was not on the agenda in any form. A few weeks later Moscow announced that it could accept a unified but demilitarized and neutral Germany. When this was rejected by West Germany, Gorbachev in early 1990 proposed that Germany remain in both NATO and the Warsaw Pact for a transitional period. This proposal also received no support from Bonn or its Western allies, especially the United States. The West German counteroffer, however, did attempt to deal with Moscow's major security concerns by proposing to reduce the size of the army and not allow NATO forces or its nuclear weapons to be stationed on the territory of the former East Germany.

East Germany's fate was decided between December 19, 1989, when Kohl went to Dresden to meet with the GDR's prime minister, Hans Modrow (who had succeeded Egon Krenz two weeks earlier), and February 13, 1990, when Modrow returned the visit. In the interim Kohl and Foreign Minister Hans-Dietrich Genscher had met with Gorbachev in Moscow. At that meeting the Soviet leader assured them that the Soviet Union would not stand in the way of German unification.

Kohl was surprised by the hundreds of thousands of cheering East Germans who greeted him in Dresden with calls for unity. That experience, he later reported, convinced him that unification would and should come quickly.[19] The Modrow government had little legitimacy. A "Round Table" in East Berlin, composed of representatives of the various opposition groups and the old National Front, became the de facto government. Free elections, scheduled for May 1990, were moved up to March. The economy continued to deteriorate, and thousands of East Germans left for the west each day. In Bonn, Modrow asked for an emergency grant of about $7 billion to shore up his regime. Kohl refused any expenditure of this magnitude, contending that the GDR's socialist economy and bloated bureaucracy would waste the money. Aid would come only after a freely elected government changed to a market economy. A disappointed Modrow returned to East Berlin empty-handed.[20]

The March 18, 1990, parliamentary election, the first and last free election in the GDR's history, confirmed that the great majority of citizens wanted unification as soon as possible. The surprise winner was the "Alliance for Germany," a coalition of center-right groups, including the Christian Democrats, the one-time puppet party in the National Front. The Alliance had been hastily assembled by Chancellor Kohl as a forum for his appearances in the GDR. The Alliance, together with the Free Democrats and the Social Democrats, received over three-fourths of the vote.[21] These parties formed a Grand Coalition that governed until unification in October 1990.

The last remaining international obstacle to unification was removed when President Gorbachev announced after a two-day meeting with Chancellor Kohl in mid-July 1990 that a unified Germany would be fully sovereign and free to join whatever alliance it desired. In exchange, Germany agreed to reduce its total troop strength to 370,000 from the then-combined level of 640,000, as well as to complete a major treaty with the Soviet Union addressing all aspects of their relationship—political, military, cultural, and scientific. The treaty, ratified in 1991, regulated the withdrawal of 385,000 Soviet troops from East Germany, a process that was completed on schedule in 1994. In addition, the Federal Republic agreed to provide more than $30 billion in economic and technical aid to the USSR.

Legal and Constitutional Dimensions of the Unification Process

Also in July 1990 the West German deutsche mark became the sole currency for both states, and their economic and social welfare systems were merged. A few weeks later a second unification treaty was concluded that regulated most, but not all, of the remaining issues between the two states. East Germany, reorganized into five states (Länder), entered the Federal Republic according to Article 23 of the West German Constitution, which allows new states to join the federation.

Unification took place largely on West German terms. Few if any of the "social achievements" of the GDR, such as cheap, subsidized housing, full employment, and the extensive system of child- and day-care facilities, were carried over into the enlarged Federal Republic. However, there were two issues that the two states could not resolve—the abortion question and the problem of the Stasi files. In East Germany abortion had been allowed on demand during the first trimester of pregnancy. Since 1972, in West Germany a woman has been required to prove that a "social" emergency—that is, poverty, medical, or other problem, such as a pregnancy due to rape—exists before an abortion could be performed in the first trimester.[22] The certification of such an emergency had to be obtained from a family planning service approved by the government. A different physician from the one certifying the emergency then carried out the abortion.

The great majority of easterners wanted to retain the former GDR's liberal law, and the issue threatened to delay the completion of the unification process. Finally, the question was resolved by passing it on to parliament. According to the treaty, a unified law had to be passed by December 1992. In the meantime, each part of the country retained its own law, and women from the west who traveled to the former east could avail themselves of the East German law without penalty. In June 1992 the parliament passed a new law that was similar to the pro-choice East German law. A year later, however, the Constitutional Court (see chapter 8 for a description of this institution) declared the new law unconstitutional. In 1995 still another law was passed that allows abortions during the first trimester but requires the woman to visit a counseling center before the procedure can take place. The counseling must be oriented to the "protection of unborn life." The courts have upheld this law.

The question of what to do with the millions of files collected by the secret police (Stasi) also remained a source of division between the two regions. The West Germans, less affected by the files than the East Germans, wanted them transferred to the Federal Archives in Koblenz (West Germany), with limited public access. As in the case of abortion, the issue was resolved or postponed by assigning it to the all-German parliament. The documents remained in Berlin under the supervision of a special commissioner responsible to parliament. East Germans wanted these materials to be the special responsibility of the five new states.

In November 1991, parliament passed new legislation that allows citizens to examine their files and identify those individuals who were spying on them. The opening of the files yielded new information about the extent of secret police activity in the former GDR and led to further resignations of party and government officials. The president of Humboldt University in the former East Berlin, the chairman of the Party of Democratic Socialism (PDS), as well as the minister-president of Brandenburg were all under investigation because of documents found in the Stasi archives. Critics of the new law claimed it unleashed a witch hunt that would ultimately do more harm than good to the development of democratic values in the former GDR.

By 2004 more than two million Germans had gained access to their files, and the Gauck Office, as it was commonly called, had conducted background checks on over 750,000 East Germans. Joachim Gauck, the current federal president (see chapter 7) was the first director of the office until 2000. But public support for the work of the Gauck Office among easterners has waned: between 1991 and 2006 the proportion that wanted to "wrap up" the last forty years, by drawing a final line under communism, increased from 36 percent to 78 percent. Thus by 2006 only about 20 percent of easterners wanted the office to continue its investigative work.[23]

UNIFICATION: A BRIEF ANALYSIS

Why did this entire process occur so rapidly, yet so peacefully? Certainly the West German government must be given high marks for seizing the initiative and completing the process before East Germany collapsed and a mass exodus westward could begin. The attempted coup in the Soviet Union in August 1991 and the subsequent decline of Gorbachev's influence supported the German decision to move quickly on the unification issue. Internationally, of course, the key to unification rested in Moscow and specifically in the hands of Gorbachev and his foreign minister. As Robert Gerald Livingston has observed, both men "had the sense to see that outsiders could not halt unification, the audacity to change Soviet policies totally, and the skill to gain substantial concessions for what by any measure is the greatest setback for the Soviet Union since Hitler's invasion a half century ago."[24] Moreover, Germany's Western allies, above all the United States, were generally cooperative and supportive throughout the entire operation. The initial lack of enthusiasm about unification demonstrated by British prime minister Margaret Thatcher and French president François Mitterrand did not delay or hinder the course of events.

West Germany's economic wealth and power was another important factor in the unification process. International support for unification was smoothed by a steady flow of deutsche marks to Germany's allies and neighbors in Eastern and Western Europe and the United States. Germany's "higher than expected" financial support for the Gulf War in 1990–1991 was in part an expression of the Kohl government's appreciation for the strong support of the first Bush administration during the unification process.[25] In return for its consent to unification and Germany's continuing membership in NATO, the Soviet Union and its successors received over $44 billion from 1990 to 1995. In essence, the Soviets were "bribed out" and NATO was moved into the former East Germany and eventually Eastern Europe.[26] The crucial negotiations in which Gorbachev agreed that a reunified Germany could stay in NATO happened without Washington's input at Gorbachev's retreat in the Caucasus in the summer of 1990. French apprehensions about unification were eased by Kohl's promise to introduce a common European currency by the end of the decade. Earlier in the process smaller players such as Hungary, which opened its borders to Austria in September 1989, received generous loan and aid packages from Bonn.

Finally, through their peaceful, "gentle" revolution, the East Germans made the prospect of a unified Germany less disturbing to all of Germany's neighbors. Because so many of the East German "successes" did not find their way into the final unification treaties, and because the courageous East German opposition once again found itself on the margins of political life, many observers have asked what exactly the East Germans contributed to unity—what they "brought" into unified Germany. The answer, of course, is that they brought themselves. Without their willingness to challenge the Stasi state, to put their lives on the line when certain party hard-liners were urging a "Chinese solution" to the unrest, the unification process would never have proceeded as smoothly as it did.

THE AFTERMATH OF UNIFICATION

For the rest of the world the German revolution of 1989–1990 ended on October 3, 1990, when the former German Democratic Republic ceased to exist and, reconstituted into five Länder, merged with the Federal Republic. For the new citizens of the unified state and, indirectly, the old as well, the revolution continued. In the east, unification has meant unemployment; anxiety about possible unemployment; rising rents; restructured schools, colleges, and universities; countless new forms to be filled out; social isolation; depopulation; and rising crime rates.[27] There was not a single revolution in the fall of 1989, but the beginning of 16 million individual revolutions. With West Germany supplying most of the resources, the former East Germany was fast-forwarded through the period from 1949 to 1989. The west is also paying for much of this change. Westerners' empathy and sympathy, however, proved to have limits.

In this section we will briefly review the first twenty-three years of the unification process. We will focus on the economic, environmental, and psychological dimensions of putting Germany back together again.

The Economy

By the standards prevalent in Eastern Europe and the Soviet Union, the East German economy was a model of efficiency. The GDR's industrial products such as Trabant and Wartburg automobiles, Ruhla watches, and Praktica cameras were widely distributed throughout the communist world. The shipbuilding and railroad car industry produced largely for the huge Soviet market, and there was never a shortage of demand. Admittedly outmoded in construction and design and often inferior in quality, East German industrial products were affordable and did not require hard currency to purchase.

This changed suddenly after unification and the collapse of communism. Now the purchase of goods from the eastern region required hard currency, which people in the former communist countries rarely had. Moreover, even if potential eastern customers had the currency, they now preferred western goods that were of much better quality and usually even less expensive than eastern products. Thus, the GDR's industrial economy went into an unprecedented tailspin between the currency union of July 1, 1990, and mid-1992. Approximately 60 percent of the country's industrial plants shut down. Out of a workforce at the time of reunification of more than 9 million men and women, only 6.2 million still had jobs in 1992.

Following a 30 percent decline in gross domestic product (GDP) in 1990 and 1991, the economy in the new states began to grow rapidly. As figure 2.1 shows, growth rates in the east between 1991 and 1996 were far higher than similar rates in the west. Annual net growth during this period in the east averaged almost 8 percent, as compared to less than 2 percent in the west. Much of this growth was the result of sharp increases in construction (particularly in the public sector) and the service industries (banking, insurance, and retail sales). But after 1997 the growth rates in the east slowed dramatically and in most years have lagged behind western levels. This means that the economic gap between the two regions has actually become somewhat larger over the last fifteen years. A decline in construction activity and a lack of export-oriented economic enterprises in the new states are the primary factors in the relative slowdown. But the sluggish national economy until the mid-2000s also hindered growth in the east.

Although the situation is more encouraging today, the economy of the former East Germany still lags behind the west. Three chronic problems have dominated: (1) persistently high unemployment levels of about 16 to 19 percent—although down to between 9 and 13 percent after 2011; (2) the lack of a diverse industrial base; and (3) the continued out-migration of younger, well-trained, and largely female easterners to the west.

Poor employment prospects at home and the promise of jobs and high wages in the western states have prompted a significant out-migration and population

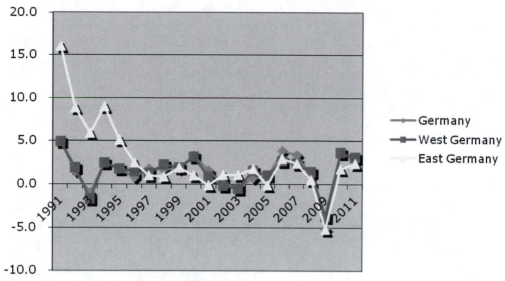

Figure 2.1.   Economic growth in East and West Germany, 1991–2007 (percent increase in gross domestic product adjusted for inflation). For 1991–2007, Deutsches Institut für Wirtschaft (DIW); for 2008–2011, http://www.vgrdl.de/Arbeitskreis_VGR/ergebnisse .asp?lang = de-DE#LA-GDP.

decline in the eastern regions. Between 1990 and 2010 the population in the former GDR (excluding Berlin) dropped from approximately 15 million to under 13 million, a reduction of about 15 percent. During this period, deaths exceeded births by 779,000, and between 1991 and 2008 net migration resulted in a further drop of 1.1 million. Those leaving tended to be younger, well educated, and female. Between 1991 and 2005, for example, 400,000 females under thirty left the region as compared to 273,000 men. This loss of human capital in the eastern states has had a negative impact on economic development. About 20 percent of new jobs in this region requiring advanced educational qualifications have gone unfilled.

Under these circumstances, assistance from the west has been crucial. For example, there has been a staggering amount of infrastructure investment. By 1995 the former East Germany was the largest rail construction site in the world. The "Germany Unity" transportation plan involves seventeen railroad, Auto-bahn, and waterway construction projects at a total cost by 2012 of almost $50 billion.[28] With most of these projects completed, the eastern region has one of the most modern and efficient transportation systems in the world. The largest single infrastructure investment was for the telephone system, which involved the installation of almost six million telephone lines, completed in 1998 at a cost of more than $27 billion; the eastern region now has a phone system that is actually technologically superior to that of West Germany.[29] Connecting East Germany to the European natural gas supply system has cost another $7 billion. The work was completed in June 1995, more than four years ahead of schedule.

Who has paid for all of this investment? The bulk of it has come from the West German taxpayer. By 2010 the net cost of the 1990 unification to westerners had grown to more than $2 trillion. This amounts to about $29,000 for every man, woman, and child in the west. Every easterner in the first sixteen years of unification has received western transfers amounting to almost $100,000.[30] Indeed, rarely in history has there been such a massive transfer of resources. West-to-East transfers as a percentage of western GDP have averaged about 4.5 percent since 1990. Thus, to finance these transfers without reducing the western standard of living would require growth levels in the west equal to or greater than the transfer payments. In over twenty years since reunification, this has rarely happened.

In addition to investment funds, many of these transfers have been grants to finance state and local governments in the east, as well as to supplement the social security system (unemployment payments, pensions, and health care).[31] Approximately half of the transfers have been financed through increased taxes, and the other half has been borrowed.[32] The taxes included a 7.5 percent "solidarity surtax" levied on income and corporate taxes from 1991 until 1992, and then reinstated in January 1995. After 1998, the rate was lowered to 5.5 percent, and the tax is expected to expire in 2019. Few other taxes have been as resented by westerners. Fuel oil and gasoline taxes were increased by 63 percent between 1991 and 1994. Between 1991 and 1995, taxes on insurance policies increased from 7 percent to 15 percent. Since 1991 the financial burden on western households caused by these transfers has totaled over $230 billion. By 1999, unification was costing the average German household about $225 per month in increased taxes and social insurance contributions. Moreover, the burden has been distributed proportionately across all income groups; that is, the upper income groups have not been paying more for unification than the lower income groups.[33]

The large sum of transfers, the generous tax breaks for investors in eastern projects, and the pressures to produce an economic upturn led in some cases to waste and inefficiency in the expenditure of these funds. Generous tax write-offs, for example, yielded a glut of rental apartments and office buildings in the new states. In 1995 approximately $147 billion was invested in the east, with roughly 25 percent of this amount spent on the construction of rental apartments. Some eastern cities now have twice as much retail store space as do their western counterparts. Investors who finance such projects could deduct 25 to 50 percent of the construction costs from their taxable income. Thus, a $240,000 investment could yield a net tax savings of almost $70,000 for those in the top tax bracket. Furthermore, the fragile administrative structures in many eastern regions have also led to poor investment decisions for projects such as wastewater and sewage treatment facilities.

The massive investments and transfers, however, have also paid dividends for many easterners. By 2008 the monthly income of the average eastern household amounted to about 75 percent of the western level, an almost 50 percent gain since unification.[34] However, substantial regional differences remain. In 2011, per capita buying power in Hamburg (Germany's richest city) is approximately 75 percent greater than in the poorest eastern state, Saxony-Anhalt.[35]

The largest group of unification winners in the east has been the pensioners. From 1991 to 1998 the average pension for East German males increased from 47 percent of the western level to 103 percent. The corresponding proportions for female pensioners were 80 percent and 135 percent. By 2008, eastern males were receiving 98 percent of the western level, but eastern women were getting 132 percent.[36] These gains were in part the result of the longer employment history for easterners. On average, males in the east worked six years longer than their western counterparts; eastern females worked on average nine years longer. Since the pension payment is based in large part on the number of years worked, rather than the gross amount of contributions, easterners benefited disproportionally. An additional factor in the eastern pensions was the higher inflation levels and hence higher cost-of-living increases in the eastern region in the early years of unification. Even in 2012, the cost-of-living increase was slightly higher in the east than in the west. Financially, these pensioners have profited more from unification than those eastern workers who kept their jobs or found new employment.

This development also illustrates some of the problems of the unification process and the integration of easterners into the country's comprehensive and generous welfare state. A system that rewards pensioners more than those who are working can hardly be viable in the long run, one of the reasons for pension reform in recent years (see chapter 8).[37] Most of the west–east transfers since 1990 have indeed been spent on consumption rather than investment. The second stage of the major transfer program, Solidarity Pact II, which began in 2005 and will run until 2019, however, is focused on investments in infrastructure and the development of new technologies.

As figure 2.2 shows, worker productivity in the east has increased from only 35 percent of that in the west in 1991 to almost 80 percent in 2010, where it has stagnated for several years.[38] Wage levels have also risen sharply. By 2011 the average eastern worker was also earning roughly 83 percent as much as his or her western counterpart.[39] In some white-collar positions such as accounting, sales, and marketing, parity in salaries has almost been achieved.[40] Nevertheless, eastern wages in some areas such as manufacturing and construction are still higher than eastern productivity—which means that these easterners are being paid more than they produce. Unit labor costs in the east have declined from 141 percent of the western level in 1991 to 107 percent in 2005 (see figure 2.2). By 2008, they were 73 percent of the western level per hour worked.[41] Despite this overall improvement, lower productivity still makes eastern goods relatively expensive to produce. These persistent problems have not helped to resolve the east's biggest economic problem: unemployment.

Before unification there were approximately 9.2 million jobs in East Germany. By 1992 the figure had dropped to 6.2 million, where it has since stabilized. What happened to the 3 million lost jobs and—more important—the people who filled them? In 2006 roughly 1.3 million were officially unemployed and drew benefits (heavily subsidized by westerners) from the unemployment insurance system, or welfare. Another 900,000 took some form of early retirement, which was offered to workers as young as fifty years of age. Around 300,000 to 400,000 easterners, or 5 to 7 percent of the workforce, commuted to the west. The

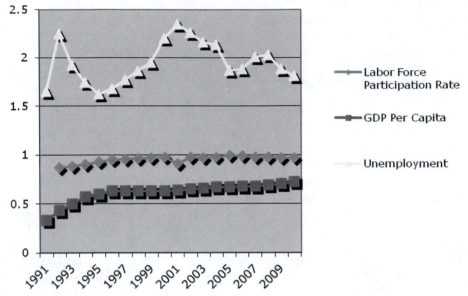

Figure 2.2.   The economic catch-up process in the former East Germany, 1991–2011; Eastern German indicators as a proportion of Western German indicators (Western Germany = 1).

Source: http://www.spiegel.de/fotostrecke/ost-vs-west-so-steht-es-um-die-wirtschaft-fotostrecke-48649-2.html; http://statistik .arbeitsagentur.de/Navigation/Statistik/Statistik-nach-Regionen/Politische-Gebietsstruktur/Ost-West/Ost-Nav.html?year_ month = 201208.

remaining 200,000 were in government-subsidized retraining programs, are working in part-time positions, or have moved permanently to the west. Thus, through a variety of programs, usually involving government subsidies, the number of officially unemployed stagnated at around 17 percent of the workforce for most of the post-reunification period.

The last few years have seen substantial improvement, and the current economic situation is probably the best since reunification. There were 650,000 unemployed in July 2012 and an additional 885,000 underemployed. The regional unemployment rate was thus just under 10 percent, and the underemployment rate was 13.2 percent.[42] These gains may be fragile, and it is unclear if this better performance will continue in light of economic uncertainties. Secure jobs for easterners will only come when the economy is self-sustaining—that is, no longer dependent on western aid. Moreover, one of the most commonly cited weaknesses in eastern Germany—a lack of corporate headquarters—needs to be overcome.[43] Here, too, Eastern Germans have made some progress. Western subsidies as a percentage of eastern GDP have dropped from 51 percent in 1991 to about 27 percent by 2010.[44] Thus, easterners now produce almost 75 percent of what they consume as compared to less than half in 1991.

All of this leads to a clear conclusion. By 2013, after more than twenty-two years of reunification and the transfer of over $2 trillion from West to East, the economic convergence of the two regions as measured by per capita income, labor productivity, capital investment, and hourly wages was about 80 percent complete. Thus, the glass is not half full, but 80 percent full. That 20 percent, or "last mile," as the German economist Michael C. Burda put it, will take longer.[45] Nonetheless there are several reasons for optimism. The eastern states are well positioned to benefit from the rapidly growing markets in Eastern Europe, especially Poland, the Czech Republic, and Russia. Second, the eastern labor market has become more flexible and efficient as a result of the difficult transformation from a planned economy to a market economy. Third, the investments in the universities and research institutes in the eastern states are beginning to bear fruit. New start-up companies led by young, eastern entrepreneurs are beginning to make their mark. "Silicon Saxony," for instance, is finally producing some self-sustaining growth.[46] And in 2011, an eastern German Land, Saxony, actually increased its population.

The Environment

The German Democratic Republic was an environmental disaster area. Water, ground, and air pollution levels were among the highest in Europe. Since unification, the closing down of many of the worst industrial polluters, largely for economic reasons, and extensive western-financed cleanup projects have produced substantial improvement in air and water quality.

In 1991 only 3 percent of the former East Germany's rivers and streams were ecologically intact, and only 1 percent of the region's lakes were free from pollution. Almost 80 percent of the rivers, streams, and lakes were either biologically dead or heavily polluted.[47] The most important river in the east, the Elbe, which flows from the Czech Republic through Germany before emptying into the North Sea, was one of the most polluted rivers in Europe.

In terms of air pollution, in the Leipzig area, autumn and winter were virtually nonstop smog seasons. In the notorious industrial city of Bitterfeld, thirty miles north of Leipzig, children suffered from respiratory diseases at a rate two to three times greater than elsewhere in the former eastern state. The major cause of air pollution in this area was the brown coal, or lignite, used in heating, power plants, and the chemical industry. When burned, lignite emits sulfur dioxide, an irritant gas that affects the nose, throat, and lungs. Used as a domestic fuel, the coal met almost 70 percent of East Germany's energy needs, as compared to only 8 percent in the west. Lignite, because of its high water content, has a much lower heat yield than anthracite or hard coal. But it was East Germany's sole indigenous energy source. Oil, natural gas, and hard coal had to be imported and paid for in scarce hard currency. East Germany's chemical industry was also a major consumer of lignite. Fuel, lubricants, fertilizers, pesticides, medicines, and synthetic fibers were all produced from the coal in outmoded prewar plants. Even the plastic body of the Trabant, East Germany's two-stroke car, was made from lignite.

Uranium mining operations in Thuringia and Saxony also contributed to extensive environmental damage. Beginning in 1946 a joint East German–Soviet company, under tight security, supplied the Soviet Union with the uranium needed for its nuclear weapons and power plants. From 1946 until 1990, over 220,000 tons were shipped to Soviet weapons plants and power stations. As a result a 1,200-square-kilometer area was heavily contaminated.

Since unification, almost 300 mine shafts, 3,000 radioactive waste dumps, 18 processing plants, and numerous storage facilities have been cleaned up by 4,000 specially trained workers and technicians. The entire operation was completed in 2006 at a cost of about $10 billion. Much of the area is now used for recreation, including several spas. In this case, former Chancellor Kohl's promise of "flowering landscapes" in the former East Germany was fulfilled.[48]

The major focus of the environmental cleanup has been on water and air quality. Modern water treatment facilities have been constructed in eastern cities where the problem has been most acute.[49] Water quality in rivers, lakes, and streams has also improved. A study of the Elbe found that over two hundred species of mussels have reappeared since reunification. Within the first five years of reunification alone, the concentration of heavy metals such as lead, cadmium, zinc, and nickel in the river dropped by over 45 percent, and the copper and chrome traces now found in the Elbe are down almost 50 percent since unification. Environmentalists, however, remain very concerned about the amount of toxic materials present in the river's sediments, as well as relatively high levels of nitrogen from agricultural runoff.[50] The situation will further improve as Germany moves toward its much touted "energy turn" toward more renewable forms of energy in the coming decades.

By 2010 the enormous cleanup operations have largely been concluded, and the environment in eastern Germany had been transformed.[51] Since 1990, air quality has improved nationwide, and the eastern regions have air as clean as in the west.[52] In Brandenburg the amount of dust declined by 99 percent and sulfur dioxide by 94 percent between 1990 and 2000.[53] Water quality has risen markedly and the Elbe is currently cleaner than the Rhine. The condition of the forests improved in the 1990s, but has stagnated since then—affected, however, by larger forces such as increased temperatures. Nevertheless, as of 2009 (see table 2.1) and

Table 2.1. Percentage of Trees with Noticeable Damage, 2009

Baden-Württemberg	42
Saarland	35
Thuringia	**35**
Schleswig-Holstein	30
Hesse	30
Bavaria	29
Berlin	29
Rhineland-Palatinate	28
North Rhine–Westphalia	21
Mecklenburg–West Pomerania	**19**
Saxony	**18**
Lower Saxony	**18**
Saxony-Anhalt	**15**
Bremen	9
Brandenburg	**6**
Hamburg	No data

Source: Statistisches Bundesamt Deutschland; Angaben für 2009; accessed from http://www.stepmap.de/landkarte/waldschaeden-127852.

with the exception of Thuringia, the eastern Länder now have the healthiest forests in the country. In addition to the financial resources devoted to cleaning up the environment, the unexpected deindustrialization of the region has, ironically, been a major cause of the improvement.

The "Wall in People's Heads"

Not long after the happiness over reunification subsided, a seemingly deep cleavage between easterners and westerners—a "wall in the head"—became evident. Many in the west began to consider *Ossis* (easterners) to be welfare-dependent, passive ingrates who fail to realize that prosperity only comes through hard work. Some westerners came to resent the stiff tax increases, large deficits, and diversion of resources needed to finance the rebuilding of eastern Germany. For instance, in 2007, 69 percent of westerners wanted to get rid of the "Solidarity Surcharge" versus 25 percent of easterners.[54] These critics have viewed the *Ossis* as whiners, "wanting it all" without being willing to sacrifice "as they did" following World War II.

On the other side, many citizens of the former East Germany began to perceive Western Germans as rich, arrogant know-it-alls (*Besser-Wessis*) who treated the former GDR like a colony. These East Germans also considered the westerners selfish, materialistic, and manipulative.[55] Many felt that their condition was an accident of history. They had neither a sense of guilt nor a sense of responsibility for the communist regime. According to polls conducted in 2009 almost twenty years after unification, 42 percent of easterners still felt they were treated as second-class citizens (although down from 57 percent in 2002).[56]

In short, many East Germans feel discriminated against. Even though as of 2013, easterners held the two highest offices in the country, they have a sense of being an irrelevant population. Particularly affected are the following groups: (1) forty- to sixty-year-old men who have lost their jobs and are unlikely to find new positions in the near future; (2) twenty-five- to thirty-five-year-olds who are optimistic about new possibilities in the market economy but are nonetheless fearful of being fired; (3) people with minor handicaps or behavioral problems; (4) the unemployed, for whom any previous job had social significance; and (5) the former *Nutznießer* (beneficiaries) of the old regime (this group receives no help or sympathy).

Clearly, the psychological pressures of unification have been stronger for residents of the former GDR than for those in the west. The East Germans lost their state and entire social system and with it a part of their identity. Unlike westerners, they had to radically redefine themselves; abandon their old values, beliefs, and verities; and adapt to western ways or become marginalized. Unlike westerners they had to confront and "overcome" the past forty years in order to preserve some aspects of their own identity. Even many noncommunists regretted the quick demise of the GDR and searched for positive elements in its history, such as antifascism and the ideal of socialism. Easterners are also more likely to be anxious about their economic future. These psychological pressures are differentially present among the various age groups or political generations in the east. Older generations are having more difficulty adjusting than are younger age groups. In fact, eastern Germany is experiencing a generational cleavage unlike anything in the west since the 1960s.

The alienation of large segments of the eastern population has also resulted in divergent voting behavior. As table 2.2 shows, there is substantially more support for protest, even antisystem parties in the eastern regions compared to the west. Both the Left Party and right radical parties are disproportionally supported in that region.

For some analysts, the dominance of westerners means that the social needs of easterners are not being met. In politics, economics, and society they have lacked opportunities to make decisions.[57] Most of the centers of power and influence—politics, the media, academia, business—are still controlled by *Wessis*. Some of the consequences include a concentration on the material-need level—individual acquisition—or a withdrawal into the private sphere. Moreover, if economic needs are not fulfilled, a substantial aggressive potential can be developed. This can manifest itself in aggression against foreigners and support for right radical parties.

As we discuss in chapter 4, although there have been outbreaks of violence against foreigners throughout the country particularly in the early and mid-1990s, most of these have occurred in the new eastern states. When Germany hosted the 2006 World Cup of soccer, several parts of eastern Berlin and eastern Germany were declared "no go" areas for foreign, especially African, fans. In 2010 about 40 percent of all reported acts of violence committed by right-wing groups took place in the east, even though only about 15 percent of the total German population lives in the five new states.[58] In 2009, just over 2 percent of eastern residents are foreigners as compared to 10 percent in the west.[59] It was not a

Table 2.2.   Protest Voting in Eastern and Western German Länder (in percent)

	Year of Election	Left Party	NPD
Baden-Württemberg	2011	2.8	0.9
Bavaria	2008	4.4	1.2
Berlin (West)	2011	4.3	1.6
Bremen	2011	5.6	1.6
Hamburg	2011	6.4	0.9
Hesse	2009	5.4	0.9
Lower Saxony	2008	7.1	1.6
North Rhine–Westphalia	2012	2.5	0.5
Rhineland–Palatinate	2011	3.0	1.1
Saarland	2012	16.1	1.2
Schleswig-Holstein	2012	2.3	0.7
Berlin (East)	2011	22.7	2.9
Brandenburg	2009	27.2	2.6
Mecklenburg–West Pomerania	2011	18.0	6.0
Saxony-Anhalt	2011	24.0	4.2
Saxony	2009	20.0	5.6
Thuringia	2009	27.0	4.3

Source: Bundeswahlleiter.

coincidence that easterners were responsible for the so-called National Socialist Underground terrorist cell (discussed in chapter 4). These behaviors could represent an extreme reaction to the psychic and economic stress of unification among a minority of the population. Young easterners with low levels of education have been especially susceptible to the appeals of radical right-wing organizations. Anti-Semitism, nationalism, and a general hostility to foreigners decline among young people at academic secondary schools.

Indeed, as the data in table 2.3 show, there remain substantial differences between easterners and westerners. In 2006, over 80 percent of *Wessis*, but only about 40 percent of *Ossis* agreed that "Easterners have to show more patience." Easterners by a two-to-one margin still wanted more willingness to sacrifice from their western cousins. In spite of billions in direct transfers and a state-of-the-art infrastructure, 70 percent of easterners still agreed with the statement that "reunification brought more advantage to the west than the east." Not surprisingly, only 25 percent of the western Germans who paid for most of the reconstruction shared this sentiment. In 2010, East Germans remained skeptical about their equality with their western counterparts. Although 59 percent of East Germans did not want the GDR back, they also did not feel fully part of the Federal Republic. Only 25 percent of easterners felt like equal citizens, and 9 percent

Table 2.3.   The Wall in People's Heads (percent who agree with each statement, 2006)

Statement	West Total	West Post-Wall Generation	East Total	East Post-Wall Generation
Citizens in the West (old states) have to show a greater willingness to sacrifice in order to improve the lives of the people in the East (new states).	20	25	42	47
The people in the East should show more patience when it comes to improving their lives.	82	76	39	45
For citizens in the West, reunification has brought more advantages than disadvantages.	25	33	70	53
For citizens in the East, reunification has brought more advantages than disadvantages.	82	83	54	58
What happens to people in the East essentially depends on what they are ready to achieve themselves.	75	78	52	70
Many citizens in the East cannot deal with the pressure to achieve in a free market economy.	55	37	35	29

Source: Der Spiegel, no. 45 (November 5, 2007), 74ff (Infratest Survey).

actually wanted the GDR back. Additionally the value placed on democracy varied between the regions. In the west, 82 percent of citizens believed that democracy is important, while only 69 percent of those in the east shared this view. Finally, 37 percent of westerners and 42 percent of easterners perceived some or a lot of benefits from reunification, whereas 35 percent of westerners and 24 percent of easterners saw some or a lot of disadvantages.[60]

Nevertheless, this "wall in the head" is not insurmountable. Table 2.3 also shows that among younger Germans the differences in some areas are significantly smaller than among older age cohorts. When we consider the "Post-Wall Generation" of those respondents born since 1977—that is, those who were no older than twelve at the time the Wall came down—we find some different patterns. Younger easterners are more likely to advocate continued patience than older East Germans. They are less likely to see unification as largely benefiting the west. The biggest area of convergence is on the item that the "future of the east depends on achievement." On this item younger respondents, regardless of region, are more likely to agree than older age groups. There is only an eight-point difference among the post-Wall generation of the east and west, as compared to a twenty-three-point difference among the older age group. Finally, the post-Wall generation in both regions is more likely than its elders to reject the idea that easterners cannot handle the pressures of a free market economy.

With the passage of time and generational change, positive memories of communism have declined. Between 1998 and 2009, the proportion of easterners who considered the German Democratic Republic a "state based on the rule of law" (Rechtsstaat) dropped from 27 percent to only 14 percent. Between 1998 and 2007, agreement with the statement "The GDR was a kind of democracy" dropped from 43 percent to 24 percent.[61] Moreover, in spite of all the problems associated with unification, easterners are increasingly proud of what they have accomplished. Between 1996 and 2007, the percent of easterners expressing pride in what has been achieved in their region since reunification has increased from 36 percent to 62 percent. Those with no sense of pride in the development of the former eastern region dropped during this same time period from 32 percent to 11 percent.[62]

Thus, in spite of these continued problems, the great majority of easterners, over 80 percent in 2007, have a positive orientation toward unification—that is, they believe it was the right thing to do.[63] Approximately one-half believe they are doing better or much better than before unification, and less than one-fourth state that their condition has gotten worse or much worse. They want to live in a unified state, but they also want to be respected and appreciated by their western cousins. When asked when the easterners will be fully integrated and their "complaining" will stop, the first and last freely elected GDR prime minister, Lothar de Maizière, once replied,

Remember that Moses led his people through the desert for 40 years, and that after 20 years people began to complain. . . . They told Moses that life in the desert was too difficult, and that at least when they were slaves they had food and water and places to sleep. Moses' friends asked him how long he thought people would be complaining like this and he replied, "Until the last person born under slavery has died." Our situation here is very similar. The psychological gap between Eastern and Western Germany will last for at least a generation, or perhaps until the last person born under Communism has passed away.[64]

NOTES

1. When we discuss the GDR, East Berlin is included. For the post-reunification period, unless stated otherwise, eastern Germany refers to the five new states and not the eastern portion of Berlin.

2. For each East German there was a *Kaderakte,* a type of personnel file that began in elementary school and followed the person throughout his or her life. The Stasi had access to all Kaderakte; the subject of each file did not.

3. Cited in Karl Wilhelm Fricke, "The Inherited Burden of the East German State Security Apparatus," *Aussenpolitik* 41 (1990): 408.

4. The Stasi was by no means the only security institution in the country. There was one police officer for every 170 residents, as compared to one for every 385 West Germans. All police personnel were under the direct control of the national Interior Ministry, which in turn was controlled by the party.

5. For an excellent analysis of the June 17, 1953, uprising, which is based on new evidence from party and state archives, see Armin Mitter and Stefan Wolle, *Untergang auf Raten. Unbekannte Kapiteln der DDR Geschichte* (Munich: Bertelsmann Verlag, 1993), 27–162. The authors contend that the uprising actually saved the Stalinist Ulbricht regime, which the Soviet Union, in the wake of Stalin's death in March, was preparing to abandon.

6. See Hope Harrison, ed., "The Berlin Wall after Fifty Years: 1961–2011," special issue, *German Politics and Society* 29, no. 2 (2011).

7. Included in West Germany's humanitarian aid was money paid to the GDR for the release of political prisoners. From 1964 to 1990 the Federal Republic paid more than $2 billion for the freedom of 34,000 prisoners held in deplorable conditions in East German jails. An additional 200,000 East Germans, usually relatives of the released prisoners, were included in the ransom deal. East Germany considered the payments as reimbursement for the expenses it incurred in educating its former citizens. This top-secret ransom program was an important source of hard currency for the GDR. Indeed, it became an item in the country's annual budget. The average cost per prisoner increased from about $12,000 in the 1960s to over $50,000 by the 1980s. To reduce the chances of negative publicity, both sides agreed to use the offices of the Protestant Church to transfer the payments, which were made either in cash or commodities, from West to East. For one account of the beginnings of this program, see Craig R. Whitney, *Spy Trader* (New York: Times Books, 1993), 51–80. There are also reports of an "unofficial channel" that was used to bring other East Germans to the west. This involved direct payments to an East German lawyer with close ties to Stasi chief Erich Mielke and to Honecker (*Frankfurter Allgemeine Zeitung,* June 3, 1992, 3).

8. For an analysis of public opinion data on the question of a GDR identity, see Peter Förster and Günter Roski, *DDR Zwischen Wende und Wahl* (Berlin: LinksDruck Sachbuchverlag, 1990). Political socialization in the former GDR is examined in Christiane Lemke, *Die Ursachen des Umbruchs 1989. Politische Sozialisation in der ehemaligen DDR* (Wiesbaden: Westdeutscher Verlag, 1991).

9. Honecker had planned to visit West Germany several years earlier, but Moscow, fearing an intra-German rapprochement, forced him to cancel the trip.

10. In all, from 1961 to 1989 more than six hundred East Germans were killed by GDR border troops and police as they attempted to flee the country either through Berlin or at other border crossings. In several trials after 1989, former border guards and some of the East German communist leadership responsible for the shoot-to-kill order were sentenced to prison terms. Many leaders, however, including Erich Honecker, escaped prosecution for reasons of health, old age, and lack of evidence that met West German legal standards (*Frankfurter Allgemeine Zeitung*, August 13, 1993, 6). By late 1998 German authorities had investigated more than 22,000 cases of alleged criminal activity and human rights violations during the communist regime. These investigations yielded 211 convictions of state and party officials, border guards, judges, and prosecutors (*Süddeutsche Zeitung*, December 8, 1998, 3).

11. Hungary's decision was, of course, enthusiastically supported by the West Germans, and Bonn's promise of substantial aid to the new democratic government in Budapest did not hurt the cause of the East Germans.

12. See Helmut Müller-Enbergs et al., eds., *Von der Illegalität ins Parlament. Werdegang und Konzept der neuen Bürgerbewegungen* (Berlin: LinksDruck Sachbuchverlag, 1991) for a detailed examination of the various GDR opposition groups that emerged at this time.

13. The sequence of events that led to the opening of the Wall on the evening of November 9, 1989, is still not clear. Apparently the communist leadership had intended to announce only more liberal and simplified procedures for GDR citizens desiring to travel to the west; they would still have to apply for exit visas. But when the communist official making the announcement was asked by reporters to clarify his statement, he said that the borders were open. Quickly the news spread that the Wall was open. GDR border guards, faced with thousands of people waiting to cross over, made a decision not to require any visas or identity cards; they simply let people cross. See Günter Schabowski, *Das Politbüro* (Reinbek bei Hamburg: Rowohlt Verlag, 1990), 134–140.

14. Daniel Hamilton, "After the Revolution: The New Political Landscape in East Germany," *German Issues*, vol. 7 (Washington, DC: American Institute for Contemporary German Studies, 1990), 11. This section of the book owes much to Hamilton's excellent analysis.

15. Hamilton, "After the Revolution," 11.

16. Cited in Hamilton, "After the Revolution," 11.

17. Forschungsgruppe Wahlen survey cited in Erwin K. Scheuch, *Wie Deutsch sind die Deutschen?* (Bergisch Gladbach: Gustav Lübbe Verlag, 1991), 352.

18. EMNID surveys cited in *Der Spiegel*, June 25, 1990, 48.

19. Personal interview, November 29, 1990, Bonn.

20. Peter Christ and Klaus-Peter Schmid, "Hauptsache guter Wille," *Die Zeit*, February 23, 1990, 10. Note that all US dollar conversions were done either at the time that the figure was generated or at the time of writing. For the latter, the current daily rate was used, which ranged from 1 Euro = $1.23 to $1.29.

21. Not all East Germans, of course, were dissatisfied with the regime. At the March 1990 parliamentary election, over 16 percent voted for the former Communist Party (renamed the Party of Democratic Socialism, or PDS). In East Berlin the PDS received over 30 percent of the vote. Much of this support came from the beneficiaries of the system: the hundreds of thousands of party and state bureaucrats, secret police officials, informers, artists, intellectuals, and privileged athletes.

22. Abortions are also allowed for "eugenic" reasons (hereditary physical or mental illness).

23. ALLBUS surveys 1991–2006. By 2006 over 60 percent of westerners also wanted to wrap the Stasi investigations.

24. Robert Gerald Livingston, "Relinquishment of East Germany," in *East Central Europe and the USSR*, ed. Richard F. Starr (New York: St. Martin's, 1991), 83.

25. James Baker (former American secretary of state), cited in *Der Spiegel*, June 14, 1998, 24.

26. Mary Elise Sarotte, "Perpetuating U.S. Preeminence: The 1990 Deals to 'Bribe the Soviets Out' and Move NATO In," *International Security* 35, no. 1 (Summer 2010): 110–137.

27. Detlef Landua, "Magere Zeiten," *Aus Politik und Zeitgeschichte*, July 10, 1992, 29–43.

28. http://www.bmvbs.de/cae/servlet/contentblob/68032/publicationFile/58125/sach standsbericht-verkehrsprojekte-deutsche-einheit-stand-mai-2012.pdf.

29. Stephen Economides, "Rebuilding the Telecommunications System in the New German States," unpublished manuscript, Telekom Fachhochschule Berlin, 1994, 5.

30. http://www.bpb.de/geschichte/deutsche-einheit/lange-wege-der-deutschen-einheit/47534/kosten-der-einheit?p=all.

31. From 1990 to 1993 the pensions of eastern Germans increased from 47 percent to 86 percent of the western level (Federal Labor Ministry Statistics).

32. In the first year of unification the federal budget increased a phenomenal 31 percent, with approximately one-third of the new spending coming from federal borrowing.

33. Ullrich Heilemann and Wolfgang Reinicke, *Welcome to Hard Times: The Fiscal Consequences of German Unity* (Washington, DC: Brookings Institution and American Institute for Contemporary German Studies, 1995), 48.

34. *Datenreport 2011*, chap. 6, p. 138.

35. http://www.gfk.com/group/press_information/press_releases/009132/index.en.html.

36. Authors' calculations, based on average pension payments; http://www.spiegel.de/wirtschaft/soziales/laenderuebersicht-so-viel-rente-gibt-es-in-west-und-ost-a-709284.html.

37. But western pensioners, while now receiving comparatively less than easterners, have far more capital resources (savings, stocks, bonds, real estate, insurance policies) than easterners. Forty years of saving and investing in a market economy produced far higher yields than under the eastern socialist economy. On average, western pensioners have about three times more savings than easterners. About half of western pensioners in 1998 owned real estate with an average value of about $205,000, as compared with a third of eastern residents whose real estate holdings had an average value of $75,000 (Klaus-Dietrich Bedau, "Zur materiellen Lage der Senioren in West- und Ostdeutschland," Deutsches Institut für Wirtschaft, *Wochenbericht* 39 (September 1999): 4–6.

38. http://www.bmwi.de/BMWi/Redaktion/PDF/W/wf-wirtschaftsdaten-neue-laender, property=pdf,bereich=bmwi2012,sprache=de,rwb=true.pdf, p. 9.

39. http://www.bmwi.de/BMWi/Redaktion/PDF/W/wf-wirtschaftsdaten-neue-laender, property=pdf,bereich=bmwi2012,sprache=de,rwb=true.pdf, p. 3.

40. *Jahresbericht zum Stand der deutschen Einheit 2007* (Berlin: Transportation Ministry, September 2007), 20.

41. https://www.destatis.de/DE/PresseService/Presse/Pressemitteilungen/2010/07/PD10_262_624.html.

42. http://statistik.arbeitsagentur.de/Navigation/Statistik/Statistik-nach-Regionen/Politische-Gebietsstruktur/Brandenburg-Nav.html?year_month=201207.

43. http://www.economist.com/node/15640987.

44. http://www.bmi.bund.de/SharedDocs/Downloads/DE/Broschueren/2011/jahresbericht_de_2011.pdf?__blob=publicationFile.

45. Michael C. Burda, "Wirtschaft in Deutschland im 21. Jahrhundert," *Aus Politik und Zeitgeschichte*, nos. 30–33 (2010), p. 32.

46. http://www.silicon-saxony.de/en/index_mikro.html; http://www.manager-magazin
.de/politik/deutschland/0,2828,791148,0 0.html.

47. Environmental Ministry statistics cited in *Der Bürger im Staat 41*, no. 3 (August
1991): 162.

48. Reiner Bürger, "Schlemas Wässer wirken wieder Wunder," *Frankfurter Allgemeine
Zeitung*, August 12, 2006, 3.

49. *Der Spiegel*, September 4, 1995, 139.

50. The findings of the Elbe River study are cited in the *Frankfurter Allgemeine Zeitung*, July 26, 1995, 1.

51. http://www.lanuv.nrw.de/liki-newsletter/index.php?mode = liste&indikator = 0&
aufzu = 0.

52. http://www.umweltbundesamt-daten-zur-umwelt.de/umweltdaten/public/document/
downloadImage.do;jsessionid = F52551021DB4C6DA148DF136307011DE?ident = 21845.

53. http://www.bpb.de/apuz/27550/umweltschutz-in-ostdeutschland-versuch-ueber
-ein-schnell-verschwundenes-thema?p = all.

54. *Allensbacher Jahrbuch der Demoskopie 2003–2009*, vol. 12 (Berlin: Walter de
Gruyter, 2009).

55. EMNID surveys cited in *Der Spiegel*, July 22, 1991, 28. Over 90 percent of easterners, but only 7 percent of westerners, agreed with the statement that Germany is using
the East as a new market and is less interested in developing the economic independence
of the region.

56. *Allensbacher Jahrbuch 2003–2009*, vol. 12, 53.

57. Ingrid Stratemann, *Psychologische Aspekte des wirtschaftlichen Augbaus in den
neuen Bundesländern* (Göttingen: Verlag für angewandte Psychologie, 1992).

58. http://www.zeit.de/politik/deutschland/2011-06/linke-gewalt-straftat.

59. http://www.statistik-portal.de/statistik-portal/dejb01_jahrtab2.asp.

60. http://www.spiegel.de/politik/deutschland/sozialreport-ostdeutsche-fremdeln-mit-
der-bundesrepublik-a-714860.html.

61. *Jahrbuch*, vol. 12, 48–49.

62. *Jahrbuch*, vol. 12, 54.

63. Forschungsgruppe Wahlen, "Politibarometer/Deutsche Einheit," September 2007, 1.

64. Cited in Craig Whitney, "Instead of Barbed Wire, Resentment Now Divides Germans," *New York Times*, October 14, 1994, A6.

③

The Social and Economic Setting

Neither people nor states function in a vacuum. Historical, geographical, and socioeconomic contexts influence political attitudes and behavior as well as policy-making institutions. This is especially true of the Federal Republic, where important postwar geographical, social, and economic changes have created a setting for politics quite different from that experienced by past regimes. This chapter surveys these contextual changes in relation to modern German politics.

AREA AND POPULATION

The unified Federal Republic, with an area of approximately 138,000 square miles (about half the size of Texas), now comprises roughly 75 percent of the pre–World War II territory of the Reich. As we will discuss later, this loss had several important consequences for postwar politics. Germany has more neighbors than any other European nation. On the north it is bordered by Denmark, on the east by Poland and the Czech Republic, on the south by Austria and Switzerland, and on the west by France, Luxembourg, Belgium, and the Netherlands. The Federal Republic extends 530 miles from the Danish border in the north to the Bavarian Alps in the south, 270 miles from the Austrian border in the southeast to the border with France in the southwest, and 300 miles from the border with Poland in the northeast to the border with the Netherlands in the northwest (see figure 1.1).

Unified Germany now has a population of about 82 million, making it by far the largest country in Western and Central Europe. A little more than a fourth of this current population (22 million) can be attributed to postwar migration into West Germany. This migration included expellees from German territories annexed or occupied by Poland and the Soviet Union in 1945, Germans expelled from what was then Czechoslovakia (the Sudetenland), as well as other East European countries, and additional refugees—almost three million—from the former East Germany from 1949 until the construction of the Berlin Wall in 1961. Since then, there has been substantial immigration from southern Europe, Turkey, and the former Soviet Union. In 2011, there were also about seven million foreign residents, most of whom consist of long-settled "guest workers" (*Gastarbeiter*) and their families in the former West Germany.[1] Almost 20 percent of the current population has a migration background, and the country is still a major target for immigrants, especially from the Mediterranean region, Russia, the Middle East, and Africa.

The five new eastern German states (Saxony, Saxony-Anhalt, Thuringia, Brandenburg, and Mecklenburg–West Pomerania) have a combined population of about 13.3 million, down from 16 million at the time of unification in 1990. (Including the eastern districts of Berlin would bring the 2006 total of the former East Germany to about 15 million.) The territory of the former GDR in 1948 had a population of 19.1 million. When the Berlin Wall was completed in 1961 the population had dropped to 17.1 million. By 1986 a relatively low birth rate had reduced this still further to 16.6 million. The emigration that triggered the collapse of the communist regime reduced the population even more to an estimated 16 million at the time of unification. Since unification, interregional migration has resulted in a net loss of about 1 million eastern Germans.[2] Finally, about 300,000 residents of the new states commute daily or weekly to jobs in the old states.[3]

The enormous economic, social, and cultural adjustments being made by easterners after forty years of division have had a depressing effect on such basic life decisions as marriage and childbirth. Between 1989 and 1993 the number of marriages in the eastern region dropped from about 131,000 to 49,000, and the number of births from about 200,000 to only 80,000. By the early 2000s, the number of births had stabilized at around 100,000 per year. Demographic changes of this magnitude are usually associated only with traumatic events such as war and economic depression.[4] They indicate the extent of fear and uncertainty felt by many in the former East Germany. Since 1993, however, there is a slow trend toward normalization; marriages and births have increased and now are converging with those in the west. The postunification decline in population has concerned some eastern governments. One eastern state, Brandenburg, pays parents a $650 premium for every new child.

In 2011 the national birth rate dropped to its lowest level since World War II. Indeed, there were more live births in Germany during 1945, the chaotic final year of the war, than in 2011. The birth rate of native Germans is even lower, since about a fourth of live births in 2011 were to foreign residents. More than half of Germany's 30 million households are without children, and about half of families with children have only one child. Less than one family in four has two or more children. Modern contraceptive techniques, the growing number of women opting for the workforce instead of the traditional housewife (*Hausfrau*) role, and the lack of affordable preschool and day-care programs are the major reasons for the low birth rate.

The birth rate in 2010 of 1.38 children per female (or 678,000) is well below the replenishment level (equilibrium) of 2.1. This German figure is similar to that in Spain, Sweden, Greece, and Italy. To increase this birth rate, the Grand Coalition government of Chancellor Merkel in 2006 passed a family leave program that pays working new mothers staying at home as much as $2,500 monthly for up to a year (fourteen months if the father also takes time off from work for child care). The government spent $5.7 billion on this program in 2010. Another new program will greatly expand day-care facilities. Other proposals include higher taxes and lower pensions for childless couples.[5] Unless these programs increase birth rates, most Germans will have to retire later to maintain the solvency of the pension system.[6]

Indeed, Germany is one of the most rapidly aging societies in the world. Currently, approximately 20 percent of the population is over 65, a figure that is expected to rise to 33 percent in 2060. If current trends continue, the overall population will decline to 65 million by 2060. The rapidly growing elderly portion of the population is already straining welfare programs and will only worsen the budgetary situation. Given the low birth rates among the native population, any population growth is due entirely to immigration. Thus, Germany faces a demographic crisis: an aging and shrinking native population and a foreign-born community that reproduces at a faster rate.

URBANIZATION AND INDUSTRIALIZATION

With ninety inhabitants per square mile, Germany is one of the most densely populated countries in Europe. It is also a heavily urbanized society, with half of its population living on less than 10 percent of the land. The large urban areas, however, are distributed throughout the country and make for considerable diversity. As table 3.1 shows, Germany currently has eleven metropolitan regions containing approximately 70 percent of the country's population.

Many of these metropolitan regions encompass rather large boundaries and many rural areas. Also, with the exception of Berlin and Hamburg, the central

Table 3.1.   Metropolitan Regions in Germany

Metropolitan Region	Population (millions, 2008)	Major Cities (population, millions 2010)
Rhine-Ruhr	11.7	Cologne (1.0), Düsseldorf (0.6), Dortmund (0.6), Essen (0.6), Bonn (0.3)
Ruhr	5.2	
Cologne/Bonn	3.5	
Middle Germany	6.9	Dresden (0.5), Leipzig (0.5)
Berlin-Brandenburg	5.9	Berlin (3.5), Potsdam (0.2)
Munich	5.6	Munich (1.4)
Frankfurt/Rhine-Main	5.5	Frankfurt (0.7), Wiesbaden (0.3), Mainz (0.2)
Stuttgart	5.3	Stuttgart (0.6)
Stuttgart Alliance	2.7	
Hamburg	4.3	Hamburg (1.8)
Hanover-Braunschweig-Göttingen-Wolfsburg	3.9	Hanover (0.5)
Nuremberg	3.6	Nuremberg (0.5)
Bremen/Oldenburg	2.7	Bremen (0.5)
Rhine-Neckar	2.4	Mannheim (0.3)

Source: http://www.metropolregion.de/meta_downloads/18243/ikm_monitoring2010.pdf.

cities themselves are actually quite small. The metropolitan regions in the south and west, especially Munich, Stuttgart, and Frankfurt, have grown disproportionally in recent decades. Although German cities are hundreds or thousands of years old—Munich was founded in 1158, Berlin in 1237, and Cologne was founded by the Romans in AD 50—much of this urbanization took place during the last quarter of the nineteenth century. In 1870, only 17 percent of the population was urban, but by 1900 it was over 50 percent, and by 2010, 76 percent.[7] Within one generation, Germany became not only predominantly urban, but also one of the world's leading economic powers. Today the Federal Republic is the world's fourth-largest industrial power (after the United States, China, and Japan) and the largest in Europe.

AN EXPORT-ORIENTED ECONOMY

Lacking self-sufficiency in food and raw materials, Germany's economic well-being, like that of other modern societies, is heavily dependent on successful competition in the international economic arena. In essence, Germany imports food, raw materials, and manufactured products and pays for them by exporting its own manufactured goods. Almost 90 percent of German exports are manufactured goods—automobiles, chemicals, heavy machinery—sent in 2010 to its European neighbors (71.2 percent, 60.3 percent to other EU countries); North and South America (10.4 percent); Asia (15.4 percent); and Africa (2.1 percent).[8] Food, raw materials, and semifinished products account for about 30 percent of Germany's imports. Currently, about 10 percent Germany's food is imported (about 7 percent of all imports). Over 60 percent of Germany's energy—especially oil and natural gas—has to be imported. Success in this exchange depends on the ability of German industry to sell its manufactured goods at a price greater than the costs of its raw materials and production. Successful production is in turn strongly related to an adequate supply of skilled industrial labor, management expertise, and scientific know-how.

The Germans have been very successful in the business of international trade. The balance of trade—that is, the value of exports minus the costs of imports—has been positive since 1955. In 2011 it reached a record high of over $200 billion. The value of exports in 2011 at over $1.3 trillion was exceeded only by China and the United States.[9] Overall, German enterprises receive about 25 to 30 percent of their gross sales from exports. In some industries—automobiles, steel, chemicals, and machine tools—almost half of total sales come from the foreign market.

This is an extraordinary achievement when one considers that the German population is only about 27 percent as large as that of the United States and the economy between 2001 and 2005 hardly grew at all. The export component of the economy is reaping the benefits of the extensive restructuring of the last decade, which included downsizing the labor force, outsourcing of some manufacturing to countries with lower wages (like Slovakia), and the importation of low-value-added manufactured products especially from China. This export performance has also been achieved with about 7 to 10 percent of the workforce unemployed.

In spite of the post-reunification difficulties, the overall performance of postwar Germany in foreign trade cannot be equaled by any other advanced industrial society during this period, with the possible exception of Japan. It is little wonder that *die Wirtschaft* (the economy) and its representatives have been an important power factor in politics and policy making. German business has a record of accomplishment that ensures it respectful consideration by any government.

The Rural Sector

The significance of agricultural production for the economy has rapidly declined in the postwar period. The postwar loss of the predominantly agrarian eastern territories reduced the amount of arable land, but even within the western region the percentage of the gross national product contributed by agriculture and the size of the agricultural work force has also dropped steadily. Between 1950 and 2010 the proportion working in agriculture declined from 25 percent to 2 percent; agricultural production contributed only 12 percent of the gross national product in 1949; and by 2010 this figure had dropped even further to less than 1 percent.[10]

Previously, German agriculture was inefficient in its use of land, labor, and capital. Although the number of farms of less than four acres in size had declined by over a million between 1950 and 1995, 30 percent of German farms in 1999 (as compared to 80 percent in 1949) were still in this size category. Farms in the west were, on average, the smallest of any non-Mediterranean region of the European Union. Their small size meant a high labor input and an uneconomical use of modern machinery. Since the early 1950s, the policies of German governments have been directed toward the restructuring of agriculture through land consolidation (fewer but larger farms) and the improvement of farm buildings, roads, land, and drainage. Also, the size of farms in the east is higher than in the west, affecting the overall average. Overall, the average size of German farms increased to 138 acres in 2010 (see table 3.2).

Agriculture long remained in a poor competitive position compared to Germany's more agrarian-oriented neighbors such as France and Italy. Recently this has changed, with profit margins per hectare for small farms in 2007 exceeded by only seven of twenty-seven EU member states, and for large farms by nine countries. German farms are about as profitable as in France, but less productive than in Italy.[11]

In spite of their problems, farmers and their interest organizations, unlike agrarian groups earlier in German history, have not shown any inclination to support antisystem parties. This is due in part to the integration of agrarian interests into the democratic political parties, but it also reflects the changed structure of rural interests. During the empire and the Weimar Republic, the aristocratic Prussian landowners (Junkers) with their large estates had a major influence on agricultural policy and often conflicted with the policy claims of small and medium-sized farmers. In contrast, the structure of German agriculture today is more homogenous, and the interests of farmers can be more easily integrated into party and government programs.

Table 3.2.   Average Farm Size, Acres, 2010

Mecklenburg–West Pomerania	706
Saxony-Anhalt	687
Brandenburg	588
Thuringia	532
Saxony	359
Schleswig-Holstein	174
Lower Saxony	153
Saarland	146
Hesse	106
North Rhine–Westphalia	101
Rhineland-Palatinate	85
Bavaria	79
Baden-Württemberg	78
Berlin, Bremen, Hamburg	61
Germany	138
EU 15 (2007)*	54
EU 27 (2007)**	31

Source: https://www.destatis.de/DE/Publikationen/Thematisch/LandForst
wirtschaft/Querschnitt/BroschuereLandwirtschaftBlick.html; for EU,
http://ec.europa.eu/agriculture/agrista/economic-briefs/03_en.pdf.
*First fifteen member states.
**Current twenty-seven members.

REGIONALISM

The enormous postwar migration of expellees, Europe's largest movement of people since the sixth century; the 1949–1990 division of the prewar Reich; the loss of the eastern territories to the Soviet Union and Poland; and the general modernization of German society have greatly reduced regional differences in lifestyles, including political behavior and values. Regional dialects and customs remain, of course, but the economic, social, and political characteristics of the Federal Republic show less of the regional variation common before 1933. Germans today read national newspapers, listen to national radio stations, and watch national television programs. The extensive geographical mobility of postwar Germans has also reduced regionalism in the sense that Germany comprises separate, distinct subcultures.

Although Germany is a federal system with sixteen states, or Länder, having considerable authority in areas such as education, police, and urban development, the geographical boundaries of these states (with the exception of Bavaria, Saxony, and the city-states of Berlin, Hamburg, and Bremen) have few historical roots and were created in most cases by the edicts of military government. By forcing regions together into states to form a federal system, the Allies ironically further reduced regional differences in the Federal Republic. Moreover, all states administer the same national legal codes and procedures; administrative practices are also generally uniform throughout the Republic.

The development of particularistic and regional sentiments is further inhibited by constitutional provisions (Article 107) requiring a "unity of living standards" throughout all Länder. This equalization takes place through (1) federal redistribution of a proportion of the states' share of certain taxes to poorer states (vertical equalization), and (2) direct payments by the richer states to the poorer ones (horizontal integration).[12] In 2012, for example, the three richest states paid just over $10 billion to the thirteen poorer states, including the five new eastern states, which have been part of this system since 1995.

OCCUPATIONAL AND CLASS STRUCTURE

Being a highly developed industrial society, the Federal Republic has an occupational structure similar to that of other advanced industrial societies. The largest single occupational group (63 percent in 2010; see table 3.3) comprises white-collar and service occupations. Like manual workers, people in these occupations are employees—that is, they are dependent on wages and salaries—but unlike manual workers, they have had on the average more extensive academic training and enjoy a considerably higher social status and, in many cases, higher income than manual workers. The next-largest group (30 percent) is made up of manual workers, most of whom are skilled and have completed extensive vocational training. The third-largest occupational group (9 percent) is composed of those in "independent" nonmanual positions (owners and directors of enterprises, doctors, lawyers, small businessmen, and independent artisans). Finally, about 2 percent of the workforce is employed in agricultural, forestry, and fishing occupations.

This occupational structure is largely the result of an extensive industrialization and modernization process that began during the last quarter of the nineteenth century, was intensified by the demands of the two world wars, and continues to the present day. The main characteristics of these changes are common to all advanced industrial societies:

1. A steady decline in the proportion employed in the "primary sphere" of the economy (agriculture) and independent nonmanuals, including the professions. At the turn of the century, 36 percent of the workforce was still in these occupations, but as table 3.3 shows, by 2010 they comprised only 13 percent of the workforce.
2. A relative stagnation or even slow decline in the proportion employed in the secondary or production sphere of the economy (industrial manual occupations). Its relative position declined from 57 percent in 1882 to 24 percent by 2010.

Table 3.3.   Occupational Composition of the Workforce, 1882–2010 (in percent)

	1882	1925	1950	1974	1986	2010
Agricultural, independent, and self-employed	36	33	28	14	13	13
Manual workers	57	50	51	45	39	24
Salaried nonmanual (white-collar and service)	7	17	21	41	48	63

Source: *Statistisches Jahrbuch für die Bundesrepublik Deutschland*, 1971, 1975, 2011 (Stuttgart: Kohlhammer Verlag); Emil Hübner and Horst-Hennek Rohlfs, *Jahrbuch der Bundesrepublik Deutschland 1987–1988* (Munich: Deutscher Taschenbuch Verlag, 1988).

3. Rapid growth among those in the tertiary sphere: the white-collar and service occupations. The size of this group has increased from only 21 percent in 1950 to 63 percent (75 percent if professionals are included) by 2010. The tertiary sector overtook manual workers by the late 1970s. The United States reached this point by the mid-1950s.[13]

Such structural changes have increased social mobility in Germany. In international comparisons, Germany is in the middle. It does, however, have more mobility than the United States today.[14] That said, upper-class and high-status occupations requiring extensive academic training still remain challenging to enter for the offspring of manual and low-level white-collar workers. The tiered structure of the German educational system also has a large impact on career and income chances.[15]

THE ECONOMY

Germany is one of the world's most prosperous societies. Its per capita GDP in 2011 of about $40,000 ranked seventeenth in the world. The sophisticated industrial economy staffed by a highly skilled workforce has made the Federal Republic an affluent, mass-consumption society. It is also a country with substantial capital resources, although, as we discuss below, these are by no means equally distributed. In 2011, the capital stock amounted to almost $10 trillion.[16]

It is a market-based or capitalist economy, but with an important difference from the market economies of the United States and even the United Kingdom: capitalism German style has included a strong social welfare component. The Germans term this a "social market economy." The free enterprise system has been tempered by comprehensive social welfare programs designed to protect all citizens from hardships caused by the exigencies of life: sickness, accident, unemployment, childbirth, and old age. These core risks are thus shared or assumed by the larger society through government programs. All parties have supported this system. There is little similarity between an American conservative and his or her German counterpart. In terms of social welfare policy, Germany's largest "conservative" party is far to the left of the American Republican Party as well as the free market wing of the British conservative party. Indeed, many of the major elements of the contemporary welfare state—health insurance, pensions, housing subsidies, nursing care programs—were introduced not by Germany's "leftist" party, the Social Democrats, but by the country's "right-leaning" party, the Christian Democrats.

But the "social" in social market has also included not only a comprehensive welfare state, but also a dense web of laws and regulations ostensibly designed to "order" and "protect" the participants in this economy: workers, consumers, manufacturers, and businessmen. In an age of rapid technological change and global competition, many of these regulations now restrict the economy and hold down growth and job creation.

The decade between 1995 and 2005, a period of high unemployment, slow growth, and cuts in the fabled social welfare system, took a toll on popular attitudes toward Germany's "social market economy." Between 1999 and 2006, the proportion of adult Germans who stated that the social market economy was still a reality dropped from 46 percent to only 24 percent, while those who no longer saw the system as "social" increased from 39 percent to 62 percent. Thus, a solid majority of Germans in 2006 doubted that the social market economy was still working.[17]

But the strong economic recovery following the 2008–2009 banking crisis has improved citizen perceptions of this social market economy. According to a 2012 Pew Research Poll, almost 70 percent of the adult population supported a "free market economy." This figure even exceeded the support level in the United States, where 67 percent of Americans liked the market economy. By contrast, a free market economy was endorsed by 50 percent of Italians and only 47 of Spanish respondents. In the same 2012 study, 53 percent of Germans were satisfied with the country's direction, far higher than the level in the United States (29 percent), Italy (11 percent), and Spain (10 percent). The latter two nations have been severely impacted by the Euro crisis (see chapter 10).

As table 3.4 shows, the postwar West German economy between 1950 and 1990 went through four rather distinct stages. Since unification there have been three additional phases. The first postwar stage occurred during the 1950s, the years of reconstruction and the "economic miracle," and it paved the way for later decades. Economic growth averaged a phenomenal almost 8 percent per year during the 1950s. Inflation, which averaged less than 2 percent during the 1950s, was among the lowest in the industrialized world. During this reconstruction phase, unemployment was substantial—especially during the early 1950s. But the ten-year average of 1.2 million still represented less than 5 percent of the workforce.

Heavy investment in capital equipment during reconstruction bore fruit in the second stage: the "golden 1960s." Economic growth averaged a healthy 5 percent; inflation remained nominal at only 2.4 percent, and more important, unemployment practically disappeared, dropping to less than 1 percent. In fact, Germany during the 1960s had such a labor shortage that almost two million

Table 3.4. German Economic Trends since 1950

Period	Economic Growth (percent)*	Inflation Rate (percent)	Total Unemployed (average)**
1950–1959	7.9	1.9	1,200,000
1960–1969	5.0	2.4	223,000
1970–1979	3.2	4.9	647,000
1980–1989	2.2	2.9	2,000,000
1990–1999***	2.4	2.5	3,700,000
2000–2009	0.9	1.6	4,034,000
2009	−5.1	0.9	3,410,000
2010	3.7	1.7	3,240,000
2011	3.0	2.1	2,980,000

Source: Statistisches Bundesamt; https://www.destatis.de/DE/Startseite.html; http://de.statista.com/statistik/daten/studie/1223/um frage/arbeitslosenzahl-in-deutschland-jahresdurchschnittswerte.
*Adjusted for inflation (real growth).
**Average annual level.
***After 1991 figures include the former East Germany.

foreign workers had to be brought in. This impressive performance throughout the 1960s also took place in spite of the 1966–1967 economic slump, the first in the Republic's history.

A sharp increase in oil prices and the resultant worldwide recession affected the German economy during the 1970s. These were the "difficult years" of stagflation—low growth and high inflation. Yet the economy remained strong relative to other Western European nations and the United States. Economic growth averaged 3.2 percent annually throughout the period—a very respectable performance, especially in light of the 1974–1976 recession. However, inflation jumped sharply to almost 5 percent, a high figure by German standards. Finally, unemployment became a serious problem for the first time since the early 1950s. From the mid-1970s to the end of the decade, between 800,000 and one million Germans found themselves out of work. This increase in unemployment was partly attributable to the general worldwide recession, but much of it had structural origins as well. Certain industries were no longer competitive: textiles, shipping, consumer electronics, and even cameras were lost to low-wage exporting countries such as Japan, Taiwan, and South Korea.

From 1980 to 1989 the economy experienced slow but steady growth. Following the 1981–1983 recession, real increases in the gross national product averaged 3.3 percent per year, or 2.2 percent for the entire decade. Unemployment remained persistently high until the 1988–1989 period, when it began a slow decline. One of the few bright spots of the 1980s was the low inflation rate, which because of the strong deutsche mark and falling oil prices dropped to only about 2 percent in 1988. Lackluster economic performance was a major reason for the collapse of the Schmidt government in 1982. Unemployment, for example, was considered to be an important issue by 88 percent of the voters in the 1983 election.[18] The belief or hope that the Christian Democrats could do a better job than the Social Democrats was a decisive factor in the party's victory.

Since unification, there have been three economic phases: a brief unification-led boom, a period of poor performance from about 1995 to 2005, and since then a modest boom, the 2008–2009 financial crisis and resulting economic downturn notwithstanding. Moreover, in the first two phases there were differences in the east and west, with the west experiencing modest success and the east mired in a prolonged depression. Only in the third phase have both parts of the country been doing better, even though performance in the east still lags. In any case, after 1990, unemployment once again became Germany's most serious economic problem. Unemployment averaged about 3.7 million in the 1990s and over 4 million in the decade after 2000. About a third of this total is from eastern Germany, but the economy in the west has also been unable to produce enough new jobs to compensate for the losses due to global competition and the export of German capital to cheaper foreign labor markets.

From 2000 to 2005 the economy declined even further. From 2001 through 2003 the economy hardly grew at all (on average, less than 1 percent per year). Only inflation remained under control, averaging only 1.6 percent between 2000 and 2009. Unemployment continued to grow; by 2005 more than 10 percent of the workforce was out of work. It was not until 2006 that unemployment began to decline. After two relatively good years, the global financial and economic crisis struck in 2008, leading to a 5 percent contraction of the economy and high deficits. Then, in 2009, the Euro crisis hit (see chapter 10). But, as Germany's European neighbors continued to experience poor economic performance, in 2010 the German economy came roaring back with 4.2 percent growth, and in 2011, 3.0 percent. There are two factors behind this post-2005 turnaround: a period of difficult policy reform and hidden economic strengths.

From Economic Basket Case to Savior of the Euro

By 2010 German economic growth was among the strongest in the European Union. Since 2005 over two million jobs have been created, and unemployment has dropped from over 10 percent to under 7 percent, and by 2012 to just over 5 percent. Berlin became the key player in the efforts to save the Euro (see chapter 10). A few years earlier, however, the economy was the mirror opposite. The German economy was one of the worst performing in Europe: low or nonexistent growth, rapidly rising unemployment, and soaring debt put the country near the bottom of the European leader board. By 2002, writes the *Economist*, the country was a "basket case."[19] The economy in 2004 for example grew by only 1.2 percent. Scholarly and journalistic commentaries were universally negative. "Bye-bye made in Germany," for example, was the lead story in a very influential newsmagazine.[20] Responding to some of these problems, German firms since the 1990s have more than quadrupled their investments overseas, producing hundreds of thousands of jobs in Eastern Europe, Latin America, Asia, and the United States. Many marquee companies such as Daimler-Benz, Siemens, Volkswagen, and BMW now have more employees outside of Germany than they do in their homeland. Moreover, two-thirds to three-fourths of their income is earned in foreign markets.

After years of economic stagnation, in December 2003 the government of Chancellor Schröder, with the support of the major opposition party, the Christian Democrats, passed a number of laws designed to revitalize Germany's stagnant economy. This legislative package, termed "Agenda 2010," included accelerated tax cuts, reduced spending on social welfare programs, and fewer regulations for business. It became easier for small firms to dismiss employees and for workers to start their own small businesses. As part of what are called the Hartz IV reforms (named after the chairman of the labor market reform commission), unemployment compensation, which amounts to about 65 percent of previous income, is now generally limited to eighteen months for workers over fifty, and the long-term unemployed have seen their benefits cut to the level of welfare recipients. The right of the unemployed to reject a new job on the basis of its "suitability" was also restricted. Subsidies and tax breaks for home buyers and commuters were reduced, but the big-ticket subsidy items were not touched. Most economists supported Agenda 2010 as a step, albeit small, in the right direction. Whether Germans will accept further cuts in long-cherished social programs remains to be seen. The introduction in 2004 of a quarterly ten-Euro (about $13) copayment for visits to the doctor angered many citizens who were accustomed to "free" medical care. The copayment requirement was dropped in 2012.

By early 2006 the reform measures of Agenda 2010 began to show positive results. While it was too late to save Schröder, the Merkel Grand Coalition had no problem claiming the credit. Between December 2005 and July 2012 unemployment dropped from 11.7 percent to 6.8 percent, the lowest level since 1991. More than 2.7 million new jobs were created during this period, many of them coming from the Agenda 2010 measures.[21] Older unemployed workers, for example, when faced with the prospect of losing their unemployment benefits, reentered the labor market. By late 2007 the proportion of Germans over fifty-five with jobs was above the European Union average for the first time in a decade. Ironically, had Chancellor Schröder not called for new elections in May 2005 and instead toughed it out until the regularly scheduled election in 2006, he might well, given the improved economy, have been reelected. The improving economy also eased the deficit problem in the public sector.

The Economy's Hidden Champions: The Mittelstand

Another major reason for the rapid comeback following the 2008–2009 recession was the fundamental strength of the country's small and medium-sized companies. While Germany has its share of giant global companies such as Deutsche Bank, Bayer, and SAP, 60 percent of all jobs are provided by the economy's "hidden champions": the thousands of small and midsized manufacturing firms that produce niche products for the world market such as state-of-the-art lighting and ventilation systems, specialized valves, commercial kitchen equipment, giant cranes, tiny screws, tunnel-drilling machines, industrial cleaning equipment, specialized printing presses, and computer-driven laser metal-cutting equipment. Many of these products are capital goods; they are needed by producers of other industrial products throughout the world.

None of these firms are household names, but they are critical to Germany's economic success. Although they produce a bewildering variety of products, they share at least six common characteristics: many are family owned, with little or no debt; most of their products are exported; their most important asset is the know-how of their highly skilled and trained workforce; and consensual labor relations, including a high level of mutual trust and respect between owners and employees; cutting-edge technology; an ability to adapt quickly to changing market conditions; and exceptional quality and service. Their products, of course, are expensive, but many of these firms have made themselves indispensable.

Following the global recession of 2008–2009, firms throughout the world that were attempting to gear up production had first to purchase the necessary capital equipment. German firms quickly found their order books filling up again. Thus a combination of wage restraint, the reforms of Agenda 2010, high-quality products, the global thinking of the Mittelstand, and a focus on investment goods that others need to make their end products fueled a remarkable swing in economic growth from a record decline of over 5 percent in 2009 to a robust 3.6 percent growth rate just one year later. This performance was the envy of the world, but it also made it easier for Germany to assume a leadership-by-example role in the Euro crisis (see chapter 10).

Continued Challenges

In spite of Germany's impressive comeback since 2006 and its quick recovery after 2009, there are still problems as the economy moves forward. These challenges need to be addressed to sustain the recent positive performance of the economy.

1. Many economists contend that there is still too much regulation and inflexibility throughout the economy. Government involvement in the postal and telecommunications fields, although declining, has inhibited innovation or expansion in these areas, whereas in countries such as the United States the same areas have been the source of high growth rates and many new jobs.

2. A second problem is the shortage of venture capital. The German capital market has been dominated by large banks that work well with established industries but have been slow to fund innovative, high-risk projects. German business culture is still averse to risk and possible bankruptcy.

3. Laws and regulations still make it difficult to lay off employees even if the companies are losing money. Even in periods of expansion, many firms increase overtime or hire temporary workers instead of adding to the regular workforce. A job protection law makes it difficult and expensive to dismiss workers. Employers are thus reluctant to add new employees. One index, for example, ranked Germany 19th worldwide in the ease of doing business—but 98th in terms of starting a business.[22] Another ranked it 125th in 2011 on labor market flexibility.[23]

4. Long-term subsidies to declining industries such as coal, steel, and shipbuilding as well as agriculture have had a negative impact on growth. Germany's coal-mining industry, for example, still receives annual subsidies amounting in 2010 to $2.5 billion or about $70,000 for each of the remaining 35,000 miners.[24] These funds could be better spent in funding new, high-tech projects with growth potential. (In 2007 the Grand Coalition government and the states of North-Rhine Westphalia and the Saarland, home to the remaining coal mines, finally agreed to end all subsidies by 2018.)

5. Finally, the service sectors of the German economy could grow at a faster rate were it not for trade union opposition and rigid regulations from both the government and professional guilds. Many small businesses and trades such as pharmacy, carpentry, roofing, and painting are still subject to a variety of licensing and work rules that deter expansion and the opening of new businesses. Economists estimate that removing these various regulations and restrictions would increase the growth rate substantially and create hundreds of thousands of new jobs.[25]

INCOME STRUCTURE

Although almost all gainfully employed Germans enjoy a relatively high standard of living, there remain persistent and growing gaps in income and capital resources between different occupational and class groups. Modern Germany is still a stratified society. In addition, easterners, regardless of occupation, lag behind their western counterparts. Income parity between the two regions is not expected for many years to come. The Gini coefficient of income inequality, for instance, worsened from approximately .260 to .300 from the mid-1980s to 2008, one of the most rapid increases in inequality among OECD (Organisation for Economic Co-operation and Development) countries. Generous social transfers, however, reduced inequality by 29 percent from .420 to .300 in 2008.[26] Compared to OECD countries, where income inequality has increased everywhere, Germany is just below the average. The United States is the most unequal society (except for Chile). The percent of the German population living with less than 50 percent of the median income (a measure of poverty) increased from about 6 percent to 11 percent from the 1980s to the late 2000s.[27] Some of the causes behind this trend include the increase in single-income households, the doubling of part-time workers to 22 percent since the 1980s, the gap between east and west, and the rise in capital income as a proportion of total income to over 15 percent.

The average monthly income of different occupational groups is presented in table 3.5. At the top is the group of civil servants (*Beamte*). One group that is not commonly included in these figures is referred to by German sociologists alternatively as "independents" or "employers" (the owners and directors of enterprises, farmers with their own landholdings, and free professionals: doctors, lawyers, small businessmen, and artists), which constitutes just over 10 percent of the workforce. In 2009, they earned approximately $5,200 per month.[28] White-collar employees, who constitute 58 percent of the workforce, had monthly incomes of about $5,000 in 2010 in the western states, and manual workers (24 percent of the workforce) had net monthly incomes of approximately $4,200.

In the eastern region, as table 3.3 shows, a gap has emerged between the civil servants and other groups. There are marginal differences in the income of this group and of the unemployed in east and west. Interestingly, the gap between white-collar and manual workers is less than in the west, and both of these groups earn significantly less than their western counterparts. An independent class of small businessmen, entrepreneurs, and professionals is still only in its

Table 3.5.   Monthly Net Income by Occupation, Dollars, 2010

	West	East*
Civil servants (Beamte)	5,809	5,356
White-collar employee (Angestellte)	5,028	3,995
Manual worker (Arbeiter)	4,267	3,479
Unemployed	1,580	1,569
Retired	2,842	2,296

Source: https://www.destatis.de/DE/ZahlenFakten/GesellschaftStaat/EinkommenKonsum Lebensbedingungen / EinkommenEinnahmenAusgaben / EinkommenEinnahmenAus gaben.html.
Note: 1 Euro = $1.29.
*Including Berlin.

infancy in the East. Few eastern German independents can afford to pay themselves the salaries earned by their western counterparts. As a market economy continues to develop, however, the differences between East and West should become smaller.

Capital Resources

In view of the pattern of income distribution in the western region we should not be surprised to find substantial differences in capital resources between the various occupations. For example, ownership of private property in the form of family homes will not be experienced by the majority of manual workers. Although they make up almost 40 percent of the workforce, manual workers buy only about 20 percent of the private homes. Independents, only about one-tenth of the workforce, own over 40 percent of all private homes.

As figure 3.1 shows, the richest 10 percent of the population holds about 60 percent of the country's wealth (stocks, bonds, real estate, savings accounts, and other capital). The top 5 percent commands 46 percent, and the top 1 percent owns 23 percent of the wealth. More than two-thirds of the population have little or no capital resources; 27 percent have no wealth or are in debt.[29] The only change in this general pattern over the past twenty-five years has been that the very rich have become slightly richer. Compared to 2002, for example, the top 10 percent increased their share of wealth, and all other groups saw their share

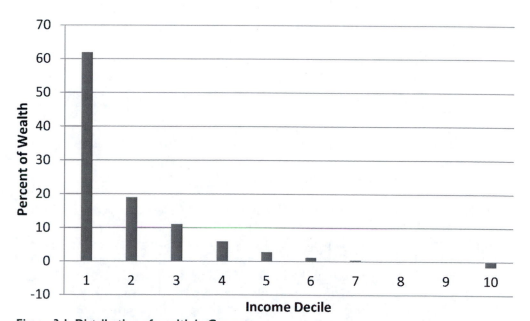

Figure 3.1. Distribution of wealth in Germany

Source: Sachverständigenrat "Analyse: Einkommens- und Vermögensverteilung in Deutschland," Jahresgutachten 2009/10, 325.

decline. This indicates that German governments have not pursued policies designed to redistribute the country's increasing wealth more equitably. On the other hand, given the above-average level of social transfers, the government has also not significantly decreased the level of redistribution.

While the mean (average) level of west German capital resources in 2007 was $110,000 per individual (older than seventeen), the median level (half above and half below) was only $19,000 per individual. As in the case of incomes, there are substantial differences in capital resources between the eastern and western regions. The average household in eastern Germany in 2007 had only about 31 percent of the net worth of the average western household.[30] After about two decades of unification, however, these eastern capital resources were about as unequally distributed as they have been in the west. Some easterners have adapted to the competitive market economy more easily than others.

This economic inequality, which has also been reinforced by the educational system, is largely the result of postwar government economic policy that gave free rein to market forces and created a very favorable atmosphere for investment capital. The 1948 currency reforms, for example, which abolished the reichsmark and installed the famous deutsche mark, to a large extent wiped out the savings of lower- and middle-income groups, who received only about one new mark for every seven old reichsmarks. Landowners and holders of stocks, securities, and capital in foreign countries lost nothing. Indeed, they gained. Moderate tax rates on profits and income from investments, generous subsidies for new plants and equipment, and lucrative tax write-offs also helped to prime the investment pump.

The major economic structures of prewar Germany—business, banking, and industrial firms—were not destroyed by the war or the military occupation but survived fairly intact to provide institutional leadership and support for economic reconstruction.[31] But these institutions of capitalist economic development could perform only if political leadership in the Federal Republic decided to take the free market rather than the socialist path to economic reconstruction. The desire to rebuild as quickly as possible in the face of a perceived Soviet threat meant a decision in favor of the capitalist market economy.

The general success of this system during the postwar and postunification decades is apparent. The political arena continues to grapple with the long-run consequences, particularly in producing and sustaining inequality and rigid social stratification. The potential influence of the issue of inequality on politics can be seen in many surveys in which solid majorities of Germans state that economic rewards have not been justly distributed in the Federal Republic.

West Germany's Left, especially during the 1960s and 1970s and more recently with the PDS/Left Party, was sharply critical of the postwar decision to restore a capitalist system, which had proven so helpless in the face of the Nazi onslaught and in some cases had even collaborated with the Nazis. For the New Left, with its emphasis on identity politics, rights, and the environment (see chapters 5 and 6 for more details), Germany had missed the opportunity between 1945 and 1949 to lay the foundations for a truly socialist society. After 1945 the Old Left, beholden to Marxist notions of class struggle, extensive social welfare redistribution, and nationalization, advocated the expropriation and socialization of industry, banks, and other commercial institutions and the creation of a state-controlled planned economy. According to this view, there is a close connection between capitalism and the Hitler dictatorship, and by restoring capitalism, the Western Allies and postwar German leaders also restored the fascist potential.

It is difficult to evaluate this interpretation of postwar German development. There is little doubt that for the sake of rapid economic reconstruction, a decision was made to use established economic resources rather than to build a new economic order from scratch. There is also little doubt that the free market or capitalist approach was, from many perspectives, extraordinarily successful. However, the German economy hardly qualifies as a "pure" capitalist system. As in other advanced Western countries, government has played a major economic role through subsidies, regulation, and in some cases capital investment.[32] For example, the Land of Lower Saxony is a major stockholder in the Volkswagen automobile firm. National and state governments have also been heavily involved in communications and the coal and steel industries, as well as in housing and transportation. In spite of the trend toward privatization of state-owned enterprises (discussed in chapter 8), there is still a considerable mix of public and private components in the economy.

Germany's postwar economic elites have assumed a more active political role than at any other time in the country's history. But this role has been distinctly supportive of the liberal democratic Republic. Business and industrial elites once subordinate to traditional Prussian and then to radical Nazi political leadership finally found political responsibility thrust upon them in the Federal Republic. Like their counterparts in other advanced industrial societies, they have been concerned above all with maintaining stable political conditions and have supported the pragmatic, middle-of-the-road policies the Republic has thus far pursued. In this sense Germany's economic elites did after 1945 what they should have done in 1871: assumed their share of responsibility for the conduct of politics, instead of deferring to the traditional Prussian elites in political matters. In the Federal Republic, the economic elites have shown no inclination to support or be associated with any extremist political movement or philosophy. More fundamentally, economic and political leaders shifted from a strategy of conflict with other groups to one emphasizing inclusion and consensus. These traditions, although strained after 1990, continue into the present.

RELIGIOUS COMPOSITION

At birth most western Germans become members of either the Roman Catholic or the Protestant Church. This division, an aftermath of the Reformation, follows regional lines: northern and eastern Germany was predominantly Protestant, whereas in the southern and western regions adherents of the Roman Catholic faith were in the majority. In the prewar Reich, Protestants outnumbered Catholics by a ratio of about two to one. The loss of the heavily Protestant (80 percent) eastern territories and the postwar division of the remaining (also predominantly

Protestant) territory meant that both confessions had about equal strength in the former West Germany. This parity brought Roman Catholicism out of its minority status and ended Protestant preeminence among political elites. Nonetheless, Catholics remained underrepresented among western business, cultural, and educational elites.

As one of the few social institutions to survive Nazism and the war with its reputation fairly intact, the churches actually increased their political influence after the war in spite of the increasingly secular, materialistic character of West German society. Because the churches were regarded by military occupiers as untainted by Nazism, the best way to get permission during the occupation period for opening or reopening a business or starting a newspaper or a political party was to have ample references from, or some affiliation with, one or both churches. According to one authority, "The immediate postwar years saw the German churches at their most influential since the Reformation."[33]

It was a far different picture in the former East Germany. By 2010 only about 33 percent of the population reported any religious affiliation, with Protestants (26 percent) far outnumbering Catholics (6 percent). Thus in the unified country the ratio of Protestants to Catholics is still about even, 32 percent Protestant and 31 percent Roman Catholic; the remainder of the population is not affiliated with either church.[34] These changes have important implications for the relative strength of the political parties and the outcome of certain major issues such as abortion.

More than one hundred Jewish congregations also receive state financial support. The largest communities (those with more than 5,000 members) are in Berlin, Munich, Düsseldorf, and Frankfurt. In the wake of the collapse of the Soviet Union in 1991, Germany offered Jews from the former Soviet bloc the right to settle in the country. By the end of 2003, about 190,000 Jews had accepted the offer, which more than tripled the size of the German Jewish community. Many of these immigrants, however, do not practice the Jewish religion and are not members of a synagogue. In 2004 the Schröder government decided to reassess its policy, because the number of Soviet Jews coming to Germany was now higher than the number migrating to Israel. In that year, for example, 9,400 Russian Jews immigrated to Germany and only about 8,000 went to Israel. In 2007, the number of Jewish immigrants had dropped to 2,500, and by 2011 to about 1,000. In 2011, the Jewish community was estimated to be about 200,000, although only about half of that number is affiliated with a religious community.

Since the influx of foreign workers and residents, which began in the 1960s, Germany has also become home to one of Europe's fastest-growing Muslim populations. By 2012 there were about four million practicing Muslims in Germany, making Islam the third-largest religion.[35] Approximately a third have become German citizens.[36] Germany's Muslims are organized into over three hundred mosques, all but two of which are in the western region. North Rhine Westphalia alone has a third of the country's Muslims—the five eastern states, less than 2 percent. The largest communities are in Berlin, Hamburg, and Cologne (12 percent of the city's population). Many new mosques have been built in recent years, with the largest being in Berlin, Duisburg, Mannheim, and Cologne. The controversial new Central Mosque in Cologne, which will be Germany's largest, is slated to open in 2013.[37] The two eastern mosques are in Leipzig and Dresden. Unlike the Protestant, Catholic, and Jewish religions, Muslim religious organizations receive as yet no financial support from the federal government, but several of the states, most notably Hamburg and Berlin, support Islamic religious instruction in the public schools.

The political effectiveness of the Muslim community is hindered by its deep divisions: 75 percent are Sunni, 13 percent Alevi. These divisions are especially prevalent within the largest group, which consists of Turkish Muslims, approximately two-thirds of the total.[38] A wide variety of Islamic organizations exist in the Federal Republic, but no single "umbrella" structure attempts to coordinate and speak for the entire Islamic population—despite the efforts of organizations such as the central Council of Muslims in Germany and the Islamic Council. In spite of these problems, various governments have tried to reach out to the Muslim community. The federal government, for instance, created an Islamic Conference in 2006, and the Interior Ministry has had an Office for Migration and Refugees since 1953 (entitled the Office for the Recognition of Foreign Refugees until 2005).

The importance of religion in the lives of native-born Germans and their attachment to the respective Christian churches, as measured by church attendance, is at best moderate. In 2010 only 12 percent of Protestants and 32 percent of Catholics reported "regular" church attendance, that is, at least once a month. About 30 percent of both religions stated that they went to services "several times" a year. Thus the remaining 60 percent of Protestants and 40 percent of Catholics "seldom" or "never" attended services. Church attendance also varies strongly by age and gender; women and older individuals are far more likely to attend regularly than are men and young people. The strength and character of religious beliefs also vary significantly by confession and eastern/western residence. Indeed, since unification, a plurality of Germans has no confession.

Interconfessional (Protestant-Catholic) differences appear minimal, with solid majorities of both Catholics and Protestants supporting some sort of union between the two churches. The presence of subcultural "in-group" values within the two confessions has been declining. In 1901, 91 percent of all marriages were between couples of the same faith; in 1938, same-faith marriages had declined to 81 percent; and by 1987, only 53 percent of newly married couples belonged to the same faith, and even fewer today.[39] Numerous surveys have found that the majority of the population does not perceive any significant conflict between Catholics and Protestants.

Though religion may not play a prominent role in the lives of most Germans, the two churches, as social institutions, are closely involved in politics. Unlike the United States, Germany has no strong tradition of church-state separation. Since the Reformation, the religious and regional division of the country has meant that the dominant church in any given area was dependent on existing state authority—that is, on the respective princes who acted as protectors of the faith in their territories. This dependence on state authority made both churches (but especially Protestantism, having no international ties) essentially conservative institutions oriented to preserving the status quo. In exchange for the churches' support, the princes also granted a variety of special privileges to the churches (tax-free land, bishops' residences, and salaries), many of which are still in effect.

Certainly the most important privilege, and one that makes German churches among the most affluent in the world, is the church tax. This is computed as a percentage (about 8 percent) of an employee's income tax that is automatically withheld from paychecks and then transferred to the churches' coffers.[40] The tax guarantees churches a steady, inflation-proof flow of funds because it is linked to the income tax, which rises with wage and salary increases. To avoid payment of this tax, a citizen must officially "contract out" of his or her church by filing the appropriate documents with state officials.[41] By so doing, however, the citizen will probably have a difficult time securing the services of clergy for baptisms, weddings, and funerals, as well as gaining admission to church-run homes for the aged or securing help from the churches' charities.

Nonetheless, the number of members choosing to opt out of the church tax has increased sharply in recent years. Between 2000 and 2010, almost three million left the two major churches. In 2010 alone, 180,000 members left the Catholic Church.[42] The tax increases instituted in the 1990s to finance reunification also sparked a wave of withdrawals from the churches. In many cases, the amount of church tax they saved was about equal to the new required taxes.

The former East Germany has been termed "the most secularized society in the world today" and "the most atheistic society ever."[43] Eastern Germans are far less likely to belong to any church or to accept any basic beliefs of Christianity than are westerners. Only 7 percent of westerners have not been baptized or have left the church, as compared to 66 percent of easterners. Belief in God is held by 61 percent of westerners, but by only 21 percent of easterners. It is remarkable that about one-third of the eastern population retained an affiliation to the church in spite of forty years of official opposition—if not hostility—to religion. The schools, youth organizations, media, and of course the Communist Party pressured citizens of the former GDR to leave the churches or avoid any contact with them.

There are no signs of a postcommunist religious revival in the former East Germany. In fact, the eastern region is apparently becoming more secular than the western. Between 1991 and 2006 the proportions of easterners who stated that they were either "not religious" or convinced atheists grew from 65 percent to 69 percent. In the west the corresponding proportion of secularists increased from 11 percent to 17 percent.[44] Thus, unification has clearly made Germany overall a more secular society.

AGE AND FAMILY STRUCTURE

The frequent and sudden changes in modern German political history have affected the present age distribution of the population. As figure 3.2 shows, low birth rates occurred during and at the end of the two world wars and during the

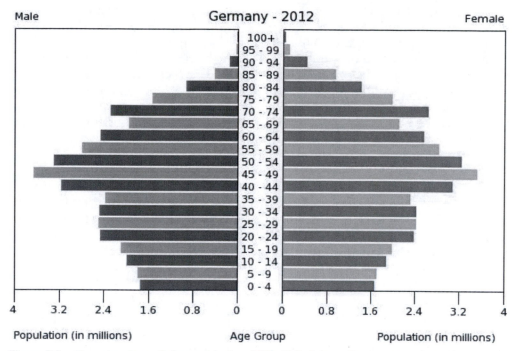

Figure 3.2.   Age structure of the population, 2012. U.S. Census Bureau, International Database.

economic depression of the 1930s. These low birth rates affected the distribution of both men and women; thus, by the 1990s the 40–50, 55–65, and 70–75 age groups were all underrepresented in the population relative to other groups.

Casualties from the two world wars also produced a shortage of males, which was especially noticeable among those over age fifty-five. In the immediate postwar period, the combined effect of war losses and low birth rates produced an underrepresentation and shortage of younger males in the workforce, hence the need to import foreign workers to alleviate a severe labor shortage. In 1946–1947, for example, in the twenty- to twenty-five-year-old age bracket there were 171 women for every 100 men; in the thirty-five- to forty-year-old group there were 153 women for every 100 men. Between 1939 and 1946 the proportion of males between the ages of fifteen and forty dropped from 59 percent to 49 percent.[45] A constant feature of the German age structure throughout the postwar period, then, has been a shortage of males in the economically productive stages of the life cycle and a surplus in the "dependent" age groups. The low birth rates of the past decades have further increased the dependent proportion of the population.

Modern Germany is thus overall a rapidly aging society. Low birth rates, longer life spans, and migration have produced an absolute and relative increase in the elderly population. Between 1955 and 2004 the number of residents over sixty years of age increased by almost 60 percent. By 2009, 26 percent of the population was over sixty, and if present trends continue, by 2030 more than one of every three Germans will be over sixty.[46] This is one reason for the need to reform the pension system, which is discussed in chapter 8.

Major generational differences in political attitudes and behavior have become noticeable only since the late 1960s. The various generations, according to most analyses, exhibited a high degree of agreement on major political and social topics during at least the first two decades of the Republic's history.[47] This cohesiveness was due in large part to the familial solidarity and almost exclusive concentration on material reconstruction that characterized the postwar period. As a result, little political communication and hence conflict took place between generations. For most Germans, the family "came to be regarded as the last stable focus in a world of vast destruction, and vital interests returned to the sphere of the family."[48] Given the overriding concern for maintenance of the nuclear family, politics as a subject of possible disagreement between parents and children and hence a threat to familial solidarity was a taboo topic. Also, the concern for economic betterment extended across all age groups and left little room for discussions about political issues, much less political participation.

The confrontation and "overcoming" of the National Socialist past, urged by Western occupiers and German intellectuals and an obvious topic for intergenerational discussion and debate, was postponed until the student and youth protest movement of the late 1960s. Many students, mostly from middle-class backgrounds, defended their radical views in debates with their parents by reminding them of their parents' support for the National Socialists.

Generational differences in other political areas also became apparent during the late 1960s. Younger age groups, generally those under age thirty, were far more likely to support the Brandt government's innovative foreign policies, begun after 1969, than were older age groups. Differences in more basic political dispositions such as liberalism and conservatism were also discovered by researchers. For example, a 1970 study found Germans under age thirty almost three times more likely to describe their basic political position as "Left" than were their fellow citizens over age sixty.[49]

This period also saw the reduction of the voting age to eighteen and an increasing tendency on the part of younger voters to prefer the Social Democrat (SPD) and Liberal (FDP) parties over the Christian Democrats (CDU). In the 1983 and 1987 federal elections, young voters provided the new Green political party with the majority of its support. In recent elections both the Greens and the SPD did well among younger voters. Among under-twenty-five-year-olds, for example, in 2005 the combined SPD-Green share of the vote was about 48 percent as compared to 38 percent among voters over sixty.[50] After 2009, the Pirates are also resonating with younger voters.

Younger Germans are also more likely to be critical of the United States than their elders. In 2003, opposition to the Anglo-American war in Iraq was strongest among the under-30 cohort. Older citizens remember the United States in terms of the postwar aid and security Washington gave to the fledgling West German state. For younger age groups, the CARE packages, the Berlin Blockade, and the hundreds of thousands of American troops are not memories, but topics studied in history courses.

But as the "student rebel" generation of the late 1960s has aged and younger generations have grown to political maturity, the conflict between the older and younger age groups in the west has lessened. In eastern Germany, the situation is different. Since reunification in 1990, a cleavage between the older generations who were socialized during the communist period and the younger postcommunist generations has developed.

Family Structure

The postwar period witnessed an increase in the importance of the family as a social institution, as well as a change in authority relations within the family. As we have discussed, most Germans after 1945, in the face of the widespread collapse of traditional beliefs and values, withdrew to the family, "the last outpost of social security."[51] Yet this was a different, less authoritarian family structure than had existed earlier in German political history. Parental, especially paternal, authority had suffered a decline through National Socialism and the war. In some parts of postwar Germany, up to one-third of all children were being raised in fatherless homes. If the fathers did return from war and imprisonment, they were in many cases:

> largely dispirited and unable to orient themselves in the post-defeat conditions, thus further impairing their prestige. . . . Men having been indoctrinated to feel as "supermen" were, in varying degrees, unable to deal in a dignified manner with the occupation forces in the role of subordinates, often discrediting themselves in the eyes of their wives through awkward obsequiousness.[52]

These postwar changes have had important consequences for German politics. Wartime and postwar research on the family, especially that conducted by American social scientists, contended that the typical family was father dominated and had not changed significantly since the Industrial Revolution.[53] Father domination and authoritarianism were then linked to the success of the Nazi movement and the apparently strong emotional support that Hitler could count on until almost the last months of the war.

Postwar research on the family has challenged this argument, as well as the assumption that there is a clear-cut relationship between the power structure within the family and levels of support or nonsupport for specific political systems. Most of this research has found a consensual style of decision making to be the most frequent.

Public opinion on the topic of "who should run the marriage" also has changed significantly since the 1950s. In 1954 only 40 percent of males and 54 percent of females felt that both husband and wife should have "equal rights" in a marriage, and 42 percent of the men questioned and 28 percent of the women thought that the "man should have more say." By 1979, however, two-thirds of the males and almost three-fourths of the females took the "equal rights" position. The "male chauvinist" proportion had dropped to 10 percent among men and only 6 percent among women in the survey. Thus, the general climate of opinion on this topic changed markedly over that quarter-century period and has remained there ever since.[54]

This steady increase in a decision-making style based on partnership, which has apparently been taking place since the turn of the century in spite of rapid and sudden changes in political systems, suggests that there is no direct relationship between familial authority relations and the specific structure of the political system. The "authoritarian-father thesis" cannot explain Nazism. Most students of family authority relations attribute the partnership style not to any political system or policy but to the effects of industrialization and modernization—specifically the entrance of married women into the labor force and the larger socioeconomic environment, which, it is argued, increased their power within the family. Thus, the present style of decision making is a further indication of the modernization of postwar social structure.

Two other trends are important. First, the number of single people in Germany has increased dramatically in recent years. In 2009, over 17 million people were single (one in five), an increase of 18 percent over a decade.[55] This has implications for birth rates as well as income and wealth distribution. Second, in recent decades there has been a marked increase in single parent households. In 2009, almost 20 percent of the country's families were headed by a single parent, 90 percent of whom were women.[56] In addition, single parent households were more frequent (27 percent of all families) in the poorer eastern states than in the more affluent western regions (17 percent).[57]

THE EDUCATIONAL SYSTEM

The stratified character of German society is in part the result of an educational system that historically has given a basic education to all, but advanced academic training to only a few. Both the German academic high school (*Gymnasium*) and the universities were designed to educate members of a small elite for leadership positions, with the rest of the population being given only a general education sufficient to enable them to perform satisfactorily at lower levels of the society and economy. This traditional system and the manner in which children were selected for attendance at the higher schools reflected and perpetuated the existing class alignment.

Basic Structure

Most German educational institutions continue to operate on the traditional three-track pattern once common to many European societies. After four years (ages six to ten) of compulsory primary school, the ten-year-old child continues on one of three tracks:

1. Five to six more years in a general school (*Hauptschule*) followed by three to four years of both part-time classroom instruction and vocational training in a company. Between the ages of eighteen and nineteen this group then enters the workforce on a full-time basis. They cease full-time education at the age of sixteen or seventeen.[58]

2. Attendance for up to six years at a general high school (*Realschule*), which combines academic and technical training. Depending on the student's aptitude and course of study, Realschule graduates can transfer to the Gymnasium (academic high school) and the university.
3. Entrance into a Gymnasium for eight (previously nine) years of university preparatory education culminating in the *Abitur* (a degree roughly comparable to an American junior college diploma) and the right to attend a university.

The first two years in any track are considered an orientation period; transfers between various tracks are possible. Until the late 1960s, only about 40 percent of German children pursued tracks 2 or 3, and less than 20 percent ever reached the university. Thus for most children full-time schooling ceased after only nine to ten years of school. The early school-leaving age meant that a career decision had to be made relatively early in life. Many working-class children, who had to make such a decision at age fifteen or sixteen, had few options and probably had little input in the decision. By the 1980s, however, the proportion of the youngest age cohort in tracks 2 and 3 had risen to over 60 percent as the various reform policies of the state and national governments began to have an impact.[59]

In spite of these changes, the system remains heavily class biased. The chances of a child going to college if his or her parents did not go are at 8 percent, the lowest level in Europe. The social background of the parents remains the decisive factor. A child of an unskilled laborer must have test scores that are twice as high as the scores of an offspring of academically trained parents to be selected for attendance at a Gymnasium and the college-prep track. For children of foreigners the barriers are even higher. Over two-thirds of foreign children are in schools with little or no chance of entrance into an academic track. It should thus not be surprising when surveys reveal that about three-fourths of manual workers are the sons of manual workers and that only about one out of every four holders of nonmanual occupations (white collar, civil servant, self-employed, or free professional) comes from a working-class family.

Both the Gymnasium and the university have been largely preserves of the middle class. According to one study conducted in 2001, working-class children had only a 25 percent chance of attending a Gymnasium, as compared to a 60 percent chance for the offspring of middle-class parents.[60] Moreover, once in the academic secondary school, working-class children were less likely to continue into university than their middle-class cohorts. In the 2000–2001 school year, only 24 percent of university students were the children of working-class parents, one of the lowest percentages among industrial societies.[61]

During the immediate postwar years, the Allied occupiers, together with reform-minded Germans, planned extensive changes in this system through the introduction of comprehensive secondary schools designed to provide greater educational opportunity. Yet, for a variety of reasons—not the least of which was Allied reluctance during the Cold War to support radical social and economic changes because western leaders thought that such transformations might hinder needed economic reconstruction and rearmament in West Germany—traditionalist, antireform forces prevailed. The movement for change soon dissipated. Anti-reform elements also saw a relationship between the planned comprehensive school and the Unified School system introduced in the Soviet zone (East Germany).

By the mid-1960s public concern with the quality and performance of the educational system rose to unprecedented levels. The federal government, which, according to the constitution, was clearly subordinate to the states in the field of education, began to seek a larger role in educational policy. The result was a 1969 constitutional amendment that assigned to the national government some responsibilities for overall educational planning and innovation—from kindergarten to the university. Ironically, in the country that gave the institution of the kindergarten to the world, there is sufficient space and personnel for only two out of every three *Kinder* (children).

For some reformers, especially among Social Democrats, a single comprehensive school (*Gesamtschule*) was touted as the key component for restructuring and modernizing secondary education. All children, regardless of social background, would attend this school until at least the age of sixteen. At that point, children with a more vocational orientation would graduate with a first-level *Abitur* and would then proceed to vocational training and full-time occupations. The second level (upper secondary) of the *Gesamtschule* would consist of three more years of academic study and would culminate with a higher-level *Abitur*, followed by university attendance or full-time employment. Thus, the tracking of students would be avoided until at least the age of 16 rather than the present age of 10 in some states. The purpose, of course, is more equality of educational opportunity and hence greater social mobility.

By 2010 there were approximately 1,000 integrated comprehensive schools with about 550,000 students, of which roughly 80 percent were in states governed by the SPD.[62] Comprehensive schools were also introduced in the five new states of the former East Germany.[63] Overall, however, only about 12 percent of all secondary school students are in comprehensive schools. In many states the traditional academic high schools, fearing competition from the comprehensive schools, have become more accessible.

The general trend in all states is toward more flexibility between the tracks. Between 1960 and 2009 the proportion of all Germans with some educational experience beyond the basic level (track 1) increased from 30 percent to almost 60 percent.[64] In the under-thirty age group, about 80 percent had completed programs beyond the general school. Already by 1991, for the first time in German history there were more young people attending colleges and universities than there were in vocational (trainee) programs.[65] Nonetheless, as a recent study has found, this enormous expansion of educational resources in Germany has not improved the "educational opportunity of children from disadvantaged backgrounds." As in the United States and the UK, "the main beneficiaries of the education expansion in Germany were children of parents with high levels of education." Equitable access to education has yet to be achieved.[66]

MASS MEDIA

As a highly developed society, Germany has an extensive mass media structure that has made Germans among the most politically informed people in the world.[67] Approximately 97 percent of the population views television news or listens to radio newscasts. Political news comprises about one-third of the half-hour evening telecasts on the major networks. Also, political reports in daily newspapers are read by roughly 80 percent of the adult population at least once a week.[68] The introduction of private television via cable and satellite systems now offers viewers a greatly expanded range of programs, but it has also arguably reduced the quality and quantity of political information.

Computer and Internet use has proliferated in recent years. In 2011, there were approximately 67 million Internet users, a penetration rate of 83 percent, one of the highest in the world. In 2010, 75 percent of the population reported using the Internet regularly, ranging from 41 percent of the sixty-five to seventy-four age group and 98 percent of the sixteen to twenty-four group.[69] But only 37 percent of Germans use social media, mainly due to sensitivities about privacy and security.[70] Interestingly, at over 6 percent, German is the second-highest language for Web content. English is first at 55 percent and Russian is third at 5.1 percent.[71]

The Press

Germany has approximately 350 daily newspapers with a combined daily circulation of about 20 million. However, only one-third of these have their own complete editorial staff. The remainder have local staff and advertising facilities and rely on wire service reports or reports from other papers for local, national, and international news. Moreover, almost 22 percent of the media market is controlled by the Springer publishing company.[72] Until his death in 1985, Axel Springer used his press empire to oppose left-wing politics, especially as they affected business interests and the possibility of German unification. Similar to other countries, newspapers have struggled financially due to the rise of the Internet.

Newspapers

In terms of national newspapers, Germany is limited to one mass-oriented tabloid, the *Bild Zeitung* (literally, "Picture Newspaper"), and several quality, "elite" papers. *Bild*, the flagship of the Springer chain with a daily circulation of 3.3 million and an estimated daily readership of approximately 12 million (about one-fifth of the adult population), is a skillfully edited blend of sensational sex, crime, and populist politics. Claiming to speak for the average citizen in advocating "commonsense" politics, the paper has generally supported Christian Democrats and other conservative groups. But *Bild* can also take conservative politicians to task, as it did Chancellor Kohl in 1991, when he reneged on his campaign pledge of "no new taxes" to finance unification. The paper also left little doubt in 1998 of its position that, after sixteen years in power, the Kohl government ought to be replaced. Then in 2011–2012, *Bild* was instrumental in the scandal that led to the resignation of Federal president Christian Wulff (see chapter 7).

While generally ignored by intellectuals, politicians take the *Bild Zeitung* very seriously as the true voice of the common man. Chancellor Schröder, for example, was reported to be very sensitive about the impact of a *Bild* headline story. In November 2001 he accepted the resignation of his top foreign policy adviser over a relatively minor matter, in large part because of the way *Bild* treated the story.[73] In the 2002 campaign, the SPD was convinced, with some justification, that *Bild* was actively working against the Schröder government's reelection. Another favorite target of the Springer press has been "radicals" and "leftists" in the schools, universities, and political parties such as the Left Party and Greens.

The major national elite daily newspapers, all with circulations between 275,000 and 500,000, are the conservative-to-middle-of-the-road *Frankfurter Allgemeine Zeitung*; the more reformist *Süddeutsche Zeitung* (published in Munich); the avowedly left-liberal *Frankfurter Rundschau*, although close to bankruptcy; and *Die Welt*, which was a highly respected publication before Springer undertook his active involvement in politics.

Although their editorial orientations differ, these papers present a high level of reporting with strong coverage given to politics as well as business and financial news. In recent years, Berlin's *Tagesspiegel* (with a circulation of 185,000) and *Die Tageszeitung*, or simply *Taz*, have become more important. *Taz* has become the major voice of the alternative media with its editorial position close to the Greens and the environmental, feminist, and peace movements.

Prior to unification, all of East Germany's major daily papers were under the control of the Communist Party and its allied organizations: trade unions, women's and youth groups, and the bloc parties. With unification, most of the GDR's seventy dailies were bought out by or were merged with West German media organizations. By 1998 more than half of the eight million daily newspaper circulation in the former GDR was accounted for by five German publishing companies. The old communist newspaper *Neues Deutschland* still has a circulation of nearly 50,000.

Periodicals

The best-known political periodical is the weekly newsmagazine *Der Spiegel* (The Mirror), with a circulation of over 1.1 million. Similar to *Time* magazine in appearance, *Der Spiegel* prides itself on a crusading, critical, iconoclastic style. Its founder and publisher, Rudolf Augstein (1923–2002), the liberal counterpart to Axel Springer, was active in politics as an adviser and parliamentary candidate. In recent years the magazine has become the leading practitioner of aggressive investigative reporting in the Federal Republic. The various scandals dealing with the financing of political parties, including the Flick affair in the early 1980s, began with extensive exposés in *Der Spiegel*. To the dismay of the West German Left and some of his own editors, Augstein strongly supported Chancellor Kohl's "rush to unity" in 1989–1990. In 2010, *Der Spiegel* was part of an international consortium that published information from Wikileaks.

Since 1993 *Der Spiegel* has had to contend with a strong competitor, *Focus*, a product of the Burda publishing group. Within a year the new weekly, published in Munich, attained circulation of 600,000 and currently is at nearly 800,000. *Focus* aims at a younger audience, is less opinionated than *Der Spiegel*, and makes much greater use of graphics. The more mass-market *Stern* (Star), with a circulation of one million, is another widely read magazine with some political content.

Television and Radio

Public Media

Mindful of the Nazis' abuses of the airwaves, the Constitution assigned sole responsibility for radio and television to the constituent states. Both of these public media are administered by state-based, nonprofit public corporations, which are to be free from direct political influence. These corporations, however, are supervised by boards of control representing the major "social, economic, cultural, and political forces," including political parties and interest groups.

There are currently ten such broadcasting corporations acting for the sixteen Länder. They form the Association of Public Broadcasting Corporations in the Federal Republic (ARD), constitute the first network of German television, and also produce cooperative radio programs. A second television network (ZDF) was established in 1962. Both public radio and television are financed largely through fees paid by each household. These fees for television and Internet access are currently about $270 a year for the average household.

The political parties exert considerable influence on broadcasting corporations through the presence of their representatives on the stations' governing councils. Some of the regional corporations are identified as either "red" (SPD), such as Bremen or Hesse, or "black" (CDU/CSU), such as the Bavarian and Southwest (Baden-Württemberg, Rhineland-Palatinate) broadcasting corporations. Proportional CDU-SPD-FDP-Green influence characterizes the North German Broadcasting Corporation (NDR). The Second National Television Network (ZDF) generally tends toward a pro-CDU position. Thus far only the West German Corporation (WDR), financed largely by the state of North Rhine–Westphalia, has remained relatively free of significant party influence.

All of these corporations, with the exception of the Second Network, are responsible for producing a common national program. The contribution of each regional corporation is determined by its size and income. This sometimes causes conflict between the regional networks. Programs produced by "red" stations critical of Christian Democratic political leaders or policies have been rejected by stations in CDU-dominated states. The "black" stations, or commentators close to the Christian Democrats, have at times returned the favor with programs critical of the Social Democrats.

Following unification, the five new eastern states established their own public broadcasting corporations.[74] The states of Saxony, Thuringia, and Saxony-Anhalt formed the Middle German Network (MDR), which became part of the First Network (ARD). This new network is based in Leipzig. The small northern state of Mecklenburg–West Pomerania joined the North German Network (NDR). Significantly, the only eastern state that did not join a network with other new states or with those in the "old" Federal Republic was Brandenburg, the sole eastern state in 1991 not governed by the Christian Democrats. It formed the

East German Network (ORB). The Second Network has also established studios in the five new states.

Private Media

In 1983 the government of Chancellor Kohl introduced a variety of proposals for private radio and television stations and began to install cable facilities throughout the country. In 1984 a private channel, renamed SAT-1 in 1985, began telecasts. Its main output was light entertainment and feature films, with some news material. The Springer Company and the Leo Kirch organization jointly owned the new channel. Kirch had become a major figure in the new private television market.[75] Shortly after the introduction of SAT-1, a second private station, RTL-plus, began its programs. The public networks have also added cable-satellite stations. By 2012, approximately 90 percent of German households received cable or satellite television.[76] In the past the Social Democrats have generally opposed private radio and television networks, fearing excessive commercialization of the media. The notion that the mass media have a responsibility for educating citizens and elevating the cultural level of the nation, rather than merely providing entertainment, is still supported by many Social Democrats.[77]

Since their introduction, however, the private and cable networks have been very successful in drawing viewers away from the public stations. Many Germans seem to prefer American-style entertainment programs over traditional cultural and educational offerings ("MTV over Wagner"). The popularity of the commercial networks has forced the public stations to adapt their programming to the mass entertainment or American model, much to the disappointment of many intellectuals. Ratings and advertising revenue are now closely watched by the public networks even though the core of their revenues still comes from user fees.

Like their public counterparts, the large private networks have been identified with specific parties and candidates. Most media observers consider SAT-1 to be pro-CDU. It was especially positive toward the Kohl government (1982–1998), whereas RTL was more critical of the chancellor. According to one study, SAT-1 during the 1994 election campaign gave almost four times more television coverage to Kohl than to his opponent.[78] In 1998, however, there was a consensus in the media that it was time for a change. In 2002 and 2005 the Springer press and its allied television stations showed a clear bias against the incumbent Schröder government.

The success of the private media companies has put the public stations on the defensive. Why, critics ask, should Germans pay monthly fees, set by law, to finance stations they increasingly do not watch? The Christian Democratic Party has been at the forefront of the current dissatisfaction with the public stations. Many Christian Democrats advocate privatizing the state-run stations or greatly reducing their budgets.[79]

Recent trends, however, indicate that the "publics" are making a comeback. Driven by their investors to show ever greater profits, some of the private stations have scaled back on their coverage of news and public affairs. In 2007 the oldest of these, SAT-1, was sold to an international private equity group. Soon thereafter the staff was cut from 270 to 170, mainly in the news departments. According to one analyst, this is good news for the public stations as the private channels are becoming "commercial platforms devoid of real content."[80]

A final dynamic has to do with the move of the capital back to Berlin. This change resulted in a sharp increase in media coverage of politics. The number of people employed in the electronic media grew to about 5,300 in Berlin. There are now over 3,000 accredited print journalists in Berlin. Daily newspaper circulation in the capital is over 1.3 million. Berlin has increasingly become the media capital of the country.

SUMMARY AND CONCLUSION

The Federal Republic of Germany today is a more socioeconomically modern, integrated society than was Germany before 1945. The postwar loss of territory in the east to the Soviet Union and Poland and the 1949–1990 division of the nation also meant the loss of several major headaches that had plagued political systems in the past: the dominance of Prussia; regional conflicts; an inner-directed Catholic subculture; an antidemocratic, militaristic landed nobility; and Great Power pretensions in foreign policy. Wartime destruction and postwar refugee migration meant a new, modern postwar economic plant staffed by an abundant supply of proficient labor, in many cases composed of expellees from the "lost territories." Economic success and prosperity brought an easing of class tensions and the end of working-class social isolation. Ironically and albeit at a frightful cost, the Nazis left West German society in a condition more favorable to liberal democracy than they had found it.[81]

Germany has resembled the West for many decades. In fact, in many ways—infrastructure, embrace of new technologies, environmental consciousness, gender issues—the country is leading many older democracies. The dominance of achievement-oriented, materialistic, and individualistic values may cause intellectuals to dismiss the Federal Republic as provincial and philistine, but they have made Germany more governable as a political democracy. As we will discuss in the next chapter, a consensus on the key values and norms of political democracy, not present in 1949, has developed in the Federal Republic during the past six decades. As a result of this consensus, the leaders and those who are led are better prepared to deal with the social, economic, and political challenges of unification and the other policy problems of the twenty-first century than were earlier generations.

NOTES

1. http://www.focus.de/politik/deutschland/freizuegigkeit-lockt-einwanderer-hoechster-auslaender-zuwachs-seit-15-jahren_aid_732630.html.

2. http://www.berlin-institut.org/online-handbuchdemografie/bevoelkerungsdynamik/regionale-dynamik/ostdeutschland.html.

3. http://doku.iab.de/kurzber/2008/kb0608.pdf.

4. See the comments by historian Jürgen Kocka in *The Economist*, May 21, 1994, 10.

5. The Christian Democrats proposed higher pensions for parents with children that would be financed by increased pension taxes from childless couples. Susanne Gaschke, "Black-Out im Bett," *Die Zeit* 49, December 24, 2003. Citing court decisions ruling that the existing nursing care program benefited childless couples more than those with children since it made them "free riders" on a program that is financed via generational transfers on a pay-as-you-go basis, the government in 2004 passed legislation raising the nursing care insurance taxes for childless couples by about 2.5 Euros monthly. The Greens wanted to take the program even further and tax retired childless couples at a higher rate.

6. Nicholas Kulish, "Falling German Birthrate Dispels Baby Miracle Myth," *New York Times*, September 23, 2007; Frank Bruni, "Persistent Drop in Fertility Reshapes Europe's Future," *New York Times*, December 26, 2002; Richard Bernstein, "Aging Europe Finds Its Pension Is Running Out," *New York Times*, June 29, 2003.

7. http://www.cepr.org/meets/wkcn/1/1679/papers/Malanima-Volckart-Chapter.pdf; http://www.berlin-institut.org/online-handbuchdemografie/bevoelkerungsdynamik/aus wirkungen/entwicklung-von-urbanisierung.html.

8. Federal Statistical Office, *Datenreport 2011*, https://www.destatis.de/DE/Publika tionen/Datenreport/Downloads/Datenreport2011Kap4.pdf?__blob=publicationFile, 253. Among individual countries in 2011, France, the United States, and the Netherlands are Germany's most important markets for exports, whereas the Netherlands, China, and France are the most important countries for imports.

9. Since unification in 1990 exports have grown by more than 86 percent. This increase shows the importance of the emerging market economies of Eastern Europe and the former Soviet Union to unified Germany's export performance. The end of the Cold War enabled Germany to once again become a major player in Eastern Europe. Export figures for 1990 are from the Federal Statistical Office, *Datenreport 2002*, Federal Center for Political Education, Bonn, 2002, 254. The figures for 2011 are from the *Datenreport 2011*, Federal Statistical Office.

10. Organization for Economic Cooperation and Development, *Economic Surveys: Germany* (Paris, 1991), 48; Agrarbericht 1995, cited in *Frankfurter Allgemeine Zeitung*, February 8, 1995, 1; Federal Statistical Office, "Strukturwandel in der Landwirtschaft setzt sich 2001 fort," January 16, 2002; *Datenreport 2011*.

11. http://epp.eurostat.ec.europa.eu/cache/ITY_OFFPUB/KS-SF-11-018/EN/KS-SF-11-018-EN.PDF.

12. Arnold J. Heidenheimer, *The Governments of Germany* (New York: Thomas Y. Crowell, 1971), 197–198. See also Arthur Gunlicks, *Local Government in the German Federal System* (Durham, NC: Duke University Press, 1986), chap. 7.

13. Daniel Bell, *The Coming of Post-Industrial Society* (New York: Basic Books, 1973), 17.

14. http://www.nytimes.com/2012/01/05/us/harder-for-americans-to-rise-from-lower-rungs.html?pagewanted=all.

15. "A Family Affair: Intergenerational Social Mobility across OECD Countries," OECD, 2010.

16. https://www.destatis.de/DE/ZahlenFakten/GesamtwirtschaftUmwelt/VGR/Verm oegensrechnung/Aktuell.html.

17. Institut für Demoskopie data cited in *Frankfurter Allgemeine Zeitung*, December 20, 2006, 5.

18. David P. Conradt, "The Electorate, 1980–1983," in *Germany at the Polls: The Bundestag Elections of the 1980s*, ed. Karl H. Cerny (Durham, NC: Duke University Press, 1990), 48.

19. April 14, 2012, 17.

20. *Der Spiegel* 44 (October 25, 2004), 94–109.

21. The job creation numbers run from early 2005 to May 2012 (26.2 million to 28.9 million). These numbers refer to "real" jobs with the full range of benefits (pensions, health care, sick leave) paid through employee and employer contributions. Federal Labor Institute data cited in "Deutschlands größte Sozialreform als Dauerbaustelle. Zehn Jahre 'Hartz IV,'" *Frankfurter Allgemeine Zeitung*, August 15, 2012; http://www.faz.net/ aktuell/wirtschaft/wirtschaftspolitik/zehn-jahre-hartz-iv-deutschlands-groesste-sozial reform-als-dauerbaustelle-11855926.html.

22. http://www.doingbusiness.org/rankings.

23. http://www3.weforum.org/docs/WEF_GCR_CountryProfilHighlights_2011-12.pdf.

24. http://green.blogs.nytimes.com/2010/06/28/europes-enduring-co al-subsidies.

25. Jack Ewing, "In Germany, a Limp Domestic Economy Stifled by Regulation," *New York Times*, February 12, 2012.

26. http://www.oecd.org/els/socialpoliciesanddata/49177659.pdf.

27. http://www.oecd.org/els/socialpoliciesanddata/41525346.pdf.

28. http://de.statista.com/statistik/daten/studie/5742/umfrage/nettoeinkommen-und-verfuegbares-nettoeinkommen.

29. http://www.bpb.de/nachschlagen/zahlen-und-fakten/soziale-situation-in-deutsch land/61781/vermoegensverteilung.

30. http://www.bpb.de/nachschlagen/zahlen-und-fakten/soziale-situation-in-deutsch land/61781/vermoegensverteilung.

31. Karl W. Roskamp, *Capital Formation in West Germany* (Detroit, MI: Wayne State University Press, 1965), 53ff.

32. German governments have also played an active role in organizing rescue operations for industries and major corporations facing a severe economic crisis. Although such bailouts are relatively rare in the United States (e.g., the Lockheed and Chrysler loan guarantees), German national and state governments since the early 1960s have come to the aid of the coal and steel industry, shipbuilding, automobile companies, and major electronics firms. Governments have used devices such as loan guarantees, tax write-offs, subsidies, and even direct grants to major industries in order to save the companies and the jobs they provide. In some cases political officials, together with business, labor, and banking leaders, have formed a "crisis cartel" to fashion comprehensive, long-term solutions to the problems of key industries such as shipbuilding and electronics. For an analysis of several corporate crises in West Germany, see Kenneth Dyson, "The Politics of Corporate Crises in West Germany," *West European Politics* 7, no. 1 (January 1984): 24–46.

33. Frederic Spotts, *The Churches and Politics in Germany* (Middletown, CT: Wesleyan University Press, 1973), x.

34. ALLBUS 2010.

35. Federal Office for Migration and Refugees data cited in *Religionswissenschaftler Medien-und Informationsdienst e.V.* (www.remid.de/statistik), accessed July 16, 2012. By 2012 over one-third of practicing Muslims had become naturalized German citizens.

36. http://www.bmi.bund.de/cae/servlet/contentblob/566008/publicationFile/3171 0/ vollversion_studie_muslim_leben_deutschland_.pdf; see also http://www.soros.org/sites/ default/files/ museucitiesger_20080101_0.pdf.

37. http://www.guardian.co.uk/world/2012/mar/05/row-over-cologne-mega-mosque.

38. Jytte Klausen, "From Left to Right: Religion and the Political Integration of German Muslims," *Religion, Politics, and Policy in the United States and Germany* (Washington, DC: American Institute for Contemporary German Studies, 2005), 26–33.

39. M. Rainer Lepsius, "Sozialstruktur und soziale Schichtung in der Bundesrepublik Deutschland," in *Die Zweite Republik*, ed. Richard Löwenthal and Hans-Peter Schwarz (Stuttgart: Seewald Verlag, 1974), 264; and John Ardagh, *Germany and the Germans* (New York: Harper and Row, 1987), 231.

40. Receipts from the tax amount to about $11 billion annually. The government retains about 3 percent of these revenues to cover the administrative expenses related to the collection of the tax.

41. Germans have to apply to leave a church and pay a fee that varies according to the Land.

42. http://www.spiegel.de/panorama/gesellschaft/missbrauchsskandal-zahl-der-kirchenaustritte-2010-deutlich-gestiegen-a-755497.html.

43. Paul Froese and Steven Pfaff, "Explaining a Religious Anomaly: A Historical Analysis of Secularization in Eastern Germany," *Journal for the Scientific Study of Religion* 44, no. 4 (2005): 397–422, here 397.

44. ALLBUS surveys, 1991 and 2006.

45. http://www.spiegel.de/panorama/gesellschaft/missbrauchsskandal-zahl-der-kirchenaustritte-2010-deutlich-gestiegen-a-755497.html.

46. http://www.bpb.de/wissen/1KNBKW,0,Bev%F6lkerungsentwicklung_und_Altersstruktur.html; Olga Pötzsch and Bettina Sommer, *Bevölkerung Deutschlands bis 2050* (Wiesbaden: Federal Statistical Office, 2003), 31.

47. Elisabeth Noelle-Neumann and Erich Peter Neumann, *The Germans: Public Opinion Polls, 1947–1966* (Allensbach: Verlag für Demoskopie, 1967), 34ff.

48. O. Jean Brandes, "The Effect of War on the German Family," *Social Forces* 29 (1950): 165.

49. Institut für Demoskopie, study no. 2060.

50. Federal Statistical Office, *Wahl zum Deutschen Bundestag am 18. September 2005*, Heft 4 Wiesbaden, February 2006, 15. For the 2002 election, see Tim C. Werner, "Wählerverhalten bei der Bundestagswahl 2002 nach Geschlecht und Alter," *Wirtschaft und Statistik* 3 (2003): 187.

51. Helmut Schelsky, "The Family in Germany," *Marriage and Family Living* 16, no. 4 (November 1954): 332.

52. Brandes, "The Effect of War on the German Family."

53. See, for example, Bertram Schaffner, *Fatherland: A Study of Authoritarianism in the German Family* (New York: Columbia University Press, 1949), 15ff; David Rodnick, *Postwar Germans: An Anthropologist's Account* (New Haven, CT: Yale University Press, 1948), 123ff; David Abrahamsen, *Men, Mind, and Power* (New York: Harper, 1947), 154ff.

54. Institute für Demoskopie, *Allensbach Report*, June 1979, 6.

55. *Datenreport 2011*, chap. 2, p. 29.

56. *Datenreport 2011*, chap. 2, p. 28.

57. http://www.spiegel.de/politik/deutschland/single-eltern-in-deutschland-die-alleingelassenen-a-709034.html.

58. Germany has a highly developed system of vocational education, which some observers consider a key to its postwar economic success. Vocational training combines both classroom instruction and on-the-job training. The trainees are paid a modest wage by the sponsoring company. Training is offered in about four hundred occupations or trades ranging from baker to computer specialist. The vocational program is completed when the trainee passes a theoretical and practical examination conducted by an examining board of experts in the field. See Susan Stern, ed., *Meet United Germany* (Frankfurt: Frankfurter Allgemeine Zeitung Information Services, 1991), 151–153.

59. Statistisches Bundesamt, *Datenreport 1989* (Bonn: Bundeszentrale für politische Bil-dung, 1989), 56.

60. Statistisches Bundesamt, *Leben und Arbeiten in Deutschland: Ergebnisse des Mikrozensus 2001* (Wiesbaden, 2002), 31–32.

61. Statistisches Bundesamt, *Leben und Arbeiten in Deutschland*, 32.

62. Federal Statistical Office, *Schulen auf einen Blick, 2012* (Wiesbaden, 2012), 37.

63. The five new states in the former East Germany had to restructure their educational systems after 1990 to fit the West German pattern. This was a massive task involving the establishment of new schools and curriculum, as well as teacher retraining. At the college and university level, communist influence was pervasive. By 1995, after extensive evaluation procedures, about two-thirds of the 140,000 employees of the old system had retired or had been dismissed because of their conduct during the communist regime, their inability to meet western standards, or for budgetary reasons.

64. Federal Statistical Office, *Datenreport 2011*.

65. *Der Spiegel*, December 9, 1991, 36.

66. Guido Heineck and Regina T. Riphahn, "Intergenerational Transmission of Educational Attainment in Germany—the Last Five Decades," German Institute for Economics Research, Berlin, August 2007, 18–19. One of the other big issues in German education has been the length of the traditional school day. Premised on the presence of stay-at-home mothers, most German schools ended instruction around noon. With the increasing number of women working or wanting to work full time, this structure has been deeply criticized—also in light of the relative lack of day cares. As a consequence, there have been increasing attempts to implement all-day school schedules (*Ganztagschulen*) in many Länder.

67. See Interuniversity Consortium for Political Research, *1991 World Values Study* (Ann Arbor, MI, 1991).

68. *World Values Survey, 2006*, http://www.wvsevsdb.com/wvs/WVSAnalizeQuestion.jsp.

69. https://www.destatis.de/DE/ZahlenFakten/GesellschaftStaat/EinkommenKonsumLebensbedingungen/_Grafik/Internetnutzung.png?__blob=poster.

70. http://www.economist.com/blogs/dailychart/2011/07/europe%E2%80%99s-social-media-hotspots.

71. http://w3techs.com/technologies/overview/content_language/all.

72. http://www.ejc.net/media_landscape/article/germany.

73. *Frankfurter Allgemeine Zeitung*, November 21, 2001, 3.

74. For an excellent account of the changes in the media of the former GDR from the collapse of the communist regime through the unification process, see Joseph E. Naftzinger, "Transitioning from Communist to Free Media in Central Europe: The Example of East German Television and Radio," unpublished manuscript, Washington, DC, December 1991.

75. Nathaniel Nash, "A Dominant Force in European TV," *New York Times*, August 28, 1995, D1.

76. http://news.bbc.co.uk/2/hi/europe/country_profiles/1047864.stm#media.

77. Former Chancellor Helmut Schmidt (1974–1982) was especially critical of private, commercial television. In 1979 he attempted to halt the installation of an experimental cable television network and the broadcast of German-language television programs from Radio Luxembourg's satellite. Schmidt contended that a "flood" of commercial television programs would be damaging to German family life and "change the structure of our democratic society." His antitelevision campaign included a proposal that Germans abstain one day each week from watching television. There was little interest in his plan.

78. Institut für Demoskopie, survey no. 6033, cited in *Information zur politischen Bildung* 260 (Fall 1998): 47.

79. Alan Cowell, "Germans, Too, May Trim Public TV," *New York Times*, February 9, 1995, A6.

80. Michael Hanfeld, "Ran an die Rendite," *Frankfurter Allgemeine Zeitung*, July 21, 2007, 33.

81. Michael Bernhard, "Democratization in Germany: A Reappraisal," *Comparative Politics* 33, no. 4 (2001): 379–400.

4

Political Culture, Participation, and Civil Liberties

According to many historians, Germany's first experiment with political democracy at a national level, the Weimar Republic, failed because it was a "republic without republicans." The formal structures of political democracy—representative institutions, free elections, constitutional guarantees of civil liberties—were present, but the political attitudes and values of many Germans were not supportive of these structures. According to this view, most Germans during Weimar longed for either a restoration of the monarchy or a similarly strong authoritarian system to return the country to economic prosperity and Great Power status. As discussed in chapter 1, the founding of the Federal Republic likewise met with little popular enthusiasm initially. Hence some Germans and foreign political leaders, as well as scholars, were quite uncertain in 1949 about the prospects of the postwar system. Once again, as during Weimar, the constitutional structures of democracy were present, but what about the political attitudes that lay behind the constitution? Would Germans, through their attitudes and behavior, accept and support this new system, or would they remain indifferent or even embrace antisystem ideologies and movements? And what about the present? How democratic does German political culture remain in the twenty-first century? How does current German national identity affect the unexpected rise of German influence over the last few years and especially during the Euro crisis?

This chapter explores these questions by examining the development of German political culture—that is, German attitudes and values toward politics and German political behavior—since the founding of the postwar system. We seek to determine how Germans think and feel about the Republic and how they have acted or behaved toward the democratic order over the past six decades. Of particular importance are the support and maintenance of civil liberties and human rights as well as the treatment of minority groups.

In this chapter we also examine the political culture of the Federal Republic's newest citizens: the 15 million inhabitants of the former German Democratic Republic who lived for forty years under a one-party dictatorship, but who, through West German television and radio, were well informed about the development of democracy among their western cousins. Are easterners different in their political attitudes and values? Or did they experience vicariously the changes that took place in West Germany and need only an opportunity to express freely their support for democratic values and institutions? Did they become "republicans without a republic"? What changes have taken place in the two decades since reunification?

POLITICAL VALUES

National Identity

As a linguistic, ethnic, and cultural unit, the German nation is one of Europe's oldest. Indeed, for centuries Germany was understood as a "cultural nation" (*Kulturnation*). The United Kingdom, France, and other European states had resolved the questions of political and geographical boundaries as well as the criteria for membership in the national community by the late eighteenth century. Yet the questions of what Germany is and who the Germans are have never been resolved in a political sense. A single state incorporating all peoples who identify with the German nation has never really existed, with one possible exception: Hitler's short-lived and ill-fated *Grossdeutsches Reich* (Great German Reich), established after Nazi annexations of Austria, Alsace, and the Sudetenland of Czechoslovakia. Even the much-heralded unification and establishment of a Second Reich under Prussian leadership in 1871, which brought twenty-five German political entities into one federation, united most but by no means all German-speaking peoples in Europe. The successors to the Second Reich, the Weimar Republic and the Nazi Third Reich, maintained the territory of the unified nation-state and, in the Nazi case, briefly extended its borders. Yet by 1945, after only seventy-five years as a unified nation-state (albeit with three different types of political systems), the problem of national identity and the future of the German nation as a political unit had to be resolved once again.

National identity—the sense of belonging to a particular national community, usually sharing a common physical territory, language, history, and cultural values—has been present among Germans for at least as long as it has among many other European nations. This general national identification has not been linked, however, with a stable, unified state. Thus, to ensure its own stability, each succeeding political system has sought unsuccessfully to broaden the scope of national identification to include a commitment to the given state. An attachment to a particular political system has been the missing component in the German sense of national identity. National identification in the United States, for example, includes identification with and support for certain political symbols (the Constitution, flag, and national anthem) and ideals (individual liberty, property, and equality). To be an American also has meant support for a particular political system: a liberal, democratic republic. Socialism, communism, and monarchy—or all other possible political options—are not a legitimate part of the American national identity.[1] Such a linkage between national identity and a specific state form has never been present in Germany. For example, Germany had three (four if one counts East Germany) different flags in the twentieth century.

The Federal Republic proclaimed in 1949 was, like its predecessors, faced with the problem of creating and fusing a commitment to a particular political form with an existing national identity. The presence of a competing German state (the GDR) within the same territory as that of the prewar Reich and its capital in the communist part of the historic center of the Reich complicated the task. West German leadership compounded the problem at first by officially encouraging support for the values of the liberal democratic constitution but not for the specific West German state. Thus, in effect, West German leadership until the late 1960s was urging citizens to become democrats but not to develop too strong an attachment to the Federal Republic, because it was only "provisional" until all Germans were reunited within a single democratic state with Berlin as its capital. Until that time, however, this provisional West German state also claimed to be the only legitimate representative of all members of the German nation within or outside its borders. The leaders of communist East Germany did not share this viewpoint, but apparently it had widespread support among East German citizens.[2]

In spite of these difficulties, to what extent has a national identity with a political component developed since 1945? In the immediate postwar period, for understandable reasons, many wanted to forget about being German. A few enthusiastically embraced the "European idea," a politically united Europe with no national borders, or gladly submitted to the Americanization that was so apparent in popular culture. Most simply reduced their scope of allegiance to the self, the family, and perhaps their Land (e.g., Bavaria) or local community. This mass withdrawal to the primary sphere (or privatization, as some social scientists have termed it) gave German leaders considerable freedom of action but also imposed limits on the intensity of commitment or identification they could require from their citizens.

This condition could not last indefinitely, and there were signs already in the 1960s that Germans were rediscovering the larger national community and at the same time developing a specific identification with the Federal Republic.[3] As table 4.1 shows, the proportion of West Germans proud of the postwar political system has increased substantially since the early years of the Republic. In 1959 only 7 percent expressed pride in some aspect of the political system. Among Americans at that time, the level of pride in political institutions was 85 percent; among British respondents, 46 percent were proud of their country's political order. By 1978 the German level of pride in their political system had risen to 31 percent, and in 2000 fully 60 percent of respondents expressed pride in the postwar constitution and political order. By 1988 the political system was the area in which Germans had the most pride; it had overtaken the economy, which until then had been the greatest source of postwar German national pride.

In a 2008 survey, when asked what they were most proud of, "political institutions, the Constitution, and parliament" came out on top (39 percent) while "economic success" was a distant second (26 percent). Support for specific national symbols has also grown since 1949. The proportion of West Germans stating that they feel "joyful" or "happy" when they see their black, red, and gold

Table 4.1.   Sources of National Pride, 1959–2008 (in percent)

	1959	1978	1988	2000	2008*
Political institutions, constitution	7	31	51	60	54
Economy	33	40	50	53	41
Social welfare programs	6	18	39	39	28
Characteristics of the people	36	35	n/a	n/a	n/a
Contributions to science	12	13	37	44	45
Contributions to the arts	11	10	22	36	34
Other, none, no answer	43	39	50	34	70

Source: For 1959 and 1978, David P. Conradt, "Changing German Political Culture," in *The Civic Culture Revisited,* ed. Gabriel Almond and Sidney Verba (Boston: Little, Brown, 1980), 230; for 1988, German General Social Survey, cited in Peter Mohler, "Der Deutschen Stolz: Das Grundgesetz," *Informationsdienst Soziale Indikatoren,* no. 2 (July 1989): 1–4; ALLBUS 2000, 2008; http://isysweb.gesis.org/isysnative/RjpcaHRkb2NzXHNob3J0Y3V0 LnBkZlxhbGxiX2NiXFpBNDYwMF9jZGlucGRm/ZA4600_cdb.pdf#xml = http://isysweb.gesis.org/isysquery/irl 1ecb/5/hilite.
Note: 1959–2000 West Germany only.
*Sum of first- through third-ranked items.

national flag has increased from 23 percent in 1951 to 69 percent in 2006 and then fell back to 53 percent in 2008. Only 43 percent of eastern Germans expressed such sentiment in 2008.[4] Solid majorities of Germans now consider national feelings of patriotism and pride to be important.

For many years, Germans were at or near the very bottom of international surveys of national pride. In 1995–1996, West and East Germany were second and third from the bottom in terms of general national pride. By 2003–2004, both had only marginally increased by two spots.[5] But with each year, levels of pride rose. In a 2009 survey, approximately 70 percent of Germans expressed trust and admiration in their country, above the UK, but below the United States.[6]

Another indication of the growing sense of identity is that Germans also have become increasingly critical of the United States, the once protective big brother who could do no wrong. For example, in a 2002 Pew survey, 67 percent thought that the spread of American ideas and customs was a bad thing (50 percent in the UK, but 71 percent in France).[7] Criticism of the United States was especially pronounced during the administration of George W. Bush with his "global war on terror" and invasion of Iraq in 2003. But such sentiments had begun already during the Vietnam War when criticisms of American foreign policy became, for Germans, quite vocal, even reaching the point where the then–finance minister and later chancellor Helmut Schmidt, while in the United States in 1971, criticized American policy. Differences over policies in the Middle East first became apparent as Germany attempted to maintain a posture of neutrality throughout most of the 1970s.[8] A similar pattern can be seen in the German reaction to American policies following the Soviet invasion of Afghanistan in 1979. The Schmidt government did not unconditionally support Washington's request for sanctions against the Soviets, including a boycott of the 1980 Olympic Games. Instead, it warned against "overreaction," "alarmism," and a "backslide" into a cold war. The widespread opposition in the early 1980s to the stationing of new NATO intermediate-range missiles in Germany was also an expression of this emerging national identity.

In the mid-1980s, one of the most influential discussions about German national identity took place. Several conservative intellectuals and political figures, some with ties to the Christian Democrats and the Free Democrats, argued that the Federal Republic was hindered in its dealings with other nations by its lack of a national identity and pride comparable to those found in other European countries.[9] They contended that the major obstacle to the development of such an identity was an excessive focus on the Third Reich by historians, educators, and the media, which burdened younger generations with an unjustified sense of guilt. The conservatives stressed that German history is long and complex and that even during the period 1933–1945 there were phenomena other than National Socialism. A country that is obsessed with guilt, they argue, would be incapable of dealing with the challenges of the future. To counteract this, they wanted to create and stress common positive historical memories and traditions. One result of these intellectual currents was the Bitburg affair, when Helmut Kohl and Ronald Reagan decided to commemorate the anniversary of the end of World War II in 1985 at a military cemetery that contained several SS members' graves. There was also the so-called House of the History of the Federal Republic opened in 1994 in Bonn with a very positive narrative of post-1945 German history.

Many liberal and social democratic intellectuals criticized what they believed was an attempt by conservatives to gloss over, or to relativize, the singularity of the Nazi experience and especially the Holocaust. The debate was particularly intense from 1986 to 1989 among several leading historians and social scientists. This *Historikerstreit* (historians' dispute) attracted national attention when a leading social philosopher, Jürgen Habermas, accused two historians of seeking to trivialize the Nazi period. He linked their efforts to a larger movement among conservative historians to create a new view of the past that would "limit the damage" done by the Third Reich and give Germans confidence and pride.

Although he did not deny the need for a sense of national identity, Habermas urged Germans to focus their patriotism and pride on the open, democratic society that has been created since 1945:

> The creation of such a society was the greatest achievement of the postwar generation, for it opened Germany unconditionally to the political culture of the West. . . . The only patriotism that will not alienate us from the West is constitutional patriotism. Unfortunately, a tie to universal constitutional principles that is based on conviction has only been possible in Germany since, and because of, Auschwitz. Anyone who wants to drive the blush of shame over that deed from our cheeks by using meaningless phrases like "obsession with guilt," anyone who wants to call Germans back to a conventional kind of identity, destroys the only reliable basis of our tie to the West.[10]

Habermas's charges were sharply denied by the historians, and the debate continued in the pages of West Germany's leading newspapers and periodicals. This *Historikerstreit* and the Bitburg incident illustrate how difficult and sensitive the question of national identity had become in the Federal Republic. It also showed the growing importance of collective memory of Nazism and the Holocaust as an influence on German political culture.[11] Even into the present this collective memory is one of the most important formative influences on German identity, values, and policies. For example, in 2012 as many Germans were debating the legality of circumcising minors, there were constant references to the country's special responsibility that its terrible history has generated.[12]

Legitimacy

Like many new states, the Federal Republic was also confronted with the problem of acquiring legitimacy. Would the inhabitants of the western occupation zones accept and obey the authority of the new state? Would the policies of the new state be consistent with what most citizens regard as right and wrong? In spite of national division from 1949 to 1990 and a constitution (Basic Law) never subjected to direct popular approval, there has been no serious challenge to the authority of the Federal Republic. Indeed, the overwhelming majority of West Germans consider the institutions and processes of the Federal Republic as legitimate. Support for this statement can be found in part in the high levels of voter turnout and the concentration of electoral support in the parties committed to the Republic. Extremist, antisystem sentiment is confined to small percentages of the electorate. Direct challenges to the Federal Republic's authority have been limited to communist and neo-Nazi parties in the 1950s and 1960s, to the small but active left-wing terrorist groups that plagued police and courts from the late 1960s until the late 1990s (discussed in greater detail later in this chapter), and to some right radical violence, especially in eastern Germany after reunification.

The legitimacy of the Federal Republic, particularly in its early years, was based in part on the absence of any credible alternative. After experiences in this century with monarchy, the Weimar Republic, and Nazism, postwar Germans had no historically successful alternative to put forward. They were quite willing to take, in essence, what the Allies offered: a liberal, parliamentary system in only part of the former Reich. However, this decline in support for past political systems and the resultant increase in support for the current regime were part of a developmental process affected by both the passage of time and the positive performance of the new system.

Through opinion surveys in which West Germans were questioned periodically about their attitudes toward two of the past political systems—monarchy and the Hitler dictatorship—and their support for key principles of the current regime, we can examine the character and sources of this process. In 1951, thirty-three years after the collapse of the Hohenzollern dynasty, almost one-third of the adult population favored its restoration. Nevertheless, fourteen years later, support for the monarchy had dropped to only 11 percent. Much of this decline, according to one analysis, was due to the simple passage of time; those with living memories of the Hohenzollerns constituted an ever-smaller segment of the population.[13] Some of this decline, however, was related to the policy successes of the postwar system.

These changes are even more apparent in attitudes toward Hitler and the Nazi Party. When asked whether Hitler would have been one of the greatest

German statesmen had it not been for the war, almost one-half of the adult population in 1955 answered affirmatively; by 1967 this number had dropped to less than one-third, with a majority flatly rejecting the proposition. Age is an important factor in explaining this change. Each age group socialized since 1949 was progressively less likely to support the Hitler dictatorship than were older generations who grew up under earlier regimes.[14] But even older generations changed their views as time went on. In West Germany, the percent who thought that Hitler was the greatest German declined from 10 percent in 1950 to 2 percent in 1971, 1 percent in 1992, and did not register in 2000.[15]

Also, when national samples on nine different occasions between 1953 and 1977 were asked how they would react if a new Nazi party attempted to come to power, a similar trend was apparent. Potential support for neo-Nazism dropped from 16 percent in 1953 to only 7 percent in 1977. The percentage of respondents who would actively or passively oppose such a party increased from 62 percent to 79 percent over the same period. Perhaps more important, by 1977 almost 60 percent of the adult population stated that it would do "everything possible" to see that a new Nazi party would not come to power. In addition to age, the steady drop in support was a result of economic prosperity and other policy successes of the first chancellor, Konrad Adenauer: German acceptance into the European Community and NATO and the integration of 10 million postwar refugees. The effects of political education in the schools apparently also were a factor in producing this decline. In short, there was some support for past regimes in the early 1950s, but it diminished over time with the growing effectiveness of the Bonn system. By the 1960s the Republic, originally legitimated by Allied occupation, could stand on its own by virtue of its performance. By the 1990s, pollsters had even stopped regularly asking such questions.

Thus far we have accounted for the legitimacy of the postwar system through the absence of a credible alternative to what the Western Allied occupiers established in 1949 and the performance of the postwar system—above all, economic prosperity, effective executive leadership, and policy successes. What, however, would happen if for some reason its performance faltered? Does the regime now have some reserve of citizen goodwill it could fall back on in crisis situations? These hypothetical questions are difficult to answer. Nevertheless, the available material suggests that this rain-or-shine support has developed and that the postwar Republic is more than a fair-weather democracy. Our evidence for this assertion comes from two general sources: the ever-present public opinion poll and the actual behavior of Germans at both elite and mass levels during political and economic crises of the recent past.

Democratic Values, Processes, and Institutions

The decline in popular support for past political regimes has indeed been paralleled by a steady increase in support for the values, processes, and institutions of the Federal Republic. The essentially passive acceptance of the postwar system for a basically negative reason—because everything else had failed and because there were Allied troops on the ground to ensure a democratic system—was displaced by a more active, positive orientation to the new Republic. Moreover, by the late 1960s the levels of popular support had become sufficiently high and diffuse that some observers were describing the Federal Republic as "institutionalized" and "established."[16] The process can also be illustrated through public opinion data covering key values of liberal democracy (acceptance of political conflict and competition) and its central institution and process (representation of the popular will via a legislative assembly).

Conflict and Competition

Many scholars explained the inability of liberal democracy to take root in Germany in the first half of the twentieth century as the result of an absence of popular understanding of the role of conflict and competition in democratic politics. Germans, it was said, longed for no-conflict solutions to social and political problems. Unlike citizens in the classical democracies of the United States and the UK, Germans in the past, according to the German sociologist Ralf Dahrendorf, would not recognize that differences of opinion and interest in politics are inevitable. Instead of learning to manage conflict through the creation of institutions and rules, they sought instead to eliminate the causes of conflict by searching for "absolute solutions" to social and political problems without ever considering whether such solutions actually exist.[17] This aversion to conflict made them "expert oriented" and "legalistic," with an administrative, perfectionist conception of politics.[18] Moreover, many of the institutions adopted after 1949 were aimed at achieving consensus. Some scholars even characterize Germany as a "Grand Coalition state."[19]

Evidence suggests, however, that if aversion to political conflict was characteristic of attitudes in the past, this aversion has diminished greatly. National samples of adult citizens were asked on eighteen separate occasions between 1950 and 1997 whether "it is better for a country to have several parties, so that a variety of different opinions can be represented, or only one party, so that as much unity as possible exists." By the late 1970s, 92 percent of the public supported the principle of party competition. These trends suggest that the value of political competition is now firmly established in the political culture.

Representation and Parliament

According to most theories of democracy, the central institution for political democracy in large societies is the legislative assembly in which the various interests and opinions are represented. Do Germans feel they are represented in parliament? Do they support, in theory at least, this important institution? Support for key political values, a central political process (representation), and the major republican institution (parliament) had by the late 1960s reached levels at which it was possible to speak of a consensus on liberal democracy in modern Germany. And although the increase in support for the system and the decline in positive feelings for past regimes have been the result of both generational changes and the performance of the postwar system, the important point is that all major social, economic, and political groups ranked high in their support of political competition, their sense of representation, and their support of parliament. Support for the liberal Republic established in 1949 has become even more diffuse in the last decades and is not significantly related to any particular group or policy of the government. These principles and processes have become accepted norms for the conduct of politics in the Federal Republic.

However, while support for democratic principles and values remains high, Germans have become increasingly critical of the performance of their political institutions and representatives and more distant from political parties. "Disappointment" with the political parties rose from 33 percent in 1991 to 62 percent by 1998, but fell to 45 percent by 2009. In 2008, only 15 percent of Germans had a lot or some trust in the parties.[20] Ironically, much of this increased criticism is an expression of the maturity and sophistication of German citizens. They expect more from their political institutions and leaders than they did a generation ago. Nonetheless the major unknowns about German politics no longer revolve around the possibility of reverting to an authoritarian or even a fascist past but, rather, to the future scope and quality of democracy. Indeed, in light of recurrent social movements and protests, there are calls for more (direct) democracy, not less.

Democratic Support in East Germany

With the collapse of the communist regime in East Germany in 1989 and the subsequent unification of the two German states, the Federal Republic of Germany was once again, as in 1949, faced with the task of integrating millions of citizens whose only concrete political experience had been with authoritarian and totalitarian regimes. After 1933, citizens in East Germany were governed by either the Nazis or the communists. Did a distinct East German political culture emerge during the forty-year division of the nation? Do East German attitudes and values show the impact of decades of indoctrination in Marxist-Leninist ideology? Or did East Germans vicariously experience the democratic development of their cousins in the west and then demonstrate their own commitment to democracy in their revolution of 1989–1990?

Since unification these questions have been the subject of extensive scholarly research. The evidence presents a somewhat mixed picture. Eastern Germans since 1989 have voted in large numbers for democratic parties. The relative success of the former Communist Party, the Party of Democratic Socialism (since 2007, the Left Party), has been restricted largely to easterners who had benefited from the old system or who felt they had been unjustly treated in the economic and social dislocations of the unification process, that is, the "losers" of unification. In the 2009 election, for example, support for the Left Party among unemployed easterners was about 45 percent.[21]

Surveys conducted in 1990 before unification found few differences between the two populations in their general support for democratic values. Approximately 90 percent of East and West Germans agreed that democracy required a political opposition, civil liberties, the rule of law, freedom of speech and expression, and free elections.[22] Easterners also have about the same level of national pride, but the sources of that pride are different from those of westerners. The easterners' pride emphasizes the Federal Republic's economic achievements and the former GDR's athletic successes. Eastern responses are not unlike those found in West Germany during the 1950s. The greatest difference between the two regions is in the area of political institutions as a source of pride. While about 35 percent of West Germans consider the Constitution or the Bundestag (parliament) as the single most important source of their national pride, only about 12 percent of East Germans share this view.[23]

Since reunification, as easterners have confronted the harsh realities of unemployment, increased crime rates, and the indifference, if not hostility, of some of their western cousins, their support—both specific and abstract—for political democracy has declined, whereas westerners remain very supportive of liberal democracy as practiced in the Federal Republic. In May 1990 almost 80 percent of eastern Germans agreed with the statement that "democracy is the best form of government," and over 40 percent considered the democracy "that we have in the Federal Republic" the best form of government or state. By July 1991, abstract support had dropped to 70 percent, and only 31 percent of easterners considered the Federal Republic the best form of government. Among westerners, both abstract support (86 percent) and specific support (80 percent) were about equal. Among younger Germans, these differences were even greater: only 25 percent of easterners under age thirty, as compared to 72 percent of young westerners, considered the Federal Republic's democracy to be the best form of government.[24] Years later, in 2009, the east-west divide remained. While 76 percent of westerners considered democracy as practiced in the Federal Republic to be the best form of government, only 36 percent of easterners agreed.[25]

Another 2009 survey found that regional differences continued, especially when evaluating political objects. When asked about the sources of national pride, westerners were more likely to mention the postwar democratic order and Germany's restored international status (80 percent) than were easterners (62 percent). The "political system and the rule of law" were considered a source of pride by about 80 percent of westerners, but by only about 50 percent of easterners. There were few regional differences regarding German culture, its economic achievements, and unification as sources of pride. Clearly after over two decades of unification the former residents of East Germany remain more skeptical and detached about politics and democracy in the Federal Republic than their western countrymen.[26]

The effects of a forty-year division are also noticeable in the differing conceptions of German history held by citizens of the two regions. In several surveys since 1988, westerners were asked whether there was anything in their history that distinguished them from other countries, "something that can really be termed German history." As table 4.2 shows, among those westerners who believed there was something that distinguished German history, about half mentioned National Socialism, Hitler, and the Third Reich. The many wars in German history and the country's postwar division were the second and third most frequently mentioned distinguishing characteristics. When easterners were asked the same question in 1990, 1992, and 2000, however, a much smaller percentage mentioned the Third Reich or National Socialism as a distinguishing feature of German history.[27] Table 4.2 also indicates a convergence between east

Table 4.2. Historical Identity: Western-Eastern Germany

Question: Is there anything in our history that distinguishes us from other countries—I mean, something that can really be termed *German* history?

	West			East		
	1989	1992	2000	1990	1992	2000
Yes (percentage)	59	59	69	67	60	68

Question: And what do you think is special about our history: what distinguishes our history from the history of other countries?

	West			East		
	1989	1992	2000	1990	1992	2000
The Third Reich, National Socialism, Hitler	52	52	47	5	11	23
Germany was a divided country, the Berlin Wall	11	11	20	36	30	31
Many wars in the history of Germany; Germans have started wars, German military leaders	23	22	29	36	36	44
Reconstruction after the war	6	8	8	2	3	2
Character traits (love of order, hard-working, etc.)	5	4	4	13	5	4
Other, don't know	22	18	6	16	24	6
Total*	119	115	114	108	109	110

Source: Institut für Demoskopie, survey nos. 5014, 9010; *Jahrbuch,* vol. 9, 385; *Jahrbuch,* vol. 11, 542.
*Multiple responses were possible.

and west on this question, as the eastern reference to the Third Reich has increased while the western level (at least between 1992 and 2000) has declined. For easterners, the country's frequent wars and postwar divisions were the most important factors setting Germany apart from other nations. These differences reflect, in part, the divergent approach the two regimes took to the past. East Germans were told by their leaders that they bore no responsibility for the Third Reich. Hitler and the Nazi regime were portrayed as the inevitable result of German and international capitalism. The German Democratic Republic, as the first socialist state in German history, represented a clean break from this militaristic and fascist past. In the west, attempts were made in the postwar period to confront the legacy of Hitler and National Socialism and to accept responsibility for the Holocaust. Western German media and schools, especially in the past thirty years, have given extensive coverage to the Third Reich. At least publicly, westerners appear more sensitive about this period in German history than do easterners.

Easterners still retain more positive attitudes toward "socialism" and a more class-oriented conception of society than do westerners. Table 4.3 presents recent 2010 responses from western and eastern Germans to selected questions. In 2010, nearly 75 percent of easterners as compared to 57 percent of westerners agreed with the statement that "socialism is basically a good idea that was only badly carried out." The economic dislocations of the unification process, especially the sharp jump in unemployment and the many plant closings, have taken their toll on easterners' views of the market economy. Moreover, the volatility of this sentiment shows that a reserve in trust and support for the market economy has not sufficiently developed. These negative experiences with the market system also extend into other attitudes toward western society. Over 90 percent of easterners, for example, consider one's social background (i.e., the social class of one's parents) to be the most important factor in determining where one will end up on the social ladder. They are less likely than westerners to consider the Federal Republic an open society in which ability and education count more than the social class of a person's parents. Since unification in 1990, the proportion of easterners who state that they sometimes feel they are second-class citizens has increased; 57 percent of easterners in a 2002 poll reported this feeling, although this declined to 42 percent by 2009.[28] As table 4.3 also indicates, by 2010, after twenty years of unification, when asked to compare their living standards with others, almost two of every three easterners still feel that they are getting somewhat less or much less than their fair share. Among western respondents, only 35 percent take this position.

There are also signs of convergence in the political culture of the once-divided nation. Although easterners are generally less trusting of the basic institutions of liberal democracy, such as the parliament, the courts, and local government, than are their western cousins, the gap has narrowed considerably, as table 4.4 indicates. Among easterners, trust in the police and the Federal Constitutional Court have increased dramatically since unification. Like their western counterparts, easterners are less trusting of the federal government and their local administration. A 1999 survey, which once again asked about respondents' trust in the government and parliament, found that east-west differences were narrowing, especially among younger Germans. Among those under twenty-five, there was, for example, only a three-point difference in the level of their trust in parliament, but in the fifty-five-and-older age group, the east-west difference grew to fifteen points.[29] Younger easterners are also more likely to have a "German identity," as opposed to thinking of themselves first as easterners, than their elders. The east-west identity gap in 2002 was only thirteen points among respondents under thirty as compared to a thirty-six-point difference among those over sixty.[30]

Even though they were able to watch democracy in the west on television, easterners are still new to participation in democratic politics. Their memories of the political, social, and economic system under which they lived from 1949

Table 4.3. Attitudes toward Socialism and Inequality, Western-Eastern Germany, 2010 (percent agreement)

Question	West	East
Socialism is basically a good idea that was only badly carried out	57	74
The state should seek to reduce income differences between rich and poor	45	69
In comparison to the living standard of others, I am getting somewhat less, or much less than my fair share.	35	64

Source: Allgemeine Bevölkerungsumfrage der Sozialwissenschaften (Cologne: Zentralarchiv für empirische Sozialforschung, 2010, Study No. 4611).

Table 4.4.   The Trust in Institutions Gap, Western-Eastern Germany, 1990–2008 (in percent)

Institution	1990			2008		
	West	East	Difference	West	East	Difference
Police	71	35	36	87	79	8
Constitutional Court	87	49	38	85	80	5
Local administration	42	22	20	51	46	5
Federal government	75	55	20	59	49	10

Source: For 1990, Institut für angewandte Sozialforschung (INFAS) surveys cited in Ursula Feist and Klaus Liepelt, "Auseinander oder Miteinander? Zum unterschiedlichen. Politikverständnis der Deutschen in Ost und West," in *Wahlen und Wähler. Analysen aus Anlaß der Bundestagswahl 1990*, ed. Hans-Dieter Klingemann and Max Kaase (Opladen: Westdeutscher Verlag, 1994), 601; for 2008, ALLBUS (General Social Survey).

to 1989 will probably distinguish them from citizens of the former Federal Republic for some years to come. But as the social and economic integration of unified Germany—including, of course, new generations of easterners who have only experienced a unified country—continues, these differences should diminish. This assumes, of course, that the unification process, especially its economic dimension, moves the east toward the western level. As in West Germany during the 1950s and 1960s, the performance of the new democratic order will be a key factor in the political integration of the former East Germany.

POLITICAL INTEREST AND INVOLVEMENT

The General Pattern

The formal, legal rules of the Federal Republic have thus far placed few participatory requirements on citizens beyond periodic voting. For example, there has never been a national referendum. This has left most responsibility for system maintenance, policy innovation, and development to political elites. Most Germans in 1949 probably did not want it any other way. After the war and the hyperpoliticization of the Nazis, the immediate postwar period witnessed a widespread withdrawal from public and political matters and an almost exclusive concern with private and familial affairs—and above all with material acquisition. Many Germans at that time had their first political experiences during the Weimar and Nazi periods; these experiences were for the most part not positive. Ordinary Germans who joined the party after 1933, caught up in the initial enthusiasm for National Socialism and Hitler, may well have found themselves after 1945 unemployed and their bank accounts and other assets frozen during denazification, in addition to the myriad other calamities suffered by all Germans in the immediate postwar years. In short, many "little people," political innocents, got burned by politics and were reluctant to try again. Hence, beyond the limited and hardly taxing act of voting, there have been relatively low rates of participation in activities such as party organizations, election campaigns, and public causes.

Formal participation in elections, however, has been high by both European and American standards. Turnout in national elections has ranged from 91 percent in 1972 to 70.8 percent in 2009, averaging above 80 percent over seventeen postwar elections. Turnout in state and local elections has averaged 50 to 70 percent, also much higher than for corresponding subnational elections in other advanced industrial societies. Yet participation in elections, although high in frequency, was low in intensity. Survey research conducted in the 1950s and 1960s found that most German citizens traditionally went to the polls more from a sense of duty or because "it is the usual thing to do" than from a belief that they were in fact helping to decide the personnel and policies of government.[31] Moreover, most studies of German political behavior found that those citizens who were interested in politics and discussed political issues with any frequency restricted such activity to their families and very close friends.[32] The overall pattern throughout the 1950s and 1960s was to focus on private matters, with little political involvement beyond voting.

This pattern has changed. Economic prosperity and rising educational levels in the 1960s and 1970s gave more people the resources of knowledge, conceptual ability, and time necessary to participate in politics. Trend data on a variety of items—interest in politics, "talking politics," and an inclination to join a political organization—show a steady increase in the politicization of German citizens.[33] But this has been accompanied by declining interest in conventional politics. The 2005 and 2009 Bundestag elections witnessed the lowest participation rates since 1949, at 77.7 and 70.8 percent, respectively. Today, Germans have become renowned for social and political mobilization outside of traditional political institutions.

Social Capital

In recent years, political scientists have focused on a country's social capital—the level of trust and cooperation among its citizens—as a key measure of a democracy's health and vitality. Social capital, it is argued, is developed through widespread membership and participation in voluntary organizations of all types and sizes: labor unions, business groups, trade associations, civic organizations, sports clubs, and leisure groups such as choral societies, stamp collectors, and arts and crafts societies. The purpose of the group is far less important to social capital formation than the members' participation in it. Members learn to work together, to share, bargain, discuss, debate, and compromise. Out of these interactions they learn to trust one another. This social trust and cooperation, frequently learned in a completely nonpolitical activity, will then spill over into the larger society and polity. Such societies will find it easier to maintain democracy and to get through hard times and crises.

The amount of social capital in West Germany has grown substantially since the 1945 collapse of the Nazi regime.[34] The West German level is now comparable to or higher than that found in other advanced democracies. As table 4.5 shows, almost 60 percent of westerners are members of some organization as compared with 40 percent of easterners. The participation in pure interest groups (labor unions, business associations, and religious organizations) and sports and leisure groups is also higher in the west. In the west, labor unions, despite declining in significance, have been the most frequent form of membership, followed by sports groups and professional business associations. Although rising markedly

Table 4.5.   Social Capital, East-West Germany, 2010 (in percent)

	East	West
Membership in some organization	50	59
Interest group	17	23
Sports group	22	32
Leisure group	33	45

Source: ALLBUS 2010, Datenreport 2011, 375.

in recent years, the lower levels of social capital in the east, as measured by membership in organizations, can be explained partially as a reaction of easterners to forty years of forced mobilization and participation under communism—not unlike the situation in West Germany after 1945. Easterners were under strong social, economic, and political pressure to join communist-controlled trade unions, farm organizations, professional societies, and women's groups. Schoolchildren came under heavy peer and school pressure to enroll as early as six years of age in the dense network of communist youth organizations.

The weak postunification economy and the social dislocation caused by unification are additional factors accounting for the lower level of social capital in the east. The unemployed, for example, have few resources or little motivation to participate in activities that their families may consider a waste of time. Getting a job or making ends meet on unemployment payments become far more important than participation in a choral society or sports club. Social trust is, consistent with this thesis, also lower in the eastern regions. If and when the east reaches economic parity with the west, many of these differences should decline or disappear.[35]

New Forms of Political Participation: Citizen Groups and Movements

The emergence of widespread citizen initiatives and action groups outside the party system is another phenomenon indicative of confidence in the role of the citizen. Some of these groups were in evidence as early as the mid-1960s and in some cases even earlier, as revealed by the substantial opposition to the rearmament of the Federal Republic in 1955, but they were voter initiative groups in support of particular parties and candidates, and in some cases their spontaneity and freedom from the existing parties were in question. These movements were led by nationally prominent writers and artists, not by average concerned citizens. Of greater interest for our purposes are the local initiative groups organized by citizens to protest and remedy a particular local problem, such as arbitrary increases in mass transit fares; inadequate children's playgrounds, kindergartens, and schools; and air and water pollution. These groups represented new patterns of political participation that contradict the traditional characterization of Germans as politically passive, relying only on intermittent, indirect participation through voting or formal contact with the state bureaucracy. Most of the groups concentrate on one issue and tend to be free from any encompassing ideology. Nevertheless, they reflect the inability of the established party system and the institutions of local government to meet key needs of the citizenry. Petitions, demonstrations, and protest marches are all part of their tactical arsenal.

These groups had their precedent in the widespread demonstrations during the late 1960s over the Emergency Laws,[36] the Vietnam War, and university reform; they were to some extent the adult version of the student protest movement.[37] The focus then shifted to the local level, the one least penetrated by the national political parties, where the problems of outmoded school systems, environmental decay, inadequate zoning, and land use regulations exceeded the capacities of most local governments and officials.

In the early 1980s a nationwide peace movement emerged, initially directed against the proposed deployment of middle-range nuclear missiles in Germany. The peace movement, allied with some elements of the Social Democratic Party, played a major role in the eventual collapse of the Social-Liberal government in 1982. These new social movements were soon joined by increasingly assertive women's rights organizations and especially by antinuclear and environmental groups. All of these movements have had close ties to the Green political party, but they have also been careful to guard their independence. Also common to all groups is dissatisfaction with the established institutions and processes of the postwar system. Many of these groups—especially the antinuclear and environmental ones—have had a marked impact on policy, including some of the most successful recycling programs in the world (recycling more than 70 percent of all waste in 2008) and the so-called "energy turn" that will phase out nuclear power and increase substantially the proportion of renewable energy sources over the next decades.

The success of citizen initiative groups and the new social movements, together with the increases in unconventional forms of political participation already described, seem to indicate that Germans are ready for a more direct democracy than that envisioned in the Basic Law. Proposals have indeed been made for more citizen involvement and influence, especially at the local level through referenda, petitions, the right to recall public officials, and even state financial support for citizen groups. Surveys indicate that the public supports a less elitist constitutional structure. In a 2004 study, for example, over 80 percent of the adult population in both the former East and West Germany endorsed referenda for important policy issues. Over half felt that "democracy works best when people have the opportunity to directly represent their interests and concerns."[38] Thus most Germans now want more opportunities for political participation than are permitted under the current constitution. In 2011–2012, pressure was mounting to conduct a national referendum on the Euro and bailouts for struggling countries like Greece.

CIVIL LIBERTIES AND HUMAN RIGHTS

Unlike the United States, the UK, or France, Germany did not have a strong civil libertarian tradition. German political and legal theory has for the most part emphasized the duties of the individual vis-à-vis the state rather than the state's responsibilities to protect individual liberties. Indeed, as Leonard Krieger has pointed out, German political thinkers have defined liberty largely in collectivist terms.[39] That is, the individual was considered "free" only within the confines of the collective or state, and obedience to its rules and regulations ensured his or her freedom and personal development. To be sure, this state, according to German political tradition, was to be a *Rechtsstaat*, a state based on the rule of law, and great attention was given to the detailed legal codes that defined individual rights and duties and delimited state authority. The interpretation of these laws and their social and political effect traditionally restricted, rather than enlarged, individual freedom. The *Rechtsstaat* tradition also produced excessive legalism, which resulted in many unjust statutes that were steadfastly adhered to in the name of the rule of law. The Nazi seizure of power, the persecution of Jews, and many other acts of the Nazi dictatorship were thus all considered "legal."

During the extensive student demonstrations of the late 1960s, courts used the old provisions of the penal code against disturbance of the public order to punish protesters who were exercising rights of free expression guaranteed in the Basic Law. Furthermore, the postwar prosecution of war criminals was consistently delayed and complicated by the retention of laws and regulations passed before and during the Nazi era that protected judicial and bureaucratic wrongdoers. Finally, as in many other countries such as the United States, lower-status or disadvantaged groups, particularly residents with a migration background, have experienced difficulties receiving equal access to and outcomes from the welfare and judicial system.

Nevertheless, public awareness and sensitivity to the importance of civil liberties is substantial in the Federal Republic, with large majorities supporting civil and political liberties. In its first twenty articles, the Constitution or Basic Law lists an impressive array of fundamental and inalienable rights and liberties. Equality before the law—the prohibition of any discrimination based on gender, race, language, national origin, religion, or political persuasion—is guaranteed in Article 3. Freedom of religion (broadly defined to include any belief system) and the right to refuse armed military service for reasons of conscience are granted in Article 4. Civil rights related to freedom of expression and information via speech, writing, pictures, broadcasts, and films are enumerated in Article 5. Censorship is rejected, although "general laws" dealing with the protection of youth (obscenity) and "personal honor" (slander and libel) limit this freedom. Explicit academic freedom (teaching and research), conditional on loyalty to the Constitution, is granted in Article 5 (paragraph 3). Article 5 also clearly guarantees freedom of assembly, association, and movement; the privacy of mail and telephone messages; and the right to petition.

Finally, in an extraordinary departure from German constitutional tradition, Article 20, as amended in 1968, declares that "all Germans shall have the right to resist any person or persons seeking to abolish the constitutional order, should no other remedy be possible." In a 1974 speech commemorating the July 20, 1944, plot to assassinate Hitler, Chancellor Helmut Schmidt specifically referred to this article as one that would legalize armed resistance against any authority that violated the individual liberties enumerated in the basic rights of the Constitution.

Civil Liberties Controversies

In its first sixty-three years, the Federal Republic has had several major controversies involving alleged government violations of these basic constitutional freedoms.

The Spiegel Affair

The most publicized and dramatic civil rights case during the past fifty years involved a government raid in 1962 on the offices of the newsmagazine *Der Spiegel* and the arrest of its two major editors. The government charged that the magazine had illegally procured and published secret defense documents and planned to publish more—hence the police raid and arrests. The minister of defense, Franz Josef Strauss, responsible for the police action, had been a frequent target of the magazine. Perhaps not coincidentally, the magazine had also begun an exposé of alleged corruption involving the minister in connection with aircraft purchases and government-sponsored military housing projects.

The government argued that a strong suspicion of treason justified extreme measures. The German press, the opposition party in parliament, and sizable segments of the governing coalition felt otherwise. The minister of justice, who had not been informed of the action, resigned; his party, the Free Democrats (FDP), threatened to leave the government if the defense minister did not resign. His subsequent resignation and the quashing of the government indictment by the Federal Appeals Court closed the case for all practical purposes. The nearly unanimous opposition of the press and the response of some, but not all, elements of public opinion were indicative of considerable support for freedom of the press, or at least opposition to overt, heavy-handed attempts at censorship reminiscent of an earlier era. Clearly, after this incident any government would be more reluctant to use such tactics against a critical press; and indeed there has not been a recurrence of this type of government behavior.

"Radicals" in Public Service

A civil liberties controversy in the 1970s involved the employment of "political radicals" (e.g., communists, neo-Nazis) by the state. The issue became political when New Left groups within the Social Democratic Party supported the radicals' right to public employment and successfully opposed the party establishment's hard line in this area. This enabled the conservative Christian Democrats to charge that the Social Democrats were allowing left-wing teachers and bureaucrats to flood the civil service and ultimately undermine the constitutional order. Most cases in the 1970s involved allegedly radical teachers in elementary and secondary schools. In a high school geography class in Bremen, the teacher sent his pupils into various neighborhoods to photograph homes and apartments and

interview their occupants about their lifestyles, finances, and sociopolitical attitudes in order to illustrate the class structure of the community. Irate homeowners in the city's more affluent sections protested the "Nazi-like tactics," and
the instructor was suspended. Many of these young teachers had attended universities during the "salad days" of student protest and New Left influence. Now
active as teachers and administrators, they embarked, in their own way, on the
"long march through the institutions."

In 1972 the federal government and the Ministerpräsidenten (chief executives) of the states issued an executive decree that was supposed to establish unified national policy in this area until formal legislation could be passed by the
parliament. Although each case was to be examined and resolved separately,
some general guidelines were given. An applicant for public employment who
was engaged in "anticonstitutional" activity was not to be hired. If an applicant
was a member of any organization that was unconstitutional, that alone was to
be grounds for doubting whether he or she would support the "free democratic
order." Thus any member of such a group, usually the Communist Party or the
radical-right National Democratic Party (NPD), would normally have his or her
employment application rejected.

This decision represented a hard-line approach to the question of political
extremists in the civil service. It also reflected the fears of the Social Democrats
of being portrayed by the opposition as "soft on radicalism." Critics charged that
the decree could be interpreted to mean that even ordinary or nominal membership in groups such as the Communist Party or NPD would mean a denial of or
dismissal from employment. The entire decree, it was argued, would encourage
denunciations and petty spying of civil servants on one another, reminiscent of
the Nazi era. Opponents of the decree also charged that it violated Article 3 of
the Basic Law, which prohibits discrimination on the basis of political views and
grants equal access to public jobs. In spite of these objections, a 1975 decision of
the Federal Constitutional Court (see chapter 8 for a description of this court)
essentially upheld this policy, although the court emphasized that membership
in radical groups would have to be substantiated by other "anticonstitutional"
activity to justify dismissal from public service.[40]

In practice, the "unified" statement was differentially applied in the various
states. In those governed by the Social Democrats, no civil servants were dismissed for mere membership in radical organizations, although a leadership or
office-holding function was grounds for removal. In states governed by the Christian Democrats (CDU), on the other hand, membership alone was sufficient for
dismissal. One CDU-governed state, the Rhineland-Palatinate, advocated a
nationwide system of security checks. Another, Bavaria, maintained dossiers on
teachers and college professors.

By the late 1970s, an increasing number of party and government officials at
all levels had become convinced that the 1972 decree was a mistake and that the
existing security clearance practices were unfair and in need of major revision. A
combination of experience with the policy; the reaction of public opinion (especially among the younger, educated segment of the population); and foreign criticism of the Federal Republic had produced a trend away from the policy. On
balance, however, the entire controversy inhibited the expression of unpopular

ideas and the support of minority political movements. It illustrates the capacity of even democratic regimes to produce authoritarian policies. However, the eventual abandonment of the policy also shows that the postwar democracy could learn from its mistakes.[41]

Civil Liberties and the Census

In the early 1980s a planned national census became another major civil liberties issue. The last complete census had been taken in 1970. For budgetary reasons a new census, planned for 1980, was postponed until 1983. The law authorizing the census was unanimously passed by the parliament with little debate or controversy. But citizen initiative groups and the newly established Green political party (see chapter 5) initiated a campaign against the census, which they regarded as an unnecessary intrusion by the state into the private lives of citizens. Specifically, the anticensus groups were critical of provisions in the law that would allow officials, including police and security agencies, to compare the new data with domicile registration information already collected by local and regional authorities. In short, information given by individuals to the census takers could be shared with the police and other public bodies.

The interior minister denounced the anticensus movement as a "minority of extremists seeking to undermine the system."[42] But in 1983 the Federal Constitutional Court, responding to a petition by census opponents, issued an injunction halting the census, which had been scheduled to begin that same month. Finally, in December 1983, the Court in a major decision unanimously struck down many of the provisions of the 1982 law. The Court objected to the open-ended character of the law's language, which it ruled did not set sufficient limits on the state's authority to question its citizens. The Court also ruled unconstitutional the statute's provision for the sharing of data among government agencies. In addition, the introduction of a single identification number for each citizen, which could be used to retrieve personal data from a variety of files, was rejected by the Court. The government and parliament had to draft a new law that satisfied the constitutional standards set by the Court. Most civil libertarians and constitutional lawyers praised the decision as an important advance for civil liberties in the Federal Republic.[43]

In 1985 a revised law, which met the objections of the Court, was passed by the parliament, and the census finally took place in 1987. Some Green leaders continued to oppose the new law and called for citizens to boycott the census. The Greens contended that the law still did not offer protection against misuse of the data. The other parliamentary parties, including the Social Democrats, strongly criticized the Green boycott as a clear violation of the law. Since that time, privacy rights have become even more enshrined, especially in light of the proliferation of the Internet and social media. For example, in 2010, when Google Street View maps were launched, the government gave homeowners the right to have images of their properties blurred out.

"The Great Bugging Attack"

The major civil liberties case of the 1990s was the issue of electronic surveillance by police and security forces. Since the end of the Cold War, Germany, as well as other Western European countries, has experienced sharp increases in organized crime activity including drug trafficking, automobile theft, and extortion. Existing laws, which reflect the postwar German effort to avoid the abuse of police power that took place during the Nazi era, greatly restricted the ability of security forces to undertake the types of investigations common in other European democracies. Wiretaps, search warrants, and other surveillance techniques could be conducted only after extensive judicial examination. German police forces felt handicapped by these procedures and requested help from the Kohl government.

The result was a 1998 constitutional amendment (Article 13) and subsequent law, which were also supported by the Social Democrats (then the opposition), granting police greater powers to plant bugging devices in private homes. Such eavesdropping practices had been constitutionally prohibited. In the view of the police, however, such bans on telephone taps and mail intercepts had hindered efforts to combat terrorism and organized international criminal bands. Following protests from the media and civil liberties groups, the legislation was amended to exclude journalists, lawyers, members of parliament, clergy, and medical doctors from any electronic snooping. This was still not enough to satisfy some critics, including the minister of justice, who resigned in protest over the legislation.

Same-Sex Marriage

Since the turn of the century another civil liberties issue—the legalization of same-sex relationships—has moved up on the policy agenda. In the 1990s a majority in both east and west opposed such unions. In 1993 the Constitutional Court declined to hear a case filed by gay couples requesting a state-sanctioned marriage.

But after the 1998 election, the Green political party, which had been supporting legal protections for gay marriages since 1990, made this a condition of their participation in the Schröder government. The Social Democrats, however, were divided on the issue. The SPD's traditionalist wing, with its base in the trade unions, considered this a marginal issue of little interest to the party's blue-collar core. Within the SPD-Green government, both the justice and interior ministers had doubts about the constitutionality of the proposal since it would no longer put traditional marriage under the special protection of the law as called for in the Constitution. The interior minister was also concerned about the financial costs of granting gays full access to the extensive social welfare system.

But the Greens were persistent. They had already compromised on the nuclear power and citizenship issues by accepting weaker versions of two of their "essentials." They stood firm on this core campaign promise. Chancellor Schröder assented to this position, and in July 2000 a bill was submitted to parliament that gave gay couples "virtually all rights that married couples enjoyed except the right to adopt children and the right of the surviving spouse to collect Social Security benefits."[44]

As expected, the Christian Democrats opposed the proposed law on moral grounds. The Bavarian CSU, which still has strong ties to the Catholic Church, argued that the law would "hollow out the most significant foundations of our society." One CSU leader even contended that since a majority opposed same-sex relationships, the homosexual minority should not be granted this legal right. Others objected on constitutional grounds. The Free Democrats, traditionally liberal on civil rights questions, argued that same-sex marriages would violate Article 6 of the Constitution, which places traditional marriage under the special protection of the state. They wanted same-sex relationships to be treated as a separate form of association with accompanying changes in the existing laws governing inheritance, powers of attorney, and prenuptial agreements. FDP opposition was thus largely technical and legal, and the party was open to negotiation.

In November 2000 the Life Partnership Law was passed by parliament. The law went into effect in 2001. In 2002 the Federal Constitutional Court rejected a constitutional challenge to the legislation. The Court ruled that the law did not violate the "special protection" of marriage provision of the Constitution since gay couples by definition would not seek any special protection for a traditional marriage.

The implementation of the Life Partnership Law has varied among the states. The more liberal states such as Hamburg and Berlin allow gay couples to register their union in a Registry Office (*Standesamt*) just like heterosexual couples. (None of the churches allow same-sex marriages.) Conservative states such as Bavaria and Baden-Württemberg have denied same-sex couples the use of the Registry Office; they must go to offices used to register "other" relationships and groups such as foreign residents. In some states same-sex couples receive a marriage certificate while in others they receive only a "receipt" documenting their partnership. States opposed to such unions also charge same-sex couples two to three times the normal fee of about $40. It would require an additional law for a unified procedure for these unions. Nonetheless the Partnership Law is now the law of the land. Public opinion polls show that solid majorities of heterosexual men and women consider the law a "good" or "very good" idea. Indeed, in 2007, 65 percent supported the current policy, with 26 percent supporting full legal marriage rights.[45] During the three national election campaigns since the passage of the law, the Christian Democrats and their Bavarian sisters made no mention of repealing the law in the event of their election. It would be "absurd," they said, to "change the facts"—that is, the Constitutional Courts' approval of the legislation. Clearly, the Christian Democrats had also seen the public opinion polls.[46]

Civil Liberties after 9/11

The broad consensus on civil liberties that developed over the decades was tested by the emergence of Al Qaeda and its allied organizations. Germans were shocked that the September 11, 2001, attacks on the United States were largely planned in Hamburg by militant Muslims, but thus far no legislation has been passed that infringes on the Federal Republic's generally strong record of protecting individual rights. As the terrorist threat continued, there has been some sentiment for new policies that could constrain civil liberties. Since 9/11 there have been several major incidents in Germany that appear to have been planned by Al Qaeda–like groups. In July 2006 a pair of suitcase bombs was placed on commuter trains. The bombs did not explode, and several suspects were arrested and tried in Germany and Lebanon. In 2007 police and security officials prevented what they termed a major terrorist attack directed at American and German targets including a large American airbase and the Frankfurt International Airport. Three Islamic militants, members of a German cell of the Islamic Jihad Union, had collected large quantities of bomb-making materials and were in the process of transporting them for final assembly when they were arrested. All three had traveled to militant training camps in Pakistan. One of the three was a native-born citizen who had converted to Islam. Like the UK and Spain, Germany apparently has also become a target for homegrown terrorism.[47]

In the wake of these events, the interior minister in the Merkel-led Grand Coalition government proposed legislation making it a crime for any German national to participate in any overseas activity that could be considered terrorist training. Other proposals included secret searches of computer hard drives, banning terrorist suspects from using mobile phones, and detaining potential terrorists. The minister also advocated legislation allowing security forces to shoot down aircraft hijacked by terrorists. He even proposed allowing security forces to assassinate terrorist leaders in other countries. While these proposals drew heavy criticism from governing and opposition parties as well as civil liberties groups, they illustrate the changed post-9/11 climate in the Federal Republic.

Although these more extreme proposals were not passed, the bugging of telephones and monitoring of computer IP addresses have been approved, albeit with safeguards such as a strict limit on how long the data can be kept. Another controversy involved sharing airlines' passenger lists with U.S. security authorities. In this case, German reservations were trumped by a European Union agreement in 2012. German civil liberty preferences are increasingly coming into conflict with European-level agreements and directives.

Another recent conflict surrounded legislation that attempted to block certain offensive websites, for example those that contained child pornography, and to restrict minors' access to certain sites (the Zugangserschwerungsgesetz). Originally passed in 2009 on the initiative of Family Minister Ursula von der Leyen with strong support from the SPD, this law raised the ire of civil libertarians and Internet activists and was one of the issues that empowered the new Pirate Party. After the change in government, the liberal FDP first insisted on passing a nonimplementation clause and eventually had the law rescinded in late 2011. This example shows how strongly many Germans value their civil liberties today.

Nevertheless, there are still some constraints on civil liberties that citizens of other countries may find difficult to comprehend. Understandably, the founders of the Federal Republic banned the Nazi Party and Nazi symbols (paragraph 86a of the criminal code). Thus, it is a criminal offense to fly the Nazi flag or perform the Nazi salute in public. There were warnings before the World Cup of Soccer in 2006 that international fans engaging in such behaviors would be arrested and prosecuted. The sale of Hitler's book *Mein Kampf* is still banned (although English translations are available in many bookstores), and there are special forms that have to be filled out if a library patron borrows the book. The borrower has to attest that the book is being read for "scientific or research purposes." Holocaust denial has been a criminal offense since 1985. Moreover, big majorities of Germans support such restrictions. In 2006, 75 percent thought that the media should be banned from denying or whitewashing the Holocaust, and 66 percent supported censoring those who would defend Nazism.[48] Recent years have also seen the German government advocate European-wide bans on Nazi symbols and Holocaust denial.

THE STATUS AND ROLE OF KEY SOCIAL GROUPS

Residents with a Migration Background

The most significant minority group in the Federal Republic comprises individuals with a migration background, currently approaching 20 percent of the population. This is a diverse category, including ethnic Germans who emigrated from the former Soviet Union after 1990, as well as refugees and their descendants, such as Croats and Bosnians who fled to Germany in the early 1990s. The biggest portion of this group consists of foreign workers, once referred to as "guest workers" or *Gastarbeiter*, their families, and their descendants. Germany is currently home to about seven million foreign residents, although the liberalization of citizenship laws about a decade ago has led to many from this group gaining German citizenship and thus no longer being classified as "foreigners" (*Ausländer*).

In spite of declines in the number of foreign workers coming to Germany, their higher birth rate and the arrival of family members have actually increased the total number of individuals with a migration background.[49] In 2007 the Federal Statistical Office reported that one-third of the children under five years of age were born in Germany with at least one foreign-born parent. In cities such as Stuttgart and Frankfurt, 60 percent of children under five years of age had a migration background.[50] The number of dependents from such families has grown from 1.4 million in 1973 to over 5 million by 2005. Thus, there are now two and even three generations of individuals with migration backgrounds in Germany. After the United States and the United Kingdom, Germany has been the world's most popular haven for immigrants. Yet many native residents long refused to accept the reality that "worldwide migration is a typical and unavoidable feature of modern societies."[51]

The first generation of immigrants was invited, indeed actively recruited, as "guest workers" by business firms, with strong government support. The country's famous postwar economic miracle was due in part to a large labor supply created by the forced migration of almost 10 million refugees from territories annexed by the Soviet Union and Poland, together with the influx of 3 million additional refugees from East Germany that continued until the Berlin Wall was put up in August 1961. These additions to the labor supply initially compensated for the loss of labor from the war. Yet by the early 1960s the economy's need for labor could no longer be met internally, and workers from Europe's poorer regions were recruited extensively by businesses with government assistance. The first wave came from Italy and Yugoslavia, but by the late 1960s, the majority of "guest workers" came from Turkey. Indeed, in popular consciousness, most Germans think first of Turks when they think of "guest workers," foreigners, or people with a migration background. Turks are by far the largest minority group, with 2.5 to 4 million residents of Germany today having full or partly Turkish ancestry.

Overall, the number of guest workers increased from about 110,000 in 1957 to more than 2.5 million by 1973. Although the recessions of 1974–1976 and 1981–1983 reduced their number to about 1.7 million, foreign workers still account for approximately 8 percent of the total workforce and roughly 15 percent of the total manual workforce.[52] In 2008 and 2009, more people actually left Germany than entered, but in 2010 there was a net plus of 127,000, and in 2011, 279,000, the highest number since 1996.[53] In 2010 the three largest "exporting" countries were Poland (18 percent of immigrants), Romania (11 percent), and Bulgaria (6 percent).[54] In 2011, the effects of the Euro crisis led to a 90 percent increase in the number of Greeks and a 52 percent increase in Spaniards migrating.

In many large German cities, such as Frankfurt, Munich, Stuttgart, and Hamburg, foreign workers constitute from 15 to over 20 percent of the total workforce and probably 30 to 40 percent of the manual workforce. Foreign workers have usually been assigned tasks that Germans are no longer willing to perform, for example, street cleaning, common labor, and grave digging. About 50 percent of Frankfurt's and 80 percent of Munich's sanitation workers are foreign laborers. Although those in major industries receive the same pay as German workers, wage discrimination in smaller firms is not uncommon.

Even in large firms, foreign workers are usually found in the lowest-paid manual occupations. This is due partly to their poor vocational training (by German standards) and language difficulties, and also to discrimination on the part of German employers. Nonetheless, many foreign workers, especially those in large firms, are covered by government health, security, and pension programs. Some authors call this social citizenship. German churches, labor unions (by requiring equal pay for equal work), and charitable organizations have also alleviated some of the more pressing problems of foreign residents.

When foreign workers bring their families into Germany, problems can be compounded. The education of their children has been particularly difficult. Should the children be educated and socialized completely as Germans, or should special school classes with native teachers be established—at least in language and social studies? In many cases the parents themselves are not able to indicate their preferences or future plans, much less those of their children. Many of the children have spent most or all of their lives in Germany. Yet their parents cling to the goal of someday returning to their home country and thus want their children to retain its language and values. As a result the children grow up in a sort of twilight zone—they master neither the culture and language of their parents nor of the Germans. Many drop out of school and, urged on by their parents, attempt to secure some kind of employment to augment the family's finances. These individuals have also had some problems adjusting to life in their home countries when they visit or return more permanently. Indeed, their identities can also be problematic, being caught between and not really belonging to any national group.[55]

Young people with a migration background have been ill prepared for the job market. Their educational experience is well below that of the native population (see table 4.6). In the 1990s, over 90 percent of all native Germans between fifteen and nineteen were enrolled in school, but only 66 percent of foreign children were in school. Among those who were twenty to twenty-four years old, 39 percent of native-born residents were still in school as compared to only 15 percent of foreigners. At the university level, Germans were four times more likely to be students than foreigners were.[56] One of the reasons for the low numbers of such individuals going to university is that many have been placed in the mediocre secondary schools, the much-criticized general school (Hauptschule).

In 2010, 72 percent of foreign residents between the ages of twenty and sixty-four had not completed job training. At best, they are prepared for unskilled or semiskilled jobs and thus are very unlikely to take positions as doctors, lawyers, or police officers.[57] Young foreign residents are also less likely to complete an occupational training or apprenticeship program. Among female foreign residents, the lack of any academic or vocational training is even greater. With neither academic nor vocational training, it is not surprising that the unemployment level among foreigners is twice the national average. Thus there is a growing body of unemployed, young foreigners especially in the large western cities (50 percent live in the large western cities and Berlin), many of whom are living in poverty or near poverty (defined as 60 percent of the median household income). Many are bored, unemployed, and resentful, with little contact with the native population. They are alienated from the rest of society and increasingly form a kind of underclass. The potential for social unrest in this situation is high.[58]

The condition of young Germans of Turkish origin is of particular concern to policy makers. Among this group, by far the largest migratory group, almost 60 percent drop out of school before completing any vocational or academic program.[59] Many will go on the welfare and unemployment rolls. They will be more likely to have emotional problems. Native Germans do not want their children to attend schools with a high proportion of children with a migration background. The flight of many native German families creates further educational challenges in terms of language acquisition for those left in these schools. Yet the country, in the view of many economists, will in the long term need this talent pool and cannot afford to waste so much potential.

Indeed, in spite of the millions of residents with migration backgrounds in their midst, Germans have been slow to recognize that their country is a multicultural society. Helmut Kohl and other CDU/CSU politicians long stated that

Table 4.6.   Educational Attainment 2010 (in percent)

	German	Foreign
No high school diploma	5.4	12.8
Hauptschule	19.0	37.6
Realschule*	41.1	35.6
Technical college certificate	1.6	1.6
General college certificate	33.0	12.4

Source: http://de.statista.com/statistik/daten/studie/73753/umfrage/schulabschluss-anteil-auslaender-und-deutsche.

*A more practically oriented high school not necessarily designed to prepare pupils for university.

"Germany is not a land of immigration," and government policy followed this formula. The integration of foreign residents has been a slow and difficult process not least because of major differences of opinion among Germans. In general, the Right demands integration, including stringent language and citizenship tests, and the Left advocates the acceptance of multiculturalism, even parallel societies. These issues are among the most contentious in Germany today. In 2010, SPD politician and the Bundesbank board member Thilo Sarrazin published a book entitled *Germany Does Away with Itself* in which he criticized Turks and Muslims for their inability and unwillingness to integrate into German society. Although the inflammatory treatise was widely condemned, it sold over one million copies and became the best-selling political book in a decade. Even if solutions are vigorously debated, there is a wide consensus that a problem exists.

One major obstacle behind resolving some of these tensions has been the difficulty of obtaining citizenship. As in many other European countries, citizenship in Germany has historically been based more on lineage than on residency. While residents of European Union countries can vote in local elections, foreign residents from non-EU countries cannot vote regardless of how long they have lived in Germany. It was not until 1999 that a German government finally passed legislation that made it easier for foreign residents to acquire German citizenship. The new citizenship legislation replaced the 1913 law, as amended in 1990, which based citizenship on lineage or blood. German-born children of foreigners now have an automatic right to citizenship if at least one of their parents has been living in Germany since age fourteen.[60] The waiting period for naturalization of foreign residents has been reduced from fifteen to eight years, and dual citizenship is allowed until the child reaches adulthood (age twenty-three), at which time a single citizenship must be chosen. Since passage of the new law, more than a million foreign residents have become citizens, but about three million additional immigrants are eligible. Two criticisms of the new law included the explicit prohibition of dual citizenship, which is especially important for many residents of Turkish origin given inheritance laws in Turkey, and the increased fees that were part of the law. Nonetheless, the rate of naturalization has greatly increased under this legislation.[61]

Current Immigration Policy

Although foreign workers are no longer actively recruited, it is possible to enter the country with the full blessings of the government as long as the potential immigrant is highly qualified and/or prepared to invest one million Euros and create ten new jobs.[62] This is the essence of the latest immigration law passed in 2004, which took effect in 2005. The road to passage was long and rocky and included several opposition vetoes and a rejection of an earlier bill by the Federal Constitutional Court (see chapter 8).

Assuming the potential immigrant meets the educational or investment requirements, there are some improvements to overall immigration policy. Newcomers and other foreign residents now have access to free or low-cost language classes as well as instruction in the justice system, culture, and history. This new law, unlike earlier programs, does not assume the immigrant is only a "guest" but a resident who intends to stay and should be introduced to the language and culture of the potential new homeland.

In its first year of operation (2005) the new law had little impact on the overall level of immigration. Only about nine hundred "top-notch experts" were recruited from abroad, "a figure that countries such as the United States and the United Kingdom would laugh at."[63] Under the policy, the spouses of these experts do not automatically receive a work permit. Nonetheless, most analysts consider the new policy a step in the right direction. Recognizing the need for still more skilled and educated workers, Germany, unlike many of its neighbors, has in recent years adopted policies to encourage *foreign students* to study and then remain in the country. The severe recession and Euro crisis in the southern European countries has accelerated this program. Foreign students, for example, at the universities do not pay any extra tuition but pay the same rates as their native counterparts, which depending on the state means they may pay no tuition at all. Following graduation, they have up to eighteen months to seek employment before their visas expire. If they succeed in finding a job, they will usually be granted a long-term visa, the so-called EU blue card, which allows them to live and work indefinitely in Germany and other countries in the European Union.

Foreign Residents and Political Asylum

In addition to recruiting foreign workers and their families, Germany from about 1984 to 1995 became the target country for hundreds of thousands of foreigners fleeing economic and political oppression. In 1991 alone, almost a quarter of a million foreigners sought political asylum in the Federal Republic, three times the level of any other European country. Article 16 of the Basic Law contained one of the most liberal asylum laws in the world. The framers of the constitution in 1949, many of whom became political refugees themselves during the Third Reich, wanted the country's borders to remain open to any refugee from political persecution. Most of the current asylum seekers, however, are fleeing for economic rather than political reasons. All applicants are entitled to due process; and even though most applications are rejected, the legal process can last for months or even years. In the interim, the foreigners are the beneficiaries of Germany's generous welfare state and are barred from working.

The growing number of asylum seekers, the poor economic situation in the former GDR (especially for young people), and a general shortage of affordable housing throughout the country were important factors in outbreaks of violence against asylum seekers that erupted in 1991 and persisted sporadically for several years. Starting in the region that was formerly East Germany, gangs of skinheads and young neo-Nazis attacked the hostels and apartment buildings that housed foreigners. In October 1991 alone, authorities registered over nine hundred attacks on foreign residents, the most extensive violence against foreigners seen in Germany since the Third Reich. Particularly egregious incidents occurred in Hoyerswerda (1991), Rostock (1992), Mölln (1992), and Solingen (1993).

The incidents sparked demonstrations by many Germans against the violence and in support of the foreigners. Responding to growing public pressure, the government, with the support of the opposition Social Democrats, passed a constitutional amendment (Article 16) in 1993 that restricted asylum rights. The legislation retained the constitutional guarantee of protection against political persecution, but it sought to exclude persons who attempt to enter the country for largely economic reasons. It also speeded up the administrative procedures at the borders. Persons from countries where there is no internationally recognized political persecution can be turned away at the borders. Also, asylum seekers who enter the Federal Republic from any European Union country can be denied asylum. Thus, a legitimate political refugee living in France cannot apply for asylum in Germany; he or she must remain in France. Numerous human rights groups in Germany opposed the amendment, but it brought Germany's policy into line with that of most of its European neighbors and the United States. Passage of the amendment took the wind out of the sails of xenophobic far-right groups. By 1994 the number of asylum applications had dropped by 60 percent. The 2004 law mentioned above also contained provisions making it easier for those who have already been granted asylum to acquire permanent residency permits.

Women

Politics in Germany, as elsewhere, has traditionally been a man's business. German women have been less likely to participate in all political activities— voting, "talking politics," party membership, campaigning, candidacy—than men. The classic functions assigned to women in German society, neatly summarized by the three K's—*Kinder* (children), *Kirche* (church), and *Küche* (kitchen)— left little room for explicit political roles and have been slow to change. Mothers who worked outside of the home were long demonized and much policy was based on the assumption that most women would be stay-at-home mothers. The traditionally subordinate status of women in politics was also evident in surveys that found most women expressing more confidence in a man as the representative of their political interests than a woman. Only approximately 30 percent of a national sample in 1975 felt that women could represent women's political interests better than men; among university-trained women, however, the proportion was higher. A 1983 study among the nations of the European Community found German respondents more likely to take a male chauvinist position on the question of women in politics than were citizens in other major West European countries.[64]

Yet since the late 1960s a greater awareness and visibility of women in politics has become apparent. Elections in the 1970s showed that the Christian Democrats could no longer count on receiving lopsided majorities from female voters. It was especially among Catholic women that the Social Democrats were able to make exceptional gains. Public attitudes toward women in politics also showed significant change; between 1965 and 1987 the proportion of men who "liked the idea" of a woman becoming politically involved rose from 27 to 68 percent. Between 1966 and 1988 the proportion of men who agreed that "politics is a man's business" dropped from 44 percent to 23 percent; among women during the same period, agreement declined from 32 percent to 15 percent.[65] Large majorities of both men and women now reject the notion that "politics is a man's business."

There are negligible differences in the voting turnout rate between men and women: 0.8 percent for the Bundestag election in 2009 and 0.4 percent in 2005.[66] Although women continue to be underrepresented among the membership of the political parties, there is a trend toward increased female involvement. From 1971 to 1985 the number of active women members in the political parties increased from about 200,000 to 440,000. By 1985 about one-fourth of all SPD members were female and more than one-fifth of CDU/CSU members were women. In the smaller parties women made up over 40 percent of the Green membership and about one-fourth of the FDP membership.[67] Currently, a little over a quarter of all party members are women. In the 2009 election, 204 women, 33 percent of the total, were elected to parliament, the highest proportion in the history of the Federal Republic. In the UK and the United States, by contrast, women make up only about 10 percent of the national legislature.

Angela Merkel's initial election in 2005 as Germany's first female chancellor further demonstrated the changing role of women in German politics. Her election continues a process seen in other European countries: a steady increase in female involvement in politics at all levels and a growing convergence of political behavior between males and females. In recent years women have increasingly risen to top posts, including the leadership of a major political party, the presidency of the national parliament, and the presidency of Germany's version of the American Supreme Court, the Federal Constitutional Court. Five of the sixteen judges on this court are also women. Since 1983 the proportion of women in the national parliament, the Bundestag, has more than tripled. Women now make up a majority of the deputies from the Green and PDS parties thanks partially to gender quotas. In 1988 the Social Democrats adopted a rule that at least 40 percent of party officials be female; since 1998 the party rules call for a 40 percent female quota for all legislative seats. This quota system now applies at all levels—local, state, and national—of the party organization.[68] Even the CDU/CSU has had a gender "quorum" since 1996. Recent innovations have included ensuring that enough women are toward the top of the list to increase the likelihood of being sent to Berlin. The federal government and many states now have cabinet ministries to address specifically the discrimination against women and the more general problem of ensuring equal opportunity for both men and women.

These changes at the elite level of the political system were preceded by fundamental shifts in attitudes. The increased political prominence of women is the result of a fifty-year trend that began with growing female interest in politics and exposure to political information; increased participation in voting and other basic forms of participation followed throughout the 1960s. For example, while the proportion of males reporting an interest in politics has remained relatively constant over the past half century, female interest has risen continually. The same trend can be found in exposure to political information as measured by reading the political sections of the daily newspaper. Between 1955 and 1999 the proportion of males reporting that they regularly read political news increased only slightly from 70 percent to 76 percent; among females, however, readership of political news grew from only 23 percent in 1955 to 63 percent by 1999.[69] Nevertheless, in 2009 only 15 percent of German women stated that they were interested in politics and 8 percent in the economy, versus 31 percent and 24 percent of men.[70]

Income differences between men and women remain substantial. In 2010 male workers in both white- and blue-collar occupations earned about 20 percent more in wages than their female colleagues. These differences are largely the result of the high proportion of women in lower-paying and part-time jobs, especially the so-called "mini-jobs" that the Agenda 2010 reforms facilitated. In western Germany in 2009, 70 percent of men had full-time jobs, whereas only 34 percent of women did. By contrast, 6 percent of men had part-time jobs, but among women this was 34 percent.[71] At 16 percent, women are about 4 percent more at risk of poverty than men.[72] Among white-collar employees, 11 percent of females were in supervisory positions, as compared with 35 percent of men.[73]

The German executive suite is still overwhelmingly a male preserve. One study found that the country's 626 largest companies had approximately 2,300 men, but only 7 women, on their managing boards.[74] Women's total entrepreneurial activity is less than half that of men's.[75] In 1993 a law was passed that was designed to increase female representation at the top levels of government agencies. The legislation required government agencies to create and carry out plans to promote women in each department, with the goal of "eliminating the underrepresentation of women in hiring and promotion." But there has been little change in the private sector. Not a single major DAX company (the German equivalent to the Dow Jones) is headed by a woman, and only 2 percent of the leadership of other leading companies is female.

There is mounting pressure to legally require corporate boards to include a set number of women, as is the case in France and Norway. In 2012, the European Union considered such legislation. Then in fall 2012, the Bundesrat passed a law that would mandate 40 percent women on the boards of directors of large companies by 2023. This development should compel the Bundestag to take action.[76]

Women in Eastern Germany

The condition of women in the GDR differed from that of West German women in two important respects. First, almost all women (about 90 percent) in East Germany, as compared to about half in West Germany, were in the paid workforce. Second, state support for child care was more comprehensive and more generous in East Germany than were corresponding programs in West Germany. East German women could leave their jobs after the sixth month of pregnancy and remain at home with full pay for up to one year after the birth of a child. Free or low-cost child care was usually available at the women's workplaces because many firms operated child care facilities for their employees. In addition, East Germany had a liberal abortion law that allowed abortion on demand through the first trimester of pregnancy. Of course, pay levels in the east were about two-thirds of those in the west. Women in the east also had to contend with long lines at stores and chronic shortages of many consumer goods.

Since unification the declining economic situation in the east has been especially difficult for women. In many cases they have been the first to be laid off or put on part-time status. By early 1992 almost 60 percent of female workers in some industrial cities were out of work. Yet, even as the economy began to improve in the east, women were still among the last to be rehired. This is one of the major factors behind the disproportional emigration of women, especially those under the age of thirty, from the eastern to the western regions. Moreover, most formerly state-owned firms have closed their child care facilities in an attempt to cut costs and make their enterprises more competitive. Thus, women employees must search on their own for adequate and affordable child care. The pro-choice East German abortion law expired in December 1992, and a generally pro-choice all-German abortion law was declared unconstitutional in 1993. This decision was considered particularly unjust to eastern women; it is little wonder that they are more likely to consider themselves "worse off" since unification than are eastern males.

In any case, the transformation in the lives of women over the last half century has been overwhelmingly positive. Germany ranked eleventh globally in 2011 in terms of having closed the gender gap (75.9 percent of the gap has been closed).[77] The United Nations ranked Germany seventh in its 2011 Gender Inequality Index, well above the UK (thirty-fourth) and the United States (forty-seventh), noting, however that only 53.1 percent of women participate in the labor force versus 66.8 percent of men.[78] As high as these figures are, there is obviously room for improvement. Germany still lags other countries in several issues that directly affect many women's lives, such as all-day schools, the availability of child care, or counting housework for pension purposes. These issues drive the very low birth rate in Germany.

Certainly, attitudes have not completely changed. On the one hand, a 2007 study showed that 88 percent of Germans rejected the stereotype of a woman being a bad mother if she worked outside of the home.[79] On the other hand, in 2005, 66 percent of Germans thought that cleaning windows, doing the laundry (85 percent), and ironing clothes (82 percent) are women's work. In 2008, only 23 percent of women (42 percent of men) thought that equal rights had been achieved.[80]

Youth

Germany's postwar baby boom, which did not begin until after 1948, coupled with a relatively high birth rate during the 1960s, produced a large "postwar generation" that during the past thirty years has assumed the leadership of the country's economic, social, and political systems. For the great majority of Germans today the traumatic experiences of depression, war, defeat, and foreign military occupations are events to be studied in history classes, not living memories. After all, the postwar generation has grown up in a politically stable and economically prosperous society.

The low birth rates of the past thirty years and ever-increasing life spans have put today's youth in a distinct minority position. Between 1965 and 2009, the under-twenty proportion of the population dropped from 29.2 percent to 18.8 percent while the proportion of Germans over sixty-five increased from 12.6 percent to 20.7 percent. The percentage of those under twenty as a proportion of the group between twenty and sixty-four years of age has dropped from 50.1 percent to only 31 percent during this period.[81] Germany has become an older society.

But like their counterparts in other Western societies, young Germans in general are not a hyperpoliticized, ideologically radical element in a staid, middle-class society. Their rate of participation in elections is below that of older age groups. In 2009, for example, 61 percent of voters under twenty-five years of age went to the polls, as compared with approximately 74 percent of voters over age forty-five.[82] In the former East Germany in 2005, only 53 percent of voters under age twenty-five cast their ballots. Further, for decades the youth organizations of the major parties in the west have counted less than 5 percent of the eighteen-to-twenty-nine-year-old group among their ranks.[83] Surveys of young people show that they are concerned above all with employment prospects, the quality of their education, vocational training, individual happiness, and a sense of fulfill-ment—goals with which their elders could hardly disagree.

Although they are not particularly involved in political matters—much less radical causes—young Germans have long been more likely to have opinions sup-portive of liberal democratic values and innovative reform policies than are older age groups. In recent decades, young people have also been more likely to vote for the Social Democrats and, above all, Green political parties rather than for the more conservative Christian Democrats. Not surprisingly, these parties have campaigned strongly for the youth vote. Some states have lowered the minimum voting age for local elections from eighteen to only sixteen. Recent years have shown less youth support for the Greens (now considered an establishment party) and a surge of support for the Pirates. In 2009, 7 percent of Germans under the age of twenty-five voted for the new party.

Official concern about youth questions and the organization of young people has been evident in all German governments. This is expressed through several major white papers on youth, and a variety of legislative programs involving the activities and problems of young people (e.g., vocational education, mental health, scholarship programs, child labor laws). Most traditional solutions to the problems of drug abuse, crime, school truancy, and unemployment among young people that are proposed by various governments tend to revolve around the orga-nization of youth in a variety of cultural, religious, recreational, labor, and educa-tional associations, all subsidized by the state. Approximately 40 percent of young Germans age fifteen to twenty-four belong to at least one of these types of organizations.

Attempts at political education designed to create a "critical, active citizen" are characteristic of most of the groups; indeed, some political educational pro-grams are required to receive state subsidies for their other activities. Whether this extensive state concern with young people is effective is difficult to deter-mine. Given the reported increases in drug abuse, alcoholism,[84] and crime, the traditional official youth programs appear to be insufficient.

Young Germans, both eastern and western, have been less concerned about unification than their elders. Indeed, in the former East Germany the students, who were a privileged group in the GDR, were not as involved as other young people in the events that eventually toppled the communist system. Only politi-cally reliable young people were allowed entrance into East German universities. Many younger East Germans were also more likely to have developed identifica-tion with the communist state than were older age groups.[85] Young people in West Germany benefited from the postunification economic upturn in the "old" Federal Republic, whereas their counterparts in the east experienced sharply increased unemployment and rapidly changing educational conditions. By the end of 1994, unemployment among young people in the eastern states reached almost 35 percent. By 2012, however, this had dropped, thanks to the strong economy, to about 10 percent.[86] High unemployment among eastern youth was frequently cited as a major factor in their proclivity to support right-wing radical groups and engage in violence against foreigners.

Surveys over the last few years, however, have also found signs of a convergence in attitudes between young people in the eastern and western states. The proportion of young people fourteen to twenty-four years of age who consider themselves "unification winners" is 41 percent in the eastern states and 45 percent in the west. Among Germans between the ages of thirty-five and fifty, however, 29 percent of easterners thought of themselves as "winners" as compared to 57 percent of westerners. Support for the idea of socialism in 2007 was also far lower among eastern young people (47 percent) than older residents (73 percent). The east–west gap among young people was only 3 percent, as compared with 37 percent for the thirty-five-to-fifty age group.[87]

Refugees and Resettlers

Over 20 percent of West Germans came to the Federal Republic as refugees or expellees from Germany's eastern territories lost to the Soviet Union and Poland after World War II, other parts of Eastern Europe, or—between 1949 and 1989—the former East Germany. The absorption of this mass of almost 14 million homeless (and in many cases impoverished) people was a major problem for the young German state, which was already overcrowded and unable to adequately feed and house its pre-1945 population. But within two decades this group had become integrated into German society—a major accomplishment of the postwar system. At times, this group and its various representative organizations such as the League of Expellees were able to influence policy, especially regarding the Eastern European states. Their pressure is one reason why the Federal Republic did not formally recognize the post-1945 eastern border with Poland until 1990–1991. Today, however, they represent neither a social nor an economic problem; hence, as refugees, they have little political relevance.

Since 1988 almost three million ethnic German "resettlers" from Eastern Europe and the former Soviet Union have immigrated to the Federal Republic. For decades the Federal Republic had urged Poland, the Soviet Union, and other Eastern European countries to allow their nationals who by virtue of their language, ancestry, or education profess to be German to resettle in the Federal Republic. Article 116 of the Basic Law makes these settlers, many of whom do not speak German, eligible for immediate and full citizenship. Thus the descendants of eighteenth- and nineteenth-century German settlers can appear in Germany and become citizens. Many of them, however, have suffered persecution and discrimination as the price for maintaining their German heritage. Considering the problems of unemployment and housing shortages, the arrival of these distant cousins has evoked some resentment among native Germans. Others, pointing to Germany's low birth rate and aging population, welcome them as a positive demographic development.

Political Radicals and Extremists

The legitimacy threshold for extremist movements has been higher in the Federal Republic than in other Western European societies. Citing the Weimar, Nazi, and East German experiences for support, both West Germany's postwar occupiers and the political elites of the Federal Republic have had a relatively low tolerance for any individual, group, or movement that advocated radical changes in the basic structure of the political, social, or economic order. In short, it has been difficult to be an extremist in Germany and—in comparison with France, Italy, and the UK—relatively easy to be labeled as such by the established parties, courts, and other institutions.

In addition to constitutional prohibitions against extremism (defined as opposition to the "basic free democratic order"), Germany and its constituent states have established offices for the Protection of the Constitution (*Verfassungsschutz*); these are charged with investigating individuals and groups suspected of undermining the system. The national office is housed in the Interior Ministry. It publishes an annual report to parliament that catalogs extremist activity (political parties, acts of political violence) and assesses any trends. At times, critics have charged that the government has misused the office for political purposes.

The Radical Right

Between 1949 and 1969 a variety of right-wing parties and organizations, many of which were led by former Nazis or people with close ties to former Nazis, came to and departed from the political scene. Most of the groups were small, but they could be very noisy and, given Germany's past, drew considerable attention, especially from foreign observers.

At the 1969 election, one of these organizations, the National Democratic Party (NPD), made a strong effort to gain representation in the national parliament. Securing only 4.3 percent of the vote, it failed to clear the 5 percent hurdle necessary for entrance into the legislature. After 1969 the party quickly faded; at the 1976 election it received less than 1 percent of the vote, and between 1970 and 1974 it lost all its seats in several state parliaments. During the 1970s various other nationalist and right-wing organizations mounted protests against the government's policy of détente with the Soviet Union, East Germany, and Eastern Europe, but little was heard from them following ratification of the treaties.

In 1989 a new radical right party, the Republicans, burst onto the political scene at state elections in Berlin, a local election in Frankfurt, and the election of deputies to the European Parliament. Led by a former member of the Waffen-SS (the military wing of the elite guard), the party attracted enormous media attention. Its success was due largely to its strong antiforeigner theme—that is, the party's hostility to foreign workers, residents, and even ethnic Germans who had been allowed to emigrate from the Soviet Union and other Eastern European countries. Voter interest in the Republicans, however, dropped quickly in the wake of the unification movement in 1989–1990 (see also chapter 5).

Since unification, groups of young skinheads and neo-Nazis have formed in the new eastern states. Although constituting only a small proportion of eastern youth, they have attracted widespread media coverage for their attacks on foreigners and for noisy, sometimes violent rallies at which racist and extremist nationalist themes are presented.[88] Their appearance, however, underscores the importance of economic and social reconstruction to the maintenance of democratic stability in the new states.

Concern with right-wing terrorism increased in November 2011 with the discovery of a small neo-Nazi group, the National Socialist Underground (NSU), in the eastern state of Saxony. Between 2000 and 2007 this three-member cell, with the support of allied organizations, murdered seven small businessmen with Turkish backgrounds, one Greek, and one female German police officer in various states throughout the country. In addition, in order to finance their operations, the group robbed several banks. Following the final bank robbery they were about to be apprehended when the two male members committed suicide. The third member, a female, blew up their apartment and then surrendered to the police.[89]

The entire case was badly handled by police and security organizations at both the state and national levels. The group and many of their supporters were well known to officials in Saxony, but this information was not shared with national and other state security agencies; nobody connected the dots. Since the crimes were committed throughout the country, police viewed them as isolated, or since most of the victims were Turkish migrants, the police dismissed the crimes as being related to some internal Turkish mafia dispute—they were dubbed "Döner murders" by police and local media. The case has triggered a series of parliamentary investigations, and most of the leading security officials have since resigned or been dismissed. Generally this case indicates that security officials, especially since September 11, 2001, have been more focused on Islamic and left-wing terrorists and have neglected the terrorist threat from the extreme right.[90]

In spite of its ability to grab some headlines at state elections, the far right has held little interest for voters in national elections. None of the radical-right parties came close to entering the national parliament in recent elections; the combined percentage for all radical right-wing parties has averaged about 2 to 3 percent. Indeed, Germany, unlike France, Italy, Austria, and some other members of the European Union, is not represented in the European Parliament by any delegates from far-right parties. Despite this lack of electoral success, the authorities still closely monitor such groups. In 2003 the Schröder government attempted to ban the NPD, but its indictment was rejected by the Federal Constitutional Court on the grounds that many of the party's leaders were in fact government informants. In 2011–2012 several politicians once again proposed to outlaw the NPD for its alleged ties to "terror cells," in particular the National Socialist Underground. One NPD official was arrested and accused of providing the cell with weapons, and more action may occur in the near future.

The Radical Left

In the late 1960s, the focus of media and public attention shifted from right-wing, neo-Nazi movements to the various revolutionary Marxist groups and radical terrorist organizations that emerged mainly in large cities and on university campuses.

In the immediate postwar period, the remnants of what had been Germany's ideological left wing during the Weimar Republic—old-guard socialists, radical intellectuals, pacifists, and socially committed church members (especially on the Protestant side)—were frustrated as the anticipated moral regeneration and drastic change in the structure of society, economy, and polity did not take place. Original hopes for a "humanistic socialism" were thwarted as a middle-class, materialist, and elitist ethos came to dominate the politics of the new Federal Republic. The radical dissenter became isolated and alienated in the affluent society.

Isolated, its ideology spurned by all major parties and leaders, the New Left in the 1960s developed a socialist theory that rejected and denied legitimacy to the liberalism embodied in the postwar system. The Cold War, West German rearmament, Vietnam, the Social Democrats' (SPD) acceptance of the market economy, and Adenauer's foreign policy all intensified the Left's opposition to the parliamentary system. The SPD's entrance into a Grand Coalition in 1966 with its longtime adversary, the Christian Democrats, was the last straw and marked the beginning of significant radical left activity.

By 1969 the internal divisions over ideology and tactics, the massive indifference if not opposition of the West German "proletariat," and the increasing tendency to violence among factions of the movement greatly weakened the New Left. The Socialist-Liberal election victory of 1969 and the end of the Grand Coalition also took the wind out of the radical argument that the Federal Republic was on the verge of a fascist takeover. Especially once the SPD was in government, many of the more radical actors engaged in what was called "extra-parliamentary opposition" (APO). Nonetheless, the New Left in its own way contributed to the increased politicization of West German citizens. The emphasis on "discussions" rather than speeches by political leaders, as well as the readiness of a traditionally passive citizenry to use the rights of free expression to protest unpopular governmental action and seek redress and reform, was to some extent influenced by the New Left of the 1960s.

Where have all the radicals gone? Like their American and British counterparts, many took teaching and research positions at colleges and universities; and some became active in the Social Democratic Party, the Greens, the trade unions, churches, journalism, and other middle-class occupations. Many refer to this as the "long march" through the country's institutions. Several splinter groups from the movement, called the Red Army Faction (RAF), however, resorted to guerrilla-type violence in an apparent attempt to bring down the state. Terrorist activities began in the 1970s with bank robberies, kidnappings, and murders. By June 1972, with the capture of the so-called Baader-Meinhof gang (named after two leading figures in the movement), terrorist activity subsided. In 1974 the death in prison of one of the terrorists, through the consequences of a hunger strike, touched off the murder of a West Berlin judge. In 1975 another splinter group kidnapped the leader of the Christian Democrats in West Berlin shortly before the city elections and as ransom demanded the release of several terrorists from West German jails.

In 1977 terrorist activities assumed new dimensions when, over a five-month period often called the "German Autumn," a series of well-planned attacks on major government and business leaders took place. The chief federal prosecutor (equivalent to the American attorney general or the British director of public prosecution) and the head of a major bank were assassinated, and in September the director of the Federation of German Industry was kidnapped and later murdered. The terrorists had the support of numerous sympathizers who provided them with falsified identification papers, escape automobiles, conspiratorial hideouts, and other logistical support. Money was secured largely through periodic bank robberies.

Following the collapse of the East German communist regime in 1989–1990, another aspect of the West German terrorist scene became known. For almost fifteen years the East German Secret Police (*Stasi*, see chapter 2) sheltered, trained, and gave extensive material support to terrorists in the Red Army Faction. At least two RAF attacks in 1981—one at the U.S. airbase in Ramstein that injured seventeen people, and an attempted assassination of a U.S. Army general—were led by terrorists who had been trained for the operations in East Germany. Terrorists involved in the 1977 murders of a leading banker and industrialist were provided with new identities and lived for twelve years in the former GDR.

In 1989 the RAF claimed responsibility for the car-bombing murder of Germany's leading banker, Alfred Herrhausen of the Deutsche Bank. A close adviser to Chancellor Kohl, Herrhausen was an early and enthusiastic supporter of German unity. In 1991 the RAF struck again when the director of the Trusteeship Authority (Treuhand), the huge agency charged with privatizing the former GDR's economy, was murdered at his home in western Germany. But by the early 1990s the Red Army Faction had only about twenty hard-core or commando-level members living underground. Officials estimated that they were supported by roughly two hundred militants and four hundred sympathizers who distributed propaganda and provided logistical support.

In 1998 the Red Army Faction suddenly announced that it had disbanded. Authorities considered the statement authentic. In its history the RAF was responsible for the deaths of at least thirty people, including prominent political and business figures. Five fatal attacks dating from 1985 remain unsolved. In its statement the RAF expressed no regret toward its victims.

SUMMARY AND CONCLUSION

The much-discussed postwar political stability of the Federal Republic is now deeply rooted in a solid attitudinal consensus on the values, processes, and institutions of liberal democracy. The "Bonn-Berlin Republic," in contrast to Weimar, is not a republic without republicans. Moreover, in the past sixty-three years there has been an ever closer fit between citizen attitudes and values and actual behavior. Germans at elite and general public levels have become more interested in politics and more inclined to use politics as a means of social change and personal development. Consider the following: Since 1966, five alternations of government and opposition have taken place without straining the system; widespread citizen initiative groups have emerged to campaign for social and political issues (housing, education, the environment), especially at the local level; election campaigns have seen extensive citizen participation and involvement; the party system has become more polarized and conflictual within the rules of the game; the intensity of political debate, both inside and outside of parliament, has increased as major innovations in foreign and domestic policies were attempted. Finally, none of the economic recessions after 1945 produced any noticeable increases in antisystem sentiment or movements. Even the Great Recession of 2008–2009 and the Euro crisis, the worst economic crisis since the Great Depression, had no significant impact on support for democratic values, processes, and institutions. This was in direct contrast to the rise of antisystem right- and left-wing movements in the late 1960s. In short, the institutions and processes of liberal democracy are being used extensively without any perceptible stress on the basic structure of the political order. Moreover, the stability of the German political system has been supplemented by a vitality in political life not apparent during the Republic's early years.

Can this democracy truly integrate the millions of new citizens in the eastern states who lived under Nazi and communist regimes for almost sixty years, as well as the millions of residents with a migration background? Can it successfully open its borders and its culture to the diversity of the global economy and society? Will German women finally achieve full gender equality? These are the challenges facing the Federal Republic into the twenty-first century. East Germans have shown substantial support for the institutions and processes of liberal democracy despite the twenty-year depression in the region and dire demographic prospects. Even with the 1999 citizenship reform, the integration of the country's millions of residents with a migration background remains challenging.

A crucial factor in the further democratic development of the former German Democratic Republic and the integration of foreigners will be the capacity of the party system and interest groups to channel the demands of these citizens and produce meaningful policy outcomes. We turn next to an examination of the Federal Republic's party system and its interest groups.

NOTES

1. Donald J. Devine, *The Political Culture of the United States* (Boston: Little, Brown, 1972), 347ff.

2. Walter Friedrich, "Mentalitätsswandlungen der Jugend in der DDR," *Aus Politik und Zeitgeschichte*, April 13, 1990, 25–37.

3. This takes several forms. There has been, for example, a renewed interest among historians and the media in Prussia and its influence on German history. The immediate post–World War II period, during which the "switches were set" (Weichenstellung) for the formation and evolution of the Federal Republic, also has attracted the serious attention of historians.

4. Allensbach 2009, 39.

5. http://www-news.uchicago.edu/releases/06/060301.nationalpride.pdf.

6. http://www.economist.com/node/14536817.

7. http://www.economist.com/node/1511812.

8. From 1976 to 1988 the proportion of foreign oil that the Federal Republic imported from the Middle East declined from 90 percent to 49 percent.

9. Elisabeth Noelle-Neumann and Renate Köcher, *Die verletzte Nation* (Stuttgart: Deutsche Verlagsanstalt, 1987).

10. Jürgen Habermas, "Eine Art Schadensabwicklung," *Die Zeit*, July 11, 1986, reprinted in *Historikerstreit* (Munich: Piper Verlag, 1987), 75–76.

11. Eric Langenbacher, "From an Unmasterable to a Mastered Past: The Impact of History and Memory in the Federal Republic of Germany," in *The Federal Republic at 60*, special issue of *German Politics* 19, no. 1 (2010), pp. 24–40.

12. http://www.nytimes.com/2012/09/18/world/europe/18iht-letter18.html.

13. G. Robert Boynton and Gerhard Loewenberg, "The Decay of Support for Monarchy and the Hitler Regime in the Federal Republic of Germany," *British Journal of Political Science* 4 (October 1974): 488.

14. Boynton and Loewenberg, "The Decay of Support for Monarchy," 485.

15. *Allensbach* 2002, 546.

16. Lewis J. Edinger, "Political Change in Germany," *Comparative Politics* 2, no. 4 (July 1970): 549–578; Robert Rohschneider, *Learning Democracy: Democratic and Economic Values in Unified Germany* (Oxford: Oxford University Press, 1999).

17. Ralf Dahrendorf, *Society and Democracy in Germany* (New York: Doubleday, Anchor, 1969), 137–138.

18. Dahrendorf, *Society and Democracy in Germany*, 146.

19. Manfred G. Schmidt, "Germany: The Grand Coalition State," *Political Institutions in Europe*, ed. Josep M. Colomer (London: Routledge, 2002), 55–93.

20. *Allensbach* 2009, 194, 120.

21. David P. Conradt, "The Shrinking Elephants: The 2009 Election and the Changing Party System," *German Politics and Society* 28, no. 3 (Autumn 2010): 32.

22. Petra Bauer, "Freiheit und Demokratie in der Wahrnehmung der Bürger in der Bundesrepublik und der ehemaligen DDR," in *Nation und Demokratie*, ed. Rudolf Wildenmann (Baden-Baden: Nomos Verlagsanstalt, 1991), 99–124; Institut für Demoskopie, "Die Unterstützung der Demokratie in den neuen Bundesländern" (unpublished manuscript, Allensbach, 1991), 26–29.

23. These pride differences have remained relatively unchanged since 1991. The figures cited are from the 2000 ALLBUS survey. For similar findings from another 2000 poll, see Elisabeth Noelle-Neumann, "Die Deutschen haben die Probe als Nation bestanden," *Frankfurter Allgemeine Zeitung*, September 27, 2000, 5. This study found a 30 percent difference in pride in the political system and Constitution (west: 71 percent; east: 41 percent).

24. Institut für Demoskopie, survey no. 5050.

25. Elisabeth Noelle-Neumann and Renate Köcher, eds., *Allensbacher Jahrbuch der Demoskopie 1998–2002*, vol. 11, 595; Allensbach 2009, 116.

26. *Renate Jahrbuch*, vol. 12, 40–41.

27. In some areas, however, the east-west conceptions of history remain quite different. In a 1995 study, about 70 percent of westerners stated that the United States had played the decisive role in the defeat of the Nazis in World War II; 24 percent credited the Soviet Union with the victory. Among easterners, however, 87 percent considered the Soviet Union's role decisive and only 23 percent viewed the United States as the decisive factor in the defeat of the Nazis. See Elisabeth Noelle-Neumann, "Der geteilte Himmel," *Frankfurter Allgemeine Zeitung*, May 3, 1995, 5, for additional survey data on differing east-west conceptions of history.

28. Allensbach 2009, 53.

29. *Eurobarometer*, no. 51 (March–April 1999).

30. *Jahrbuch*, vol. 11, 525.

31. Sidney Verba, "Germany: The Remaking of Political Culture," in *Political Culture and Political Development*, ed. L. W. Pye and S. Verba (Princeton, NJ: Princeton University Press, 1965), 130–170.

32. Erwin K. Scheuch, "Die Sichtbarkeit politischer Einstellungen im alltäglichen Verhalten," *Kölner Zeitschrift für Soziologie und Sozialpsychologie*, Sonderheft 9 (1965): 169–214.

33. David P. Conradt, "Changing German Political Culture," in *The Civic Culture Revisited*, ed. Gabriel Almond and Sidney Verba (Boston: Little, Brown, 1980), 231–240.

34. For early postwar data on group membership and involvement see David P. Conradt, "Changing German Political Culture," 255.

35. In 1991 shortly after unification there were substantial differences in social trust between the two regions. By 2003 there was evidence of convergence in social trust, but this was found largely among easterners with stable employment. See Helmut Rainer and Thomas Siedler, "Does Democracy Foster Trust?" German Institute for Economic Research, discussion paper, no. 609 (Berlin, June 2006).

36. In 1968, after years of discussion and debate, the parliament passed a series of laws and constitutional amendments prescribing the conduct of government in emergency situations. Mindful of how the conservative nationalists and later the Nazis had abused the emergency provisions of the Weimar Constitution after 1930, various groups such as trade unions, student organizations, and some intellectuals mounted a vigorous opposition to the proposed legislation. Strong criticism was also leveled against the Social Democrats who while in the parliamentary opposition had vetoed previous attempts at emergency provisions, but who in 1968, as a governing party, supported the laws.

37. Horst Zillessen, "Bürgerinitiativen im repräsentativen Regierungssystem," *Aus Politik und Zeitgeschichte*, March 23, 1974, 6.

38. *ALLBUS* 2004, variable 848.

39. Leonard Krieger, *The German Idea of Freedom* (Chicago: University of Chicago Press, 1957).

40. *Der Spiegel*, July 28, 1975, 28–29.

41. For a thorough analysis of this issue, see Gerard Braunthal, *Political Loyalty and Public Service in West Germany* (Amherst: University of Massachusetts Press, 1990). The relevant decisions of the Federal Constitutional Court are discussed in Donald Kommers, *The Constitutional Jurisprudence of the Federal Republic of Germany* (Durham, NC: Duke University Press, 1989).

42. Interior Minister Zimmermann, quoted in *Die Zeit*, December 30, 1983, 5.

43. Hans Schuler, "Der Staat darf nicht alles wissen," *Die Zeit*, December 30, 1983, 5. The Court's decision and strong opposition from civil libertarians also caused the government to reconsider the proposed introduction of a computerized identification system for all citizens. Under the plan each adult would receive a coded plastic card containing a variety of personal data that could be read out by any authority with the appropriate computer terminal. Opponents argued that the identification system, like the census data, could be easily abused by police and security forces.

44. Louise K. Davidson-Schmich, "Germany's Same-Sex Partnership: Elite Political Tolerance and Political Institutions in Post-Communist Eastern Europe," *American Political Science Association*, Boston, MA, September 2002, 10.

45. Allensbach 2009, 651.

46. Davidson-Schmich, "Germany's Same-Sex Partnership," 21.

47. Mark Lander, "German Police Arrest 3 in Terrorist Plot," *New York Times*, September 6, 2007, 1.

48. Allensbach 2009, 432.

49. Since the onset of the current Euro/debt crisis there has been a modest increase in the number of workers, usually very skilled, from other European Union countries such as Spain and Italy. The strength of the German economy has created labor shortages in a variety of technical occupations.

50. The data come from the 2005 microcensus and are cited in *Frankfurter Allgemeine Zeitung*, May 5, 2007, 4.

51. Marion Schmid-Drüner, "Germany's New Immigration Law: A Paradigm Shift?" *European Journal of Migration and Law* 8, no. 2 (July 2006): 191.

52. In 1973 the Federal Republic, in cooperation with other European Community states, stopped recruiting foreign workers.

53. https://www.destatis.de/DE/PresseService/Presse/Pressemitteilungen/2012/05/PD 12_171_12711.html.

54. http://www.bamf.de/SharedDocs/Anlagen/DE/Downloads/Infothek/Forschung/Studien/migrationsbericht-2010-zentrale-ergebnisse.pdf?__blob = publicationFile.

55. http://www.spiegel.de/international/world/leaving-germany-for-turkey-ethnic-turks-encounter-kueltuerschock-a-703805.html.

56. Wolfgang Jeschek, "Schulbesuch und Ausbildung von jungen Ausländern—kaum noch Fortschritte," *DIW Wochenbericht* 10 (2001): 1–17. See also Jeschek, "Integration junger Ausländer in das Bildungssystem kommt kaum voran," Deutsche Institut für Wirtschaft, *Report No. 24* (1998).

57. *Der Spiegel*, September 13, 2010, 22.

58. For evidence on the influence of Islamic fundamentalism on the 450,000 Turkish young people (fifteen to twenty-one years of age) in the Federal Republic, see Wilhelm Heitmeyer, Helmut Schröder, and Joachim Müller, "Desintegration und islamischer Fundamentalismus," *Aus Politik und Zeitgeschichte*, February 7, 1997, 17–31.

59. *Der Spiegel*, October 31, 2011.

60. The old law allowed the children (under age twenty-three) of foreign residents to become naturalized citizens provided that they had lived in the Federal Republic for at least eight years and had attended German schools for at least six years.

61. Figures provided by the Federal Statistical Office. See Marc Morjé Howard, "Germany's Citizenship Policy in Comparative Perspective," *German Politics and Society* 30, no. 1 (2012): 39–51.

62. Immigrants with high potential, such as scientists, professors, high-income managers, and specialists, receive "red carpet" treatment (i.e., they can receive an immediate residency permit). Lesser-qualified applicants are admitted if the Labor Ministry certifies that there is a need for and a shortage of workers with their skills. Unskilled workers are generally denied the right to residency. See Schmid-Drümer, "Germany's New Immigration Law," for a detailed analysis of the legislation.

63. Hardy Graupner, "German Immigration Law Marks One Year," *Deutsche Welle World*, January 2, 2006, www.dw-world.de. The new integration courses (language, history, and culture) have been more successful. In the first nine months of the new law, 220,000 foreigners had signed up.

64. *Eurobarometer*, no. 23 (April 1983).

65. Elisabeth Noelle-Neumann and Renate Köcher, eds., *Jahrbuch der Öffentlichen Meinung*, vol. 9 (New York and Frankfurt: K. G. Saur Verlag, 1993), 620.

66. http://www.bpb.de/nachschlagen/zahlen-und-fakten/wahlen-in-deutschland/555 97/nach-gechlecht.

67. Beate Hoecker, "Politik: Noch immer kein Beruf für Frauen," *Aus Politik und Zeitgeschichte*, February 28, 1987, 5; and *Das Parlament* 32 (August 10, 1985): 11.

68. Since the 1980s many local, regional, and state governments have appointed Frauenbeauftragte (ombudswomen) to oversee antidiscrimination and equal opportunity programs.

69. *Jahrbuch*, vol. 11, 395. These trend data refer only to West Germany.

70. Allensbach 2009, 637.

71. *Datenreport 2011*, 110.

72. http://tk.eversjung.de/www/downloads/Gender_Equality_National_Report_Germany.pdf.

73. *Datenreport 2011*.

74. Manager magazine cited in Ferdinand Protzmann, "In Germany, the Ceiling's Not Glass, It's Concrete," *New York Times*, October 17, 1993, 16. A similar study eleven years earlier found only two women at the top level of German companies.

75. http://tk.eversjung.de/www/downloads/Gender_Equality_National_Report_Germany.pdf.

76. http://www.dw.de/dw/article/0,,16253512,00.html.

77. http://www.weforum.org/issues/global-gender-gap.

78. http://hdr.undp.org/en/media/HDR_2011_EN_Table4.pdf.

79. http://www.welt.de/politik/article1171149/Rabenmuetter-sterben-aus-Rabenvaeter-keinesfalls.html.

80. Allensbach 2009, 644, 638.

81. Datenreport 2011, 14.

82. http://www.bpb.de/wissen/C11SZM,,0,Wahlbeteiligung_nach_Altersgruppen.

83. Walter Jaide and Hans-Joachim Veen, *Bilanz der Jugendforschung* (Paderborn: Ferdinand Schoningh Verlag, 1989), 202.

84. http://www.ias.org.uk/resources/papers/europe/phproject/bingedrinking-report.pdf.

85. Bettina Westle, "Strukturen Nationaler Identität in der DDR und der BRD," unpublished manuscript, Mannheim University, July 1991, 14.

86. http://de.statista.com/statistik/daten/studie/189105/umfrage/jugendarbeitslosenquote-nach-bundeslaendern.

87. "Spiegel Umfrage: Generation Deutsche Einheit," *Der Spiegel*, October 29, 2007, 22ff.

88. *Frankfurter Allgemeine Zeitung*, September 19, 1998, 3.

89. http://www.washingtonpost.com/world/germany-refocuses-on-neo-nazi-threat/2012/08/11/b11af85e-e2fd-11e1-98e7-89d659f9c106_story_1.html.

90. A döner or döner kebap is a shaved meat sandwich originating from Turkey but ubiquitous in German cities today.

91. Judy Dempsey, "The True Threat to Integration in Germany," *New York Times*, August 6, 2012.

5

The Party System and the Representation of Interests

The postwar party system differs substantially in structure and function from that of the empire and the Weimar Republic. Structurally, the number of political parties seriously contending for parliamentary representation has dropped to five or six, in contrast to the twelve to twenty-five parties represented at various times in the Reichstag between 1871 and 1933. The extremist, regional, and small special-interest parties that made stable coalition government so difficult during the Weimar Republic either did not reappear in 1949 or were absorbed by the major parties by the elections of 1953 and 1957. Functionally, postwar German parties have become key carriers of the democratic state and have assumed an importance and status unprecedented in German political history. Before the creation of the Federal Republic, democratic political parties, fragmented and narrowly based, were not, for the most part, major forces in political life. The executive, the bureaucracy, the military, and the economic elites—not the democratic political parties—made many of the important decisions. Frustrated and thwarted in their quest for governmental and specifically executive power, the parties concentrated more on ideological differentiation and the construction of their extraparliamentary organizations than on the more practical matter of organizing government. The presentation of meaningful alternatives to the electorate, the ability to translate party policy into governmental programs, and the control of governmental leaders were functions that the parties rarely performed.

THE PARTY STATE

The Federal Republic, by contrast, has been termed a *party state*. German political scientist Kurt Sontheimer provides a clear definition of this term:

> All political decisions in the Federal Republic are made by the parties and their representatives. There are no political decisions of importance in the German

democracy, which have not been brought to the parties, prepared by them and finally taken by them.[1]

Political parties in the Federal Republic became agencies that made nominations and fought elections with the goal of controlling the personnel and policies of government. They no longer stood on the sidelines.

The postwar parties antedated the Republic. In fact, they created it and have penetrated key institutions as never before in German history. Relatively untainted by Nazism (they were all outlawed in 1933), the parties began work early. Between 1945 and 1950, with considerable amounts of patronage at their disposal, they ensured that not only parliament, but also the bureaucracy, the judiciary, the educational system, the media, and later even the military, were led directly or indirectly by their supporters. Even today, few German civil servants would dare attempt to "go public" with criticism in any controversial area without the protection of a party/political figure. Moreover, these democratic parties were distrustful of what an American would term "independents." In Germany, to be independent has historically meant to be "above the parties," and those "above the parties" have usually sided with the authoritarian-statist tradition. Hence the parties opposed the efforts of American occupiers to establish a Federal Personnel Office along the lines of the nonpartisan American Civil Service Commission to staff, especially the upper levels of the bureaucracy, with "independents." To postwar German party leaders, a nonpartisan civil service meant at best a bureaucracy indifferent to the democratic system, and at worst one opposed to it. Today, after almost sixty-five years of democratic politics, the highest positions in the state bureaucracy, the educational system, and even the radio and television networks are mainly given to people who are active party members.

The strength of this party system was also shown during the unification process. When it became apparent that the indigenous East German democratic forces could not compete with the well-organized Communist Party apparatus during preparations for the country's first free election in 1990, the West German parties quickly moved across the recently opened border and organized the campaign. In the March 1990 election, East Germans could choose from the full range of parties available to West Germans. The losers in this process, however, in addition to the communists, were the native East German democratic revolutionaries, who had risked their lives to bring down the communist regime. Only about 5 percent of East Germans supported these groups in the election.

The constitutional source of this strong position held by the parties is found in Article 21 of the Basic Law, which states that "the political parties shall take part in forming the political will of the people. They may be freely established. Their internal organization must conform to democratic principles. They must publicly account for the sources of their funds." It is rare for any democratic constitution to mention political parties in such detail, much less assign them a function. Article 21 goes on in paragraph 2, however, to grant the Federal Constitutional Court the right to prohibit any party that does not accept the Constitution:

Parties that by reason of their aims or the behavior of their adherents seek to impair or abolish the free democratic basic order or to endanger the existence of the Federal Republic of Germany, shall be unconstitutional. The Federal Constitutional Court shall decide on the question of unconstitutionality.

In other words, a political organization, exercising the rights of free speech and freedom of assembly but that opposes the constitutional order may be outlawed. Indeed, in the 1950s two political parties—the communists and a neo-Nazi party—were banned by the court under this provision. Many constitutional scholars and political scientists questioned the wisdom of this action, arguing that the ballot box is the best place to defeat extremist groups in a democracy. But its inclusion in the Constitution indicates the determination of the leaders of Germany's democratic parties to avoid a recurrence of Weimar conditions and to close the system to all extremist movements.

The constitutional recognition given to the parties is the major rationale for the extensive state support they receive, especially for election campaigns (see chapter 6). Each of the major parties also has a quasi-official foundation that sponsors extensive domestic political education projects and engages in "political developmental" work in several less-developed countries (see chapter 10). The overall thrust of the foundations' overseas work tends to be directed toward establishing goodwill for the Federal Republic, especially in the Third World, by supporting the training and development of native democratic parties and interest groups. Political education in the sense of training party and interest group officials and functionaries is also included in this overseas work. The SPD's Friedrich Ebert Foundation supported the Social Democratic parties of Spain and Portugal while those countries were still under dictatorial control. The training and support of trade unionists in developing countries is another area of activity for the foundation. Similar projects, in some cases oriented to more centrist or conservative political movements, are sponsored by the CDU's Konrad Adenauer Foundation, the CSU's Hanns Seidel Foundation, and the FDP's Friedrich Naumann Foundation. Since 1989 the Green Party has established its own foundation, the Heinrich Böll Foundation, which support projects identified with the Green program (i.e., environmental problems, women's issues, and human rights organizations). In 1999, the Party of Democratic Socialism (PDS), the successor to the former ruling Communist Party of East Germany (now the Left Party), also received funds to establish a foundation, the Rosa Luxemburg Foundation, named after one of the founders of the German Communist Party. Almost all of the funds for these party foundations come from the state.

This system of strong parties, or the "party state," is not without its shortcomings or critics. It can be, for example, difficult for new interests, parties, and movements to gain a political foothold. The influence of the grassroots is also limited by the parties' hierarchical structure. The emergence in the 1970s of a significant citizen initiative movement and later a new political party, the Greens, outside the boundaries of this party system illustrates the extent to which some important issues, such as nuclear power, housing, and urban planning, have not been dealt with by the parties to the satisfaction of large groups of involved citizens. The emergence of the Pirate Party in the 2009 election and its entrance into several state parliaments in 2010–2012 is another indication that issues such as privacy and Internet freedom have not been sufficiently addressed by the established parties.

There is also increasing evidence that the established parties have abused and manipulated the laws governing their financing. In the 1980s several leading officials from the Free Democrats were indicted for illegally receiving campaign funds. In 1992 the Federal Constitutional Court (see chapter 8) ruled that the parties were far too liberal in their allocation of public funds for their activities. It also ruled that state subsidies cannot exceed the amounts the parties raise themselves.

By 2006 public subsidies to political parties in the Federal Republic accounted for more than a third of their total income; no other democracy is so generous in its support of parties through public funds. There is a complex system in place that calculates a party's financing based on votes won at various levels, the number of seats, membership, and donations (see the more extensive discussion in chapter 6).[2] Because the parties control both the state and national parliaments, which allocate these funds, there are few means to control independently their ever-increasing demand for taxpayer support. Party finance scandals have been blamed for the growing distrust of political leaders and institutions and the decline in voter turnout. None of these scandals has thus far had any major impact on the way the major parties raise money.

But finance scandals, the policy performance of recent governments, as well as socioeconomic and cultural change have taken their toll on public support for the parties. Party membership is down, and a generalized sense that the parties have lost touch with the public is clearly evident in recent polls. In a 2004 survey, more than 80 percent of Germans said they "tended not to trust" the political parties. In a more recent survey, almost two-thirds of respondents stated that the parties offered them no real alternatives, and only 20 percent felt that the parties encouraged political activity.[3] Since 1990 the SPD has lost 40 percent of its members, and the CDU/CSU 25 percent.

In the 2009 national election, the two largest parties, the Christian Democrats and the Social Democrats, saw their combined share of the vote drop to its lowest level in the history of the Federal Republic. The three opposition parties secured the highest totals in their histories, and new protest movements and parties, such as the Pirates, may be further complicating the situation. This party system, so successful in the first six decades of the Federal Republic's history, may be on the verge of a major transformation that will see the further decline of the once-large parties and the emergence of a more fragmented multiparty system.

THE PARTY SYSTEM

The Christian Democrats

For most of its history (forty-four out of sixty-four years), the Federal Republic has been governed by a political party that—like the Republic itself—was a distinctly postwar creation. The center-right Christian Democratic Union (CDU) and its

Bavarian affiliate, the Christian Social Union (CSU), represented the efforts of widely divergent groups and interests to seek a new beginning following the Nazi catastrophe and postwar occupation.

Between 1945 and 1948, small groups of political activists made up of former Weimar Center, Liberal, and Socialist party members, together with Catholic and Protestant laity, organized throughout Germany. The dominant theme motivating these disparate interests was the need for a new party based in part on the application of general Christian principles to politics. It was felt that the traditional differences between Protestants and Catholics had to be bridged, at least at the political level, to create a new movement that could be a powerful integrating force in the new political system. Also, by stressing its ties to the churches, this new party linked itself to the one pre-Nazi social institution that survived the war with some authority, legitimacy, and organizational strength.[4]

In its early years, the CDU was programmatically committed to wide-ranging socioeconomic reform, particularly in the British zone. The major statement of the party, the Ahlen Program of 1947, indeed called for the nationalization of large industries and rejected the restoration of many prewar capitalistic structures in the Federal Republic. In addition, Article 15 of the Basic Law—which permits, with proper compensation, the socialization of land, natural resources, and the means of production—was supported by the chairman in the British zone and future chancellor, Konrad Adenauer.

What happened between 1947 and 1949? Essentially the success of Ludwig Erhard's 1948 currency reform, which ended postwar inflation and the black market; the end of Allied dismantling of German industry; American opposition to "socialist policies"; and the realization that the Christian Democrats, given the strength of the socialists, had little freedom to maneuver on the left of the political spectrum—all of these factors together shifted the CDU toward a more center-right than center-left position. In short, there was by 1949 room for a middle-of-the-road, centrist party with a conservative economic policy and a major party to the right of the SPD, but not for another center-left party. The Union's performance at the first federal election in September 1949, the economic boom that began with the Korean War in 1950, and the foreign policy successes of Chancellor Adenauer solidified the more conservative course.

Nonetheless, the party remained remarkably open to a wide variety of political viewpoints. Apart from a general commitment to the "social market economy" (capitalism with a heart) and a pro-Western, anticommunist foreign policy, the Christian Democrats avoided any specific policy orientation, much less ideology. To its critics, this was opportunism; to supporters, however, the party's pragmatic, bargaining approach to politics represented a welcome relief from the ideological rigidity that had characterized many Weimar parties. The CDU thus provided a home for liberals, socialists, and conservatives; Catholics and Protestants; north and south Germans; rural and urban areas; and industrial and labor interests, all held together by, above all, the electoral successes of Chancellor Adenauer. The CDU became a prototype for what Otto Kirchheimer termed a "catchall party," a broadly based, programmatically vague movement that capitalized on the mass economic prosperity of postwar Europe.[5]

The stunning victories of the party in the 1953 and 1957 elections were essentially personal triumphs for Adenauer. Adenauer represented stability, economic success, and continuity. He also was adept at capitalizing on his reassuring, grandfatherly image with the famous campaign slogan, "No experiments." The CDU's dependence on the popularity of the chancellor, however, would prove to be a short-run advantage but a long-run liability. In riding the crest of his personal popularity, the Union did not take the necessary steps to strengthen its organization and depersonalize its appeals to retain its position after Adenauer's inevitable departure. At the 1961 election, Adenauer's age (eighty-five), thirteen years of governmental responsibility, and a "new look" SPD began to erode the party's electoral base. The Christian Democrats lost their absolute majority, and as a condition for a coalition with the Free Democrats, Adenauer had to agree to step down by 1963. His successor, Ludwig Erhard, had never been a party leader and had little real political power within the Union. But as the architect of postwar economic prosperity, he did possess an electoral appeal that the Union gratefully employed in the 1965 election. With the 1966 recession, however, Erhard's status as an "electoral locomotive" declined, and with it his position in the party and his chancellorship.

With no strong, electorally successful chancellor to hold it together, the party's numerous factions and wings began to struggle among themselves for control of the organization. Taking the SPD into the government in 1966 (forming the Grand Coalition) kept the party in power until 1969 under the chancellorship of Kurt Georg Kiesinger but failed to halt the steady decline in its image among many voters as the only party capable of governing at the national level. For the first time in its history, the CDU/CSU in 1969 found itself without a leader, without a program, and, above all, without power.

The Union in Opposition, 1969–1982

Yet the closeness of the CDU/CSU defeat in 1969 (the party fell only thirteen seats short of an absolute majority) provided the Union with sufficient reasons not to prepare for its new role as the parliamentary opposition. Although its percentage of the vote declined, the CDU/CSU in 1969 remained the largest single party. The Union's leadership insisted that, as the largest party, it was entitled to form the government, a privilege denied them by the "manipulations" of a "desperate" FDP and SPD. Thus, the party concentrated much of its effort between 1969 and 1972 on short-range tactical maneuvers designed to split the coalition parties or at least gain enough support from discontented government deputies to erase the coalition's small majority and return the Union to power without new elections. To this end, the party attempted unsuccessfully to unseat the Brandt government in May 1972 by means of a "constructive vote of no-confidence" (see chapter 7). Instead of concentrating on the development of its organization, program, and leadership, the party sought to topple the government and take a shortcut back to political power.

After the decisive SPD-FDP victory in the 1972 election, however, the CDU/CSU could no longer deny the necessity of accepting its role as the opposition party. Yet the Union in opposition still lacked leadership, policy, and organizational consensus. After several years of intraparty maneuvering, Helmut Kohl, the young Ministerpräsident of the state of Rhineland-Palatinate, emerged in 1973 as the party's new leader and 1976 chancellor candidate. In the 1976 election the CDU/CSU made impressive gains but nonetheless narrowly missed returning to power.

The Bavarian Challenge, 1976–1980

The Christian Social Union is the Bavarian affiliate of the Christian Democratic Union. While the CSU has its own leadership, organization, and fund-raising structures, it does not run candidates outside of Bavaria, Germany's largest state in terms of area and second in population. The CDU returns the favor and does not compete in Bavaria. At the national level both parties agree on a single candidate for chancellor. In seventeen elections between 1949 and 2009, the CDU/CSU has only twice, in 1980 and 2002, nominated a Bavarian.

Electorally the CSU has consistently outperformed the CDU by a wide margin. In the sixteen national elections held between 1953 and 2009, the Christian Democrats averaged about 34 percent of the party vote. Their Bavarian sister, however, has averaged a phenomenal 54 percent of the vote. Were it not for this Bavarian bonus, the CDU/CSU would have lost rather than won most of these national elections.

The CSU anchors the right wing of the combined parties. It is more conservative than the CDU, especially on social issues such as abortion, church-state issues, immigration, and the rights of Germany's eight million foreign residents. In foreign policy the Bavarians also tend to take a more nationalist position. In the 1970s the CSU opposed the efforts of the Social Democratic government led by Willy Brandt to normalize relations with Eastern Europe and the then Soviet Union. It has also been less supportive of the European Union than the Christian Democrats. CSU leaders were prominent opponents of the Euro and of the various bailouts since 2009 for weaker Eurozone countries.

Although they have cooperated closely at the national level, the relationship between the two parties has at times been fraught with conflict. The key figure in the Bavarian party's history is Franz-Josef Strauss (1915–1988). Strauss, a federal minister from 1953 to 1969 and Bavarian minister-president from 1978 to 1988, is credited with building the party into an electoral powerhouse with a modern grassroots organization long before Kohl did the same for the CDU. Strauss considered the 1976 result a defeat for Kohl. He believed that he should have a chance at the chancellorship in 1980.

With his Bavarian CSU solidly behind him, Strauss was able to convince the more conservative elements within the CDU that he could indeed win. Many CDU activists, ideologically opposed to the Bavarian, nonetheless also began to accept the idea of a Strauss candidacy. They reasoned that given the high popularity of Chancellor Schmidt and the solid record of his government, the CDU/CSU, regardless of its candidate, was bound to lose in 1980. Why not let Strauss have his chance and thus, after his inevitable defeat, be rid of this source of so much tension and division within the Union? This argument was quite persuasive for a sufficient number of moderate and liberal party leaders, and Strauss was elected as the Union's 1980 chancellor candidate.

The Union's decisive defeat in 1980 was absorbed at the leadership level with relatively little intraparty rancor. Strauss returned to Bavaria, and Kohl retained his position as national chairman of the CDU and parliamentary floor leader. His loyal support of Strauss in the campaign increased his stature within the CSU and among CDU conservatives.

The Return to Power

By early 1982 it was apparent that the Social (SPD)–Liberal (FDP) (Red-Yellow) coalition would not last until the next scheduled election in 1984. Now the unchallenged national leader of the party, Helmut Kohl carefully maintained his good relations with the Free Democrats and especially their leader, Hans-Dietrich Genscher. In September 1982 the Free Democrats left the Schmidt cabinet. Shortly thereafter they joined with the CDU and removed Schmidt, replacing him with Kohl. After thirteen years in opposition, the Christian Democrats had returned to power.

Six months later, at the March 1983 election, the CDU/CSU had all the advantages of incumbency without any of its disadvantages. From the chancellor's office, Kohl could campaign against the thirteen years of Social Democratic rule and optimistically point to the new beginnings that his government now wanted to make if the electorate would give it the opportunity. Although the economy continued to decline after October 1982, the Union disclaimed any responsibility, dismissing even the record high unemployment levels of early 1983 as the burden it inherited from the Social Democrats.

In the 1987 election, the Christian Democrats campaigned on the record of the Kohl government. The party emphasized that it had brought Germany back to economic prosperity, reduced the federal deficit, cut taxes, and restored the Federal Republic's status both as a dependable ally of the United States and as a major force in the European Community. Nonetheless, attaining 44 percent of the vote, the CDU/CSU dropped to its lowest level since 1949. By 1989, there was growing voter fatigue with Kohl's leadership, and the next election, scheduled for 1991, was widely expected to be won by the opposition.

The Christian Democrats and Unification

As West German political parties began to participate in the East German political process in early 1990, the outlook for the Christian Democrats was bleak. The East German CDU, which for a brief period after 1945 was an independent party with some association to Christian Democrats in other parts of the country, became a puppet or "bloc" party, one of four that the communists allowed to operate as a democratic facade for the regime. It did count among its members some East Germans who tried to improve the existing system from within, or who saw the party as a refuge from the one-party system, that is, a means for expressing a small degree of independence without being pressured to join the

Communist Party. There were also some devoutly religious East Germans among the party's members. The leadership, however, was totally corrupted by the communists. In exchange for obediently following the communist line, they were given luxurious (by East German standards) homes, automobiles, generous salaries, and some patronage.

The West German CDU at first avoided any formal contact with this "bloc CDU" in the east. But after the east CDU changed its leadership in the wake of the GDR's collapse and as the date for East Germany's first free parliamentary election approached, Chancellor Kohl and the west CDU began to reassess their relationship to their errant East German cousin. Kohl and his advisers contended that while the old leadership was hopelessly compromised, the rank-and-file membership was basically sound.

Once opinion polls in the east showed that the Social Democrats, a new but "clean" party, held a commanding lead, Kohl put together an "Alliance for Germany" composed of two new opposition groups—the German Social Union and the Democratic Breakthrough—and the "reformed" East German CDU. With Kohl as the de facto leader, the Alliance won a solid victory in the March 1990 East German parliamentary election. The East CDU's large membership and organizational infrastructure served the Alliance well at the subsequent state elections in October 1990 and the all-German poll in December. The CDU became the dominant party in four of the five East German states, and with 44 percent of the vote, it remained the largest party in unified Germany. Kohl masterfully led the unification process (see chapter 2), as well as reviving his party's electoral fortunes through it. Due to a variety of factors such as lackluster SPD leadership, a well-timed economic upturn, and disproportional support in eastern Germany, Kohl's coalition also barely won the 1994 election.

The End of the Kohl Epoch

By 1998, Kohl and the Christian Democrats showed the effects of their sixteen-year tenure in office. The chancellor's dominance of the national organization left little room for new leaders to emerge. At the state level the party continued to decline. By 1997 they were the major governing party in only four of the sixteen states. Younger party leaders wanted Kohl to step down before the 1998 election, but Kohl, Western Europe's senior statesman, insisted on running again. It was a huge mistake. The party ran an uninspired campaign and could not overcome the "Kohl must go" theme of the opposition. After Kohl's sixteen years in power, many Germans were simply tired of the "old man." Also, unlike 1994, the economy did not improve in 1998, and the unemployment issue badly hurt the CDU. In the eastern states, now mired in a prolonged depression, voters turned on Kohl and the CDU with a vengeance. After giving the Christian Democrats lopsided support in the elections of 1990 and 1994, which were still dominated by the unification theme, eastern voters deserted the Union in droves; CDU support in the east in 1998 dropped by more than 30 percent. Kohl accepted defeat gracefully and stepped down as leader of the party shortly after the election. He was replaced by Wolfgang Schäuble, the longtime crown prince of the party.

The party appeared to be recovering well from the 1998 defeat. In early 1999 it won a narrow victory at an important state election and regained control of the Bundesrat, the second parliamentary chamber representing the states. The myriad problems of the new SPD-Green government were helping the party in public opinion polls, along with populist tactics in various Länder such as Hesse and North Rhine–Westphalia. Then disaster struck. In late 1999 details of a massive scandal involving millions of marks in illegal campaign funds rocked the party. The key figure in the scandal was none other than the party's icon, Helmut Kohl, who for decades had illegally collected and dispersed funds to his supporters. The scandal soon spread to Kohl's successor, Wolfgang Schäuble, who had to resign as the national chairman when it was revealed that he had known of the secret donations. With the entire Kohl leadership group badly damaged, the Union went in search of fresh faces untouched by the scandal.

In April 2000 the party broke new ground when it selected a female from the east, Angela Merkel, as its national chairperson. Ms. Merkel became the first female to ever lead a major political party. Merkel, trained as a physicist in the communist east and hence untainted by any association with the communist regime, first attracted national attention when Kohl appointed her to his cabinet in 1992 as environmental minister. General secretary of the CDU since 1998, her low-key, unassuming personality and her indifference to media image enabled the Union to claim that it had made a clean break from the Kohl era.

After Merkel had spent several months as chairperson, however, doubts emerged about her ability to control the now-feuding factions within the party and her viability as a chancellor candidate. By mid-2001 it was apparent that many in the party could still accept her as chairman but not as the chancellor candidate in 2002.

With the 2002 election fast approaching, the Union turned for only the second time in its history to Bavaria for a chancellor candidate. Like his political godfather, Franz-Josef Strauss, Edmund Stoiber was a conservative. He had taken hard-right positions on immigration; European unity, including the Euro; and education. But he was a winner. Indeed, his selection was due in large part to the extraordinary success of the Christian Social Union, the Bavarian affiliate of the CDU. Bavaria, governed exclusively by the CSU since 1954, has consistently enjoyed higher growth rates and lower unemployment rates than any other region. By late 2001 the country was once again in an economic decline. Perhaps with an election campaign focused on the economy, Stoiber would have a chance.

The Merkel Era

Stoiber officially became the CDU/CSU candidate in early 2002. Soon thereafter the party overtook the Social Democrats in the polls. With a team of campaign advisers from outside Bavaria, Stoiber was able to soften his hard-right image. The economy worsened throughout the year and Stoiber looked like a sure winner. By early August the Union enjoyed what looked like an insurmountable lead over the SPD. But on August 12 the Union's fortunes began a dramatic reversal. A major flooding of the Elbe and Mulde rivers in the eastern region gave Schröder the opportunity to demonstrate decisive leadership and dominate the headlines. Stoiber and the CDU/CSU were slow to respond to the disaster. For the first time in the campaign they were confused. Then Chancellor Schröder's opposition to the Iraq policy of the Bush administration—that is, the American intention to launch a preemptive war to overthrow the regime of Saddam Hussein—struck a responsive chord among many German voters. Finally at the last debate, two weeks before the election, Stoiber was bested by Schröder, who emphasized his national and international experience in contrast to the alleged provincialism of Stoiber. While Stoiber and the CDU/CSU were able to make solid gains and pulled even with the SPD on polling day, they fell short of the votes necessary to replace the government. Their potential coalition partner, the Free Democrats, could not secure more votes than the SPD's partner, the Greens. The SPD-Green coalition was reelected with a razor-thin majority of only eleven seats.

The CDU's near miss in 2002 was due largely to unique events that could not have been foreseen by the best campaign planners. Nonetheless, Stoiber was not given a second chance. Following the election, Merkel assumed the leadership of the party's parliamentary delegation in addition to her role as national chairperson. Like Helmut Kohl in 1980, she was a good soldier and deferred to the older and more experienced Bavarian. But she also steadfastly sidelined the CDU old guard and regional bosses, promoted her supporters, developed close ties with Schäuble, and worked for programmatic renewal. Thus, in 2005 she had little difficulty becoming the party's chancellor candidate.

As the 2005 election approached, Merkel and the CDU enjoyed a large lead over the incumbent SPD-Green government. Yet voter anxiety over her proposals for further cuts in social programs and increased taxes and a surprisingly skillful campaign by Chancellor Schröder caused her lead to disappear by election day. When the votes were counted, the CDU/CSU received only 35 percent of the party vote as compared to 34 percent for Schröder's Social Democrats. Neither party could find enough partners among the smaller parties to form a coalition. After weeks of difficult negotiations, the CDU/CSU, still led by Merkel, formed a Grand Coalition with the Social Democrats, the second such alignment in the Republic's history. Angela Merkel became the first female chancellor in German history. But since the CDU/CSU had to share power with its chief rival, the Social Democrats, it was an ambiguous victory.

Nevertheless, the Grand Coalition was rather successful from a policy perspective and lasted the entire parliamentary term. Both Merkel and the SPD were ideologically moderate, and the Social Democratic ministers were competent administrators. The Merkel-led coalition was also helped by an economic upswing after 2006, which made policy making less contentious than in periods of scarcer resources.

As the 2009 election campaign approached, Merkel showed that she would not repeat her mistakes of 2005. This time her campaign would avoid any major policy proposals. She also benefited from the economic recovery that was already under way by the summer of 2009, as well as a weak competitor from the SPD. She won the September 2009 election and was able to form a coalition with her preferred partner, the FDP.

The first one hundred days of the new coalition went badly. There was infighting on economic and foreign policy, as well as widespread allegations of cronyism, chaos, corruption, and incompetence. FDP leader Guido Westerwelle's nosedive in the polls and his party's stunning losses in North Rhine–Westphalia in 2010 and Baden-Württemberg in 2011 sharply reduced the party's clout in the coalition to the point that Merkel could act unilaterally. Shortly after the May 2010 North Rhine–Westphalia election, for example, she announced that there would be no tax cuts in the current parliamentary period. Thus the signature issue of the FDP was off the table not long after the party's strongest electoral performance in its history. A few weeks later following the abrupt resignation of Federal President Köhler, Merkel and the CDU, with no input from the FDP, selected the CDU minister-president of Lower Saxony, Christian Wulff, as the coalition's candidate to succeed Köhler (see chapter 7). Clearly, decisions were made in the Chancellery without FDP consultation.

In spite of the tensions within her coalition and the disappointing results of her party in various Länder elections since 2009, Merkel has spearheaded some major changes in the CDU program, including ending conscription, abandoning nuclear power, and grudgingly accepting a European transfer union. These core principles of the "old CDU," as well as a more critical relationship to the Catholic Church, have raised the ire of the old guard and some quarters of the CSU. Nevertheless, Merkel's promotion of her own supporters and sidelining of previous opponents left the critics with few alternatives within the party. Moreover, Merkel apparently thought that some short-term costs should result in longer-term benefits by reaching out to younger, more urban voters and becoming more attractive to the Greens, perhaps even as a coalition partner. Even in light of the problems of the last years, Merkel approached the 2013 elections as strong as any eight-year incumbent could hope to be. But soon, the Union will have to have a discussion about what and who will come after Merkel.

The Social Democrats

One of the oldest parties in the world (founded in 1875), the Social Democratic Party of Germany (SPD) was the only major Weimar political party to reemerge almost entirely intact in the Federal Republic. The SPD maintained an executive committee in exile throughout the Nazi period. Together with members who had survived within Germany, it was able to reestablish its national organization in relatively short order after 1945. The SPD is the main center-left catchall party in Germany, traditionally advocating a stronger state role in the economy and a robust, redistributive welfare state. More recently, it has come to advocate social and gender rights. Its core constituencies have been wage earners, the industrial working class, trade unions, urban residents, and public sector employees (e.g., teachers).

In view of the party's unequivocal opposition to National Socialism (the SPD was the only party to vote against Hitler's Enabling Act in March 1933), its strong organization, and its large number of industrial workers, it appeared that the SPD would soon become Germany's natural governing party with the resumption of democratic politics at the national level. These expectations were not fulfilled, because the party at the first parliamentary election in 1949 fell far short of an absolute majority (29.2 percent of the vote versus 31 percent for the CDU/CSU) and by 1953 was clearly subordinate to the enormously successful CDU under Adenauer.

Why did the SPD fail during the immediate postwar period to become Germany's major governing party? Most analysts attribute this to (1) the party's leadership and, specifically, its national chairman after 1945, Kurt Schumacher, who died in 1952; (2) its incorrect reading of German public opinion on key foreign and domestic policy issues; and (3) the unexpected appeal of Adenauer and the free market economic policies of Economic Minister Ludwig Erhard.[6]

Following the disastrous 1953 (28.8 percent) and 1957 (31.8 percent) federal elections, major changes in policy, leadership, and strategy were advocated by an increasing number of SPD state leaders, particularly in Hamburg, Frankfurt, and Berlin. They flatly argued that the party would be permanently consigned to the "30 percent ghetto" unless it made major changes. Their analysis of the election defeats and public opinion polls showed that the SPD had several substantial electoral barriers to surmount.

First, large segments of the electorate had doubts about the SPD's foreign policy, specifically, its tepid commitment to NATO and the pro-Western, anticommunist policy initiated by Adenauer and strongly supported by the electorate during the 1950s. By 1960 the great majority of West Germans accepted the Western orientation of the Bonn Republic, and the reformers were convinced that the SPD must also commit itself to NATO and the Western alliance as opposed to some ambiguous form of neutrality that might lead to German reunification. Second, there were doubts about the patriotism of the socialists. Were they really "German" enough or still "wanderers without a country," as Kaiser Wilhelm II had once termed them? Third, the party's working-class image, its formal commitment to Marxism, including the nationalization of industry, and its generally proletarian style made it difficult for middle-class voters to identify with it. Fourth, the SPD's commitment to the "social market economy" was still questioned by large segments of the electorate who feared that the party would experiment with the highly successful economic system and thus endanger prosperity. Finally, the party's anticlerical past remained a significant obstacle among many religious, especially Catholic voters. The SPD's attempt to integrate its members via numerous suborganizations—youth, women, adult education, mutual assistance, sports, newspapers, and magazines—made it appear to many as an ersatz religion, a whole way of life competing with the churches for the hearts and minds of the working class. Although this was a successful strategy during the imperial and Weimar periods, the reformers thought this was costly and outmoded and wanted to deemphasize this dimension of the SPD's public image.

At its 1959 convention in Bad Godesberg near Bonn, the SPD formally abandoned many of the policies and procedures that had hindered its support among Catholic and middle-class electors. Its commitment to the Western alliance and anticommunist policies, seen in the administration of Berlin mayor Willy Brandt, who was elected national chairman a year later, were underscored at this convention. Moreover, the party at Bad Godesberg dropped those sections of its program calling for the nationalization of the means of production and compulsory national economic planning. Finally, the party repeated its 1954 statement on Christianity and socialism, in which it maintained that Christianity together with classical and humanistic philosophy were the intellectual and moral roots of socialist thought. In short, the SPD now saw no contradiction between socialism and Christianity; the party was firmly committed to the constitutional guarantees respecting freedom of religion as well as state support for religious institutions.

The electorate rewarded the SPD's new look with increased support in 1961 (36.2 percent) and 1965 (39.3 percent). But, despite gaining on the Christian Democrats, the socialists remained well behind the Union and had no national political power or responsibility. The SPD during the 1960s was concerned above all with "embracing the middle," that is, appealing for middle-class support by stressing its allegiance to the free market economy and the Western alliance. Major policy differences with the Christian Democrats were avoided. Instead of policy, the SPD focused on its leader, Willy Brandt. Much younger than Konrad Adenauer, Brandt was projected as a dynamic, reform-oriented, yet reliable personality who would build on the accomplishments of the (aging) postwar leadership. While this strategy brought electoral gains, national political responsibility came only after the collapse of the Erhard government in 1966 and the subsequent Grand Coalition with the Christian Democrats.

Coming to Power

By entering into a coalition with its longtime opponent, the Social Democrats propped up a severely divided and leaderless Christian Democratic Union. The pact with the CDU, in which the Union still retained the chancellorship, was opposed by a sizable proportion (about 40 percent) of the SPD's membership and some top leaders, among them Willy Brandt. The main strategist of the party during these years and the key architect of the Grand Coalition, Herbert Wehner, successfully argued that such a coalition would finally give the party the opportunity to show its critics that it could govern Germany efficiently and responsibly, indeed better than the Christian Democrats. Moreover, successful performance in the coalition could set the stage for becoming the largest party after the elections of 1969 or 1973.

These arguments prevailed, and the Social Democrats in 1966 entered a national government for the first time since 1930. The party used its opportunity well. Almost all of the SPD ministers in the coalition performed successfully; one of them, Economics Minister Karl Schiller, had spectacular policy successes that even surpassed those of Brandt, who had become foreign minister. Applying essentially Keynesian policies of increased government spending, tax reductions, and lower interest rates, Schiller by 1969 had restored the economy to full health. Mainly through these efforts, for the first time in German history, economic prosperity and the Social Democrats were closely associated by large segments of the electorate.

Complementing Schiller's successes in economic policy, Foreign Minister Brandt began what was to become known after 1969 as *Ostpolitik*, the normalization of relations by West Germany with Eastern Europe and the Soviet Union.

Social Democratic ministers in justice and social welfare also got high marks for their work. The party was rewarded in 1969 with a further 3.5-percent increase in its share of the popular vote (to 42.7 percent). Much of this increase came from middle-class electors supporting the Social Democrats for the first time in their lives. The 1969 gains enabled the party to become the dominant partner in a "small coalition" with the Free Democrats under the chancellorship of Willy Brandt.

With their foreign policy successes after 1969, the strong personal appeal of Brandt, and continued economic growth and prosperity, the Social Democrats in 1972 became the strongest party (45.8 percent) and, together with the Free Democrats, increased their parliamentary majority from twelve to almost fifty seats. The long march out of the "30 percent ghetto" of the 1950s was over. Political power and responsibility, however, brought new tensions.

Electoral success and governmental power had come largely through the party's conscious move into the center of the political spectrum, where, as we shall discover in chapter 6, "the votes are." But success also brought increased criticism from both young and old socialists that the SPD had sold its ideological or Marxist soul for political power. Dormant since the Bad Godesberg reforms, the SPD's Left had sprung to life in 1966 over the coalition with the bourgeois CDU. The Left argued that the party, instead of trying to persuade the electorate of the need for an extensive restructuring of the economy and society, had taken the easy route to political power by being content simply to represent diverse social groupings and classes without changing the power relationships between them. In short, the party had been opportunistic and not much better than the Christian Democrats. This division deepened still further after Helmut Schmidt became chancellor in 1974. It played a major role in the party's fall from power in 1982.

Electoral Decline and Opposition

In 1976 the SPD suffered its first decline in support in a national election since 1957 (42.6 percent). The 1974–1976 recession and disillusionment with the slow pace of détente with Eastern Europe and the Soviet Union, together with the party's internal organizational and programmatic disputes, had a negative impact on its electoral fortunes. With the prospects of a return to the opposition looming larger, the party's leadership attempted to unite behind the Schmidt government, whose parliamentary majority was reduced to only ten seats. The key integrating figure in the party became its national chairman, Willy Brandt, who had retained this post after his resignation in 1974.

The party was also disappointed with the results of the 1980 election. In spite of the high personal popularity of Chancellor Schmidt, the SPD gained less than 1 percent over its 1976 total. It was the Free Democrats, the junior partner in the governing coalition, who profited the most from Schmidt's popularity. The SPD Left sharply criticized the Schmidt government for cutting social programs but raising defense expenditures in the new budget. At one point in 1981 Schmidt threatened to resign unless the Left factions within his own party ceased to undermine his government's policies.

In September 1982 the Schmidt government collapsed, and the Social Democrats, after almost sixteen years as a governing party, went into opposition. This was followed five months later, in the 1983 election, by the party's worst electoral performance (38.2 percent) in almost twenty years. The party's leadership responsible for the campaign held to the belief that there was a majority "to the left of the CDU." By emphasizing the "new politics" issues of the environment, nuclear power, and opposition to the NATO decision to station new intermediate-range nuclear missiles on German soil, they believed that sufficient support could be attracted from Green voters and new voters to make an SPD-Green alignment numerically if not politically possible. But by moving to the left to attract Green support, the SPD lost important segments of its traditional core electorate: skilled workers and lower- and middle-level white-collar and technical employees.

In 1987 a new candidate and more centrist campaign did not improve the party's performance. Johannes Rau could not duplicate his success at the state level in North Rhine–Westphalia in the national campaign. Rau also pledged that he would not allow himself "to be elected chancellor with the votes of the Greens." The party's share of the vote in the 1987 election dropped to 37 percent, its lowest level since 1961. For the second time in the 1980s the party remained in opposition.

The SPD and the Unification Process

The 1989–1990 unification both surprised and divided the SPD. For years the party had sought to improve the concrete living conditions of East Germans by negotiating with the communist regime. The contact with the GDR leadership, however, also gave the communists a certain legitimacy and status in the view of many Germans. When the revolution began, the SPD was ill prepared. While the party had good contacts with the now-beleaguered GDR "elite," it had few if any with the "street" (i.e., the fledgling democratic opposition, including the churches). The "rush to unity" that followed the opening of the Wall also divided the party. Many members under the age of forty-five, like most younger Germans, had no living memories of a united Germany. They had accepted, at least tacitly, the permanence of the division, or believed that it could be overcome within a united Eastern and Western Europe. The SPD, in short, was outmaneuvered by Kohl and the CDU, who early on understood how the collapse of the GDR could benefit them.

In the 1990 election, these SPD activists, including the party's chancellor candidate, Oskar Lafontaine, were unable to recognize the appeal German unity had in the west and its fundamental importance for the new voters in the east. Older Social Democrats, such as former chancellors Willy Brandt and Helmut Schmidt, enthusiastically supported unification and had few problems with the euphoria this issue generated. Lafontaine's lukewarm approach to this issue hurt the SPD in the 1990 election, especially in the east, where the SPD received only 24.5 percent of the vote. Overall, its total of 33.5 percent represented the party's worst performance since 1957.

But while the SPD was hurt in 1989–1990 by the "upside" of the unification issue, by mid-1991 it was benefiting from its "downside," namely voter discontent in the western region over the tax increases needed to finance unification and voter unhappiness in the east with the slow pace of economic reconstruction. In 1994 the SPD attempted, with Rudolf Scharping, the chief executive of the state of the Rhineland-Palatinate and the party's fourth candidate since 1983, to avoid its fourth straight loss. In the early going, Scharping did well on the campaign trail. His campaign focused on the economy and record-high unemployment. But an upturn in the economy in early 1994 took the wind out of the party's sails. The SPD did increase its vote over 1994 (to 36.4 percent) but still fell short.

Scharping was removed from his position as party leader at the SPD's 1995 party convention. Although he had been elected by a vote of the party's members in 1993, several other SPD leaders, led by Oskar Lafontaine, pushed through a change in the party's rules at the convention and dumped Scharping. The SPD, the rebels argued, was badly in need of new leadership and direction. The SPD was unable to take advantage of a weak and aging Kohl government. Something had to be done. Lafontaine replaced Scharping, but the question of who would lead the party in 1998 was left open.

Following the 1995 "putsch" convention, the party's fortunes in state elections and in public opinion polls improved. Lafontaine had unified the party, but the SPD still needed a candidate to challenge Kohl in 1998. The prime contenders were Lafontaine and the popular chief executive of Lower Saxony, Gerhard Schröder. Both men wanted the job. Lafontaine yearned for another chance at Kohl, and Schröder was convinced that he was the only Social Democrat who could defeat Kohl. Lafontaine also enjoyed the support of the party's rank-and-file activists, but Schröder's poll numbers were much better. The candidate question was not resolved until March 1998, six months before the national election, when Schröder was reelected decisively in the state election in Lower Saxony.

The New Center

In 1998 the SPD tried for the fifth time to defeat Kohl. How did they finally get it right? The party decided that job one was to win the election. Internal ideological and policy squabbles were put aside as the SPD concentrated on winning. A professional campaign organization was set up, modeled on the efforts of Bill Clinton in the United States and Tony Blair in the United Kingdom. A new advertising agency was employed to give the party a new look. In Schröder, the party also had a strong candidate. Young, but not too young (fifty-four), media savvy, compatible with the party's new pragmatic style, Schröder fit nicely. Schröder left much of his program purposefully vague. He promised to build a "new center" that would get the economy moving without causing too much pain for voters used to the generous welfare state. Finally, relying heavily on polls, the Schröder campaign was focused above all on the incumbent chancellor: "Kohl must go!" was the chant that drew the loudest response at his rallies. This approach was successful. With 41 percent of the party vote and 298 seats, the SPD achieved its best result since 1980. And for only the second time in the history of the Federal Republic, the party received more votes than the Christian Democrats.

The 1998 victory, however, did not end the conflict between Schröder and Lafontaine. Their differences were put aside for the sake of the election campaign, but soon after the victory they resumed their struggle, this time within the new government. Lafontaine was appointed finance minister, and as chairman of the party, he was the strongest single member of the Schröder cabinet; many within the party actually considered Lafontaine more powerful than Schröder.

The differences between the two leaders were most apparent in economic and tax policy. Lafontaine, with the support of the party's Old Left and the trade unions, advocated an unabashed demand-side approach to economic growth: higher wages, increases in social welfare payments, lower interest rates. While advocating tax cuts for lower- and middle-income groups, he did little to relieve high labor costs for business and actually planned to increase taxes on large business firms. Schröder's policies were aimed at making business more competitive in the global economy: lower taxes, more investment incentives, and fewer government regulations.

The conflict finally came to a head in March 1999 when, at a cabinet meeting, Schröder, in a statement apparently directed at Lafontaine, announced that he would not support any new legislation that was directed against business. He was referring to Lafontaine's proposal to tax the cash reserves of energy and insurance companies. The next day Lafontaine abruptly announced his resignation from the government and the leadership of the party. A few weeks later a special party congress elected Schröder to succeed Lafontaine as party chairman. Lafontaine resigned all his positions and went into an ostensible early retirement. He would return, but not as a leader of the SPD.

Lafontaine's departure and the CDU/CSU finance scandal gave the Schröder government a second chance after its fitful and ineffective start. In 2000 it passed a major tax reform, and in 2001 the pension system was changed. The economy also improved in 2000 and through the first part of 2001. The reelection chances for the SPD looked good.

The September 11, 2001, terrorist attack on the United States, however, sent the German economy into a tailspin. Instead of a projected growth rate of 3 percent, the economy in 2001 rose less than 1 percent. Unemployment increased, and by early 2002 the SPD had lost its lead in the polls. More Germans trusted the CDU/CSU over Schröder's Social Democrats to improve the economy.

In early August 2002 the party appeared headed for defeat. But a unique series of events late in the campaign—a major flood in the east, the looming Iraq war issue, and the first-ever one-on-one debate between the chancellor and his challenger—enabled the SPD to survive. Although its vote total declined to 38.5, a tie with the Union, it was able with the help of the Greens to return to power with a narrow eleven-seat majority.

It was a precarious victory. Shortly after the election a series of tax hikes and cuts in social programs sent the party's standing in public opinion polls into a free fall. In February 2003 it was badly defeated in two state elections it usually wins in Hesse and Lower Saxony. Schröder's Agenda 2010 reform program, announced in 2003, deeply divided the party. For many in the party, Agenda 2010 was a betrayal of the core values of German Social Democracy, which emphasized the attainment of social justice through a comprehensive welfare state. By early July 2004, support for the party had dropped to 20 percent. Thousands of members left, and the SPD's relationship to the trade unions—a core of its clientele—deteriorated. Frustrated by the lack of support from within his own party, Schröder in February 2004 resigned as party chairman. In May 2005 the Social Democrats suffered a major defeat in the party's heartland, North Rhine–Westphalia. After the results were announced, Schröder announced his plans to call for an early election in September 2005.

The 2005 and 2009 Elections

While the party was able to remain in power after the 2005 election as a partner of the CDU/CSU, it lost the chancellorship to Angela Merkel, and Schröder withdrew from the public stage. As the economy and job market improved in 2006 and 2007, in part because of the Agenda 2010 reforms, it was Merkel's party that received the lion's share of the credit. The SPD's support in polls dropped below 30 percent while the CDU gained popularity.

Internal divisions continued to hinder the party, and it went through six chairmen between 2004 and 2009. The rise of the Left Party reminded the SPD of the heavy costs of Agenda 2010. Led by Lafontaine, the Left was taking voters and members away from the Social Democrats. The SPD's left wing wanted to form an alliance with the Left Party, while the center and right advocated continuation of the reform policies of the Schröder era. By late 2007 the SPD leadership outside of the Merkel government had begun to advocate a restoration of some of the programs cut by Agenda 2010. The SPD leaders in the Grand Coalition, however, strongly opposed any turning back on the reform course. As the next federal election approached, the party was in danger of hemorrhaging voters both to the CDU on the right and to the Left Party.

In the 2009 election, the Social Democratic vote dropped to 23 percent, its worst performance since late in the nineteenth century. Although it performed well in the Grand Coalition and certainly deserved some of the credit for the improving economy, voters rewarded Merkel. Also, the party's chancellor candidate, Frank-Walter Steinmeier, had been Merkel's foreign minister in the Grand Coalition and was in the awkward position of having to criticize the actions of a government he had been part of. As one of the biggest figures in the SPD's reform wing, no one was more associated with the controversial Agenda 2010 than Steinmeier, who had been head of Schröder's chancellery from 1999 to 2005. Steinmeier, a successful lawyer and administrator, had never run for public office before and held no important party posts until 2005. He was inexperienced in campaigning and lacked the charisma of Schröder or the reassuring charm of Merkel. Moreover, there was a disconnect between the party leadership and the base/core constituencies. Most of the SPD leadership grew up in the 1970s when the party had already been transformed from a working-class movement to a governing center-left party that became even more pragmatic by 2009, after eleven years in power. The SPD still has not worked through the question of how the party should adapt to a postindustrial world, globalization, an aging society, asymmetrical wars, and growing international responsibility. Most importantly, the party, especially economic pragmatists like Steinmeier, were unable to respond effectively to the fears of average people, especially as the financial and economic crisis began to hit in 2008. The SPD rank and file had turned on Agenda 2010. As a result of these tensions, the SPD presented itself as a more left party, emphasizing issues such as child care, education, a minimum wage, and a wealth tax—yet it did so with a pragmatic, centrist leadership. Many voters were not convinced.

Following the 2009 debacle, the task of picking up the pieces went to Sigmar Gabriel, the new party chairman; Steinmeier, now the leader of the parliamentary party; and Andrea Nahles, general secretary. Absent from this group was the party's leading finance expert and nominal leader of the SPD's conservative wing, Peer Steinbrück. In the aftermath of the 2009 defeat, Steinbrück, who as finance minister had worked closely with Merkel in dealing with the financial crisis, showed little interest in assuming any major party role. Indeed, after the election he made it very clear that he was displeased with the direction the party was taking in opposition and especially its revision to some of the key components of Agenda 2010, such as the labor market reforms and a higher retirement age. But as the financial crisis mutated into a Eurozone sovereign debt crisis by 2010, Steinbrück's star began to rise. Nahles, on the other hand, did little to improve her status either within the party or nationally. Her longtime association with the SPD left, which brought her to prominence, was now a liability. Thus, as the 2013 election approached, the SPD had essentially three contestants for the chancellor nomination to take on the formidable Merkel: Gabriel, Steinmeier, and the party's prodigal son, Steinbrück.

This leadership troika became a quartet following the impressive victory of Hannelore Kraft and the SPD at the May 2012 state election in North Rhine–Westphalia. This region also contains the core of the traditional SPD electorate, blue-collar workers. Whoever decisively wins in this state will generally vault into the top echelon of the party. Kraft became the first female minister-president, and immediately the speculation about her possible chancellor candidacy began. If she decides not to try for the chancellorship in 2013, she will at a minimum play a major role in determining who will lead the SPD in the 2013 campaign. In any case, by July 2012 she was the third-highest-ranked politician, at 62 percent (behind President Gauck and Chancellor Merkel). Would 2013 become a battle of the "Power Frauen" for Germany's top job?

In the end, this did not come to pass because in September 2012 the SPD chose Steinbrück to be their chancellor candidate for the 2013 Bundestag election. At the time of his selection, most commentators lauded the choice of such a seasoned pragmatist as representing the Social Democrats' best competitor to defeat Merkel and the CDU/CSU. However, in October and November 2012, his popularity in the electorate sank as it came to light that he had earned over two million Euros in secondary income from speaking engagements and author royalties.[7]

The Free Democrats

Traditionally located ideologically somewhere between the CDU/CSU and the SPD is the only small party to survive the steady reduction in the number of serious contenders for parliamentary representation from 1949 to 1983: the Free Democratic Party (FDP). The FDP is a classically liberal party that has always emphasized free markets, civil liberties, and democratic rights. Its core clientele have been urban professionals, entrepreneurs, and small business owners. It has never aspired to become a catchall party, and despite trying to monopolize its bourgeois clientele, it traditionally maintained ideological flexibility and different coalition options. This has changed recently. The FDP is now a staunchly center-right party that advocates deregulation, privatization, and tax and spending cuts.

The Free Democrats have never received more than 15 percent of the vote in any national election. Yet the FDP has played a role in the German political system far out of proportion to the size of its electorate. It has participated in 16 of the 21 cabinets formed at the national level since 1949. From 1949 to 1956 and from 1961 to 1966, it was the junior coalition partner of the CDU/CSU; between 1969 and 1982 the Free Democrats were in a coalition with the SPD; from 1982 to 1998 the party was again aligned with the Christian Democrats; and since 2009 it is again in a coalition government with the Christian Democrats. Thus the FDP has been in power for forty-five of the Federal Republic's first sixty-four years. In government it usually receives about twice as many seats in the cabinet as it would be entitled to based on its vote. According to one analysis, the FDP has also had a disproportionate influence on government spending policies. The authors conclude that "the most useful document a German voter should consult at election time in order to anticipate the shape of public spending under the next government is the program of the FDP."[8]

The party owes its *survival* to an electoral system that ensures parliamentary representation on a proportional basis to any party that secures at least 5 percent of the popular vote. But its extraordinary *success* has been a result of its position as the needed "pivot" party in parliament. Simply put, traditionally, the FDP has held the balance of power in the Bundestag following most federal elections. Because both major parties have, with one exception (the CDU in 1957), failed to win an absolute majority of seats, they are faced with three alternatives in the postelection coalition negotiations: (1) a coalition with the FDP, (2) a "Grand Coalition" with the other major party, or (3) opposition. Obviously the first of these has been far more attractive to the major parties than the latter two. This gave the FDP an enviable bargaining position, assuming that the party is willing to consider a coalition with either major party and that the major parties have roughly the same number of parliamentary seats. Recent years have witnessed some changes to this pattern with the arrival of the Greens and later the PDS/Left Party in the Bundestag, as well as with the FDP moving farther to the right.

The party regards itself as the legitimate heir to the tragic German liberal tradition. Historically, German liberals have been divided between (1) a conservative, nationalist wing with strong ties to large industrial interests, the professions, and the bourgeoisie and an ambivalent commitment to parliamentary democracy, and (2) a progressive, or left, wing centered in the southwest and in the Hanseatic cities (Hamburg, Bremen), whose support for parliamentary government and civil rights took precedence over nationalism and the authoritarian imperial system. Thus, unlike liberals in the UK or France, German liberals as a whole were not unequivocal supporters of parliamentary government and the liberal state. During the turbulent last years of the Weimar Republic, the vast majority of the liberal parties' supporters defected to the right-wing parties, including, above all, the Nazis.

It was not until the formation of the FDP in 1948 that the two tendencies in German liberalism were united within one organization, and unity in terms of policy has remained a rare commodity in the party's postwar history. The nationalist or right wing held the upper hand during the 1950s when, in coalition with the CDU/CSU, the party was to the right of the Union, especially in economic policies. Even at this time, however, its opposition to Catholic Church influence within the CDU/CSU and to Adenauer's pro-Western orientation, which the Free Democrats claimed neglected if did not abandon reunification, differentiated the party from its much larger partner.

The FDP's drift to the center-left and hence toward the SPD in the mid-1960s took place as much for tactical as for policy reasons. As a junior coalition partner, it always ran the risk of suffering a fate similar to that of the other small parties: absorption by the CDU/CSU. Thus, it had to seek to retain its identity vis-à-vis the CDU/CSU by either pulling out of the coalition, as it did in 1956 and 1966, or stressing its differences with its major partner, especially prior to elections.

Following the Grand Coalition between the SPD and CDU/CSU in December 1966, the FDP became the sole opposition party for the first time in its history. Key party leaders at this time, such as Walter Scheel, foreign minister from 1969 to 1974 and federal president from 1974 to 1979, and Hans-Dietrich Genscher, foreign minister from 1974 to 1992, sought to demonstrate through a series of policy and leadership changes that the party was not a mere satellite of the CDU/CSU. Their purpose was not only to gain votes from SPD and CDU/CSU supporters discontented with the Grand Coalition, but also to demonstrate to the Social Democrats that it could at some future time be an acceptable and reliable coalition partner. In moving toward the SPD, the Free Democrats lost much of their "old" middle-class clientele but gained the support of younger, "new" middle-class voters living in large metropolitan areas who wanted an end to two decades of CDU/CSU rule.

This approach worked. After the four elections from 1969 to 1980, the FDP formed a governing coalition with the Social Democrats. After the 1980 election, however, it became apparent that the party was attempting to loosen its ties with the Social Democrats in preparation for another switch in coalition partners— this time back to its old ally from the 1950s and 1960s, the Christian Democrats. The shift took place in 1982 and was ratified by elections in 1983 and 1987.

With 11 percent of the vote in the 1990 all-German election, the FDP achieved the fourth-best result in its history. This success was largely a tribute to the role the party's de facto leader, Hans-Dietrich Genscher, the longtime foreign minister and vice chancellor, played in the unification process.[9] As FDP campaign speakers never tired of reminding voters, "Bismarck unified Germany with blood and iron. Helmut Kohl did it with Hans-Dietrich Genscher!" The Free Democrats, moreover, benefited from their "no new taxes" theme and did especially well in East Germany, from which Genscher had fled in the 1950s.[10]

In 1998 the Free Democrats, after twenty-nine years in power, went into opposition. While the party was able to surmount the 5 percent barrier, it ran a lackluster campaign devoid of popular leaders or an attractive program. Many in the FDP saw the defeat as an opportunity to rejuvenate the party. Freed from its ties to Kohl and the Christian Democrats, the FDP was able to strike out on its own.

The Liberals after 1998

After the 1998 election, no party attempted to change its image as much as the Free Democrats. Starting from the premise that for a small party any publicity was better than none at all, the FDP wanted to make waves. Its energetic national chairman, Guido Westerwelle, declared that the Free Democrats were Germany's "Fun Party," committed to the concerns of young people and the young at heart. The party boldly proclaimed that its goal was 18 percent of the vote. It fell well short of its goal in 2002 but with over 7 percent of the vote did improve slightly on its 1998 performance.

After 2002 the party carefully cultivated the Christian Democrats and Angela Merkel, leaving no doubt that it wanted to join them in the next government. Merkel and the CDU also targeted the Free Democrats as their preferred partner. As a dress rehearsal, the FDP and CDU in 2004 cooperated in securing the election of Horst Köhler to the federal presidency (see chapter 7 for a description of this office). But when the 2005 votes were counted, the dream coalition fell far short of an absolute majority. The FDP held up its end of the bargain as its vote increased from 7.4 percent to almost 10 percent, but the CDU/CSU vote dropped from 38.5 percent to 35.2 percent. Thus a deeply disappointed FDP found itself once again in opposition.

Westerwelle used these opposition years to sharpen the FDP's neoliberal economic profile and solidify its urban, young professional support. By the 2009 campaign, he was able to count on this base, but he also successfully leveraged the party's opposition status to channel a kind of protest vote against both members of the Grand Coalition. Tactically, the FDP emphasized the importance of ticket splitting with CDU voters and exploited the fatigue that Bavarian voters had with the post-Stoiber CSU. It was a brilliant campaign, and Westerwelle's party achieved its most stunning result ever, with 15 percent of the vote. This result also increased the FDP's leverage in the cabinet formation process, receiving five of sixteen posts (over 30 percent), including the powerful ministries of foreign affairs, economics, and justice.

Starting almost immediately after the triumph of the 2009 election, however, the Free Democrats have been in a veritable free fall. They have done rather poorly in Länder elections (only 5.3 percent in Baden-Württemberg in 2011), and by 2013, national polls even had the party hovering below the 5 percent threshold, which would eliminate them not only from government, but also from the Bundestag for the first time in its history. There were several factors at play in the post-2009 collapse. First, Westerwelle was an effective campaigner but has been a disappointing foreign minister and vice chancellor who committed some unforced errors, for example, attacking welfare recipients. In May 2011, he stepped down as party leader and as the vice chancellor of government. His decade-long domination of the party left a leadership vacuum, with his thirty-eight-year-old successor, Philipp Rösler, lacking experience. Other potential leaders such as Daniel Bahr, the health minister, or Christian Linder in North Rhine–Westphalia are even younger. Second, the party's profile has increasingly centered on neoliberal economic policies, especially tax cuts. The financial and Euro crises, as well as the necessary accommodations of coalition governments, have made the implementation of this program difficult, leading to dissatisfaction from FDP voters. Moreover, such a singular focus meant that the Liberals have little else to negotiate with in the coalition or to offer voters. Third, much of the FDP's support in 2009 was soft. Many of their voters were actually CDU supporters who split their votes. Westerwelle had become the least popular political figure in Germany. By July 2012, only 25 percent of Germans wanted him to play an important role in the future versus 68 percent for Merkel, whose approval ratings have remained high since 2009.

Finally, there was the hotel tax scandal. During the 2009 election, the Free Democrats received about $1.4 million, one of the largest donations in its history, from the Substantia AG. The owner of Substantia is one of Germany's richest citizens, August Baron von Finck, who is a major shareholder in the Mövenpick Group, which owns a chain of hotels in Germany and abroad. During the coalition negotiations, the FDP leaders pressed for a cut in the value-added tax (VAT) for hotels from 19 percent to 7 percent, which was indeed added to the new CDU-FDP government's Economic Growth Acceleration Law. This legislation made small cuts in overall taxes and was billed as the first stage in a comprehensive program of tax reform that had been the cornerstone of the FDP's 2009 campaign. The big tax break for hotels went into effect on January 1, 2010. While the FDP vehemently denied that there was any connection between the von Finck donation and the tax cut, the great majority of the public disagreed. The opposition SPD and Greens charged that the FDP was a "clientele party," only interested in providing lucrative tax breaks and other public largesse to a few narrow interests, and demanded that the FDP return the donation. One commentator opined, "The hotel tax sticks to this coalition like an old piece of chewing gum."[11]

The Greens

In 1983, for the first time since the 1950s, a new political party—the Greens—secured representation in the parliament. As a "New Left" group, the Greens have stood for environmental policies and pacifism in foreign policy, as well as opposition to nuclear weapons and power. They are strong advocates of rights for women, gays and lesbians, and minorities. Their core supporters have come from the better-educated, urban middle classes.

The party began as the political arm of the citizen initiative group movement discussed in chapter 4. In the late 1970s those groups concerned with the environment and especially with the danger of nuclear power plants established a national political party. In 1979 and 1980, the Greens entered two state parliaments but fared poorly in the national elections, receiving less than 2 percent of the vote. After 1980, however, the Greens' cause was greatly aided by the emergence of the NATO missile question, the planned deployment of new middle-range ballistic missiles in the Federal Republic. The nationwide peace movement that arose in response to the missile deployment plan was a major source of new support for the party. The peace movement also brought the Greens additional activists, many of whom had acquired extensive political experience in the student protest movement of the 1960s, and various left-wing splinter groups. These new supporters, who came to the Greens less out of a concern for the environment and more because of the arms race and various socioeconomic problems such as inner-city housing and education, gave the movement its badly needed organizational and tactical expertise. The Greens soon entered several state parliaments, and in 1983 the Green Party entered the national parliament with 5.6 percent of the vote and twenty-eight seats.

With the twin issues of the environment and the NATO missile or "peace" question, the party became attractive to young voters, especially those in colleges and universities. In university towns, the Greens received over 20 percent of the vote. Following this initial national success, the Greens' advance stalled. Divisions within the movement became an issue. The critical problem was the party's relationship to the Social Democrats. Should the Greens seek power through a coalition with the SPD, or should they remain a protest movement uncontaminated by any association with the old, established parties? Most Green voters supported an alignment with the SPD. The party's activists and leaders, however, were divided. One group, the Fundamentalists (*Fundis*), has rejected any cooperation with the established parties, whereas a second wing, the Realists (*Realos*), were willing to form coalitions with the SPD at state and national levels in order to achieve Green goals, if only in piecemeal fashion.

The 1986 accident at Chernobyl in Ukraine, where a reactor complex broke down and caused many deaths and injuries, gave renewed life to the environmental movement throughout Germany and Europe. In the wake of the disaster, support for the Greens in public opinion polls doubled to over 12 percent. For a time it appeared that had the Greens decided to coalesce with the SPD, the two parties would have had an absolute majority after the 1987 election. By mid-1986, however, the effects of Chernobyl began to wane, and the potential Green-SPD vote dropped from 53 percent to 43 percent. Although the Greens clearly gained support because of the accident in Ukraine, they also lost voters due to their radical positions on foreign policy, defense, and domestic issues. In spite of these problems, the Greens were able to increase their share of the vote in the 1987 election from 5.6 percent to 8.3 percent, and the size of their parliamentary delegation grew to forty-two deputies.

The Greens and Unification

Of all the parties, the Greens proved to be the least interested in and the least prepared for the political impact of unification. The great majority of their young electorate—and more importantly, their leadership—had no memories of a Germany that was not divided. They were the least likely to have a sense of German national identity, thinking of themselves more as Europeans or even "citizens of the world." On November 9, 1989, when the Berlin Wall was breached, most members of parliament in Bonn rose spontaneously and sang the national anthem. Most Greens did not, and those who did were criticized by their colleagues for this emotional display of "outmoded" national feelings. The Greens opposed the Kohl government's "rush to unity," which they argued disregarded the interests and needs of East Germany's indigenous democracy movement. They advocated a more evolutionary approach to unification within the context of the movement toward European unification.

The Greens' leadership failed to understand the political impact of the widespread support that unification had in the electorate, even among its own voters. In 1990 two-thirds of Green voters supported unification. This stood in sharp contrast to the opposition of the party's parliamentary leadership, which voted against both unity treaties in the Bundestag. This issue dominated the 1990 campaign, and the Green message was lost. With only 4.8 percent of the vote in West Germany, down from 8.3 percent in 1987, the party failed to gain representation in the all-German parliament. The Greens in the former GDR, running in coalition with East German citizen reform groups, did surmount the 5 percent barrier—the only election for which there were separate 5 percent thresholds in both regions. Generally, the Greens in the east were more attuned to the importance of the unification issue than their counterparts in the west. Had the two parties run a combined list in 1990, the West German Greens, under the special provisions of the electoral law in effect for the 1990 election, would also have been represented.[12]

The End of the Long March: National Political Power

By 1994, with the euphoria of unification long gone, and now formally united with their eastern German equivalent—the *Bündnis90*/Green Party—the Greens were well positioned to reverse the 1990 defeat. The Realo wing of the party, led by Joschka Fischer, was now firmly in control, and since 1990, the Greens had been able to demonstrate in several state-level coalitions that they could govern. Also, environmental issues continued to trouble more than enough voters to put the party over the 5 percent mark.

With 7.3 percent of the vote in 1994, the Greens became the first party ever to return to parliament following a failure to surmount the 5 percent mark. As expected, the party did very well among younger, middle-class voters and students in the western states. Their eastern wing, however, declined to less than 5 percent. After 1994 the Realo-Fundi cleavage in the Greens was replaced with an even deeper division between the western and eastern wings of the party: the postmaterialist, middle-class western Greens have little understanding for their eastern counterparts. The core of the eastern group was the *Bündnis90*, the former dissidents who played such a critical role during the 1989–1990 collapse of communism. They were still deeply concerned about coming to terms with the communist past, including a vigorous investigation and, if possible, prosecution of communist officials. The western Greens, with no personal experience of living under communist rule, wanted the party to reach out to former communists, especially the rank and file, who were relatively innocent of any association with the abuses of the communist regime.

In 1998 the Greens, after twenty years, finally achieved what many of the early Greens had never wanted: national political power. The original Greens of the 1980s were a protest party, an antiparty, with little interest in traditional party politics. Their "long march" to national political responsibility began in earnest in the mid-1980s when the more radical "ecosocialists" and peace movement supporters began to leave the party. The Greens began to test the waters by entering state governments as a partner of the Social Democrats. This experience further strengthened the Realists in their intraparty struggles with the Fundamentalists.

The party's 1998 campaign, after a rocky start, aimed at forming a coalition with the Social Democrats. The party's major campaign slogan, "The Change Must Be Green," was designed to remind voters that only in coalition with the Greens could change—that is, the removal of the Kohl government—take place, because the Social Democrats alone could not do it. Clearly, the party, in tandem with the SPD, wanted to ride the anti-Kohl wave into power. With 6.7 percent of the vote and forty-seven seats, the party achieved its goal.

In government from 1998 to 2005, the Greens had a mixed record of implementing their policy agenda. Their demand for an end to the use of nuclear power as an energy source was met in a 2001 law that planned to phase it out over a period of twenty years. They also were the major supporter of alternative energy sources such as wind and solar power.[13] The 1999 Citizenship Law was not as strong as the Greens wanted but still represents the most liberal and tolerant approach to citizenship in German history.[14] In 2002 another key Green issue, the Life Partnership Law legalizing same-sex marriages, was passed and upheld by the Federal Constitutional Court. But the party also abandoned its pacifist, nonviolent heritage by voting to deploy military forces in Kosovo (1999) and Afghanistan (2001). The party was also unable to persuade the Social Democrats to modernize and slim down the welfare state or to discontinue state subsidies for declining industries such as coal mining and shipbuilding.

In this context the Greens expanded into other policy areas. From 2000 to 2005 a Green led the agriculture ministry, which was renamed in the wake of the mad cow disease scandal as the Ministry for Consumer Protection, Agriculture and Nutrition. Civil liberties and the rights of minorities such as children, gays, and foreign residents are now prominent Green issues.

The party also began to address several economic issues, paying special attention to the traditional welfare state and the many state subsidies to declining industries such as coal mining and shipbuilding. This agenda has brought the Greens into conflict with the Social Democrats' trade union wing and other traditional welfare state supporters—the so-called "social welfare mafia." Many Greens come from middle-class socioeconomic backgrounds and are fiscally conservative. Unlike the Social Democrats and the Christian Democrats, they are not attached to deficit spending and the traditional pension and health care systems. Thus, they were allies for Chancellor Schröder in his efforts to modernize his own party.

The Return to Opposition

With its expanded program and popular leaders, the Green Party in 2002 garnered over 9 percent of the vote in the western states (8.6 percent nationally), the best election results in its history as the party compensated for the decline of the Social Democrats. Indeed, the Greens in 2002 provided the government with its razor-thin margin of victory. But the woes of the Social Democrats after 2002, described above, also spread to the Greens. In the 2005 election the party received 8.1 percent of the vote, far short of the support needed to stay in power with the Social Democrats. Rejecting any alliance with the Christian Democrats, the party went into opposition. Its most prominent leader, Joschka Fischer, retired after the election, and the party had to regroup, rebuild relations with a dissatisfied base because of the compromises necessary during the years in power, and adjust to a changing party system.

In opposition, the Greens indeed sought to broaden their appeal beyond their signature issue of the environment. They now emphasized the economic benefits of renewable energy sources and the millions of "green jobs" created by solar, wind, and biomass technology. They have also become critical of the welfare state. Some even charge that they are becoming too business oriented, "like the FDP on a bicycle," as one critic put it.[15]

The Greens were able to parlay their strong showing at the 2009 election (almost 11 percent) into a series of state election victories and soaring numbers in national opinion polls. Without question the biggest post-2009 success for the party was its stellar performance in the March 2011 state election in Baden-Württemberg. For the first time in its history the Greens with over 24 percent of the vote assumed governmental leadership in one of Germany's largest and most prosperous states. The vote was heavily influenced by the nuclear disaster in Japan, but the Greens were also able to attract moderate middle-class voters through their emphasis on the economic benefits of clean, renewable energy as well as their opposition to the controversial Stuttgart 21 train station project. This seems to be paying off nationally with the Greens consistently at 13 to 15 percent in the polls since 2009 and at some points over 20 percent.

This new look—a liberal, probusiness, middle-class party with a Green tint— also sparked speculation about a possible CDU-Green coalition at the national level after the 2013 election (inspired by a precedent set in Hamburg from 2008 to 2010). For a time, the Greens in national polls became the second-most-popular party after the CDU. With a weakened FDP probably unable to bring the current coalition over 50 percent of the seats, Chancellor Merkel may have to consider either the Greens or the SPD as her next coalition partner. Whether either party is seriously interested in helping the CDU remain in power, however, is an open question.[16]

The Left Party

The party system became more complicated in 2007 with the formation of the Left Party. The party represents a merger of the former communist party of East Germany, the Party of Democratic Socialism (PDS),[17] with a western group formed in 2005, the Electoral Alternative for Labor and Social Justice (WASG), led by former SPD leader Oskar Lafontaine. In the 2005 election, the two groups conducted a common campaign that yielded almost 9 percent of the vote and fifty-four seats in parliament. The PDS/Left Party has been the most ideological left-wing party standing for "democratic socialism." It advocates a heavy state hand in the economy, social justice through much higher taxes and welfare redistribution, solidarity with the dispossessed, and uncompromising pacifism. Largely based in the former East Germany with some support from disaffected SPD supporters in the west, it has long had an eastern regional identity. Moreover, when in government, as in Berlin and Brandenburg, it has been more pragmatic.

The party represents a curious marriage between many former western Social Democrats and the old communists in the former East Germany. For the westerners, Agenda 2010 was the last straw. Meanwhile, the eastern PDS looked lost in unified Germany. It had no foothold in the western states and was struggling on its eastern home turf. It failed to clear the 5 percent hurdle in 2002 and was left with only two members in the parliament, representing the only two districts in which it won a plurality of votes. The PDS also suffered in 2002 when its most popular figure, Gregor Gysi, resigned from the party leadership and, like Lafontaine with the SPD, retreated to the sidelines. Both men, however, saw Schröder's troubles as an opportunity for their own political comeback. It was an ideal campaign alignment. The PDS badly needed western support, and the Electoral Alternative had few voters in the eastern states. The PDS also had more funds and a much stronger organization than the newly founded Electoral Alternative.

The Left Party is thus far purely a protest party. Its program in 2009, which it frankly admitted had no chance of being implemented, contained the usual left-wing panaceas: "soak the rich" tax plans, a massive and very expensive public works campaign for the unemployed, and a repeal of all the "antilabor" policies of Agenda 2010. But the party already in 2005, largely because of Lafontaine, also took a page from the playbook of Germany's small radical right groups and criticized the government's immigration policies, which it charged allowed too many foreigners into the country and cost native Germans their jobs. In one speech, Lafontaine even used a former Nazi term, *Fremdarbeiter* (alien workers), to describe such immigrants. This blatant appeal to the far right was one reason why no right-wing party in 2005 came even close to entering the parliament.

With 8.7 percent of the vote in 2005, fifty-four seats, and the leadership of two of the most talented political speakers in the country, the Left Party has attracted much media attention. It was a major reason for the Social Democrat attempt to repeal some of the Agenda 2010 program. But mutual suspicions abounded in this alliance, with the majority PDS fearing a western takeover by Lafontaine and the westerners wary of the former communists whose organizational strength is far greater than that of the western component. Many in the PDS also fear that Lafontaine was merely using the Left Party as a platform for a comeback in his old party, the Social Democrats. Indeed, there have been periodic calls for a merger of these two leftist parties. The party has been especially strong among those voters in the eastern states who are unemployed. In 2005 it received 40 percent of the vote among unemployed easterners and 12 percent among jobless voters in the western regions.

At the 2009 election the party achieved the best results in its short history with 11.9 percent of the vote and seventy-six seats. Like the FDP and Greens, the

Left was able to capitalize from both the CDU/CSU and SPD being in government, as well as from the long-term decline of those catchall parties. This result, however, may have been the high point of their success. Following the 2009 election, programmatic and leadership conflicts intensified and took their toll on the party's electoral status. In spite of the international financial and Euro crises, the Left with its strident critique of international capitalism has failed to make any gains in state elections, especially in the west. In May 2012 a full-scale dispute erupted when the erstwhile SPD leader Oskar Lafontaine, who resigned from his leadership post in 2010 apparently for health reasons, again changed his mind and in the face of opposition from the eastern wing of the party withdrew his candidacy for the leadership of the party. The longtime parliamentary leader Gregor Gysi has declining influence. Moreover, the core eastern electorate is aging, and the party does not resonate as much with younger voters socialized after 1989, especially as the economy has picked up in parts of the eastern region.

Other Parties

The Pirates

The newest component of the increasingly complex party system is the Pirate Party. The name derives from a 2006 lawsuit in Sweden in which computer hackers were charged with illegally pirating content and software (mainly music and videos) from the Internet. In response the Swedish defendants formed their own political party in an attempt to change Swedish and European copyright laws. The German version was also founded in 2006. The Pirates first attracted national attention in 2009 when they attempted to gain representation in the national parliament. With only 2 percent of the vote they failed, but among young and new voters they their support reached double digits, and they had growing momentum.

The typical Pirate supporter is male, eighteen to thirty-four years of age, and well educated, with a background in the natural and computer sciences. One Berlin Pirate calls them "cyber-hippies." Obviously, their number-one issue is free, unrestricted, uncensored Internet access. One of their major targets has been the then family minister, Ursula von der Leyen, who passed legislation restricting access to alleged child pornography sites. Dubbed "Zensursula" (a play on the German word for censorship, *Zensur*), their campaign brought the party much-needed media attention and was a factor in their first breakthrough in September 2011 when they gained representation in the Berlin parliament with 8.9 percent of the vote and fifteen seats. This was followed by good showings—that is, more than 5 percent—in elections during 2012 in the Saarland (7.4 percent), North Rhine–Westphalia (7.8 percent), and Schleswig-Holstein (8.2 percent). Soon national polls had the party between 7 and 9 percent, and at one point over 10 percent.

What do the Pirates want besides Internet freedom? This is difficult to determine since the party's program is driven by its constantly changing "liquid democracy" software. If enough supporters or "friends" endorse a particular proposal, it is voted on by the other Pirates on the Internet. But whether the Pirates in legislatures actually introduce corresponding legislation is not clear. Indeed, much of the Pirates' appeal is procedural and not programmatic. Nonetheless, currently the Pirates appear to support a basic income for all adults without any work requirements, reform of the Hartz IV laws, free education, and ticketless public transportation. It is also difficult to place the party on the ideological spectrum, although classifying them as left-libertarians is probably the best. They are also technological fundamentalists, believing in the direct democratic potential of the Internet and social media.

This lack of programmatic clarity both hurts and helps the party. It is difficult for opposing parties to attack them since they really have no program. "Dealing with the Pirates," one Green leader said, "is like boxing against Jello." But without a program the party has little chance of rising above the level of a pure protest movement, which can do well in polls and state elections but falls short in the national election or in parliament. As one Pirate in North Rhine–Westphalia put it, "We Germans were never the greatest revolutionaries. . . . Instead of burning barricades, we go out and found political parties."[18] The Pirates also have a dearth of female candidates and members and have had some problems with right-radicals.

The Radical Right

There are also a variety of radical right parties—such as the Republicans, the German People's Union (DVU), and the National Democrats (NPD)—that have competed in elections since the foundation of the Federal Republic. The right-radical and neo-Nazi parties consider themselves to be patriotic, nationalist parties that are racist, anti-immigrant, anti-Semitic, and historically revisionist, at times advocating the creation of a greater Germany. They do not necessarily support the democratic order and have harbored violent tendencies. Economically, their proposals are an odd mixture of conventional left and right positions. Their color, like the Nazis before them, is brown.

Nationally, they have never made it over the 5 percent threshold, which was largely designed to prevent exactly these parties from gaining representation. The NPD came the closest in 1969 with 4.3 percent of the vote. Nevertheless, these parties have done better in Länder elections, such as the Republikaner in Baden-Württemberg in the early 1990s. In recent years these radical right protest parties have had their most recent successes in some of the most depressed regions of eastern Germany, such as the DVU in Saxony-Anhalt in the 1990s and the NPD in Saxony more recently. These regions have also given rise to a radical and violent neo-Nazi scene (see the discussion of the NSU in chapter 4).

Part of the explanation for their lack of national success has been the inability of the various parties to unify. Besides programmatic and tactical differences, one factor is that various state agencies constantly monitor these groups and have had agents infiltrate the parties. There was even an attempt between 2001 and 2003 to have the constitutional court ban the NPD as a threat to the democratic order. But in the future there is a danger that these parties will gain support and expertise from the much more successful radical right parties abroad.

But the German protest vote market is crowded. The right radicals have to compete with the Left and even the Pirates for the support of the discontented. Improving economic conditions in the east and greater vigilance from the authorities after the horrifying NSU incident may sap them of strength. Above all, the complete rejection of these parties and their platforms by all mainstream parties and by the vast majority of average Germans will likely keep these tendencies in check.[19] Certainly, these parties have had much less success in Germany compared to other European countries—like the National Front in France or the Freedom Party in Austria.

THE REPRESENTATION OF INTERESTS

Extent of Interest Groups

Germany is a densely organized society. Germans are used to organizations and accustomed to working with them for the satisfaction of individual and group needs. Numerous international surveys have found Germans to be more likely to use interest groups as a means of influencing government than citizens in other Western democracies such as the United States or the UK.[20] Currently, there are 674 voluntary associations for every 100,000 inhabitants of the Federal Republic, or almost 550,000 in all.[21] This includes, however, thousands of local sports clubs and singing societies, whose explicit political activity is very limited and restricted to the local level. There are also various politically latent interests, such as those of consumers and immigrants, that remain poorly organized and represented.

Importance and Style of Interest Representation

German political tradition and values, the consensual style of the mainstream political parties, and the structure of the Federal Republic have all combined to make interest groups a vital factor in the policy-making process. Germany had interest groups long before the formation of the Reich, indeed before the formation of any sovereign political entity on German soil. A variety of associational groups representing occupations and economic interests can trace their origins to the corporate guilds of the Middle Ages. Composed of practitioners of a particular trade or craft (e.g., carpenters, bakers, cabinetmakers, butchers), these groups still perform regulatory functions for the state such as licensing and the supervision of training, and membership is compulsory for those desiring to practice the occupation legally. Almost all skilled artisans, in addition to those in the "free" professions (law and medicine), belong to these chambers, which also determine and enforce standards for the craft and control the recruitment of new members.

This tradition has had many benefits. Self-regulation, for example, means that fewer government officials are necessary. Nevertheless, there are also costs. Many of the occupational associations monopolistically restrict the admission of new members, reducing competition and thereby keeping prices (and members' incomes) high. The quality of goods and services may also suffer. This behavior has also reduced productivity. In fact, Germany has some of the most regulated professions in the OECD group of developed countries. By 2007, productivity in services had actually declined to 95 percent of the 1995 figure while manufacturing productivity was up to 125 percent.[22]

Their legal responsibility for membership recruitment and conduct gives the chambers important political as well as economic power. They are all organized hierarchically from the local to the national level. Thus their national leaders have considerable authority in dealing with the ministerial bureaucracy. The hierarchical, quasi-governmental character of these associations makes individual members dependent on the group's leadership for the furtherance of their interests. The national-level interest group leadership thus becomes part of a larger elite structure within which informal bargaining plays a key role.

Most of the major occupational chambers also have members in parliament, mainly in the delegations of the CDU/CSU and FDP. The Christian Democrats, for example, have a parliamentary group with direct affiliations with one or several of the chambers. It is estimated that about a third of the members of parliament represent their occupations (see chapter 6). Either they are professional interest group employees assigned to represent their groups, or they are associated with certain trade, occupational, or professional interests on a part-time basis. The influence of interest groups in the recruitment of parliamentary candidates is to a great extent the result of the parties' dependence on groups for financial and electoral support. The electoral system, as we discuss in chapter 6, also facilitates the nomination and election of these interested parliamentary deputies. Their efforts are particularly noticeable in committee work.

Perhaps more important than their role in the recruitment of parliamentary deputies is the access of interest groups to the ministerial bureaucracy. Such access allows them to influence the design of legislation. Major interest organizations are consulted in the drafting of laws affecting them as a matter of administrative procedure. The practice dates back to the early nineteenth century and reflects the strain of corporate or group, instead of individual, representation in the German political tradition, as well as the government's interest in the expertise of these groups and their cooperation in the implementation of policy.[23] During the Weimar Republic, access to the ministries was limited to nationally organized interest groups. This practice was also adopted in the administrative rules of the federal ministries. It tends to accentuate the hierarchical character of German interest groups and the formal, quasi-legal character of their activity.

This pattern of strong government/interest group/political party integration became more institutionalized during the late 1960s when the top representatives of government, business, and labor met in a "Concerted Action," a regular conference at which general economic conditions were discussed and guidelines for wages, prices, and economic growth were set. At these meetings, business, labor, and the national government sought to reach a consensus on (1) what a reasonable wage increase would be for various workers, (2) the acceptable level of price increases, and (3) the amount of government spending and taxation necessary to ensure stable economic conditions and moderate—that is, noninflationary—economic growth. Although the Concerted Action disbanded in the late 1970s as labor interests became dissatisfied with what they felt were the unreasonable sacrifices they were called on to make, informal labor/business/ government contacts continued. The record levels of unemployment since unification prompted Chancellor Kohl and later his successor, Gerhard Schröder, to call for an "Alliance for Jobs"—a cooperative program involving business, labor, and government that resembled the Concerted Action of the 1960s.

The Concerted Action, Alliance for Jobs, and other formal interest-group and government contacts have prompted some observers to term Germany a "neocorporatist" state.[24] *Corporatism* is an old term in social and political thought referring to the organization of interests into a limited number of compulsory, hierarchically structured associations recognized by the state and given a monopoly of representation within their respective areas.[25] These associations become in effect quasi-governmental groups, training, licensing, and even exercising discipline over their members with state approval. The power of these associations is not determined by a group's numerical size alone but also by the importance of its function for the state and community.

In addition to parliamentary recruitment and extensive consultations between government and interest groups, the practice of appointing group representatives to the many permanent ministerial advisory commissions and councils affords the interest groups still more input into the policy-making process. Finally, the highly developed system of semipublic institutions and administrative courts, discussed in chapter 8, offers interest associations an additional opportunity to influence the policy process.

Major Interest Alignments

Business and Industrial Interests

In a society in which the stability and legitimatization of postwar political institutions have been closely connected with economic prosperity, business and industrial interest groups enjoy considerable cultural support when they enter the political arena and make policy demands on the system. Regardless of which party or parties form the government, the interests and claims of German business will receive a thorough hearing. Indeed, a frequent charge of the left is that even the Social Democrats, when in office, are too receptive and accommodating to the interests of business.

In addition to their own national offices, the numerous local and state employer organizations are represented by three umbrella organizations with extensive facilities and staffs in the capital: the Federation of German Industry (*Bundesverband der Deutschen Industrie* [BDI]), the Federation of German Employer Associations (*Bundesvereinigung Deutscher Arbeitgeberverbände* [BDA]), and the German Industrial and Trade Conference (*Deutscher Industrie und Handelstag* [DIHT]).

The BDA tends to specialize in wage policies, whereas the Industrial and Trade Conference concentrates most of its efforts on maintaining the economic viability of small independent business owners and artisans. Thus, neither organization is as politically active or visible on as broad a front as the Federation of German Industry, which focuses its activities on the government's national and international economic policies and is clearly the most influential and effective voice of business in national politics.

The BDI is a federation made up of thirty-nine individual industrial associations, which together have a membership of more than 90,000 firms. During the first decades of Christian Democratic rule, it enjoyed very close ties to the government and tended to get the edge in competition with trade unions for political advantage. Yet, given the commitment of all major parties to the social free market economy, the BDI has had little difficulty putting its proposals to the government when the Social Democrats have been in power.

Apart from its general support of German industry, the BDI evaluates all proposed legislation in any way related to business during all stages of policy making, from ministerial drafting through parliamentary debate and even administrative implementation. In addition to sympathetic parliamentary deputies and general cultural support by virtue of its accomplishments, business interests command considerable financial resources, and their support or nonsupport—especially of the middle-class parties, the CDU and FDP—gives them added weight in electoral politics.

The BDI consistently resists extensions of the social welfare system that would increase employer contributions, and like its counterparts in the United States and the UK (the National Association of Manufacturers and the Federation of British Industry), it constantly implores the government to "hold the line" on spending. The BDI, as expected, has been very critical of labor unions, Young Socialists, intellectuals, and any other "radical" group that would weaken industry's position in German society or undermine the market economy.

Most BDI activity takes place in direct, small-group consultations with ministerial officials, parliamentary deputies, and governmental leaders. The BDI has an extensive research department that supplies information to its member associations, the media, schools, and universities. Only rarely has it engaged in advertising campaigns to influence large groups of voters.

Since unification, the BDI and other interest groups have attempted to assist the government in the conversion of East Germany's planned economy to a market economy. It also supports a variety of tax breaks and investment incentives to stimulate economic growth in the region. Its critics have charged that it has been more interested in securing lucrative opportunities for large western German firms than in helping create an indigenous entrepreneurial class in the eastern regions.

German business has strongly supported the attempts of the Schröder and Merkel governments to make Germany's economy more competitive in a global environment. Schröder's Agenda 2010, with its promise of reduced costs for labor and nonwage benefits such as pensions and unemployment compensation, received high marks from most business interests. During the Grand Coalition, business has also sought major changes to, if not the elimination of, codetermination, which is the practice of giving labor representatives up to half the seats on a firm's supervisory board. In no other European country are labor and management so closely connected to a firm's governance. Indeed, only thirteen of the EU's twenty-seven members have any requirements for labor participation, and all of them are much weaker than codetermination.[26]

Critics charge that the program encourages collusion and corruption between labor and management. They cite the major scandals at two of Germany's leading firms, Siemens and Volkswagen, that were connected to codetermination. The problem at Volkswagen resulted in the conviction of Peter Hartz, the same person who chaired the commission charged with reforming the labor laws. A growing number of firms are seeking to get around codetermination by incorporating in other countries or registering as European Union corporations (SEs or Societas Europae). A major insurance company (Allianz) became an SE in 2006, and several other large firms are planning a similar change. Not surprisingly, labor unions, who consider codetermination to be one of their premier postwar achievements, oppose any change in the system. The prolonged crisis situation after 2008 has put many of these proposals and changes on hold.

Labor

The major German labor organization, the German Federation of Labor (*Deutscher Gewerkschaftsbund* [DGB]) is also a postwar creation. Previously, the German labor movement had been closely tied to political parties and their respective ideologies. In the Weimar Republic, socialist, communist, liberal, and Catholic unions all vied for the support of workers, thus politicizing and fragmenting the labor movement. Western Allied occupiers, particularly in the American zone, strongly urged the separation of the unions from the political parties and the establishment of a single, unified trade union federation that would emphasize the basic economic objectives of improving wages and working conditions rather than implementing radical social and economic change. Many German labor leaders also wanted an organization less attached to parties, and in 1949 the DGB was founded. The DGB is composed of eight separate unions with a combined membership of about seven million; the two largest units of the federation are the metalworkers' union (steel, automobiles, machinery) and the government employees and service workers union *ver.di* (see below). These two unions now make up about 70 percent of the DGB's total membership.

Although the DGB's initial programmatic statements in 1949 had a decidedly Marxist tone (socialization of key industries, central economic planning), which reflected the majority position held in the new organization by former leaders of the Weimar socialist unions, the major emphasis in the union movement's work soon shifted to more pragmatic goals of a shorter workweek and higher wages. In the DGB's new basic program of 1963, Marxist elements were abandoned for all practical purposes. Like its American counterpart, the AFL-CIO, the DGB now emphasizes collective bargaining to improve the economic status of the worker gradually within the existing social, economic, and political framework. Unlike American business unionism, the DGB has given strong backing to workers' representation and input into the decision making of the industrial firm through the codetermination system discussed above.

Labor is represented in the parliamentary delegations of both major parties, but its influence and sympathies lie more with the Social Democrats than the CDU. Most SPD members (about 70 percent) eligible to join labor unions are members of the DGB-affiliated groups, and the unions indirectly account for a large portion of SPD revenue. Generally the labor unions have supported Social Democratic policies, although at times they have been impatient with the slow pace of the party's domestic reform programs. On balance, the DGB's relationship to the SPD is not as close as that of the British unions to the Labour Party but closer than the American AFL-CIO's relationship to the Democratic Party.

By the end of the Kohl era (1982–1998) the trade unions wanted a change. Under CDU-FDP governance the unions felt that labor had not received its fair share of the economic pie. While income from investments had increased sharply during the Kohl years, labor's share had actually declined. The unions raised millions in extra funds to help finance the Schröder campaign. In 2002, labor again strongly supported the reelection of the SPD-Green government with money and campaign workers.

The climate between trade unions and the Social Democrats, however, changed dramatically with the passage of the Schröder government's Agenda 2010 program. Cuts in pensions and especially the reduction in unemployment protection were too much for many trade union leaders and members. They felt betrayed by the SPD and the Schröder government. By 2004 some union leaders were calling for a new party to the left of the Social Democrats. Wahlalternative Arbeit und soziale Gerechtigkeit (Electoral Alternative for Labor and Social Justice) was formed in part on the initiative of the major white-collar union ver.di. As we discussed earlier in this chapter, it later became part of the new Left Party. The decline in trade union support because of Agenda 2010 was one factor in Schröder's decision to step down as SPD chairman in 2004. In the 2005 and 2009 elections, the Social Democrats lost trade union votes to the Left Party. Although there is a labor wing in the Christian Democratic Union led by deputies from the Rhine-Ruhr region, there is little or no labor influence in the Bavarian CSU, and over the past two decades the power of the labor wing has declined in the Union's internal councils.

Unions in the Federal Republic are now faced with the necessity of branching out into new areas of activity if they are to continue as a major force in German social, economic, and political life. Because the Constitution (Article 9, Section 3) prohibits the closed shop, new members must be recruited through the unions' ability to offer concrete benefits that come only through union membership. Many of these benefits, such as unemployment, health, disability, accident, and pension programs—once private goods that could be obtained only through union membership—are now the province of the state, and as public goods are available to all without affiliation with the union. Support during strikes is still provided by the unions, but given the low strike rate in Germany, this is a marginal benefit. Unions must seek ways to provide their members with programs that are not public goods.

In the 1990s, relations between labor and management became more conflictual. Higher unemployment levels, reduced rates of economic growth, the weaker competitive position of German goods in some export markets, and automation have all contributed to this development. Unions have given greater priority to job security than to direct wage increases. For example, in the 1980s as unemployment spiked, the unions began a campaign for a thirty-five-hour workweek as one way to provide more jobs. The conflict level has also been heightened by the German employers' extensive use of the lockout in strike situations. This practice, legal in the Federal Republic, means that many workers not directly affected by the strike are barred from working.

The collapse of the GDR also meant the end of the East German trade organization, the Free German Trade Union (FDGB), which had been under the complete control of the Communist Party. Membership was compulsory, but the unions had no significant power. Strikes were forbidden, and collective bargaining was unknown. The GDR trade unions did administer a vast network of vacation homes and organized holidays for most of their nine million members. After the 1989–1990 revolution, the leader of the FDGB was arrested and later tried and convicted on charges of corruption and misuse of union funds.

The West German unions moved quickly to organize eastern workers. German trade union leadership has found itself in a difficult position in the eastern region. Given the lower productivity prevailing in the east, wage parity with western workers would mean that many former GDR firms would price themselves out of the market. Thus the unions have negotiated contracts that on average pay easterners about 70 to 75 percent of what their western colleagues earn, an amount that by 2012 had only slightly increased. This discrepancy has upset many eastern workers, especially those in the service industries. Hospital workers, for example, have staged wildcat strikes, and some have left for higher-paying jobs in the west. Until the eastern economy improves, the unions will have great difficulty in delivering the benefits their new members expect.

Trade unions have experienced a steady membership decline. Between 1991 and 2011, total membership dropped from 13.7 million to about 8 million. Overall about one in five workers is unionized today. Much of this decline has come from the east, where trade union membership was artificially high in the first years of unification. The original rush to membership in the east was in part based on the mistaken notion that trade union membership could somehow ensure job security. But union membership has also declined in the west, due mainly to the loss of blue-collar jobs.[27]

One of the few growth areas for labor unions has been among white-collar, service, and government workers. Until 1999 many of these employees were organized into five different unions. These unions—the public employees (ÖTV); post office employees (DPG); trade, banking, and insurance (HBV); media (IG Medien); and white-collar union (DAG)—with a combined membership of 3.2 million, merged in 2001 to form a single organization, the United Service Sector Union (ver.di), which replaced the metal workers as the largest single component of the DGB (with 2.2 million members). Representing over a thousand different professions, the service sector union seeks to give more weight in the bargaining process to the specific needs of each profession rather than following the "one size fits all" approach of the industrial trade unions.

In June 2003 the trade union movement experienced another reminder of its declining status. The Metal Workers Union for the first time in almost fifty years had to abandon a strike. The work stoppage in the eastern German automobile industry began over the issue of the length of the workweek. The union sought to have the western level of thirty-five hours applied to the eastern auto plants, which had been at thirty-eight hours. The Schröder government, a solid majority of the public, and many trade union members opposed the strike. By reducing the workweek with no reduction in pay, the union was essentially demanding a 9 percent hike in wages at a time when the country was in a recession and unemployment in the east was at almost 20 percent. Moreover, the work stoppage soon forced western auto plants to shut down for lack of parts from their eastern factories. In the face of widespread and growing opposition, the union leadership called off the strike. The failed action sparked a major conflict within the union as many local union officials demand the resignation of the leaders responsible for the "disaster."[28] The labor unions are now fighting on three fronts: against business, against governmental policy since at least 1998, and against a negative public image.

More fundamentally, as in most other advanced economies, labor has lost leverage compared to management. An increasingly deregulated European and global market means that there is more competition for jobs and thus less ability for unions to demand higher wages. It is true that unlike most other rich countries, Germany has been able to maintain a healthy industrial and export sector, which is one of the most productive and competitive in the world today. But this situation came about predominantly by reducing unit labor costs since the mid-1990s. Companies demanded and unions agreed to restrain wages. Unions understand that current economic circumstances do not allow for achieving higher wages and secure jobs simultaneously. There has also been a decline in industry-wide wage agreements and an increase in sector- and even factory-specific wage contracts. Moreover, public sector unions grasp that burdened taxpayers are reluctant to support generous wage increases.

The level of tension among the various actors should not be overstated. Certainly, after a decade or more of stagnant wages, there is pent-up demand for some increases. Even some neoliberal economists have advocated for higher wages in Germany after 2008 to increase domestic consumption and jump-start the faltering Eurozone economy. This would also address current account and trade imbalances. During the post-2008 economic crisis, there was unprecedented cooperation among unions, business, and government to defend jobs and maintain incomes. Strong institutions including codetermination—so strained since 1990—were able to manage economic turbulence and maintain social peace.

Agriculture

As analysts of interest groups have long known, the effectiveness of a group's efforts is closely related to its internal cohesiveness and unity of purpose. The experiences of German agrarian interests, the so-called Green Front (not to be confused with the Green political party discussed earlier in this chapter), substantiate this thesis. The vast majority of the Federal Republic's roughly 850,000 farmers belong to three organizations that constitute the front: the German Farmers League (*Deutscher Bauernverband*); the Association of Agricultural Chambers (*Verband der Landwirtschaftskammer*); and the *Raiffeisenverband*, a cooperative association involved in banking, mortgage loans, and retailing. In part because of their steadily dwindling number and increasing social isolation, agrarian interests are closely integrated and, unlike American rural interests, do not for the most part pursue conflicting aims. This united Green Front is probably the country's best-organized lobby. In addition, there are about a dozen—down from around fifty in previous decades—parliamentary deputies (most of whom are in the CDU/CSU) who form a relatively cohesive farm group within the legislature and dominate parliament's thirty-four-member committee for food, farming, and consumer protection.[29]

How can such a small and dwindling group—less than a million people now work on the 350,000 farms, of which only 150,000 are run full-time[30]—develop such substantial political influence and privileges? Farms are subsidized when they produce too much, but also when they cut production. They receive about $8.5 billion per year in subsidies, with the eastern Länder benefiting disproportionally from the European Union's Common Agricultural Policy (CAP), along with special tax concessions; for example, even the diesel oil for their tractors was until recently not taxed. The German state pays about 80 percent of their pension contributions (about $3 billion per year), and they collect value-added taxes that they do not have to pay the state. And if they do pollute, they receive additional subsidies to clean it up. Most of these programs benefit primarily larger farmers and cooperatives.

Mindful of past agrarian support for right-wing radical groups, including the Nazis, all parties have made major efforts to placate agriculture and meet its demands. Indeed, the influence of farm organizations probably increased under social-liberal governments (1969–1982). In an effort to secure the support of the FDP's right wing, the post of agricultural minister was assigned to a Bavarian conservative in 1969. Fearful of a break in the coalition, the Social Democrats, with little rural support themselves, were very generous and conciliatory to their strange bedfellow.

After more than fifty years of large subsidies and structural change, there has only been marginal improvement in the German agricultural sector. The focus of farm interests has thus been on the protection and maintenance of the farm market through price supports and direct subsidies. Currently, almost half of the income of German farmers comes from national and European subsidies and price supports.[31] Germany's farmers want above all the continuation of the European Community's Common Agricultural Policy.[32] Recent data, however, show an increase in the performance of German agriculture due mainly to the addition of the very large and relatively efficient eastern regions.[33]

The CAP program (see chapter 10) ensures farmers high prices in a protected market. This is good news for the farmers but bad news for consumers. In 2009, Germans spent about 11.4 percent of their income on food, whereas Americans spent about 6.9 percent and the British were at 8.8 percent, but the French spent 13.5 percent.[34] Most of this difference is due to the price-support program.[35] In countries with larger sectors of the workforce in agriculture, such as France and Italy, support for CAP is strong. But in the Federal Republic, which must import much of its food, why does this policy encounter no significant opposition? Indeed, the high food prices caused by this policy have never been a major item on the German political agenda.[36] There are two major reasons for this paradox: (1) despite declining economic significance, there is policy inertia, and the highly organized agricultural interests in the Federal Republic constitute a critical voting bloc in many districts; and (2) there are overall net gains to the Federal

Republic from membership in the European Community. The Green Front has been a significant force in the parliamentary delegations of both the Christian Democrats and the Free Democrats. Generally, German policy makers, regardless of party, accept the CAP because the losses to agriculture have been more than compensated for by profits from industrial exports to other European Union countries.

Since reunification, agriculture in the former East Germany has undergone a difficult transition. Under the communists, almost all farmers were forced to join collective farms. But in the post-1990 economy, about 20 percent have reclaimed their land and are now attempting to become independent, while about 60 percent are now reorganized into cooperatives. The remainder have left agriculture. Some farmland has also been leased or purchased by western German interests or is under the control of the successors to the Trusteeship Authority. In some cases the former members of the collective farms sold their shares to the new cooperatives at prices far below the actual market value of the land and equipment. Many former directors of the collective farms emerged after unification as the new and very prosperous leaders of these cooperatives. There have been a variety of lawsuits and investigations into these sales. Many sellers claim they were cheated by the former communist collective farm directors.[37]

Eastern Germany contains some of the country's richest soil and has become a productive and profitable agricultural region. But like other sectors of the economy, the collective farms were overstaffed. Before unification, over 850,000 East Germans were employed in agriculture; by 2003 the total had dropped to only 167,000. Most of these former collective farmworkers either retired, moved to other occupations, or are unemployed.[38] Those remaining on eastern farms, however, saw their incomes increase rapidly in the years following unification. By 1994 the average income of farmers in the east was actually higher than their colleagues in the west. This was due ironically to the larger size of eastern farms inherited from communist collectivization, special unification subsidies, and a reduced reliance on unprofitable livestock breeding in the former East Germany.[39]

In 2000 the agricultural establishment in Germany and Europe was shaken by an outbreak of "mad cow disease" that quickly became a mad cow scandal. Contaminated animal feed had been given to beef cattle, causing a form of bovine encephalitis. Consumption of the meat by humans was linked to a potentially fatal brain disease. The German agricultural leadership attempted to downplay the entire issue and assured consumers that the meat sold in Germany was safe. But further revelations about the scope of the problem increased public anxiety. The sale of meat, especially beef, sank sharply. Public and media criticism of agricultural authorities finally forced Chancellor Schröder to fire his agriculture minister. His replacement, Renate Künast, was a Green Party leader from Berlin with no ties to the traditional establishment. She emphasized consumer protection and organic farming, two issues that were usually dismissed by the agrarian lobby. But she quickly became one of the country's most popular political figures. Her success could be a sign that the days of Green Front dominance are numbered.

After the 2005 election, the traditional establishment regained the federal ministry. But the two Bavarians from the CSU have continued the stronger emphasis on product safety and consumer protection. Further scandals over dioxins in animal feed and an outbreak of *E. coli* in organic sprouts in the summer of 2011, which killed nearly fifty people, have underscored the necessity for the new policy focus. Moreover, budgetary pressures throughout the European Union should eventually affect the generous subsidies of the agricultural sector.

The Churches

In Germany as in other European countries, religious pluralism—state acceptance of equal rights and privileges for all religions and state neutrality in religious matters—has been a difficult concept to realize. Indeed most European societies have or have had state churches that occupy privileged positions in law, culture, and politics. While the Basic Law guarantees religious freedom, all faiths do not receive equal treatment from the state. The two established churches—the Protestant or Evangelical and the Roman Catholic—receive a variety of state benefits and subsidies. The state grants a wide variety of subsidies, some dating back to the early nineteenth century, and benefits including the collection of a church tax, a surtax on the income tax. In 2010, the amount collected was over $11 billion. State aid also includes funding for religious instruction in the schools, conducted by teachers approved by the churches but paid by the state; the training of clergy; and the construction and maintenance of church buildings. Church officials appointed by the state, such as military and hospital chaplains, are considered civil servants and are paid by the state.

The much smaller Jewish religious community also receives most of the benefits accorded the two established Christian denominations. By 2010 there were also about 105,000 Jews, out of a total Jewish population of almost 200,000, who were members of over seventy Jewish congregations. New synagogues have been built in a number of cities including Munich, Dresden, and Postdam. Germany now has one of the fastest-growing Jewish populations in the world due mainly to immigrants from the former Soviet Union. The Jewish congregations also receive state support.

Unlike the Christian and Jewish religious organizations, Germany's over four million Muslims and their more than 300 mosques receive no financial support yet from the federal government. With the 1999 citizenship law (see chapter 4), which has eased the restrictions for foreign residents to become naturalized German citizens, the proportion of Muslims who can vote has increased. With the franchise, it is expected that these new voters will then press for state support of their religion. In 2012, for example, the city-state of Hamburg passed legislation that would allow Muslims to take time off for certain holidays, as well as providing for more religious instruction in schools.[40] Hamburg is home to one of Germany's largest Muslim communities.

Income from the church tax and additional state subsidies finances a wide variety of charitable activities. The two major churches through their social welfare organizations—the Catholic *Caritas* and the Protestant *Diakonie*—operate over 50,000 hospitals, nursing homes, nursery schools, and other care facilities for children, women, the elderly, and the unemployed throughout the country. These institutions employ over 700,000 people and make the churches Germany's largest private employer and provider of health and welfare services. The churches operate about 75 percent of all child-care and elderly support agencies and one of every three hospitals. Charitable work among foreign workers and foreign missionary activity also benefit from public support.

All church-owned properties are tax exempt. Both churches are by law represented on the boards of control of radio and television networks. Representatives of the churches are also found on numerous advisory commissions at both federal and state levels. Finally, both church bodies maintain offices in Bonn and Berlin that are responsible for ensuring that the churches' position is well represented in the government and parliament.

Although they share this common legal and political status, the two churches have differed in their approach to public policy. The German Catholic Church has traditionally been more active in pursuing specific policy aims than its Protestant counterpart has been. Well organized, with extensive lay organizations of more than 3 million members and a press with 25 million readers, German Catholicism has sought output from the political system consistent with its goal or claim that the church has a right to intervene in certain political, social, and spiritual matters.

From 1949 to the mid-1970s the Catholic Church made a major effort to secure state financial support for separate Catholic and Protestant school systems. The church insisted that parents had the right to send their children to a state-funded Catholic school. Unable to get a clear statement supporting separate schools for Catholics and Protestants in the Basic Law, the Catholic hierarchy relied on the 1933 *Reichskonkordat* (treaty) between the Vatican and the Nazi government, which guaranteed a state-supported religious school system. Most Protestant states, however, exercising their newly restored rights in the education field, established biconfessional public schools after the war, in some cases abolishing previously separate Catholic systems.[41] By the 1970s these confessional schools had largely been phased out due to lack of support by parents and evidence that this "separate but equal" approach was inefficient and detrimental to educational quality. The Catholic Church lost the battle not because of the strength of the opposition but through massive desertions by its own troops, Catholic parents.

In addition, the Catholic Church has actively sought extensive state support and recognition of the family, stiffer divorce laws, strict control over "obscenity" in films and magazines, and the prohibition of abortion for all but the most pressing medical reasons. As in the case of the church school issue, the church has been losing the battle in all these areas. The Ministry of Family Affairs (a pet project of the Catholic Church since 1949) was abolished in 1969 and became part of the Health and Youth Affairs Ministry. During the Grand Coalition (1966–1969), criminal penalties for homosexual relations between consenting adults, blasphemy, and adultery were removed. From 1969 to 1982, the Social-Liberal government, over strong and vocal Catholic opposition, liberalized divorce, abortion, and pornography laws. Civil unions for same-sex couples were introduced in 2001. In all these cases, the church leadership was unable to mobilize its membership to oppose the new policies. Germany's very low birth rate, which is roughly the same for both Catholic and Protestant families, is a further indicator of the gap between the teachings of the Catholic Church hierarchy and the practices of its members.

In contrast to Roman Catholicism, German Protestantism—or more specifically its political arm, the Evangelical Church in Germany (EKD)—has placed greater emphasis on supporting the basic political values of the Federal Republic than on matters directly affecting the immediate interests of the church. Its major policy concerns, which it pursues less intensely than does the Catholic Church, have been social welfare issues, the treatment of foreign residents, peace and disarmament, civil liberties, educational reform, and aid for the developing world. Traditionally conservative on social-economic policies, the postwar Protestant leadership, if not its members, has turned almost 180 degrees and now has the reputation of being a center-left progressive movement in domestic policies. Unlike the Catholic leadership, however, the Protestant hierarchy has been unwilling to make any of its policy pronouncements binding on its members and has kept lines of communication open to all parties.

In the former GDR, however, the Protestant Church pursued a more active political role. In the early postwar years it strongly opposed the communist attempts to eliminate religion as a force in East German society. Throughout the 1970s and 1980s it provided a base and a refuge for the country's small dissident movements. When mass opposition to the regime finally emerged in 1989, the church again provided the initial base of support. The famous Monday demonstrations in Leipzig began after a prayer service in the Nicholas Church. Many of the early democratic East German leaders were Protestant ministers. During the GDR's first and last freely elected government, the foreign minister, defense minister, and development minister were members of the Protestant clergy.

Some members of the East German clergy, however, apparently collaborated in some way with the communist regime. One study of the East German church contended that about 3,000 clergy cooperated with the *Stasi* and allowed some church organizations to be infiltrated with secret police informers. Several bishops and the administrative chief of the Protestant Church, Manfred Stolpe, Ministerpräsident of Brandenburg until 1999, are alleged to have had ties to the Stasi. Since unification, some churches have begun to investigate the clergy and church administrators. Knowledge of the full extent of church involvement in the regime's security apparatus must await the opening and review of the church's archives.[42]

Both churches today find their traditional relationship to state and society in flux. The historically close relationship between the churches and state bodies, which has its roots in the aftermath of the Reformation, has brought most Germans to accept the traditional character of church-state relationships as legitimate. Criticism of state financial support and the advocacy of a clear separation of church and state have been restricted to small groups of liberal intellectuals centered in the larger metropolitan areas such as Hamburg and Berlin. Nonetheless, the sentiment that at least the church tax must be reduced or eliminated is growing.

In recent years, high unemployment coupled with an increase in the number of Germans leaving both churches have affected church revenues. Budgets for charitable work and day-care centers have been cut, and some churches have been forced to close. Their buildings and real estate have been sold and converted into schools, restaurants, museums, offices, apartment buildings, and even banks.[43] Some estimate that up to a third of all churches will close in the next two decades.[44] Not surprisingly, fewer young people are entering the clergy. In the Catholic Church, for example, between 1998 and 2011 the number of newly ordained priests dropped from 368 to only 86.[45] In 2011 only 764 men were preparing for the priesthood as compared to 3,627 in 1990.[46] Part of this decline is due to the various abuse scandals that have rocked Catholicism in recent years. Given the growing secularization of German society, which has been accelerated by unification, the restructuring of church-state relations will clearly be a subject of continued and increased debate in German politics.

SUMMARY AND CONCLUSION

The traditional, established interest groups in German society have, for the most part, adapted well to the ever-changing circumstances of political life. They have all become less attached to and less dependent on specific parties and now tend to concentrate on policy goals directly related to their major area of concern. As we have seen, business interests have discovered that they can flourish under Social Democratic governments just as they did under Christian Democratic governments. Agricultural interests, more pragmatic than in the past, saw the subsidies and protectionist policies so vital to their survival continued under different governments. In short, there has been a high degree of consensus and cooperation between major interest alignments and the established parties. Many professions continue to self-regulate and have successfully rebuffed calls for greater competition.

But what of those interests not accommodated by the existing structures? To what extent is the institutionalized, hierarchical character of German interest groups, parties, and—as we discuss in chapter 8—the bureaucracy a help or hindrance to the development of popular attitudes favorable to participation and involvement in the political process? The emergence and success of citizen initiative groups and new social movements, discussed in chapter 4, testifies to the presence of demands that neither established parties nor interest groups have met. The interests of foreign workers and residents, consumers, and working women have also been inadequately represented by existing institutions. Because membership in many occupational and professional groups is compulsory or automatic, the constitutional provisions for intragroup democracy should be, but have not been, enforced. The same absence of democratic procedures also applies to decision making within the political parties.

These are by no means uniquely German problems. To some extent they are the result of a constitutional order that has put little confidence in the ability of the ordinary citizen to meet the participatory requirements of political democracy. If established parties and interests have adapted well to this constitutional system, which has been so cautious and conservative in its approach to popular participation, their next task may well be to respond and adapt to new demands from a citizenry that is no longer willing to defer to others.

NOTES

1. Kurt Sontheimer, *The Government and Politics of West Germany* (New York: Praeger, 1973), 95.

2. http://www.bundestag.de/htdocs_e/bundestag/function/party_funding/index.html.

3. Renate Köcher, *Allensbacher Jahrbuch der Demoskopie*, vol. 12 (Berlin and New York: De Gruyter Verlag, 2007), 425.

4. Many of the CDU/CSU founders had roots in political Catholicism. The Catholic Center Party (Zentrum) existed from 1870 until it was dissolved after the Nazi takeover in 1933. It was one of the most successful parties during the empire and Weimar Republic, garnering as much as 20 percent of the Reichstag vote in 1903 and 12 percent in 1930.

5. Otto Kirchheimer, "Germany: The Vanishing Opposition," in *Political Opposition in Western Democracies*, ed. Robert A. Dahl (New Haven, CT: Yale University Press, 1966), 237–259.

6. Adenauer also received the unqualified endorsement of the United States throughout the 1950s. See Gordon Craig, "Die Bundesrepublik Deutschland aus der Sicht der USA," in *Deutschland Handbuch*, ed. Werner Weidenfeld and Hartmut Zimmermann (Munich and Vienna: Hanser Verlag, 1989), 672ff. During the 1953 Bundestag election campaign, the then–American secretary of state, John Foster Dulles, declared that Adenauer's defeat would be a "catastrophe" for Germany.

7. Melissa Eddy, "Merkel's Ex-Finance Minister to Oppose Her," *New York Times*, September 28, 2012, http://www.spiegel.de/politik/deutschland/buchhonorare-steinbrueck-verdiente-insgesamt-zwei-millionen-euro-a-865145.html.

8. Richard I. Hofferbert and Hans-Dieter Klingemann, "The Policy Impact of Party Programs and Government Declarations in the Federal Republic of Germany," *European Journal of Political Research* 18, no. 3 (May 1990): 300.

9. Genscher was the principal architect of the 1982 collapse of the Schmidt government. He was also involved in the 1984 plan to grant amnesty to those individuals and business firms under investigation for violating the party finance laws. Because of their smaller membership base, the Free Democrats are more dependent on larger contributions (and contributors) than the large parties. Only about 30 percent of the party's income comes from membership dues, as compared to about 40 percent for the major parties.

10. Like the Christian Democrats, the FDP also had a "bloc problem" in the former GDR. The Liberal Democratic Party (LDPD) was one of the four satellite parties in the GDR's National Front. When it merged with its West German counterpart in 1990, the unified FDP's membership and finances improved dramatically; in fact, for a time the east FDP had more members than the West German party.

11. Andreas Mihm, "Das Schwarz-gelbe Herbst dauert schon ein Jahr," *Frankfurter Allgemeine Zeitung*, October 28, 2010, 13.

12. The two Green parties failed to form an alliance at the 1990 election primarily because western Greens did not want to dominate their eastern counterparts as the Christian Democrats and the Free Democrats did. There were also policy disagreements. The eastern Greens, who were allied with the former GDR's democracy movement, were more concerned about unification than were the western Greens.

13. During the SPD-Green years Germany became Europe's largest producer of wind-generated electricity. Over 14 million of the country's 83 million residents receive electricity from wind-powered generators. This will increase in coming years with offshore units in the North Sea. By 2010 approximately 22 percent of Germany's electricity and 12 percent of all energy came from renewable sources. Marlise Simons, "Wind Turbines Are Sprouting Off Europe's Shores," *New York Times*, December 8, 2002, 7.

14. See Marc Morjé Howard, *The Politics of Citizenship in Europe* (Cambridge: Cambridge University Press, 2009).

15. *Der Spiegel*, no. 16 (April 18, 2011): 18.

16. Jack Ewing, "Germany's Greens Prepare for Power, and Major Tests," *New York Times*, April 1, 2011.

17. The former ruling East German Socialist Unity (Communist) Party changed its name during the revolution of 1989–1990 as well as its leadership and program.

18. Nicholas Kulish, "Direct Democracy 2.0," *New York Times*, May 6, 2012.

19. See David Art, *The Politics of the Nazi Past in Germany and Austria* (Cambridge: Cambridge University Press, 2006).

20. Samuel Barnes, Max Kaase, et al., *Political Action: Mass Participation in Five Western Democracies* (Beverly Hills, CA: Sage, 1979).

21. Federal Statistical Office, *Datenreport 2011*, 2008 data (Bonn: Federal Center for Political Education, 2006), 358–359.

22. "German Services: Protected and Inefficient," *Economist*, February 18, 2012.

23. Gerhard Loewenberg, *Parliament in the German Political System* (Ithaca, NY: Cornell University Press, 1967), 285–286.

24. Gerhard Lehmbruch, "Liberal Corporatism and Party Government," in *Trends toward Corporatist Intermediation*, ed. Phillipe C. Schmitter and Gerhard Lehmbruch (Beverly Hills, CA: Sage, 1979), 147–188; and Helmut Willke, "Zur Integrationsfunktion des Staates. Die Konzertierte Aktion als Paradigma in der neuen Staatstheoretischen Diskussion," *Politische Vierteljahresschrift* 20 (September 1979): 221.

25. Phillipe Schmitter, "Interest Intermediation and Regime Governability," in *Organizing Interests in Western Europe*, ed. Suzanne Berger (Cambridge: Cambridge University Press, 1981), 300ff.

26. G. Thomas Sims, "German Industry Would Alter Law Requiring Labor Seats on Boards," *New York Times*, April 6, 2007.

27. *Das Parlament* 7–8 (February 10–17, 1995): 7; Statistisches Bundesamt, ed., *Datenreport 2002* (Bonn: Bundeszentrale für politische Bildung, 2002), 602.

28. *Frankfurter Allgemeine Zeitung*, July 1, 2003, 1. Critics of the strike also pointed out that it was directed at the one industry, automobile manufacturing, that had done far more than any other to promote economic development in the eastern regions. Since unification more than 100,000 new jobs had been created in the eastern automobile industry.

29. http://www.bundestag.de/bundestag/abgeordnete17/mdb_zahlen/Berufe.html. Two-thirds of the agriculture committee is composed of agricultural interest group officials. See Ferdinand Müller-Rommell, "Interessengruppenvertretung im Deutschen Bundestag," in *US-Kongress und Deutscher Bundestag*, ed. Uwe Thaysen et al. (Opladen: Westdeutscher Verlag, 1990), 312.

30. http://www.bmelv.de/SharedDocs/Downloads/EN/Publications/GermanAgriculture.pdf?__blob=publicationFile.

31. Federal Statistical Office. In the United States, subsidies account for 30 percent of farm income.

32. The CAP was originally conceived at a time when Western Europe still had to import food. European farmers were encouraged to produce by fixed prices and guarantees

from the European Community to purchase whatever the free market could not absorb. Once Europe became self-sufficient in food production, however, the program was not modified but continued under the original assumption of a dependency on imported food.

33. Laure Latruffe, "Competitiveness, Productivity and Efficiency in the Agricultural and Agri-Food Sectors," *OECD Food, Agriculture and Fisheries Papers*, no. 30, OECD Publishing (2010); http://dx.doi.org/10.1787/5km91nkdt6d6-en, p. 10.

34. http://civileats.com/2011/03/29/mapping-global-food-spending-infographic.

35. Erich Andrlik, "The Farmers and the State: Agricultural Interests in West German Politics," *West European Politics* 4, no. 1 (January 1983): 104.

36. Andrlik, "The Farmers and the State," 108.

37. *Der Spiegel*, June 12, 1995, 133.

38. Federal Statistical Office, *Landwirtschaft in Zahlen 2003* (Wiesbaden, 2004), 8.

39. *Frankfurter Allgemeine Zeitung*, February 8, 1995, 1.

40. http://www.dw.de/dw/article/0,,16169442,00.html.

41. In biconfessional or community schools, children of both Catholic and Protestant faiths attend the same school but are given separate religious instruction (usually two to three hours per week) by representatives of the two faiths.

42. Gerhard Besier and Stephan Wolf, eds., *Pfarrer, Christen und Katholiken* (Berlin: Neukirchener Verlag, 1992) cited in *Der Spiegel*, February 3, 1992, 40–41, 44–45; see also Ralf-Georg Reuth, *IM Sekretär. Die Gauck-Recherche und Dokumente zum "Fall Stolpe"* (Frankfurt-Berlin: Ullstein Verlag, 1992).

43. *Der Spiegel*, no. 13 (March 26, 2005): 46–47.

44. *Der Spiegel*, no. 13 (March 26, 2005): 47.

45. http://de.statista.com/statistik/daten/studie/200021/umfrage/priesterweihen-der -katholischen-kirche.

46. Data cited in Daniel Deckers, "Klasse staat Masse?" *Frankfurter Allgemeine Zeitung*, June 18, 2004, 4.

6

Elections and Voting Behavior

The most common and extensive form of political participation in Germany, as in other industrialized societies, is voting. Indeed, in the absence of any significant plebiscitary components in the Constitution, voting affords the German citizen the major formal means of influence in the policy-making process. Elections were held at the local and state levels as early as 1946 in the British and American zones, and the first national election in 1949 was regarded as a quasi-referendum on the Constitution. Subsequent West German claims to be the sole legitimate representative of the German nation (East and West Germany) were based on the freely elected character of these governments. Thus the results of early local, state, and national elections were viewed primarily as indicators of system support and legitimacy. How many citizens would actually vote? And how many would support the democratic parties? The high turnout and the general rejection of neo-Nazi, communist, and other extremist parties evidenced in these early elections were seen as securing the legitimatization of the postwar system. The first free election in East Germany in March 1990 also legitimated the interim government and the subsequent unification process.

The other major functions that elections have for a political system—providing succession in leadership, influencing and controlling the policy decisions of government—were of lesser importance in the early years of the Federal Republic. The elections of the 1950s and even the 1961 vote were largely referenda on Adenauer's leadership; the policy and personnel alternatives of the opposition parties played a subordinate role in these campaigns.

Since the mid-1960s, however, the policy, leadership succession, and control functions of elections have become more prominent at both the national and the state levels. In 1969, for example, the electorate precipitated the first alternation of government and opposition in the history of the Republic, ending twenty years of Christian Democratic rule. The near miss of the Christian Democrats in 1976 and the Schmidt-Strauss "duel" in 1980 continued this pattern of hard-fought election campaigns, the outcome of which can directly influence the policies and personnel of government. In 1983 the electorate strongly endorsed the Christian Democratic–Free Democratic coalition that had taken office six months earlier when the government of Chancellor Schmidt collapsed. German voters in 1983 also brought the first new party since 1957 into parliament, the Greens. In 1987, for the first time in the history of the Republic, both major parties lost support in the same election. Voters returned the coalition government of Helmut Kohl, but with a reduced majority.

In December 1990 at the first free all-German election since 1932, German voters strongly endorsed the unification policies of Chancellor Kohl and Foreign Minister Genscher. The government was returned with a record majority of 134 seats in parliament. In 1994 Kohl and his governing coalition were reelected for a fourth term, but with a greatly reduced majority of only ten seats. In 1998 German voters for the first time in the fifty-year history of the Republic replaced an incumbent chancellor and his entire government. The Social Democrats returned to national power after sixteen years in the opposition and ended the Kohl era in German politics. In 2002 this government was reelected by a very narrow margin of only three seats, thanks to several unusual last-minute campaign developments (see chapter 5). In 2005 the voters denied the two major parties the ability to form a coalition with a small party. The share of the vote of the combined "major parties" (CDU-SPD) dropped to only 69 percent, the lowest total since 1949. After a long period of negotiations, the two erstwhile rivals had no choice but to form a Grand Coalition, the first since 1966, under the chancellorship of Angela Merkel, the first woman and easterner to hold that office. In the 2009 election, the Christian Democrats and Free Democrats led by the popular Merkel replaced the Grand Coalition. But the proportion of the electorate supporting the "elephants," as the Germans call the two largest parties, dropped to the lowest level since the first election in 1949. As the electorate gets ready for the eighteenth postwar election in 2013, the party landscape has become even more complicated with the potential emergence of a new party, the Pirates.

ELECTORAL MECHANICS

Elections to the national legislature must be held at least every four years but can be held sooner if the government loses its majority and requests the federal president to dissolve parliament and call new elections. This has occurred three times in the Republic's history: in 1972, when the Brandt government, through the defection of several FDP and SPD deputies, lost its majority but the opposition was unable to secure a majority for a new government; in 1982, when the Kohl government called for elections to legitimize the parliamentary developments that ended thirteen years of Social Democratic–Liberal rule; and in 2005, when then-chancellor Schröder determined that he could no longer govern after major defeats in state elections and opposition to his reform agenda. Elections to the various Länder parliaments are held every four or five years, but elections can be called earlier. Often state elections are held in off years, a procedure especially favored by the opposition party at the national level to mitigate "coattail" effects.

For elections to the national parliament, the Federal Republic is divided into 299 constituencies with an average size of about 275,000 residents and 205,000 registered voters. Each district must be a contiguous whole, while respecting state and, if possible, county (Kreis) boundaries. The size of each district must not deviate by more than one-fourth from the national average. Thus there is some variation in district size. Due to worries that the size of the parliament was unwieldy, for the 2002 election the number of districts was reduced from 328 to 299. This required an extensive redrawing of district boundaries.[2] An equal number of list seats were also cut for a total reduction in the size of parliament from 656 to 598. Yet, because of excess and now compensatory mandates (see below), the overall size of the parliament changes after each election and usually exceeds the 598 minimum.

The Basic Law, as amended in 1970, grants universal suffrage and the right to hold public office to citizens eighteen years of age or older (reduced from twenty-one).[3] Germany has automatic registration based on residence records maintained by local authorities. If a citizen has officially reported his or her residence in the constituency (as required by law), he or she will automatically be placed on the electoral register, provided that the age requirement is met. Before election day, the voter will be notified of registration and polling place.

THE ELECTORAL SYSTEM

The procedures by which popular votes are converted into parliamentary seats—a country's electoral system—are more than just a technical problem best left to constitutional lawyers. Most political scientists and political leaders assume that the electoral law will affect the character and structure of a country's party system and hence its politics. Generally, there are two basic types of electoral systems: (1) a plurality system, usually with single-member districts, as in the United Kingdom and the United States, according to which the party or candidate securing the most votes wins, and (2) a proportional electoral system, by which a party's share of parliamentary mandates is proportional to its percentage of the popular vote. Most political scientists have argued that a plurality system encourages a concentration of popular support among a small number of parties and enables clear decisions to emerge from an election, making postelection coalition negotiations unnecessary. The proportional system, on the other hand, although more equitable in providing representation to small segments of opinion and group interests, is said to produce a fractionalization of the party vote and hence a multiparty system in which no single party usually secures a majority of the parliamentary seats and government by coalition often results. Some authors prefer the closer relationship between a territorial representative and the electorate, and others think that proportionality creates a parliament more representative of the society that comprises it.

The assumption that a certain type of electoral law is related to a particular type of party system and hence favors some parties more than others makes the electoral law question a partisan political issue. Small parties generally favor a proportional system because it guarantees them some parliamentary representation even if their percentage of the popular vote is far less than a plurality. Large parties tend to support a winner-take-all system, confident of their ability to mobilize the marginal voter.

The German system, innovative in 1949, has been widely copied in many countries such as Japan, Italy, and Mexico because of its combination of territorial representatives with proportionality. The system has been termed a "personalized proportional" or a mixed-member proportional system, with half of the 598 parliamentary deputies elected by plurality vote in single-member districts and the other half by proportional representation from Land (state) party lists. Each voter casts two ballots—one for a district candidate and the other for a party. The party vote is more important because it is used to determine the final percentage of parliamentary mandates a party will receive.[4] The seats won in the district contests are then deducted from this total. Thus the more district mandates a party wins, the fewer list seats it will receive. But if a party wins more district mandates than its party vote would allow, it is able to keep these "excess" mandates. Finally, only parties that obtain at least 5 percent of the national vote total are eligible for the proportional seat allocation process.

As an example, the 2009 election should illustrate these procedures. As table 6.1 shows, the CDU/CSU received 33.8 percent of the second ballot vote (proportional list). But 6 percent of the second votes went to small parties below the 5 percent threshold. So the percentage of the second vote is recalculated once these smaller parties are eliminated, giving the CDU/CSU 35.9 percent. Instead of being entitled to 202 proportional seats, it gets 215: 13 seats came from the "wasted" votes of the smaller parties. However, because it won 194 direct mandates from the first vote (excluding the 24 excess mandates) it received 21 representatives from the party lists (215 minus 194) and ended up with 239 members in the Bundestag (194 plus 21 plus 24). The SPD and Left Party received their seats in a similar manner, but the FDP and the Greens received all (minus one direct mandate for the Greens) from the proportional list candidates. All of the parties that made it over the 5 percent threshold benefited from the 6 percent of second votes that were "wasted" on the small parties.[5]

Table 6.1.   Seat Allocation after 2009 Bundestag Election

Party	Percent on first ballot	Percent on second ballot	Corrected second ballot percentage*	Number of seats earned**	Number of district seats won (excess mandates)***	Number of list candidates elected	Total seats (of which excess mandates)
CDU/CSU	39.4	33.8	35.9	215	194 (24)	21	239 (24)
SPD	27.9	23.0	24.5	146	64	82	146
FDP	9.4	14.6	15.5	93	0	93	93
Left Party	11.1	11.9	12.6	76	16	60	76
Green	9.2	10.7	11.4	68	1	67	68
Other	3.0	6.0	—	—	0	0	0
Total	100	100	100	598	299	323	622 (24)

Source: Federal Statistical Office.
Note: SPD = Social Democratic Party; CDU/CSU = Christian Democratic Union/Christian Social Union; FDP = Free Democratic Party; PDS = Party of Democratic Socialism.
*Percentage of second votes only for parties surpassing the 5 percent electoral threshold.
**Under proportional representation.
***In first ballot.

In practice, then, because of the overwhelming importance of the second vote in determining the composition of the Bundestag, this is a proportional representation system. Nevertheless, there are four exceptions to "pure" proportionality, all of which have played important roles in recent elections:

1. *The 5 percent clause.* As mentioned above, a party must receive at least 5 percent of the vote in order to be proportionally represented in parliament; hence the minor parties in our example, with a total of about 6 percent of the vote, received no seats, and the approximately thirty-six mandates they would have been allotted in a pure proportional system were given to the parties that cleared the 5 percent mark. Moreover, the 5 percent threshold is based on national not Land votes, even though seat allocation is done at the Land level. If a party gets 40 percent of the Land vote but only 35 percent nationally, it will get only 35 percent of the seats in that Land.

2. *The Three-Mandate Waiver.* If a party wins at least three district (first-ballot) seats, the 5 percent clause is waived and the party participates in the proportional distribution process.[6] The former East German Communist Party, the Party of Democratic Socialism (PDS) that since 2007 has been the Left Party, owed its return to parliament in 1994 to this little-known and seldom-used provision of the law.[7]

3. A party or candidate that wins any direct mandate keeps that seat even if the 5 percent threshold or three direct mandate provisions are not achieved. The PDS received only 4 percent of the national vote in 2002 but won two direct mandates in eastern Berlin and thus had a parliamentary delegation of two.

4. *The excess mandate (Überhangmandate) provision.* If a party wins more direct mandates than it would be entitled to under proportional representation, it retains these "excess" seats, and the size of parliament is increased accordingly. Let us assume, for example, that the SPD in 2009 had won all 299 district contests but had received only 40 percent of the second-ballot vote. In a pure proportional system it would be entitled to only 40 percent, or 239 seats. According to the German system, however, it would retain all 299 district seats but receive no mandates from the proportional lists, and the total size of the parliament would be increased from 598 to 658. An enlargement of the parliament to this extent has never occurred.

Until 1990 the excess mandate provision was a relatively inconsequential component of the electoral system. Before unification the largest number of excess mandates was five in 1961, and in several elections there were none at all. But in 1990 the CDU won six such seats, and in 1994 the number increased to sixteen: the Christian Democrats received twelve, and the Social Democrats four. Because of this provision, the government's "true majority" of only two seats grew to ten when all the first-district ballots were counted, and the Bundestag was "enlarged" from 656 to 672 members. In 1998 the number of excess mandates dropped to thirteen, all of which went to the Social Democrats. The complete redistricting after 2002 was expected to reduce the number of excess mandates to around five, but the strong showing in 2005 of the Left Party in the eastern regions caused a sharp increase of excess mandates to sixteen (nine for the SPD and seven for the CDU). The Left Party turned many eastern races into three-party contests, which meant that the larger parties could win pluralities with far less than an absolute majority. In 2009, as discussed above, there was a record twenty-four excess mandates, all for the Union parties (twenty-one for the CDU and three for the CSU). Some even feared before the election that a CDU-FDP majority would only occur because of excess mandates. In its 2012 electoral law decision, the Federal Constitutional Court (see chapter 8) ruled that in the new electoral law the number of excess mandates cannot exceed fifteen.

This electoral system—through its provisions for two ballots and the extra seats in the event a party wins more direct district contests than it would be entitled to under proportional representation—can also facilitate a great deal of ticket splitting, or "lending" of votes by supporters of two coalition or prospective coalition partners. Supporters of one party could cast their first-ballot vote for the party's coalition partner, thereby ensuring it a high number of district victories; voters of the second party could return the favor by casting their second ballot for the coalition partner, thereby increasing its share of mandates from the state lists.

Ticket splitting of this type has become fairly widespread. In national and state elections during the Social Democratic–Liberal era (1969–1982), many SPD voters, fearing that their junior coalition partner, the Free Democrats, would not surmount the 5 percent hurdle, "lent" their second-ballot votes to the FDP. Because the FDP's district candidate had little chance for direct election, the Free Democratic voters in turn lent their first-ballot votes to the SPD. In 2009, ballot splitting reached record levels as about 25 percent of the electorate split their ballots. The combined total of almost 40 percent for the three smaller parties (FDP, Greens, and the Left) was in large part the result of this behavior.[8] Indeed, about 40 percent of FDP second-ballot voters supported the CDU with their first ballot, and about a third of Green second-ballot voters used their first ballot to vote for an SPD candidate.[9] Ballot splitting has become a key factor in the survival of the Free Democrats and the Greens. In 2009 about a fourth of the Greens' national total of 12 percent came from SPD splitters. In 2005 about 57 percent of the Green national second ballot came from first-ballot SPD voters.[10] The Greens now appear to be as dependent on SPD ballot splitters as the FDP is on CDU first-ballot voters. For the FDP in 2005, support from first-ballot Christian Democratic voters made up about 52 percent of their second-ballot vote.[11] In 2002 the FDP, in contrast with 2005, did not indicate a preelection preference for a coalition partner. This cost the party the support of many potential CDU splitters. In 2009 the FDP did indicate a clear preference for the Christian Democrats, and its support from CDU splitters increased by about 15 percent.

In light of the many quirks of the electoral system, proposals for change have periodically surfaced, usually advocating a plurality system of the Anglo-American type—that is, plurality elections in single-member districts. Such a system, it is argued, would eliminate the need for coalition governments by creating clear majority winners (and losers) and would thereby increase the electorate's role in the selection of a governing party; it would also eliminate the possibility of extremist parties, even those securing above 5 percent, gaining parliamentary representation with only a small percentage of the vote.

The Free Democrats and Greens have mainly opposed these proposals, because their survival as a serious political force depends on the retention of the proportional system. Thus, before either party enters into any coalition with one of the major parties, it secures a pledge from its potential partner that the electoral law will not be tampered with. A number of analysts argue that the proportional electoral system was partly responsible for the lack of more comprehensive social and economic reforms over recent decades. The necessity of coalition governments means that fundamental reform proposals frequently become weakened through the demands of coalition politics.

In 2008 the Federal Constitutional Court added further controversy to the debate about the electoral system when it ruled that parts of the law are unconstitutional because in some cases involving excess mandates, all votes are not equally weighted. A vote for a particular party can actually have a negative impact on its total number of seats because of the complexities of the seat allocation process. In other words, voting for a party can reduce its total number of seats. Although it was not specifically mentioned in the opinion, many observers consider the excess mandate provision to be a major factor contributing to the law's defects. The Court did not invalidate the 2005 election result; rather, it gave the parliament until June 30, 2011, to correct the law or pass a new one. The 2009 election, therefore, was conducted under the old law including the excess mandate clause. That year Germans went to the polls according to an electoral law that in 2008 its highest court had declared, in part, unconstitutional.

In September 2011, the parliament, or more specifically the governing majority, passed a new law that it claimed met the objections of the court regarding the "negative vote." The opposition disagreed, and in June 2012 the Constitutional Court once again heard arguments for and against the electoral system, finding that the government's proposal did not pass constitutional muster. Another proposal was agreed upon by the parliamentary parties (except for the Left) in October 2012 for the fall 2013 elections. This law would add "off-setting" or "compensatory" mandates to the system—equaling the number of excess mandates to ensure that no party is disadvantaged and thus greater overall proportionality. The size of the Bundestag would be increased commensurately, reaching as many as 700 seats. Not only would this create one of the largest parliamentary chambers in the world, but it would also cost approximately 40 million Euros more per year.[12]

NOMINATION AND CANDIDATE SELECTION

The electoral system is also an important structural factor influencing the recruitment and nomination of candidates to parliament. The party list section of the ballot allows parties to bring into parliament, through a high position on the list, representatives of interest groups and experts with specialized knowledge who would for various reasons (personality, background) have a difficult time winning a grassroots campaign. This is also a "closed" list, meaning that the parties and not the voters determine the composition of the list and the order of the names. Parties have used their lists to increase the number of women elected through the use of quotas and a requirement to have enough women candidates placed higher on the list.[13] A district campaign, on the other hand, affords candidates an opportunity to establish their personal vote-getting appeal and can provide a second chance for personalities left off the state list or given a hopelessly low position. Moreover, a strong district following gives an incumbent a measure of independence from the state or national party organization.

Yet, in spite of one-on-one district contests (the personalized part of the electoral system), most Germans vote for a party label rather than a personality. In 2002, for example, about 60 percent of a representative sample of the electorate stated that the most important factor in their vote was their attachment to a party rather than a particular candidate "with whose basic policies I agree."[14] Moreover, some authors assert that district representatives have a lower stature than the pure list candidates because the rigors of constituent service are considered a distraction from policy formation and the legislative process.

Constituency candidates, by law, must be nominated after a secret ballot election, either by all party members in the district or by a district selection committee that has itself been elected by the vote of the entire membership. This nomination must be made not more than one year before the election. The official nomination papers must also contain minutes of the selection meeting, together with attendance records and voting results. The enforcement of these legal provisions, however, has thus far been left to the parties.

The selection of candidates for state lists takes place at party conventions held six to eight weeks before election day. The construction of these lists is usually a controversial matter in which the various factions struggle and bargain to receive positions high enough to ensure election or, in most cases, reelection—because if a party gets, for example, ten members from a list, the top ten names will go to Berlin. There is a tendency for even those candidates running in supposedly safe districts to seek the safety net provided by a high list position.

At the district level, the entire process of candidate selection is, according to most observers, a relatively decentralized procedure in which local party oligarchies and issues play a more important role than the construction of state lists. The grassroots organizations are very sensitive to pressure from above and jealously seek to maintain their power. Indeed, there are reports that, especially at recent elections, national "prominents" seeking a district nomination feel handicapped by the so-called local matadors and under pressure to prove themselves to be sufficiently in touch with the base. Moreover, the district selection process is becoming more conflict laden. This development reflects the influence of new members in the local party organizations and the emergence of contending ideological factions at the grassroots level.

In addition to a focus on gender issues, in recent years all parties have begun to recruit some candidates with a migration background (i.e., immigrants). In 2005 almost 200 naturalized citizens, or slightly more than 5 percent of the total, ran for parliament, and 13 percent were elected. The proportion of immigrant candidates ranged from 3 percent for the CDU/CSU to 7 percent for the Left

Party. Immigrant candidates from the city-states of Hamburg, Bremen, and Berlin were most likely to be nominated.[15] As much as this is a step in the right direction, given the almost 20 percent of the population with a migration background, only fifteen members after 2009 (2.4 percent of the total) actually had such a background.

Criteria for Selection

How does an aspiring German politico become a candidate for parliament? Because most nominees are incumbents, the most obvious qualifications are previous experience and performance. In the absence of national experience, however, a good record in some local or Land office is an important qualification. About half of all district candidates have held local office, and about one-fourth have had some experience at the state level. Having a reputation as a good party man or woman (i.e., being a loyal, hardworking partisan, especially in local party work) will further enhance the aspirant's prospects. The political culture values expertise, so occupational and educational experience is a further qualification. Finally, the degree of interest group support for a particular candidate and the character of the expected opposition are also at work in the local nomination process.

A good position on the state list (second part of the ballot) usually requires one or more of the following: state or national prominence; the support of top leaders of interest groups vital to the party (especially important in the CDU/CSU); leadership positions at the state or national level in auxiliary organizations of the party (youth, women, farmers); and the support of important ideological groupings within the organization. Because the top three names on each party's state list will be printed on the ballot, most state party organizations try to have the most prominent national or state leaders in these slots to aid in voter recognition. The use by some district candidates of the list as a safety net, and the ability to do so, usually also requires senior leadership status in the party. In some cases a candidate in a hopeless district who has nonetheless done a good job of campaigning in the area over several elections will eventually be rewarded with a good list position.

Proposals for reform of the nomination system have focused on the introduction of American-type primary elections, stricter enforcement of the provisions of the party law governing the selection process at both district and state levels (secret ballots, public announcements of meetings), and establishment of nationwide candidate lists at the parties' national conventions. Given the growth in grassroots participation in party affairs, reform proposals are likely to gain increasing support.

ELECTORAL POLITICS AND CAMPAIGN STYLES

As in other advanced Western societies, the style of election campaigns in Germany has become strongly influenced by professional advertising and public relations techniques. All major parties contract with ad agencies for the design of their campaign appeals: slogans, posters, television spots, and newspaper and magazine advertisements are pretested to achieve, if possible, the desired effect on the target group of voters.[16] Nonetheless, it would be erroneous to assume that the German version of Madison Avenue is a behind-the-scenes power. The message, or main themes, of a campaign are for the most part the decision of the parties, with the public relations and advertising experts largely determining the manner in which these themes are presented. Still, there is a long tradition of artistic and provocative campaign posters that stretches back to the empire.

Media

Use of the mass media, above all television, has become a key factor in the German political process. The ability or inability to frame issues and personalities through skillful use of the media has become critical in the success or failure of policies and candidates. The "media democracy" is a term frequently used by political observers to describe this process. Issues and personalities have to be *"vermittelt"* or "sold" via the media to be successful. The intrinsic worth of a policy proposal or candidate means little without this media-based process.

Extensive, well-developed media structures and close, well-financed relationships between major interest groups and the parties ensure that the voters will be subjected to a massive barrage of electoral propaganda. In addition to daily press, radio, and television news coverage, parties are given free time for political spots on radio and television. Special election previews, with commentary and analysis, are standard fare during the final four to six weeks before an election. From 1972 to 1987, televised debates between the leaders of the parties represented in parliament highlighted the final stage of the campaign. Prior to the elections from 1990 to 1998, however, Chancellor Kohl and the Christian Democrats declined to take part in the "elephant round"—as the Germans term the debate between the top leaders—fearing that the media exposure would enhance the standing of the postcommunist PDS, which was entitled to participate.

During the 2002 election campaign, for the first time in German history, the two top candidates—Chancellor Schröder and his challenger from the CDU/CSU, Edmund Stoiber—engaged in two American-style televised debates. The leaders of the other smaller parties cried foul, but to no avail. These debates were touted as American-style duels between the two top guns. The first debate, according to public opinion polls, was essentially a draw. But since most observers considered Stoiber to be the weaker debater and hence had lower expectations for him, it could also be interpreted as a Stoiber victory. But in the second debate, the chancellor clearly came out on top. Most polls gave Schröder about a two-to-one advantage over Stoiber. The second debate probably added to the momentum that the government was building after the flood and the Iraq issue.[17] In 2005, mindful of the telegenic Schröder's debating skills and with a large lead to protect, Angela Merkel agreed to only one debate with the incumbent chancellor. As expected, Schröder was generally considered the winner, albeit by a small margin. Unlike 2002, this debate did little damage to the CDU/CSU campaign. The 2009 election also witnessed a televised debate between Merkel and Steinmeier, indicating that this format may have become a new electoral tradition.

In the last four decades electoral politics have also been characterized by a steady increase in public involvement during the campaign. Traditionally, German voters have been rather passive and reticent during campaigns, dutifully absorbing information channeled to them by the media and party organizations. Discussions among family and friends, attendance at election meetings, and the public display of partisan preferences were restricted to only a part of the electorate. Since the late 1960s, however, public interest and involvement in elections have taken on new forms and reached higher levels than during previous campaigns. The proportion of voters reporting that they discussed the elections with family or friends almost tripled between 1969 and 1976 and has remained at these higher levels ever since. New forms of public involvement include widespread voter initiative groups and the public display of partisan preferences through bumper stickers.[18] By the 1972 federal election, citizen groups were working for all parties, although most of them tended to favor the Social Democratic–Liberal government.[19] These groups organized rallies, staffed information booths in downtown shopping areas, sponsored advertisements, distributed literature and campaign buttons, and generally attempted to stimulate voter interest and activity in the campaign. Such activities have since become commonplace during campaigns. These various signs of interest, popular concern, and involvement indicate that Germans have acquired a fuller understanding of the citizen's role and of the potential for political change available through political participation.

The German parties have increasingly adopted Internet-based forms of campaigning, even if their use of such technology lags compared to other systems. One contrast from the United States is that the German parties are less dependent on individual donations than are American candidates. Online donations have been responsible for much innovation in the United States. Nevertheless, all of the parties do currently have sophisticated websites with substantial information and some interactivity.[20] Websites such as "Direct to the Chancellor" (www.direktzurkanzlerin.de) and "Representative Watch" (www.abgeordneten-watch.de) try to facilitate more direct communication between voters and politicians. Other websites, such as "Wahl-O-Mat," ask for voters' preferences on various issues and then match them with parties' platforms.[21] More interactive platforms are not as commonly used as in other countries. In 2009, for instance, the two chancellor candidates combined had only 10,000 supporters on Facebook, compared to Barack Obama's six million in 2008.[22]

The Pirates stand out, not only in Germany but also internationally, for their intensive use of the Internet and comprehensive interactivity. Their online "liquid feedback" platform provides a mechanism for Pirate members to constantly interact in real time and continuously debate and modify the party's positions.[23] Although it is difficult to predict how much staying power the Pirates will have in the party system beyond 2013, their innovations will most certainly affect the way other parties and campaigns operate. The Internet is already the primary source for information for heavy computer users, indicating the decline of print and television-based communication. Moreover, younger Germans are much heavier computer and Internet users, so these trends will only intensify thanks to the process of generational replacement.

Campaign and Party Finance

As in the United States, election campaigns in Germany have become very expensive. Unlike those in many other modern democracies, however, German political parties are the recipients of extensive governmental subsidies with which they finance a large part of their organizational and campaign work (see table 6.2). In 2005, for example, public subsidies constituted over one-third of the total income reported by the parties represented in parliament and over half of that received by the smaller parties. By 2011, public financing totaled almost $185 million.

State subsidies began in 1959 with a modest annual allotment of about $2 million. By 1965 this had increased to $20 million, including the addition of subsidies from some Länder. In 1967 a new law provided a public subsidy of about a dollar for each vote received by any party gaining at least 2.5 percent of the popular vote in the preceding election. Thus, by 1976 the federal government alone paid out over $60 million to the parties contesting federal elections. The 1967 law also required the parties to file annual statements of their finances and to disclose the names of all individuals contributing more than $10,000 in any year, as well as all corporations contributing more than $100,000. The Federal Constitutional Court (see chapter 8) later ruled that the law was unconstitutional in a number of ways. It ordered the minimum percentage needed for a party to receive subsidies to be dropped to 0.5 percent (about 250,000 votes) and also required that the disclosure ceilings be lowered. The reduction of the minimum percentage means that public subsidies are an important source of funds for smaller parties, especially for those that do not gain representation in a parliament.

In spite of public financing, the parties' need for additional funds is insatiable. The parties continue to solicit large, tax-deductible contributions from businesses and other interest groups. As in other developed democracies, there is a real danger that political favors will be anticipated or actually promised by the parties in exchange for financial support. In late 1999 a major scandal involving

Table 6.2.   State Funding of Parties, 2011

Party	Amount of Funding (million $)
CDU	58.0
SPD	55.1
Greens	17.9
FDP	17.7
Left Party	15.7
CSU	13.5
Republikaner	1.8
NPD	1.7
Ecological Democratic Party	0.9
Pirates	0.8
Other	1.3
Total	184.5

Source: http://www.bundestag.de/bundestag/parteienfinanzierung/festsetz_
    staatl_mittel/finanz_11.pdf.
Note: 1 Euro = $1.30.

the Christian Democrats and former chancellor Kohl again focused public atten-tion on the role of money in election campaigns. Kohl admitted that he kept special secret bank accounts to finance campaigns and strengthen his hold on the party. It was alleged that these funds came largely from arms dealers and other firms that profited from government contracts. The scandal eventually spread to Kohl's successor as CDU leader, who was forced to resign in 2000. In 2002 the Social Democrats had their own finance scandal. In several large cities in the Rhine-Ruhr region, SPD government officials routinely raised large sums of money from firms seeking lucrative contracts for garbage disposal and waste incineration. Needless to say, the Social Democrats did not make the Kohl scandal an issue in the 2002 campaign. Following the 2009 campaign (see chapter 5), the Free Democrats had their turn in the scandal spotlight when a large dona-tion from a hotel chain was later linked to an even larger tax break for hotel owners.

THE PATTERN OF FEDERAL ELECTIONS

The results of the seventeen national elections held since 1949, including the six (1990–2009) all-German elections, are presented in figure 6.1. These data reveal six major characteristics of German voting behavior over the past sixty-four years:

1. The hegemonic position of the CDU/CSU in the party system from 1953 to 1965, due above all to the party's spectacular electoral victories in 1953 and 1957.

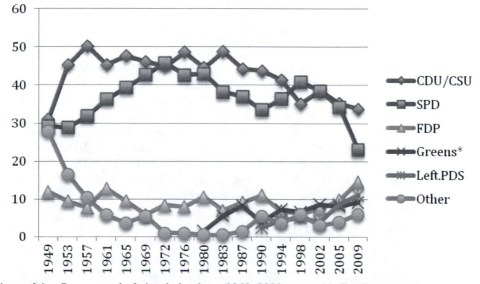

Figure 6.1.   Party vote in federal elections, 1949–2009, second ballot (in percent).

2. The steady increase in support for the SPD between 1953 and 1972, averaging about 3 percent in each election, which brought the party up to parity with the Christian Democrats.
3. The gradual decline of smaller parties ("other") between 1949 and 1980, whose percentage of the poll dropped from 28 percent in 1949 to about 2 percent in 1980.
4. The competitive and less predictable character of elections since 1983. Long-term trends have been replaced by short-term fluctuations from election to election.
5. The decline of the two largest parties since the late 1980s and the slow but steady increase in smaller parties, as well as declining turnout rates.
6. The increasing complexity of forming governmental coalitions and the proliferation of acceptable combinations.

In the first federal election in 1949, twelve parties secured parliamentary representation, but only two—the CDU/CSU and the SPD—received more than 25 percent of the popular vote. The CDU/CSU campaigned on the twin issues of the Federal Republic's integration into the Western alliance abroad and the market economy at home. "We don't want any socialism in Germany" was its major slogan. With the exception of the Communist Party, which secured 5.7 percent of the vote and fifteen parliamentary seats, all other smaller parties generally agreed with these two Christian Democratic positions. The differences between them and the Union were far less than between them and the Social Democrats. If one combines the CDU/CSU's 1949 vote and that of the smaller, nonleftist parties in that first election, the total—44.3 percent—is similar to the total achieved by the Union alone in the elections of 1953 and 1957.

The elections of 1953 and 1957, which brought the Christian Democrats to the pinnacle of their electoral success, represented the continuation of the 1949 pattern. By this time, however, the policy successes of the Adenauer-led government began to take their toll on the small, regional, special-interest parties, whose support steadily dwindled. Also, the Constitutional Court banned the far-right Socialist Reich Party in 1952 and the Communist Party in 1956. The CDU gains resulted above all from its absorption of many of these smaller parties rather than from gains from the SPD. One of the most significant of the smaller parties represented the interests of expellees from the east. The CDU was increasingly able to absorb these interests. Indeed expellees became one of the most important CDU/CSU clienteles in the 1960s and 1970s. The Social Democrats' policy alternatives—neutralism in foreign policy and a socialist planned economy at home—were rejected decisively by the majority of the electorate. By absorbing the smaller parties, the CDU/CSU greatly simplified the party system and reduced the possibility of a reversion to the unstable multiparty system of the Weimar Republic.

The early successes of the Christian Democrats provided the impetus for the SPD's transformation from a narrowly based, ideologically committed socialist movement to a heterogeneous, pragmatic, center-left party of reform. This process, described in chapter 5, produced steady electoral gains after 1953 and by 1972 gave the SPD a larger share of the popular vote than the CDU received.

Most of the SPD gains over these years, however, came from Christian Democratic voters and new voters, not from the ranks of the minor parties. Until 1972 the CDU was able to compensate for losses to the SPD by gains from minor parties. Had it not been for this reservoir, the Union's decline between 1965 and 1972 would have been even more apparent.

The 1976 federal election saw the return of the Social Democratic–Liberal coalition that had governed Germany since 1969, but with a majority of only ten seats, down sharply from the advantage of forty-six seats held after the November 1972 poll. The opposition Christian Democrats, led for the first time by their new chairman, Helmut Kohl, not only regained their status as Germany's largest single party but also achieved their highest proportion of the party vote since 1957 and reversed the steady gains the Social Democrats had achieved at every election since 1957.

In the 1980 federal election, the SPD-FDP coalition, due largely to a strong performance by the Free Democrats, won a decisive victory over the Christian Democrats led by the controversial Bavarian Franz-Josef Strauss. The Free Democrats increased their share of the vote from 7.9 to 10.6 percent. The electorate decisively rejected the Strauss candidacy but did not endorse the Social Democrats, preferring instead to return a stronger FDP as a "liberal corrective" to the SPD. The CDU/CSU, in spite of a 4.1 percent drop in its vote, remained the strongest party.

In 1980 the three established parties also had to contend with a nationwide environmentalist political party, the Greens. The Greens had a strong protest component to their image, and this helped them skim votes from all the established parties—but especially the SPD and FDP—in state and local elections. In 1980 they were unable, however, to overcome the charge of being simply a single-issue protest movement with no capability to assume or share responsibility for the myriad tasks and problems of government.

After the 1980 election, the NATO missile question and the resultant nationwide peace movement gave the Green Party new momentum. In the March 1983 elections the Greens, with 5.6 percent of the vote, became the first new political party to enter the parliament since the 1950s. Their electoral success in 1983 was due above all to the strong support they received from younger voters, especially those with college or university backgrounds. The Greens' success in 1983 and, after reunification, those of the PDS/Left Party also indicate that the electoral system does not place insurmountable barriers to new political parties.

In the 1987 election, voters returned the ruling Christian Democratic–Free Democratic coalition, but with a reduced majority. For the first time in postwar German electoral history, both major parties lost support in the same election. The combined CDU (44 percent) and SPD (37 percent) share of the vote dropped to 81 percent, the lowest since 1953. The Free Democrats increased their vote to 9 percent, and the Greens' proportion of the vote rose to over 8 percent.

Elections after Reunification

On December 2, 1990, German voters elected 662 deputies to the parliament (Bundestag). Among these were 140 new members who now represented the 16 million inhabitants of what had been, until October 3, 1990, the German Democratic Republic. Although this election was the twelfth for the Federal Republic, it was the first time that the eastern citizens participated in a federal election and the first free "all-German" vote in fifty-eight years. The election was also the culmination of a unification process that had begun in November 1989 with the opening of the Berlin Wall and the subsequent collapse of the East German regime.

Two quite different electorates went to the polls on December 2, 1990. West Germans had been participating in democratic elections at the local, state, and national levels for over forty years. East Germans, following the collapse of the communist regime, had participated in only three free elections: the parliamentary elections in March 1990, the local elections in May, and the state parliament elections in October.

After a year of unprecedented political developments, many voters were tired of politics, and the campaign was generally routine, if not dull. As expected, the Kohl government was returned, with an increased majority of 134 seats in the expanded parliament. Within the governing coalition the big winners were the Free Democrats, who achieved one of their best results in their history.

The opposition parties were the big losers in 1990. The Social Democrats, securing only 33.5 percent of the vote, dropped to their lowest level since 1957. SPD losses were heavy among middle-class voters—including skilled manual workers, the traditional core of the party's electorate. In the new eastern states the party received less than one-fourth of the vote. This poor performance of the SPD in the east was in part a reaction to Oskar Lafontaine's lukewarm attitude toward unification (see chapter 5). But it also reflected the party's organizational weakness in the new states.

In the east, the former Communist Party, now renamed the Party of Democratic Socialism/Left List (PDS/LL), did secure enough votes under special provisions of the electoral law to enter the new parliament. Eastern German parties needed to receive only 5 percent of the vote in the former territory of the GDR to enter parliament. With about 11 percent in the east, but only 2.4 percent nationwide, the PDS cleared this barrier, as did a coalition of East German Greens and former GDR dissidents (Alliance 90). With the exception of the PDS, the West German party system was successfully transplanted into the east with little disruption.

The 1994 election, only the second national election for easterners and the first since the social and economic upheavals of unification began in early 1991, produced mixed results for all parties, large and small. There was neither a clear winner nor a clear loser. The ruling coalition returned to power, but with a greatly reduced majority of only ten seats, down from 134 in 1990. To carry their small and weakened partner, the Free Democrats, over the 5 percent line, the Christian Democrats had to give up about 4 percent of their vote to the Liberals. The Social Democrats, with 36 percent of the vote, finally ended their string of three straight declines in national elections. But they nonetheless lost their fourth straight national election.

In September 1998 the Social Democrats and Greens finally succeeded in toppling the Kohl-led CDU-FDP coalition that had governed for sixteen years. For the first time in the history of the Federal Republic an entire sitting government was replaced. Previous power shifts, such as those of 1969 and 1982, had involved only one of the coalition parties leaving after an election. The 1998 election was also the first time that German voters replaced an incumbent chancellor.

Unemployment was by far the major campaign issue and the area in which the Kohl government was most vulnerable to opposition criticism. By early 1998 over 4.8 million Germans, or about 11.5 percent of the workforce, were officially unemployed. This represented an increase of almost 100 percent over the 1990 level. High unemployment has also meant increases in poverty and welfare recipients.

But the poor economy was not the only reason for Kohl's defeat. After sixteen years, German voters had grown tired of Chancellor Kohl and wanted at least a new face, if not new policies. Kohl's younger and more telegenic rival, Gerhard Schröder, was consistently ranked ahead of the chancellor in polls throughout the campaign. Indeed, Schröder's appeal cut across party lines, with about 10 percent of Christian Democrats preferring Schröder over their own candidate.[24]

Kohl and the Christian Democrats suffered massive losses in the east. With an unemployment level approaching 20 percent, almost double the national average, eastern voters who had supported Kohl and the Union in 1990 and 1994 were now looking for alternatives. Many felt betrayed by Kohl's vision of flowering landscapes, full employment, prosperity, and high-tech-powered growth. Manual workers, those hit hardest by unemployment, left Kohl and the CDU in droves; between 1994 and 1998 the proportion of eastern workers voting for the Christian Democrats dropped from 52 percent to only 32 percent, about the same level of support that western voters gave the CDU.[25] Generally, there were signs of a convergence in the two electorates in 1998 that had not been noticeable in 1990 and 1994. The 1998 election also showed how important eastern Germany had become for election outcomes.

In 2002 a series of unique events late in the campaign, discussed in chapter 5, saved the Schröder government from certain defeat. The final result was a dead heat between the major parties, but the Greens, due mainly to the popularity of their leader, Foreign Minister Joschka Fischer, received a record 8.6 percent of the party vote. The potential partner of the Christian Democrats, the Free Democrats, came in at 7.4 percent. When all the votes were counted and the excess mandates were calculated, the SPD-Green government was returned with a majority of only eleven seats.

The last-minute swing to the government in 2002 was a further indication of the growing volatility of German voters. In the final weeks of the 2002 campaign, almost a fourth of the electorate were still undecided. This is the group that can be swayed by media events such as U.S.-style "presidential" debates and the mistakes of tired candidates such as the comparison one SPD cabinet member made between U.S. president George W. Bush and Adolf Hitler.

The 2005 and 2009 Elections: The End of Two-Party Dominance?

In 2005 and 2009 the two largest parties—the Christian Democrats and the Social Democrats—were actually the losers of the election. In 2002 each party secured about 38.5 percent of the vote; in 2005 the SPD dropped to 34.2 percent and the CDU/CSU to 35.2 percent. For the Christian Democrats, 2005 was the third-poorest result in their history; only the 1949 and 1998 elections were worse. The Social Democrats in 2005 dropped to their lowest level since 1990. The combined two-party share of the vote was the smallest since 1949. The two smaller opposition parties, the Free Democrats and the PDS, made the largest gains. Escaping relatively unscathed were the Greens—the junior partner of the Social Democrats—who declined only slightly. The 2005 elections also marked the first time since 1949 that neither major party was able to form a coalition in which one would be the dominant partner. All sorts of coalition possibilities that previously were unthinkable were now being discussed. A minimal winning coalition would have required that both the FDP and the Greens agree to join either the SPD in a "Traffic Light" (Red, Green, Yellow) coalition, or the CDU/CSU in a "Jamaica" coalition, named after the colors Black (CDU), Yellow (FDP), and Green of the Jamaican national flag. A third possibility, a Red (SPD)–Red (PDS)–Green alignment, was never even remotely likely since long before the elections both the SPD and the Greens categorically rejected any alliance with the PDS. In any case, this party ran a campaign of "fundamental opposition" with no interest in governing, at least in the short term.

As the campaign began, the SPD expected to lose. Following the intraparty tumult over Schröder's Agenda 2010, the party was more interested in holding its base against the expected challenge from the left than in reaching voters in the center of the electorate. While Schröder initially viewed the election as a referendum on his reform policies, many of which were opposed by the traditionalists in his party, other factions in the SPD considered both the election and Schröder's Agenda 2010 to be lost causes. They were focused on unifying what was left of the SPD and preparing it for the opposition role.

As the short campaign began, Merkel's Christian Democrats enjoyed almost a twenty-point lead. But with about six weeks until election day, the CDU shifted its focus from the failures of the Schröder government to its own plans for further reform, which included higher taxes and additional cuts in social programs. This gave the Social Democrats the opportunity to change the campaign themes from defending their own governing record to zeroing in on the dangers of the "heartless, cold" plans of Merkel. The "Merkel tax" (a proposed increase in the value-added tax) and the radical proposals of her designated finance minister became the focus of the SPD's campaign. This approach worked. By the end of the campaign, Merkel's huge lead had dwindled to almost nothing. The major beneficiary was the Free Democratic Party. But since their gains came at the expense of the Christian Democrats, their combined total fell short of the majority needed to govern. To govern as the dominant party, both the CDU and the SPD would have needed not one but two partners. This quickly proved to be politically impossible. There was then no viable alternative except a Grand Coalition.

In September 2009, the seventeenth postwar election and the fifth since unification, voters gave a majority of the parliamentary seats to the Christian Democrats and their old coalition partner, the Free Democrats. Merkel remained chancellor, and the Social Democrats went into opposition for the first time since 1998. The Christian Democrats' new partner, the Free Democrats, returned to government after eleven years out of power. Many voters, however, stayed home, dropping the turnout rate to 70.8 percent, the lowest level in the history of the Federal Republic. The SPD campaign largely ignored the Agenda 2010 program and former Chancellor Schröder that had so divided and weakened the party. Instead, it returned to the traditional themes of social justice and unwavering support for the welfare state, partially motivated by the desire to outmaneuver the new Left Party. It attempted to project itself as the guardian of social trust and an anchor in the world economic crisis. The CDU, its partner since 2005, was portrayed as the party of rich capitalists and managers, which would dismantle the welfare system that had given Germany social peace and prosperity for sixty years. Voters, however, did not buy this argument, and SPD support dropped from 34.2 percent to 23.0 percent, its worst performance in the history of the Federal Republic. Contributing to this defeat was the low turnout. Although Merkel's Union parties won the election, they also saw their vote total decline, albeit far less than the Social Democrats. Nevertheless, the CDU/CSU's 33.8 percent was its worst performance since the Federal Republic's first election in 1949. Much of this was due to the disappointing performance of the CSU in Bavaria and to Union supporters giving their second votes to the FDP.

This decline of the once dominant "major parties" indicates that many voters have lost their ties to these "elephants" and are looking for new alternatives. The combined vote of the elephants in 2009 reached its lowest level in the history of the Federal Republic. The Social Democrats' 23 percent was not just the lowest level of support since 1949, but since 1893. The big winner in 2009 was the Free Democratic Party, which received almost 15 percent of the vote, by far the best result in its history. The FDP's clear message of tax cuts and reduced government spending resonated especially among younger middle-class voters. But the other "small" parties also did well. Both the Left Party and the Greens, with 12 percent and 10.7 percent, respectively, achieved record highs in voter support. Among the "other" parties, the Pirates (advocating civil and privacy rights online), which did not even exist until 2006, received the support of about one in every ten new, first-time voters or 2 percent of the second ballot vote.

This trend is not confined to Germany. Europe's once-dominant catchall parties—both traditional center-right and center-left alternatives—are in decline. In addition to Germany, France, the UK, Austria, Ireland, and the Netherlands have seen these parties' electoral support drop by about 30 percent from postwar highs. Likewise, their organizations, as measured by membership, have weakened. The key factor, according to many observers, is the changing European social structure, specifically the steady drop in trade union membership and church attendance. Social Democratic and Christian Democratic support was rooted in dense milieus associated with the church, especially the Roman Catholic and the trade unions. To be integrated into these subcultures meant a lifetime of voting left or center-right. Just as the pews are empty and labor union rolls are shrinking, so is the vote for the parties associated with these social groups. In this context, which has been developing for decades, voting becomes more of a "consumer choice rather than an expression of loyalty."[26] People no longer spend twenty years in a job; why should they stick with the same party for decades?

But as much as the elephants have their troubles, the smaller parties also face challenges. While the Greens in 2009 failed in their goal to return to government, the postelection decline of the Free Democrats and their increasing conflicts with Merkel's Christian Democrats led some in the CDU to openly speculate about an eventual national coalition with the Greens, a party the Union once derided as a collection of left-wing radicals who represented a threat to the Republic's democratic stability. The Greens returned the favor by openly discussing a possible alignment with the Union. But this is a risky strategy that could alienate their core electorates. Both the FDP and the Left in 2009 became single-issue parties, and they experienced both the advantages and the disadvantages of this strategy. For the FDP it was tax cuts; for the Left it was reform of the Hartz IV welfare/unemployment program. The FDP hoped for a surge in middle-class support, the Left from disgruntled SPD voters and the unemployed, especially in the east. Both were successful in achieving the highest vote totals in their history (for the FDP largely because of vote splitting). But shortly after the election, issues changed to emphasize debt reduction, the Euro crisis, nuclear power, and unrest in the Middle East and North Africa (e.g., Libya). Neither party had any convincing answers to the new items on the public agenda. Also the rapidly improving economy after 2010 brought unemployment down to levels not seen since 1992. Even in the east, by mid-2011 unemployment was in the single digits for the first time since unification.

BASIC ORIENTATIONS OF THE ELECTORATE

Ideology

In light of deep antidemocratic traditions and the twelve years of Nazi socialization, most observers were quite pessimistic about the political orientations of postwar West Germans. Yet the absence of major electoral support for parties proposing drastic changes in the political and economic order of the Federal Republic, as well as the success enjoyed by the Social Democrats since they moved more to the center of the political spectrum decades ago, indicates that the electorate had little interest in extremist or ideological parties and politics. This lack of support for extremist parties and the early stability of the Federal Republic came as a surprise to many. Recent research has shown, however, that the areas of Germany that became the Federal Republic were among the most modern and industrialized of prewar Germany and thus were more supportive of democracy.[27] The Christian Democrats during the 1950s and 1960s were a middle-of-the-road party par excellence, and they were essentially joined by the Social Democrats in the early 1960s. Survey data on the ideological orientations of the electorate tend to substantiate this interpretation. Figure 6.2 presents the ideological self-image of the electorate in 2012. As the figure shows, the great majority of voters are somewhere in the center; over 90 percent are either "moderate" left, center, or "moderate" right. Given these orientations, electoral success in the Federal Republic clearly resides in the vital center of the political spectrum.

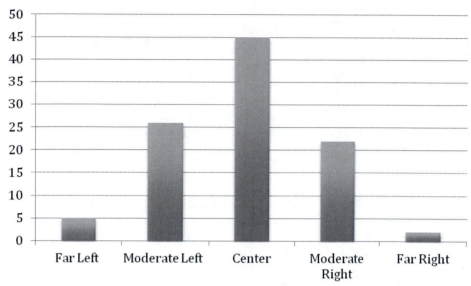

Figure 6.2.   Ideological self-estimate of the electorate, 2012 (in percent).

Source: Forschungsgruppe Wahlen, Politbarometer, August 2012.

Party Preference

As table 6.3 indicates, most Germans still tend to vote for the same party from election to election. The consistency of support is roughly similar for the major parties, with both managing to retain approximately 75 percent of their supporters between elections. The Free Democrats, however, have had the most unstable electorate by far; the party has generally been able to hold only about 40 percent of its voters from the previous election. But in recent elections the Green electorate has also shown substantial volatility. Overall volatility, the change of party preferences between elections, has steadily increased and now stands at the highest level in the history of the Federal Republic.

DETERMINANTS OF VOTING BEHAVIOR

Sociodemographic Factors

Social class, usually measured through occupation, and religion have traditionally been the most important demographic factors structuring the party vote in western Germany. The hard core of the Social Democratic electorate has been composed of manual workers. The Christian Democratic Union, on the other hand, enjoys a high level of support among independent nonmanuals (professionals, the self-employed), including farmers. The Free Democrats have received their strongest support from white-collar workers or salaried nonmanuals, sometimes referred to as the "new middle class," in contrast to the CDU's "old middle class."

Table 6.3. Continuity and Change in Voting Behavior, 1990–2009 (in percent)

	1990/1994	1994/1998	1998/2002	2002/2005	2005/2009
Supported the same party at both elections	54	55	55	58	54
Changed party choice between elections	24	23	34	31	34
New voters/nonvoters	22	22	11	11	12

Source: Forschungsgruppe Wahlen survey nos. 720, 864, Forschungsgruppe Wahlen, Bundestagswahl 1998. For 2002, 2005, and 2009 computed from exit poll data provided by the Forschungsgruppe Wahlen. We are indebted to Dr. Dieter Roth for these materials.

In terms of the religious factor, the overall relationship in the west has also been quite clear: Christian Democratic support is greatest among Catholics, especially those with a strong attachment to the church, which is usually measured by church attendance. On the other hand, the Social Democrats and Liberals receive disproportionate support from Protestants with moderate or weak attachment to their religion. Because Protestants, as compared to Catholics, are less likely to attend church regularly and are less attached to their church, it may well be more accurate to term SPD and FDP supporters as more *secular* than CDU/CSU voters. But, given that church attendance is declining rapidly even in Catholic areas, perhaps it is better to speak about individuals being only nominally or even culturally Catholic.

Thus far in the still brief electoral history of the eastern states, the relationships of social class, religion, and voting found in the western region have yet to develop. In the east, most working-class voters in various elections from March to December 1990 supported the Christian Democrats. In the March 1990 parliamentary elections, for example, approximately 55 percent of manual workers in the east supported the CDU or its conservative allies. In the December 1990 federal election, approximately 60 percent of manual voters voted for the CDU or the FDP.[28] In the industrialized southern regions of Saxony and Thuringia, worker support for the western German middle-class parties was higher still. In 1998, however, these differences diminished as eastern voters began to converge with their western cousins. The Social Democrats, for example, made substantial gains in 1998 among eastern blue-collar voters.

But in 2005 many manual workers in the eastern states left the Social Democrats for the Left Party. Indeed, among eastern manual workers in 2005, the SPD and the Left Party each received about 30 percent of the vote. Their combined eastern total of 58 percent was considerably higher than their western level of 46 percent. Thus, thanks to the Left Party, the class cleavage has finally become significant in the eastern states.

Religion in the east and west continues to play different roles in structuring the party vote. The religious cleavage in the east falls between Protestants and Catholics on the one hand, and those with no religious affiliation on the other. Both eastern Catholics and eastern Protestants have given strong support (50 to 60 percent) to the Christian Democrats. But three-quarters of the eastern states' population, as compared to over a third in the west, have no religious affiliation today. This group is far more likely to vote for the Social Democrats or Left Party. These differences may well change as the eastern electorate matures and the Social Democrats, together with the trade unions, organize and mobilize eastern workers. Over twenty years after reunification and despite the reorganization of the churches in the east, there has not been an increase in religious affiliation, or even a return to precommunist levels. In fact, the eastern electorate has become even more secularized.

Some analysts have also argued that "normal" elections for easterners only began after 1998. The elections of 1990 and 1994 were influenced by the exceptional atmosphere created by reunification. Easterners temporarily forgot their forty years of socialization under a system that emphasized a strong state and social and economic equality. Even though an economic depression had set in almost immediately after 1990, many easterners were patiently waiting for the "blossoming landscapes" that Helmut Kohl had promised. But in 1998, easterners returned home to the "left" parties, Social Democrats and the PDS. In 2002 the Social Democrats increased their lead over the CDU in the east. Indeed, without their 11.5 percent advantage over the CDU in the east, the Social Democrats would have lost the 2002 election.

Three other demographic factors of some importance are age, gender, and place of residence (rural community, urban-metropolitan area). Generally, younger voters entering the electorate for the first time (especially since 1980) have been more likely to support the SPD or the Greens than the CDU/CSU. Since 1983 the overall importance of the age factor increased sharply as the Greens made a successful appeal to new and young voters. Approximately one of every five new voters in 1983 supported the Greens; among the rest of the electorate, the party received the vote of only about one of every twenty voters. Age, rather than class or religion, was the most important determinant of support for the Greens. In the 2005 election, however, support for the Greens was highest among the thirty-five- to forty-five-year-old group. Almost 12 percent of this middle-aged group voted Green. In 2009 and likely in 2013, the youngest voters have begun to support the Pirate Party. The elephants have done best with voters over the age of sixty.

There were sizable differences in the party vote of men and women, at least until 1972. In four elections held between 1957 and 1969, the percentage of women supporting the CDU/CSU exceeded that of males by about 10 percentage points. Female support for the SPD, however, was on the average about 6 percent below that of males. It is ironic indeed that Germany's "left" party, which consistently fought for women's suffrage, was not rewarded at the polls. If the electorate had been composed only of males, the SPD would have become the strongest party by 1965 instead of 1972.

This tendency toward disproportionate support for the CDU among females was halted in the 1972 election as the difference in male-female support for the CDU/CSU dropped to only 3 percent. In the case of the SPD, the male-female difference declined to only 1 percent in 1972 and 1976. In 1980 the Social Democrats for the first time actually received more support from females than from males. In the 1990 and 1994 elections there was no significant gender gap in the unified German electorate. This pattern has continued in subsequent elections.

In 2005 and 2009, for example, there were once again only minor gender differences within the CDU or SPD electorates. For example, both women and men abandoned the SPD at about the same level.

These demographic variables, then, form the major structural determinants of voting behavior. Yet by themselves they do little to explain the dynamics of this behavior and, specifically, the factors that produce social changes in party support between elections and over the course of several decades. To explain these aspects of voting behavior, most analysts explore the dynamic interrelationships of *social change* and *electoral choice*, together with opinions of candidates, party policies, and issues. A fuller understanding of voting and its function in the political system must also take these factors into account.

Voter Dynamics

Social Change

As we have seen, the core of the Social Democrats' vote has been among manual workers, while the Christian Democrats do best among Catholics. What, then, of Catholic workers? Or unionized, low-paid, white-collar workers? SPD support is strongest among younger voters, manual workers, Protestants with marginal attachments to their church, and residents of large metropolitan areas. CDU/CSU support is centered in older age groups, middle-class workers, Catholics with strong attachments to the church, farmers, and voters in small towns. What about young Catholic women living in metropolitan areas? Social scientists refer to these groups of voters as *cross-pressured*: their socioeconomic positions expose them to conflicting political communications. Their support for any one party tends to be less constant than that of voters with consistent attributes, such as older Catholic women living in villages or young manual workers with little interest in religion living in metropolitan areas. The size of the cross-pressured segment of the electorate has been estimated at approximately one-third and growing as German social structures become more complex.

Another important source of change can be found in the class and religious composition of the electorate. As discussed in chapter 3, the size of both manual worker segments of the workforce has declined in the postwar period, whereas the number of Germans in new middle-class occupations has increased greatly. Members of the new middle class are university-educated professionals such as teachers, engineers, managers, and middle-level administrators. New middle-class voters are generally more likely to change their vote from election to election than are voters in manual or old middle-class occupations such as small business owners. This development is shown in table 6.4, which presents the party preferences of the three class groups since 1994. The old middle class remains largely the preserve of the CDU and the FDP, with these two parties combined receiving about 70 percent of the vote. In 1994 the smaller parties, especially the Greens and in the east the PDS, took some votes away from the established parties among this group. The long-term decline in the size of the old middle class, however, reduces its importance in explaining aggregate change.

Table 6.4.   Party Vote by Class, 1998–2009 (in percent)

Party	Old Middle Class				New Middle Class				Working Class			
	1998	2002	2005	2009	1998	2002	2005	2009	1998	2002	2005	2009
CDU/CSU	56	51	53	47	31	36	37	34	30	37	32	31
SPD	21	18	23	15	42	40	34	25	48	44	37	25
FDP	12	11	14	19	7	7	18	13	3	6	8	13
Greens, others	14	17	10	19	20	17	11	18	19	13	23	31

Source: For 1998, Forschungsgruppe Wahlen, *Bundestagswahl 1998* (Mannheim, 1998), 22; for 2002, 2005, and 2009, Forschungsgruppe Wahlen, exit poll data.

The expanding new middle-class part of the electorate has been more volatile since the 1980s than has the old middle class or the working class. In 2005 and 2009 many voters in this group turned to the FDP as its vote increased. But soon after the 2009 election many of these voters moved away from the FDP. In 2005, the SPD lost its narrow advantage over the CDU among this swing group, and this continued in 2009. The Green proportion of the new middle-class vote remained above the party's national average. In 1983, when the Greens first cleared the 5 percent mark and entered parliament, they received only 6 percent from this group.[29] The Greens are clearly more a middle-class than a working-class party.

Among working-class voters there are also signs of growing volatility. Traditionally, the Social Democrats have done best among blue-collar workers. But as table 6.4 shows, since 1998 the proportion of manual workers supporting the SPD has dropped from 48 percent to only 25 percent. This sharp drop was largely due to discontent among trade union members with the Agenda 2010 program. The Left Party has been the major beneficiary of the declining working-class support for the large parties.

The growing secularization of the Federal Republic has also changed the significance of the religious factor in voting behavior. In the 1950s more than 40 percent of the electorate attended church on a weekly basis; by the time of the 1994 election less than 20 percent attended church as regularly, and by 2009 less than 10 percent did.[30] Among German Catholics, regular church attendance declined from 54 percent in 1953 to 20 percent in 2002.[31] In 1953, six of every ten Catholics reported attending services every Sunday or almost every Sunday. By 2005 only two out of ten Catholics regularly attended services.[32]

This trend can be seen in table 6.5, which presents the support level for Christian Democrats since 1983 among Catholics and Protestants. The CDU/CSU remains the preferred party for German Catholics, but their support has declined from 65 percent in 1983 to only 44 percent in the 2009 election. Overall, the importance of religion for the CDU vote has dropped. In 1983 the CDU/CSU received 25 percent more support among Catholics than among non-Catholics; by 2009 this gap had narrowed to only 12 percent. As fewer voters are exposed to the social and political cues of a religious milieu, they are more likely to turn to some other source in making their voting decisions.

Table 6.5.   Support for the CDU/CSU by Religion, 1987–2009 (in percent)

	1987	1994	1998	2002	2005	2009
Catholics	51	55	47	49	48	44
Protestants	33	40	32	36	34	32
Difference	18	15	15	13	14	12

Source: Forschungsgruppe Wahlen, election surveys. Because of the small number of Catholics in the eastern states, these figures refer only to West Germany.

Candidates: The Chancellor Bonus

As in other Western societies, the incumbent government has a distinct advantage over the opposition. Its ability to dominate the news, announce new programs such as tax reductions and pension increases, and proclaim foreign policy successes, all timed to the campaign and election, are well-known tactics in British and American politics that are also practiced in Germany. The announcement of new policies, subsidies to various interest groups, and trips to major European allies for special conferences (and lots of photographs) are standard pre-election procedures for any chancellor.

The government also benefits from certain features of the political culture. Germans like to perceive their government as strong and decisive, as something certain in a world of uncertainty, something they can count on to protect and maintain the social order. These orientations provide an advantage for any incumbent government, and any chancellor quickly learns to tap these cultural supports of governmental authority.

When Willy Brandt challenged Adenauer for the chancellorship in 1961, the electorate (according to public opinion polls) preferred the incumbent by a three-to-two margin. When Brandt ran against the then-popular Chancellor Ludwig Erhard in 1965, Brandt fell further behind; Erhard was preferred by a five-to-two margin. Even in 1969, when Brandt as foreign minister campaigned against Chancellor Kiesinger, Brandt could not overcome the handicap of opposition; Kiesinger was the electorate's favorite as chancellor by an almost two-to-one margin. In 1972, however, Brandt, as the incumbent, enjoyed a similar advantage over his Christian Democratic rival, Rainer Barzel. From 1949 to 1969 it was the CDU/CSU that benefited from this bonus, whereas from 1972 to 1980 the SPD and its chancellor candidates, Brandt and Helmut Schmidt, were the beneficiaries. In 1998, however, the chancellor bonus disappeared as Kohl's challenger, Gerhard Schröder, maintained a strong lead over Kohl throughout the campaign.

In 2002 the incumbent Gerhard Schröder maintained a substantial lead over his challenger, Edmund Stoiber, throughout the campaign. Indeed, until the last-minute swing to the government in mid-August, the chancellor's greater popularity was the only bright spot for the SPD. German voters considered the chancellor to be more credible and sympathetic than his opponent, but when it came to concrete economic policies, above all jobs, these same voters opted for the challenger. They liked Schröder more than Stoiber, but they believed that Stoiber would be able to deal more effectively with the economy than the incumbent would.

Three years later in the 2005 election, Schröder looked like a sure loser. Indeed, his party had essentially given up on him. But CDU mistakes enabled him to go on the offensive, and by the end of the campaign, 53 percent of the electorate wanted him to remain as chancellor while only 39 percent supported Merkel.[33] In 2009, Chancellor Merkel became the beneficiary of the bonus. Throughout the campaign she consistently held a lead of about 30 percent over her SPD rival, Steinmeier. But her high level of popularity was not enough to significantly lift the fortunes of her party.

Party Policies

The policies and programs of a party are another dynamic factor affecting voting behavior. The SPD between 1957 and 1972 made steady gains of about 3 percent in each federal election. Most of this increase came from new voters and from middle-class voters who had previously supported the bourgeois parties. This growth in support was related to changes in SPD policies since the late 1950s. The party made a major effort to attract middle-class support by abandoning the more radical or Marxist components of its programs (nationalization of industry and banks, and national economic planning) and attempting to project itself as a modern, innovative party that nevertheless accepted the basic characteristics of the postwar social and economic order. Moreover, when the Social Democrats did come to power at the national level through the 1966 Grand Coalition (discussed in chapter 5), they assumed the Ministry of Economics and thus were afforded the opportunity to demonstrate to the electorate that the party could outperform the CDU/CSU and was not a group of irresponsible radicals who could not handle money and finances. Thus the policies and behavior of the party, as surveys have shown, reduced the impact of social class and spurred changes in voting behavior to the net benefit of the SPD.

The personnel and strategy decisions of the parties can also influence electoral outcomes. For example, the selection of Franz-Josef Strauss by the CDU/CSU as its chancellor candidate in 1980 was a major factor in the party's subsequent electoral defeat.[34] The SPD's decision in 1983 to all but ignore the unemployment issue and emphasize noneconomic issues such as the NATO missile decision was another strategic error that cost the party sizable blue-collar support.[35] During the 1987 campaign, both parties made questionable strategy choices. The Christian Democrats underestimated the extent of discontent among farmers, many of whom stayed home.[36] The SPD's decision to seek an absolute majority lacked credibility in the view of most voters.[37] To compound the problem, the party essentially abandoned this approach about two months before the January 1987 vote. In 1990 the SPD badly misread public opinion on unification. Its ambivalent approach was out of step with the generally positive attitude most voters had about the unification process. In 1998 the CDU/CSU should have replaced Helmut Kohl as its chancellor candidate. Kohl's decision to run one more time was a critical factor in their defeat. The Union in 1998 was also unable to convince voters that it had a solution for the problem of mass unemployment. In 2002 the CDU decided to focus its campaign almost exclusively on the economy. For most of the campaign it looked like a winner until the last six weeks when events that the party leadership had not anticipated derailed Stoiber's victory express. The Union had no alternative to the Iraq war issue and the floods.

During the 2005 campaign, as discussed above, the CDU and Merkel made some fundamental policy and strategy mistakes that enabled a rejuvenated SPD to almost close a twenty-point deficit in the polls. First it stopped focusing on the failures of the Schröder government, an approach that had given it a commanding lead since 2002. Second, its "campaign of honesty," featuring above all a promised tax increase and cuts in subsidies, was "all gloom and no hope. There was no over-arching positive, warm future perspective within which these sacrifices could be softened."[38]

But without question the single biggest mistake of the 2005 Merkel campaign was the appointment on August 17, with only a month left in the campaign, of Professor Paul Kirchhof to Merkel's "Competence Team" or shadow government. Although he had no party affiliation, Merkel made him her choice for finance minister, one of the key positions in any government. Although he was a highly respected jurist and academic, Kirchhof was new to politics and the practice of the media. Not content to restrict himself to tax policies, which are the responsibility of the finance minister, he began to expound on pensions, family policy, and education. His positions on these issues, however, were at odds with Merkel and the CDU program. The CDU with the Kirchhof caper allowed the SPD to change the focus of their campaign from "defense to offense." In the last weeks of the campaign, Schröder's biggest applause line was his riff on this "Heidelberg professor" with his "strange ideas about taxes and social welfare, which treated people as objects, as test animals." Clearly unsettled by the SPD's portrayal of the plan, the CDU banished Kirchhof to obscure provincial venues for the remainder of the campaign. Not surprisingly, in election day surveys, almost 70 percent of voters stated that Kirchhof had damaged Merkel and the CDU.[39] As mentioned above, Merkel did not repeat these mistakes in 2009, which was widely considered "the shortest and softest" campaign in the Federal Republic's history. When asked about the campaign in postelection surveys, over 80 percent of voters stated that it was of little or no help to them in reaching a decision.[40] Even the debate in 2009 between Merkel and her opponent, Frank-Walter Steinmeier, who had been her foreign minister, was labeled more of a "duet" than a confrontation.

Issues

In preelection surveys, national samples of voters were given a list of policy issues or problems. Each voter was asked to name the issues that were personally "very important" to him or her. Table 6.6 ranks the issues according to the percentage of respondents stating that the particular issue area was personally "very important." If 60 percent or more of the sample regarded the issue as very important, its salience was coded as high; if 40 to 59 percent rated it so, its salience was medium; and if 0 to 39 percent gave it this rating, its salience was low.

In both 2002 and 2005, economic issues, above all unemployment, topped the list of voter concerns. Environmental protection, a major concern in the 1990s, was nowhere to be found by 2002. The post-1990 revelations of widespread

Table 6.6.   Rank Order of Major Campaign Issues by Salience to the Electorate, 2002 and 2005

Salience	Issue		
	2002	2005	2009
High (above 60%)	Unemployment	Unemployment	
Medium (40%–59%)			Unemployment
Low (0%–39%)	War/terrorism	Prices/wages	Economic conditions
	Economy	Pensions	Banking/finance crisis
	Immigrants	Taxes	Education/schools
			Prices/wages
			Health

Source: For 2002, Forschungsgruppe Wahlen, *Bundestagswahl 2002* (Mannheim, 2002), 42; for 2005, *Bundestagswahl 2005*, 52; for 2009, Forschungsgruppe Wahlen as reported in http://www.kas.de/wf/doc/kas_18443-544-1-30.pdf.

environmental damage in the eastern region had made this question "very important" to almost three-fourths of the voters in earlier campaigns. By 2009, the proportion choosing unemployment as the most pressing issue had declined to 58 percent, whereas it was above 80 percent before the last three elections. That election was noteworthy for no one issue overwhelming voters' concerns, but rather a variety of smaller concerns.

As in many other modern democracies, most German elections tend to be focused on domestic issues, particularly the economy. In survey after survey preceding the 1998, 2002, and 2005 elections, voters in the west overwhelmingly considered unemployment the most important problem. Of course in the east it has been the top problem almost since reunification in 1990. Whereas in past elections—especially those of 1990 and 1994—noneconomic issues such as the environment, "law and order," or "peace" (missiles, disarmament) have equaled or surpassed economic issues in importance, this was not the case in 2002 until the last weeks of the campaign. In 2005 these noneconomic issues were nowhere to be found, but they did return in 2009 with, for example, 12 percent mentioning education, 6 percent families/youth, and 5 percent pensions.

At the depth of the economic problems in 2002, public confidence in Schröder's economic policies was very low, and many voters doubted if either party could turn the economy around. In one of the last preelection polls, 33 percent of the electorate believed that CDU candidate Stoiber could deal better with the country's economic problems as compared to only 24 percent for Schröder, but 37 percent had no confidence in the economic competence of either candidate.[41] In 2005 the CDU/CSU early in the campaign held a major advantage over the SPD in this area of economic competence. But it quickly disappeared under the impact of Merkel's campaign mistakes. By 2009, 40 percent of the electorate trusted the Union to solve the country's major problems, almost twice the percent who thought that the SPD would do better.

The 2002 election was also unique because for the first time since the 1983 election a foreign policy issue—the looming Iraq war—played a significant role in a national election. Chancellor Schröder's opposition to any German participation in military action against the Saddam Hussein regime had three important benefits for the government. First, it diverted voter attention from the core economic issues that had previously dominated the campaign. Second, it mobilized many dormant SPD supporters—especially the party's traditionalist left wing. Finally, polls showed that it boosted SPD support among women. The 2002 election was also the first time since the 1961 building of the Berlin Wall that unanticipated events late in the campaign, the flooding in eastern Germany, played a critical role. In 2005 and 2009, voters showed little interest in foreign policy problems.

In 2009 in spite of the worldwide economic downturn and public concern about jobs, the economy was not a major issue. Indeed, as one analysis put it, "It was the dog that barked, but did not bite."[42] One reason was that the dog's two owners—the Christian Democrats and the Social Democrats—had muzzled it during the campaign. Their Grand Coalition alignment meant that neither party had any incentive to politicize the financial, credit, and economic distress of the country. Sharing governmental responsibility also meant that it was difficult to stake out an advantageous campaign position. Moreover, the measures that were taken by the Grand Coalition after September 2008—a multibillion-Euro bank bailout, deposit guarantees, two stimulus packages, and "cash for clunkers" (Abwrackprämie), together with well-established safety nets—have enabled Germany to weather the storm in better condition than most of its neighbors and trading partners.

But only Merkel and her CDU, and not the SPD, received any credit for these policies. The voters gave the chancellor's party the credit for the economic upturn during the Grand Coalition and punished the Social Democrats who six years earlier had enacted the very programs that made the quick economic recovery possible. The Social Democrats in 2009 could certainly cite the old adage that "life is not fair."

SUMMARY AND CONCLUSION

German voters from 1949 to 2002 concentrated their support on two major parties and two small but important "third" parties. In fact, from the 1950s to mid-1980s there was only a single third party, the FDP. After two decades of governments dominated by the Christian Democrats, the electorate in 1969 used the ballot to give the longtime opposition party, the Social Democrats, the major share of political responsibility for the first time. Throughout the 1950s the center-right parties (the CDU plus small middle-class parties) secured about 70 percent of the popular vote, and the center-left SPD secured only 30 percent, but by 1980 the distribution of preferences had changed to about 55 percent for the center-left and 45 percent for the center-right. Yet in 1983 the SPD monopoly over the center-left segment of the electorate was broken as the first new party in thirty years, the Greens, gained entrance to parliament.

Voters have also increasingly turned away from both major parties; the Christian Democrats and the Social Democrats together now command the allegiance of under 60 percent of the electorate. There are now two reasonably large parties and three established smaller parties that in 2009 receive 40 percent of the vote.

Finally, since 1990, Germany's new voters in the east have further complicated the electoral landscape. About one eastern voter in five has supported the former communists (now part of the Left Party), and eastern voters are more inclined to change their vote between elections than are their western counterparts. In 2009, 20 percent of the electorate in the five eastern states supported the Left Party.

These changes in voter behavior have been accompanied by a growing politicization and mobility of the electorate. Interest in elections, knowledge and concern about issues, and readiness to switch party allegiance have increased. Voters are drifting from their once-firm demographic moorings as the concrete performance of parties, their leadership, and their treatment of policy issues become relatively more important in determining voting behavior than are social class or religion. This is, then, an electorate that is in transition in the sense of becoming more sophisticated about issues and policies and more willing to use the ballot to achieve political change and secure the desired policy outputs.

NOTES

1. In addition, after unification, the Bundestag election scheduled for 1991 was moved up to December 1990.

2. The redistricting for the 2002 election resulted in changes in 167 districts. Because of population shifts since unification, the eastern states lost disproportionately more seats than the western Länder.

3. In seven states—Bremen, North Rhine–Westphalia, Rhineland-Palatinate, Baden-Württemberg, Schleswig-Holstein, Brandenburg, and Berlin—the voting age for local elections is sixteen.

4. This was not true, of course, for the voters in the few districts the PDS was trying to win in 1994 and 1998. In those seats, the first ballot was more important.

5. Most voters do not understand this system. In one survey, only 30 percent correctly identified the second ballot as more important than the first; 14 percent believed the first was more important than the second; 48 percent stated that the two ballots were equally important; and the remaining 8 percent of the sample knew nothing about the system. Institut für Demoskopie survey cited in *Frankfurter Allgemeine Zeitung*, October 5, 1994, 5.

6. This is, strictly speaking, not an exception to proportionality but the application of proportionality if the three-district victory requirement is met.

7. For the 1990 election, a one-time-only modification of the electoral law was in effect. In order for the smaller parties in the former East Germany to have a better chance to enter the national parliament, they were required to secure a minimum of 5 percent in the new eastern states, the "old" West Germany, or the country as a whole. East German parties were also allowed to submit joint or combined lists in order to increase their chances of meeting the 5 percent minimum. These special provisions were added to the electoral law at the insistence of the Federal Constitutional Court, which threw out a law favored by the large West German parties that the Court ruled was unfair to voters in the former GDR.

8. Author's calculations from official statistics. The media and political education outlets also now routinely inform voters about how they can split their ballots. This system is ideally suited for tactical voting.

9. Der Bundeswahlleiter, Wahl zum 17. Deutschen Bundestag am 27. September 2009, Heft 4 "Wahlbeteiligung und Stimmabgabe der Männer und Frauen nach Altersgruppen" (Wiesbaden, 2010), 18–19.

10. Federal Statistical Office, "Wahl zum 16. Deutschen Bundestag am 18. September 2005," Heft 4 (Wiesbaden, 2006), 19.

11. Federal Statistical Office, "Wahl zum 16." See also Forschungsgruppe Wahlen post-election surveys cited in *Bundestagswahl 2002* (Mannheim, 2002), 108, 101. Thus far the new Left Party is not as dependent on split-ballot voters. In 2005, 72 percent of its second-ballot vote came from its first-ballot supporters; the respective figure for the FDP was 29 percent and for the Greens 35 percent. Federal Statistical Office, Heft 4, 19.

12. http://www.spiegel.de/politik/deutschland/vergroesserung-des-bundestags-durch-neues-wahlrecht-wird-teuer-a-862032.html. A related proposal might reduce the number of territorial constituencies perhaps to 250 to limit the overall size of the chamber. As of February 2013, this proposal had not yet become law.

13. See Louise Davidson Schmich, "Gender Quota Compliance and Contagion in the 2009 Bundestag Election," in *Between Left and Right: The 2009 Bundestag Election and the Transformation of the German Party System*, ed. Eric Langenbacher (New York: Berghahn Books, 2010).

14. Forschungsgruppe Wahlen 2002 postelection surveys.

15. See Sonia Alonso and Sara Claro da Fonseca, "Immigration, Left and Right," paper presented at 2009 American Political Science Association Annual Meeting, Toronto, Canada; Sara Claro da Fonseca, "New Candidates? Candidate Selection and the Mobilisation of Immigrant Voters in German Elections," in *The Political Representation of Immigrants and Minorities*, ed. Karen Bird, Thomas Saalfeld, Andreas M. Wüst (New York: Routledge, 2011).

16. See D. M. Farrell and M. Wortmann, "Party Strategies in the Electoral Market: Political Marketing in West Germany, Britain and Ireland," *European Journal of Political Research* 15 (1987): 297–318, for an account of the role of marketing specialists in German campaigns.

17. Forschungsgruppe Wahlen, "TV-Duell, Umfrage vom 08.09.02," Mannheim, 2002.

18. Max Kaase, "Die Bundestagswahl 1972: Probleme und Analysen," *Politische Vierteljahresschrift* 14, no. 2 (May 1973): 158. For more recent campaigns, see David P. Conradt, "The 1994 Campaign and Election: An Overview," in *Germany's New Politics*, ed. David P. Conradt et al. (Providence, RI: Berghahn Books, 1995), 1–18.

19. Institut für Demoskopie, *Jahrbuch der öffentlichen Meinung, 1968–1973*, vol. 5 (Allensbach: Verlag für Demoskopie, 1975), 337. For corresponding 1976 data, which show that CDU groups were about as frequent as those campaigning for the Social Democrats, see Elisabeth Noelle-Neumann, "Kampf um die öffentliche Meinung" (manuscript, Institut für Demoskopie, Allensbach, Germany, 1977), 25.

20. http://www.cdu.de; http://www.spd.de/aktuelles; http://www.fdp.de; http://www.gruene.de/startseite.html; http://www.die-linke.de.

21. http://www.bpb.de/politik/wahlen/wahl-o-mat.

22. Hartwig Pautz, "The Internet, Political Participation and Election Turnout: A Case Study of Germany's www.abgeordnetenwacth.de," in Langenbacher, *Between Left and Right*, 186.

23. https://lqfb.piratenpartei.de.

24. Forschungsgruppe Wahlen, *Bundestagswahl 1998*, 55–63.

25. Kai Arzheimer and Jürgen W. Falter, "Annäherung durch Wandel? Das Wahlverhalten bei der Bundestagswahl 1998 in Ost-West Perspective," *Aus Politik und Zeitgeschichte*, December 18, 1998, 39.

26. *Economist*, April 30, 2011, 66.

27. Michael Bernhard, "Democratization in Germany: A Reappraisal," *Comparative Politics* 33, no. 4 (2001): 379–400.

28. Forschungsgruppe Wahlen, *Bundestagswahl 1998*, 22ff.

29. Although the Greens have had an antitechnology image that is partially deserved, the party does better among white-collar employees in high-tech occupations than it does among those working in low-tech or traditional technology occupations.

30. Institut für Demoskopie, survey no. 061; Renate Köcher, "Nachhut oder Vorhut?" *Frankfurter Allgemeine Zeitung*, April 5, 1995, 5.

31. Forschungsgruppe Wahlen 2002 exit poll data.

32. For 2002, see Forschungsgruppe Wahlen, "Zweite Runde für Rot-Grün: Die Bundestagswahl vom 22. September 2002," in *Wahlen und Wähler. Analysen aus Anlass der Bundestagswahl 2002*, ed. Jürgen Falter et al. (VS Verlag für Sozialwissenschaften: Wiesbaden, 2005), 15–49. Dieter Roth and Andreas W. Wüst, "Abgang ohne Machtwechsel: Die Bundestagswahl 2005 im Lichte längerfristiger Entwicklungen," *FGM* (Mannheim, 2005), 16.

33. Forschungsgruppe Wahlen, *Bundestagswahl 2005* (Mannheim, 2005), 45.

34. Jürgen W. Falter and Hans Rattinger, "Parteien, Kandidaten und politische Streitfragen bei der Bundestagswahl 1980" (unpublished manuscript, Bundeswehr Hochschule, Munich, June 1981), 85.

35. David P. Conradt and Russell J. Dalton, "The West German Electorate and the Party System: Continuity and Change in the 1980s," *Review of Politics* 50, no. 1 (January 1988): 6.

36. Institut für angewandte Sozialforschung, *Politogramm: Bundestagswahl 1987* (Bonn–Bad Godesberg: INFAS, 1987), 114.

37. Surveys cited in *Der Spiegel*, May 14, 1986, 42, 43.

38. Frank Brettschneider, "Bundestagswahlkampf und Medienberichterstattung," *Aus Politik und Zeitgeschichte*, nos. 51–52 (December 19, 2005): 19–26.

39. *Bundestagswahl 2005*, 55. Even 60 percent of CDU voters agreed that Kirchhof had hurt their party. In his memoirs, former chancellor Schröder termed the Kirchhof appointment "a gift from heaven." Gerhard Schröder, *Entscheidungen. Mein Leben in der Politik* (Hamburg: Hoffmann und Campe Verlag, 2006), cited in *Der Spiegel*, no. 43 (October 23, 2006): 60.

40. University of Mannheim, postelection survey, 2009, variable pos 034, cited in David P. Conradt, "Shrinking Elephants: The 2009 Election and the Changing Party System," *German Politics and Society* 28, no. 3 (Autumn 2010): 27.

41. Forschungsgruppe Wahlen, *Bundestagswahl 2002*, 37.

42. Robert Rohrschneider and Rüdiger Schmitt-Beck, "Understanding the 2009 Election Outcome" (unpublished presentation, Rice University Conference on Germany, Houston, October 2009).

7

Policy-Making Institutions I
Parliament and Executive

In the preceding chapters we have surveyed the historical, socioeconomic, cultural, organizational, and behavioral contexts in which the German political process takes place. We now turn to an examination of the process itself and to its outcomes: governmental policies. The provisional character of the new state created in 1949, the traditional weakness of representative institutions in Germany, the particular circumstances of Allied occupation, and the authoritarian character of the first chancellor, Konrad Adenauer, led to a decision-making process in the early years of the Federal Republic that was clearly dominated by the executive. Since the early 1970s parliament and the judiciary have become more assertive. Unification, the move of the government and parliament to Berlin, and the growing importance of the European Union have also produced new patterns of policy making.

At the outset it must also be kept in mind that Germany is a less centralized state than either the United Kingdom or France and that the sixteen Länder that constitute the Federal Republic play important roles, which are more fully discussed in chapter 9. In addition, at the national level, which concerns us in this chapter, the states have direct influence on policy making through the *Bundesrat*, or Federal Council, an institution whose role has undergone considerable change in recent years. Finally, like other members of the European Union, the Federal Republic has transferred policy-making authority to European institutions in some areas such as agriculture and (since 1999) monetary policy.

There are three major national decision-making structures: (1) the parliament, or *Bundestag*; (2) the Federal Council, or *Bundesrat*; and (3) the federal government, or executive (the chancellor and the cabinet). In addition, a federal president, indirectly elected and having little formal authority for policy making, serves as the ceremonial head of state. Each of these institutions has some precedent in the German political tradition, and their contemporary roles reflect in part the influence of this tradition.

LEGISLATIVE INSTITUTIONS

The Bundestag: The Main Political Battleground

In theory, the center of the policy-making process in the German political system is the Bundestag, or parliament. The Basic Law assigns to it the primary functions of legislation, the election and control of the federal government (chancellor and cabinet), the election of half of the membership of the Federal Constitutional Court, and special responsibilities for supervision of the bureaucracy and military. Its 598 (or more if there are excess mandates) members are elected at least every four years and are the only directly elected political officials in the constitutional structure. In practice, however, this parliament, like its predecessors—the *Reichstag* of the empire (1871–1918) and the Weimar Republic (1919–1933)—has had a long uphill struggle to realize the lofty authority assigned to it in the constitutional documents. Prior to 1949, parliamentary government had both a weak tradition and a poor record of performance in the German political experience.

During the empire, the Reichstag was hindered in the performance of its control and legislative functions by a Prussian-dominated upper house and a government whose chancellor was appointed by the monarch. This, together with executive control of the military (especially its budget) and bureaucracy, left parliament with the partial power of the purse as its main source of influence, but with little direct initiative in the policy-making process. The chamber's posture toward the government was defensive and reactive, and although the government had to seek some accommodation with Reichstag opinion, there was little parliamentary control over the government. The policy successes of the legendary Bismarck, particularly in foreign policy, awed even the most antimonarchical deputy and intensified the reputation of the executive as a branch that *acted*, whereas parliament only *talked*. Nevertheless, there was some evolution toward greater parliamentary power over the course of the empire's existence, and many authors believe that the country was on the cusp of achieving a fuller democracy when World War I broke out.[1]

The Weimar Constitution of 1919 greatly enhanced the power and function of parliament. The executive branch (chancellor and cabinet) was now directly responsible to the lower house and could be removed by a vote of no confidence. In what most analysts regard as a major error, however, the framers of the Weimar system also created a strong, directly elected president independent of parliamentary control. This dual executive of president and chancellor, only one of which could be directly controlled by parliament, created the conditions for conflict and competition between the chancellor and parliament on the one hand, and the president and mighty state bureaucracy on the other. The former became identified as republican institutions; the latter, especially after the 1925 election of the authoritarian monarchist Paul von Hindenburg (a successful general before and during World War I) as president, as antirepublican. This arrangement also put the cabinet somewhere between the chancellor and the president, which encouraged both executives to vie for its support. Thus executive responsibility was not clearly fixed.

In addition, the growing polarization of politics during the Weimar period steadily reduced the strength of prorepublican parties in parliament. After the first parliamentary election in 1919, about three-fourths of the deputies belonged to parties more or less committed to the Republic, but in the last elections of 1932, most deputies belonged to parties (Nazi, Nationalist, and Communist) committed to the destruction in one way or another of the very institution and constitution they were supposed to support. Parliament became increasingly immobile; successive governments in the early 1930s had no parliamentary majority supporting them, yet neither could the parliamentary opposition secure a majority for a new government. The strong president, however, at the request of the chancellor, could and did rule by decree, hardly an ideal situation for a fledgling democracy. Through the incessant attacks of the antirepublican parties, especially the Nazis and communists, but also through their own inexperience and ineptness in the ways of democratic politics, the prorepublican parties and the parliament itself became identified in the public mind as weak, ineffective, and indecisive—a gossip chamber, as the Nazis' propaganda chief, Josef Goebbels, termed it.

The world economic collapse between 1929 and 1930, combined with the government's feeble response, all but ended the parliamentary system. Lacking a majority, the government was unable to act without the crutch of presidential decrees. Government by executive fiat made the legislature superfluous. Finally, by approving Hitler's Enabling Act in March 1933, it ceased to function as a law-making body and became merely an occasional forum for the dictator's public pronouncements.

The Bundestag, established in 1949, inherited this tragic parliamentary tradition. Unlike earlier parliaments, however, in theory at least it no longer had to compete with an executive over which it had no direct control. For the first time in German constitutional history, the Basic Law assigned sole control over government and bureaucracy to parliament. Although this control function of parliament was undercut by the strong leadership of Chancellor Adenauer during the early years of the Federal Republic, the Bundestag since the mid-1960s has begun to assume a role in the policy-making process more congruent with its formal and legal position.

Postwar Germany's Two Capitals

German legislators in Bonn met in the most unpretentious surroundings of any modern parliament. The chamber itself was first built in 1949 as an addition to a former teachers' college. Until 1970 most deputies had to share offices, which were once classrooms, with one or two of their colleagues. From 1988 to 1992, parliament convened in a restored waterworks building while the old chamber was being completely rebuilt, which was then used for only seven years. The city of Bonn, with 300,000 inhabitants crowded into an area suitable for 150,000, was by no means a capital city in the classic European sense, rather the "small town in Germany" of John Le Carré's novel. Conveniently located in the most populous state of North Rhine–Westphalia about seventy kilometers from the Belgian border and five kilometers from Adenauer's home in Rhöndorf, "Bonn was a beginning, a city without a past," as Adenauer once opined about the capital that was intended to be provisional.[2]

The Bonn-Berlin Debate

After unification in 1990 a lively debate began over whether the Bundestag should move to Berlin, always considered the official capital, or remain in Bonn. A growing number of political leaders from other states and cities contended that the postwar federal system would be weakened by moving all government offices from small Bonn to Berlin, the country's largest city. The cost, estimated at over $70 billion, was also frequently cited as a factor against a move. In spite of its disadvantages, Bonn was associated with West Germany's postwar transformation into a stable democracy, a model member of the European community of nations and firmly rooted in and oriented toward the West. For some, Berlin was a symbol of Germany's militaristic, authoritarian, and totalitarian past: the Prussian kaisers and Hitler all waged war from Berlin. Berlin's supporters countered that it was unfair to blame an entire city for the acts of a few individuals many years ago. They pointed to Berlin's steadfast commitment to Western values during the darkest days of the Cold War. The city, surrounded by the former GDR and containing eastern and western halves, also needed the economic boost that parliament and government would bring.

On June 20, 1991, following an emotional eleven-hour debate, the Bundestag voted by a narrow margin to return the seat of government and parliament to Berlin. In the vote, the deputies were not bound by party discipline, but only by their individual consciences. Support for both cities cut across party lines. The decision for Berlin was one of the most important in the chamber's history, affirming parliament's commitment to integrate the eastern states into the larger Federal Republic as soon as possible. It was not until 1996, however, that concrete plans for the actual move to Berlin were finalized. Parliament, the chancellor, and ten of the government's fifteen ministries finally moved to Berlin in 1999. Although this division of ministries is still official, there has been a steady tendency toward relocation and centralization in Berlin, such as the Justice Ministry and the Federal Intelligence Service (Bundesnachrichtendienst).

Mindful of Berlin's past image as the city where the emperor and Hitler attempted to dominate Europe by military force, the city's planners, together with Germany's political leadership, have attempted to design the old/new capital in an open, international, and avant-garde style. The design of many buildings has been entrusted to renowned international architects such as Sir Norman Foster, Daniel Libeskind, and Frank Gehry. Foster was in charge of renovating the old Reichstag, the home of the "new" Bundestag. The chancellery, the president's office, and other governmental structures are adorned with numerous works of art commissioned after international competitions. This "public-art spending spree," according to one authority, was "unrivaled in modern times." The total budget from 1995 to 2005 for Berlin's artwork exceeded the amount that the U.S. government had spent during the previous thirty-five years. Over 140 artists from around the world were involved in creating new pieces for the public buildings. The main facade of the parliament, for example, features a $1 million mural by the renowned American artist Ellsworth Kelly.

Part of the reconstruction of Berlin has also involved confronting the city's history through a variety of museums and memorials. The German Historical

Museum was completely redone and reopened in 2006, and a new Jewish Museum was opened in 2001. The Topography of Terror (site of Gestapo and SS headquarters during the Nazi period) was reopened in 2010. Above all, there is the Memorial to the Murdered Jews of Europe, which opened in 2005. Located in the very heart of Berlin, near the Brandenburg Gate, the memorial takes up more than five acres and consists of about 2,700 concrete stelae or slabs of varying heights arranged to form a waving grid. A study and research center has also been built on the site.[3] As divisive as the issue of moving the capital back to Berlin was, and despite the huge expense—which continues in light of new projects like the new central train station that opened in time for the World Cup of soccer in 2006, a subway line in the center of the city, or the reconstruction of the Hohenzollern's old city palace—there has been little regret. Indeed, Berlin has been celebrated inside and outside of the country as one of the top sights on the continent and a national capital of which Germans can be proud.

Structure and Organization

The key organizing agents of the Bundestag are the parliamentary groups of the political parties, or *Fraktionen* (caucuses). A Fraktion is a group of parliamentary members all belonging to the same party. From an organizational and operational standpoint, the parliament is composed of these Fraktionen and not individual deputies. The size of a party's Fraktion determines the size of its representation on committees, the number of committee chairpersons it can name, and the amount of office space and clerical staff it receives, as well as its representation on the important executive bodies of the chamber, the Council of Elders and the Presidium.[4] Although there have been a few independent deputies not formally affiliated with any party, they have invariably had "visiting rights" with a Fraktion.

The importance of the political parties in organizing the work of the chamber also extends to the relationship between the leadership of the parties and the individual deputy. As in the UK, party discipline, and hence party voting, is high in parliament: approximately 85 to 90 percent of all votes are straight party votes, with all deputies following the instructions of the Fraktion leadership or the results of a caucus vote on an upcoming bill. Free votes, when the party gives no binding instructions to its deputies, are rare. Nonetheless, the Constitution guarantees that a deputy who cannot support his or her party can leave its Fraktion and join another without having to resign, at least for the duration of the legislative period.

The daily agenda of the chamber is determined by the Council of Elders—in essence a steering committee—composed of the Bundestag's president (always a member of the largest Fraktion), the four vice presidents, and twelve to fifteen representatives of all Fraktionen. The council schedules debates, allots time to each party, and assigns committee chairmanships to each in proportion to its parliamentary strength. A second executive body in the Bundestag is its Presidium, consisting of the president and vice presidents of the chamber. The Presidium is responsible for the overall administration of the chamber, from its furnishings to the recruitment of clerical and research personnel. In theory, partisan factors play a lesser role in the conduct of its business than they do in the Council of Elders.

Committees

Parliamentary committees are more important in Germany than in the UK or France, yet less important than in the U.S. Congress. The Bundestag has twenty-two standing committees, devoted to issues like the budget, defense, internal affairs, and scrutiny of elections.[5] Both the partisan composition and leadership of these bodies are proportional to party strength in the chamber. Thus, unlike in the American system, the opposition party or parties have a share of committee chairmanships. In addition, German committees cannot pigeonhole or reject bills but must examine them, take testimony, and if necessary propose amendments to the entire house. The activities of committees generally reflect parliament's self-image as a responsible critic of the government but not a rival force. Committees do not have the large independent staffs of their American counterparts. In meetings, most of which are closed to the public, the ministerial officials who wrote a bill frequently explain the drafts of legislation to the lawmakers. Until recently, parliamentary committees were not aggressive in the use of their investigatory and information-gathering powers. This resulted in part from the chamber's traditional deference to the government and state bureaucracy and in part from the party loyalty of the committee majority to the government. This latter phenomenon is common to committees in parliamentary systems, where support for the government inhibits the independence of the committee and parliamentary majority, especially in the exercise of their control function. That said, approximately 60 percent of bills are modified through the Bundestag's committees.

The Members

The members of the Bundestag constitute part of Germany's political elite. All but two chancellors, almost all cabinet ministers, and all parliamentary state secretaries (the minister's political assistants) are drawn from its ranks. Thus the social backgrounds of these members reveal something about the quality and characteristics valued by the prevailing elite culture and by that relatively small group of party leaders at national, state, and district levels who, through their control of the nomination process, play a key role in Bundestag recruitment.

The social background of Bundestag deputies has changed dramatically between the first Bundestag in 1949 and the seventeenth Bundestag, elected in 2009. Almost half of the first parliament (1949–1953) was composed of employees (manual and lower-level white-collar workers) dependent on wages for a livelihood.[6] The value placed on this type of individual declined rapidly after 1949, and by 1961 less than 15 percent of parliamentary deputies came from this relatively modest occupational background. Since 1961 and even after the Social Democratic victories of 1969 and 1972, this proportion did not increase.

Two specific occupational groups that by the 1980s were especially prominent in the chamber were civil servants and interest group leaders. Together these two occupations accounted for over 60 percent of the membership.[7] In fact, civil servants are represented at a rate about five times greater than their proportion in the population at large. Unlike the situation in the UK or the United States, a German civil servant can be elected to legislative office (local, state, or national) without resigning from the service. Indeed, the existing civil service regulations encourage standing for public office. A government employee desiring to run receives a six-week leave of absence with full pay during the election campaign. If elected, he or she takes additional leave for the duration of the legislative term. Moreover, while on parliamentary leave, the civil servant receives pension credit and normal promotions. The potential conflict of interest between civil servants serving as parliamentary deputies with, among other duties, the responsibility for setting civil service salary scales has as yet not prompted any change in the laws.[8]

Apart from these incentives, the strong representation of state officials in parliament is also consistent with the expert, administrative orientation to politics that characterizes German political culture. As Gerhard Loewenberg has pointed out,

> In a society noted for the early development of a modern bureaucracy, government is still widely regarded as a purely administrative matter. From this, it is an easy step to the conclusion that administrators are the best qualified occupants of any governmental position, and that the parliamentary mandate is a type of administrative office.[9]

Interest group leaders and functionaries from business, industry, agriculture, and labor constitute another major part of the chamber's membership. Like civil servants, they have had extensive experience with bureaucratic structures and procedures. One study found that over half of all members of parliament from 1972 to 1987 had some paid or unpaid (voluntary) function in an interest group.[10] Among the middle-class parties (the CDU and FDP), almost 70 percent of their deputies held some office in an interest group.[11] Interest group representatives were also very prominent in the labor, transportation, and family and health committees.[12] Thus, almost 70 percent of the deputies can be said to have essentially bureaucratic backgrounds as civil servants or interest group representatives. This leaves workers, housewives, farmers, and even those in business and professional occupations heavily underrepresented in the chamber. Unable to take temporary leave from a job or career, they are at a comparative disadvantage to those in occupations strongly related to the activities of parliament.

The deputies from the former East Germany who entered parliament following unification in 1990 had occupational backgrounds quite distinct from their western colleagues. Almost one-third of this group, including the current chancellor, were either natural scientists, engineers, physicists, or chemists, as compared to only about 5 percent of the members from the west. Easterners in these positions were less likely to be tainted or discredited by associations with the Communist Party and above all the secret police (Stasi).[13] Many lawyers and civil servants in the former East Germany, as well as intellectuals and university professors and teachers in the social sciences and humanities, were in some way compromised by the Stasi regime.

In addition to changes in occupational backgrounds, the educational level of the deputies has steadily increased. Between 1949 and 1983, the proportion of Bundestag members with some education beyond the basic eight-year *Volksschule* increased from 70 percent to 95 percent; by 1998, about 30 percent of the members held doctoral degrees. Younger deputies are most likely to enter the chamber with this higher educational background. Lawyers are the largest group at 20 percent, followed by teachers at 5.6 percent. Finally, the proportion of women in parliament has increased steadily from less than 10 percent in 1949 to over 30 percent in 2005 and 33 percent after 2009. This is one of the highest proportions of female members in any European parliament or worldwide. Moreover, about 32 percent of the seventeenth Bundestag were new members.

These trends apply to all parties in the chamber from 1949 to the present. Indeed, in terms of social background, the first Bundestag in 1949 was actually more representative of the total population than were succeeding parliaments. German parliamentarians have become an internally unified professional elite, distinct from the general population by social background and training. These developments certainly facilitate a consensual policy-making style at the elite level and are indicative of a certain political maturity. They also relate to the increased assertiveness of the chamber vis-à-vis the executive in recent years. Yet the increasingly closed character of the membership also raises serious questions about democratic representation and the access of especially disadvantaged social

Table 7.1. Occupational Background of Members of the Seventeenth Bundestag, 2009–2013 (in percent)

Occupational Group	Overall	West	East	CDU/CSU	SPD	FDP	Greens	Left
Officials*	29.6	30.5	27.5	32.2	43.2	19.6	17.7	18.4
Public service**	5.0	4.6	7.7	4.2	7.5	2.2	5.9	5.3
Pastors	0.5	0.4	1.1	0.4	—	1.1	1.5	—
Employees of political and societal organizations***	16.6	16.1	20.9	8.8	19.9	5.4	26.5	39.5
Employees from business	13.4	13.4	13.2	18	10.3	18.3	7.4	5.3
Self-employed****	9.7	10.3	6.6	15.5	0.7	19.6	2.9	2.6
Free professions*****	16.3	17.8	6.6	15.9	11.6	26.1	23.5	7.9
Housewives	0.5	0.6	—	0.4	1.4	—	—	—
Workers	0.3	0.4	—	—	0.7	—	—	1.3
Other******	4.4	3.5	7.7	2.9	2.1	4.4	7.4	10.5
No answer	3.9	2.7	8.8	1.7	2.7	4.4	7.4	9.2

Source: Melanie Kintz, "Die Berufsstruktur der Abgeordneten des 17. Deutschen Bundestages," *Zeitschrift für Parlamentsfragen,* Heft 3/2010.
*Beamte, including teachers, professors, judges.
**Öffentliche Dienst.
***Party and union employees, etc.
**** Small business owners, including farmers.
*****Lawyers, doctors, engineers, journalists, etc.
******Students, unemployed.

groups to the decision-making centers of the system. Individuals with a migration background, comprising 18 percent of the population, were only 2 percent of the sixteenth Bundestag (2005–2009) and 2.4 percent of the seventeenth (2009–2013). There were three Muslims in the seventeenth Bundestag. The addition of members from the former East Germany may have changed this pattern in the first years after unification, but the backgrounds of representatives from this region have started to converge with those from the west. Nevertheless, regardless of party, they have tended to emphasize the unique problems faced by their constituents in the new eastern states.

Electing and Controlling the Government

The Bundestag elects the federal chancellor.[14] Unlike the procedures under the Weimar Constitution, the chamber does not elect specific ministers but only the chancellor, who then appoints the cabinet ministers. Although this election is by secret ballot, it follows strict party lines and has, with the exception of the CDU/CSU's unsuccessful attempt to bring down the Brandt government in 1972, provided few surprises.

Parliament's efforts to control the government and state bureaucracy are, of course, far more complex than the election of the chancellor. One important control procedure is the "question hour," adopted from English parliamentary practice, in which a deputy orally questions the relevant minister or the minister's representative about a particular problem. These questions vary considerably in tone and content. Many deal with citizen complaints, which a deputy can take for mutually beneficial publicity to the "highest level." Others deal with more fundamental questions about the direction of governmental policy. Since 1949, use of the question hour has increased dramatically. During the first Bundestag—in retrospect, the pinnacle of executive domination—members asked the government only about 400 questions over four years. By the fifth Bundestag (1965–1969), this had increased to about 10,500; and during the seventh Bundestag (1972–1976), almost 19,000 questions were put to the government by the deputies. During the 2005–2009 session, 15,492 questions (12,789 written and 2,703 oral) were issued.

To supplement the question hour, an *Aktuelle Stunde* (an hour devoted to current developments) procedure was added in 1965. According to this procedure a group of deputies (usually from the opposition) can petition the Bundestag leadership and the government for a question period about a particularly pressing problem. Deputies may also submit to the government written questions to be answered in writing and inserted in the record. If twenty-five to twenty-nine deputies submit such a petition, it is regarded as a minor inquiry needing no parliamentary debate; if thirty or more deputies submit a written question, it becomes a major inquiry, and a plenary debate must be held on the question and the government's reply. Almost 40 percent of all major inquiries were made during the first Bundestag (1949–1953). This was a time of great debates about the fundamental principles and policies of the Republic: the Western Alliance, European integration, federalism, rearmament, and the market versus a planned economy.

A further control procedure is the chamber's right to investigate governmental activities and its power to demand the appearance of any government or state official. Upon the request of at least one-fourth of the deputies, an investigating committee must be formed, with partisan composition proportional to party strength in the entire house. Therein lies one of the major problems of parliamentary investigating committees in a parliamentary system with disciplined parties. The possibility that its findings may embarrass the government and hinder the committee members' own political careers is an impediment to the more freewheeling investigatory practices found under separation-of-power systems with loose party discipline, as in the United States. Nonetheless, hearings have become an important part of the parliament's activities. In 2005 the first-ever televised hearing took place. Millions watched as the foreign minister was intensely questioned about the visa-granting practices of his ministry.

Finally, the most drastic form of parliamentary control is a formal vote of no confidence in the chancellor and his cabinet. Because of the stable, disciplined parties and the Basic Law's positive or constructive vote of no confidence (discussed later in this chapter), this procedure has been used only twice in the chamber's history, in 1972 unsuccessfully and in 1982 successfully. There have been five other votes of confidence, most recently used by Schröder to call early elections in 2005.

The Parliament in Action

Since the 1960s, parliament's use of its investigative powers and its efforts to increase public knowledge and involvement in its work have become more extensive. Although public committee hearings on proposed legislation, for example, have been possible since 1952, little or no use was made of this provision until the mid-1960s. In the fourth Bundestag (1961–1965), only four bills were given public committee hearings, but in the fifth parliament (1965–1969) about sixty public hearings on proposed legislation were held. Public debates have become more lively and focused, partly because of increased issue conflict between the parties and the reduction of time limits for speakers. Television coverage of important debates has also enhanced the image of the chamber. Debates can now be scheduled according to policy areas—for example, one week on foreign policy, the next on education. Thus the government can be questioned about a specific set of problems over an extended period.

The overall effect of these changes has been to make parliament a more independent institution, but this outcome should not be exaggerated. The initiation of legislation is still for the most part the responsibility of the chancellor and the cabinet. Party discipline and the hierarchy within the Fraktionen still limit the impact of the lone deputy. Only about 40 percent of bills introduced by individual deputies, most of a private and marginal character, are passed, in contrast to 85 percent of those introduced by the government.[15] In addition, the conditions associated with the often-discussed decline of parliaments in other countries—the increasingly technical character of government that requires expertise available only in the executive branch, the alleged necessity for speedy decisions, and the strict discipline imposed by modern mass parties—are also prevalent in Germany.

In terms of its influence vis-à-vis the executive, the Bundestag now occupies a middle position in comparison with the U.S. Congress and the British parliament. It is not as independent of the executive as the U.S. Congress, but neither is it as dominated by the government as the British House of Commons. The Bundestag supplies the government with a working majority, but through a strong committee system and the prevalence of coalition governments, it has also been able to maintain some independence from the executive. In the preparation of bills, even government bills, the Bundestag has more influence than the House of Commons. The German chancellor, in contrast to the British prime minister, also has less influence on the day-to-day schedule and agenda of parliament. The German executive must engage in more informal negotiations with the leadership of the parliamentary parties than in the UK. The Bundestag in committee can make major changes in a government bill without forcing the government to resign; numerous bills submitted by the government have in fact been extensively rewritten by parliament with both government and opposition parties influencing the bills' final form.[16]

The Bundestag has secured a firm position in the Republic's political life. The great majority of Germans regard it as a necessary and important political institution.[17] Citizens' belief in the responsiveness of the institution has also grown over the past decades. When asked in 1951 whether a parliamentary deputy would respond to their letter, almost half of a national sample thought they would receive no answer; by 1983 the proportion of the electorate with such a pessimistic assessment of parliamentary responsiveness had dropped to only 19 percent.[18] As the data in table 7.2 show, the German parliament has also fared well in comparison with the legislative assemblies of other major European countries, most of which have stronger democratic and parliamentary traditions than Germany. The proportion of Germans who believe they can trust the Bundestag is higher than in the UK or France. The level of trust in Germany is also well above the average found in the twenty-seven European Union countries. Noticeable is the decline in trust across Europe as a result of the global financial and

Table 7.2.   Trust in Parliament among Major European Countries, 2007 and 2012

		Tend to Trust	Tend Not to Trust	Don't Know
Germany	2007	51	45	13
	2012	46	49	5
United Kingdom	2007	43	50	7
	2012	23	72	5
France	2007	44	49	7
	2012	42	47	11
Italy	2007	30	55	15
	2012	8	84	8
EU-15*	2007	41	49	11
EU-27	2012	28	66	6

Source: Eurobarometer (Spring 2007), B9; Eurobarometer 2012.05; http://ec.europa.eu/public_opinion/cf/step1.cfm.
*Fifteen original members.

Euro crises, especially in the UK and Italy. Given the history and pre-1949 record of German parliaments, such sustained levels of support are a substantial achievement.

In spite of this progress, parliament faces continued challenges to its autonomy. First, the European Union plays an increasingly important role in the national policy-making process. Agricultural policy, for example, is largely the province of the EU's Common Agricultural Policy (CAP). Much of fiscal policy is constrained by the Stability Pact of the European Monetary System, which limits the taxing and spending ability of any member nation. The Basic Law was also amended in 2009 to prohibit structural deficits. Trade issues are also largely decided at the European level.

Second, parliament must also deal with the increasing tendency of the executive to turn to extraparliamentary commissions to fashion policies which the legislature must either rubber-stamp or blindly obstruct. In 2002, for example, parliament was scheduled to debate the controversial issue of genetic engineering. In preparation for the debate, a special Committee of Inquiry on the Law and Ethics of Modern Medicine had held hearings and prepared an extensive report. The votes on any proposed legislation were to be free of party discipline. Nonetheless, the chancellor, prior to any parliamentary actions, formed his own National Ethics Council, an extraparliamentary, corporatist group, to advise him—and presumably parliament—on ethical issues involved in genetic engineering. The presiding officer of parliament, a Social Democrat, sharply protested this usurpation of the legislative function by the executive. Schröder was especially fond of using neocorporatist commissions, councils, and experts to find consensual solutions to complex problems. Unlike Kohl, who relied upon an extensive network of personal contacts to secure support for his programs, Schröder sought to engineer consent via these ostensibly nonpartisan extraparliamentary bodies. Merkel has combined both methods, utilizing personal contacts, but also engaging in activities such as her two "integration summits" in 2006 and 2007. Frequently, parliament has been called upon to ratify policy proposals worked out in these commissions. The 2001 decision to phase out nuclear power was the result of extensive negotiations over a three-year period between the power companies, the energy ministry, and the chancellor's office. Conspicuously absent was parliament, although it was more involved in the 2010 decision to delay the phase-out and then the 2011 decision to return to the 2001 timetable. Merkel had also assigned this issue to an expert commission.

The Bundesrat: The "Quiet" Second Chamber

Located close to the Bundestag in Berlin is Germany's second legislative body, the Bundesrat or Federal Council.[19] Few non-Germans are aware of its existence, much less its importance, and even many Germans do not know how powerful this institution can be in the legislative process. Klaus Schütz, a former lord mayor of Berlin, called it the "most boring" institution ever invented because all the decisions were made before the formal sessions began.[20] Passionate speeches, interruptions of the speaker, and loud applause from the floor are all very rare.

During the week when preparations for the plenary sessions are made, the Bundesrat consists of civil servants among themselves. They prepare the issues for a final decision by their political superiors, the minister-presidents of the states and their cabinet members.

The purpose of the Bundesrat is to represent the interests of the states (Länder) of the federation in the national legislative process. It is the continuation of a tradition that extends back to the Bundesrat of the empire. The unified Reich established in 1871 was possible only after Bismarck and the Prussians had made certain concessions to the other states—specifically, a strong representation in Berlin and the right of states to implement state-related national policy. In effect, this bargain of 1871 meant that Berlin would rule but that the states would administer the rules. The framers of the Basic Law, many of whom were state officials themselves with strong Allied and especially American encouragement, returned to the federal structure of the empire and Weimar Republic and in some ways gave the Länder, now without Prussia, more influence than either of the two earlier regimes had.

Each state has three to six votes in the Bundesrat, depending on the state's size, for a total of sixty-nine. The votes are apportioned as follows: the four most populous states (North Rhine–Westphalia, Bavaria, Baden-Württemberg, and Lower Saxony) each receive six votes; Hesse has five votes; the middle-sized states (the Rhineland-Palatinate, Schleswig-Holstein, Berlin, and four of the new eastern states, Saxony, Thuringia, Saxony-Anhalt, and Brandenburg) have four votes each; and the four smallest states (the Saarland, Hamburg, Bremen, and the eastern Land of Mecklenburg–West Pomerania) receive three votes each. The degree of malapportionment in the Bundesrat ranges from one vote for every 182,500 inhabitants of Bremen to one vote for every 3 million citizens of North Rhine–Westphalia. Thus, although the Bundesrat does not represent the states as equal units (as the U.S. Senate does), the smaller states are still clearly favored in the distribution of votes.

There are no dedicated representatives elected from each state. Rather, the delegation from each state, usually headed by the state's chief executive or premier (Ministerpräsident), must cast the state's votes as a unit based on the decision of the state's government. When states are governed by coalitions, as they frequently are, the state's vote in the Bundesrat can become more complicated, since one coalition partner may support the national governing party while another supports the national opposition. This problem is usually addressed in a coalition agreement that the parties conclude before assuming power. These agreements typically stipulate that if the government cannot agree on the state's Bundesrat vote, it will abstain. Other agreements leave the question open and call only for ad hoc negotiations. The national Constitution requires that if the state cannot agree, it is recorded as an abstention.

The most celebrated case of a state government's indecision took place in 2002. On a vote dealing with a new immigration law, the state of Brandenburg, governed by the SPD and the CDU, through its SPD minister-president voted for the law, but the state's interior minister, a member of the CDU, voted against the law. When the presiding officer (SPD) asked for clarification, the minister-president repeated his yes vote while the interior minister simply stated, "Mr.

President, you know my position." The presiding officer then ruled that Brandenburg had voted in favor of the law and it therefore passed. The opposition strongly
protested the chair's ruling. A somewhat staged tumult ensued and the session
was adjourned. The CDU appealed to the Federal Constitutional Court (see
chapter 8 for a discussion of this institution), which ruled that the presiding
officer had incorrectly recorded Brandenburg's vote. Brandenburg had in fact
abstained, and the law was declared unconstitutional.

Thus while all federal states have a second legislative body, which represents
the constituent units of the federation, none is constructed like the German federal council. When voters elect a state government, they are also determining the
state's representation in the second national chamber. Moreover, the composition and thus partisan voting blocs in the Bundesrat change periodically when-
ever there is an election at the Land level. These elections are not aligned with
those for the Bundestag. Between the 2009 Bundestag election and mid-2012, for
example, there were elections in ten of the sixteen states, and these resulted in
five different state-level partisan coalitions (as well as different combinations of
the parties as junior or senior coalition partners). Also, because there is much
more parliamentary flexibility at the Land level than nationally, early elections
are rather common (recent examples include North Rhine–Westphalia, Hessen,
and Hamburg), making Bundesrat majorities quite unpredictable. Indeed, most
chancellors have had to deal with lack of support in the Bundesrat, usually
divided into progovernment, opposition, and neutral blocs. This is not even to
mention that the almost constant stream of elections at the Land level are frequently seen as plebiscites of the national coalition's performance.

Functions

According to the Basic Law, the Bundesrat can initiate legislation, and it must
approve all laws directly related to the states' responsibilities, such as education,
police matters, state and local finance questions, land use, and most transportation issues. In addition, any legislation affecting state boundaries, national emer-
gencies, and proposed constitutional amendments requires Bundesrat approval.

In practice, however, the Bundesrat, at least until 1969, has rarely initiated
legislation or exercised its veto powers.[21] Its influence in the policy-making
process has nevertheless increased since 1949, and especially since 1972 it has
become a more politicized institution. This somewhat paradoxical development
is due largely to changes in (1) the actual composition of the chamber's membership, (2) the determination of those areas in which the Bundesrat has an absolute
veto, and (3) the party control of the two chambers of parliament, as seen in the
divided government of Germany between 1972 and 1982, 1991 and 1998, 1999
and 2005, and 2010 to the present.

Formal vs. Actual Composition of Membership

In its early years, the Bundesrat was more an administrative than a policy-making
institution—or, as one authority has said, it was "between" politics and administration.[22] Because the states have to administer much of federal law, the Bundesrat has been mainly concerned with examining governmental legislation from

the standpoint of how the states would implement it. This function of the institution was related to the types of people who actually did the work of the chamber: state-level civil servants who had been deputized by the formal members, state political officials.

Most civil servants come from the ministries of the formal Bundesrat members. Originally the framers of the Basic Law included this deputation provision (contained in Article 51) with the expectation that it would be used only rarely, when regular members could not attend committee and plenary sessions because of state commitments. In practice, however, in the Bundesrat's committees, where most of the work takes place, bureaucrats outnumber politicians (the ministers sent by the states) by about a fifteen-to-one ratio.[23] Thus, at a typical Bundesrat session there are few, if any, political heavyweights.

When ready for a formal vote, the draft legislation is presented to the plenary session, which usually approves pro forma the result of the committee's work. Thus, in practice, the Bundesrat does not reject bills outright; but early in the policy-making process, after committee study, it would recommend changes in legislation designed to facilitate its implementation at the state level. In most cases, the expert advice of the Bundesrat does produce revisions or withdrawal by the government of the proposed legislation, thus making an outright veto unnecessary but also testifying to the influence of the states, through their governmental administrations, on the national policy-making institutions.

Expansion of Veto Power

The framers of the Basic Law anticipated that only about 10 percent of all federal legislation would require Bundesrat approval and hence be subject to the chamber's veto. In practice, however, through bargaining in the legal committees of each house and judicial interpretation, the scope of the Bundesrat's absolute veto power was enlarged to the point at which by the early 1970s it could veto roughly 60 percent of all federal legislation.[24] This unforeseen development occurred largely because many federal laws that refer to matters not subject to Bundesrat veto nonetheless contain provisions that set forth how the states are to administer and implement the legislation. Citing Article 84 of the Basic Law, the states have argued that because they are instructed as to how the federal legislation is to be administered, the legislation requires Bundesrat approval in both its substantive and procedural aspects. The courts have generally supported this coresponsibility theory. Thus, if the law affects the states, even if only in its administrative aspects, the entire law falls under the Bundesrat's veto power. This has also, in most cases, applied to any subsequent extension of or amendments to the legislation that the Bundesrat may propose. Administrative decrees and regulations issued by the government require Bundesrat approval under this interpretation.

This enlargement of Bundesrat power was a major factor in the federalism reform package (see below and chapter 8 for a further account) passed in 2006 by the Grand Coalition government. The changes presumably reduce the veto power of the states via the Bundesrat, although currently approximately 50 percent of laws still need Bundesrat approval.[25] In exchange the states received more power to administer federal laws as they see fit and greater independence in establishing education and regulatory policies. For example, store closing hours and tuition fees at universities are now solely the responsibility of the individual states.

Divided Parliamentary Control

Since the early 1970s, different parties have frequently controlled the Bundestag and the Bundesrat. Although in opposition in the Bundestag, the Christian Democrats from 1972 to 1982 held a majority in the Bundesrat. During this period some Christian Democratic leaders argued that the Bundesrat would be an ideal instrument with which the party could block, or at least force revisions on, government programs. In spite of its slim advantage in the chamber, the CDU/CSU delegates voted *en bloc* against many of the government's major proposals. In areas where the Bundesrat had an absolute veto, the CDU/CSU delegations forced major compromises on the government and in some cases—such as the higher education planning law (1974)—completely blocked the proposed government bill. Although it was in the majority, however, the CDU/CSU did not attempt to draft and introduce alternative programs to those offered by the government in the Bundestag. Its efforts were concentrated largely on delaying legislation and forcing changes on the government.[26]

Between 1991 and 1998 the roles were reversed. The Social Democrats were the majority party in the Bundesrat, although the Christian Democratic government held a slim majority in the Bundestag. The Social Democrats used their majority to block or force changes in a variety of government initiatives. The 1993 Solidarity Pact, which refinanced the costs of unification and increased taxes, was passed only after concessions were made to the Social Democrats. In 1994 the chamber rejected the abortion law passed by the Bundestag because it required women seeking an abortion in the first trimester of pregnancy to be counseled. The constitutional amendments proposed by the Constitutional Commission in 1994 (see chapter 8 for a description) were also blocked by the Bundesrat even though they passed the Bundestag.

In the latter years of the Kohl era, the SPD's use of its second-chamber majority continued. In 1997 in a controversial vote, the Bundesrat rejected Kohl's tax reform legislation. The government had proposed a very comprehensive tax reform package designed to make German business more competitive in the global economy. It was the cornerstone for Kohl's response to record-high unemployment and stagnant economic growth. The government charged the SPD with pursuing a "blockade policy" with its Bundesrat majority and with acting against the interests of the states, including those that it governed, in order to pursue a national strategy designed to defeat Kohl in the 1998 election.

In 2000 and 2001 the Christian Democrats attempted to return the favor. Party discipline is, however, significantly weaker in the Bundesrat than in the Bundestag. When faced with choosing between the best interests of their state or the best interests of their national party, state-level German leaders not infrequently chose the former. In 2000, for example, the national CDU leadership expected CDU state governments to oppose the SPD-Green tax reform in the Bundesrat. However, in those states where the CDU governed in coalition with the SPD, the Schröder government was able—thanks to a generous infusion of funds—to persuade three states to vote for the tax package against the wishes of their national party leadership. When the tax reform package passed, these states were sharply criticized by CDU loyalists.

During the 2005–2009 Grand Coalition, of course, there was no divided government. The two governing parties had lopsided majorities in both chambers. One of the major accomplishments of the Grand Coalition was the 2006 Federalism Reform legislation, which promises to change the relationship between the two chambers. The ability of the states to veto federal legislation has been reduced. In exchange, the national government has given up its rights in a number of areas including education. However, the critical question of the federal-state distribution of tax revenues (the Financial Constitution) was not resolved, but rather made part of the Federalism Reform II program. If the reformers succeed, the Bundesrat's ability to block national legislation could be reduced. Ultimately, however, some independent taxing authority must be given to the states if they are to agree to any further reduction in their ability to veto national legislation.

After 2010, Merkel's CDU/CSU–FDP coalition lost its majority in the Bundesrat. By early 2013, the national government could count on only 3 of 16 state governments or 15 of 69 votes. This made policy making during the Euro crisis all the more complicated and is one of the reasons for Merkel's seeming intransigence on various proposed responses at the European level. Unlike many other chancellors, Merkel has had to actively court opposition or neutral support in the Bundesrat. In the end, the chamber was sufficiently supportive of the various policies—also because often the biggest opponents of the various bailouts and other policies have come from her own coalition, especially the FDP and CSU.

The increase in the power of the Bundesrat and the frequency and intensity of divided government over the past thirty years has prompted one leading analyst to term the German system (and the European Union's institutional structure) a "joint decision trap." With so many veto points in the system it is difficult to make major innovations of the type that are required to address the economic and demographic challenges facing contemporary Germany. A single, small coalition partner in a small state government can force major changes in major national legislation. The Bundesrat has turned into a veritable bazaar where states offer to sell their votes in exchange for some extra benefit, usually monetary, from the national government.[27] It would be difficult, however, to develop the Bundesrat into a coequal second chamber. Neither the Constitution nor the structure and tradition of the house favors such a development. The Constitution does not provide any legal mechanism for the Bundesrat to bring down the government elected by the Bundestag. In addition, the strength of each party group always depends on state-level political conditions, which can change rapidly.

EXECUTIVE INSTITUTIONS: CHANCELLOR AND CABINET

Chancellor Democracy

In framing the Basic Law of the Federal Republic, the delegates to the parliamentary council centered executive authority in the chancellor. Unlike the governmental structure under the Weimar Constitution, the chancellor does not share executive power with a strong president, nor do the provisions of the Basic Law make the chancellor as vulnerable to shifting parliamentary alignments as were the Weimar executives. In some respects the German chancellor's constitutional position is similar to that of the chancellor under the Imperial Constitution, although her powers over cabinet ministers and the *Länder* are not as extensive.

The position of the chancellor as the chief executive of state is defined in Article 65 of the Basic Law:

> The Federal Chancellor shall determine, and be responsible for, the general policy guidelines. Within the limits set by these guidelines, each Federal Minister shall conduct the affairs of his department autonomously and on his own responsibility. The Federal Government shall decide on differences of opinion between Federal Ministers. The Federal Chancellor shall conduct the affairs of the Federal Government in accordance with rules of procedure adopted by it and approved by the Federal President.

The chancellor also appoints and dismisses cabinet ministers, whose primary political responsibility is to the chancellor's policies and not to parliament. The power of the chancellor to set guidelines and her sole responsibility for the appointment and removal of ministers place her in a stronger position than her Weimar counterparts. Although ministers are not subordinate to the chancellor, as under the Imperial Constitution, she supervises their work and has veto power over their decisions if they contradict her general guidelines. Moreover, unlike the case in the Weimar system, parliament cannot remove individual ministers, but it must successfully conduct a no-confidence vote in the chancellor before the cabinet is also dismissed.[28]

The framers of the Basic Law also made it more difficult for the parliamentary opposition to bring down a chancellor than was the case during the Weimar Republic. A parliamentary majority against him or her does not suffice; the opposition must also have a majority in favor of a new chancellor before the incumbent chancellor is dismissed. This constructive or positive vote of no confidence was added to protect the chancellor from the changing and unstable parliamentary alignments that brought down many Weimar chancellors.

In practice, as discussed in chapter 5, the unstable multiparty system of Weimar, which the framers of the Basic Law had in mind when drafting the constructive vote of no confidence, has not reemerged. The concentration of electoral support in two large, well-disciplined parties and two or three smaller parties has ensured most chancellors firm parliamentary majorities. The positive vote of no confidence has been attempted only twice. In April 1972 the Christian Democrats filed a no-confidence motion against Chancellor Brandt and nominated their parliamentary leader, Rainer Barzel, as the new chancellor. The CDU's leadership was convinced that it had enough support from its own ranks and from dissatisfied members of the Free Democrats to remove Brandt. The motion failed, however, as parliament in a dramatic secret ballot split 247 to 247, with two abstentions. Apparently one or two of the CDU members either abstained or voted for Brandt. In October 1982, however, the Christian Democrats, with the help of the Free Democrats, did successfully employ the constructive no-confidence vote when an absolute majority of the parliament voted to remove Helmut Schmidt and replace him with Helmut Kohl. About five months later, the electorate gave its stamp of approval to this change as the Kohl government (CDU/CSU–FDP) was returned with a large majority.

The Constitution in Article 68 also permits the chancellor to ask for a vote of confidence. Unlike the "constructive vote of no confidence" (Article 67), which is initiated by the opposition to replace the chancellor with its own candidate, this vote enables the chancellor to strengthen his or her position by stabilizing the majority—that is, compelling dissidents in his or her party and/or the coalition partners to support the government or risk new elections. It can, however, also be used to trigger new elections. If the chancellor loses the confidence vote, either deliberately or not, he or she can resign, ask the president to dissolve parliament, remain in office as the head of a minority government until the end of the legislative term, or be removed through a constructive vote of no confidence.

The stable postwar party system has given most governments firm majorities for their four-year terms, thus making both confidence and no-confidence votes a rarity. Article 68 has been invoked only five times in the Republic's history. In 1972 (Willy Brandt) and 1982 (Helmut Kohl), the provision was used to force new elections. Both chancellors lost the vote (in Kohl's case intentionally) and then requested the president to dissolve parliament and call new elections, which they subsequently won with comfortable majorities. Helmut Schmidt, while chancellor, in 1982 used the vote to stabilize his government. Although he won the vote, his coalition government with the Free Democrats lasted only seven more months.

In 2001 Chancellor Schröder became the first leader to link the confidence vote with a specific piece of legislation. He stipulated that the parliamentary decision on the deployment of military forces to Afghanistan was also a confidence vote. By fusing the two issues he compelled opponents of the Afghanistan deployment to choose between the survival of the government and their opposition to German participation in the antiterrorism war. He gambled that ultimately the government's survival would be more important to his intracoalitional critics than the military deployment. At least in the short run Schröder was right. On November 6, 2001, he won the confidence vote, albeit by a narrow majority of only two votes. One Social Democratic member of parliament and four Greens voted against the confidence/deployment measure.[29] In the view of many constitutional experts, Schröder's case was weak. The chancellor's argument—he is no longer able to govern properly because he has lost so much support—was political and not due to any loss in his parliamentary majority.

Four years later in 2005, Schröder again used the no-confidence vote, this time to force new elections. Following a major defeat in a state election, Schröder and some of his closest advisers decided that he could no longer govern in the face of so much opposition to his program. He essentially wanted the voters to send him and the country a clear message: keep my government in office or get rid of it. Schröder "lost" the vote when his own party deliberately abstained, and then he asked the federal president to dissolve the parliament and set new elections.

Schröder's decision had multiple goals. First, he hoped the early campaign would unify the party and stop the intraparty conflicts that could well have brought down the government before the scheduled 2006 election. Before his decision, the chancellor was facing nothing less than a putsch within his own party's left wing, parts of which did in fact leave the party to join the WASG led by Lafontaine (see chapter 5). Some on the left viewed Schröder as the grave digger of the SPD. Second, with this decision he hoped to seize the initiative from the CDU/CSU and force it to delay the nomination of Merkel as its chancellor candidate. A CDU/CSU thrown off stride might also make some campaign mistakes. Third, the early election would spare the country sixteen months of further deadlock.

Building a Cabinet

In forming a cabinet, the chancellor has to consider (1) the commitments made to his or her coalition partner, (2) the demands of the various factions within his or her own party, and (3) the objective needs of each position in relation to the qualifications of the various candidates. Most students of German leadership would agree that the first two criteria have outweighed the third criterion in the cabinet selection process. Cabinet size has ranged from thirteen during the second Schröder cabinet (2002–2005) to twenty-two in the Erhard governments (1963–1966). Expansion of cabinet size beyond fifteen seems invariably connected to coalition and other major political considerations—that is, some important faction or personality demands to be accommodated. For example, after unification in 1990, Kohl had to find room in his new cabinet for several representatives from the former East Germany. To create more cabinet posts, an existing ministry may also be divided. In the current CDU-FDP coalition government, the Free Democrats, thanks to their record 15 percent performance in the 2009 election, received five cabinet posts with an additional four going to the CDU's Bavarian sister, the Christian Social Union. This left only seven for the CDU. Six of the sixteen (about 38 percent) cabinet members are women.

Nonetheless, the chancellor is constitutionally superior to the cabinet, whose members serve at his or her pleasure and not that of parliament. Yet the exact division of responsibility between chancellor and minister is, in theory, difficult to determine. After giving the chancellor responsibility for the overall direction of government policy, Article 65 goes on to state that "within this policy, each minister conducts the affairs of his department independently and under his own responsibility." This directive has been interpreted to mean that the chancellor cannot interfere in the day-to-day affairs of a department, deal directly with a civil servant within a department, or bypass a minister and issue direct instructions to a department.[30] But the chancellor can dismiss a minister or order him or her directly to rescind or abandon a particular policy or planned policy on the basis of this guideline authority. In addition, in times of war the chancellor assumes supreme command of the armed forces from the defense minister.

In practice, the chancellor will rarely give formal instructions to a minister. The communication of chancellor guidelines usually takes place through cabinet discussions, informal face-to-face contacts, and advisory memoranda from the

Table 7.3.   The Cabinet of Angela Merkel, 2013

Position	Incumbent	In Office Since	Year of Birth	Party	Official Location of Ministry
Chancellor	Angela Merkel	2005	1954	CDU	Berlin
Vice chancellor and minister of economics and technology	Philipp Rösler	2011	1973	FDP	Berlin
Foreign minister	Guido Westerwelle	2009	1961	FDP	Berlin
Minister of finance	Wolfgang Schäuble	2009	1942	CDU	Berlin
Minister of justice	Sabine Leutheusser-Schnarrenberger	2009	1951	FDP	Berlin
Minister of the interior	Hans-Peter Friedrich	2011	1957	CSU	Berlin
Minister of defense	Thomas de Maizière	2011	1954	CDU	Bonn
Minister for special tasks and head of the chancellery	Ronald Pofalla	2009	1959	CDU	Berlin
Minister of health	Daniel Bahr	2011	1976	FDP	Bonn
Minister of labor and social affairs	Ursula von der Leyen	2009	1958	CDU	Berlin
Minister for environment, nature conservation, and nuclear safety	Peter Altmaier	2012	1958	CDU	Berlin
Minister of education and research	Johanna Wanka	2005	1955	CDU	Berlin
Minister of food, agriculture, and consumer protection	Ilse Aigner	2008	1964	CSU	Bonn
Minister for family affairs, senior citizens, women, and youth	Kristina Schröder	2009	1977	CDU	Berlin
Minister of transport, building, and urban development	Peter Ramsauer	2009	1954	CSU	Berlin
Minister of economic cooperation and development	Dirk Niebel	2009	1963	FDP	Bonn

chancellor's office to the ministries. The ministries, in turn, are required to keep the chancellor's office informed of developments in their areas, and the chancellor must clear all ministerial statements. Thus the ministers are constitutionally more than civil servants but less than British cabinet ministers. They do, however, have legal and administrative responsibility, and in practice, through their positions in the party and coalition and through procedures such as the question hour in parliament, they have also acquired political responsibility.

Generally, the classic ministries—foreign affairs, defense, finance, interior, and justice—are the most important cabinet posts. Their incumbents are correspondingly viewed as the strongest cabinet members and the heirs apparent to the chancellor.

The Special Role of the Finance Minister

In Germany as in other parliamentary systems the finance ministry is responsible for drafting the government's budget and overseeing how the various government departments spend the appropriations. In most cases the finance minister is the financial watchdog over the other government agencies. The finance ministry must approve all government proposals dealing with money, and it has veto power over any spending programs, including those that may be favored by the chancellor. This extraordinary authority is clearly grounded in the Constitution, which formally makes the finance minister the most important member of the government after the chancellor.

Cabinet Ministers

German cabinet ministers, like their counterparts in the UK and France, have usually achieved their rank after an extensive and successful apprenticeship in parliament, a party, or a professional career. Of course, chancellors must also take into consideration regional and gender balance, as well as fostering new generations of leadership (*Nachwuchsarbeit*). As table 7.3 shows, Merkel currently has two cabinet members in their forties and three in their thirties, with the average age at fifty-two. Analyses of the social and political backgrounds of cabinet members have found four major pathways to ministerial office:

1. through a successful rise within the *party* hierarchy and into the circle of ministerial candidates;
2. through successful *occupational* experience, especially in business, the free professions, or interest group administration;
3. through *local and state officeholding or civil service* experience, especially in areas such as justice, finance, and economics; and
4. through *expert status* in an important field such as science or education.[31]

Given the number of qualified applicants, achieving ministerial office is in itself a considerable accomplishment and brings a variety of additional political and administrative responsibilities as well as substantial personal power and prestige. A minister inherits the traditionally strong German respect for state authority. Responsible for the "house," as a ministry is commonly termed, he or she receives a substantial salary (about $200,000 annually as of 2013, plus a generous expense allowance) and pension, not to mention a chauffeur-driven limousine. Moreover, the minister's power and influence within the party are also usually enhanced by the ministerial office. A minister's power within the cabinet depends on his or her political support within the party, his or her relationship to the chancellor, and the nature of the specific issue.

As a cabinet member, the minister belongs to the top governmental elite and is, together with the chancellor and ministerial colleagues, collectively responsible for all acts and policies of the government. Yet in practice the necessity of coalition governments and the heterogeneity of German parties have greatly reduced cabinet solidarity. On numerous occasions, cabinet ministers have disagreed publicly with their colleagues. For example, in early 2012, the interior minister Hans-Peter Friedrich (CSU) openly contradicted government policy by calling for Greece to leave the Euro. Merkel has also publicly disagreed with Westerwelle on the Israeli-Palestinian conflict. It is not unusual for a chancellor, through top aides, to leak criticisms of the ministers to the news media.

The German cabinet, unlike the British, is not a "working cabinet" in which government policy is openly discussed, debated, and finally determined. As one authority has observed, "Its role is limited to a final political check on the general lines of governmental policy. Decisions are approved, rather than made, by the cabinet."[32] The strong constitutional position of the chancellor and the ambition of most cabinet ministers to achieve still higher status in the government combine to give the institution a relatively low profile. Thus, the cabinet is more a loose board of managers than a policy-making body.[33] The cabinet minister is aided by at least two state secretaries: (1) a career civil servant responsible for the administration of the ministry and (2) a parliamentary state secretary (similar to a junior minister in the British system) who assists in the political and representational tasks of the minister. Yet German ministers, unlike their British counterparts, must be both policy specialists and politicians. The Germans do not have the neat British division between the politically responsible cabinet minister and the administratively responsible permanent secretary.

The Chancellor's Office

Consistent with his or her constitutional position, the chancellor has facilities and staff that exceed those of the British and French prime ministers but are less than those of the American or French presidents. The chancellor's office has a staff of about 500, headed by either a cabinet minister without portfolio or a high-ranking civil servant. The office is organized into departments, usually directed by senior civil servants that correspond to the cabinet ministries and act as a liaison between the chancellor and the respective ministry. The chancellor's office has above all a right to information, and its key officials, with daily access to the chancellor, are among the most influential members of the government. The office is also a type of institutional watchdog over the various ministries to ensure that the chancellor's guidelines and cabinet decisions are indeed being carried out.

Chancellor, Parliament, and the Military

Throughout most of German history the military has played a major role in state and society. From the rise of Prussia in the eighteenth century to final military defeat in 1945, "the army, rather than the political forces of the society, traditionally provided the impetus toward national independence and greatness, and thus the army has always been the dominant partner in its relations with civilian authorities."[34] Military values of order, obedience, dedication to duty, and hierarchy were also diffused throughout the rest of society. The army (at least its leadership) thought of itself as "the school of the nation," an institution uniquely qualified to inculcate the proper values of citizenship and patriotism in succeeding generations of German youth.

Germany's conquerors in 1945 were determined to eliminate the political and social influence of the military and to prevent the reemergence of Germany as a significant military power. By the early 1950s, these same wartime Allies, now split into opposing camps, were in the process of rearming their former enemy. The Cold War had made Germany too important a territory to remain unarmed or neutral.

In the immediate postwar years, however, there was little public support for an independent army or even one integrated into a supranational European defense force. Rearmament, which began in the mid-1950s, was strongly rejected by opposition parties in parliament but also by significant elements in the ruling Christian Democratic Union, the churches, labor unions, and many intellectuals. The army, in view of its collaboration with the Nazis, was a discredited institution. Fears of a reemergence of militarism and a new military elite, which would attempt to play an independent political role, were also widespread.

Civilian control of the military was thus of prime importance when parliament, after long and sometimes bitter debate, finally approved the establishment of a West German army in 1956. During peacetime, supreme command of the armed forces is vested in the defense minister, who is expected to work closely with the defense council, a subcommittee of the cabinet. In wartime, the chancellor becomes commander-in-chief. Parliamentary control operates largely through its supervision of the military budget and the Bundestag's commissioner for military affairs, a type of ombudsman who is empowered to hear the complaints and grievances of soldiers and to protect their constitutional rights. The officer corps has not become a politically powerful elite, and its influence in policy matters has been subordinate to elected political leadership. By the 1970s most Germans perceived the military as another public service institution with specific functional tasks, somewhat like the railways, police, or post office.[35]

In the 1980s, however, the emergence of a nationwide peace movement and the widespread protests over the deployment of new missiles in the Federal Republic had an impact on the status of the military in society. Public induction ceremonies for new recruits were the scene of sometimes violent demonstrations by peace movement activists. The number of petitions for exemption from military service also increased. In some areas, teachers and school authorities have denied recruiting officers access to school classes unless peace groups receive equal time.

The Military since Unification

Unification and the related end of the Cold War dramatically changed the military. The former East Germany's National People's Army (NVA) became part of the Federal Army (*Bundeswehr*) in October 1990. The NVA was once considered one of the strongest and most effective armies in the Warsaw Pact. But following the collapse of the communist regime, the East German army also began to disintegrate. Between the fall of the Berlin Wall and unification, the army's size dropped from 170,000 to about 100,000. Many high-ranking officers resigned, took early retirement, or were dismissed because of their association with the communist system. The remainder were put on probationary status pending a review of their backgrounds and qualifications for service in the Federal Army.

As a condition of unification, the Federal Republic, in treaties with the Soviet Union and the Western occupying powers, agreed to reduce the combined size of unified Germany's armed forces from 600,000 to 370,000 by 1994. This reduction was accomplished largely at the expense of the former East German army. By 1995 only about 12,000 officers and troops of the old NVA had survived the review process and had been assigned a place in the downsized, unified army. The Federal Republic also took over huge stockpiles of military equipment, supplies, and ammunition, including some of the most advanced armaments in the military arsenal of the former Soviet Union. By 1995 most of these supplies and equipment had been destroyed, sold, or given to allies.[36] Currently the role of the military is being fundamentally redefined (see chapter 10 for a fuller discussion).

The Chancellors of the Federal Republic

Konrad Adenauer, 1948–1963: Founding Father

When one considers the constitutional position of the chancellor described above and adds to it the strong personality, popular appeal, and authoritarian style of its first incumbent, Konrad Adenauer, the origins of the term *chancellor democracy* become evident. With presidential-like control over the cabinet, the bureaucracy, and his political party, Adenauer was able to bypass parliament in many policy-making cases. Adenauer, supported by Article 65 (which he interpreted liberally to his benefit), dominated his cabinet and led the government unlike any chancellor during the Weimar Republic. His relationship to his ministers was not unlike that of an American president to his cabinet members or that of the imperial chancellor to his state secretaries.

During his fourteen-year tenure, Adenauer, already a successful statesman during the Weimar Republic, established the procedures and style of chancellor government, with which all subsequent incumbents of the office have had to contend in some way. His early successes in dealing with the Western occupation powers, the integration of West Germany into Europe, the reconciliation with France, and the rapid economic recovery that began shortly before his first term and became an economic boom by the mid-1950s gave him a record of accomplishment that enabled him to dominate parliament on many important matters, especially foreign policy. Impatient with the delays and indecisiveness of government by committee, he frequently made commitments (e.g., to the Allied occupiers on German rearmament) without any prior consultations with his cabinet, much less parliament. He was also very adept at keeping the various wings and factions of the Christian Democrats in balance and under control, while at the same time discouraging their organizational and programmatic development. For all practical purposes, the party was run from the chancellor's office.

In Adenauer's chancellor democracy, the general public played a minor role. Deeply pessimistic about the capacities of the German people to measure up to the demands of democratic citizenship, Adenauer wanted their support but not their involvement. In short, Adenauer wanted to govern, and he did not want parliament, his party, his cabinet ministers, or the public to bother him while he went about his business. His message to the electorate was, in essence. "Go about your private affairs, rebuild your lives, concentrate on regaining and improving your economic position, and leave the politics to me." Many citizens accepted and indeed welcomed this approach, even though it meant that much of the state building and the resolution of major problems, such as reunification and social reforms, would have to be postponed until after the Adenauer era.[37] However, Adenauer did make a major contribution toward the institutionalization of the Federal Republic: he convinced most citizens that the new political system could be strong, effective, and democratic and give West Germans what they desperately wanted in the postwar period: security and economic prosperity. Through his authoritarian, paternalistic style, he sold West Germans on the Second Republic.[38] But Adenauer also stood for continuity with the better traditions of German history. His funeral in 1967 was one of the biggest events of the postwar period.

The Heirs of Chancellor Democracy

None of the three chancellors after Adenauer—Ludwig Erhard, Kurt-Georg Kiesinger, and Willy Brandt—lasted more than five years. As table 7.4 shows, there also has been a trend toward younger political leaders. Helmut Kohl became chancellor at the age of fifty-two and exceeded Adenauer's tenure, governing for a record sixteen years. Angela Merkel is the first chancellor since Helmut Schmidt who has spent a significant part of her adult life under a nondemocratic regime (communist East Germany).

Adenauer's immediate successor was Ludwig Erhard, the father of the economic miracle, who had been a self-designated heir ever since the late 1950s and whom Adenauer ceaselessly criticized publicly and privately as ill suited for the top job. Erhard never had any close contact with his party organization and did not consolidate his position within the CDU/CSU. He was, as one observer put it, more of a guest in the CDU.[39] Proud of his accomplishments as economics minister and aware of his great electoral appeal, he considered the party secondary to his government and never attempted to gain the support of its key factions. He attempted to project himself as a *Volkskanzler*, a people's chancellor,

Table 7.4.   German Chancellors, 1949–Present

Name	Party	Tenure	Age at Assumption of Office	Age at Nazi Seizure of Power
Konrad Adenauer	CDU	1949–1963	73	57
Ludwig Erhard	CDU	1963–1966	66	36
Kurt-Georg Kiesinger	CDU	1966–1969	62	29
Willy Brandt	SPD	1969–1974	56	20
Helmut Schmidt	SPD	1974–1982	56	15
Helmut Kohl	CDU	1982–1998	52	3
Gerhard Schröder	SPD	1998–2005	54	Not yet born
Angela Merkel	CDU	2005–present	51	Not yet born

someone who was above the parties. This posture left him in a very vulnerable position when Germany's first serious postwar recession in 1966 took the luster off his reputation as the guarantor of economic prosperity. After Christian Democratic defeats in key state elections in 1966, the Erhard government fell—ostensibly because of the departure of the junior coalition partner, the Free Democrats, but more through the internal maneuvering for power within the various factions of the Union. A stunned, disbelieving Erhard, still somewhat of a political innocent, retired to elder statesman status.

The chancellorship of Erhard's successor, Kurt-Georg Kiesinger, was inextricably connected with the rise and fall of the Grand Coalition between the SPD and the CDU/CSU. Kiesinger had been a Bundestag deputy from 1949 to 1958, specializing mainly in foreign policy. Finding the road to national prominence in Bonn too crowded, he returned to his native state of Baden-Württemberg and became its chief executive. When the Erhard government collapsed eight years later and the CDU/CSU desperately needed a new chancellor candidate who would also be acceptable to the Social Democrats in the likely event of a Grand Coalition, Kiesinger became the ideal person simply because he had the fewest outright opponents in either party.

As chancellor, Kiesinger had the very difficult task of leading a government in such a way that none of the three main players—he, his party, and its partner, the Social Democrats—would be too successful. Partisanship might have caused the strange alignment to break up before 1969, something both parties feared. This honest-broker style of leadership gave some of his ministers considerable freedom of action, and as discussed in chapter 5, the Social Democrats in the government took full advantage of the opportunity. After the 1969 election and the SPD-FDP government, Kiesinger became a liability to the Christian Democrats. After a decent interval he stepped down from the titular leadership of the party in 1971 (replaced by Rainer Barzel and then Helmut Kohl in 1973). Whether he could have been an effective national leader was never determined because, given the character of the Grand Coalition, he never had a chance.

Willy Brandt, 1969–1974: Visionary

In 1969, Willy Brandt became the fourth chancellor of the Federal Republic. In terms of policy innovation, controversy, foreign stature, and significance for the political system, Brandt ranks as one of Germany's most important postwar leaders. Born in the north German city of Lübeck, he became active in social democratic politics as a teenager and was forced to flee Germany for Norway and later Sweden shortly after the Nazi seizure of power, when he also changed his name from Herbert Frahm to Willy Brandt. He thus is the only chancellor born before or during World War II not to have lived in Germany during the Third Reich. Returning to Germany in 1945 as a Norwegian press attaché in a Norwegian military uniform, he resumed German citizenship and became active in Social Democratic politics in Berlin. Identified with the reformist, pragmatic wing of the party, Brandt rose rapidly in the organization and became lord mayor in 1957. Soviet pressure against the isolated city of Berlin intensified in the late 1950s and made it a major source of East-West tension. As its mayor, Brandt acquired a national and international reputation as a young, dynamic, progressive, yet non-Marxist and anticommunist leader.

This image coincided with the SPD's new look after 1959. Brandt was elected national chairman in 1964 and became the party's chancellor candidate in 1961 and again in 1965. His defeats in these two elections, during which he was subjected to numerous personal attacks regarding his illegitimate birth and his wartime activity—which to some Germans made him a traitor—almost caused his retirement from national politics. The collapse of the Erhard government and the Grand Coalition, however, compelled his return to the national scene as foreign minister in the Kiesinger government. As foreign minister, he laid the foundations for the new relationship that the Federal Republic would develop with East European states—*Ostpolitik*. Although limited somewhat by the demands of coalition politics, Brandt was able to establish himself as a competent, innovative foreign minister and in so doing erased much of the "loser" image he had acquired in his unsuccessful bids for the chancellorship.

Immediately after the 1969 election, Brandt seized the initiative and formed a coalition government with the Free Democrats in spite of an SPD-FDP majority of only twelve seats. He thus became the first SPD chancellor since 1930. Between 1969 and 1972, Brandt and Foreign Minister Walter Scheel (FDP) effected a major transformation of West German foreign policy through treaties with the Soviet Union, Poland, and East Germany. During this period, some domestic reforms were also made in social welfare programs, the pension system, and the criminal legal code. But although Brandt had promised a government of internal reform, most of the government's domestic program was postponed because of its weak and dwindling parliamentary majority. Following the 1972 election, which gave the government a solid working majority of almost fifty seats, the unfinished domestic projects (e.g., codetermination, capital resources reform, urban renewal, education, and tax reform) were placed high on the political agenda.

Yet to the considerable disappointment of SPD supporters, the government in the first year and a half following the 1972 victory did not use its parliamentary majority to move forward in the domestic field with the same decisiveness it had demonstrated three years earlier in foreign policy. This relative inactivity was explained in part by the government's attempt to curb inflation through ceilings on government expenditures and the postponement of new programs. After 1972, it also became apparent that neither Brandt nor Scheel had expertise or interest in domestic affairs. Brandt had little knowledge of economics or finance and disliked much of the detail work and bargaining associated with domestic politics. In addition, unlike their cohesiveness in foreign policy, there were serious differences between the coalition partners over major domestic issues such as codetermination, taxes, and education reform.

The arrest of East German spy Günter Guillaume on Brandt's personal staff in April 1974 was the final blow in a series of setbacks since his triumph in November 1972. The East German agent, a resident of the Federal Republic since 1957, had been under suspicion by security agencies for almost a year before the actual arrest. Brandt had been privately informed of this but apparently acceded to the requests of security officials to keep the agent on his staff. Brandt assumed full responsibility for all errors connected with the affair and resigned as chancellor in May 1974.

Brandt's five-year tenure was distinguished above all by his foreign policy of reconciliation with Eastern Europe and the Soviet Union, for which he was awarded the Nobel Peace Prize in 1971, only the fourth German so honored. As the first chancellor with an impeccable record of uncompromising opposition to Nazism, he contributed greatly to the Federal Republic's image abroad as a society that had finally overcome its totalitarian past. Some authors even talk about Brandt presiding over a "second" transition to democracy in which "daring more democracy" meant more memory and justice.[40] In spite of shortcomings in domestic policies, the Brandt chancellorship at least was one in which many innovations and long-overdue reforms began to be discussed and programs formulated. After his tenure, Brandt remained active as SPD chairman until 1987 and as president of the Socialist International from 1976 to 1992. Brandt, a constant supporter of reunification, made one of the most famous speeches at the time, stating, "Now what belongs together, grows together." Many mourned his death in 1992, and in 2009 it was decided that the new Berlin-Brandenburg international airport would be named after him.

Helmut Schmidt, 1974–1982: The Enforcer

Less than two weeks after Brandt's resignation, Helmut Schmidt, the only chancellor who had fought in the Wehrmacht during World War II, became the fifth chancellor of the Republic. Schmidt had been the strongest figure in Brandt's cabinet and was his designated successor. He had been finance minister (1972–1974), defense minister (1969–1972), chairman of the SPD's Fraktion (1966–1969), and interior minister in his native Hamburg (1961–1965). In these posts Schmidt acquired the reputation of a very capable—some would say brilliant—political decision maker. He was also criticized for having what some regarded as an overbearing, arrogant, and cold personal style. Schmidt clearly lacked the emotionally warm image of Brandt, yet he received higher marks for his concrete performance.

Schmidt was identified with the Federal Republic's mainstream. A pragmatic, problem-solving approach to politics, with a basic acceptance of the main features of the economic and political system, characterized his political philosophy. Schmidt assumed the chancellorship in the midst of the worldwide economic recession that followed the 1973 Arab oil embargo and subsequent astronomical rise in oil prices. His expertise and experience in national and international economic affairs and his ability to take charge in crisis situations, such as the 1977 terrorist hijacking and commando raid (see chapter 4), soon became apparent. Within two years, inflation was brought under control and unemployment was reduced.

Unlike Brandt, Schmidt had little patience with the SPD's left. A strong supporter of the market economy, he maintained a close relationship with the Federal Republic's economic and industrial elite. Indeed, in 1980 he was even seen by many CDU voters as more capable than the Union's own candidate. Schmidt's electoral and policy successes, however, were not matched in his relationship to his party, the Social Democrats. Specifically, he was unable to overcome and integrate the opposition of the SPD left and especially the Young Socialists. He also underestimated the intensity of the opposition within his own party, and in the country as a whole, to nuclear energy.

Soon after the 1980 election victory, Schmidt was once again confronted with opposition to his leadership by segments of the SPD. Budget cuts in social programs, due in large part to the worsening economic situation; the planned deployment of new middle-range nuclear missiles in Western Europe; and arms sales to Saudi Arabia were issues that prompted sharp criticism from the SPD left. The Schmidt government by 1981 also became a prime target for the peace movement—a loose collection of environmentalists, religious pacifists, and elements of the SPD left—which strongly opposed the NATO missile decision. The movement accused Schmidt of deferring to the alleged American military strategy of attempting to confine at least the first stages of a nuclear conflict to Europe and, specifically, to the Federal Republic. Schmidt rejected this charge, but the peace movement had gained significant support among SPD activists and became a force that seriously weakened the governing coalition.

On September 17, 1982, Helmut Schmidt lost his parliamentary majority when the Free Democratic Party, the junior party in the governing coalition with the SPD since 1969, left the government. Two weeks later, in the first successful use of the constructive vote of no confidence procedure, Helmut Kohl became the Federal Republic's sixth chancellor. Active but largely out of the public eye since 1982, Schmidt in recent years has seen his popularity surge as he has taken on an elder statesman/commentator role.

Helmut Kohl, 1982–1998: The "Unity Chancellor"

Helmut Kohl first became a significant figure on the German political scene in 1969, when he was elected chief executive of the state of the Rhineland-Palatinate. His success at the state level coincided with the decline of his party, the CDU, in national politics. After CDU/CSU defeats in 1969 and 1972, Kohl moved from his provincial power base, and in 1973 he assumed the leadership of a divided and weakened CDU. He is credited with initiating a thorough modernization and revitalization of the party's organization. In 1976, as the chancellor candidate of the CDU/CSU, he conducted a well-planned campaign that almost toppled the Schmidt government.

Born in 1930, Kohl was the first chancellor who had not experienced the Third Reich and World War II as an adult. Following the completion of his university studies in the 1950s, receiving a PhD in history in 1958, he began a political career. In contrast to earlier CDU chancellors, Kohl was an active party leader who carefully attended to the tasks of political fence-mending and coalition building within the diverse Christian Democratic Union. This control of the party was a major factor in his political longevity.

The most difficult problem confronting the first Kohl government (1982–1987) was the economy. Like other West European states, Germany was slow to recover from the 1981–1983 recession. Cuts in social programs, tax incentives for business investment, and a general tax reform were the chief means he used to stimulate the economy. From 1983 to 1988 the economy did expand, albeit at a slow rate. And although inflation was reduced, unemployment remained high. Kohl's policies were a German version of supply-side economics, but he was generally identified with the moderate wing of the Christian Democrats, which supports both the market economy and an extensive welfare state.

In foreign affairs Kohl was a firm supporter of the transatlantic relationship and was the most pro-American chancellor since Adenauer. In spite of widespread protests and the opposition of the Social Democrats and the Greens, the Kohl government secured parliamentary approval for the stationing of new intermediate-range missiles in the Federal Republic in November 1983. This strong position against the peace movement was vindicated by the 1987 United States–Soviet treaty eliminating these middle-range nuclear missiles in Europe. Kohl's support for American policies, however, did not prevent his government in 1989 from entering into open diplomatic conflict with the United States over the question (now moot) of when and if a generation of short-range missiles should be developed and stationed in the Federal Republic.[41]

More than any of his predecessors, Kohl attempted to appeal to traditional patriotic symbols and national pride. Terms such as *Vaterland* (fatherland) and *nation* and an emphasis on post–World War II German history as an object of pride were frequent themes in Kohl's speeches. Although not denying the country's responsibility for the Third Reich, the Holocaust, and World War II, Kohl urged that Germans in general, and postwar generations in particular, develop a positive sense of German history. Germany, Kohl believed, had earned the right to be accepted as an equal in the Western community, and the past should no longer limit the capability of the Federal Republic to act. Nevertheless, Kohl's memory and history politics in the 1980s were controversial. For example, in 1984, he made a speech in Israel in which he stressed his generation's "grace of late birth," and he attempted to celebrate Western unity with President Ronald Reagan on the anniversary of the end of World War II in 1985 at a military cemetery in Bitburg that contained graves of SS members.

Kohl and the Unification Process

Kohl seized the initiative on the unification issue with a ten-point program for German unity that he announced in parliament on November 28, 1989, less than three weeks after the opening of the Berlin Wall. Although many of his proposals, such as a network of treaties between the two states as a preliminary stage to a confederation, were overtaken by the rapid pace of events, his initiative established a pattern of decisive and timely action throughout 1990.

His crowning achievement occurred at a July 1990 summit meeting with Soviet president Gorbachev at the Soviet leader's summer retreat in the Caucasus. In exchange for German economic aid, a sharp reduction in the size of the German army, and a comprehensive treaty regulating the two nations' future economic, technical, and political relations, Gorbachev agreed that a unified Germany could remain in NATO; he further pledged that all 400,000 Soviet troops in East Germany would leave by 1994. This agreement earned Kohl the praise of even his harshest critics. During the 1990 all-German election campaign, Kohl was at the zenith of his popularity, power, and influence both domestically and internationally. He promised eastern Germans western-style economic prosperity within five years and assured West Germans that unification could be financed without any tax increases. For the first time in the chancellor's many election campaigns, his popularity exceeded that of his party.

After the election, however, the eastern German economy continued to deteriorate, and Kohl had to concede that his prediction of a rapid economic upturn had been overly optimistic. With rising unemployment in the east, his support dropped. Then, in 1991, contrary to his campaign promise, he announced major tax increases to finance unification. This prompted a strong voter backlash in the west, and support for Kohl and the Christian Democrats in state elections and public opinion polls dropped sharply. The 1992–1993 recession further weakened Kohl's standing with the voters. As in the past, there were calls for his resignation both from within and outside the government. The opposition's new candidate, Rudolf Scharping, outranked Kohl in most polls during this period. But by early 1994 the economy was reviving, and as the election approached, most German voters did not want a change in the chancellor's office. In October 1994, Kohl won his fourth straight national election—equaling the record of his idol, Konrad Adenauer.

1998: Kohl's Last Hurrah

Following the 1994 victory it was widely expected that Kohl would step down sometime before the 1998 election in favor of his designated successor, Wolfgang Schäuble, the leader of the CDU in the Bundestag. But the chancellor hesitated and did not heed the warnings from within his own party and from his declining status in public opinion polls after 1994. Kohl believed that given the divisions within the Social Democratic Party, he could probably win one more election. He believed that his 1998 opponent would be Oskar Lafontaine, whom he had soundly defeated in 1990.

When the Social Democrats decided in March 1998 to nominate Gerhard Schröder, Kohl and the Christian Democrats were slow to react. Record-high unemployment, the inability to pass major reform legislation, and the general perception that it was time for a change were major handicaps from which Kohl and his party could not recover. Helmut Kohl, who had led his party to a record four consecutive victories, suffered his worst defeat in 1998 as the CDU received only 35 percent of the vote. Europe's last great heavyweight had to make way for a new leader and the coming to power of a new generation. Not long after he left office, a wide-ranging party-financing scandal broke, which tarnished his reputation and led to the resignation of his handpicked successor as CDU chairman, Wolfgang Schäuble.

The 1998 defeat and the party-financing scandal will likely have little effect on history's assessment of Kohl's chancellorship. He succeeded in fulfilling the Basic Law's primary mandate: the unification of Germany in peace and freedom. This is a goal that had eluded his five predecessors. Equally important was his unrelenting commitment to the unification of Europe. Without his leadership, the pace of European unity, especially the introduction of a common European currency, would have been much slower. He left to his successors a united Germany surrounded by neighbors who now share common political, economic, and social values.

Gerhard Schröder, 1998–2005: The Reluctant Reformer

The man who toppled Helmut Kohl, unlike any of his six predecessors, is fully a child of the Federal Republic. Born in 1944, Gerhard Schröder, of course, had no living memory of the Third Reich or World War II. Both his supporters and opponents considered Schröder to be intensely ambitious and even ruthless in his pursuit of Germany's top job. Much of his drive can be traced to his impoverished childhood. He never knew his father, who was killed in World War II, and his mother had to support five children on her meager earnings as a cleaning lady. Forced to leave school at the age of fourteen to work as an apprentice salesman, Schröder was able to complete his university preparatory studies by taking night classes. In 1978, at the age of thirty-three, he graduated with a law degree from Göttingen University.

While still a student, Schröder became active in the Social Democratic Party and by the late 1970s was the leader of the Young Socialists, who were considered radical neo-Marxists by their more conservative elders in the party. In spite of his radical rhetoric, Schröder was able to maintain good relations with all factions of the party, and by the early 1980s he began to move toward the center while a member of the Bundestag (1980–1986). In 1990 he became the Ministerpräsident or governor of Lower Saxony, one of Germany's largest states. As governor he was very supportive of business interests. In spite of his state's high unemployment, he was reelected in 1994 and 1998. With this victory he became the SPD's chancellor candidate.

Schröder's performance in his first term (1998–2002) was mixed. After a difficult start, which was due in part to the conflict within the SPD between the modernizers, led by Schröder, and the traditionalists, led by Oskar Lafontaine, his government was able to pass major changes in the tax and pension systems. But he was unable to deliver on his campaign pledge of reducing unemployment, which had been high since the mid-1990s, especially in stagnant eastern Germany. The economic slowdown following the September 11, 2001, terrorist attacks in the United States made his government vulnerable. Unemployment rose steadily throughout late 2001 and 2002. The cornerstone of the government's plan to reduce unemployment, the "Alliance for Jobs," a combined business-labor-government effort, was unsuccessful.

Throughout most of the 2002 campaign, it appeared that Schröder would be the first chancellor in the history of the Federal Republic who failed to be reelected. It was not until mid-August, about six weeks before the election that the SPD and Greens finally cut into the lead of the Christian and Free Democrats with their Bavarian candidate Edmund Stoiber (CSU). The floods in the eastern regions, Schröder's performance in the second television debate, and his staunch opposition to the Iraq policy of the Bush administration were critical for his last-minute come-from-behind victory.

Following the election, however, his woes continued. The weak economy and the resultant decline in tax revenues forced his government to announce a variety of tax increases and budget cuts. His popularity dropped sharply. Charging that he had deliberately withheld the bad economic news during the campaign, the opposition launched a parliamentary investigation of the SPD campaign. In 2003 after an extensive struggle with his own party, Schröder was able to push through major cuts in spending for social programs and labor market reforms (Agenda 2010). In foreign policy, his unconditional opposition to the Iraq war damaged Germany's relations with the United States, its most important ally.

Schröder paid a heavy price for his reform programs. His own party and much of its trade union core opposed the reduction in social programs, above all his elimination of the second tier of unemployment compensation, which dropped hundreds of thousands of jobless Germans into the welfare system. The creation of a low-wage sector also drew the opposition of the trade unions. In 2004 Schröder stepped down as the leader of his party, but this did little to improve his status or that of the SPD. In 2005 his troubles continued when dissident SPD members formed a new party, the Left Party, by merging with the postcommunist PDS under the leadership of his rival, Oskar Lafontaine.

With Agenda 2010 yielding few positive results and unemployment at record-high levels, the SPD suffered a major defeat in May 2005 in one of its traditional strongholds, North Rhine–Westphalia. When the results were final, Schröder went on national television and announced that he had asked the president to dissolve the parliament and set a date for early elections. In essence, he took a gamble, attempting to bring his own party into line. Despite high levels of unpopularity, Schröder, the best campaigner of his generation, almost won. In the end, his party did well enough to enter a Grand Coalition with the CDU/CSU, but Schröder had to resign. Ironically, not long after his fall from power, the German economy started to do much better, and unemployment started to decline. This positive performance has continued to today and is largely credited to the Agenda 2010 and Hartz IV reforms that he pushed through.

Angela Merkel, 2005–: Accidental Chancellor or Iron Frau?

In November 2005, after two months of difficult postelection negotiations, Angela Merkel became the Federal Republic's eighth chancellor. Not only her gender and age—she is the first female chancellor and the youngest in German history—but her personal biography set her apart from her predecessors. She came to politics late and by an accident of history. Born in 1954 in Hamburg, she became an easterner when her father, a Protestant minister, in the same year accepted a call from a congregation on the other side of the Iron Curtain. Her religious environment insulated her from much of the communist socialization of East German youth. Although she was discriminated against because of her religion, her exceptional academic record enabled her to study physics at the graduate level. After completing her doctorate, she began a career at a physics research institute in East Berlin. Merkel has stated that she does not believe that she would have gone into politics "under western conditions."[42]

Her career path abruptly changed with the fall of the Berlin Wall and the unification of Germany in 1990. She volunteered in one of the prodemocracy groups that sprang up in the wake of the opening of the wall. She became a top aide to East Germany's first (and last) freely elected prime minister. By 1992, now a member of the Christian Democrats, she was named environmental minister in the Kohl government. Indeed, she owed her successes to Kohl's patronage and was even known demeaningly as "Kohl's *Mädchen*" (Kohl's girl). After the CDU/CSU defeat in 1998, she remained in parliament and became the party's general secretary. The finance scandal of 1999–2000 moved her career a step further as she assumed the leadership of the Christian Democrats when Schäuble also became involved in the scandal. Thus, by 2000 she was the national leader of her party and an automatic chancellor candidate. While she did not get the nomination in 2002, she could not be denied in 2005.

Merkel's emergence as a national figure was due largely to a series of unique events—the end of the Cold War, rapid German unification, a major scandal in her own party, and the weakness of the Schröder government following Agenda 2010. Competent easterners were needed at the national level, but it was difficult to find candidates who had not been compromised by contacts with the East German secret police. Her background as a physicist meant that she was clean of any Stasi involvement. Since she had grown up in the east, she also had made few enemies within her own party—but also few friends or allies. That said, she has also proven adept at outmaneuvering almost all of her intraparty rivals—Friedrich Merz, Christian Wulff, Edmund Stoiber, and Roland Koch to mention just a few.

As discussed in chapter 6, Merkel ran a poor campaign in 2005 but was saved by some unusual conditions. Although her party suffered record losses, her main political opponent lost even more. When on election night Chancellor Schröder, in a joint television appearance, rudely dismissed her claim to the chancellorship, her party had no choice but to rally behind her.

As chancellor of a Grand Coalition, Merkel was careful to avoid blatant partisanship while at the same time looking out for the interests of her own party. During the first years of her chancellorship the record of her government was mixed. There have been some successes such as federalism reform (see chapter 9), cuts in wasteful subsidies, the beginning of change in the health care system, further changes in the pension system, and the establishment of a major family leave program. In foreign policy she has restored at least normal relations with the United States following the tumult of the Schröder years. Unlike her predecessor, she has also adopted a more realistic approach to Russia and the growing authoritarianism of the Putin regime. Both she and her government have benefited greatly from a stronger economy and the positive effects of Schröder's Agenda 2010, but have also put public finances in order by raising the value-added tax (VAT) and pushing through a balanced budget amendment to the Constitution.

But her greatest success thus far has been her personal popularity. Her approval ratings are the highest of any chancellor since the advent of public opinion polling. Over most of her time in office, around 75 percent of Germans have consistently stated that they like her and think she is doing a good job. As the 2013 election year opened, her approval ratings were still between 65 and 70 percent. Even her political opponents give her high marks. Her calm, analytic approach to policy problems and aversion to the slogans and posturing of many politicians is a welcome change to many voters. Again events have helped. In the first year of her chancellorship, Germany successfully hosted the World Cup soccer tournament in 2006. Some of its success transferred to her. In 2007, she chaired the European Council (the heads of government of the European Community members) and successfully negotiated several key compromises. In the wake of the post-2008 global financial and economic crisis, Germany's economy went into a deep recession, but her management received high marks and the economy was recovering nicely by the time of the election in September 2009. She retained power, but with a presumably more desirable "bourgeois" coalition partner, the FDP.

Merkel's second term as chancellor has been dominated by the Euro crisis (see chapter 10), the biggest challenge to the European Union in its history. She has arguably become the most controversial chancellor in the history of the Federal Republic. None of her predecessors has been the subject of so much international and domestic pressure and criticism. For the media in countries such as Greece, Portugal, Spain, and even Italy, she is "Frau Nein," the "Sauer Kraut," for her alleged refusal to commit the Federal Republic fully to the rescue of the troubled countries of southern Europe. The pressure on Merkel also comes from Washington and London, which think that a more expansive EU monetary policy would benefit them. The *Economist* cover featured a ship labeled "The World Economy" sinking rapidly toward the bottom of the ocean, with the caption, "Please can we start the engines now, Mrs. Merkel?"[43]

But while she is heavily criticized, the great majority of Germans and many Europeans give her high ratings for her handling of the Euro crisis. In a 2012 survey, solid majorities of voters in France (76 percent), the Czech Republic (67 percent), Poland (66 percent), and the UK (66 percent) thought she was doing a "good job." Only the Greeks (84 percent) considered her leadership to be poor. The Germans repay the favor with 60 percent stating that the Greeks are the least hardworking and most corrupt country in Europe. Merkel's appeal is widespread, cutting across gender, ideological, and generational lines.[44]

Domestically, in the wake of the 2011 Japanese nuclear disaster, Merkel announced a shutdown of seven of the country's seventeen reactors and ordered a "moratorium" on the planned extension of reactor use beyond 2021. It was a complete U-turn from the position of her government six months earlier. No other country using nuclear power took such drastic action. She also appointed a commission to examine whether nuclear power had a future in the Federal Republic. Many observers attributed the speed and extent of her decision to the critical March election in Baden-Württemberg. Terming it a "catastrophe of apocalyptic dimensions," she took 25 percent of the power generated by nuclear offline immediately.

If the decision was political, it did not work. The Greens and SPD ended fifty-eight years of CDU rule in that state, with turnout jumping from 53 to 66 percent. The Greens even overtook the SPD as the largest leftist party; with 23.1 percent, the SPD suffered the worst result in its history. Winfried Kretschmann is the first Green minister-president in German history. All of this occurred despite the strong economy in the state. With 13.2 percent of the country's population, it accounts for 14.5 percent of GDP and 16 percent of exports. Unemployment is 4.2 percent as compared to 7.3 percent nationally. Almost 36 percent of its workforce is still in manufacturing as compared to 28.7 nationally. But the voters were not interested in rewarding the incumbents for their economic record but rather in punishing them for their support of nuclear power and the unique problem of the ambitious reconstruction of Stuttgart's train station (Stuttgart 21).

THE FEDERAL PRESIDENT

The framers of the Basic Law were determined to avoid the problems created by the dual executive of president and chancellor during the Weimar Republic and thus made the office of federal president clearly subordinate to the chancellor and parliament in the policy-making process. In contrast to the Weimar system, the president is not directly elected but is chosen every five years by a federal assembly (*Bundesversammlung*) of all Bundestag deputies and an equal number of delegates elected by the state parliaments. The president is the ceremonial head of state; he or she formally proposes the chancellor and the cabinet for election by the Bundestag; he or she signs all laws and must certify that they were passed in the prescribed manner; and he or she formally appoints and excuses national civil servants and federal judges. If the federal government and the Bundesrat request it, the federal president can declare a state of legislative emergency that would enable the government, but not the president, to rule by decree. In all these functions, however, the president is merely implementing the will of the government or parliament. The question of whether the president has the power to refuse to accept the recommendation of a chancellor for a particular cabinet appointment has never been legally resolved. Yet on those few occasions when the president has in various ways indicated his reservations or objections to a particular candidate, he has seldom been able to block the appointment.

The president does, however, have the right to be consulted and thoroughly informed about planned governmental actions. In the event of a parliamentary crisis, the president is expected to be a mediator and conciliator. Thus, in selecting candidates for this position, emphasis has been placed on personalities with fairly nonpartisan images who evoke few strong negative feelings among the parties and whose backgrounds and personal styles would make them appropriate representatives of the Republic. Most importantly, the president has taken on important symbolic tasks. He or she is expected to be the conscience of the country, the mourner in chief, and a visionary leader.

The first president, Theodor Heuss (1949–1959), had all these qualities. A former journalist and parliamentary deputy of the left liberals (Democratic Party) during the Weimar Republic, he had played a major role in the founding of the Free Democratic Party and in the drafting of the Basic Law. Heuss carefully avoided any partisanship during his two terms and was an effective symbol of the new, democratic state both at home and abroad. Heuss also began the tradition

Table 7.5.   Presidents of the Federal Republic of Germany

President	Tenure	Party
Theodor Heuss	1949–1959	FDP
Heinrich Lübke	1959–1969	CDU
Gustav Heinemann	1969–1974	SPD
Walter Scheel	1974–1979	FDP
Karl Carstens	1979–1984	CDU
Richard von Weizsäcker	1984–1994	CDU
Roman Herzog	1994–1999	CDU
Johannes Rau	1999–2004	SPD
Horst Köhler	2004–2010	CDU
Christian Wulff	2010–2012	CDU
Joachim Gauck	2012–present	Independent

of public atonement and contrition for the crimes of the Nazi past. His successor, Heinrich Lübke (1959–1969), had been minister of agriculture in the Adenauer government and generally followed in the traditions established by Heuss. He became, however, a frequent target of media criticism for his occasional lapses into partisanship and his alleged participation as an architect in the construction of concentration camp buildings during the Third Reich. This latter charge was not substantiated, and Lübke steadfastly denied any involvement.

The third president of the Republic and the first Social Democrat was Gustav Heinemann, elected with the help of the Free Democrats in 1969. Heinemann was also the first president whose general political philosophy was clearly left of center. During his tenure, he raised the prestige of the office and distinguished himself by his concern for the underprivileged in German society and by his support for the conciliatory foreign policy of the Federal Republic toward its Eastern neighbors.

In 1974, Walter Scheel became the Republic's fourth president and the second Free Democrat to hold the post. At the time of his election, Scheel was also at the height of his career as party leader and foreign minister. As president, Scheel explored briefly the possibilities of enlarging the power of the office. He delayed signing some legislation and refused to sign a few other bills on the grounds of their questionable constitutionality. His efforts were firmly blocked by the chancellor and parliament, and there was little support for Scheel's exploration of the constitutional limits of his office. The majority in the federal assembly held by the SPD and FDP at the time of Scheel's election in 1974 disappeared by 1979, and Scheel stepped down. His successor was Karl Carstens, a former chairman of the CDU's Fraktion and top-ranking civil servant in the foreign ministry and chancellor's office. In May 1979 Carstens was elected on a straight party vote by the federal assembly as the fifth president of the Republic.

In 1984 Carstens declined to run for a second term. As his successor, the Christian Democrats nominated Richard von Weizsäcker, the former governing mayor of West Berlin. A lawyer by training, he had been a leading lay figure in the Protestant Church and a prominent member of the Christian Democrats' moderate wing. In acknowledgment of his nonpartisan image, the Social Democrats did not nominate their own candidate. One of President von Weizsäcker's most notable achievements was his address on the fortieth anniversary of Nazi Germany's unconditional surrender on May 8, 1945. For the first time a major German political leader directly challenged the traditional explanation used by older, ordinary Germans that they "knew nothing" about the Holocaust:

> [E]very German was able to experience what his Jewish compatriots had to suffer, ranging from plain apathy and hidden intolerance to outright hatred. Who could remain unsuspecting after the burning of the synagogues, the plundering, the stigmatization with the Star of David, the deprivation of rights, the ceaseless violation of human dignity? Whoever opened his eyes and ears and sought information could not fail to notice that Jews were being deported. . . . When the unspeakable truth of the Holocaust then became known, all too many of us claimed that they had not known anything about it or even suspected anything.[45]

This speech, which attracted worldwide attention, illustrates the capacity of the federal president to bring public attention to important questions that transcend party politics. Into the present, von Weizsäcker remains the most popular and respected president.

In 1994, after serving the maximum of two terms (ten years), von Weizsäcker was succeeded by Roman Herzog, president of the Federal Constitutional Court. Herzog was the personal choice of Chancellor Kohl, whose ruling coalition held a narrow majority of seats in the federal assembly. Herzog was not the first choice of the Christian Democrats. They had hoped to nominate someone from the former East Germany but were unable to find a suitable candidate.

During his tenure (1994–1999) Herzog became a strong advocate for change. In 1997 he strongly criticized the entire German political and economic establishment for its inability to make the reforms necessary for the country to compete in the twenty-first century. For Herzog this *Reformstau*, or stalled reform, was the responsibility of all major groups and institutions in the Republic— business, labor, government, the universities, and churches.

Herzog declined to run for a second term. In May 1999 Johannes Rau, the former minister-president of North Rhine–Westphalia and the SPD's chancellor candidate in 1987, was elected by the federal assembly as his successor. Rau was only the second Social Democrat to hold the post. In 2002 he was at the center of the controversy surrounding the Federal Council's vote on immigration. He signed the legislation in spite of opposition claims that the presiding officer had violated procedures. The Constitutional Court later invalidated the law that Rau had signed.

In 2004 the Christian Democrats and Free Democrats once again held a majority in the federal assembly and nominated Horst Köhler as the Republic's ninth president. Köhler had been a high-ranking civil servant specializing in finance matters before becoming head of the International Monetary Fund (IMF) in Washington, D.C. His image was that of a nonpolitical technocrat who would make no waves. Generally the federal presidents have avoided any direct involvement with partisan politics. But the unusual circumstances surrounding the demise of the Schröder government in 2005 thrust Köhler into the political spotlight. After Schröder deliberately lost a vote of confidence in parliament, he then asked the president to dissolve parliament, thus putting Köhler on the political hot seat. Two of Köhler's predecessors had been in similar situations: Gustav Heinemann in 1972 and Karl Carstens in 1982. After weeks of deliberation, Köhler, in a nationally televised speech, announced his decision to dissolve the parliament.

Indeed, Köhler became the most political president since von Weizsäcker. To the chagrin of party and government leaders, he was outspoken on a number of issues and did not refrain from criticizing specific policies and cabinet members. In 2007 he expressed his concern over the interior minister's plan for increased blanket surveillance of Internet communication. The minister's proposals to give police and intelligence forces more "freedom in the struggle against terrorism," including the suspension of certain constitutionally guaranteed civil liberties, were also criticized by Köhler. He targeted all parties, but especially the Grand Coalition, for not moving fast enough to liberalize labor markets, slim down the welfare state, and balance the budget. He supported Chancellor Schröder's Agenda 2010 and expected the Grand Coalition to finish the job of making Germany competitive in the global economy.

Reelected in 2009, while visiting German troops in Afghanistan in 2010, Köhler stated in a radio interview that the Federal Republic's military involvement was ultimately about protecting its worldwide economic interests. He apparently took the ensuing round of media and opposition criticism personally and promptly resigned. A few weeks later, Merkel and the CDU, with no input from the FDP, selected the CDU minister-president of Lower Saxony, Christian Wulff, as the coalition's candidate to succeed Köhler. The June 30, 2010, vote in the federal assembly turned into a kind of no-confidence vote on the Merkel-led CDU-FDP coalition. In an unprecedented turn of events, three ballots were needed to get him elected, despite Merkel's coalition having enough votes. This unexpected development occurred, on the one hand, because Köhler's resignation took place in the middle of the political shock waves set off by the government's defeat in the May 7 state election in North Rhine–Westphalia. On the other hand, the opposition candidate, Joachim Gauck, was widely respected.

Only a year and half into the job, Wulff was enveloped by a scandal over an undeclared private loan he had received from a wealthy political supporter in 2008, with rumors of political favors being offered in return. Things became worse in early 2012 when it came out that he had angrily demanded that a tabloid newspaper withhold the story. As state prosecutors tried to have his immunity lifted, he resigned in February 2012. Politically bruised by the resignations of Köhler and Wulff (and the recent memory of Wulff's divisive election), and with the strong backing of the SPD, the Greens, and the Free Democrats, Merkel and the CDU reluctantly agreed that Joachim Gauck would be best suited for the job. Gauck was quickly and overwhelmingly elected as the eleventh federal president in March 2012. Gauck is a Protestant clergyman by training, but after unification he led the office charged with investigating the crimes of the Stasi. Admired for his conscientiousness, Gauck is widely respected except by the Left Party, which detests him for pursuing many old communists because of their Stasi connections. He is the first president with no political party affiliation, and the first easterner to hold the office.

SUMMARY OF THE FORMAL LAWMAKING PROCESS

Preparliamentary Stage

About three-fourths of all bills submitted to parliament are conceived and drafted by the government. The impetus for such legislation, however, may come from outside—from interest groups, the European Union, the governing coalition parties, parliamentary delegations, or programs. In some cases, a proposal from the parliamentary opposition may even find its way into a bill, as was the case with the revision of the tax system in 1988 and the 1992 abortion law. Some idea of the mix of ministerial bureaucracy, party, and parliament can be seen in the replies of two cabinet ministers to the question of where and how policy proposals originate. According to one minister,

> The overwhelming number of bills submitted by me can be traced to my and my ministry's conceptions and preparatory work. In one or another case, the suggestion to prepare a specific bill came from the coalition Fraktionen, but was limited to their suggestion for a ministerial initiative. The way in which such initiatives were then considered and formulated was left up to me.[46]

According to the other minister,

> The source of bills nearly always goes back to multiple impulses and demands, thus making rare a "monocausal" explanation. Parliamentary decisions, resolutions and electoral programs of parties, discussions among the public about long-range development trends or suddenly emerging problems, preparatory work in the ministries, the chancellor's decision about the government program and, last but not least, the personal interest of the minister produce the most diverse combinations, which often make it impossible subsequently to sort out the decisive factors for the origin of a law.[47]

During the ministerial drafting process, the rules of procedures in governmental departments also allow civil servants to consult with the affected interest groups. This is done as a matter of course, and the interest group–state bureaucracy relationship is well established. However, in order to ostensibly simplify the consultation process, ministries are generally required to negotiate only with the leadership or national offices of these interest groups. In practice, this procedure contributes to the centralized, hierarchical character of both governmental and interest group bureaucracies.

If a policy area is the concern of more than one ministry, such as economics and finance or defense and foreign policy, interministerial negotiations take place. In cases of conflict due to overlapping responsibilities, the chancellor's office is also informed and, if necessary, mediates and resolves the dispute. This is consistent with the chancellor's responsibility for the overall direction of policy. Most bills requiring new or increased appropriations also are cleared with the finance ministry at the drafting stage. This planning and drafting stage, as Gerard Braunthal has found, involves in many cases a "protracted bargaining process among specialists and politicians" within the ministries and governing parties.[48] Extensive revisions are very common.

Following ministerial approval, the draft legislation is presented to the full cabinet for approval before its submission to parliament. Most internal (governmental) opposition to the legislation is resolved before formal discussion in the cabinet. Although most cabinets have pursued a consensual style of decision making, the chancellor has veto power over any ministerial proposal; similarly, the support of the chancellor virtually ensures cabinet approval.

In practice, however, the chancellor's power can be affected by the size of the government's parliamentary majority, his personal interest in the policy area, the demands of the coalition partner, and the internal pressures from his party and the state bureaucracy. Governments with a relatively small majority have had difficulty in getting their proposed legislation through the chamber. The first Brandt government (1969–1972), with a majority of only twelve (which dwindled to zero by 1972), was able to pass a relatively low 75 percent of its proposed legislation. After the 1972 election, which gave the SPD-FDP coalition a majority of about fifty seats, the government's success rate rose to 93 percent, the highest percentage since the third Adenauer government (1957–1961).[49]

Chancellors such as Adenauer and Brandt had little interest in many domestic policy areas and were willing to exchange concessions in these areas for support in foreign policy and defense matters. Brandt's indifference to or even disdain for issues such as a liberalized abortion law—an issue of considerable importance to elements in the SPD—was a major factor in the long delay before its passage.

During their coalitions with the Free Democrats, both major parties had to make concessions to their junior partners. The Christian Democrats, especially after Adenauer's departure, were urged by the FDP to pursue a more dynamic foreign policy toward Eastern Europe. In collaboration with the CDU's conservative business wing, the Free Democrats were also able to block several social welfare programs advocated by the Union's labor wing. From 1969 to 1982, the Free Democrats played a major role in the delay that plagued the SPD's commitment to internal reform in areas such as codetermination and the reform of vocational education. The SPD-Green government (1998–2005) was also divided on several domestic and foreign policy issues including nuclear energy and the use of German ground troops in NATO operations in Kosovo and the 2001 deployment of German troops to Afghanistan.

Parliamentary Stage

After cabinet approval, draft legislation (that affects the states) is presented to the Bundesrat for a first reading. The Bundesrat at this point can approve, reject, or amend the bill. Regardless of Bundesrat action at this stage, however, the bill will be submitted to the Bundestag—for even if the Bundesrat rejects a bill, this rejection can still be overridden by the Bundestag. In the Bundestag, the bill is discussed in the Fraktionen. At this point, party strategy and policy toward the bill are formally discussed and determined. The bill is then given its first reading, during which only introductory formal debate is held, with no amendments allowed. Referral to the appropriate committee follows this first reading.

Because the government parties have a majority in each committee, a bill is rarely returned to the floor with a negative report. Committees also cannot pigeonhole a bill. In many cases, however, after consideration of a bill the committee does propose amendments.

After the committee report, a second and more thorough debate takes place in the Bundestag. At this time, amendments to the bill are considered. House debate is led by specialists in the policy area who act as spokesmen for the committee. If, after the second reading and debate, a bill is approved without amendment, the third and final reading follows immediately. If the bill has been amended and passed in the second reading, a waiting period of at least two days after the distribution of the revised bill to all deputies is observed before the final vote.

Following Bundestag action, the bill returns to the Bundesrat for a second reading. If the policy area involved requires Bundesrat approval and if the Bundesrat vetoes the policy, the bill is dead. When the policy area is not one affecting the states (defense, for example), a simple Bundestag majority can override a Bundesrat veto. If the Bundesrat veto is by a majority of two-thirds or more, the veto must be defeated by a Bundestag majority of two-thirds.

In most cases, as discussed earlier in this chapter, the Bundesrat objects to parts of a bill affecting the states, and these differences are then referred to a joint conference committee for resolution. In some cases, Bundesrat objections are already incorporated in amendments introduced in the Bundestag. The report of the conference committee is then submitted to both houses for approval. Finally, the bill is examined for constitutionality by the chancellor's office, justice ministry, and president's office before being signed and promulgated by the president.

The entire process is executive dominated, and our examination of the state bureaucracy in chapter 8 should make this even more apparent. Nonetheless, there are instances when the government does meet resistance from its parliamentary delegations after the submission of legislative proposals. In most of these cases, interest groups disappointed in their preparliamentary bargaining with the ministries attempt to mobilize their parliamentary contacts for one last try at revision. During the current Merkel CDU-FDP coalition, interest group activity has increased especially in policy areas where the Free Democrats have substantial influence. The hotel tax scandal, discussed in chapter 6, was an example of the type of clientele politics associated with the party.

But other interest groups that traditionally have expected a friendly hearing from the Christian Democrats have been disappointed. Above all the energy industry, which was not consulted prior to the 2011 decision to abandon nuclear power, has suffered substantial financial losses and has been unable to persuade the government to delay or revisit its policy. Sometimes lobbyists will attempt to persuade the chancellor's own party to revise a policy already approved by the cabinet. One such case occurred in July 2012 shortly before the parliament adjourned for the summer recess. The government had approved a new domicile registration law under which the personal data supplied in the registration process would not be sold to third parties such as mail-order firms without the explicit consent of the citizen. Displeased with the decision, CDU/CSU deputies with ties to the merchandising industry succeeded in reversing the policy during the final readings of the bill in parliament; that is, citizens' data would be automatically released to commercial interests unless the citizen made a specific request not to have the information released. The Merkel government was put in the embarrassing position of having to ask the second chamber, the Bundesrat, to correct the actions of its own party in the Bundestag.

NOTES

1. Margaret Lavinia Anderson, *Practicing Democracy: Elections and Political Culture in Imperial Germany* (Princeton, NJ: Princeton University Press, 2000).

2. Michael Z. Wise, *Capital Dilemma: Germany's Search for a New Architecture of Democracy* (New York: Princeton Architectural Press, 1998).

3. Richard Bernstein, "Germany Opens Holocaust Memorial in Berlin," *New York Times*, May 10, 2005, 1.

4. A party must have a minimum of 5 percent of the total membership, currently thirty-one deputies, to receive Fraktion status. A party with less than 5 percent can be given "group" status. A group cannot make any procedural motions, but it can have members on every committee and can introduce legislation. Groups are allotted speaking time in proportion to their size.

5. http://www.bundestag.de/htdocs_e/bundestag/committees/index.html.

6. John D. Nagle, "Elite Transformations in a Pluralist Democracy: Occupational and Educational Backgrounds of Bundestag Members, 1949–1972" (manuscript, Syracuse University, 1974).

7. Adalbert Hess, "Berufstatistik der Mitglieder des 10. Deutschen Bundestages," *Zeitschrift für Parlamentsfragen* 14 (December 1983): 487–489. In the 2005 parliament, civil servants, interest group representatives, and political party employees constituted about two-thirds of the membership. Manual workers and housewives made up less than 1 percent of the body. Melanie Kintz, "Daten zur Berufstruktur des 16. Deutschen Bundestages," *Zeitschrift für Parlamentsfragen* 37 (September 2006): 461–470.

8. In the eleventh Bundestag (1987–1990), the committee that dealt with most civil service questions (Domestic Affairs) was composed largely (80 percent) of civil servants, and the informal subcommittee that specialized in civil service salaries was made up solely of civil servants.

9. Gerhard Loewenberg, *Parliament in the German Political System* (Ithaca, NY: Cornell University Press, 1966), 46.

10. Ferdinand Müller-Rommel, "Interessengruppenvertretung im Deutschen Bundestag," in *US Kongress und Deutscher Bundestag*, ed. Uwe Thaysen, Roger H. Davidson, and Robert G. Livingston (Opladen: Westdeutscher Verlag, 1989), 305.

11. Müller-Rommel, "Interessengruppenvertretung im Deutschen Bundestag."

12. Müller-Rommel, "Interessengruppenvertretung im Deutschen Bundestag," 309.

13. The opening of the Stasi files in early 1992 apparently revealed that individuals in these occupations were by no means immune from contacts with the secret police.

14. The chancellor does not have to be a member of the parliament, but all but one, Kurt-Georg Kiesinger (1966–1969), have been sitting members at the time of their election.

15. Peter Schindler, ed., *Datenhandbuch zur Geschichte des Deutschen Bundestages* (Bonn: Presse und Informationszentrum des Deutschen Bundestages, 1983).

16. Kurt Sontheimer, *Grundzüge des politischen Systems der Bundesrepublik Deutschland* (Munich: Piper Verlag, 1984), 162–163.

17. Institut für Demoskopie surveys cited in Schindler, ed., *Datenhandbuch*, 1048.

18. Institut für Demoskopie, survey nos. 0040 (1951) and 4036 (1983).

19. Shortly after the Bundestag's 1991 vote to move to Berlin, the Bundesrat decided to remain in Bonn as an expression of its commitment to the states. But in 1996 the Bundesrat changed its mind and by a 13–3 vote decided to join the Bundestag in Berlin. Remaining in Bonn with the government in Berlin, it was argued, would have weakened the influence of the chamber and thus the states. Even Bavaria, once a strong supporter of Bonn, citing the presence of the media in Berlin, voted to move. In July 2000, one year after the Bundestag's move was completed, the Bundesrat held its final session in Bonn. In Berlin it now resides in the renovated chambers of the old Prussian upper house of parliament.

20. Quoted in Klaus Stüve, "Konflikt und Konsens im Bundesrat," *Aus Politik und Zeitgeschichte*, nos. 50–51 (December 6, 2004), 25.

21. Heinz Laufer, "Der Bundesrat," *Aus Politik und Zeitgeschichte*, January 22, 1972, 50–52.

22. Karlheinz Neunreither, *Der Bundesrat zwischen Politik und Verwaltung* (Heidelberg: Quelle und Mayer Verlag, 1959), 84–86.

23. Uwe Thaysen, *The Bundesrat, the Länder and German Federalism* (Washington, DC: American Institute for Contemporary German Studies, Johns Hopkins University, 1994), 9.

24. Peter Schindler, "Der Bundesrat in parteipolitischer Auseinandersetzung," *Zeitschrift für Parlamentsfragen* (June 1972), 148–149.

25. http://www.tatsachen-ueber-deutschland.de/en/political-system/main-content-04/the-bundesrat.html; see also Simone Burkhart, Philip Manow, and Daniel Ziblatt, "A More Efficient and Accountable Federalism? An Analysis of the Consequences of Germany's 2006 Constitutional Reform," *German Politics* 17, no. 4 (2008): 522–540.

26. Ingo von Münch, "Der Bundesrat als Gegenregierung?" *Die Zeit*, April 5, 1974, 5.

27. Fritz W. Scharpf, "No Exit from the Joint Decision Trap? Can German Federalism Reform Itself?" (working paper 05/8, Max Planck Institute for the Study of Societies, Cologne, September 2005).

28. This has not prevented opposition parties from attempting to dismiss individual cabinet ministers through no-confidence resolutions. Such resolutions have been introduced at various times since 1949. They have all been rejected, tabled, or withdrawn. This is a political tactic designed to embarrass the chancellor and the cabinet member. Even if a resolution against an individual minister passed, it would have no legal effect. For a discussion of these resolutions, see Peter Schindler, ed., *Datenhandbuch zur Geschichte des Deutschen Bundestages, 1949 bis 1982* (Bonn: Presse und Informationszentrum des Deutschen Bundestages, 1983), 418–421.

29. The SPD member formally resigned from the party before the vote and was technically an independent when she cast her ballot.

30. F. F. Ridley, "Chancellor Government as a Political System and the German Constitution," *Parliamentary Affairs* 19, no. 4 (February 1966): 446–461; Kenneth Dyson, "The German Federal Chancellor's Office," *Political Quarterly* 45, no. 3 (July–September 1974): 364–371.

31. Rolf-Peter Lange, "Auslesestrukturen bei der Besetzung von Regierungsämtern," in *Parteiensystem in der Legitimationskrise*, ed. Jürgen Dittberner and Rolf Ebbighausen (Opladen: Westdeutscher Verlag, 1973), 132–171.

32. Gerard Braunthal, *The West German Legislative Process* (Ithaca, NY: Cornell University Press, 1972), 112–134. For an excellent account of the development of the chancellor's office, see Ferdinand Müller-Rommel, "The Chancellor and His Staff," in *Adenauer to Kohl: The Development of the German Chancellorship*, ed. Stephen Padgett (London: Hurst and Company, 1993), 106–126.

33. Ferdinand Müller-Rommel, "Federal Republic of Germany," in *Cabinets in Western Europe*, ed. Jean Blondel and Ferdinand Müller-Rommel (London: Macmillan, 1988), 166.

34. H. Pierre Secher, "Controlling the New German Military Elite: The Political Role of the Parliamentary Defense Commissioner in the Federal Republic," *Proceedings of the American Philosophical Society* 109, no. 2 (April 1965): 63.

35. Public opinion surveys generally find that the military is considered a rather unimportant institution compared to parliament, the chancellor, the courts, and the Federal Bank. See Elisabeth Noelle-Neumann, ed., *The Germans: Public Opinion Polls, 1967–1980* (Westport, CT: Greenwood Press, 1981), 188.

36. Peter Joachim Lapp, "Der Preis der Einheit: Kapitulation und Auflösung," *Das Parlament*, June 17, 1994, 16. See also Peter Schneider, "Die neuen Kameraden," *Der Spiegel*, June 13, 1994, 74ff; and Frederick Zilian, *From Confrontation to Cooperation: The Takeover of the National People's (East German) Army by the Bundeswehr* (Boulder, CO: Praeger, 1999). There was widespread opposition in the West German army to accepting any former NVA personnel, especially officers, into the service. Over 90 percent of the NVA officer corps had been members of the Communist Party, and their commitment to serving a democratic state was suspect. Prior to the 1990 unification, all East German generals had been required to resign or be demoted. None chose the latter course.

37. Kurt Sontheimer, *The West German Political System* (New York: Praeger, 1973), 131.

38. Karl-Dietrich Bracher, *The German Dictatorship* (New York: Praeger, 1973), 499–500.

39. Klaus Bölling, *Republic in Suspense* (New York: Praeger, 1965), 74.

40. Jeffrey Herf, *Divided Memory: The Nazi Past in the Two Germanys* (Cambridge, MA: Harvard University Press, 1997).

41. The Kohl government's opposition to any modernization of the short-range missiles was based in part on its experiences with the medium-range weapons issue in the early 1980s. The government had no interest in another conflict with Germany's peace movement. In this sense the message of the movement had finally reached, albeit belatedly, the inner councils of the government.

42. Alexander Osang, "Die Schläflerin," *Der Spiegel*, no. 46 (September 9, 2011): 69.

43. *Economist*, June 9, 2012.

44. Pew, 2012, 39.

45. For key excerpts from von Weizsäcker's speech, see *New York Times*, May 9, 1985, A20.

46. Cited in Gerard Braunthal, "The Policy Function of the German Social Democratic Party," *Comparative Politics* 9, no. 2 (January 1977): 143.

47. Braunthal, "The Policy Function of the German Social Democratic Party," 143.

48. Braunthal, *The West German Legislative Process*, 231.

49. Braunthal, *The West German Legislative Process*, 231.

8

Policy-Making Institutions II

Administration, Semipublic Institutions, and Courts

The policy process neither begins nor ends with the formal decision making of government and parliament that we examined in the preceding chapter. The implementation and adjudication of policy decisions are also an integral part of government. In modern, developed political systems, these functions are largely the responsibility of the state's administration, courts, and semipublic institutions. Our concern in this chapter is with these institutions and their role in the policy process.

Although Germany did not invent bureaucracy or courts, it certainly contributed to their refinement and development. The Prussian civil service of the Hohenzollern emperors became a model of efficiency, dedication, and incorruptibility adopted not only throughout the Reich, but in other countries as well. Assessing this famous bureaucracy during the reign of Frederick the Great, one author wrote, "It managed to support the army of a first-rate power on the resources of a third-rate state and at the same time accumulated a large reserve in the public treasury."[1] The German judiciary and the massive codification of civil and criminal law, completed in the late nineteenth century, influenced legal developments in such diverse settings as Greece, Korea, and Japan.

During the past century, specific governments and regimes have come and gone, but the civil service and judiciary have remained largely unchanged in structure and procedures. It is little wonder that Germans at both elite and mass levels have had more confidence in dealing with their bureaucracy and courts than with other branches of government.[2] The legalistic-bureaucratic mentality attributed to the political culture is in part a result of the far greater stability of these institutions, and hence, the more extensive experiences Germans have had with them.

The Federal Republic also has an extensive network of semipublic agencies that are either independent of both national and state governments or have their own separate administrative structures. These institutions—most notably the Federal Bank (Bundesbank), which in 1999 became part of the European Central Bank system; the social security and health systems; and the Federal Labor

Agency—play key roles in economic, social, and welfare policy making and implementation. The unification process brought forth still another semipublic institution, the Treuhandanstalt, or Trusteeship Authority, which became the single most important economic institution in the former East Germany. From 1990 to 1994, the Treuhand was the world's largest holding company. It controlled approximately 14,000 formerly state-owned enterprises, thousands of small businesses (restaurants and shops), 30 percent of the farmland, and two-thirds of the forests in the east. These enterprises at one time employed almost nine million people.

DEVELOPMENT OF THE GERMAN ADMINISTRATIVE AND JUDICIAL SYSTEM

The performance of the courts and state bureaucracy, defined in a narrow technical sense of getting the job done, has been good. Historically, at least, the commitment of the bureaucracy and the judiciary to the values and processes of liberal democracy, however, was less than satisfactory. During the Weimar Republic, both institutions were at best ambivalent toward and at worst hostile to the new regime. Given their monarchical origins and the nationalist, upper-class character of their personnel, together with the association of the Weimar Republic with military defeat and foreign humiliation, these orientations should not be surprising. During the Third Reich, whatever independence and sense of integrity the judiciary and bureaucracy had possessed were soon lost as both became tools of the dictatorship. Arnold Brecht, himself a former high-ranking civil servant in Prussia until he was driven out by the Nazis, observed,

> By the end of the Hitler era the German civil service had become a worldwide epithet for irresponsible servility, for turncoat opportunism, for bureaucratic self-preservation and for an utterly undemocratic type of authoritarianism. Its renowned incorruptibility had been shown to have an unexpected limit. While its members would not be bribed individually, as a group they had surrendered to the corruption of their work by the governing party. Gone with the storm was the admiration of the world.[3]

After 1945 the Western Allies intended to purge both institutions of Nazi Party members and sympathizers and reorganize them to facilitate their democratization. Yet the occupation authorities soon found that the dismissal of all party members from the bureaucracy and judiciary would have brought administration to a standstill.

Thus, although Nazis were removed from top-level leadership positions and replaced by known antifascist or "clean" civil servants, the middle and lower levels of the civil service remained essentially intact and were transferred to the various local and state governments being formed by the military occupation. In all, about 53,000 civil servants were dismissed for party membership in the immediate postwar period, but only about 1,000 were permanently excluded from any future employment.[4] In 1951, after the restoration of partial sovereignty to the Federal Republic, a Reinstatement Act gave even most of the dismissed party members full pension credits for service during the Third Reich and reemployment in civil service. The result was that by the early 1950s, 40 to 80 percent of officials in many departments were former party members.[5]

A similar development took place in the judiciary. Initially all courts were closed, and all Nazi party courts and special tribunals were abolished. Only those courts then devoid of Nazi influence and personnel and sanctioned by occupation authorities were reopened. At first, adjudication practically came to a standstill. By 1946, however, the regular system was functioning much as it had before the Nazi seizure of power.[6]

The elimination of Nazi Party members from the judiciary was never accomplished. The problem was that the occupation authorities soon found that the great majority of all judicial officials, judges, and prosecutors had been in the party. Each case was decided on an individual basis, and distinctions were made between fellow travelers of varying degrees and committed Nazis. The occupation authorities also discovered many non-Nazi judges seeking to protect colleagues who had been only nominal party members.[7] In spite of party membership, "if a man was a good judge, his redemption and readmission to the depleted ranks were made easy. The judicial caste had not failed its members."[8] At most, about 2,000 judicial officials lost their jobs, and only a few fanatics were permanently disqualified.

The abandonment for all practical purposes of the denazification and democratization of the civil service and judiciary was due to the Allies' desire to return to stability and normality as soon as possible. Countering the perceived Soviet threat to Western Europe, which heightened after the fall of Czechoslovakia and the Berlin Blockade in 1948, became more important than major internal reform in the Western zones.

Denazification could also be abandoned with little short-run risk because the great majority of former party members were more than willing to accept the rule of the new masters. Very few had actually been committed party members, and many of these had learned their lesson and were hardly inclined to subvert the new state. But this generation of civil servants and judges could not be expected to show a genuine commitment to the ideals of liberty, equality, and the democratic process. The reform of the state administration was thus postponed. Moreover, only in recent years have important government ministries such as the Foreign Office, Justice, and Interior finally addressed their role during the Third Reich. In 2005, for instance, then–foreign minister Joschka Fischer convened a commission of historians to investigate the actions of the Foreign Office during the Nazi period, and in 2010 the resulting report was published (*Das Amt und die Vergangenheit*; The Office and the Past).[9]

STATE ADMINISTRATION

Structure

German civil servants may work at one of several governmental levels: national, state, regional, district, county, or local. In spite of the decentralized structure of the state, civil servants generally share a common background and training, and they work within a similarly structured bureaucratic framework. The occasional coordination and integration of these multiple governmental layers is, in part, the result of this common training and administrative framework.

German administrative units are very hierarchical but not centralized. The bureaucratic pyramid is very steep, but there is little actual direct control from the top of the activities in the middle and at the base. At the national level there are fourteen federal ministries, ranging in size from the ministry of finance, with about 3,000 employees, to the ministry for the family, with 325 employees.

All ministries have a common structure. They are divided into four levels: executive (the minister and the state secretaries), departments, subdepartments, and sections (bureaus). The ministry's personnel are classified into five groups: (1) political officials, (2) higher service, (3) elevated or upper-middle service, (4) intermediate service, and (5) simple or lower-level service. Also within groups two to five, but usually in the lower three levels, a public employee can be classified as a *Beamter* (official) with lifetime tenure, a white-collar employee, or a manual worker. Almost all civil servants at the top two levels are officials, whereas most of those in the intermediate and lower-level service are either white-collar employees or manual workers. The elevated service, group three, is about equally divided between officials and white-collar workers.

Within each organizational level, however, different types of personnel with varying ranks, job titles, and responsibilities can be found. The minister's state secretaries and department heads are all "political" civil servants. Thus, although they are the highest-ranking employees in the ministry, they can be removed, transferred, or pensioned by the minister if necessary.[10] In spite of their formal political status, most state secretaries and ministerial directors (the rank of most department heads) are longtime tenured civil servants. If the minister does not retain them, they must by law be transferred to another position suitable to their status. If Germany had an administrative class or *grands corps* of civil servants, as in the United Kingdom and France, they would be at this level. But there are no graduates of elite schools whose members are distributed throughout the various ministries. There are also parliamentary state secretaries (in some cases called ministers of state), who are simultaneously members of parliament and are similar to deputy ministers in other systems. Merkel's post-2009 cabinet has approximately thirty parliamentary state secretaries.

Although they function at two different organizational levels, the subdepartment heads (with ranks of ministerial *dirigent* or councilor) and the section, or bureau, chiefs are part of the higher service. They all have academic training and decision-making responsibilities within their bureaus or subdepartments and are personally and legally responsible for decisions that bear their signatures. The section assistants constitute the lowest group in the higher-level service. These are comparable to junior executive positions. Their titles vary depending on the length of their service and the size of their section.

The elevated service is composed largely of caseworkers, or *Sachbearbeiter*. Because the higher service (section assistants to state secretaries) requires an academic degree, few caseworkers will ever enter it, even though their experience and job knowledge may make them more qualified than some of their superiors.

The intermediate-level service is made up of clerical and secretarial staff and comprises about 35 percent of most ministries' total personnel. At the bottom of the organizational ladder are those in the simple services (e.g., messengers, drivers, custodians).

Thus about 30 percent of a typical ministry's staff hold executive or junior executive positions; another 25 percent are caseworkers; and the remaining 45 percent perform clerical, secretarial, or custodial functions. The key unit is the section, or bureau, and the key personnel are the section heads. Each section is assigned responsibility for a particular policy area. The development, initiation, and supervision of ministerial policy are centered in these sections. They are the powerhouses of German administration; as one frustrated reformer observed, the section heads are the "princes" of the policy-making process within the ministries.[11] The average section is small, with only three to seven members: a section head, one or two assistants, caseworkers, and clerical personnel. Overall there are about 2,000 such sections at the national level. To a large extent, national policy, as formulated in the ministries, is the sum of what these 2,000 parts produce.

Critics of Germany's administration have focused on this hierarchical yet decentralized structure. It is, they contend, highly fragmented and discourages comprehensive policy planning or major reform initiatives that require extensive interdepartmental, interministerial, or federal-state cooperation. Small sections tend to work best with small problems.[12] Because the top political officials in each ministry have so little staff, they cannot in practice exercise the control they have in theory. Expertise is concentrated at the bottom, in the sections.

The small size of each section and the practice of making the section head personally and legally responsible for the section's decisions make success or failure highly visible. Promotion is related to success. Hence sections tend to concentrate on limited, short-run projects that will, in effect, yield only minor modifications in an already existing policy but that will be judged successful by superiors who approve of the existing policy. Risky projects are avoided in part because they exceed a section's limited capacity but also because their failure can be easily attributed to specific individuals.

At the ministerial stage of policy development, a complex process of bargaining and negotiation takes place among the experts at the base, the section head, the department and subdepartment chiefs, and the executive (minister and state secretary). The influence of outside forces—such as interest groups, parties, and consultants—is most directly felt at the executive and departmental levels. The sections are relatively insulated and secure in the knowledge that they have as much, if not more, expertise as anyone else in the house, even with the outside specialists whom the executive may call in. Shoring up the top to contend with the princes in the sections is, according to many students of the system, its most pressing need. Political leadership is supposed to initiate, oversee, coordinate, and integrate policy programs, but it does not have the necessary resources. The problem is not an unwillingness of the middle and lower levels to respond, but an inability of political leadership to formulate and operationalize policy goals because of a lack of staff and planning capability. Similar structural frameworks at the state and local levels compound the problems of fragmentation and hierarchy at the national level.

Personnel

When the Federal Republic was established in 1949, many of its first civil servants came directly from either the unified (American, British, and French zones) Economics Administration in Frankfurt or the Länder bureaucracies. Early coordination between the central government and the states was thus facilitated by the common background and training of civil servants at both levels. From the beginning, the Bonn Republic had a well-trained, relatively intact bureaucracy in its service.

As of 2011 about 13.6 percent of the German workforce was employed by the government (or public corporations, excluding military personnel), down from 16.5 percent in 2000 and decreasing since the peak in 1991. This is similar to the proportion of public employees in the United States (14.6 percent), but smaller than the public sector in the UK (18.6 percent), France (24.4 percent), or Norway (34.8 percent).[13] The privatization of the postal and telecommunication systems and the partial privatization of the railroads have decreased the number of public employees by almost one million. Out of the approximately 4.6 million people working for government, only about 34 percent of public employees have tenured civil servant status. About 11.4 percent now work at the federal level, as compared to 51 percent for the Länder (the vast majority of whom are teachers or professors), 30 percent for local government, and 8 percent for the social security system (including the Federal Labor Agency).[14] Moreover, most of the national civil servants are not employed in the federal ministries, but in various offices (tax administration, weather service, air traffic control, economic agencies). Only about 25,000 civil servants are directly employed in the federal ministries. Moreover, as we have seen, most of these are not in policy-making positions. Considering the 2,000 section chiefs and their assistants as policy makers, and adding subdepartment and department heads, the total number of civil servants with policy-making initiatives is about 3,000. All others are administrators in the strict sense of the term: they carry out the decisions of others.

German public officials at all levels are by law and custom a special group with unique privileges and obligations. The civil servants are expected to be loyal and obedient to the state and their superiors and willing to adjust their private lives to the demands of the service. In exchange for this commitment to the state, officials may receive lifetime tenure and salaries and benefits that enable them and their families to maintain a lifestyle commensurate with their status. In 2012, for instance, annual salaries for federal officials ranged from $26,000 for the lowest officials to $175,000 for the highest.[15] In short, for loyal and correct service, the Beamte receive a guarantee of lifelong security. Other occupational groups must take their chances in the free market economy, but the civil servants are risk free. Both the American occupation authorities and the Social Democrats opposed the postwar restoration of this privileged status, which has its origins in the age of monarchy. Nonetheless, civil servants, through energetic and effective lobbying, were able to secure the restoration of the service to its traditional position.[16]

The conception of the civil servant as an official with a special and privileged relationship to the private citizen has certainly changed since 1949. The modern executive, unlike those during previous regimes, is now more dependent on social and political forces, specifically political parties, than on a politically independent "supreme authority." Yet the fact that Germans have traditionally viewed the state as an institution above and superior to society still persists to some degree and gives powerful support to the acts of the German bureaucrat.

Recruitment

Recruitment to the service is closely tied to the educational system, with each level having specific educational requirements such as a master's degree. The higher level, still the monopoly of the university educated, was once even more restricted in that a legal education was required. Today, lawyers still dominate the upper ranks, and surveys have shown that they remain the most privileged of the privileged.[17]

Although the Constitution (Article 36) calls for higher-level national civil servants to be selected from all constituent states on a proportional basis, some regions are disproportionately represented at the top of the federal bureaucratic pyramid. One study found that 36 percent of all high-level civil servants in office from 1949 to 1984 had come from what was then East Germany (that is, they had fled after 1945), the "lost" provinces east of the Oder-Neisse line, or Berlin. These areas were historically part of Prussia, or were Prussian dominated. Generally, northern Germans were far more likely to be higher-level civil servants than were southern Germans (from Baden-Württemberg and Bavaria).[18] The traditional high-level German civil servant was male, the son of a civil servant, Protestant, from northern Germany or "Prussia," and a lawyer.

This profile may be changing. Already in 2000, 51.4 percent of public employees were women (including military personnel). Among civil servants and judges, women made up 39 percent; in the group of salary earners, 68 percent; of wage earners, 37 percent; and in the case of military personnel, 2.1 percent.[19] Although Germany has no specific elite school (such as the French Ecole Nationale d'Administration or Cambridge and Oxford universities in the UK) that produces a large percentage of high-level civil servants, the universities of Frankfurt, Bonn, Munich, Tübingen, and Hamburg are very well represented in the senior bureaucracy. The Berlin universities may also be starting to supply candidates for the civil service.

Entrance into the service, especially at higher and elevated levels, is normally limited to young candidates who are expected to make a long-term if not lifetime commitment. Most candidates must pass entrance examinations that, like those in most other European countries, test not for ability in specific positions but for general career aptitude. After admittance to the service, there is a probationary period of two to three years, during which systematic in-service training is given before a final examination and eligibility for the coveted status of *Beamter auf Lebenszeit* (public official for life).

These procedures apply to all public positions that have civil service status. Sharp distinctions are made within the service between those with Beamte status and those without (manual workers and white-collar employees), as well as between the career civil servant and the outsider. If we add these features of the recruitment process to the hierarchical structure described earlier, we have a further explanation for the absence of major programs of innovation emanating from the established bureaucracy. The still-dominant influence of lawyers in the higher service and the pervasive influence of legal norms and practices do, however, aid in the integration of local, state, and federal bureaucracies. Practices and procedures within the bureaucracy are explicitly prescribed both in law and in the Common Code of Administrative Procedure, which is a revised version of a code from the 1920s. This document—part office manual, part code of etiquette—is still used in some form in most German governmental offices.

Attitudes and Values

Given the background, recruitment, and structural environment of German civil servants, one should not be surprised that surveys have found them to be a status-conscious, somewhat cautious group of people with nonetheless a firm commitment to the Republic and to the values and processes of liberal democracy. One study of students' career plans found that those planning to enter the state bureaucracy deviated from average students in their emphasis on "the occupational values of job security, old age security, clearly structured tasks, and well-circumscribed demands on one's abilities and time."[20] The more independent, ambitious, and achievement-oriented students were less interested in a civil service career. Not unexpectedly, bureaucrats are also very promotion oriented, and most feel that special efforts are necessary to merit promotion.[21]

The civil servant's perception of the political character of the job, however, has increased. In a comparative study of top administrators (department heads) in the 1970s, German respondents were already found to be (1) as conscious of the ways in which democratic politics affect their work and, conversely, of the ways in which their work affects the stability and effectiveness of the postwar democracy as were civil servants in the UK, and (2) more aware than Italian bureaucrats.[22] A study of assistant section heads (the lowest or beginning level of the higher service) in the economics ministry found that most recognized and accepted the political character of their job; 67 percent perceived that they were involved "in politics" and were not merely administering the laws as "neutral" agents of a state above society, parties, and parliament.[23]

The civil service has also adapted to a variety of political masters since 1949 and has provided a strong element of continuity. Contrary to expectations, after twenty years of Christian Democratic rule the civil service did not attempt any sabotage of Social-Liberal reforms after 1969. The fact that many of the SPD's domestic reform programs between 1969 and 1982 did not become reality is usually attributed to factors over which the bureaucracy had little or no control: disagreements within and between the parties in the governing coalition, lack of adequate financial resources, and inadequate political leadership.

The civil service also received high marks for its work during and since the unification process, as well as in response to the post-2008 economic crisis and the post 2010 Euro crisis.[24] In fact, Germany rates as one of the best-governed countries in the world. According to the World Bank's worldwide governance indicators, the country had percentile ranks in the low to mid 90s for voice and accountability, government effectiveness, regulatory quality, rule of law, and control of corruption, but only 74 for political stability/absence of violence.[25] The Bertelsmann sustainable governance indicators ranked the country eleventh in management, noting, "Although administrative structures appear at first glance sclerotic, Germany demonstrates remarkable adaptability to international and supranational developments."[26]

Pressures for Reform

Despite its efficiency, the state bureaucracy and its role in the policy-making process have come under criticism in recent years. Much of this focuses on its inability to adapt to new policy demands and developments, especially where major innovations are needed: economic development, transportation, land use, health care, and education. Although it served the Republic well in the reconstruction phase of the postwar period, it has not been able, the critics charge, given its present structure and mode of operation, to respond to the new, more complicated policy needs of the future.[27]

Specific recommendations for change have centered on the following factors:

1. the size of the administration, in terms of both the number of public employees and the number of administrative units;
2. the outmoded hierarchy and reward system; and
3. the privatization of public services and state-run enterprises.

Within a physical space about half the size of Texas are a national government, 16 states, 45 governmental districts, 426 counties, 129 cities (independent from county government), and about 11,500 local communities. The division of labor among these units, the coordination of administrative activity, and the relationship between their size and responsibilities are insufficiently defined. Given this number of administrative units, it is not surprising that concerns over the size and cost of the public sector have increased over the last decades.

With unification, the Federal Republic inherited a bloated East German bureaucracy that had been thoroughly controlled by the Socialist Unity (Communist) Party. Most of the 1.2 million public employees in the former East Germany were put on probationary status, and eventually about 300,000 become permanent pubic employees. In 1991 the Federal Constitutional Court upheld the provisions of the intra-German Unity Treaty of 1990, which allows the dismissal of public employees in the eastern region because of their support for the communist dictatorship or in order to establish a "rational effective administration" in the new states. Since unification, the size of the bureaucracy in the eastern states has declined, but on a per capita basis there are still more public employees in the eastern states than in the western regions. Overall, however, there has been a decrease in the size of the state sector over the last twenty years, largely due to privatization (see below).

The strict distinctions of higher, elevated, intermediate, and low or simple service levels; the privileges of lifetime tenure and generous pensions; and the aversion to outside experts are expensive and outmoded and have increasingly little relationship to the actual work of administration. Much of the work done by academically trained higher-level civil servants could be done just as well by caseworkers at a lower level. In a 1997 survey, 47 percent of the adult population agreed that white-collar employees could replace Beamte; only 29 percent wanted the present system retained.[28] In some states pension costs for Beamte equal the salary costs of active personnel. Some of the poorer states, such as the Saar, spend almost all their revenue for personnel and are dependent on federal grants for capital investment.

Beyond the reduction in the number of civil servants, there have been some successful reforms in recent years including a performance-related pay structure introduced in 1997, and after 2005 the application of better techniques to measure the effect and cost of bureaucracy (standard cost model) as part of an international "Better Regulation" initiative. In 2004, it was estimated that regulations cost German business over $50 billion. After a "spring cleaning" that reduced the number of federal regulations, it was estimated that about $9 billion of such costs had been saved.[29] These initiatives may be paying off. Although 85 percent of Germans thought there was still too much bureaucracy in 2007, 26 percent thought that service had improved, and 37 percent thought that government offices were run more with the service of citizens in mind.[30]

Discontent with big bureaucratic government has existed for several decades and has greatly influenced public corporations. The state-run postal service, banks, telephone system, railroads, and the national airline, Lufthansa, have been partially or totally privatized. The postal system has been divided into three independent units: (1) letters and packages, (2) postal savings banks, and (3) telephone and telecommunications (*Telekom*). All three are run as private enterprises with no government subsidies. Indeed, by 2011, the courier company (DHL) had become one of the world's largest. Many of the employees of these enterprises have civil service status and have opposed any attempts to change in the name of free enterprise or sound business principles. In 2007 the nation's locomotive engineers went on strike in protest over further privatization plans for the railroads.

The Kohl government also proposed legislation that would phase out civil service ranks in the newly privatized enterprises. The state's near monopoly of the job placement process through the Federal Labor Agency (discussed later in this chapter) was also abandoned in 1994. Plans for the privatization of many functions now performed by local or state governments (e.g., garbage collection, libraries, and recreational centers) have also drawn the wrath of public employees and their unions, but the process of privatization and downsizing the bureaucracy has continued under the Schröder and Merkel governments, albeit at a slower pace.

SEMIPUBLIC INSTITUTIONS

Among the semipublic institutions, the German social security and health systems, like the bureaucracy and courts, have survived the frequent and sudden regime changes of the past century. Both were established in the 1880s by the conservative Chancellor Bismarck, who sought to ensure that the growing working class would support the existing monarchical regime and not the socialists. The Federal Labor Agency, located in Nuremberg, administers a nationwide network of employment offices first established during the Weimar Republic that reemerged relatively intact after 1949. The Bundesbank (Federal Bank) in Frankfurt, which has been primarily responsible for monetary policy and now represents German interests in the European Central Bank, is a postwar creation, although it can trace its origins to the Reichsbank of the Hohenzollern Empire. These institutions assume functions performed by national governments in centralized systems such as the UK and France. Even though they are nominally under the supervision of the national finance ministry, like the other semipublic bodies, they have substantial independence from the federal government. These semipublic institutions lessen the total political load carried by the national government, but they also reduce its strength. Their distance from the national and state governments has also generally shielded them from the conflicts of partisan politics.[31]

The Social Security and Health Systems

The German welfare state is one of the most generous and comprehensive in the world. Expenditures for health care, pensions, industrial accident compensation, child support, public housing, veterans' support, and (since 1995) long-term nursing care insurance consume about 33 percent of the country's gross domestic product. It also provides Germans with over one-fourth of their disposable income. The pension and health care programs are financed largely through equal employer and employee contributions. The costs of other programs (e.g., child support, housing and rent subsidies, welfare) are taken from general tax revenue. Employers must pay the costs of the accident insurance program. Yet the administration of these huge programs is not carried out by either the national or state governments but by more than 1,800 social security and health funds located throughout the country.

The 200 or so health, or "sickness," funds cover about 85 percent of the population. They are organized by economic sector (business, agriculture, professions); occupational group; and geographic area and are nonprofit. All Germans must have health insurance either through the semipublic health funds or through private insurance, which is also heavily regulated. Those citizens earning less than about $65,000 annually are required to purchase insurance from one of the semipublic funds. Premiums are based on income; after 2010 employees pay about 8 percent of gross wages up to about $63,000, while their employers contribute an additional 8 percent up to the limit. Coverage is comprehensive and includes most health care needs with the exception of long-term nursing care, which since 1995 is covered in a separate program (2.2 percent of gross income split equally by employer and employee). Self-employed workers, civil servants, and individuals earning above the $65,000 are allowed to opt out of the semipublic system and purchase private health insurance, which is generally more expensive. Private insurance companies must also conform to national health care standards.

The social security (pension and accident) programs insure about 43 million adults. Established during the late nineteenth century, these programs have undergone extensive changes since the founding of the Federal Republic. The governing boards of all the funds are now based on the principle of parity representation for the various business, professional, and labor interests most concerned with the programs. After 1949, the left, or labor, wing of the ruling Christian Democratic Union, working with the trade unions and the opposition Social Democrats and enjoying the support of Chancellor Adenauer, was able to convince business interests that the confrontational class politics of the Weimar Republic should be replaced with a new emphasis on "social partnership." This required concessions from both business and labor. The trade unions gave up their majority control of the health funds, and employers did the same for the pension and accident insurance programs. Although the officials of the funds are nominally elected by their millions of members, the turnout at *Sozialwahlen* (social welfare program elections) is very low, and the slates or candidates presented by the labor unions and business and professional associations are rarely contested.

Federal law limits the administrative independence of the funds. For example, the size of pension payments and the taxes to pay for them are determined by parliament. The funds do, however, have considerable discretion in setting the fee structure for physicians, the construction and management of hospitals, and the investment for pension fund capital. The concept of social partnership thus extends to the state as well. The funds, according to one authority, are "political shock absorbers," connecting "state with society because they leave it to the major economic interest groups to mediate the state's administration of major social welfare programs."[32]

The postwar emphasis on consensus and social partnership is seen most clearly in the landmark 1957 reform of the pension system. Previous pension legislation based the size of payments largely on the individual's contributions. The 1957 law, although retaining some elements of individual insurance, linked increases in pension payments, with some time lag, to increases in the overall national wage level. This dynamic feature enabled all pensioners, regardless of their individual contributions, to share directly in the expanding national economy. It was also expected that these pension increases would have a stabilizing, countercyclical effect. That is, in periods of rapidly rising wages the pension increases would be relatively lower than wages, reflecting the previous three-year average; but in periods of only modest wage hikes the pensioners would receive increases reflecting the previous prosperity. The 1957 law was a political compromise. Conservative business interests and the Christian Democrats accepted its dynamic provisions (i.e., indexing pensions to the national economy), and the labor unions and Social Democrats abandoned their preference for a more uniform, egalitarian system. By 1990 the average pension payment amounted to about 70 percent of the employee's preretirement net income, as compared to only 18 percent for the first recipients in 1891.[33] As discussed below, in recent years, this postwar consensus on the pension and health systems has been strained by budgetary cutbacks, rising unemployment, and the costs of integrating the former East Germany into the market economy.

The cost of pensions to retired easterners, for example, is far higher than the amount they have paid into the system. Working westerners make up the difference. In 1999 the western part of the pension fund had a surplus of about $15 billion while the eastern portion ran a deficit of about $9 billion. In 2008, approximately $17 billion was transferred from west to east.[34] Germans, like their neighbors in other West European societies, are also living longer but retiring earlier. This means that there are decreasing numbers of contributors paying for increasing numbers of recipients. In 2002, for example, there were approximately twenty-eight elderly being supported by one hundred workers, but by 2025 this will be approximately forty-two per one hundred workers.[35] There have also been issues achieving gender parity in pensions partially because of challenges in counting housewives' work.

Pension Reform

In response to the growing challenges, the Schröder government in 2001 passed new legislation that represents the most far-reaching change since the 1957 pension program. Under its terms the public or state portion of pension payments will decline and be augmented by individual retirement accounts. This, it is hoped, will enable the system to avoid drastic increases in payroll taxes as the combination of declining birth rates and longer life expectancies yields fewer and fewer workers to support more and more pensioners. The current proportion of 19.6 percent (9.8 each from employer and employee) of monthly wages will remain at or below 20 percent until 2020 and is not scheduled to exceed 22 percent until after 2030.

The new individual retirement accounts (dubbed "*Riester Rente*" in honor of the former minister of labor who is identified with the reform) are tax deferred, and families with children receive additional payments into their pension accounts. From 2006 workers could contribute 1 percent of their gross wages into their own account; after 2008 this increased to a permanent limit of 4 percent. Participants receive tax credits ($190 per person; $380 if they have children) that cost the government about seven billion Euros per year. Holders of these accounts may borrow up to $60,000 for the purchase of a home. This loan, however, must be repaid before the borrower is sixty-five.

This new legislation was opposed strongly by the trade unions, pensioner associations, the churches, and other social welfare interest groups. Many of these groups supported Schröder in 1998 with the expectation that his government would preserve the existing system and not cut benefits. Other critics charge that the privatization of the system will continue to grow as the government seeks to reduce labor costs and encourage more business investment.

Debates over the future of the pension system continue. In 2006 the Grand Coalition raised the retirement age from sixty-five to sixty-seven (to be phased in by 2029), a move already taken by some of Germany's European neighbors including Denmark and the Netherlands. Although the SPD-led Schröder government originally proposed the change, large segments of the SPD's grassroots now want to revisit this decision.

The fabled dynamic pension system is now history. Between 2004 and 2006 there were no increases in pension payments, three years of what the Germans call a *"Null Runde."* This meant, of course, that because of inflation and additional costs that pensioners must now bear for nursing care insurance, the pensions have actually declined. Since 2004 pensioners have had to pay the full premium of 1.7 percent of their pension income for nursing care insurance. Previously, the pension system picked up half of the premium. Since July 2005, pensioners must pay an additional 0.9 percent for health insurance. Those receiving private, employer-based pensions must now also pay the health insurance premium. Early retirement programs originally introduced during the boom times in the late 1960s and early 1970s have been steadily reduced during the Red-Green years. Early retirement is now defined as 63.1 years as compared to 62.1 in 1997. Eventually benefits will be reduced from 70 to 67 percent of previous net income. Finally, above a certain level, pension payments are now being taxed.[36]

The Health Care System

The health care system shares many problems with the pension program. Longer life expectancies mean additional costs for hospital care, medical procedures, and prescription drugs. As one of the biggest health care spenders in the world, Germany spent 11.6 percent of GDP in 2010 on health care, representing a 2.6 percent increase from the previous year. Almost 77 percent of spending was public.[37] According to some studies, the government will be paying 15 percent of GDP for health care by 2025 and 25 percent by 2050 based on current benefit levels and demographic projections.[38] Increased premiums paid by employers and employees have financed this heightened spending. But health care costs have been growing at a faster rate than the wages and profits that finance this system. As a result, successive governments since the 1980s have proposed a wide variety of changes to cut health care costs and the premiums that employers and employees must pay. The goal is to reduce the costs of labor and hence to create more jobs. During the first Schröder government, the costs for single-mother subsidies, maternal rest cures, and contraceptives for minors were taken out of the system and paid for with general revenue. In addition, the public insurance program no longer covers the costs of some dental care and non-job-related accident insurance. Private insurance is available for these programs, but the individual beneficiary pays the premiums.

The traditional program was thus scaled back to provide basic health care. For "extras," Germans now have to enroll in private insurance plans. This public-private mix in health care corresponds to the changes in the pension program enacted in 2001. No longer will the public program automatically cover all health care. Privatizing insurance for non-job-related accidents saves the system $10.5 billion annually. A private accident policy costs each insured family about $240 a year. Requiring Germans to pay for their dental crowns and bridges would save an additional $10 billion; private insurance to cover these expenses costs an additional $250 annually.

These changes clashed sharply with two traditional principles of the German welfare state: payroll taxes have always been *progressive*—that is, related to income, with higher-income groups paying more than lower groups—and payments have been equally *shared* by employers and employees. Private insurance premiums would not be related to income and would be paid solely by the employee. These changes are designed to reduce labor costs for business and make individuals responsible for some of the costs currently borne by the state. The introduction of a ten-Euro ($12) copayment for office visits in 2004, discontinued in 2012, was widely protested (there are also small copayments for prescriptions). The changes in the health care system also have encountered significant opposition from physicians, hospitals, drug companies, and patients' rights groups.

Further reform of this health care system was high on the agenda of the Merkel-led Grand Coalition. In February 2007, after almost a year of negotiations, the Grand Coalition's health care reform legislation was finally passed. There was no lack of criticism for the new legislation. Over fifty SPD and CDU deputies voted against their government's bill. The three opposition parties were unanimous in their rejection of the legislation. All significant constituencies—hospitals, doctors, health care funds, trade unions, and employer organizations—were critical of the final product. The key components of the reform package were (1) the introduction in 2009 of a new "Health Fund" that will distribute payments to the regional health care associations, (2) additional tax revenues to finance insurance for children, and (3) mandatory coverage for all residents after 2009. The legislation, it is claimed, will introduce more competition into the system.

After 2009, the health associations lost their financial autonomy. They will no longer set contributions for their members. Instead they will receive a per capita payment for each insured person. Employers and employees will no longer make contributions to their respective associations. These payments will now flow to the new fund. Employees will continue to pay 7.85 percent of their income up to a $4,500 monthly limit. Employers contribute 6.95 percent of gross wages with the same limit; the 0.9 percent difference covers long-term nursing care insurance. The fund will also receive a subsidy from general revenue (the 2009 subsidy is $3.8 billion). This subsidy is limited to 5 percent of the fund's total expenditures and is expected to cover about half of the costs of insuring children. If the fund's payments to the association fall short of association expenses, the association must cut costs. If the association is still in debt, it can impose an additional premium charge on its members, which cannot exceed 1 percent of income. If the association accumulates a surplus, it can issue refunds to their members. Each insured person will receive a statement detailing how much the association received from the fund, together with a report about an eventual additional payment or refund.[39]

Whether these changes will lower costs and provide for more efficient health care financing remains to be seen. The final program was the product of a series of compromises that satisfied few of the participants. An additional change was passed in 2010 to plug a $13 billion deficit, raising premiums to 15.5 percent of gross wages (evenly split between employee and employer).

The modest cutbacks in services and the increases in copayments and premiums reduced popular support for the system. Between 1994 and 2002 the proportion of Germans who considered the health care system to be "good" or "very good" dropped from 82 percent to 61 percent, but then rose to 63 percent in 2009.[40] Interestingly, in 2009, 65 percent (and 81 percent of doctors) thought that comprehensive reforms to the health care system were still necessary.[41]

The Federal Labor Agency

The Federal Labor Agency is a semipublic institution that is assigned primary responsibility for organizing the labor market (i.e., bringing jobs and job seekers together) and for administering the system of unemployment insurance. The agency also (1) administers programs financed from unemployment insurance revenues that retrain workers and (2) supplements the income of those put on a reduced workweek. In its programs, the agency must give special attention to the elderly, women, the handicapped, the long-term unemployed, and other special groups such as seasonal workers. The agency, which was established in 1952, is under the supervision but not the direct control of the Labor and Economics Ministry. It is governed by a president, an executive committee, and a supervisory board, which has representatives from the trade unions, employers, and federal and state officials. The major guidelines determining labor policy are developed in Nuremberg and are administered by branch, local, and regional offices. Most of the unemployment compensation programs are financed by equal employer and employee contributions, which amount to about 3 percent of a worker's gross income. If the unemployment level is high, however, the federal government must subsidize the agency. Thus in certain circumstances the agency can be financially dependent on the federal government.

As in the case of the pension and health systems, business and labor representatives are closely involved in the work of the agency's employment offices through their membership on the agency's local, regional, and national administrative committees. The members of these committees are proposed by the trade unions, business associations, the federal government, and local government authorities. The agency has almost 120,000 employees at its headquarters in Nuremberg and at almost 200 branch offices and 650 counseling centers. The agency is also responsible for overseeing the vocational education system, which supports over 1.6 million apprentices. The agency still has a legal monopoly on career counseling and is the largest employer of psychologists in the country.

Unification and the resultant mass unemployment in the east have severely taxed the resources of the agency. From 1989 to 1999 its annual budget increased from about $24 billion to $84 billion, and in 2010 it was approximately $67 billion. The amount of the agency's unemployment payments going to the east has been disproportional since unification—at one point about half, although the population in this region comprises only about 20 percent of the country's total. Thus the agency is also transferring large amounts of insurance premiums paid by westerners to the east. In 1993, when the western region was in a recession, total income was insufficient to cover all claims, and the government had to subsidize the agency with borrowed funds. Between 1991 and 1999 national government subsidies to cover the agency's shortfall totaled about $140 billion.[42]

Since 1994 the near monopoly of the Federal Employment Agency has been broken. Commercial agencies are now allowed to place employees in all available positions; previously they were restricted to placing managers, artists, and models. The new firms may charge for finding employees, but they may not take fees from individuals using their services to find employment (i.e., the costs are paid by the employer). Approximately 2,000 private employment agencies have opened since the 1994 law went into effect.

In 2002 the agency itself came under sharp criticism from the government's accounting office for overstating its record of securing jobs. In 2000, for example, the agency claimed that it was responsible for about 60 percent of all job placements in the country. The accounting offices said the actual proportion was less than 20 percent. The agency was taking credit for many job placements that were actually accomplished directly by job seekers and their eventual employers. In some cases the labor offices booked placements that never took place. The report undermined the credibility of the agency and damaged the Schröder government. In response to the criticism the director resigned.

The agency's administrative structure also came under closer examination. Only about 10 percent of employees are directly involved in finding jobs for the unemployed. The remaining staff members calculate unemployment benefits, direct retraining programs, issue labor permits, conduct economic research, or administer the organization.

The Agenda 2010 reform program (including the Hartz Commission reforms) of the Schröder government assigned several major new responsibilities to the Federal Labor Agency. Its field offices, renamed "job centers," were to focus on carrying out the changes in the unemployment compensation program called for in Agenda 2010. After some initial start-up problems, the agency, like the Agenda 2010 program overall, has begun to play a major role in reducing unemployment. The proportion of its staff engaged in finding employment for its clients has increased. A major overhaul of its infrastructure has yielded greater efficiency in matching jobs with job seekers, and overall payments have decreased. The Hartz reforms also shook up the system. Greater labor market flexibility has been achieved through the creation of "mini-jobs" that pay no more than 400 Euros per month but are not subject to the regular social security contributions. The Hartz IV reforms (after 2005) introduced two types of unemployment compensation (Arbeitslosen Geld I and II), reducing the time that one could receive benefits and the overall amount of compensation, while still maintaining a kind of minimum income. Recipients must also register and sign a contract, in which they pledge to find a new position. Also, previous geographical restrictions were limited so that the unemployed are encouraged to look farther afield for a new position. Although still controversial, these reforms are partially responsible for the lower unemployment and better governmental finances of recent years.

The Bundesbank

The Bundesbank, now part of the European Central Bank (ECB) system, is the German national bank, roughly equivalent to the American Federal Reserve or the Bank of England. It was an almost legendary institution in the postwar decades, chiefly responsible for establishing monetary policy and hence maintaining price stability. Given the impact of German preferences on the institutional architecture and policy of the ECB since the 1990s (see chapter 10), it is still an important institution. According to one study:

> The distinctive element in the Bundesbank ethos is a refusal to compromise on inflation. "There is no such thing as a little bit of inflation," Bundesbank officials like to say; and the Bundesbank view has been constant on this issue. Even single-digit inflation destroys a currency's value over the medium term and gradually destroys the economy as a whole.[43]

No central bank in the world guarded the value of its currency as carefully as the Bundesbank protected the deutsche mark (DM) from 1949 to 1999. The bank is legally independent of the federal government, the states, and private interest groups. Its autonomy was greater than that of its counterparts in the UK, France, Japan, Sweden, and even the United States. Since 1982 the bank has also been directly involved in reducing the national government's deficits by transferring a portion of its profits from foreign exchange transactions to the national treasury. Since the onset of the European debt crisis, however, the bank's profits have declined. In 2001 the bank transferred about $11 billion in much-needed funds to the national treasury. By 2008 the figure was roughly $8 billion, but in 2012 this dropped to only $2 billion.[44]

The power and independence of the Bundesbank reflect the strong concern about inflation held by all Germans. Twice in the previous century, following each world war, Germany experienced disastrous inflation that wiped out the savings of millions of citizens. Determined to keep monetary policy out of the reach of politicians, West Germany's postwar leaders did not make the bank subject to any national ministry or to the general supervision of the chancellor under the guideline powers (see chapter 7). Nor is it accountable to parliament. According to its 1957 constitution, the bank is obligated to support the government's overall economic policy; but this applies only as long as government policy, in the judgment of the bank's leadership, does not conflict with the bank's prime mission: safeguarding the currency. If the federal government opposes a bank decision, the government can delay implementation of the decision for only two weeks.

The bank is governed by two executive bodies, a directorate and a central bank council. Members of the directorate are appointed to eight-year terms by the federal president on the recommendation of the federal government. The central council mainly represents the interests of the regional branches of the bank. It is largely controlled by the regional bank presidents, who are appointed by the Bundesrat on the recommendation of the respective state governments. Thus the directorate has a more national perspective, whereas the bank council tends to reflect state or regional interests. Since unification, the bank has also established regional offices throughout the new eastern states to make a total of nine regional branches today.

The Bundesbank has not become a partisan political institution. In recommending appointments to the directorate, the government has usually selected individuals who are acceptable to the banking community and are generally in agreement with the main economic policy objectives of the government. Once appointed for their eight-year terms, however, the directors have tended to be independent. There is little evidence that, unlike in France or Italy, the Bundesbank responded to political or electoral pressures. In the period from 1981 to 1982, Karl Otto Pöhl, then president of the bank, clashed with Chancellor Schmidt over interest rates. Schmidt wanted lower rates to help take the Federal Republic out of a recession; Pöhl, supported by the bank, saw inflation as a more serious threat than sluggish growth and unemployment. Schmidt later blamed the bank for the collapse of his government in September 1982.[45]

The bank has not hesitated to criticize the government when it considers the government's economic policies a threat to monetary and price stability. In the late 1970s the Bundesbank initially opposed Chancellor Schmidt's plan to create a European Monetary System (EMS) linking the deutsche mark to the currencies of several other European Community nations. The bank feared for the stability of the deutsche mark in a system where it was tied to the weaker currencies of countries with high inflation, such as France and Italy. Chancellor Schmidt was able, however, to finally convince the bank that the advantages of the EMS—such as decoupling European currencies from the unstable dollar—outweighed the potential disadvantages of rising inflation. In practice, the EMS did not restrict German monetary policy or the bank's independence.[46] On the contrary, in the view of many of Germany's neighbors, the EMS imposed German anti-inflationary discipline on its participants and promoted German trade.

In 1989 the Bundesbank initially opposed the Kohl government's plan for a one-to-one exchange rate for East German marks. The Bank—and especially Pöhl—considered the currency exchange "fantastic" in the sense of having little to do with reality; on the free market, East Germany's currency had about one-fifth to one-sixth the value of the West German mark. The bank's opposition eventually led the government to limit the one-to-one rate to personal savings under 4,000 East German marks. Above that level, the exchange rate would still be a very generous two to one. The Bank reluctantly accepted the government's plan as a political necessity, which still made little economic sense. The resulting 20 percent increase in the money supply was met by only a 6 percent increase in gross national product due to the merger of the two economies. The relatively high inflation rate of over 4 percent in 1992 was related in part to this decision, as was the EMS crisis (see chapter 10).

The Bank and European Unification

In 1997 Germany's efforts to meet the criteria for membership in the currency union led to increases in interest rates and a major conflict between the Kohl government and the bank. The government attempted to reduce the budget deficit by revaluing the nation's gold reserves. The move was strongly criticized by the Bundesbank as an accounting trick that would undermine the independence of the bank and public confidence in the currency union. While other countries also used such creative bookkeeping, the Germans had insisted on strict adherence to the provisions of the Maastricht Treaty establishing the bank. The controversy drew international attention, and an embarrassed Kohl government eventually backed down.

In 1999 the Bundesbank began to cede many of its powers to the new European Central Bank, which is also located in Frankfurt. The Bundesbank is now one of the regional banks in the Eurozone, the seventeen nations that have phased out their national currencies and replaced them with the Euro. Although most Germans have consistently supported the economic and political integration of postwar Europe, the prospect of actually losing the mark did provoke some concern in public opinion.[47] The Bundesbank, together with the federal government, lobbied successfully for Frankfurt as the seat of the European Central Bank.

While the Bundesbank is now formally only one of seventeen regional units of the European Central Bank, the size and weight of the German economy in the Eurozone, not to mention the bank's physical proximity to the European Central Bank, ensure that it is an influential voice in the councils of the new central bank. The Bundesbank has contributed almost 20 percent of the ECB's capital. Indeed, the Bundesbank's "footprint" is very visible in the European Central Bank. Many observers in fact consider the European bank to be a German creation in the sense that it has been almost solely committed to the strong anti-inflationary policies of the Bundesbank.

THE JUDICIARY AND THE COURT SYSTEM

Contributing to the complexity and organized character of German social, economic, and political life are the courts and the judiciary, which play a major role in regulating the entire process. One observer has pointed out, "There is hardly an area of human relations in Germany, untouched by some rule, order or regulation."[48] For example, the opening and closing hours of shops and stores and the nighttime working hours of bakers are fixed by law. One Bavarian ordinance requires parents to keep their children quiet each afternoon between 1 and 3 p.m.[49] Some observers even say that "*Ordnung*" (order) is the ultimate German virtue. Whether Germans are simply more inclined to settle their disputes by legal means than through informal negotiations and bargaining or whether it is because of the relatively extensive court system available to them, they are a very law- and court-minded people.

The Character of German Law

Like that of most of its Western European neighbors, German law was fundamentally influenced by the Roman legal codes introduced by Italian jurists during the Middle Ages and by the Napoleonic Code enforced in the Rhineland during the French occupation in the nineteenth century. After the founding of the empire in 1871, the civil and criminal codes were reorganized and in some cases rewritten by teams of legal scholars. This massive work was completed by the turn of the century. Although relatively few changes have been made in the civil code since then, the criminal code since the early 1950s has been in a process of major revision. For example, the statute criminalizing same sex acts was modified in 1969 and rescinded in 1994.

These codes form the basis of Germany's unified legal system. Although political institutions are decentralized and fragmented, German law is the same in all states of the federation. Thus, unlike the situation under American federalism, laws regarding such matters as bankruptcy, divorce, criminal offenses, and extradition do not vary from state to state.

The codified character of German law also means that unlike in countries using the Anglo-American legal system, there is little judge-made, or common, law. The judge in a codified system (in theory at least) only administers and applies the codes, fitting the particular case to the existing body of law as found in them. The German judge may not set precedents and thus make law, but must be only a neutral administrator of the existing codes. According to this theory, judges do not have to make law; all the law that is needed is already in the codes. This conviction, that the judge is not an independent actor in the judicial process but merely an administrator, lies at the base of the still-dominant philosophy of *legal positivism*, or analytical jurisprudence. Legal positivism contends that existing general law as found in the codes sufficiently encompasses all the rights and duties of citizens. In other words, judicial review is not necessary. The law supposedly offers the citizen the best protection against the arbitrary exercise of power by political authorities. Politics, according to this philosophy, must be kept strictly distinct from law.

Although in theory the judges are neutral administrators, according to the rules of procedure they are not disinterested referees or umpires of court proceedings. They are expected to take an active role in fitting the law to the facts of the particular case and in ensuring that all relevant facts become known. Court observers accustomed to the Anglo-American system would be surprised by the active, inquisitorial posture assumed by German judges. At times they seem to be working with the prosecution against the defendant. But if one assumes, as the German legal system does, that it is the duty of all participants to discern the truth or facts of the case in order to ensure a just application of the law, this activist orientation of the judge is to be expected. Unlike the Anglo-American system, the process is not one of advocacy, with defense and prosecution each presenting their side of the case as forcefully and persuasively as possible, and with the judge or jury making the final decision. It is more inquisitorial, with all participants—defense, prosecution, and judge—expected to join together in a mutual search for the truth, the real facts of the case.

Many critics of the German legal system have focused on this legal philosophy as the root cause of the judiciary's scandalous behavior during the Third Reich. By claiming to be only neutral administrators of the law, judges disclaimed any responsibility for judging the contents of the laws they were to administer. According to legal positivism, the judge is a "cog in the wheel of judicial administration, unmoved by feeling or even conscience."[50]

This philosophy also grants no legitimacy to any other type of law, such as natural or common law, that does not emanate from the sovereign state through its official representatives. Thus the state is the only source of law. In this sense, positivism is quite supportive of the statist mentality—that is, the setting of state above society—attributed by many to the German political culture of the past.

The Judiciary

Socialization and Recruitment

In Germany, as in other continental European states, there traditionally has been a close relationship between the court system and the state bureaucracy. Nearly all judges—with the exception of those in specialized courts and the relatively few at the federal level—are appointed by the state ministers of justice. They are civil servants with roughly the same salaries, rank, tenure, and promotion structures as the Beamte in the higher service. Indeed, during the empire and the Weimar Republic, judges were not distinguished at all from higher-level civil servants. In the Federal Republic, however, a separate set of regulations for judges was introduced, designed to ensure judicial independence. Nonetheless, structurally at least, the judge remains very much a part of the bureaucratic hierarchy. Starting at the lowest level (the local courts), a judge is promoted on the basis of recommendations from superiors. Independence and individual initiative are not encouraged by this system.

A German judge, unlike many of her or his American counterparts, has in most cases chosen a lifetime career and does not enter private practice and rarely even goes into the prosecuting end of judicial administration. There is a relatively strict separation between bench and bar. After about four years of legal study, all prospective lawyers and judges take a state examination. Upon passing this test, the student becomes a *Referendar*, a sort of apprentice or junior jurist, and begins a two-and-a-half-year period of training in ordinary courts, in administrative courts, as an attorney, and in the office of a public prosecutor—thus gaining experience in all major areas of the profession. After this practical experience, prospective jurists must take a second state examination that, if passed, qualifies them to practice law. At this point (around age twenty-seven to thirty-two) the candidates must make career decisions: private practice, a business or corporation career, civil service, or the judiciary. Those who enter private practice as attorneys or who work for corporations (about 50 percent of the total) can and do switch from job to job; but those who enter state service must commit themselves to the judiciary, the prosecutor's office, or the regular civil service. Those who embark on a judicial career must go through an additional three-year probationary period before receiving lifetime tenure as a judge and beginning the ascent up the career ladder. Once committed, the German judge has little contact with other lawyers not in the judicial track, with the possible exception of those in the prosecutor's office. Judges come from predominantly middle- or upper-middle-class backgrounds, and minorities are underrepresented.

Taken together, the socioeconomic background, recruitment, and professional socialization of judges would seem to make for a rather conservative group oriented toward the status quo. In the sense of supporting the status quo (i.e., a middle-class liberal republic), the judges are conservative. Opposition to the values of liberal democracy, much less hostility to the Republic à la Weimar, are hardly to be found, at least not in studies of judges' attitudes and values. In one extensive study based on a representative sample of federal and state judges, it was found that all but 5 percent supported one or more of the mainstream, democratic political parties.[51] Almost 40 percent of the judges sampled in another study said they would personally participate in a political demonstration if they were in agreement with its goals.[52]

Judges and Justice in Eastern Germany

Following unification, the Federal Republic's legal system went into force throughout the five new eastern Länder. But neither the existing court structure nor the judges themselves were in any way comparable to the West German system. For the East German communists, law and judges were both subordinate to party control. The rule of law and an independent judiciary meant little in the one-party "dictatorship of the proletariat."

The great majority of the former judges and prosecutors had been members of the Communist Party. Their decisions included many scandalous political trials reminiscent of an earlier era. East Germans were sentenced to prison terms for wearing a white bow in their lapel as a sign that they had applied to leave the country. In 1989 a young East German received a two-and-a-half-year prison term because he attempted to hand a visiting West German leader a note appealing for help. Another East German was given a ten-year sentence for talking to West German television correspondents. But the most outrageous judicial acts involved citizens who were trying to flee the country. In some cases they were forced to give up their children, who were then adopted by parents loyal to the regime. West German authorities estimate that at least half of all East German judges and prosecutors were incriminated by evidence maintained at a West German center that monitored human rights abuses in the former GDR. The center has documented over 40,000 cases of East German maltreatment of its citizens.

Jurists from the western states are still present in some ministries of justice in the eastern states. In the years immediately following unification, retired judges from West Germany and recent graduates from western law schools filled the gap. After unification in 1990 about two-thirds of the former GDR's 1,500 judges and prosecutors were given probationary appointments. By 1998 about 400 of this group had been given permanent civil service tenure, and the remaining 600 had been dismissed or had resigned.[53] Thus, of the original 1,500 East German jurists, less than a fourth were deemed qualified to serve in the new democratic system. This relatively thoroughgoing purge of the communist legal system contrasts sharply to the "denazification" of the West German judiciary after 1945.[54] In recent years, the graduates of the law schools established in the eastern states have begun to assume leadership positions in the regional and national judiciary.

Court Structure

In addition to a unified body of law, all regular courts follow the same rules of procedure. However, the structure of the courts is decentralized. Unlike in the

United States, there is no separate system of federal and state courts. With the exception of the seven national high courts of appeal, all regular tribunals are state courts; and although national law outlines the basic organization of the judiciary, the courts are established and administered by state statutes. The other significant characteristics of the German structures are the collegial nature of most tribunals and the extensive system of specialized courts.

Regular (civil and criminal) courts are organized on four levels: local, district, appellate, and federal. About 660 to 700 local courts (*Amtsgerichte*) are usually staffed by a single judge (in criminal cases the judge is assisted by two lay judges chosen randomly from local citizens) and are located in most small- to medium-sized towns. Local courts have jurisdiction over minor civil matters and petty criminal offenses and also perform some administrative functions (bankruptcy supervision, administering estates, appointing guardians). At the next level are 116 district courts. These are appellate courts for the *Amtsgerichte*, but they also have original jurisdiction over most major civil and criminal matters. Panels of three to five judges try all district court cases. There are several panels at this level, and each tends to specialize in different types of cases. The final court of appeal below the national level is the *Oberlandesgericht* (state appellate court). These courts take cases only on appeal, with the exception of cases involving treason and anticonstitutional activity. In Germany, an appeal involves both a reexamination of the facts in a case and its procedural and legal aspects. These courts are also divided into panels of three to five judges, with each panel specializing in different types of cases. The final appellate court in the regular system is the Federal Appeals Court at Karlsruhe (not to be confused with the Federal Constitutional Court, discussed later, which is also located at Karlsruhe). This is a very large tribunal with more than a hundred judges divided into over twenty panels or senates (see table 8.1).

The specialized court system is also decentralized. Courts dealing with administrative, social welfare, and labor matters operate at three levels—district, appellate, and national—with the national court serving as the final court of appeal. Specialized courts dealing with fiscal and tax matters operate only at the state and national levels.

In their respective areas, these courts dispense relatively speedy and inexpensive justice. If a citizen or a group feels that any state official or agency has acted illegally or arbitrarily, the case goes to an administrative court. This system has been the major recourse for opponents of nuclear power.[55] The regular court system does not allow class action (*Verbandsklage*) suits and grants standing to an environmental group only when its rights and those of its members are directly affected. The numerous permits and procedures required for the construction of a nuclear plant, however, offered these groups an opportunity to challenge the government in the administrative courts on a variety of technical legal grounds. Administrative courts have ruled that safety must take precedence over economic and technical questions in the construction of nuclear plants; several plants were closed by administrative court rulings. These legal and regulatory actions helped to turn public opinion and eventually government policy against nuclear power.

Table 8.1.   The German Court Structure and Judiciary

Court	Number	Number of Judges
Regular courts*	801	14,925
Local	(661)	
District	(116)	
Appellate	(24)	
Specialized courts (state control)	257	5,144
Administrative courts	(51)	
Social courts	(699)	
Labor courts	(119)	
Fiscal courts	(18)	
State-level constitutional courts	13	140
Federal (national) courts	7	485
Federal appeals court	1	
Federal administrative court	1	
Federal labor court	1	
Federal social court	1	
Federal fiscal (finance) court	1	
Federal patent court	1	
Federal Constitutional Court	1	
Totals	1,085	20,694

Source: Statistisches Bundesamt, Statistisches Jahrbuch 2011 (Wiesbaden, 2012), 270.
*Civil and criminal cases.

Specific disputes involving the social security, health, or welfare systems are heard in a "social" court. Similarly, labor–management problems, usually involving issues arising from collective bargaining agreements, are addressed in labor courts. In the specialized courts, professional judges sit with lay members; in the case of labor courts, for example, employers and employees select these lay members.

Thus these institutions adjudicate matters that would be resolved either out of court or in the nonspecialized regular courts in the United States the or UK. To an extent, the readiness of Germans to go to court is due to the fact that there are so many available. Their presence also encourages the cautious, legalistic approach to administration so characteristic of the bureaucracy. Knowing that their mistakes may quickly find them in some court makes civil servants more concerned about the legal correctness of their actions than about the political implications.

Judicial Review and the Federal Constitutional Court

All courts and judges are engaged in politics, but a court is most political when it strikes down the acts of other governmental bodies, usually those of the executive or the legislature. In the continental legal tradition, judicial review (the authority of courts to nullify legislative or executive acts on constitutional grounds) has been an alien concept. It has been regarded as (1) an undemocratic infringement on the right of popular sovereignty as expressed in parliamentary acts, or (2) contradictory to the principles of legal positivism that assign only an administrative role to judges. Although the practice of constitutional review, whereby courts resolved disputes between different levels of government or determined the validity of constitutional amendments, had some historic precedent in Germany, the acceptance of judicial review is essentially a twentieth-century and specifically postwar development.[56]

The framers of the Basic Law, desiring to check and balance governmental authority, were in general agreement on granting the courts the power of judicial review and on establishing a specific national court as the final arbiter in constitutional questions. American occupation authorities, with the U.S. Supreme Court in mind, also supported such an institution. The result was Articles 93 and 94 of the Basic Law, which established the constitutional court, assigned its competency and jurisdiction, and defined its composition. The court was a new addition to the postwar legal system and has become the most political of all German courts. It is assigned the functions of judicial review, adjudication of disputes between state and federal political institutions, protection of individual civil rights as guaranteed in the Constitution, and protection of the constitutional and democratic order against groups and individuals seeking to overthrow it. In the latter area, the constitutional court has the right to ban such groups and their activities. Recent years have also seen a proliferation of cases regarding the constitutionality of European laws and initiatives. For instance, in the summer of 2012, the court reviewed the planned European Stability Mechanism (ESM). These powers make the court unique in German judicial history.

The constitutional court, set up in Karlsruhe in 1951, is also distinct from other courts in organization and composition. Unlike state and national courts, which are administratively dependent on their respective justice ministers, the constitutional court is administratively independent. It hires, fires, and supervises all of its employees, and justices are exempt from the administrative rules and regulations applicable to their colleagues on state and federal courts. Indeed, not even parliament can impeach a constitutional court justice; only the federal president, upon a motion from the court itself, can remove a justice.[57] The court is financially autonomous. Like the two houses of parliament, it draws up its own budget, negotiating directly with the finance ministry and parliament's judiciary committees.

The unique position of the constitutional court and its explicitly political character is most apparent in the selection of its members. Half of the sixteen judges are selected by the Bundesrat (the upper house), and half by the Bundestag (the lower house); in each case a candidate must have at least a two-thirds majority. These selection provisions ensure that both state and party/political factors play an important role and that they further enhance the unique character of the court. Moreover, a high degree of consensus is necessary to gain the necessary two-thirds of votes for any candidate. The Bundestag's candidates are nominated by a special judicial selection committee, an elite group composed of leading members of all parties in proportion to their strength in the chamber. The Bundestag parties attempt to influence the appointment of judges by presenting lists of candidates to the committee, although legally they cannot instruct their members on the committee how to vote. The Bundesrat's eight appointees are elected in a bloc vote from nominees proposed by its judiciary committee.

Because the two houses cannot nominate the same judges, there is an ad hoc conference committee that coordinates the process. In the Bundesrat, as discussed in chapter 7, each state's delegation votes en bloc on instructions from its government. This ensures that state governments have a direct influence on the selection process; moreover, interstate bargaining over nominees is quite common—especially over appointees to the court's second chamber, which hears most states' rights cases.

It is not difficult for knowledgeable students of the constitutional court to determine how each appointee got the job. Although there is considerable open political "horse trading" and occasional conflicts in the selection process, the quality of appointees has been high.[58] The Bundesrat has usually preferred high-level civil servants with excellent records in state administration. The lower house tends to nominate active politicians and judges from other federal courts. Both houses have recently drawn more candidates from their own ranks—that is, state justice ministers and leading members of the judicial selection committee. Membership on the court is regarded as a very prestigious appointment, and the quality of candidates is indicative of the status this institution has in the political system. Its strong penetration by state governments and parties also sets it apart from older German judicial traditions.

The constitutional court's sixteen members are divided equally into two senates. Election is to a specific senate, and members may not transfer. Each senate is administratively separate from the other, with its own president, and has its own areas of specialization. The first senate's jurisdiction includes all cases dealing with basic liberties covered by Articles 1 to 20 of the Basic Law and constitutional complaints involving these articles. The second senate is responsible for constitutional conflicts between different levels of government (federal–state, state–state) as well as a variety of specific political matters (political parties, election disputes, anticonstitutional activity, international law disputes). There is also a presidency of the entire court that must alternate between the two senates. Each senate is further divided into three chambers with three justices each. Chamber decisions, for example on whether the court will accept a complaint, must be unanimous. Senate decisions, by contrast, need an absolute majority or a two-thirds majority depending on the case. Members of the court must be at least forty and have prior judicial experience. They are appointed for a twelve-year term but must retire at the age of sixty-eight. Currently, approximately one-third of justices are women. The budget of the constitutional court in 2011 was approximately $30 million.

Decisions

In its sixty-two-year history, the constitutional court has made its mark as an independent guardian of the democratic Constitution, a protector of human rights, and an adjudicator of German federalism. By the early 1990s it had interpreted over half of the Constitution's 151 articles in over 2,100 cases, and in almost 800 of these cases involving the constitutionality of legislation, it had invalidated federal and state laws or regulations.[59] In its early decisions such as the Southwest case (1951), a dispute over state boundaries comparable to the landmark American cases of *Marbury v. Madison* and *McCulloch v. Maryland*, the constitutional court established its authority as the supreme source of constitutional interpretation, clearly departed from legal positivism in granting legitimacy to certain higher or natural-law values, and set forth fundamental principles (e.g., federalism, democracy, and the rule of law) that are superior to all other constitutional or legal provisions.

More than any other postwar institution, the constitutional court has enunciated the view that the Federal Republic is a militant democracy whose democratic political parties are the chief instrument for the translation of public opinion into public policy. The concept of the party state, discussed in chapter 5, owes much to the opinions of the court. The controversial banning of the communist and neo-Nazi Sozialistische Reichspartei in the 1950s was also an expression of this concept of militant democracy.

Nor has the court shirked conflict with the government and top executive leadership. When Adenauer attempted to form a second television network that would have been under national control, the court, responding to state claims that such a network violated the reserved rights of the Länder to govern their own cultural affairs, struck down the legislation. The cries of protest from the chancellor's office left little doubt that the court was doing its job.

In other significant political decisions, the court upheld the landmark 1970 "Eastern Treaties" with the Soviet Union and Poland, struck down the abortion law passed by the Social-Liberal government in 1974, ordered major changes in the 1983 census law, threw out the government's electoral law for the 1990 federal election, and ruled that citizens whose property had been confiscated during the 1945–1949 Soviet military occupation of the former East Germany are not entitled to the return of their property but may receive monetary compensation. The 1990 Unity Treaty between the two German states did not allow for the return of property seized during that period, and in 1991 the court ruled that the provisions of the treaty were indeed constitutional.[60]

In 1993 the court struck down yet another abortion law that had been passed in response to the differing West and East German laws (see chapter 2). In 1995, in a controversial unification decision, the court ruled that top East German spies could not be tried in a unified Germany if they had done their work exclusively from the territory of the former East Germany against the former West Germany. The ruling amounted to a virtual amnesty for the top leadership of the GDR intelligence agencies. However, East German spies formerly operating within West Germany (in many cases on orders from the top GDR agency leaders) could be prosecuted. The ruling drew sharp criticism from eastern civil rights groups that wanted the Federal Republic to bring their former oppressors to justice.

Later in 1995 the court was again at the center of a storm of controversy when it struck down a Bavarian school ordinance mandating that each classroom be equipped with a crucifix. The court ruled that the regulation, which in effect required all children to learn "under the cross," violated constitutional guarantees of religious freedom and the neutrality of the state in religious questions (Article 4). Catholic Church officials and the Bavarian government immediately denounced the decision as an unwarranted intrusion into the state's deeply rooted cultural traditions and a violation of Bavaria's right to run its own schools.

Some Bavarian leaders called for a boycott of the ruling. In 1998 the court ruled that Bavaria's abortion regulations violated the Constitution. The ruling sharply limited the rights of states to pass regulations and legislation that conflict with federal law. In the Bavarian case, the state administration had attempted to restrict the freedom-of-choice components of the national abortion law.

In 1999 the court in a major decision ruled that the existing tax laws for child care expenses were unconstitutional because they allowed single parents to deduct more than married parents. The existing law assumed that "intact" families would spend less for child care than single parents. The court ruled that the law violated the equal protection provisions of the Constitution as well as Article 6, which obligate the state to protect and promote the family. In 2002 the court struck down an immigration law, strongly supported by the government and business, designed to bring skilled workers into the country on a fast track. The court ruled that the vote for the bill in the Bundesrat was unconstitutional because the chamber's president, a Social Democrat, incorrectly recorded the vote of one state, Brandenburg, as supporting the legislation when in fact Brandenburg's government was divided on the issue. In that situation, the Constitution requires that the state's vote be recorded as an abstention.

The Court and the European Union

As the process of European integration accelerated after unification (see chapter 10), the constitutional court became a more important national and international actor. In several instances, the court has become the final authority for European level agreements. Although traditionally interpreting the Basic Law as compatible with the European integration process—that is, transferring sovereign powers to supranational entities—recent years have witnessed a more restrictive attitude from the court. It has increasingly emphasized the importance of democratic legitimation and German sovereignty while criticizing the extent of integration and insufficient democratic oversight.

In 1993 the constitutional court found that the Maastricht Treaty (which paved the way for the European Monetary Union) was constitutional. But it also asserted its power to decide whether a European initiative is compatible with the Basic Law and hinted that a fully federal Europe would probably not be. In 1998, the court ruled that Germany's entrance into the European Monetary System was constitutional, but reminded the government and parliament about their duties to ensure monetary stability, as well as about the "no bailout clause" of the Maastricht Treaty.

Then, in one of the most important decisions in its history, the court ruled that ratification of the Lisbon Treaty by the parliament could only take place if certain supplemental legislation accompanied the act of ratification. The Court essentially ruled that the treaty would be constitutional only with legislation that would allow the states, through the Bundesrat and Bundestag, to give direction to the national government's representatives in the European Council. In its decision, the Court was concerned that decisions at the European Union level could violate Germany's Constitution, especially its federalism provisions and extensive human and civil rights guarantees. It was critical of the democratic deficit at the EU level (see chapter 10). The court also outlined the policy areas, including fiscal policy, that ought to remain at the national level.[61] The supplemental legislation, which was passed at a special session in September 2009 just prior to the national election, is to serve as an "emergency brake" on the national government's representatives in Brussels. Before the federal government "gives the store away" in Brussels, so the supporters argued, the Bundesrat and Bundestag can pull the brake. Of course, since the Bundestag elects and controls the government, the Bundesrat would primarily invoke this supplementary legislation.

Plaintiffs from Bavaria with close ties to the Christian Social Union brought the case before the Court. Its sister party, the Christian Democrats, as well as the SPD, were critical of the Bavarians' action, viewing it as a blow to supranationalists and an attempt to reassert national, or in this case states', rights in European Union matters.[62] The decision was sharply criticized by some legal experts as anti-European. As one commentator wrote, "That the Basic Law could be viewed as anti-European was envisioned by none of its framers. Now the Court has done just that." The word *sovereign* is not used at all in the Basic Law, but this decision used it thirty-three times. Critics argued that the Basic Law clearly commits Germany to a united Europe, supported by the court's own past precedents. In this highly political decision, the court signaled its intention to keep the Bundestag, Bundesrat, and the European Union on a short leash, interpreting the pro-integration thrust of the Basic Law in a highly restrictive manner. As one commentator put it, if the "EU could endanger German democracy—that's a matter for the people and their elected representatives, not the Court."[63]

The court was also at the center of the constitutional debate surrounding the efforts to save the Euro and the troubled economies of southern Europe through various bailouts and the establishment of a European Stability Mechanism (ESM). While these measures passed both chambers of parliament by a two-thirds majority, which is required for constitutional amendments, opponents of the legislation challenged their constitutionality, and in July 2012 the Court held hearings. The issue was again whether too much German sovereignty was being transferred to nonelected European officials and institutions. Was democracy itself being weakened by the Merkel government's efforts to save the Euro and perhaps the entire European Union? The Court issued its final decision in September 2012, upholding the legality of the ESM, but once again reaffirming the necessity of obtaining approval from the Bundestag.[64]

Thus, like those of its American counterpart, the constitutional court's decisions have often provoked sharp reactions from political leaders, and charges have been made that the court has failed to exercise judicial restraint and has attempted to usurp legislative functions. To students of judicial review, especially as practiced by the U.S. Supreme Court, these charges are very familiar. Although disputes about court decisions are usually couched in legal terms, both supporters and critics of the court's decisions have ample political reasons for their positions. In other words, it all depends on whose ox is gored. Public support for the court is strong. Surveys generally find that Germans have more trust in the court than in any other public institution.[65] In 2009, 67 percent had a lot or some trust in the court (versus 20 percent that had little trust and 8 percent with none). Also that year 72 percent had some or a lot of trust in the Basic Law.[66] There is no doubt that the court has become a legitimate component of the political system and that its decisions have been accepted and complied with by both winners and losers.[67]

SUMMARY AND CONCLUSION

The administrative and judicial institutions of the Federal Republic have provided an important element of continuity between the postwar democracy and earlier political systems. As in the past, they have adapted to new political events and situations with few difficulties. The unification process of 1989–1990 was also an impressive achievement for the West German civil service—as have been the implementation of reforms after 1998 and the responses to the post-2008 economic and Euro crises. These examples belie the notion that bureaucracies cannot respond quickly and efficiently to new situations. Unlike previous phases of German history, today's civil servants and lawyers are fundamentally committed to democratic principles and ideals.

Nevertheless, the ability of the public service and judiciary to adapt to the new quantitative and qualitative demands of modern policy making has been questioned in recent years. It is the fragmented, decentralized, often ad hoc character of policy making and administration that concerns many students of German governmental institutions. Gender equality has not been fully achieved, and the number of civil servants with a migration background does not come close to this group's share of the population. Moreover, budgetary resources will likely remain scarce.

On the other hand, when one considers the circumstances of the Republic's founding, the pressures of Allied military occupiers, and the experiences with the centralized, "efficient" Third Reich, the current structure does not seem inefficient or irrational, at least to many foreign observers. Where some see fragmentation, others see pluralism; and there is little doubt that postwar decentralization has provided many opportunities for practicing the art of compromise and bargaining, which are essential to conflict management in a modern democracy. Also, some planners and reformers want a stronger, centralized political system that would be far more committed to basic social and economic change than most Germans seem to prefer. Added to this is the persistent tension between the national and European levels, as well as pressures from increasing globalization. Thus, the German public service will have to continue a delicate balancing act among competing interests and jurisdictions while simultaneously working toward increased efficiency and service in the context of budgetary austerity.

NOTES

1. Walter L. Dorn, "The Prussian Bureaucracy in the Eighteenth Century," *Political Science Quarterly* 46, no. 3 (September 1931): 404.
2. Gabriel Almond and Sidney Verba, *The Civic Culture* (Princeton, NJ: Princeton University Press, 1963), 189ff.

3. Arnold Brecht, "Personnel Management," in *Governing Postwar Germany*, ed. Edward H. Litchfield (Ithaca, NY: Cornell University Press, 1953), 264.

4. Brecht, "Personnel Management," 267.

5. Brecht, "Personnel Management," 268.

6. Karl Loewenstein, "Justice," in *Governing Postwar Germany*, 236–262.

7. Loewenstein, "Justice," 248.

8. Loewenstein, "Justice," 245.

9. http://www.auswaertiges-amt.de/EN/AAmt/Geschichte/Historikerkommission.html.

10. Following the 1969 and 1982 changes of government, approximately one-half of the government's state secretaries and one-third of the department heads were removed for political reasons and either pensioned or reassigned elsewhere in the state administration. Hans-Ulrich Derlien, "Repercussions of Government Change on the Career Civil Service in West Germany: The Cases of 1969 and 1982," *Governance* 1 (1988): 50–78. The replacement rate for the 1998 change of government appears to be higher, but this is distorted by the civil servants who chose to retire instead of moving to Berlin.

11. Reimut Jochimsen, "Integriertes System," *Bulletin: Presse-und Informationsamt der Bundesregierung*, no. 97 (July 16, 1970): 953.

12. Renate Mayntz and Fritz W. Scharpf, *Policymaking in the German Federal Bureaucracy* (New York: Elsevier, 1975), 69–76.

13. http://www.oecd-ilibrary.org/sites/gov_glance-2011-en/05/01/index.html?contentType=&itemId=/content/chapter/gov_glance-2011-27-en&containerItemId=/content/serial/22214399&accessItemIds=/content/book/gov_glance-2011-en&mimeType=text/html.

14. https://www.destatis.de/DE/ZahlenFakten/GesellschaftStaat/OeffentlicheFinanzenSteuern/OeffentlicherDienst/Personal/Tabellen/Aufgaben.html.

15. http://www.beamtenbesoldung.org/images/bund/bundesbesoldungstabelle-2012.pdf.

16. Werner Thieme, "Das Stiefkind des Staates," *Die Zeit*, September 18, 1970, 60.

17. Gerhard Brinkmann, "Die Diskriminierung der Nicht-Juristen im allgemeinen höheren Verwaltungsdienst der Bundesrepublik Deutschland," *Zeitschrift für die gesamte Staatswissenschaft* 129 (1973): 150–167; and Bärbel Steinkemper, *Klassische und politische Bürokraten in der Ministerialverwaltung der Bundesrepublik Deutschland* (Cologne: Carl Heymanns Verlag, 1974), 20. A comparative study found that over 60 percent of top German civil servants were lawyers, as compared to approximately 20 percent of high-ranking American bureaucrats. Joel D. Aberbach et al., "American and German Federal Executives: Technocratic and Political Attitudes," *International Social Science Journal*, no. 123 (February 1990): 7.

18. Jürgen Plöhn and Winfried Steffani, "Bund und Länder in der Bundesrepublik Deutsch-land," in *Handbuch der deutschen Länder*, ed. Jürgen Hartmann, 2nd ed. (Bonn: Bundeszentrale für politische Bildung, 1994), 33–48.

19. http://www.bmi.bund.de/SharedDocs/Downloads/EN/Broschueren/Der_oeffentliche_Dienst_in_Deutschland_Id_24276_en.pdf?__blob=publication File.

20. Mayntz and Scharpf, *Policymaking*, 53ff.

21. Niklas Luhmann and Renate Mayntz, *Personal im öffentlichen Dienst* (Baden-Baden: Nomos Verlagsanstalt, 1973), 56ff.

22. Robert D. Putnam, "The Political Attitudes of Senior Civil Servants in Western Europe: A Preliminary Report," *British Journal of Political Science* 3 (1973): 257–290.

23. Eberhard Moths and Monika Wulf-Mathies, *Des Bürgers teuere Diener* (Karlsruhe: Verlag C. F. Mueller, 1973), 59.

24. For a comprehensive account of the professional civil service and the unification process, see Wolfgang Seibel et al., eds., *Verwaltungsreform und Verwaltungspolitik im Prozeß der deutschen Einigung* (Baden-Baden: Nomos Verlagsgesellschaft, 1993).

25. http://info.worldbank.org/governance/wgi/sc_chart.asp.

26. http://www.sgi-network.org/index.php?page=countries_keyfindings&country=DEU.

27. In 1991 some officials in the postal and transport ministries of the Kohl government proposed the abolition of career civil service status for employees of the Federal Railroad and Post Office.

28. Elisabeth Noelle-Neumann and Renate Köcher, *Jahrbuch der Demoskopie*, vol. 10 (Munich, Allensbach: K. G. Saur Verlag, 1997), 741.

29. "Better Regulation in Europe: Germany 2010," OECD; http://www.oecd.org/regreform/regulatorypolicy/45079989.pdf, p. 22.

30. Allensbach 2009, 167, 169.

31. Peter J. Katzenstein, *Policy and Politics in West Germany: The Growth of a Semi-Sovereign State* (Philadelphia: Temple University Press, 1987), chap. 1.

32. Katzenstein, *Policy and Politics in West Germany*, 58.

33. Pension fund statistics cited in *Der Bürger im Staat* 41, no. 1 (March 1991): 22.

34. http://www.welt.de/wirtschaft/article2487176/Ost-Rentner-erhalten-mehr-Geld-als-Westdeutsche.html.

35. http://aging.senate.gov/crs/ss4.pdf, p. 8.

36. Kerstin Schwenn, "Finanzierungsakrobatik und Neuanfänge," *Frankfurter Allgemeine Zeitung*, August 23, 2005, 4.

37. http://www.oecd.org/germany/BriefingNoteGERMANY2012.pdf.

38. http://www.ncpa.org/pub/st286?pg=4.

39. *Frankfurter Allgemeine Zeitung*, July 5, 2006, 13.

40. Allensbach 2009, 754. The introduction in 2004 of a copayment for office visits met with widespread public opposition that even included death threats against the health minister and demonstrations at Chancellor Schröder's private residence in Hanover. See Gabor Steingart, "Die Wohlstands-Illusion," *Der Spiegel*, no. 11 (March 8, 2004): 22.

41. *Jahrbuch 2009*, 768.

42. DIW, *Wochenbericht*, no. 45 (1999): 6.

43. Ellen Kennedy, *The Bundesbank* (New York: Council on Foreign Relations Press, 1991), 8.

44. *Der Spiegel* online, August 22, 2012.

45. Kennedy, *The Bundesbank*, 99ff.

46. Kennedy, *The Bundesbank*, 12.

47. Forschungsgruppe Wahlen, *Politbarometer*, no. 9 (September 1998): 3.

48. Donald P. Kommers, *Judicial Politics in West Germany* (Beverly Hills, CA: Sage, 1976), 50. See also Donald P. Kommers, *The Constitutional Jurisprudence of the Federal Republic of Germany* (Durham, NC: Duke University Press, 1989).

49. Kommers, *Judicial Politics*, 34.

50. Kommers, *Judicial Politics*, 44.

51. Manfred Riegel, "Political Attitudes and Perceptions of the Political System by Judges in West Germany" (paper, IX World Congress of the International Political Science Association, Montreal, 1973), 2a.

52. Ursula Hoffmann-Lange, "Eliteforschung in der Bundesrepublik Deutschland," *Aus Politik und Zeitgeschichte*, November 26, 1983, 14.

53. There were strong regional variations in the examination process. Only a handful of East German jurists passed muster in Berlin (4) or the states of Saxony (7) or

Mecklenburg–West Pomerania (19), but 135 judges and prosecutors in the small state of Saxony-Anhalt made the grade. *Frankfurter Allgemeine Zeitung*, June 10, 1994, 4.

54. Several top former GDR judges and prosecutors have been convicted of human rights violations and of disregarding even the GDR's laws when it was politically expedient to do so. In 1994, for example, a former judge of the East German supreme court was sentenced to almost four years in prison for unjustly sentencing two East Germans to death. *Frankfurter Allgemeine Zeitung*, June 18, 1994, 4. Between 1990 and 1998, judicial authorities in the new eastern states initiated about 22,500 investigations into human rights abuses, judicial misconduct, and criminal acts (mainly fraud and misuse of government funds) committed by DDR authorities. These investigations led to 877 indictments and 211 convictions. The greatest number of convictions (seventy-eight) occurred with police and border guards. Over one hundred indictments against DDR judges and prosecutors yielded only sixteen convictions. About sixty Stasi officials were indicted and twelve convicted. About eighty former GDR officials were convicted of economic crimes connected with the unification process. German judicial officials consider this work largely completed and anticipate no major new investigations. Karl-Heinz Baum, "Justiz will Akten schließen," *Frankfurter Rundschau*, November 6, 1998 (Internet edition).

55. Dorothy Nelkin and Michael Pollak, "French and German Courts on Nuclear Power," *Bulletin of the Atomic Scientists* (May 1980), 37. It has also been suggested that administrative court judges are more likely to be concerned with citizens' rights against the state (rather than the "general" interest) than are their counterparts in the regular court system. Some of the administrative court judges were also part of the student protest movement of the 1960s. According to a leading environmental lawyer, "Judges with a left ideology will usually try to find a job in the administrative rather than the civil courts." Cited in Nelkin and Pollak, "French and German Courts," 41.

56. Kommers, *Judicial Politics*, 29. During the Weimar Republic, the *Reichsgericht* (the highest general court in the Weimar system), capitalizing on the ambiguity of the Constitution in this area, did in fact strike down legislation on constitutional grounds, especially between 1921 and 1929. Most state courts at this time also accepted judicial review in theory, although they rarely used it to nullify legislative acts. Thus there was some tradition, albeit fragmentary, for this principle.

57. Kommers, *Judicial Politics*, 85.

58. Kommers, *Judicial Politics*, 120–144.

59. In approximately three hundred cases the court ordered a revision of the unconstitutional legislation. By early 1991 it had upheld the constitutionality of about 1,400 federal or state laws and regulations. Court statistics cited in *Das Parlament*, no. 36 (August 30, 1991), 4.

60. The court did not rule out subsequent action by the government and parliament (1) to compensate those citizens whose property was confiscated by the communists from 1945 to 1949, or even (2) to return the property if it was in public ownership and still intact. *Frankfurter Allgemeine Zeitung*, September 2, 1994, 8.

61. http://www.ft.com/intl/cms/s/0/48bbec78-6f10-11de-9109-00144feabdc0.html#axzz 23v3amv9l.

62. Günter Bannas, "Länder setzen 'Weisungsrecht' in Europapolitik durch," faz.net, August 12, 2009.

63. Karl Otto Lenz, "Ausbrechender Rechtsakt," faz.net, July 7, 2009, 7.

64. http://www.nytimes.com/2012/09/13/world/europe/german-court-backs-euro-res cue-fund.html?_r=1&hp.

65. For recent data, see *General Social Survey* (ALLBUS), 1994, 2002.

66. Allensbach 2009, 208.

67. The success of the Constitutional Court is related, of course, to the performance of the overall system of which it is a part. Because the judges are selected by legislative institutions, political and ideological considerations have played a role. However, the dominant political parties have shared a consensus on the basic values, norms, and institutions of the Republic, including the types of people who are to serve on the court. A breakdown in this consensus would also over time undermine the court's representativeness and legitimacy. See Nevil Johnson, "The Interdependence of Law and Politics: Judges and the Constitution in West Germany," *West European Politics* 5, no. 3 (July 1982): 249, for a discussion of this point.

9

Subnational Units

Federalism and Local Government

The federal structure of the Republic, which corresponds to German political tradition as well as to the wishes of postwar Allied military occupiers, ensures that the formulation and implementation of policy, together with the recruitment of political leaders, are not concentrated at the national level. In 1990, prior to the formal unification of east and west, the once rigidly centralized German Democratic Republic was reconstituted with five new federal states joining the eleven from West Germany (including West Berlin, which had an exceptional status), a further testimony to the strength of the federal idea in Germany's political tradition. More than any other major European state, the Federal Republic has decentralized and fragmented political power. Indeed, as discussed in the preceding chapter, many experts have contended that power and authority are too decentralized and compartmentalized.[1] In contrast to the United Kingdom, France, Italy, and other states, the devolution of power is really not an issue in Germany; more important is its consolidation. Germany's membership in the European Union has also complicated the relationship between the national government and the constituent states.

THE DEVELOPMENT OF GERMAN FEDERALISM

The German Reich that was founded in 1871 was composed of twenty-five historic German states, which "voluntarily" entered into a federation. These entities, however, were grossly unequal in size and population. Seventeen of them combined made up less than 1 percent of the total area of the Reich and less than 10 percent of the total population. The duchy of Braunschweig, for instance, had fewer than 500,000 people in 1910, and the principality of Reuss-Greiz had about 70,000, whereas Prussia, which had absorbed many other states over the course of its history (including Hanover in 1866) was by far the largest unit in the federation, accounting for two-thirds of its area and population and 40 million people on the eve of World War I. Many Germans were attached to their state, region, or even city—their *Heimat* (homeland). Indeed, "particularism"—exacerbated by regional dialects and confessional differences—was one of the defining features of German history and had long hindered the formation of a nation-state. After the Peace of Westphalia in 1648, there were over 200 territorial units in the Holy Roman Empire, and the rationalized post-1815 German Confederation had 38 states, including Austria.

The unity of this newly formed Reich was tenuous. Some of the member states had, in fact, been forced into the federation by a combination of military defeat at the hands of Prussia and the power politics practiced with consummate skill by Bismarck.[2] Religion was a major cleavage during this period, with the predominantly Catholic areas such as Bavaria, Baden, and Alsace-Lorraine resenting the dominance of Prussia, which was about two-thirds Protestant. But the remarkable industrial and economic growth that followed unification temporarily stilled opposition to Prussian dominance and reduced particularistic sentiment. Germany's defeat in World War I, coupled with the political, social, and economic unrest that plagued the postwar Weimar Republic, brought forth a variety of individuals and groups in areas such as Bavaria and the Rhineland who demanded the end of the more centralized Reich and the restoration of full sovereignty to the constituent states. The Nazis, who ironically in their early years found common ground with the separatists in their opposition to the Republic, abolished state government in 1934 and imposed a centralized administration on the Third Reich along with thirty-four subdivisions called *Gaue*. Bavaria, for instance, was divided into five Gaue. The leaders of these divisions, the *Gauleiter*, were some of the most important figures during the Nazi period.

The destruction of the Nazi system and the postwar military occupation returned the forces of decentralization to a dominant position. All of Germany's conquerors wanted a decentralized postwar Germany in some form. The French would have preferred a completely dismantled Reich composed of several independent states, none of which would be powerful enough ever to threaten France again. The American occupiers, having considerable experience with federal structures, urged an American-type system. The British, although more supportive of centralized power than the Americans or French, also envisioned a decentralized postwar Germany. Among the Germans, opposition to a strong federal system was mostly limited to the SPD and to those Christian Democrats in the Soviet zone, which incorporated a large amount of what remained of postwar Prussia before that entity was officially abolished in 1947.

With the emerging Cold War and division of Germany, the influence of centralizing proponents waned still further, and by 1949 there was little significant West German opposition to plans for a decentralized state. Indeed, Western occupiers could count on German support for federalism in their occupation zones because the zones included the historically most particularistic and anti-Prussian segments of the former Reich: Bavaria, the Rhineland, the province of Hanover, and the Hanseatic cities of Hamburg and Bremen. The framers of the Basic Law were also largely state-level or former Weimar politicians, who since 1946 had renewed their political careers at the state level. Thus the delegates to the parliamentary council were a very states' rights–oriented group.

The Basic Law ensures the states' substantial influence in three ways:

1. through powers reserved to them (education, police and internal security, administration of justice, supervision of the mass communications media);
2. through their responsibility for the administration of federal law, including the collection of most taxes and, since 2006, their power to adopt their own regulations for the implementation of some federal law; and
3. through their direct representation in the parliament (the Bundesrat).

From 1969 to 2006 the states were also equal participants with the federal government in certain joint tasks enumerated by Articles 91a and 91b of the Basic Law: higher education, regional economic planning and development, agricultural structure, and coastal protection. In 2006 as part of the federalism reform (see below) these joint tasks were reduced to regional economic development, agriculture, and coastal protection. Thus, in addition to their own reserved powers, the states have either direct or indirect influence on all national legislation. In only a few areas, such as defense and foreign affairs, does the national government not have to consider the views of the states in either the making or the implementation of policy. Even in these areas, the states through the Bundesrat can make their views known. A series of constitutional amendments passed in 1994 is also designed to ensure state influence at the European level. The states are concerned that the national government respect their authority and prerogatives when negotiating in the European Union.

STATE-LEVEL POLITICS

Unity and Diversity among German States

The sixteen states differ in tradition, size, population, and socioeconomic resources. In the "old" Federal Republic (i.e., before unification), only three of the states—Bavaria and the two city-states of Hamburg and Bremen—existed as separate political entities before 1945. The remaining Länder were created by Allied occupiers, in many cases to the consternation of tradition-conscious Germans. That said, many of the newly formed states corresponded loosely to older entities. Lower Saxony, for instance, mirrored the old kingdom and the Prussian province of Hanover. In the American zone, two new states, Hesse and Baden-Württemberg, were formed.[3] In the French zone, on the left bank of the Rhine, another new state, Rhineland-Palatinate, was created from territories that had earlier been provinces of Prussia, Bavaria, and Hesse. In the north, some previously independent areas and still more Prussian provinces were rearranged by the British to make the two new states of Schleswig-Holstein and Lower Saxony. In 1957 the Saar region, which had been under French control since 1945, returned to Germany after a plebiscite and became the tenth Land. Finally, West Berlin, whose status as a Land was disputed by the GDR and the Federal Republic, as well as by the Western powers and the former Soviet Union until the 1990 unification, existed de facto as a state after 1949. On October 3, 1990, Berlin's division ended, and the city, east and west, is now a full-fledged member of the federation.

The five new eastern states have also had a checkered postwar history. Several of the states—Mecklenburg, Saxony, and Thuringia—had existed as political entities before World War II. The Soviet occupation authorities created a new state, Saxony-Anhalt, from parts of Saxony and Thuringia. The state of Brandenburg, which surrounds Berlin, constitutes the remains of the prewar Prussia, which was dissolved after World War II. But in 1952, only three years after the formation of the German Democratic Republic and five years after the reconstitution of the states, all five were abolished and replaced with fifteen administrative districts (including East Berlin). East Germany's first (and last) freely elected government reestablished the five states prior to the October 1990 unification.

The Big Four

The four largest states in area and population are North Rhine–Westphalia, Bavaria, Baden-Württemberg, and Lower Saxony. Of these, North Rhine–Westphalia is by far the most populous. Approximately 22 percent of Germany's 82 million inhabitants live in this state, which incorporates the Rhine-Ruhr region, once the industrial heart of the country and the largest metropolitan region in the country with 11 million inhabitants in cities such as Cologne, Dortmund, and Essen. Politics in this Land have been competitive since 1946, with relatively close elections and alternations of government and opposition parties. Since 2010 the state has been governed by a coalition of Social Democrats and Greens, first as a minority and after 2012 as a majority.

The largest state in area and second largest in population is Bavaria. Left intact after the war, Bavaria is without question the most particularistic and conservative of the states. If there are any American-style states' rights advocates left in the Federal Republic, they are in this heavily Catholic, tradition-conscious region that has been marching to a slightly different beat from the rest of Germany since long before the Federal Republic. Bavaria entered the Bismarckian Reich in 1871 only after receiving special concessions (its own beer tax among them), and it was a hotbed of separatist and extremist sentiment during the Weimar Republic. It was the only Land that did not ratify the Basic Law in 1949, although the Bavarians acceded to the will of the other states and did finally join the Federal Republic. Bavaria thus rejected the Basic Law but also refused to exclude itself from "the common German destiny"; that is, Bavaria joined but with little enthusiasm. Once a poor rural area with a weak infrastructure, Bavaria actually benefited from the postwar division of Germany, as many large firms that had been in the east, such as the giant Siemens electronics company, relocated in the south.

In spite of their particularist traditions and strong support of federalism, the Bavarians (and especially the ideologically committed among them in the Christian Social Union, the only Land-based party) in many ways consider themselves the guardians of the German nationalist tradition in an increasingly cosmopolitan and integrated Western Europe. Following unification in 1990, Bavaria went before the court in an effort to stop the Kohl government from accepting the

Oder-Neisse line as the legitimate border between Germany and Poland—perhaps partially prompted by the 20 percent of the population that consisted of expellees. Expellees had even been adopted as a Bavarian "tribe" (*Stamm*) by former minister-president Franz-Josef Strauss. Bavaria's leaders have been among the most prominent opponents of the Euro even up to the present. Bavaria is a strong one-party-dominant state. The Christian Social Union (CSU) has been the strongest single party in all but one of sixteen postwar state elections (1950) and has governed either alone or in coalition for all but four years since 1946. The 2008 election was one of the worst ever for the CSU, which lost its absolute majority for the first time since 1962 and formed a coalition with the FDP.

The third largest Land in population, with almost 11 million inhabitants, is the southwestern state of Baden-Württemberg, one of the economic powerhouses of Germany with companies like Mercedes-Benz, Porsche, and much of the Mittelstand (small and medium-sized enterprises). More religiously balanced than Bavaria, with Baden along the Rhine being traditionally Catholic and Württemberg Protestant, its politics have usually been controlled by center-right parties, most often the CDU in coalition with the Free Democrats. Grand Coalitions between the CDU and SPD, however, have also governed at various times. From 1969 to 1988 the CDU governed alone. In 2011 the Christian Democrats were defeated and entered the opposition for the first time in almost sixty years. Currently the Greens lead a coalition with the Social Democrats. Overall, it has become a somewhat more competitive state than Bavaria.

Lower Saxony is the fourth most populous state and the third largest in area. A heavily Protestant Land with a significant rural component to its economy but also with Volkswagen in Wolfsburg, Lower Saxony has had competitive party politics in the postwar period. After fourteen years in opposition, the Social Democrats returned to power in 1990 with the Greens, and between 1994 and 2003 governed alone. But in 2003 the Christian Democrats, capitalizing on dissatisfaction with Schröder's national government, returned to power in a coalition with the FDP until narrowly losing the January 2013 election to another Red-Green coalition.

The remaining six states from the "old" West Germany—Hesse, Rhineland-Palatinate, Schleswig-Holstein, Saarland, Hamburg, and Bremen—have fewer than seven million inhabitants each. Hesse, a heavily industrialized Protestant Land with some Catholic enclaves like Fulda, contains Frankfurt, one of the most important financial centers in Europe. It has generally been an SPD stronghold, but in 1999, only a few months after the national election that brought the Social Democrats and Greens to power, the Christian Democrats and Free Democrats won a surprise victory. In 2003 the CDU/CSU won an absolute majority for the first time in the state's history, and after a period of instability from 2008 to 2009 entered into a coalition with the FDP.

Both Schleswig-Holstein and Rhineland-Palatinate have significant rural, small-town populations and are two of the poorest states from the standpoint of per capita income. The CDU has frequently dominated state politics in both, usually in coalition with the Free Democrats, but in 1988 the Social Democrats for the first time in their history won an absolute majority in Schleswig-Holstein. In 2005 the Social Democrats, following yet another election defeat attributed to the weakness of the national Schröder government, had to form a Grand Coalition with the Christian Democrats. The 2009 election led to a CDU-FDP government, and the 2012 election resulted in a coalition of SPD, Green, and the South Schleswig Voter Federation (a Danish minority party with three of sixty-nine seats). Rhineland-Palatinate combines Catholic rural areas with larger cities such as Koblenz and Ludwigshafen. Helmut Kohl's home state is currently governed by the Social Democrats in coalition with the Greens. The Saarland, one of the smallest states, is primarily an industrial area with a large Catholic population. Until the mid-1980s this state was controlled by the Christian Democrats. In the next three elections, however, the Social Democrats, led by Oskar Lafontaine, won an absolute majority. In 1999 the Christian Democrats returned to power. Currently, a Grand Coalition of Christian and Social Democrats governs the state.

The city-states of Hamburg and Bremen, both historically Protestant, have been governed mainly by the Social Democrats. From 1995 to 2007, Bremen was governed by an SPD-CDU Grand Coalition, and since 2007 by an SPD-Green coalition. Hamburg is the richest state in the federation. The city has profited mightily from unification and the end of the Cold War and has long been Germany's media capital. It is the main port of entry for the many goods now imported into the east, and the Elbe, Germany's "blue-collar" river, flows into the Baltic Sea at Hamburg. Hamburg's port is the third largest in Europe and the fifteenth worldwide. A CDU majority government existed in Hamburg from 2004 to 2008, a novel CDU-Green government from 2008 to 2011, and after 2011 a majority SPD government.

The Eastern German States and Berlin

The five eastern states are relatively small. The largest Land, Saxony, with about 4.1 million residents, is only the sixth largest of the sixteen states. Saxony is also the major industrial center of the former East Germany, accounting for about a third of the area's population and gross national product. Before 1933, Saxony was a stronghold of the Social Democrats, but the Christian Democrats won an absolute majority in the state's first free election in 1990 and have been the strongest party in all subsequent elections, currently in coalition with the FDP.

The other four states are smaller and less industrialized than Saxony. Its neighbor, Saxony-Anhalt, has the shortest history as an independent political entity. The state, which contains some of Germany's most fertile farmland, is currently governed by a Grand Coalition of Christian Democrats and Social Democrats. Thuringia, with 2.2 million inhabitants, has a more mixed economy than Saxony or Saxony-Anhalt. It was the center of the former GDR's high-tech microelectronics, optics (Zeiss), and carmaking (Wartburg) industries. A Grand Coalition of CDU and SPD is currently in power. Because of its proximity to the western states, Thuringia has had one of the highest growth rates in the eastern region. About 120,000 Thuringians commute daily to jobs in Hesse and Bavaria.[4] Brandenburg is a sparsely populated Land in the northeast. Until 1920, Berlin was a province of Brandenburg; the city lies within its borders. From 1990 to 1999, Brandenburg was the sole stronghold of the Social Democrats in the eastern states. From 1999 to 2009, the SPD has had to share power with the Christian Democrats, and since 2009 with the Left Party.

The smallest of the new states in population, with fewer than two million residents, and the poorest state in the federation, is the coastal Land of Mecklenburg–West Pomerania. This region is primarily agricultural, but it has a shipbuilding industry in cities like Rostock. In 1998 a coalition between the Social Democrats (SPD) and the Party of Democratic Socialism (PDS) formed a new state government. It marked the first time since unification that the PDS (now the Left Party), the successor to the former ruling Communist Party of East Germany, had acquired governmental responsibility at the state level. Many Christian Democrats sharply criticized the Social Democrats for aligning with what they considered an antidemocratic party. In 2006 another Grand Coalition of Social Democrats and Christian Democrats replaced this "Red-Red" (SPD-PDS) government.

The final state, Berlin, is also, of course, Germany's capital. In 1990 the city, like the country, was unified after forty years of division. Divided since 1961 by a wall, East Berlin, the Soviet sector, was the capital of the German Democratic Republic, while West Berlin had a special status as a city under the official control of the United States, the UK, and France but administered by a freely elected government. Since the double unification of 1990, the two parts of the city also lost their special status and the abundant subsidies they had received as a consequence of their "showcase" position. The city, which had lost almost all of its economic base after 1945, had to fend for itself. Currently, Berlin is one of the most indebted of all the states. After unification, unemployment doubled, almost 20 percent of its population is on welfare, and 400,000 industrial jobs (mainly in the eastern section) have been lost. As Mayor Klaus Wowereit put it, the city is "poor but sexy." Recently, the economy has started to recover. In 2011, unemployment was 12.7 percent, still about double the national average but a fifteen-year low. Nonetheless, a property boom, government employment, a burgeoning high-tech sector, and tourism auger well for the future.

From 2001 to 2011, Berlin was governed by a "Red-Red" coalition of Social Democrats and the Left Party (formerly the PDS), and since then by an SPD-CDU Grand Coalition. It continues to seek special status and economic relief from the national government. In 2006, as a consequence of the Federalism Reform (see below), an amended Article 22 states that "the representation of the entire country in the capital city is the responsibility of the national government. Details shall be regulated by federal laws." This means that some additional long-term funding (and possible debt relief) for the expenses associated with being the capital city should be forthcoming. The city and the national government have been attempting, with considerable difficulty, to negotiate a "treaty" that would determine the extent of this support.

All of these new eastern states, including unified Berlin, are poor. Despite massive transfers from west to east over twenty years, per capita gross national product is still only 73 percent of the level in the west ($37,368 in the eleven western states including Berlin, and $27,431 in the five eastern Länder). Adding to their economic problems is a declining population. With the exception of Brandenburg, the eastern states between 1990 and 2009 lost approximately 12 percent of their populations, largely through migration to the west. Over this period, approximately 1.7 million people, especially young women, have left the region, and there are fewer than 13 million people in the five new Länder (excluding Berlin).[5] Brandenburg's slight increase was due to Berlin residents moving to suburbs in Brandenburg. In fact, 40 percent of Brandenburg's population lives around Berlin.

As table 9.1 shows, the sixteen states range in population from Bremen, with fewer than 1 million inhabitants, to North Rhine–Westphalia, with a population of almost 18 million. Their areas range from Bavaria's 70,600 square kilometers to Hamburg and Bremen's combined 120 square kilometers. Per capita GNP ranges from $26,875 in Mecklenburg–West Pomerania (the other former GDR states are only slightly better off) to $64,500 in Hamburg.[6] Over the entire history of the Federal Republic, the Social Democrats have been the strongest party in Hesse, Hamburg, Bremen, and Berlin; the CDU/CSU has done best in Bavaria, Baden-Württemberg, Schleswig-Holstein, the Rhineland-Palatinate, and the Saarland. Competitive party politics have been most prevalent in Lower Saxony and North Rhine–Westphalia and have increased everywhere in the last decade.

Since the late 1970s, the southern states of Baden-Württemberg and Bavaria, Germany's version of the "Sun Belt," as well as Hesse and Hamburg, have experienced more economic growth and less unemployment than the northern or western states. Most of Germany's microelectronics, robotics, and aerospace industries are in the southern states, whereas the declining coal, steel, textile, and shipbuilding sectors of the economy are concentrated in the north and west. By 2012, unemployment in the south averaged about 5 percent or less, as compared to about 7 or 8 percent in northern states such as Lower Saxony and North Rhine–Westphalia. The recent economic upturn has reduced unemployment rates everywhere, but it is unclear how long this situation will continue.

The Constitutional Structure of the States

The Basic Law requires that the "constitutional order in the Länder conform to the principles of republican, democratic, and social government based on the rule of law" (Article 28, paragraph 1). The specific form of government, including the questions of whether the legislature is to be bicameral or unicameral and the executive directly or indirectly elected, is left to the discretion of the states. All states have unicameral legislatures with an executive (minister-president and cabinet) responsible to it. Most states have also adopted the personalized proportional electoral law described in chapter 6. State-level cabinets are composed of eight to twelve ministers. In addition to the classic ministries of finance, education, health, justice, and internal affairs, each state has several ministries whose activities reflect the state's special characteristics (e.g., the Rhineland-Palatinate's wine ministry, Hamburg and Bremen's harbors ministry).

Coalition governments have been as common in the states as they have at the national level. Until the mid-1960s, coalition alignments, especially in the larger states, were usually similar to those at the national level. This ensured that the national government would have adequate support for its program in the Bundesrat. The practice was an example of the integrating effects that political

Table 9.1a.   The Länder of the Federal Republic

Land	Population (millions) 2011	Proportion of Total	Area (thousands of sq. km)	Population (per sq. km)	Gross Domestic Product 2011 (billion $)*	Proportion of Total
North Rhine–Westphalia	17.8	21.8	34.1	522	699.7	22.1
Bavaria	12.6	15.4	70.5	179	549.1	17.4
Baden-Württemberg	10.8	13.2	35.8	302	462.8	14.6
Lower Saxony	7.9	9.7	47.6	166	276.0	8.7
Hesse	6.1	7.5	21.1	289	281.0	8.9
Saxony	4.1	5.0	18.4	223	116.9	3.7
Rhineland-Palatinate	4.0	4.9	19.8	202	139.3	4.4
Berlin	3.5	4.3	0.9	3,889	124.7	3.9
Schleswig-Holstein	2.8	3.4	15.8	177	90.6	2.9
Brandenburg	2.5	3.1	29.5	85	67.8	2.1
Saxony-Anhalt	2.3	2.8	20.4	113	63.8	2.0
Thuringia	2.2	2.7	16.2	136	59.2	1.9
Hamburg	1.8	2.2	0.8	2,250	116.1	3.7
Mecklenburg–West Pomerania	1.6	2.0	23.2	69	43.0	1.4
Saarland	1.0	1.2	2.6	385	37.5	1.2
Bremen	0.7	0.9	0.4	1,750	34.5	1.1
Total	81.8	100	357.1	227	3,162.1	100

Source: http://www.statistik-portal.de/Statistik-Portal/en/en_jb27_jahrtab65.asp.
* Converted at 1 Euro = $1.23.

Table 9.1b. The Länder of the Federal Republic

Land	Per Capita GNP ($)	Percent Foreign Residents (2009)	Percent Agriculture (2010)	Percent Unemployed (2011)	Percent Catholic/ Protestant/ No Religion (2011)*	Governing Party or Coalition (2013)**	Capital
North Rhine–Westphalia	38,806	10.5	0.9	8.1	42/28/23	SPD-Green	Düsseldorf
Bavaria	43,579	9.5	2.3	3.8	55/21/20	CSU-FDP	Munich
Baden-Württemberg	42,852	11.9	1.3	4.0	37/33/24	Green-SPD	Stuttgart
Lower Saxony	34,937	6.7	2.5	6.9	18/50/30	SPD-Green	Hanover
Hesse	46,066	11.1	1.1	5.9	25/40/29	CDU-FDP	Wiesbaden
Saxony	28,512	2.7	1.9	10.6	4/21/75	CDU-FDP	Dresden
Rhineland-Palatinate	34,825	7.7	2.0	5.3	45/31/20	SPD-Green	Mainz
Berlin	35,629	13.7	0	13.3	9/19/63	SPD-CDU	Berlin
Schleswig-Holstein	32,357	5.1	2.6	7.2	6/53/38	SPD-Green-SSW***	Kiel
Brandenburg	27,120	2.7	2.7	10.7	3/17/80	SPD-Left	Potsdam
Saxony-Anhalt	27,739	1.9	2.3	11.6	4/14/81	CDU-SPD	Magdeburg
Thuringia	26,909	2.2	2.3	8.8	8/24/68	CDU-SPD	Erfurt
Hamburg	64,500	13.6	0	7.8	10/30/52	SPD	Hamburg
Mecklenburg–West Pomerania	26,875	2.4	3.6	12.5	3/18/79	SPD-CDU	Schwerin
Saarland	37,500	8.4	0	6.8	63/19/14	CDU-SPD	Saarbrücken
Bremen	49,286	12.5	0	11.6	12/41/36	SPD-Green	Bremen
Total	38,656	8.8	1.6	7.1			

Source: http://www.statistik-portal.de/Statistik-Portal/en.
*http://de.statista.com/statistik/daten/studie/201622/umfrage/religionszugehoerigkeit-der-deutschen-nach-bundeslaendern.
**The party listed first is the senior coalition partner, providing the minister president.
***The South Schleswig Voter's Federation, representing the Danish minority.

parties can have in a federal system. It began in the 1950s when Adenauer sought to compel all CDU state parties to leave coalitions with the Social Democrats and conform to the federal pattern of governing alone, if possible, or with other middle-class parties.[7] By the end of the decade, either the CDU and its allies or the Social Democrats controlled all state governments.

The waning of Adenauer's influence, CDU/CSU intraparty conflicts, and the greater acceptability of the SPD as a partner to the Free Democrats, and in some cases the Union itself, led to the breakdown of this pattern in the early 1960s. After the formation of the Grand Coalition in 1966, almost all types of party alignments possible could be found in the states. There were Grand Coalitions (SPD-CDU) in Baden-Württemberg and Lower Saxony; CDU/CSU–FDP alignments in Schleswig-Holstein, Rhineland-Palatinate, and the Saar; SPD-FDP coalitions in North Rhine–Westphalia, Hamburg, and Bremen; and single-party governments in Bavaria (CSU) and Hesse (SPD). After the formation of the national SPD-FDP coalition in 1969, coalition governments at the state level again became consistent with the Bonn pattern: either the SPD-FDP governed in coalition (Hesse, Hamburg, Bremen, Lower Saxony, and North Rhine–Westphalia), or the Christian Democrats ruled alone (Bavaria, Rhineland-Palatinate, the Saar, Baden-Württemberg, and Schleswig-Holstein). After 1976, however, a mixed pattern returned as the Christian Democrats and Free Democrats formed coalition governments in Lower Saxony and the Saar.

Although the Free Democrats governed with the Christian Democrats in Bonn, they were aligned with the Social Democrats in the Rhineland-Palatinate and in the new East German state of Brandenburg until 1994. The two largest parties were also in a Grand Coalition in Berlin and Baden-Württemberg, and from 1995 to 2007 in Bremen. Between 1990 and 1998 the Free Democrats disappeared from the parliaments in twelve of the sixteen states, thus depriving both major parties of a traditional coalition partner. The Christian Democrats in these states are now in an especially difficult situation. They could form Grand Coalitions with the Social Democrats or break new ground and take the Greens, a party they once denounced as a radical left-wing sect, as a coalition partner. Hamburg did just this between 2008 and 2011. By mid-2012, there was an almost equal distribution of center-right coalitions (CDU-FDP) in four states, center-left (SPD-Green) in five states, and Grand Coalitions in five states. There have also been novel combinations such as SPD-Left and CDU-Green, as well as the first-ever Green-led coalition in Baden-Württemberg. Of the current minister-presidents, three are women (including the popular Hannelore Kraft in North Rhine–Westphalia) and one is openly gay (Klaus Wowereit in Berlin).

Land-Level Party Systems

The simplification of the national party system, discussed in chapter 5, was paralleled at the state level. During the early postwar years and into the 1950s, small regional parties played an important role in several states, principally Lower Saxony (the Refugee Party and the German Party), Bavaria (the Bavarian Party), and North Rhine–Westphalia (the Center Party). Their disappearance by the early 1960s reduced the particularistic or regional component and intensified the nationalization of state politics. Nonetheless, it is still easier for new parties to test the water and make a national impact by first concentrating on the state level. This was the strategy pursued by the right-wing National Democratic Party (NPD) during the 1960s. By gaining representation in state parliaments, the party secured a foothold and received nationwide attention far sooner than if it had concentrated on national elections. Even in this case, the substance and direction of the party's appeal were national, and the NPD's defeat in the 1969 election also ended its string of successes in state elections. A similar strategy was followed by the Greens—more successfully—in the 1980s. In two states, Bremen and Baden-Württemberg, the party cleared the 5 percent hurdle and suddenly became a national political phenomenon. Since 1990 the Left Party (PDS from 1990 to 2007) succeeded in establishing itself as a regional party in eastern Germany. In the last few years, there have been several state-level protest parties such as the Statt Party in Hamburg, which was in government from 1993 to 1997 and then lost support; the Freie Wähler in Bavaria, who received 10.2 percent of the vote in 2008; and the Pirate Party receiving, among other results, 8.9 percent of the vote in Berlin in 2011 and 7.8 percent in North Rhine–Westphalia in 2012.

State-level party systems also increase the sociological and ideological diversity of the national parties. For example, the impetus for the transformation of the SPD during the late 1950s came from those SPD state organizations that were in power. Indeed, the SPD was able to endure twenty years (1949–1969) of national opposition without becoming a radical, extremist sect, partly because it held power in several states where it had to deal with concrete policy problems. In this sense, state-level politics kept the SPD in the mainstream of national political life. In the case of the CDU/CSU, the federal system increased the national influence of the Union's right wing by providing it with a power base in Bavaria. In a unitary system, the Bavarian component of the party would have far less impact on the national organization than it now has under a federal system.

Electoral Politics in the States

Since the early 1960s, state elections, especially in the larger Länder, have increasingly become indicators or tests of the electorate's mood toward national parties, leaders, and issues. Indeed, many analysts speak today of a perpetual campaign or a series of plebiscites in light of the steady stream of elections at the Land level. They can also have a direct effect on national politics by altering the party alignment in the Bundesrat.

As in congressional elections in the United States and by-elections in the UK, the party or parties in power at the national level generally lose support in state elections, which are usually held in off years. The results of state elections, while usually contested on local or state issues, such as the Stuttgart 21 train project in Baden-Württemberg in 2011, can also have an effect on the stability of the national governing coalition and its leadership, as well as on policy. The resignation of Willy Brandt in 1974 was partially related to poor SPD showings in state elections after 1972. The collapse of the Schmidt government in 1982 was preceded by losses in state elections. In 1999, just four months after the stunning victory of the SPD and the Greens in the 1998 national election, the two parties lost a state election in Hesse. The defeat in Hesse meant that the Schröder government no longer had a majority of votes in the Bundesrat (Federal Council). The SPD's 2005 defeat in a state election in North Rhine–Westphalia caused the Schröder government to call for new national elections. Thus changes at the state level can have a direct and immediate impact on national politics. All major transfers of power at the national level since 1949 have in fact been presaged by developments in state-level politics.

In 2010–2011 during the Greek debt crisis, the Merkel government tried to avoid committing any additional resources to the bailout funds in part because of concern about voter reaction at critical state elections in North Rhine–Westphalia (May 2010) and Baden-Württemberg (March 2011). The controversial German abstention on the UN Security Council vote to provide military support to the Libyan forces opposing Ghadafi in March 2011 was also apparently done to enable Merkel's struggling coalition partner, the Free Democrats and their then leader, Guido Westerwelle, to gain support in the upcoming Baden-Württemberg election. Westerwelle's efforts appeared to be similar to the 2002 decision of Chancellor Schröder to oppose the Iraq war. His refusal to support the war did resonate among voters, but these efforts did not help the FDP in that state. Merkel wanted to support the UN intervention but deferred to Westerwelle. Perhaps because they also understood her political problem, the reaction of the United States, the UK, and France was muted.

These consequences of state elections are largely the result of campaign strategies adopted by the parties, which have increasingly used state polls as tests of current support for national policies. In 1999, Roland Koch engaged in a signature campaign during the election in Hesse to delegitimize the SPD-Green coalition's plans for dual citizenship. The legislation was indeed watered down as a consequence. The state election of 1998 in Lower Saxony was the critical test for Gerhard Schröder's chancellor candidacy. His success in that election made him the SPD's national candidate. The infusion of national personalities and issues into state campaigns may also explain the relatively high turnout in these elections.

In some cases, a party may not want to "nationalize" a state election because of unfavorable national conditions, and its top leaders will stay away from the campaign. But the opposition may well compel national leaders to come out and fight the electoral battle in the provinces. Thus, in spite of the occasional presence of genuine state factors in elections, they have increasingly become part of the national political struggle.

Too Many Elections?

While state elections are the functional equivalents of midterm elections in the United States, they are not timed to take place at the halfway point of the national cycle but are staggered over a four-year period. Moreover, there is a much greater likelihood of early elections in the more volatile states—Hesse, Hamburg, Schleswig-Holstein, and North Rhine–Westphalia are recent examples. Thus, soon after a national vote, the new or reelected government will have to deal with one or two state elections that can become a kind of referendum on the national government's policies. The narrow victory of the Schröder government in late September 2002 was followed less than five months later by elections in two of the larger states, Hesse and Lower Saxony. The national government's low standing in public opinion polls was transferred to the SPD candidates in these states, both of which have historically been Social Democratic strongholds. The FDP since 2009 has lost much support in the states due to the unpopularity of its national leadership. The national character of the media, the absence of great geographical distances, and the integrated, interdependent nature of fiscal policies invite the nationalization of a state campaign.

For some analysts the timing of state elections has become a negative factor in the national government's efforts to develop, pass, and implement reform policies. Instead of being able to govern "undisturbed" for four years, the national government must think of the short-run impact of its actions on state-level politics. Since some of these elections occur soon after a national election, the government is restrained from starting any new initiatives that in the difficult start-up period could hurt its state-level partners. Former Chancellor Schröder even proposed scheduling eight (or half) of the state elections at the midpoint of the national cycle and the remaining eight on the same date as the national election. This would give a government at least a two-year period free of any electoral pressure. This proposal is an example of the kind of new thinking that is being called upon to deal with the so-called stalled reform process (Reformstau) in the Federal Republic.

Leaders and Policies

The style of state Ministerpräsidenten (minister-presidents) has ranged from the strong father figure to a low-key bureaucratic approach. The postwar leaders of Hesse, Hamburg, and Bremen, and the former chief executives of Bavaria, especially Franz-Josef Strauss and Edmund Stoiber, are representative of the father-figure type. Many minister-presidents, however, have been relatively colorless administrators with extensive careers in local and state party organizations as their most common background characteristic. In the new eastern states, the first generation of political leaders has passed from the scene. As in the west after 1949, East German voters initially preferred strong, fatherlike authority figures, such as Manfred Stolpe in Brandenburg, who would carefully introduce them to the world of democratic politics and market economics. Many of these leaders, such as Kurt Biedenkopf in Saxony and Bernhard Vogel in Saxony-Anhalt, were western transplants. The second generation of leaders—Mathias Platzeck in Brandenburg, Stanislaw Tillich in Saxony, Christine Lieberknecht in Thuringia, and Wolfgang Tiefensee, the former mayor of Leipzig and now transportation minister in the Merkel government—are homegrown and will eventually make their mark on national politics. Chancellor Merkel and Federal President Joachim Gauck are perhaps the most notable easterners in national politics today.

Four of the Republic's eight chancellors (Kiesinger, Brandt, Kohl, and Schröder) were state chief executives before assuming the top national spot. The SPD's chancellor candidates in 1987 (Johannes Rau), 1990 (Oskar Lafontaine), and 1994 (Rudolf Scharping) were all state-level chief executives. The former leader of Bavaria, Edmund Stoiber, was the CDU/CSU's chancellor candidate in 2002. Federal presidents Richard von Weizsäcker, Johannes Rau, and Christian Wulff were also minister-presidents. Executive leadership experience at the state level, as opposed to parliamentary experience at the national level, may become more common for future chancellor candidates.

The major issues of state politics tend to focus on those areas for which the states have primary responsibility: education, police and law enforcement, environmental questions, the supervision of radio and television, and the organization and regulation of the bureaucracy. The remainder of state activity tends to be rather routine administration of policies formulated at the national level, albeit with state input.

The states have varied considerably in their treatment of educational matters. During the 1950s and 1960s, the issue of separate schools for Protestant and Catholic children was a major problem in those states with large Catholic populations. The reform of secondary and university-level education has also varied, with CDU/CSU states such as Bavaria and the Rhineland-Palatinate being decidedly less enthusiastic about the comprehensive school and democratized universities than are SPD states such as Hesse and North Rhine–Westphalia. Also, as discussed in chapter 4, the issue of radicals in public employment was treated differently in conservative CDU states than in liberal SPD regions.

A clearer picture of state policy activities and the federal-state division of labor is provided by table 9.2, which shows the expenditures of state and national governments by policy areas. Although the national government has almost sole responsibility for defense, internal security (police) is primarily a state function. In the area of social welfare, the national government spends about four times as much as the states. Education has clearly been the prerogative of the states, and it still constitutes about one-third of all expenditures. Nonetheless, federal efforts to gain a foothold in the education area are evident by the $16.9 billion Berlin spent on education and research in 2013. Both levels are also the dispensers of public largesse to other levels of government. Approximately 35 percent of local revenue comes from the Länder budgets. The grants of the federal government

Table 9.2. Expenditures of Federal, State, and Local by Policy Area, 2009 (in percent)

	Federal	Länder	Local
General public services	30.50	25.20	14.60
Defense	7.60	0.00	0
Public order and safety	1.00	9.10	4.50
Economic affairs	8.90	10.50	11.40
Environmental protection	0.10	0.60	5.70
Housing and community affairs	1.60	2.80	6.40
Health	0.00	1.30	1.90
Recreation, culture, and religion	0.20	1.60	6.00
Education	1.20	25.40	16.20
Social protection	48.70	23.50	33.30

Source: OECD.

(about 10 percent of expenditures) go largely to the states, but local communities are also the recipients of some national grants.

Federal-State Integration: Revenue Sharing

The Basic Law commits the Federal Republic to the maintenance of a "unity of living standards" for the various states of the federation. Given the different economic levels of the states, this result can only be achieved by revenue sharing to balance the varied taxing powers of the states. The goal is a unity or parity of per capita governmental revenues, not any equality of personal incomes. Each state should have a similar per capita amount of funds for schools, roads, hospitals, environmental protection, and other infrastructure responsibilities. This policy makes financial relations between the states and the federal government very complex. They involve the following programs (see table 9.3):

1. Vertical equalization (federal payments to poorer states). In 2010, for example, the federal government paid approximately $15 billion to the twelve "poor" states to bring their level of public expenditures to 95 percent of the national average. Many of these funds have come from the "Solidarity Surcharge" on income taxes earmarked for eastern Germany. A second solidarity pact agreed in 2001 will send $193 billion to the five new states from 2005 to 2019. After that, exceptional transfers are no longer envisioned.

Table 9.3. Fiscal Federalism in Germany

	Horizontal Payments (2010, $ million)*	Vertical Payments (2010, $ million)**	Per capita Länder Debt ($, 2010)
Bavaria	−4,398.66	0	4,348.26
Hesse	−2,189.88	0	10,765.44
Baden-Württemberg	−2,134.44	0	7,615.44
Hamburg	−78.12	0	17,789.94
Saarland	112.14	137.34	18,451.44
Schleswig-Holstein	126	131.04	13,662.18
Lower Saxony	322.56	157.5	10,644.48
Rhineland-Palatinate	331.38	236.88	12,998.16
North Rhine–Westphalia	451.08	153.72	15,476.58
Brandenburg	500.22	2106.72	11,072.88
Bremen	559.44	259.56	34,182.54
Thuringia	587.16	2107.98	10,585.26
Saxony-Anhalt	618.66	2288.16	13,028.40
Saxony	1,062.18	3743.46	3,064.32
Mecklenburg–West Pomerania	1,595.16	495.18	9,356.76
Berlin	3,633.84	3293.64	21,900.06

Source: Statistisches Jahrbuch 2011, 571; https://www.destatis.de/DE/Publikationen/StatistischesJahrbuch/FinanzenSteuern.pdf?__blob
     = publicationFile; http://www.spiegel.de/politik/deutschland/bild-844855-312650.html.
Note: Converted at 1 Euro = $1.26.
*Länderfinanzausgleich.
**Bundesergänzungszuweisungen—from federal government to Länder.

2. The sharing of common tax revenues between the states and federal government.
3. Horizontal equalization (payments to poorer states by richer ones). In 2010, four states—Bavaria, Baden-Württemberg, Hamburg, and Hesse—contributed about $8.6 billion to the twelve other states.[8] Reforms of 2001 implemented in 2005 did not substantially change the system.
4. Intergovernmental grants and subsidies for various special and joint projects, as well as federal payments to the states to defray the costs of administering federal law.

The most controversial of these programs has certainly been the horizontal (state-to-state) sharing. The donor states, especially the three largest, have among the lowest debt levels in the country. They are, of course, dissatisfied with this system and argue that it penalizes them for their efficient administration by giving their citizens' Euros to the poorer, allegedly spendthrift states. As one donor state minister-president put it, "Why do we have to pay while Wowereit (Berlin's mayor) parties it up in Berlin?"[9] The "rich" states also complain that they have to contribute so much of their revenues that at the end of the process, when federal payments are included, they are worse off than the poorer states that the system is designed to help. The current system also offers no incentives for the poorer, receiving states to make their economies more efficient and productive. If they were to do so, they would become contributing states and would have to give up most of these gains to the remaining poorer states. In the view of the contributing states, the current system also hinders economic growth by rewarding consumption and penalizing savings and investments—that is, the "rich" states, instead of investing their surplus, must pay it to the consuming states.[10] Especially Bavaria, by far the biggest contributor to the scheme today—although before the mid-1980s it was a recipient—has complained. In the summer of 2012, Minister-President Horst Seehofer even threatened to take the system to the constitutional court despite the court upholding the system in 1992 and 2006. Even North Rhine–Westphalia, previously a contributor and now a small beneficiary, has criticized the system as preventing a recovery of its finances.

The recipient states respond by emphasizing that this horizontal revenue sharing is only a small part of the larger system of federal-state financial relations. The rich states, for example, receive far more in other forms of federal aid such as grants for research, support for higher education, and other subsidies than do the poorer states. Bavaria and Baden-Württemberg's booming high-tech sectors have been the recipients of huge federal grants for research. Most of Germany's newly designated "elite" universities are in these two states, which means even more federal largesse.

It has proven difficult to change this system in light of the constitutional guarantee that "the stronger help the weaker." In 2007, 67 percent of Germans supported horizontal payments (19 percent opposed), although this was down from 78 percent support in 1995.[11] Indeed, the question of federal–state financial relationships was the topic of another Federalism Reform Commission (Federalism Reform II) that concluded its work in 2009. In voting, each state—

regardless of size—had one vote. Since only four states are net contributors and the remaining twelve are net beneficiaries of horizontal revenue sharing, the paying states could be outvoted easily unless they could form alliances with several of the receiving states. Because these proposed changes required amending the Constitution, a two-thirds majority in both the Bundestag and Bundesrat was necessary. The biggest changes involved the creation of a Stability Council (comprising the federal minister of finance, the federal minister of economics and technology, and the 16 Länder ministers of finance) and the necessity of the federal (by 2015) and state governments (by 2019) to balance their budgets without taking on more debt. In the future, only the federal government may take on more debt, but this cannot exceed 0.35 percent of GDP (structural deficit). Especially indebted states (Berlin, Bremen, Saarland, Saxony-Anhalt, and Schleswig-Holstein) have been given extra funds to balance their budgets.

Vertical Equalization and Tax Sharing

Vertical revenue sharing, especially on the federal government's part, has been designed to consolidate the structure and process of policy making. Although the federal government receives about 45 percent of all tax revenues, in 2010 it was responsible for only about 42 percent of all public expenditures, including national defense, whereas the states accounted for 36 percent and local governments about 22 percent.[12] The states and local communities, on the other hand, spend more than they receive in taxes, with the federal government making up most of the difference. This financial leverage has enabled the national government to achieve some coordination in areas such as education, regional economic development, and social welfare programs.

The states, however, have steadily struggled for a larger piece of the tax pie and hence greater independence from the national government. At present, the states receive about one-third of the largest source of tax revenue, the individual and corporate income tax (currently 48 percent goes to Berlin, 34 percent to the states, 12 percent to the cities, and the remainder to the European Union). Since 1995 the states' share of the second-largest money raiser, the value-added tax, has increased from 37 percent to 44 percent (see table 9.4 for information about sources of tax revenues). The federal government receives about 95 percent of its income from taxes, but taxes account for only 70 percent of state revenues; the difference of 25 percent is, in a sense, the margin of state dependency on the national government. For the national government, on the other hand, it is a means of facilitating integration and consolidation. Neither side is satisfied with the arrangement, and the struggle over the distribution of tax revenues continues.

Until 1995 these revenue-sharing provisions were suspended for the new East German states. The old states, fearing a large drain on their treasuries, insisted that the new states would have to experience a substantial economic revival before these sections of the constitution could take effect. In exchange, the old states agreed to underwrite part of the "German Unity Fund," a bond issue to finance economic development in the new regions. In 1993 a "Solidarity Pact" was passed by the national parliament that restructured the distribution of tax revenues between local, state, and national governments and in 1995 brought the

Table 9.4.   Sources of Tax Revenues by Governmental Level (in percent)

	1980	1989	2008
Shared Taxes	**73.20**	**74.10**	**70.60**
Income tax	40.70	40.80	31.10
Capital gains tax	1.10	2.40	5.40
Corporation tax	5.80	6.40	2.80
Value-added tax	14.50	12.70	23.30
Import sales tax	11.10	11.90	8.10
Federal Taxes	**11.40**	**11.40**	**15.40**
Tobacco tax	3.10	2.90	2.40
Liquor tax	1.20	0.90	0.50
Energy tax	5.90	6.20	8.10
Insurance tax	0.50	0.80	1.90
Solidarity tax contribution*	0.70	0.70	2.30
State Taxes	**4.40**	**4.50**	**3.90**
Property/wealth tax	1.60	1.50	0.80
Road tax	1.80	1.70	1.60
Beer tax	0.30	0.20	0.10
Tax on land acquisition	0.70	1.10	1.00
Local Taxes	**9.70**	**8.60**	**9.30**
Property tax	1.60	1.60	1.80
Commercial tax	7.40	6.90	7.30
EU Transfers			0.70

Source: Statistisches Bundesamt as quoted in Wolfgang Rudzio, "Das politische System der Bundesrepublik Deutschland, 8, aktualisierte und erweiterte Auflage" (2011): 337.
*Until 1989 "other" federal taxes.

new states into the revenue-sharing system. This pact has since been extended to 2019.

The Future of Federalism

On balance, one can say that the federal system has worked well since 1949. Among West Germans, support for federalism grew from only 20 percent in 1952 to over 70 percent by the early 1990s. In 1992, when asked their opinion of federalism for the first time, easterners were actually slightly more supportive (74 percent to 72 percent) than their western counterparts. Forty years of communist centralization had apparently convinced them of the value of federalism.[13] By 2007, in contrast, 33 percent saw more advantages, 20 percent saw more disadvantages, and 34 percent saw neither, down from 42 percent, 8 percent, and 36 percent in 1995.[14]

Federalism is not without its problems. The states have jealously guarded their independence and have opposed many long-overdue administrative reforms, fearing a loss of power and funds. In the "joint projects" program dealing with higher education, regional economic development, and health care, they opposed giving the national government any significant coordinating authority but conceded it only as a planning function. They have also opposed increased authority for the national government on questions of water and air pollution. Thus, for example, the national government is being held responsible by neighboring countries such as Switzerland and the Netherlands for the pollution of the Rhine River; but because of federalism, the national government's power to make and enforce stricter pollution control laws, without the consent of the states, is limited.[15]

The weakness of the federal system was also noticeable in the inability of the police to apprehend the left-wing terrorists (RAF) responsible for robberies, kidnappings, and murders that plagued the Federal Republic for over two decades from the 1970s to 1990s, and more recently the neo-Nazi group the National Socialist Underground (see chapter 4). Since the end of the Cold War, Germany has also become a target country for organized crime groups from Eastern Europe and the former Soviet Union. Terrorism and crime are national problems, but the structure of law enforcement—largely as a consequence of experiences with the centralized Nazi police state—is highly decentralized. Police powers are largely reserved to the states, which have been reluctant to cede any major responsibility to the federal government. Because terrorists and organized crime do not respect state boundaries, the inadequate coordination and communication among the states and between them and the federal government is a major hindrance to Germany's fight against terrorism and organized crime. In the case of terrorism, only after national law enforcement agencies, such as the Federal Criminal Office and the Office for the Protection of the Constitution, were strengthened was significant progress achieved in the apprehension of terrorists, but coordination problems persist.

Finally, by insisting on a greater role in the European Union, the states have reduced the capacity of Germany to speak with a single voice in the councils of Europe. This may be comforting to Germany's neighbors, but it probably reduces the Federal Republic's effectiveness in the European arena. Before committing Germany to any major initiative, the national government must consult with the states.

One solution to these problems might be to consolidate the federal system by reducing the number of states from the present sixteen to seven or eight units of roughly equal size, population, and economic resources. Such a federal structure would greatly reduce, if not eliminate, the poor state–rich state problem and hence the need for the national government and the richer states to pay subsidies or equalization money to the poorer states. Realignment and consolidation would also end the veto power now enjoyed by even the smallest state in many federal–state undertakings. It would also mean fewer state elections. The adoption of any realignment would require the approval of both the Bundestag and the Bundesrat; thus, without bipartisan support, realignment would be very difficult. However, the addition of the five new eastern states and the increasing frequency of state opposition to the federal government's reform policies have once again focused attention on this problem.[16] The Federalism Reform Commission II (see next section) was charged with considering this possibility in their deliberations, unfortunately to no avail. Indeed, there have been numerous plans over the last two decades to reduce the number of Länder, by, for example, merging Hamburg with Schleswig-Holstein and perhaps Mecklenburg–West Pomerania. There was even an unsuccessful referendum in 1996 to fuse Berlin and Brandenburg.

FEDERALISM REFORM

Federalism—and specifically the ability of the states to block national legislation—led some critics in the late 1990s to call for a drastic overhaul of the federal system. The immediate problem was the weak economy and the inability in 1997 of the Kohl government to pass its much-heralded probusiness tax reform legislation. In the wake of the failed reform, one representative of a major business interest group, the Federation of German Industry (BDI) (see chapter 5), even called for reducing the power of the states through constitutional amendments, including ending the practice of revenue sharing.

To address these and other problems of federalism and to respond to growing criticism that federalism was in part responsible for the overall policy gridlock in the Federal Republic, a joint Federal–State Federalism Commission began its work in October 2003. Fourteen months later it suspended its work, citing irreconcilable differences, particularly over education.

But the 2005 Grand Coalition brought the commission back to life, and in July 2006 Chancellor Merkel could announce that both parliamentary chambers had finally approved the reform package, involving more than forty constitutional amendments. The changes are intended to streamline the legislative process by reducing the proportion of bills that the Federal Council (Bundesrat) can veto from over 60 percent to less than 30 percent. Some recent research doubts that this reduction will occur and estimates the percentage of bills currently to be around 50 percent. In exchange, the states will have more flexibility in implementing national legislation and have greater autonomy in a number of policy areas, most notably education, care for the elderly, pay for public employees, and that central symbol of German overregulation, store closing hours. The states now have sole responsibility in education, including higher education, which includes charging tuition or not. Yet the federal government still (co-)finances many research programs, such as the Excellence Initiative after 2006 to foster world-class research universities. Länder also can deviate from federal norms in certain environmental policy areas. Thus there is now less uniformity and somewhat more diversity in the federation.

In addition, according to the reform, the states' rights in addressing European questions will be reduced. During negotiations at the European Union level, the states can now participate only if the issues involve education, culture, or the media (radio and television). Otherwise only the national government will represent Germany in the councils of Europe.

Not surprisingly, the changes have drawn renewed criticism. The core problem is money. Giving the states more autonomy means little without a corresponding taxing power. Under the present system the income of the states depends entirely on decisions made at the federal level, albeit with considerable state input via the Bundesrat. Obviously the states will not surrender their veto power at the national level unless they have the authority to raise and collect their own revenue. Thus, while the first phase of the federalism reform agreed in principle on a clearer definition of state and federal authority, including a reduction in the issue areas where the states have a veto, it did not address the far more important question of how revenues are to be raised and distributed between the states and federal government. Powers that were transferred totally to the states—that is, those surrendered by the federal government—were relatively minor and very inexpensive.[17] Thus, the major hope for reformers shifted to the second stage or Federalism Reform Commission II, which began its work in 2007. As mentioned above, however, there was no agreement on providing more Land control over taxes. In fact, the rigid limits on debt and balancing budgets will probably constrain the Länder even more.

LOCAL GOVERNMENT

Germany has a long tradition of local self-government. Many cities proudly trace their independence to the Middle Ages, before the establishment of the nation-state. The trade-based Hanseatic League in the North and Baltic seas, including cities like Lübeck, Bremen, Hamburg, and Rostock, as well as free imperial cities such as Nuremberg, Ulm, Regensburg, Augsburg, and Frankfurt are notable examples. Vestiges of this history are still seen in the city-states of Hamburg and Bremen today. Although the consolidation of monarchical rule, especially in Prussia, later reduced the autonomy of cities, the reforms of Freiherr vom Stein, which followed Napoleon's defeat of Prussia, revived local independence. The Weimar Constitution also gave all communities the right of self-government.

During the Weimar Republic, three types of local self-government were common:

1. A single council system fusing both legislative and executive functions (most prevalent in southern Germany).
2. A strong-mayor form in which an elected council appointed a mayor with long tenure to perform executive functions—for example, Konrad Adenauer, mayor of Cologne from 1917 to 1933.
3. A bicameral municipal council in which the lower house, directly elected, invested executive power in a board of magistrates, which served as the upper chamber.

The Nazis abolished local elections and self-government, and thereafter higher-level Nazi Party or governmental agencies appointed all local officials. Committed to a grassroots approach to postwar democratization, Allied occupation powers restored and actually strengthened local self-government after 1945. The Basic Law (Article 28) guarantees local communities "the right to regulate under their own responsibility all the affairs of the local community within the limits set by law."

Structures and Functions

There are approximately 11,500 local communities in the Federal Republic, ranging in size from towns and villages of less than 2,000 inhabitants to large cities of one million or more. Until the 1960s in West Germany, the number of local communities approached 30,000, but local government reform in many states in the 1970s has consolidated most units with fewer than 8,000 inhabitants. In Bavaria, for instance, the number of rural counties (*Landkreisen*) was reduced from 143 to 71, and the number of local governments (*Gemeinden*) went from about 7,000 to 2,000. In the east the consolidation process began only after reunification. In Brandenburg, the number of Landkreisen was reduced from 38 to 14 and the number of local governments from 1,696 to 421 between 1995 and 2005. In Mecklenburg–West Pomerania the number of Landkreisen declined from 31 in 1990 to 6 in 2011, and in Saxony the number of Gemeinden was reduced from 860 to 514 from 1995 to 2005.

Generally there are four types of local government, but all have an elected council in common.[18] Within each state, local government structures are uniform: In Lower Saxony, Hesse, and North Rhine–Westphalia, this council delegates executive and administrative authority to an appointed city manager. In Schleswig-Holstein, this executive is collegial. Rhineland-Palatinate has a dominant-mayor system, with the mayor being responsible to the council. In Bavaria and Baden-Württemberg, the council has both executive and legislative functions but shares executive responsibility with a directly elected mayor. Elections to these councils, which range in size from about six to as many as seventy-five members, usually take place every four years. The electoral systems at the local level vary considerably among the Länder, and most use a form of open-list proportional representation.[19] Currently, seven Länder allow sixteen-year-olds to vote in local elections.

The primary organs of county governments are an elected council and an executive official, the county manager (*Landrat*), chosen by the council (except in Bavaria, where the executives are directly elected). Only about 130 cities (*kreisfreie Städte*) are not within the jurisdiction of a county. The county manager supervises local administration, especially those local activities performed on behalf of the state government. If a local community within a county disagrees with county policies, it can challenge them in the administrative or constitutional court. The character of local–state relations is determined by each state's local government constitution.

Local politics tend to be more focused on individual personalities than those at the state or national levels. People know more about local problems, feel they have some influence, and are more likely to vote in local elections because of the candidate's personality rather than his or her party label. About 80 percent of voters in local elections, for example, report that they personally know the candidate they supported. The occupational prestige of the local candidates is another major factor in local elections. One study in the state of Baden-Württemberg concluded that "medical doctors, above all gynecologists, are guaranteed winners." Lawyers, tax consultants, architects, police officers (especially detectives), and well-known local merchants also do very well in these elections.[20]

The belief that local government is largely a matter of nonpolitical administration and hence not appropriate for party politics is widespread. As a concession to this attitude, political parties frequently nominate well-known local figures who are not party members. Most candidates try to deemphasize their party affiliations and stress their concern for the particular community. The small size of most localities also enables personal relationships to remain determinants of political relationships. In local elections, the national parties must sometimes compete with two types of local voter groups: relatively stable local *Rathaus* (city hall) parties with a formal program and organization, and more loosely structured voter groups that are formed for specific elections and then disband. In some states these local "antiparties" (Citizen Unions, Free Voters Associations) have secured over 40 percent of the vote.

In spite of the partisan structure of local elections, especially in large cities, there is little evidence to suggest that major policy differences in cities are the result of party/political factors. Rhetorically the parties do differ in their approaches to local government. The SPD supports a so-called municipal socialism with publicly owned utilities, hospitals, and cultural centers over private control of such institutions. The SPD has also advocated municipal control of land and large housing projects, whereas—in theory at least—the Christian Democrats have supported individual property and home ownership. However, studies that have attempted to relate policy outputs in fields such as housing and education to local party control have found few differences that could be explained by party/political factors.

Many local issues are far removed from national politics, and informal coalitions are formed that would be unthinkable at the national or even state level. In several cities in the eastern states, for example, the Christian Democrats have formed alliances with the PDS (since 2007, the Left Party), the former ruling Communist Party. In western cities, coalitions, both formal and informal, between the CDU and the Greens have become quite common.

There are two types of local government functions: the so-called compulsory responsibilities (e.g., schools, fire protection, streets, and sanitation) and the transferred responsibilities, activities carried out for the Länder or national government (e.g., tax collection, health care, and housing). In spite of administrative reforms that reduced the number of communities, many are still too small to carry out these responsibilities independently. County government and regional local associations with pooled resources assume many of these functions. Regional associations of local communities are a relatively recent innovation and have been assigned an important role in plans for regional economic development.

Although local self-government is constitutionally guaranteed, this independence is considerably limited by local dependence on federal and, especially, state grants as well as tax revenues from industrial enterprises. In 2006, grants from Land and federal governments accounted for approximately 57 percent of local revenue. About 42 percent of local government revenue comes from taxes[21]— mainly its share of the income tax (15 percent) and the Gewerbesteuer, a tax on the production and capital investment of commercial and industrial firms. Property taxes, a major source of local government revenue in the United States, account for only about 7 percent of revenue for German communities. The low return on property levies is primarily a result of assessment rates that are kept artificially low by federal law for reasons of social policy. Also, large proportions of land located in the communities—such as public housing projects, defense installations, and other government-owned property—are tax exempt. Of all the taxes collected in 2005, about 34 percent came from the income tax share, 43 percent from the commerce tax (Gewerbesteuer), and 17 percent from property taxes (*Grundsteuer*).[22]

Besides taxes and grants, the fees charged by the cities for their services (e.g., water, electricity, public transportation, gas, refuse collection) constitute another major source of local government revenue. Generally, German cities offer a broader range of services than do their American counterparts: publicly owned utilities (despite a wave of privatizations), public transportation, city-run banks, markets, breweries, and an extensive range of cultural activities (operas, repertory theater, orchestras, festivals, adult education). Local, state, and federal governments heavily subsidize the latter services. Admission prices to the opera, for example, cover less than half of the costs.[23]

Challenges to Local Government

Like local communities in other advanced industrial societies, German local government is heavily indebted, is facing rising demands for goods and services, in many areas is structurally outmoded, and faces challenges due to a heavy concentration of residents with a migration background. The condition of German cities in the western region, however, is still far better than that of cities in the former East Germany.

Mounting Financial Deficits

Although the cities' share of tax revenues has increased in recent years, their expenditures, especially for personnel and construction costs, continue to increase at a faster rate than their revenues. The total debt of German cities in 2010 was almost $150 billion. Two-thirds of all local government investment is done with borrowed money, and about one-third of local tax revenues are consumed by debt service. Eastern cities were formerly completely dependent on financial allotments from the central government in East Berlin. Although they now have the legal authority and administration to levy taxes, the prolonged economic downturn, shrinking populations, and backlog of public works projects have created acute challenges. Only some cities, notably Dresden, Leipzig, Potsdam, and Eisenach have reached a semblance of sustainable development.

The increased demand for more and better public services and their increased cost, coupled with an inadequate tax distribution system, are largely responsible for these financial problems. Yet poor planning and accounting procedures on the part of local government are also involved. Cost overruns on major urban projects such as cultural centers and subways are common. There is hardly a major German city that has not had its share of scandals over the financing of major construction projects. For instance, the new Elbphilharmonie in Hamburg was originally projected to cost under $250 million and is now about $620 million (and the opening has been delayed two to three years). The new Willy Brandt Airport just outside of Berlin has experienced an almost $ 2.5 billion cost overrun and had its opening delayed repeatedly because of problems in the construction.

Long periods of one-party domination of many large cities and the right of city employees to hold legislative positions have produced a political style in some urban areas not unlike the party machine politics once characteristic of most large American cities. In Berlin during the 1970s, for example, the SPD party organization and the SPD-controlled city administration became so inter-locked that it was difficult to separate the two. Approximately two-thirds of the SPD's delegation in the Berlin parliament was employed by the city, and almost 90 percent of parliament's internal affairs committee, which plays a key role in salary and wage determination, were themselves city employees. This *Verfilzung* (literally, "entanglement") of governmental bureaucracy and party is one reason why local governments have been the least likely to hold the line against the wage demands of public officials. In 2002, long-entrenched local governments in the Cologne region were involved in scandals over the privatization of garbage collection and incineration.

Several cities, including Dresden and Düsseldorf, have been able to retire their debt by privatizing city-owned housing. This "selling of the family silver" gives them a clean balance sheet but deprives the cities of future revenue. Some have taken a "no new debt" pledge to avoid the temptation of borrowing. Improvement in the national economy, which began in 2006, has also helped the financial status of local governments. In 2006, towns and cities finished the year with a slight surplus, the first since 2000. The real test will come when the economy slows down.[24]

European cities were never built for automobiles. City planning from the 1950s to 1970s tried to accommodate a motorized society (*autogerechte Stadt*), but the efforts were inadequate and there was a backlash in light of the damage done to aesthetics and quality of life. After attempting to construct streets and freeways to accommodate cars, most urban planners believe it is financially and ecologically impossible for the city and the automobile to coexist. The historical core of many cities was badly damaged (e.g., Cologne, Berlin, Frankfurt), yet streets remain jammed and parking facilities inadequate. These conditions leave mass public transport as the only alternative, yet one that is costly and not profitable. Subsidizing public transportation in many German cities is a major budgetary item.

Existing zoning regulations and the postwar commitment to a free market economy encouraged widespread urban land speculation, and a booming economy meant that highly profitable projects such as office buildings and apart-ment houses received priority over parks, playgrounds, and low-cost public housing. City governments, greatly dependent on the Gewerbesteuer for revenue, were forced into competition for new industry. By catering to industry, cities also neglected public services such as schools, hospitals, homes for the elderly, and environmental protection. In Hanover, for example, to secure a large IBM assembly plant, the city developed large tracts of prime park and recreational land at public expense, which was then offered to the firm as a plant site. When IBM later pulled out of the deal, the pitfalls of catering to private interests became painfully apparent to the community.

In many large German cities, notably prosperous places like Munich, Stuttgart, Frankfurt, Hamburg, and recently Berlin (at least central areas like Mitte and Prenzlauer Berg), the shortage of affordable housing has become acute during recent years. The high price of land and soaring interest rates have reduced new construction and led to soaring rents (58 percent of Germans rent). The Kohl government cut back programs for government-subsidized public housing. Access to existing low-cost housing favored older families who already had been in public housing or on waiting lists. Young people moving into the cities had to face the high rents in private housing. In some cities, however, groups of homeless citizens simply occupied vacant houses and apartment buildings. This squatters' movement has also been accompanied by frequent demonstrations and in some cases clashes with police. Squatters in some cities (especially Berlin) have also been subject to mass arrests, with some accompanied by violence.

These problems are to a great extent the result of inadequate urban and regional planning in the postwar period. German urban policy makers understandably wanted to rebuild as quickly as possible in light of approximately 20 million homeless people. By some estimates, an adequate number of residences was only achieved in the 1970s and 1980s. Comprehensive long-range planning was not a priority. The postwar drabness of many cities (Cologne, Frankfurt, Dortmund) was a consequence. The emergence of urban citizen initiative groups, discussed in chapter 4, illustrates the extent to which established local political institutions have been unable to meet the more sophisticated demands for change they now face. Nevertheless, the last decades have witnessed a major movement toward the beautification and rebuilding of cities such as Dresden, Berlin, and Frankfurt.[25]

Germany's issues with migration, discussed in chapter 4, are also an urban problem. Most of the country's eight million foreign residents have settled in western urban centers. The proportion of foreigners in these cities is almost three times the national average: Cologne, 17 percent; Mannheim, 21 percent; Munich, 23 percent; and Frankfurt, 24 percent. This clustering of immigrant populations in urban areas, including many refugees who are not allowed to work, means added costs and burdens for local government, given that their social welfare needs are higher than the national average. Providing adequate housing and education for foreign residents are the most pressing problems. Local governments in many cases have done more to integrate foreign residents than the state and national governments. The cities pioneered foreign resident advisory councils and local foreign resident assemblies, which give foreign populations some voice in local politics.

The Urban Crisis in Eastern Germany

Local government in the former German Democratic Republic had little independent power. Control at the local level was in the hands of the Communist Party organization, specifically the first secretary of the party. Government merely carried out the dictates of the center or took on those assignments the party assigned to it. Many local government officials were merely party hacks or members of the puppet parties aligned with the communists in the so-called National Front. Hence the first task for local government after unification was to recruit competent officials who could be trained in the new democratic procedures. Thousands of western civil servants were sent to the east to help in the construction of a democratic civil service at the local level. Many incumbent officeholders were dismissed for their past involvement with the communist system, especially those who had worked for the Stasi as informers. Other holdovers from the communist system remained on the job in a probationary status. They would be given a chance to demonstrate their competency and commitment to the new democratic system.

The eastern cities face a myriad of problems:

1. Most towns and cities are heavily in debt and are dependent on grants from state governments and the national government. Although their dependency on these transfer payments declined from 78 percent in 1991 to 48 percent by 2006, eastern cities are still far from the West German level of 24 percent.[26]
2. The large cities in the east—those with populations over 100,000—lost about 12 percent of their populations between 1990 and 1999 alone, as compared to a loss of about 5 percent for the entire region.[27] This population loss lowered the tax base and increased the financial problems of local government. This trend continued unabated, and by 2007 the population loss in many larger eastern cities approached 25 percent. Schwerin, for example, went from 130,000 people in 1988 to 95,000 in 2010 and Magdeburg from 278,000 in 1990 to 231,000 in 2010. Some cities have recovered and are even thriving: Potsdam went from 139,000 in 1990 to 157,000 in 2010 and Dresden from 491,000 to 523,000 over the same period. Differences within eastern Germany are now probably as important as differences between the east and west.
3. Under communism the local administration was bloated. Even by 1994 there were still sixty local government employees for every 1,000 residents in the east as compared to forty for every 1,000 residents in the west. Although there has been progress since then, thousands of local government jobs still must be eliminated, which could save local governments billions annually in salary expenses.
4. The inner core of most East German cities was woefully neglected by the communists.[28] Instead of renovating existing housing in the inner cities, the communist regime built new settlements on the outskirts.[29] Now giant concrete silos, all identical, dot the landscape. These new communities have little or no social identity. Shops, recreational facilities, children's play areas, and adequate parking facilities were not a priority in the regime's housing plans. Moreover, apartment houses were built from prefabricated concrete panels. The quality of construction was poor. Almost 20 percent of all new housing built since 1981 is already in need

of repair. Much of this housing, which was built according to procedures imported from the former Soviet Union, is being torn down.

5. Local governments in the east must attempt to balance the need for economic growth in urban areas with the need for environmental protection and preservation of the cities' architectural past. Will the cities' financial problems cause them to allow unrestrained development? Will some of the same mistakes made in the west after 1945 be repeated now in the east? The eastern states' local policy makers are wrestling with these problems under severe constraints of time and money.

SUMMARY AND CONCLUSION

German federalism and local self-government are largely the expression of a historically rooted particularism and the disastrous experiences with the centralized Third Reich. Like the Basic Law of which they are a part, these structures are primarily oriented to the past and the avoidance of the errors of former regimes. Their future utility is now a topic of serious political debate. At issue is not the abolition of the federal system or local self-government, but their modernization. This involves at a minimum the consolidation and realignment of state and local units, the restructuring of their finances, and their support for more cooperative policy programs with the national government.

In many areas federalism has been a positive force in the Republic's postwar development. It has enhanced the internal diversity of the political parties, has provided at times an opportunity for policy innovation, and has enabled the national government to avoid the disadvantages of a large centralized bureaucracy. There was no hesitation or opposition when the tightly centralized German Democratic Republic restored federalism prior to unification. But Germany today is a far more integrated society than any of its predecessors, and it now confronts policy problems that are more complex and global in scope. There have been a lot of changes to the federal system over the last decade, but many critics do not see fundamental reform. Can the federal system continue to adapt to changing conditions, not the least of which come from the European arena, or will it become a further hindrance to reform?

NOTES

1. Fritz W. Scharpf, "Politische Durchsetzbarkeit Innerer Reformen im Pluralistisch-Demokratischen Gemeinwesen der Bundesrepublik" (Berlin: International Institute for Management, 1973), 33ff. Unification prompted a new discussion about the viability of the current federal structure. See "The New Federalists," *Economist*, October 6, 1990, 54–55.

2. Rudolf Hrbek, "Das Problem der Neugliederung des Bundesgebiets," *Aus Politik und Zeitgeschichte*, November 13, 1971, 3–12.

3. Between 1946 and 1951, Baden-Württemberg was divided into three separate units that were merged after a plebiscite.

4. http://www.arbeitsagentur.de/nn_29402/Dienststellen/RD-SAT/RD-SAT/A01-All gemein-Info/Presse/2011/08-Pendler-in-Thueringen.htm.

5. http://www.nytimes.com/2009/06/19/world/europe/19germany.html.

6. Note that the Euro-dollar exchange rate affects these amounts. In 2007 the exchange rate was 1€ = $1.40, and in August 2012 it was 1€ = $1.23.

7. Arnold J. Heidenheimer, "Federalism and the Party System: The Case of West Germany," *American Political Science Review* 52 (1958): 808–828.

8. The two "Sun Belt" states of Bavaria and Baden-Württemberg have been the largest contributors. From 1970 to 1994, Baden-Württemberg alone paid almost half of the national total. Not surprisingly, these two states have complained the loudest about revenue sharing. They have also challenged the constitutionality of the present program. Günter Bannas, "Arme gegen Reiche und die Länder gegen den Bund," *Frankfurter Allgemeine Zeitung*, September 17, 2007, 2.

9. Baden-Württemberg's chief executive, Manfred Oettinger, cited in *Der Spiegel*, no. 9 (February 26, 2007), 3.

10. From 1990 to 1995 these revenue-sharing provisions were suspended for the new East German states. The old states, fearing a large drain on their treasuries, insisted that the new states would have to experience a substantial economic revival before these sections of the Constitution could take effect. In exchange, the old states agreed to underwrite part of the "German Unity Fund," a bond issue to finance economic development in the new regions.

11. Allensbach 2009, 161.

12. *Statistisches Jahrbuch 2011*, 563.

13. Institut für Demoskopie, *Jahrbuch der Öffentlichen Meinung*, vol. 9, *1984–1992* (Munich, New York: K. G. Saur Verlag, 1993), 654.

14. Allensbach 2009, 159.

15. It must be noted, however, that other countries, such as Switzerland and France, also bear considerable responsibility for the condition of the river because of their discharge of wastes into it.

16. See *Der Spiegel*, May 19, 2003, 52ff, for a discussion of federalism in the context of the ongoing *Reformstau* debate. Following unification in 1990 the then–finance minister, Theo Waigel, proposed a plan for the consolidation of the states that continues to be discussed among advocates of change. He envisioned a reduction in the number of states from sixteen to nine. Four states, North Rhine–Westphalia, Bavaria (Waigel's home state), Baden-Württemberg, and Saxony, would remain unchanged. A new state in the northeast would be created through the merger of Schleswig-Holstein, Hamburg, and Mecklenburg–West Pomerania. Lower Saxony, Bremen, and Saxony-Anhalt would be combined into a new state in the northwest. In the east, Berlin and Brandenburg would be merged, a proposal that was defeated by the voters in 1996. In Germany's middle region, the states of Hesse and Thuringia would be merged. Finally the two western border states of Rhineland-Palatinate and Saarland would also be combined into a single state. This plan would give the very small states—Bremen, Mecklenburg–West Pomerania, and the Saarland—larger partners. It also has the advantage of merging four of the five eastern states with more affluent western states. In spite of its logic, it is very doubtful that such a restructuring will take place. The only realistic near-term plan would once again try to merge Berlin and Brandenburg.

17. Fritz W. Scharpf, "Föderalismusreform: Weshalb wurde so wenig erreicht?" *Aus Politik und Zeitgeschichte*, no. 50 (December 11, 2006): 6–11.

18. A rarely cited provision of the Constitution (Article 28) does permit local communities to be governed by citizen assemblies (town meetings) instead of by elected, representative bodies. Few if any communities, however, have made use of this form of direct democracy at the local level. Referenda are also permitted in most states.

19. http://www.wahlrecht.de/kommunal/index.htm.

20. The study was conducted by Professor Hans-Georg Wehling of Tübingen University and is discussed in the *Frankfurter Allgemeine Zeitung*, September 17, 1994, 4.

21. http://www.oecd-ilibrary.org/sites/9789264075061-en/02/03/index.html?content Type = &itemId = /content/chapter/9789264061651-7-en&containerItemId = /content/ serial/22214399&accessItemIds = /content/book/9789264075061-en&mimeType = text/ html.

22. http://www.bertelsmann-stiftung.de/cps/rde/xbcr/SID-69011738-800BE689/bst/F _Steuersystem.pdf.

23. Some cities, to save costs, have attempted to privatize these cultural organizations and activities. Such efforts usually provoke strong citizen opposition.

24. *Frankfurter Allgemeine Zeitung*, September 13, 2007, 16. Both cities have retained several income-producing enterprises such as the city-owned utilities works. The privatization of public housing has also provoked the opposition of residents who fear higher rents.

25. http://www.stadtbild-deutschland.org.

26. Federal Transportation Ministry, *Germany Unity Report 2007*, Berlin (September 2007), 20. See also Heinz Sahner, "Zur Entwicklung ostdeutscher Städte nach der Wende: nicht nur 'dem Tod von der Schippe gesprungen,'" *Aus Politik und Zeitgeschichte*, January 31, 1999, 33.

27. Sahner, "Zur Entwicklung," 30.

28. About three-fourths of the apartment buildings in Leipzig's inner city, for example, were in dire need of repair. An additional 10 percent were uninhabitable. Carola Scholz and Werner Heinz, "Stadtentwicklung in den neuen Bundesländern: Der Sonderfall Leipzig," *Aus Politik und Zeitgeschichte*, March 17, 1995, 17.

29. Jürgen Rostock, "Zum Wohnungs und Städtebau in den ostdeutschen Ländern," *Aus Politik und Zeitgeschichte*, July 12, 1991, 41–50.

The Return of German Power
The Federal Republic's Foreign and European Policy

Thus far, this book has discussed many of the transformations that reunited Germany has experienced since 1990. Overall, this is a successful story of integrating the former communist eastern region into the stable democracy and social market economy of the west. More recently, the country experienced a wave of institutional and policy reforms that have affected federalism, the competitiveness of the economy, and the welfare state. Germany is stronger because of these efforts, which have produced a modest economic boom domestically and world-class exports externally.

This story of transformation and growing strength would be incomplete without a discussion of Germany's foreign and European policy. Indeed, few policy areas have experienced more change since 1990 than these. Over the last two decades, Germany has deployed thousands of troops abroad, has developed strong and friendly relations with dozens of countries, and is increasingly comfortable defining and pursuing its national interest. It has become a more normal medium-sized power, while not abandoning its postwar foreign policy traditions and its commitment to never repeat its militaristic mistakes of the early twentieth century.

In European policy, Germany has helped to construct the "ever closer union" that the founders of the European Union envisioned. Not only has the EU expanded from twelve members in 1989 to twenty-seven today, but the most ambitious undertaking in recent European history, the creation of a common currency, has occurred. Embedding Germany in deeper European institutions was supposed to preclude a repetition of the terrible past by forever constraining German power. Unexpectedly, it has paved the way for an unprecedented return of German strength in Europe. The post-2009 Euro crisis has emphasized the fact that Berlin—almost alone—is making decisions for over 330 million residents of the seventeen-member Eurozone.

No one, not least the Germans, intended for this to happen. And no one is really comfortable with the situation. Despite the goodwill that the Federal Republic has generated abroad since 1949, many fears have surfaced recently

331

about Germany's renewed power. There is even a sense of déjà vu—that we have been here before and it did not end well. In short, the return of German strength has also refreshed fears about German power, what people long ago deemed the German question.

THE GERMAN QUESTION

The unification of Germany in 1871 was extremely disruptive to the European and larger international system. Former British prime minister Disraeli presciently noted, "The war represents the German revolution, a greater political event than the French Revolution of last century. The balance of power has been entirely destroyed."[1] Burgeoning German political, economic, and military power in the next decades generated what was called the "German question" or the "German problem." How could the other actors in the system accommodate this new force that was not strong enough by itself to dominate the continent, but was too strong for any one power (or several) to balance? How would Germans themselves react to their increasing strength? Certain tensions were inevitable, such as the competitive pressures created by the rapidly industrializing German economy, which had become the largest in Europe by 1900, and growing population—Germany had 41 million people in 1871 and 67 million in 1914, whereas the UK had increased only from 31.5 to 45 million—or tensions engendered between the wobbly imperial systems especially in Russia, Austria-Hungary, and Germany versus the rise of nationalisms and national liberation movements among the subordinate ethnic groups such as Poles, Czechs, and Croats and calls for more democracy and economic justice from working classes everywhere.

Deep-seated German fears and policies exacerbated the tensions. Germany, the "land of the middle," had been the battleground of Europe since the sixteenth century. Its territory, lacking natural borders, was long invaded and decimated by stronger powers from all directions. This generated what Bismarck called the *"cauchemar des coalitions"* (nightmare of coalitions), an almost paranoid fear of encirclement by hostile powers. The iron chancellor was adept at avoiding this outcome, but the bellicose and self-defeating policies of his successors, especially Kaiser Wilhelm II in power from 1888 to 1918, led to exactly this outcome by 1914. France was hostile ever since it was deprived of Alsace-Lorraine in 1871 and was forced to pay hefty reparations; Russia was locked into competition in southeastern Europe with staunch German ally Austria-Hungary and was seduced by the French; the United Kingdom, despite competition with France in colonial regions, turned against Germany as it was perceived to be the bigger threat as Wilhelm II tried to achieve a "place in the sun" through the acquisition of colonies and unleashed an expensive naval arms race. The fact that the illiberal, militaristic, and aristocratic imperial system despite some evolution toward greater democracy was trying to maintain its tenuous grip on power, partially through the populist distractions of nationalism and militarism—for instance, the *Flucht nach vorn* (escape forward) was an aggressive policy pursued to catch enemies off guard and to deflect attention away from problems at home—was also a factor.[2]

In any case, we have already recounted the disasters that were World War I, the Treaty of Versailles, and the absolute nadir of the Nazi regime and its genocidal World War II. In 1945, the country was devastated, divided—like the continent—into two antagonistic blocs, with the eastern half subjugated to communist totalitarianism. Moreover, with the exceptions of Austria, which, pledging neutrality, rapidly differentiated itself from Germany, and Switzerland, the country was surrounded by bitter countries that had suffered immeasurably during the Nazi occupation. Indeed, the first seventy-five years of German unity were disastrous, and the international environment that postwar leaders faced was about as hostile as anyone could imagine. Moreover, the "German question" was still not solved, with the country divided—one-third of its previous territory attached to Poland and the USSR, with millions expelled (a cause for potential revanchism)—and the vast majority of the population, which was still by far the largest in Europe west of the USSR, living in a bombed-out, economically devastated rump country. The future was not auspicious, and policy makers inside and outside of the country were deeply concerned.

POSTWAR TRANSFORMATION

Almost seventy years later, the situation could not be more different. Over this period, the Federal Republic has developed into one of the world's most stable democracies, has peacefully reunified with East Germany and helped to construct a united Europe, has become an economic powerhouse—fourth or fifth largest in the world depending on the measure; seventeenth based on per capita GDP—is at peace with all of its neighbors, and is deeply respected worldwide. In fact, a British Broadcasting Corporation poll (see table 10.1) has consistently found Germany to be the most respected country worldwide in recent years. What accounts for this transformation and solution to the German question?

This success was due in part to Germany's acceptance, indeed enthusiastic embrace, of a limited role on the international political stage. The Federal Republic essentially outsourced its foreign and defense policies to the United States and NATO. Even as it was becoming an economic giant, it was content to remain a political dwarf. It studiously avoided any appearance of leadership

Table 10.1.   Views of Countries' Influence in the World, 2011

	Mainly Positive	Mainly Negative	Depends/Neither/Don't Know
Germany	62	15	23
United Kingdom	58	17	25
European Union	57	18	25
Japan	57	20	23
France	52	19	29
United States	49	31	20
China	44	38	18
Russia	34	38	28

Source: http://www.worldpublicopinion.org/pipa/articles/views_on_countriesregions_bt/680.php.

because, largely for historical reasons, it feared that such leadership would be perceived as an attempt at domination. Securely embedded in multilateral military and economic organizations, the Federal Republic followed the lead of the United States, the UK, and France on most foreign policy and defense questions. All German governments displayed a marked aversion to the use of force to resolve disputes and an even greater aversion to the projection of German military power in international conflicts. Indeed, from one perspective the Bonn Republic (1949–1999) was for Germany a holiday from history. It was content to be, as one observer put it, a "sort of giant Switzerland."

But, how did the Federal Republic achieve this? There are at least four factors behind this transformation.

Institutions and Socialization

The Basic Law (Constitution) and subsequent statutes laid the basis for trust building and change through the rejection of chemical and nuclear weapons; the enshrinement of human rights as the basis of the democratic order; and after 1955 clear civilian control over the reconstituted army, the Bundeswehr, which was prohibited from deploying outside of the NATO area. More generally, there was the construction of a stable democracy, as well as the so-called social market economy, which generated broadly shared prosperity. One major, if often ignored, achievement was the integration of the approximately 12 million expellees (predominantly from what is now Poland and the Czech Republic), so that they did not become a radical group bent on revisionism. Of course, the ongoing presence of American and British forces was an additional guarantee of good behavior even after most sovereignty was regained in 1955. One of the consequences of the new institutions and the vigilant commitment of elites to democratic and liberal principles especially through pedagogical measures (schools and adult education—the Bundeszentrale für politische Bildung) and the dense network of civil societal organizations was the attitudinal transformation of the populace. Values such as tolerance, acceptance of democracy, and pacifism are today pervasive. The 2003 Transatlantic Trends survey shows how widespread such attitudes are, with over half of the population espousing dovish, pacifistic values (see table 10.2).

Table 10.2.   Orientations toward Foreign Policy, 2003

	Hawks	Pragmatists	Doves	Isolationists
Germany	4	35	52	9
United States	22	65	10	3
Europe	7	43	42	8
United Kingdom	14	63	19	5
France	6	34	49	11
Italy	4	40	45	10
Poland	6	47	41	6

Source: Ronald Asmus, Phillip P. Everts, and Pierangelo Isernia, "Power, War and Public Opinion: Thoughts of the Nature and Structure of the Transatlantic Divide," German Marshall Fund of the United States, 2003.

"*Nie wieder Krieg*" (never again war) was one of the firmest lessons learned from the past, as well as the dangers of nationalism. Indeed, part of the postwar transformation was the decline of German nationalism, national pride, and even national identity. Germans became one of the least proud nations on earth and embraced notions of "postnationalism," "Europe," or "constitutional patriotism" (see chapter 4).

Reconciliation

As several scholars have argued, the basic goal of West German foreign policy was to rebuild trusting relationships with countries and peoples that had been previously victimized,[3] a stance that has also been called the "culture of contrition."[4] In the context of the Cold War, these efforts were at first confined to western countries like the Netherlands and especially France—where a strong special relationship was prioritized and solidified by the 1963 Elysee Treaty. Making amends to Jewish communities worldwide was also prioritized, as shown through the 1952 Luxembourg Agreement and a special relationship with Israel. By the end of 2010, the Federal Republic had paid $85 billion in various forms of compensation to victims of the Nazis, some of which (e.g., pensions) are ongoing.[5] More fundamentally, at least since the mid-1980s remorse for the past has become a fundamental component of elite and mass culture. The Memorial for the Murdered Jews of Europe, opened in the heart of Berlin in 2005, is an indication of the value that Germans today place on such memories.

Reconciliation with eastern European countries had to wait until Brandt's new *Ostpolitik* in the early 1970s and in many cases until after the fall of communism in the early 1990s. Indeed, still in the mid- and late-2000s, memory-based issues, for instance over plans by some expellees to build a Center against Expulsions in Berlin, negatively affected these relationships. Although there was always tension with East Germany and the policy during the early decades was unremittingly antagonistic—the Hallstein doctrine that would not recognize the East German regime or any other country that did so—by the 1970s reconciliatory détente (change through rapprochement) eventually helped to pave the way for the peaceful fall of the communist regime and the reunification of the country.

Soft Power

Out of both necessity and choice, German foreign policy has prioritized diplomacy and soft forms of power. After its economic recovery in the late 1950s, the Federal Republic quickly became one of the largest providers of international assistance in the world. In 2011, it spent $14.5 billion on official development assistance that made it the second-largest donor after the United States ($30 billion). As a percentage of gross national income, Germany comes in at 0.4 percent (the United States at 0.2 percent), well below the UN target of 0.7 percent.[6] In addition it has transferred billions of marks and Euros to other member states of the European Union for the development of their poorer regions.

The Federal Republic has also invested heavily in a soft-power, cultural infrastructure; exchange programs with many countries run through the German Academic Exchange Service (DAAD) and other organizations, Goethe Institutes fostering German language and culture, and political foundations (the Social Democrats' Friedrich Ebert Foundation has offices in over one hundred countries and the CDU's Konrad Adenauer Foundation is in seventy countries); international television and radio broadcasting—Deutsche Welle, along with public stations such as ARD and ZDF; as well as lesser known initiatives such as support for well-regarded German schools in Latin American countries. Tourism is also a form of soft power. Germans are some of the most avid travelers in the world, and people from far-off places in Crete, Croatia, Mallorca, and Miami have all had many chances to get to know the transformed, postwar population. Indeed, Germans are first in the world in international tourism expenditures, having spent over $83 billion in 2011 alone.

Multilateralism

From the outset of the postwar period and consistently ever since, the Federal Republic has pursued a foreign policy stressing integration into and action only through various international organizations, what has been called "reflexive multilateralism." The movement toward European unity (discussed at length below) and international organizations such as GATT/WTO and the UN are pertinent, but it was the realm of security, particularly NATO, that was especially important. When NATO was first set up in 1949, it was memorably justified as "keeping the Germans down, the Americans in, and the Soviets out." Yet, after Germany joined in 1955, it became a vehicle for collective security against the feared Soviet threat and fundamentally shaped German foreign policy thinking and the very options that were considered acceptable. In addition there is the postwar role of the United States. Rarely has a dominant power acted with such forgiveness, pragmatism, and foresight in such stark contrast to the treatment of Germany by the victorious World War I powers. The United States was instrumental in transforming postwar Germany and in creating a supportive international environment in which the country could transform itself—the Marshall Plan, Fulbright exchanges, NATO, and the security and nuclear guarantee.

This record, however, is by no means entirely positive. Certainly there were many challenges and tensions that had to be overcome. Reconciliation with the UK, Poland, and especially the USSR/Russia were more problematic. The special relationship with Israel has been maintained, even strengthened under Merkel, but many Germans—especially on the left, as epitomized by Günter Grass's controversial 2012 poem—sympathize with the Palestinian cause.[7] Anti-Semitism still rears its ugly head periodically. The French could be difficult partners—such as with their veto over the European Defense Community in 1952. The Federal Republic would act in a self-interested manner, and the facade of NATO unity masked major tensions over burden sharing and strategy, such as during the peace movement of the 1970s and 1980s and the NATO double-track decision of the early 1980s. Germany's internal transformation was not perfect. There have been many critics of efforts to adequately come to terms with and make amends for the past.[8] Nevertheless, the big picture between 1945 and 1989 was very positive—the German question had been solved.

THE POSTUNIFICATION PERIOD: A NEW VERSION OF THE GERMAN QUESTION

The dramatic events that began with the fall of the Berlin wall in 1989 brought forth yet another version of the German question. German unification, the end of communist hegemony in Eastern Europe, and the collapse of the Soviet Union changed Germany's position in the international political arena. No longer was the Federal Republic a divided nation, exposed to massive Soviet power and dependent on other nations, most notably the United States, for its security. United Germany's 82 million or so residents constituted the largest single national group in the European Union, it was the strongest state in Europe, and it was the only one to emerge much stronger from the Cold War. Nevertheless, despite the "taming" of German power during the Cold War,[9] not a few observers were fearful for the future. Leaders in the UK, the USSR, and even France, as well as intellectuals across the world, were concerned that reunified Germany would turn away from its postwar domestic and foreign policy precepts and reembrace nationalism and self-interest in the context of burgeoning power of all types. Germany's neighbors were also still very mindful of what rabid German nationalism and racism did to Europe and the world. While distrust and hostility toward Germany had abated over the postwar period, especially among younger postwar generations, there remained a residual fear that Germany would once again attempt to achieve hegemony over at least the western and central parts of the continent. Some Europeans even saw the European Union as a largely German-dominated vehicle to achieve hegemony by economic means. German economic nationalism, in other words, would succeed where military conquest failed. Several authors even feared the emergence of a "Fourth Reich."[10]

These fears have not come to pass. Germany today has settled frontiers, has made no territorial claims, faces no conventional military threats from any direction, and has shown no interest in traditional nation-state maneuvering. In addition, it has continued to reaffirm many of the precepts discussed above. It emphasizes foreign aid and soft power, and all of its successful bilateral relations have been maintained, for example with the United States and Israel. In fact, it has increased its number of friends in Eastern Europe and globally with countries like China, South Africa, and Brazil. Moreover, it has tried to allay fears by redoubling efforts to integrate Europe and to embed it within transnational structures (see below). Governments have hoped that much of the country's increased international responsibilities can be accommodated through its membership in the European Union; it wants to act wherever possible with and through a united Europe.[11] But certainly the structural or institutional changes in the European and international environment have created the context for greater independence in foreign policy.

Moreover, many actors have actually lobbied Germany for greater efforts abroad. In late 2011, Polish foreign minister Radek Sikorski stated, "I will probably be the first Polish foreign minister in history to say so, but here it is: I fear German power less than I am beginning to fear German inactivity."[12] Others have seen the Germans as "free riders" in defense and security issues, letting other countries pay the price and bear the burden of military operations. During the

Cold War (1948–1989), the United States spent an average of 7 percent of its gross domestic product on defense and the United Kingdom about 5 percent; in contrast, Germany spent only about 3 percent on its military, and even less today. The operative "culture of reticence," in this view, "reflects a certain selfishness and an unwillingness to live up to the meaning and obligations of collective defense . . . and a sign that Germany remains a flawed and wounded nation when it comes to questions of war and peace."[13]

Due to these forces both internal and external, reunified Germany has slowly come to resemble other "normal" medium-sized powers in its class, such as France and the UK. This process has been constant, but also not without its challenges. Part of this transformation has been increased assertiveness and even self-interest. For instance, the Federal Republic has lobbied, discreetly but firmly, for a permanent seat on the United Nations Security Council. It has become a major diplomatic player in negotiations between Israelis and Palestinians and has been part of a six-country group negotiating with Iran over the latter's nuclear ambitions. Germany has also tried to assume more of a leadership role in the international disarmament discussion. The Schröder government wanted NATO to pledge "no first use of nuclear weapons" as part of NATO's new post–Cold War strategy. This proposal was opposed by NATO's nuclear powers, the United States, the UK, and France, but other countries such as Canada, Denmark, and Norway were supportive.

Within the European Union, Germany has exerted pressure on both the UK and France to accept a compromise on the voting rights of individual countries. The procedures now make it more difficult for a few countries to block decisions. Germany has also been a major force in the creation of the Common Security and Defense Policy of the European Union since the 1990s, even though such a defense infrastructure is one of the least developed components at the European level. But in other security-related fields, such as police cooperation, a Europe-wide arrest warrant, and common border controls around the Schengen area, more progress has been evident since the early 1990s.

One of the most controversial foreign policy decisions came in 1991 when the Federal Republic became the first European state to recognize the then-breakaway Yugoslav republics of Slovenia and Croatia.[14] The decision was made in spite of the opposition of the United States, the United Nations, and some European Union members. Earlier international attempts to halt the civil war in the former Yugoslavia were not successful, and the Federal Republic argued that recognition of the republics would increase the prospects for a peaceful resolution of the conflict. Although other western governments considered the Yugoslav conflict a civil war between rival ethnic groups, Germany viewed it as the result of Serbian aggression against democratically elected governments in Slovenia and Croatia that wanted to leave the Yugoslav federation. In early 1992 the German fait accompli forced the entire European Union to recognize the new republics.

The Croatian decision revealed an important feature of unified Germany's foreign policy: Germany is resuming its historical role as a Central European power with independent interests in the east that are as important as those in the west. The Federal Republic's policy toward its eastern neighbors, above all Poland, Hungary, and the Czech Republic, has sought to promote democratic institutions, human rights, environmental cleanup and protection (above all the shutdown of dangerous Chernobyl-era nuclear reactors), and German economic and financial interests. The country has been a staunch advocate for postcommunist countries to join the European Union, as well as NATO, and it has been the primary source of economic aid for the postcommunist countries of Eastern Europe and the former Soviet Union. Supported by strong collective memories, the great majority of Germans also believe that their country has a special responsibility to aid these nations in the transformation of their economies and political systems.[15] For business, these Eastern European societies represent new markets with a skilled yet affordable labor force, and increasing voracious consumers. Since the fall of communism, the Federal Republic has become their largest trade and investment partner—for example, accounting for approximately 26 percent of Polish exports and 22 percent of imports, and in the Czech Republic, 31 percent of exports and 32 percent of imports.

Despite the marked improvement in relations since 1990, tensions remain. Memory issues, especially those concerning the German expellees and their descendants, have periodically emerged to negatively affect relations with Poland and the Czech Republic. Historically grounded sensitivities toward German power in the region also led to some conflicts such as resentment in Poland over being bypassed by the German-Russian Nordstream gas pipeline and tensions concerning reforms to the European Union at the 2007 Summit, particularly with the Kaczynski brothers in Poland and with Vaclav Klaus in the Czech Republic. Germany has also been criticized for being too reticent in admonishing leaders and regimes that have moved away from liberal democratic norms—for example Ukraine under Yanukovych (2010–).

Most importantly, since the end of the Cold War the Federal Republic has become Russia's chief supporter in Western Europe. Chancellors Kohl, Schröder, and Merkel to a lesser extent developed close personal relationships with Presidents Mikhail Gorbachev (1985–1991), Boris Yeltsin (1991–2001), Dmitri Medvedev (2008–2012), and Vladimir Putin (2001–2008, 2012–). In the case of Schröder, the opposition Christian Democrats criticized his government for ignoring the clear trend toward authoritarianism under Putin so as not to jeopardize economic ties and needed energy exports from Russia.[16] The Merkel governments have pursued a more balanced and less personalistic approach to Russia, but have also been criticized for excessive timidity in the face of abuses of human rights and civil liberties. Nevertheless, the relationship is better than at any point in the last one hundred years. Russia, for example, currently imports more from Germany than from China. There has also been much cooperation in the energy field, epitomized by the Nordstream pipeline operational since late 2011.

Perhaps the most problematic aspect of postunification foreign policy has revolved around conventional security and defense issues. On the one hand, many Germans still believe that there is a residual distrust of the country among its neighbors because of the Third Reich, and they prefer that the country maintain a low international profile. Memories of the death and destruction caused by the world wars of the twentieth century are still very much alive and have produced pacifistic attitudes that oppose any military participation even in United Nations peacekeeping operations. Institutional and constitutional restrictions have also been seen as policy impediments. On the other hand, Germans increasingly understood that more is expected regionally and globally from their country and that fealty to allies and alliance obligations is important. Thus, even though the "culture of reticence" in defense policy—the reluctance to use force for any purpose other than national defense or for NATO and UN military operations—has continued to characterize the Federal Republic's international conduct, it has step-by-step started to develop new norms and behaviors.

From the 1991 Gulf War to Kosovo

The first postunification international crisis, the 1991 Gulf War, was really a continuation of past policy. Germany sent no combat forces into the region but did contribute generously in the form of financial aid in support of the military operation. Indeed, "checkbook diplomacy" had become a German specialty. The bloodshed in the Balkans in the early 1990s, especially the genocidal policies perpetrated in Bosnia, and the apparent inability of western powers to intervene in a timely manner led to deep soul-searching in Germany and a variety of legal and policy changes. A landmark July 1994 constitutional court decision cleared legal obstacles to the deployment of German military forces out of the NATO area in UN and other operations as long as there is Bundestag approval, as well as greatly expanding the definition of "defense." For example, in justifying Bundeswehr intervention in Afghanistan, Schröder stated, "The defense of Germany begins in the Hindu Kush." Moreover, Bosnia and Rwanda led to more support on all sides of the political spectrum except for the PDS/Left for the position that the country has a moral duty to help those in need (responsibility to protect, R2P) or that sometimes military means are necessary to prevent genocide, the *"nie wieder Auschwitz"* (never again Auschwitz) lesson from history. Then–foreign minister Joschka Fischer, a leader of the Realo faction in the Green Party, was instrumental in making this case.

The result of these legal and political changes was the 1999 decision of the Red-Green government that if necessary Germany would send troops to enforce a cease-fire in Kosovo, then an Albanian-majority province of Serbia subjected to harsh repression by Slobodan Milosevic's regime, in addition to those already deployed in Bosnia and Macedonia. In March 1999, Luftwaffe fighters left their base in Italy to join in the NATO attack on Serbia, marking the first time since 1945 that German forces had been in combat. Ironically, the attack was supported by the Social Democratic–Green government, many of whose members in the 1980s had strongly opposed the deployment of German forces overseas. Some Greens had even proposed German withdrawal from NATO.

Participation in the military attack underscored the new German international role. But the military action in the Balkans was also motivated by a desire to demonstrate the Federal Republic's commitment to the NATO alliance and to prevent a wave of refugees from heading for Germany similar to the 350,000 refugees from the former Yugoslavia that entered Germany in the early 1990s. There were also strong moral concerns about protecting the victims of persecution and aggression. The aversion to conflict during the years of the Cold War has been tempered by the sober realization that unified Germany, as the second-largest member of NATO, cannot escape its defense and security responsibilities.

INTO THE TWENTY-FIRST CENTURY

Following the September 11, 2001, terrorist attacks on the United States, Chancellor Schröder assured the Bush administration of Germany's "unconditional solidarity." A few weeks later, Schröder agreed to deploy up to 3,900 troops, including elite special forces units, to Afghanistan as part of the NATO-led and UN-endorsed International Security Assistance Force mission. The Federal Republic also supplied specialized armored equipment, reconnaissance aircraft, and medical facilities. Parliamentary approval for these deployments came in a narrow vote on November 16, 2001, which the chancellor also made a confidence vote in his government—that is, if the government had lost, it would have resigned. Since 2001 this commitment has been continually extended and in 2011 peaked at 5,300 troops. Germany has been one of the most important contributors to the Afghan mission but is scheduled to withdraw along with the rest of the ISAF forces by the end of 2014.

Despite strongly supporting the Afghanistan antiterrorist struggle and vigorously pursuing terrorists at home, the Schröder government in 2002 adamantly refused to support the planned American campaign in Iraq. Unlike the Bush administration and the Blair government in the UK, the chancellor drew a sharp distinction between the antiterrorism campaign and Iraq. This antiwar position of Schröder's tapped the continuing pacifism of many Germans and the anti-Americanism of some elements of the SPD and Green left. It also struck a positive chord among easterners who had no personal experiences with American support for Germany during the Cold War and weaker attachments to NATO and other institutions of German and American cooperation. But it also reflected the Federal Republic's growing sense of independence from Washington, which has been building since reunification.[17]

The government was strongly opposed to the unilateralism of the Bush administration. Berlin was not consulted or informed before the August 2002 speech of U.S. Vice President Cheney in which he announced America's intention to remove the Iraqi dictator Saddam Hussein, if necessary by force and unilaterally. German irritation was especially strong in light of the political price the chancellor had to pay for the decision to deploy German troops to Afghanistan. The extent of German solidarity in the antiterrorism campaign, in Berlin's view, entitled the government to be treated as a reliable and important partner whose counsel would be sought and considered before any announcement of American policy. The Schröder government thus refused to give military or financial support to the Iraq war but would allow the use of military bases and overflights of German territory.[18]

The Iraq decision marked the first time in the history of the Federal Republic that Germany had opposed the United States on a major issue. In early 2003 Berlin took its opposition to the Bush administration a step further when it openly entered into an informal alliance with France and Russia in opposition to the Iraq war. At times the relationship between Berlin and Washington became openly hostile.[19] Communication between the president and chancellor broke down as the Bush administration policy was "punish France, ignore Germany and forgive Russia," as Condoleezza Rice put it.[20] It was not until May 2003, when Secretary of State Colin Powell visited Berlin, that attempts at reconciliation began. The Merkel governments (2005–present) have made extensive efforts to restore cordial relations with Washington. Nonetheless, Berlin has made it clear that it is not interested in supporting any additional military actions in places like Iran, even though it is increasingly supportive of the hard-line approach pursued after 2011 emphasizing economic sanctions.

The unilateralist foreign policies of the Bush administration and above all the Iraq war took a toll on German support for the NATO alliance. Like its European neighbors, the Federal Republic is now less supportive of international commitments that may involve them in further foreign military action. As table 10.3 shows, German support for NATO, the attitude that it is "essential for Germany's security," dropped from 74 percent to 56 percent in 2006 and then recovered slightly. A similar pattern was found for the UK, France, and Italy. Since Iraq, pacifist sentiment among Germans and many of their European neighbors has also grown. Between 2003 and 2007, the proportion of Germans who agreed with the statement that "under some conditions war is necessary to obtain justice" has dropped from 39 percent to 21 percent. Among American citizens surveyed in this study, the proportion agreeing that war is sometimes necessary dropped from 84 percent to 74 percent.[21] These rather fundamental differences explain in part the Berlin–Washington rift over Iraq and the rejection of any further preemptive military actions in Iran.

With the change in government in 2005, relations with the United States improved considerably. Merkel got along well with Bush, and although her relationship with Obama is only cordial, the bilateral relationship is strong. Indeed, Obama is one of the most popular presidents ever in Germany, as manifested by the 200,000 who attended a 2008 rally in Berlin when he was still a candidate. By 2012, 87 percent of Germans had some or a lot of confidence in Obama, whereas Bush had only 14 percent in 2008—even though 59 percent of Germans

Table 10.3. Attitudes Toward NATO, 2002–2009 (percent agreeing with the statement "NATO is essential for our country's security")

	Germany	United Kingdom	France	Italy
2002	74	76	61	68
2003	73	64	56	64
2004	70	70	57	60
2005	61	65	58	52
2006	56	62	59	52
2007	55	64	55	55
2008	62	68	62	55
2009	63	72	56	60

Source: German Marshall Fund of the United States, "Transatlantic Trends 2006," Washington, DC, p. 6; "Transatlantic Trends 2010," Topline report, p. 37.

disapproved (38 percent approved) of Obama's heavy use of drone strikes.[22] Nevertheless, and despite the entwined transatlantic economy, revealed by the contagion that both sides of the Atlantic have experienced after 2008, the Obama administration's "strategic pivot" toward Asia has not gone unnoticed. Europeans think that China has surpassed the United States as the most important economic power.

Merkel and her defense ministers have continued and even intensified the normalization processes begun by Kohl and Schröder before her, while steadfastly adhering to the policies and precepts developed during the Cold War period. As of 2011, the Bundeswehr under United Nations and/or NATO auspices had a total of about 7,000 to 10,000 troops deployed in places such as Bosnia, Kosovo (1,500), Afghanistan (5,000), the Congo, Sudan, the Horn of Africa to combat piracy, and South Lebanon, as well as military observers in Georgia and in the border region between Ethiopia and Eritrea. Germany has lost approximately one hundred soldiers since 1994 and 3,100 since 1955, with several hundred injuries in Afghanistan alone.

In light of these current and anticipated commitments, the last few years have experienced fundamental reforms to the structure and purpose of the Bundeswehr—similar to changes in allied countries like France, Spain, and the UK. Despite opposition from some conservatives, conscription, in place for men since 1955 with a popular alternative service option, the Zivildienst, was suspended in late 2011. The army is now being transformed into an all-volunteer, professional force. Maximum troop levels will decline from 221,000 to 185,000, and the new organizational goals are to increase flexibility and reaction time through a smaller, more mobile and high-tech army. In 2007 the government also proposed employing the army at home in certain situations. "The old division between internal and external security is outdated," Merkel stated at a CDU party meeting. "We must think in entirely new categories."[23] Officials estimate savings of approximately $2 billion, which will reduce German defense spending from the already low 1.5 percent of GDP. The German defense industry—the world's third-biggest arms exporter after Russia and the United States—will also be affected. The country is also trying to align its capabilities with nascent European and NATO structures and missions.

This ongoing normalization of German military power has also given rise to other transformations and challenges. Over a decade of military intervention in Afghanistan has never been deemed a war, a stance that has hamstrung soldiers on the ground and led to terrible mistakes such as errantly calling in U.S. bombers near Kunduz in 2009 and killing approximately one hundred civilians. Bundeswehr casualties have generated debates about how such sacrifices should be commemorated. In 2009, a memorial was established at the Defense Ministry in Berlin despite many critics who thought that this rehabilitated discredited traditions of militarism. Equally contentious were plans to introduce medals for battlefield valor and the question of whether the old iron cross should be reintroduced. The CDU/CSU–FDP government's response to the unrest in the Middle East and North Africa (the Arab Spring or Arab Uprising) from 2010 onward has been lackluster, and support for liberalizers and democratizers has been inconsistent at best. There has been little action taken to avert or even manage the emerging humanitarian crisis in Syria after 2011 although reports of covert support for rebels have surfaced. Of course, all major powers in the region have had problems balancing desires for stability and supporting democratizers.

Then, in March 2011, Germany abstained from the UN Security Council vote on establishing a no-fly zone over Libya, which clearly would have helped those rebelling against Ghadafi's repressive regime. In essence, the government broke with NATO allies, the United States, UK, and France. Although the decision was widely rumored to have come from Guido Westerwelle, the FDP foreign minister, the stance was widely criticized at home and abroad as misguided unilateralism, neither fostering alliance solidarity, nor furthering German national interests, nor conforming with German values and foreign policy principles. Former CDU defense minister Volker Rühe called the decision "a serious mistake of historic dimensions, with inevitable repercussions."[24] But public opinion was a constraint that leaders had to consider: 67 percent of Germans think that the European Union should not get involved with transitions in the Middle East and North Africa because of the danger that hostile governments might come to power, and 78 percent were against Germany sending ground troops to assist Libyans who were fighting Ghadafi.[25]

There is also a domestic side to security policy. The fact that several of the 9/11 Al Qaeda plotters, including Mohammed Atta, lived in Hamburg for several years and were even under surveillance at one point was a major intelligence failing. Several reforms followed, including centralization of the Federal Intelligence Service (BND) in Berlin (a new headquarters for 4,000 employees is currently under construction), better coordination with foreign intelligence agencies, a new European-level intelligence organization, and increased funding. There have also been concerns about the methods that governments can utilize to maintain security in light of the strict postwar protections on privacy. Dating back to the Schröder era, debates over the use of wiretapping and other online surveillance, the sharing of online data (e.g., Google maps, Facebook), and antiterrorist laws have taken place. These efforts have paid off, insofar as attacks by foreign or homegrown Islamist terrorists have largely been averted. But a Kosovar did murder two U.S. servicemen in March 2011 at a military terminal in the Frankfurt airport. Nevertheless, more reform and coordination is necessary, as the 2011 National Socialist Underground incident reveals (see chapter 4).

THE EUROPEAN UNION

Recall that in 1945 a solution to the ever-present "German question" seemed as far away as ever. In addition to the domestic and foreign policy transformations, the movement toward European unity was key to solving the issues. West Germany was a charter member and an enthusiastic supporter of the postwar European movement. Whether it was the Common Market, the Defense Community, or any other European organization, German participation could always be counted on. All democratic parties supported "Europe" and expressed the hope for an eventual political unification of the continent. Through Europe, Germany sought to rehabilitate itself on the international stage and reassure its neighbors that it had changed and was no longer a threat to European peace and stability. For its neighbors, the European Union[26] was in part designed to curb and tame German power. The European Union not only offered Germany access to its classical markets, but it did so without it being perceived as threatening. From one perspective, the EU offered cover for Germany to regain its dominant economic position on the continent.

From the very beginning, a mixture of pragmatism and idealism characterized European Union policies. Motivated by the desire to stitch the continent back together after the World War II years and to overcome centuries of fragmentation into various monarchies, confessions, and nation-states, as well as by practical considerations, the first step was the European Coal and Steel Community (ECSC) established in 1952 by France, West Germany, Italy, Belgium, the Netherlands, and Luxembourg. Founders like Jean Monnet, Robert Schuman, Alcide de Gasperi, and Konrad Adenauer thought that pooling sovereignty and control over this important war materiel would make hostilities among the members impossible. Benefits achieved through economies of scale were also expected.

The momentum established by this agreement led to the much more ambitious Treaty of Rome and the creation of the European Economic Community (EEC) or Common Market in 1957, as well as Euratom to coordinate nuclear power. This was intended to reduce tariffs within and impose a common external tariff, promote standardization and the movement/exchange of people, and more generally increase commerce among member states. The Common Agricultural Policy, soon the EC's largest budgetary item—historically about 70 percent of spending percent, although projected to be about 32 percent by 2013—was established, as well as so-called regional policy through structural and cohesion funds to help less-developed areas catch up. The EEC was also given its own budgetary resources derived from transfers from member states, a part of the value-added tax (VAT, a form of sales tax) collected by member states, and revenues from external tariffs. Basic institutions were also established: the European Commission as a kind of executive where initiatives are supposed to originate, with two commissioners per country; the Council of Ministers, an intergovernmental body with weighted votes based on population; and a six-month rotating presidency, concluding with a summit of heads of government, where most major agreements were concluded.

Very soon, certain tendencies and tensions became evident. First there was the issue of membership open to all European countries that are democratic or widening. Expansions took place in 1973 (the UK, Denmark, and Ireland); 1981 (Greece); 1986 (Spain and Portugal); 1994 (Sweden, Finland, and Austria); 2004 (Poland, Hungary, the Czech Republic, Lithuania, Latvia, Estonia, Slovenia, Slovakia, Malta, and Cyprus); and 2007 (Romania and Bulgaria), for a current total of twenty-seven member states. East Germany joined when it reunified with the west, Croatia is set to join in 2013, and the other former Yugoslav countries are expected to join eventually. Turkey has had an open application since 1987, and several others may join (Iceland, Ukraine). The lure of EU membership has been a marked force in democratizing and liberalizing formerly authoritarian countries, even if the burden persists of adopting the entire corpus of EU laws, which

is now over 170,000 pages long. As much as everyone benefits from the proliferation of market-based, liberal democracies, any organization is more difficult to
manage with twenty-seven members as opposed to six. Indeed, decision making
and deals have been much more difficult in recent years (e.g., translation and
interpreters in twenty-three different official languages costs the EU about $1.25
billion a year[27]), and a tendency toward lower-common-denominator policies is
evident.

Second, there has been constant tension between supranationalism and inter-
governmentalism. Is the EU an organization representing sovereign states, or is
it truly something above and beyond preexisting states—a confederation or a federal union? For many years, the former pertained, so that the Council of Ministers
and the biannual summits were the most powerful institutions. French president
Charles de Gaulle insisted on the national veto, formalized in the 1965 Luxembourg Compromise. Recent years, however, have seen a marked shift toward a
more supranational tendency. Since the treaties of Nice (1999) and Lisbon (2009),
more decisions are made through qualified majority voting (QMV),[28] and additional powers have been granted to Brussels, especially for those members using
the Euro. But much opposition to this trend away from national sovereignty has
surfaced. Several countries have not joined the Euro. The UK and Ireland have
not joined the borderless Schengen area, yet several non-EU states—Iceland,
Norway, and Switzerland—have. Some of the new member states, notably the
Czech Republic, have also attempted to assert their sovereignty. One of the
results is a multispeed or multitier Europe with "variable geometry," in apparent
violation of the basic principles that all laws and agreements must pertain to all
members.

Third, the EU has always been an elite-driven project. The so-called democratic deficit has existed from the beginning—not just that EU institutions are
only indirectly legitimized by elections and give disproportional weight to the
smaller members, but also that many competences that used to take place within
democratic nation-states are now dictated by unelected technocrats or lawyers in
Brussels. For example, the lion's share of German agricultural policy making now
takes place in Brussels. The Bundestag and the Bundesrat now examine proposed
EU regulations in their committees. Major interest groups, especially in agriculture and business, and the states have offices in Brussels. The European Court of
Human Rights and the European Court of Justice, which have rather successfully
asserted the supremacy of the EU over national law, probably have had the biggest
impact in fields as diverse as gender and employment discrimination, the right
to strike, and environmental review. It is estimated that as much as 80 percent
of all new German domestic laws originate from the European level.

Clearly, progress toward European unification has been most apparent in the
economic field. Germany had little difficulty with either the European customs
union or the common external tariff policy of the Common Market. European
integration probably has been overall advantageous to the economy, and all governments have supported efforts to perfect the economic union, such as the
Single European Act of 1986 and the Schengen Agreement of 1985 to eliminate
border controls. But there has been increasing dissatisfaction with what has been
termed "neofunctionalism." Neofunctionalists maintain that efforts at integration in one area will spill over into other areas, thereby leading to greater overall

integration. It is widely expected that economic integration will lead to greater political integration, something that may finally be happening during the current Euro crisis. Many EU citizens, including in Germany, where there has never been a referendum on European issues, oppose such surreptitious integration without real democratic legitimation. This in turn leads to what is termed "Euroskepticism," a general feeling that the European project is moving too fast and too far and now impacts the daily lives of Europeans without their consent. Defeats in 2005 of the proposed EU Constitution in referenda in France and the Netherlands are excellent examples of such sentiments. The lack of democratic legitimation and transparency has also facilitated corruption, as evidenced by the resignation of the entire Santer Commission in 1999.

Third, a bureaucratic tendency has evolved. The European zeal to standardize has infringed on core national sensibilities. At one point, the EU tried to take away British sausages, French cheese, and German beer on health, sanitation, or standardization grounds. The famous banana controversy of the 1990s is telling. A shortage of basic consumer items like bananas in East Germany was one of the main reasons for the delegitimation of the regime. Germans have long preferred larger Central American bananas, but in 1993, French pressure led to preferential treatment of smaller bananas from former colonies in Africa and the Americas. Not only did this new policy upset consumers in Germany, but it led to a trade dispute with the United States and other producers that was settled through the World Trade Organization (WTO) only in 2009. This example illustrates the protectionist, market-distorting tendencies reminiscent of the much-derided wine lakes and butter mountains of the 1980s, which were composed of surpluses mandated by the CAP to maintain higher prices for farmers. Other EU market-distorting policies include the requirement that only wine fermented in the bottle from the Champagne region of France may legally be called "champagne," or cheese only from a certain region in Italy can be deemed "Parmesan." EU rules on privacy and antitrust regulations have also made it difficult at times for many transnational corporations like Microsoft, Facebook, and Google to operate in Europe.

All of these trends continue into the present, even though recent reforms have attempted to address them. For example, the democratic deficit has been reduced somewhat through the creation of the European Parliament, which has been directly elected since 1979. Additional powers granted to the parliament in various treaties now give it the right to approve the EU budget and commission. The Treaties of Nice and Lisbon have also endeavored to reweight votes in other institutions to better represent countries with large populations. The latter has been a particular German concern. The Lisbon Treaty (2009) also streamlined institutions by limiting each member state to only one commissioner. It also renamed the Council of Ministers to the Council of the European Union, of which member states rotate the presidency every six months; got rid of the summit system and replaced it with the European Council, not to be confused with the Council of Europe, a separate organization, which is to meet at least four times a year and which has a permanent president (Herman van Rompuy since 2009); and created a high representative of the Union for Foreign Affairs and Security Policy (Catherine Ashton since 2009), a kind of EU foreign minister who also presides since 2012 over a new External Action Service, a type of EU diplomatic corps. Although these reforms are probably steps in the right direction, the proliferation and often overlap of EU entities make the current structures far from intelligible or efficient. Certainly the tension between national sovereignty and supranational authority has not been resolved and has arguably grown more acute during the Euro crisis.

The Impact of European Integration on Germany

Overall, membership in the European Union has been positive for Germany. Today, the majority (59 percent in 2011) of German commerce is with other EU member states.[29] The large internal market has created many of the economies of scale originally envisaged, and the power of the EU globally has had a major impact on international commerce, for example, many transnational mergers need to obtain regulatory approval from EU regulators. In spite of the difficult adjustments at its introduction, most commentators view the Euro as a big plus for Germany. Most importantly, the European Union has rehabilitated the country. During the past sixty years, reconciliation and trust with its neighbors has replaced many of the memories of German aggression, as it twice in the twentieth century attempted to achieve continental hegemony through military conquest.

Nevertheless, EU membership has always come at a cost. As Germany continues to become a normal country, less influenced by its past, criticism of the EU has increased. As the largest net contributor to the European Union's budget, the Federal Republic has been keenly interested in controlling EU spending (see table 10.4).

Before unification, Germany had the resources to "walk softly but carry a big checkbook" in the councils of Europe.[30] Former chancellor Kohl was frequently considered a "rich uncle" at European Union summit meetings who could solve any pressing financial issue with a promise of additional German funding. Indeed, some landmark EU initiatives such as the Single European Market of the 1980s and the Monetary Union were greatly facilitated by German "side payments" to poorer members to gain their support. The governments of Chancellors Schröder and Merkel have not been as generous, and big-ticket items and expensive new initiatives are not high on Germany's European agenda. Recent leaders have also been adept at decreasing the most costly, inefficient, and market-distorting of all EU programs, the CAP, from 70 percent to around 30 percent, even though structural and cohesion fund spending has increased over the last fifteen years commensurately. Germany has long subsidized other EU member states, especially Italy and France, through the CAP.

Germany has also accepted its chronic underrepresentation in EU institutions. It does so largely to alleviate fears that it would somehow use its superior size to dominate the EU. As table 10.5 demonstrates, Germany, on the basis of its population, would be entitled to significantly more seats in the European Parliament and the European Council. But instead it accepts parity with France, the UK, and Spain.

Table 10.4.   Major Contributors and Beneficiaries in the EU Budget, 2009

	Absolute ($ million)	Per Capita ($)	Percent of GDP
Contributors			
Germany	10,996	134	0.37
France	8,076	126	0.34
Italy	7,558	126	0.41
United Kingdom	4,831	78	0.24
Netherlands	1,860	113	0.26
Denmark	1,454	264	0.53
Finland	758	142	0.36
Beneficiaries			
Poland	7,649	201	1.66
Greece	3,761	334	1.30
Hungary	3,325	331	2.68
Portugal	2,609	246	1.25
Romania	2,011	94	1.24
Czech Republic	1,969	188	1.11
Lithuania	1,835	548	5.33
Luxembourg	1,459	2956	3.05
Belgium	1,210	113	0.29
Bulgaria	736	97	1.76
Estonia	698	520	4.02
Latvia	619	274	2.62

Source: Nicolaus Heinen, "EU Net Contributor or Net Recipient: Just a Matter of Your Standpoint?" Deutsche Bank Research, 2011.
Note: Converted at 1 Euro = $1.25

As much as Germany supported the European Union's expansion into Eastern Europe, it was also wary of the increased costs. The addition of countries such as Poland, Hungary, and the Czech Republic, with their hundreds of thousands of inefficient yet politically powerful small farmers selling their meat, grain, and dairy products at much lower prices than in Western Europe, would have wreaked havoc on the agricultural support program. Thus, lower levels of subsidies were negotiated with Eastern European farmers. Even today, Greece and Spain benefit the most from the CAP. Germany has also long worried about jobs and its high unemployment rate in eastern Germany. Consequently, as a further condition of the 2004 expansion, Germany succeeded in securing a seven-year moratorium on the unrestricted circulation of workers from the new member countries of Central and Eastern Europe. But fears of workers from the east taking jobs from native Germans have subsided in recent years. The post-2010 economic boom has created historically low unemployment rates even as many workers from eastern and southern Europe have emigrated. Also, declining birth rates and an aging population will necessitate higher immigration in the future.

European issues have thus far had little partisan impact. For years, relations with Brussels, the administrative center of the European Union, were mainly the responsibility of one department in the economics ministry and generally were treated as a technical issue. The establishment of a common agricultural price support and marketing structure in 1967 did provoke political controversy, as farmers concerned about competition from France and other more efficient

Table 10.5.   Voting Weights in EU Institutions

	Population (2011, millions)	Percent of EU Population	Votes in European Council	Percent of Council Votes	Seats in European Parliament	Percent of European Parliament Seats
Germany	81.7	16.2	29	8.4	99	13.1
France	65.4	13.0	29	8.4	72	9.5
United Kingdom	62.6	12.4	29	8.4	72	9.5
Italy	60.6	12.0	29	8.4	72	9.5
Spain	47.2	9.4	27	7.8	50	6.6
Poland	38.2	7.6	27	7.8	50	6.6
Romania	21.4	4.3	14	4.1	33	4.4
Netherlands	16.7	3.3	13	3.8	25	3.3
Greece	11.3	2.2	12	3.5	22	2.9
Belgium	11.0	2.2	12	3.5	22	2.9
Portugal	10.6	2.1	12	3.5	22	2.9
Czech Republic	10.5	2.1	12	3.5	22	2.9
Hungary	10.0	2.0	12	3.5	22	2.9
Sweden	9.5	1.9	10	2.9	18	2.4
Austria	8.4	1.7	10	2.9	17	2.3
Bulgaria	7.5	1.5	10	2.9	17	2.3
Denmark	5.6	1.1	7	2.0	13	1.7
Slovakia	5.4	1.1	7	2.0	13	1.7
Finland	5.4	1.1	7	2.0	13	1.7
Ireland	4.5	1.0	7	2.0	12	1.6
Lithuania	3.2	1.0	7	2.0	12	1.6
Latvia	2.2	0.4	4	1.2	8	1.1
Slovenia	2.1	0.4	4	1.2	7	0.9
Estonia	1.3	0.3	4	1.2	6	0.8
Cyprus	1.1	0.2	4	1.2	6	0.8
Luxembourg	0.5	0.1	4	1.2	6	0.8
Malta	0.4	0.1	3	0.9	6	0.8

agricultural producers protested. Yet all parties made great efforts to support the farmers, so this problem did not become a partisan policy issue. The European Union has also attempted to develop common trade policies for its members. This has led to numerous European–American disputes over steel, high technology, and agriculture. As a key member of the Union, Germany plays a major role in the formulation of these policies. Yet, as Gebhard Schweigler has noted, "[Germany] is able to escape direct blame for controversial trade policies by pursuing them together with its European partners, and, if need be, by hiding, as it were, behind the decision-making process in Brussels."[31]

German Federalism and Europe

As we discussed in chapter 9, European integration has posed particular problems for the Federal Republic, the only large federal state in the European Union. The increasing delegation of national autonomy to the organs of the European Union called for in the 1986 Single European Act further complicated the future of

German federalism. For example, in order to meet the regulations of the European Union, Berlin is seeking more power in education and over the mass media, areas in which the states have been autonomous. Because Germany, until the addition of Austria, was the only federal state in the European Union, the German Länder have received little sympathy from other European countries. Ironically, in a federal or united Europe, the German states may lose autonomy to the national government. The states and local governments consistently charge that Germany's European commitments have hurt their budgets for housing, local transportation, and economic development. It appears, according to one authority, "that the . . . costs attributed to the expansion of the European Community will be paid primarily by the states."[32]

The states want to be consulted on questions of European unity that affect them. In the absence of consultation, the states, through their representatives in the Bundesrat, could veto treaties dealing with European unity that the central government negotiates. For the Länder, many European issues such as the standardization of educational systems are no longer "foreign" policy but important domestic problems. To meet these concerns of the states, in late 1992 a series of constitutional amendments was passed that explicitly grants the states the right to veto, via the Bundesrat, any commitments the Federal Republic may make to the European Union. The most important provisions are found in the constitution's new Article 23, section 4, which calls for the national government to involve the Bundesrat in European decision making "insofar as it would have to be involved in a corresponding internal measure or insofar as the Länder would be internally responsible." It is now constitutionally impossible for the national government to make any major decision involving the European Union without the approval of the Länder, especially since the 2006 Federalism Reform (see chapter 9), and recent Constitutional Court decisions further strengthen the rights of the states in European policy.

And what do average Germans think about Europe? Although the European Union has long experienced high levels of support, it has also been quite removed from the concerns of the average voter, and it still does relatively little overtly. It does not tax Europeans directly, and its expenditures are only a fraction of the funds controlled by national governments. For instance, the EU budget in 2011 was about $180 billion, whereas the German federal budget for that same year was approximately $385 billion.

The federal or subnational governments, not the European Union, provide almost all of the programs and services that affect Germans' daily lives. Moreover, the democratic deficit at the EU level remains. Why should and how can anyone "vote European"? In many countries, national leaders have not made "Europe" a political issue, with the UK being a significant exception. If there had been a referendum on the Euro in France or Germany, there would be no Euro today. Germans do not vote European; they vote national, and European Parliamentary elections have not been taken seriously. In 2009, only 43 percent of Germans actually bothered to vote, down from 66 percent in 1979, whereas turnout was 71 percent for the 2009 Bundestag election. Nonetheless, recent years have raised the profile of the EU in German political culture, and despite all of the challenges and the current crisis, public opinion is still rather supportive of EU membership.

As table 10.6 shows, Germans have long perceived more good than bad from EU membership. In 2011, 57 percent of Germans were very or fairly satisfied with how democracy works at the EU level, with 35 percent not very or not at all satisfied. Moreover, that same year, 48 percent thought that Germany had benefited, and 42 percent stated that the country had not benefited from being a member of the EU.[33]

Table 10.6.   German Attitudes toward Membership in the European Union (in percent)

	Good	Bad	Neither Good nor Bad
1973	63	4	22
1976	48	12	30
1980	65	6	18
1986	64	6	22
1990	73	5	17
1996	60	8	24
2000	41	15	33
2002	52	9	31
2006	57	12	28
2008	64	11	22
2009	60	11	25
2011	54	16	26

Source: Eurobarometer, various years.

THE EURO

The most ambitious endeavor of the European Union has undoubtedly been European Monetary Union and the establishment of a common currency, the Euro. Although long a dream of committed Europeans, it was only after German unification and the end of the Cold War that real movement toward a currency union began. It has been reported that French support of reunification was contingent on the Germans acceding to a common currency, thereby irrevocably tying them to other EU member states. The strength of the fabled deutsche mark, along with the fiercely independent Bundesbank, was one of the few postwar symbols that evoked pride among most Germans. Thus giving up this currency was controversial. In spite of public opposition to the abandonment of the mark, German leaders almost without exception supported this momentous step toward greater economic and political union. Germany in effect said to its neighbors that it was willing to sacrifice the deutsche mark at the altar of a united Europe.

The Euro has a long prehistory. During the past fifty years, Germany, together with its major European ally, France, was at the center of European monetary affairs.[34] The precursor to the 1999 European Monetary Union (EMU), the 1979 European Monetary System (EMS, also known as the Exchange Rate Mechanism or ERM), which coordinated exchange rates within a band (the "snake"), was largely the brainchild of former chancellor Helmut Schmidt and French president Valery Giscard-d'Estaing. But this was a union of unequal partners, especially after François Mitterrand linked French monetary policy in 1983 to the mark through the *"franc fort"*(strong franc) policy to restrain inflation. Because of its size and strength, Germany basically set monetary policy for the entire EU, even greatly affecting the UK, allowing others to import stability but also leading to some dire consequences. In the summer of 1992, for instance, the EMS broke down after the Bundesbank, to dampen the inflationary pressures associated with unification, raised interest rates. This forced other countries with weak economies to follow suit. Italy and the UK were driven out of the system, and British taxpayers eventually paid 3.3 billion pounds, an event that greatly weakened British support for a common currency. Such tensions shadowed the Maastricht Treaty, which went into force in 1993 and committed member states to a common currency. Germany agreed to transfer monetary and currency powers to a supranational institution, where its influence is highly diluted. In fact, there are few examples anywhere of a country so willingly giving up power.

The Germans, however, did not enter the currency union for purely altruistic purposes. The new currency architecture had a strong German footprint. While monetary policy was now firmly in the control of the European Central Bank (ECB), fiscal policies (i.e., taxing and spending decisions) remained the responsibility of the individual national members. Thus members would lose control over exchange rates and interest rates but would maintain control over taxation and spending. Although some European and German leaders wanted more, German public opinion, and the Constitutional Court, would not have it—even insisting on a "no bailout clause." Aware of the "moral hazard" dilemma—that there was a danger currency members would not behave in a fiscally responsible manner, eventually affecting all participating countries—German governments insisted on a Stability and Growth Pact (SGP) both before and after a country joined the currency. Potential members pledged to keep budget deficits below 3 percent of gross domestic product (GDP), although some exceptions in the event of a severe economic downturn were included, and total public debt could not exceed 60 percent of a country's GDP. The pact also called for a system of monetary sanctions to punish members if they breached these criteria. Moreover, the Germans insisted that the new European Central Bank be located in Frankfurt and that it embrace the Bundesbank's mandate to above all keep inflation low and maintain price stability. The new bank was not to consider a wider array of economic factors such as employment or growth as do other central banks like the U.S. Federal Reserve system.

At the time of its inception, the EMU had no lack of critics. Many economists pointed out that the European Monetary Union was not an optimum currency area, given that the composition of member states' economies differed considerably and that business cycles were not aligned.[35] But above all the Euro lacked a strong centralized political authority, which could redistribute resources between weak and strong regions. In the United States, for example, the central government in Washington, D.C., through its taxing and spending polices, can assist poorer states at the expense of more affluent states; for example, revenues from Connecticut can indirectly benefit the residents of Mississippi. The European Union does not yet have such a strong central government.

Other critics emphasized the potential moral hazard issues, problems resulting from taking away interest and exchange rate tools from national governments and the necessity of achieving fiscal as well as monetary union. Also, there was no mechanism for a member to leave the currency union. Proponents responded by stressing that economies and business cycles would align after the EMU took effect and that the Stability and Growth Pact would ensure good behavior. Responding to specific German fears, such advocates also stressed the potential benefits of the Euro—more commerce through lower transaction costs; greater mobility of capital and labor through the elimination of national currencies; and greater economies of scale and global influence. The Euro was expected to rival the U.S. dollar as a major world currency. Today, some authors assert that Germany benefits from the Euro because the exchange rate with other currencies is lower than the previous deutsche mark exchange rate. This is good for German exporters. But this argument was not common during discussions about joining the Euro.

Yet not every member state was convinced. When the Euro was implemented in 1999 as an accounting currency and went into circulation in 2002, the UK, Sweden, and Denmark did not join. Greece had not met the eligibility criteria in 1999 but was allowed to join in 2002, a move many in the European Union would later regret.[36] By 2012, seventeen countries officially used the currency, including the newer participants: Slovakia, Estonia, Slovenia, Cyprus, and Malta.

In Germany, the first years of the Euro were difficult. Even though the organizational and logistical problems were easily resolved, there were widespread complaints of increased prices. The official rate was two deutsche marks to one Euro, but many people said that old prices in deutsche marks were simply converted into Euros. More importantly, as discussed in chapter 3, the decade after 1995 was one of poor economic performance. The costs of reunification, excessive regulation, and high labor costs all contributed to stagnant growth, soaring debt, and high unemployment. It was not until 2006 that the economy, following a variety of labor market and spending reforms (Agenda 2010), finally turned the corner. Labor costs declined, welfare spending was trimmed, and deficits were reduced.

Initially, however, the Euro made change more difficult than under the deutsche mark system. As one expert has explained, "The euro, it seems, bled Germany of capital which then fueled growth in southern Europe until 2008. Until then Germany performed worse than any other country in the euro zone and the E.U. . . . Germany was the loser not winner of the euro."[37] In 2003, the *Economist* published an article concluding that the Euro was worse for Germany in reality than it would have been for the UK theoretically.[38]

In 2002, the Germans, as well as the French, were warned that the country's budget deficit was coming close to the 3 percent limit of GDP. The official warning, termed by the Germans the "blue letter," the color of warning letters sent by teachers to the parents of school children having difficulties in class, was not sent, but the publicity did not help the Schröder government in its reelection plans. The national government blamed the states, some of which had not limited their spending as they had agreed upon in the federal–state planning council. Since 2006 the deficit criteria of the Stability and Growth Pact have been met, and Merkel's reforms—raising the VAT and amending the Constitution to ensure balanced budgets—have made continued compliance quite likely. Economic recovery and even a modest boom by the mid-2000s started to change the narrative. While never strongly attached to the Euro, Germans had grown to accept it. By 2007, on the eve of the Euro crisis, over 70 percent of the adult population supported the single currency.[39]

The Never-Ending Euro Crisis?

Coming shortly after the global financial and economic crisis, which itself began in the United States in 2007 but deteriorated in fall 2008 with the collapse of Lehman Brothers, the sovereign debt or Euro crisis began in late 2009 and intensified in 2010. In late 2009, a new Greek government announced that the country's fiscal situation was much worse than reported, with a debt reaching 113 percent of GDP, and a little later reported that the budget deficit was almost 13 percent instead of the reported 3.7 percent. Interest rates on Greek government debt rose considerably, and other indebted or vulnerable countries, the so-called PIIGS (Portugal, Ireland, Italy, Greece, and Spain) or "peripheral" economies, started to come under pressure. In March 2010 the Eurozone and the IMF came up with about $30 billion in emergency money to help Greece. In May 2010 the first formal bailout of about $140 billion was guaranteed to Greece. In November it was Ireland's turn, and its troubled economy received a $106 billion bailout. Conditions placed on the bailouts included severe austerity—budget cuts, reduction in the number of government employees, privatization of public assets, and tax increases. By February 2011, the Eurozone set up the European Stability Mechanism, a $625 billion rescue fund to deal with any additional problems and to reassure markets. In May, Portugal received a $98 billion rescue, and in July 2011, increasingly threatened Greece got a second, $140 billion bailout. The fall of 2011 and 2012 witnessed much volatility as other threatened countries like Spain and Italy were downgraded by bond ratings agencies and forced to pass extreme austerity budgets as their economies and the entire Eurozone went into a tailspin. In July 2012, Spain requested another $125 billion bailout for banks.

There were periodic European-level efforts to come up with more money and to compel endangered countries to push through needed budget cuts and reforms. Among the threatened economies, Greece was especially reluctant to enact further austerity measures. Greek leaders faced two elections during the first half of 2012. Nevertheless, market volatility and general fear persisted throughout 2012 with wild speculation about Greece leaving the Euro (Grexit), financial contagion infecting other weaker or stronger countries like France and even Germany, and the Euro itself breaking up.

To paraphrase Tolstoy's thoughts that "all unhappy families are unhappy in their own way," there were specific issues in each affected country. In Greece, the problems were too much spending and public debt, real wages and pension benefits almost doubled in ten years, exacerbated by tax evasion and corruption. Portugal also suffered from too much spending and public debt. In Spain and Ireland, which actually had one of the lower public debt burdens of Eurozone members, the problems stemmed from a real estate boom and price bubble and overly indebted banks that had invested in mortgages and mortgage-backed securities. Many banks in other countries, such as France, Austria, and Germany, are also endangered because of the extent of bad loans they have made. Thus there are several components to the crisis: endangered banks inside and outside of the affected countries and sovereign debt problems, with investors demanding a higher return before lending to weaker countries. The interest rates these troubled countries have to pay make it difficult, if not impossible, for them to repay. These interrelated problems resulted in severe economic downturns. In the summer of 2012, Spain's economy was contracting by 1.5 percent, and the unemployment rate approached 25 percent, whereas Greece experienced a 6 percent decline in GDP and 23 percent unemployment. This situation has made it much more difficult to implement needed austerity or to increase tax revenues.

The issues that critics of the Euro had raised in the 1990s came home to roost. First, as optimum currency analysis predicted, the different economic cycles and dynamics in such a large currency area could not be accommodated. One interest rate for the Eurozone meant that countries' specific needs were not met. When the property market was overheating in Spain or Ireland, for example, these countries would have benefited from higher interest rates. This would have made mortgages more expensive, thereby reducing or precluding the dangerous price bubble that emerged. Second, all the Eurozone countries benefited from overall monetary stability. Investors lent to Greece as if there were the same risk as lending to Germany, thereby ignoring the profligacy and poor governance in Greece. Also at work was the global savings glut looking for places to park money generated by commodity booms and the surging Chinese economy. Third, the design flaws of the Euro became painfully apparent: a monetary rather than a fiscal union meant that there was little oversight of national finances, especially when the sanctions of the Stability and Growth Pact were eviscerated by Germany and France in 2002; there was no Euro-level banking supervision or deposit insurance; no pooling of debt (Eurobonds); and there was no procedure for a country to exit. The ECB, with only its inflation-fighting mandate, was not monitoring other economic indicators such as unemployment and private and public debt. Fourth, the inflexibilities of the Euro almost preordained severe economic difficulties in crisis countries. Unable to devalue their currencies or expand their money supply, countries could respond to deficit and debt problems only by raising taxes and cutting spending, which can hasten economic contraction.

In Germany, the effects of the 2008 global financial crisis included a large contraction in GDP in 2009 and an almost 5 percent deficit in 2009. The Merkel-led Grand Coalition passed a variety of stimulus programs, a bailout for some financial institutions, and an increase in total public debt from 65 percent of GDP in 2004 to 82 percent in 2012. Very soon, however, the Merkel government was pushing through some austerity measures at home, which included a pre-agreed balanced budget amendment in 2009 that strictly limited the size of the structural deficit.

In 2010 the German economy, in contrast to those of its neighbors, made a strong comeback. The 2009 negative growth rate of -5.1 was reversed as the economy grew by a remarkable 4.2 percent. This continued into 2011 with a healthy increase in GDP of 3.0 percent. Unemployment dropped to about 6 percent, the lowest level in almost twenty years. Seeking a safe haven, borrowers drove down the interest rate on ten-year German bonds to around 1 percent. At times in 2012 this rate dropped to near zero. In other words, investors were ready to accept practically no return in exchange for the safety of German notes.

But this robust economic performance came in part at the expense of Germany's neighbors. Spanish bonds had a 7 percent interest rate, and Greek notes carried a 25 percent interest rate. Other large Eurozone economies such as France and especially Italy, although nowhere near as threatened as Spain or Greece, also had economic vulnerabilities and thus little leverage in crisis management. During the entire crisis, only Germany was economically and financially strong. As the *Economist* succinctly summarized the crisis in late 2011, "In the end, the future of the Euro will be decided largely in Germany. It has the deepest pockets, and its postwar renaissance is intimately bound up with European integration."[40]

The Euro Stops Here

Indeed, the Euro crisis thrust Germany into the center of the greatest challenge facing the European Union since its founding. The core issue was whether the Federal Republic should use its economic and financial resources to aid those Eurozone countries whose weak economies, troubled banks, and soaring deficits were weakening the Euro and perhaps even endangering the survival of the European Union. Like it or not, the Federal Republic now had to lead. It could not duck under and defer to some stronger power such as the United States, or in the European context, France. Moreover, each passing month made it more evident that the Germans no longer wanted to defer to others but were comfortable leading and could accept the criticism that leadership necessarily entails. Merkel, her finance minister Wolfgang Schäuble, and other German leaders—perhaps for the first time since 1945—were comfortable asserting notions of self-interest overtly and sticking to their policy guns.

This newfound assertiveness did not always go over well with Germany's fellow Europeans. The French dubbed Merkel "Madame Non," and protesters in Greece often portrayed her in a Nazi uniform with a Hitler mustache. The accusations thrown around were broad: her government only pursued policies that would help heavily indebted German banks; her policies were shortsighted and would lead to the breakup of the Eurozone with calamitous consequences; Germany was not showing enough solidarity with other Europeans—many Greeks even referenced Nazi occupation as a justification for German bailout funds; the austerity policy that Germany was foisting upon others was the exact opposite of the Keynesian stimulus that was necessary; Germany was responsible for the problems in the periphery; Germany was vetoing necessary responses; flawed German preferences (the ECB) led to the problem in the first place. Most dramatically, some said it was all a German conspiracy to dominate others, to illegitimately create markets for its exports and to have a currency from which it alone benefited.[41] Some asserted that the Euro exchange rate is much lower than what a deutsche mark would have had, thus making German exports cheaper. Yet German exports to other Eurozone economies actually declined from 45 percent of all exports in 1998 to 39 percent in 2011.[42] Germany was the decisive player—indeed supplicants traveled to Berlin and not Brussels.

The Euro crisis has revealed the weakness of the European Union's supranational institutions. The critical decisions are being made above all by Germany, France, the European Central Bank, and the International Monetary Fund in Washington, D.C. Nothing can be decided without Berlin's consent, and Merkel is widely seen as the most influential leader in Europe. In 2012 she was listed as the most powerful woman in the world and the fourth most powerful person in the world. Even important U.S. leaders such as President Obama and Treasury Secretary Timothy Geithner were urging Germany to do more, since instability in Europe was negatively affecting the American economy and therefore Obama's political future.

Power within the European Union has shifted from Paris to Berlin.[43] The various bailout funds, the fiscal pact approved in January 2012 that will allow for European monitoring of national finances, the European Stability Mechanism, and the policies of the European Central Bank all require German support.

There have been many proposed remedies for the Euro crisis: joint Eurobonds (i.e., a pooling of all European debt), European deposit insurance, a debt write-down, or increasing the money supply. Thus far Germany has rejected these proposals. At the same time Chancellor Merkel has insisted that Germany will do whatever is necessary to save the Euro. Throughout the Euro crisis, Merkel and her government have been constrained by the domestic political institutions discussed earlier in this book. She must sustain coalition unity especially with more extreme voices in the FDP and the Bavarian CSU, obtain Bundes-rat approval, and receive Constitutional Court validation. Political and economic elites are divided over the proper responses,[44] and public opinion thus far has adamantly refused to support further bailouts for the troubled southern European economies. As Christopher Meyer put it, "Merkel's obsession with moral hazard at the expense of the German taxpayer is simply another way of telling the world that it's going to be Germany's way or no way . . . the Euro is not going to be debauched by bailing out profligate states like Greece."[45]

But the chancellor's bark may be sharper than her bite. Throughout this now three-year-old crisis, there has been a pattern to Merkel and Germany's many responses. The longtime British Euro analyst David Marsh has termed it Merkel's "Law of Permanent Disappointment." As fears of the Euro's demise increase, the chancellor "will always do more than she originally promised to help out errant states, but the funds committed will always be less than actually necessary to solve the euro's problems once and for all." She will thus disappoint both conservative German voters who oppose bailouts as well as the crisis-ridden countries needing German help, albeit for equal and opposite reasons.[46] Thus Merkel must somehow secure and maintain domestic support if she is to do "everything necessary to save the Euro."

SUMMARY AND CONCLUSION

This overview of Germany's foreign and European policy has highlighted several key points. First, keeping the big picture in mind, the transformation of Germany since 1945 has been remarkable. From an inauspicious starting point, the country has transformed its internal workings and external relationships to become a trusted and respected member of the international community of nations. During the Cold War years of division, it did so by taking a low profile, developing a "culture of contrition and reticence" and a willingness to sacrifice self-interest for the greater good. Steadfast German commitment to the movement toward European unity was a big part of this change. Structurally, being the "land in the middle," which for centuries had led to many foreign invasions and a corresponding fear of encirclement, has turned into a geopolitical advantage, situated as it is at the heart of a unifying continent where economic and cultural issues matter instead of "blood and iron." Indeed, Germany—with its postwar emphasis on diplomacy, economics, and soft power—has become the quintessential "geo-economic power,"[47] helping to forge and poised to benefit greatly from the current environment.

Second, the decades since reunification have witnessed a slow but steady normalization of the country's foreign policy. It is much more comfortable, albeit still reluctant, to use force to achieve foreign policy goals. But it will do so only under the auspices of multilateral organizations like NATO or the UN. As with other influential states, it is prepared to make mistakes and take criticisms of poor decisions such as the Libya decision of 2011. Ongoing reforms to the Bundeswehr and the intelligence services will continue these trends into the future.

Third, and most importantly, it is not only that German power has normalized itself and that German leaders are increasingly comfortable exercising it, but also that German power has increased, as especially evident during the Euro crisis. Many people—including numerous Germans—do not like this, and this was certainly not something that was intended, but it is a reality. As a leading CDU politician, Volker Kauder, put it in late 2011, "Suddenly Europe is speaking German."[48] It is impossible to tell if this will last or whether the dream of real European political and economic integration will occur, but whatever happens, Germany no longer aspires to be or act like a big Switzerland, and it most certainly is no longer an "economic giant, but a political dwarf."

It has been almost seventy years since the demise of the Third Reich, and this period of time is almost as long as the seventy-four, mainly difficult years between German unification in 1871 and 1945. Since then, memory of those horrible years has been a constant influence on domestic and foreign policy elites inside and outside of the country. Even during the crisis, such memory-based arguments have surfaced: "The European Union was created to avoid repeating the disasters of the 1930s, but Germany, of all countries, has failed to learn from history. As the euro crisis escalates, Berlin should remember how the banking crisis of 1931 contributed to the breakdown of democracy across Europe. Action is urgently needed to stop history from repeating itself."[49] Helmut Kohl has repeatedly exhorted his compatriots to save the Euro, in his view, the only thing that is separating the peaceful present from the terrible past. Even Merkel has said, "The euro is much, much more than a currency. The euro is the guarantee of a united Europe. If the euro fails, then Europe fails."[50]

The impact of memory is strong in Germany today, but in a meaningful way, Germany has overcome its past. A culture of contrite memory helped to forge new and resilient values stressing democracy, liberalism, and human rights. But today, as much as those values are firmly rooted, the past and the memory of past atrocities are decreasingly heard. As Theodor Adorno once wrote, coming to terms with the past means eliminating the causes.[51] This undoubtedly has occurred, but with the return of German power, or "embedded hegemony,"[52] in Europe, will these successes erode, and how will its partners react?

NOTES

1. http://www.newstatesman.com/books/2011/03/bismarck-germany-europe-hitler.
2. Fritz Fischer, *Germany's Aims in the First World War* (New York: Norton, 1968).
3. Jennifer Lind, *Sorry States: Apologies in International Politics* (Ithaca, NY: Cornell University Press, 2008); Lily Gardner Feldman, *Germany's Foreign Policy of Reconciliation: From Enmity to Amity* (Lanham, MD: Rowman & Littlefield, 2012).
4. David Art, *The Politics of the Nazi Past in Germany and Austria* (Cambridge: Cambridge University Press, 2006).
5. http://www.auswaertiges-amt.de/EN/Aussenpolitik/InternatRecht/Entschaedigung_node.html.
6. http://www.oecd.org/dac/aidstatistics/developmentaidtodevelopingcountriesfalls becauseofglobalrecession.htm.
7. http://www.guardian.co.uk/commentisfree/2012/apr/05/gunter-grass-german-anger-at-israel.
8. Ralph Giordano, *Die zweite Schuld oder Von der Last Deutscher zu sein* (Kiepenheuer and Witsch, 2000); Charles Maier, *The Unmasterable Past: History, Holocaust, and German National Identity* (Cambridge, MA: Harvard University Press, 1988).
9. Peter Kaztenstein, ed., *Tamed Power: Germany in Europe* (Ithaca, NY: Cornell University Press, 1997).
10. Jim Hoagland, "Speaking for Thatcher—at a Cost," *Washington Post*, July 17, 1990.
11. Ronald D. Asmus, "German Strategy and Public Opinion after the Wall, 1990–1993," Rand Corporation, February 1994, 47.
12. http://www.economist.com/blogs/easternapproaches/2011/11/polands-appeal-germany.
13. Asmus, "German Strategy and Public Opinion," 48ff.
14. Germany has historical ties to both Slovenia and Croatia. Much of Slovenia was part of the Austro-Hungarian Empire and was incorporated in Hitler's Greater German Reich during World War II. During the war the Nazis also set up a puppet government in Croatia, which was guilty of numerous atrocities against Serbians and Jews. Most of the 800,000 residents of the former Yugoslavia in the Federal Republic are Croatian.
15. M. Steven Fish, *Democracy Derailed in Russia. The Failure of Open Politics* (Cambridge: Cambridge University Press, 2005).
16. *Financial Times*, October 11, 1998, 3.
17. Dieter Dettke, *Germany Says "No": The Iraq War and the Future of German Foreign and Security Policy* (Washington, DC: Woodrow Wilson Center Press; Baltimore, MD: Johns Hopkins University Press, 2009).
18. While the government opposed the Iraq war, German military and intelligence authorities, according to reports leaked to the German and American press in early 2006, continued their normal cooperation with the United States. German military bases and facilities were used to transport American personnel and equipment into Iraq. After the evacuation of the German embassy in Baghdad, two German intelligence operatives remained behind and relayed important information about Iraqi military deployments, including the Baghdad defense plan, to the approaching American forces. Officials in both the new (Merkel) and old (Schröder) governments have vehemently denied these reports.

See "Liebesgrüße nach Washington," *Der Spiegel*, no. 3 (January 16, 2006), 22–35, for the initial account of the alleged German-American military cooperation. See also Dieter Dettke, *Germany Says "No."*

19. See Stephen F. Szabo, *Parting Ways: The Crisis in German-American Relations* (Washington, DC: Brookings Institution Press, 2004) for an excellent analysis of these developments.

20. http://www.brookings.edu/research/opinions/2007/09/europe-gordon.

21. German Marshall Fund, "Trans-Atlantic Trends," Washington, DC, 2007, 54. The French and Italian responses were very similar to the German.

22. http://www.pewglobal.org/2012/06/13/global-opinion-of-obama-slips-internation al-policies-faulted.

23. *Frankfurter Allgemeine Zeitung*, July 3, 2007, 1.

24. http://www.spiegel.de/international/germany/a-serious-mistake-of-historic-dimen sions-libya-crisis-leaves-berlin-isolated-a-753498.html.

25. Transatlantic Trends 2011, Country Report: Germany.

26. The organization has had several name changes over the decades: European Economic Community, European Community, and after 1993 the European Union. For ease of comprehension, we use European Union throughout this chapter.

27. http://www.independent.co.uk/news/world/europe/cost-in-translation-eu-spends -83641bn-on-language-services-407991.html.

28. QMV is a super-majority stipulation for votes in the Council of the European Union. After 2014, this will entail 55 percent of member states and at least 65 percent of the EU's population.

29. It is, of course, difficult to determine what level of integration would have been achieved in the absence of the EU.

30. Jeffrey J. Anderson, "Germany and Europe: Centrality in the EU," in *The Member States of the European Union*, ed. Simon Bulmer and Christian Lequesne (New York: Oxford University Press, 2005), 83.

31. Gebhard Schweigler, *West German Foreign Policy: The Domestic Setting* (New York: Praeger, 1984), 21.

32. Hartmut Klatt, "Forty Years of German Federalism: Past Trends and New Developments," *Publius* 19, no. 4 (Fall 1989): 202.

33. http://ec.europa.eu/public_opinion/cf/step1.cfm.

34. Karl Kaltenthaler, "German Interests in European Monetary Integration," *Journal of Common Market Studies* 40, no. 1 (January 2002): 69.

35. Economists use the optimum currency area term to refer to a geographical area in which a common currency would maximize economic efficiency and increase welfare.

36. It is now known that Italy and Portugal also engaged in creative bookkeeping. According to some reports, the Kohl government was aware of the Italian situation but did not attempt to block Italy's participation for political reasons.

37. Gunnar Beck, "Germany the Euro Winner? Hardly," *New York Times*, June 26, 2012.

38. "Germany's Euro Test," http://www.economist.com/node/1842183.

39. *Eurobarometer*, no. 67 (September–October 2006), question 27(1).

40. *Economist*, October 1, 2011, 26.

41. http://www.newstatesman.com/europe/2011/11/germany-european-economic.

42. Beck, "Germany the Euro Winner? Hardly."

43. http://www.economist.com/node/17675940.

44. In summer 2012, the so-called *Ökonomenstreit* (economists' debate) revealed deep divisions within the economics field regarding the best course of action to resolve the Euro crisis; http://www.spiegel.de/wirtschaft/oekonomenstreit-sinn-und-kraemer-weh ren-sich-a-843524.html.

45. Christopher Meyer, "The Return of the German Question," *Huffington Post*, November 23, 2011, http://www.huffingtonpost.co.uk/sir-christopher-meyer/the-return-of-the-german-question_b_1110673.html.

46. David Marsh, "Not for the First Time, Euro Optimism Starts to Decline," *OMFIF Commentary* 3, no 14 (April 2, 2012).

47. Hans Kundnani, "Germany as a Geo-economic Power," *Washington Quarterly* 34, no. 3 (2011): 31–45.

48. http://www.spiegel.de/international/europe/now-europe-is-speaking-german-merkel-ally-demands-that-britain-contribute-to-eu-success-a-798009.html.

49. http://www.spiegel.de/international/europe/the-germans-have-learned-nothing-from-history-a-838429.html.

50. "Germany: Grappling with the Euro, and Its Own Complicated History," *Time*, September 28, 2011.

51. Theodor Adorno, "What Does Coming to Terms with the Past Mean?" in *Bitburg in Moral and Political Perspective*, ed. Geoffrey H. Hartman (Bloomington: Indiana University Press, 1986).

52. Beverly Crawford, *Power and German Foreign Policy: Embedded Hegemony in Europe* (New York: Palgrave Macmillan, 2007).

Conclusion

Germany's Rise and Future Challenges

THE PAST AND FUTURE OF GERMAN EXCEPTIONALISM

In a 2009 visit to Europe, U.S. President Barack Obama stated, "I believe in American exceptionalism, just as I suspect that the Brits believe in British exceptionalism and the Greeks believe in Greek exceptionalism."[1] He should have added Germany to that list because there are few countries that have had such unique historical experiences. For many decades, however, German exceptionalism was not something to be celebrated. This "special path" (*Sonderweg*), as it was sometimes deemed, was cause for concern within the country and particularly abroad. German exceptionalism was about how it deviated from liberal and democratic developments in the West. Germans seemed to prefer more autocratic political institutions. German culture was one of discipline, provincialism, deference, hypernationalism, patriarchal authority, and aggressive expansion. It is no wonder that a "German question" plagued the European and international system for so long.

Over the last half century, this old sense of exceptionalism has ceased to exist. During the four decades of the Cold War and the two after reunification, Germans have embraced a political system and culture in which the values of liberalism, tolerance, openness, and democracy are deeply anchored. Germany has become "normal"—fundamentally similar to other highly developed western countries like the UK, France, or the United States. Every country still has its own peculiarities that create specific political and cultural forms such as presidential versus parliamentary systems or a federal versus a centralized state. But fundamental structures and values are now shared throughout the West. Thus the old fears that the German "special path" fostered—the German question—are part of the "dustbin of history."

Yet there is another sense in which German exceptionalism is still apparent. This newer conception also stresses that the country is different, but now in a positive sense. Many authors even refer to Germany as exemplary—Modell Deutschland. The German electoral system and central bank have influenced institutional reforms in countries across the world. Many people deeply respect the social market economy, which has provided much higher levels of socioeconomic equity or justice than in other capitalistic economies such as the UK or the United States. German economic virtues—price stability, sound public finances, a strong currency—are emulated across Europe and envied elsewhere. Above all, German industry, especially the export sector, is admired globally. There are few indicators in which Germany does not rank at or near the top—human development, governance, transparency, infrastructure, the status of women, or environmental issues.[2] There are even fewer countries with a sizable population that rank as highly. On many measures, Germany actually scores better than more established democracies like the UK or the United States.

As has been evident, this edition of *The German Polity* has shared much of this optimism. Yet, even five years ago, the situation appeared very different. Books with titles like *Germany's Gathering Crisis* or *Can Germany Be Saved?*[3] described a dysfunctional political system that was incapable of addressing the problems that the country faced: the ongoing depression in eastern Germany, the integration of foreigners, an aging and shrinking population, an outmoded business and banking model, overtaxed citizens, or a bankrupt welfare state. Both outside and especially inside the country, a deep sense of pessimism reigned. Germany's best years were behind it.

As Germany came out of the 2008–2009 recession, the estimates and judgments of observers changed dramatically. The media ran headlines like "Germany's New Economic Miracle" or "The Cause of the Latest German Economic Miracle." Economists also made their contribution with papers like "What Explains the German Labor Market Miracle in the Great Recession?"[4] It is said that a week is a long time in politics and five to ten years is an eternity. We might be pessimistic again in five years. Like many other observers of Germany, we are somewhat surprised at how positive the situation has become. Political and economic life is hard to predict. Forces and trends that seemed insignificant at one point can have unexpected and surprising impacts. As former U.S. secretary of defense Donald Rumsfeld once put it, "There are known knowns . . . known unknowns . . . and unknown unknowns."[5] For example, Angela Merkel was long considered a political lightweight who would be a weak interim leader at best. Instead, she has become a major world figure and a key actor in the Eurozone crisis. Or consider the Agenda 2010 and Hartz IV reforms, which were underappreciated at the time they were implemented about a decade ago. Most analysts thought they were too little, too late. But they restructured the German labor market and are responsible for the much lower unemployment rate and strong economy recently. German institutions have indeed proven to be less sclerotic than believed. As our discussions of the bureaucracy and federalism in chapters 8 and 9 showed, institutional self-correction has occurred.

The same pattern applies to the European Monetary Union. In the first years after its implementation, the Euro did not have a positive impact on the German economy. With very low levels of inflation in the early 2000s, Germany had the highest real interest rates. In light of the low level of economic growth, the economy actually needed much lower interest rates, but the currency union could not accommodate that. By the late 2000s and especially since the Eurozone crisis, however, the common currency has become a major advantage for the country. The Euro's exchange rate with other currencies, for instance, was much lower than an alternative German currency. This greatly aided the German export sector.

In sum, Germany is currently experiencing an exceptional period of political and economic momentum. Nevertheless, the current economic upturn will not continue indefinitely. Already in mid-2012, growth rates were approaching zero, and some observers were predicting a recession by the end of the year.[6] What happens next? Have the problems that plagued Germany been truly solved, or have they just been obscured momentarily thanks to what was actually a superficial boom? Merkel has been in power since 2005, making her one of the longest-serving heads of government in Europe. What comes after her? And what about the often-discussed return of German power? Is this a fundamental shift or a temporary consequence of the ever-shifting balance of international economic and political forces? Above all, will this positive sense of exceptionalism continue into the future or is the German model really spent?

REFORMING THE GRIDLOCKED REPUBLIC?

The strength of the German economy over the last several years and its leadership role in the current Eurozone crisis led many to quickly forget the decade-long poor performance of the economy and the inability of the political system to enact long-needed reforms. In the late 1990s and early 2000s, there was a sense of institutional paralysis that has prompted a number of analysts and practitioners to call for fundamental constitutional change. Despite the federalism reforms of the last five years, many still call for a further reduction in the power of the Bundesrat and the state governments to block national legislation. Others criticize the almost constant campaigning that has resulted from the steady stream of off-year state elections. Not only does this situation affect the balance of power in the Bundesrat, but arguably it has led to the nationalization of state elections to the detriment of important local issues. Moreover, the ability of the national government to govern effectively is negatively affected by fast-changing majorities in the Bundesrat.

There have also been calls for the abolition of the ceremonial presidency, checking the Constitutional Court's power of judicial review, and pushing back against an increasingly intrusive European Union. Some argue that the proliferation of levels of government—local, Land, federal, European, and international—has created even more red tape and policy confusion. Some reformers have even called for a new Anglo-American–style electoral system that would produce clear majorities for a single party and eliminate the need for coalition governments. These proposals are not new, but the intensity of the calls for major constitutional reform has not abated.

For some critics, the Constitution itself is an obstacle.[7] It not only declares that Germany is a *democratic* and *federal* state governed by *the rule of law*

(*Rechtsstaat*), but also that it is a social state in which minimal levels of social welfare are constitutionally guaranteed. Over the last five and a half decades, this "social" dimension of the Constitution has been expanded to include a wide array of welfare programs: pensions, health care, unemployment compensation, sick leave, nursing care, aid to dependent women and children, and housing subsidies. Fulfilling the social mandate of the Constitution now consumes over a third of the country's total GDP. This number is set to expand considerably as the population becomes smaller and older. What is constitutionally required under this provision is a matter for the courts to decide, but any legislation could be challenged as unconstitutional. Obviously any effort to amend the "social" principle in the Constitution would be strongly opposed by a wide variety of groups.

The political parties also present obstacles to reform. In contrast to the United States and the UK, Germany has no major political party that is fundamentally skeptical and critical of the welfare state. Both the Christian Democrats and the Social Democrats support comprehensive state-based programs providing social and economic security to all. To be sure, the parties reached this common point via different routes. For the Social Democrats, a strong system of government-sponsored social and economic security was an integral part of democratic socialist ideology. The Christian Democrats' support for the welfare state has its origins in Catholic social thought, which emphasizes the moral responsibility of the state and its wealthier groups to protect and support the less fortunate members of society. Neither party has any tradition of support for the free market, minimal-government philosophy identified with the Republican Party in the United States or the free market wing of the British Conservative Party. Even the liberal FDP, although coming closest to supporting neoliberal economic doctrines like lower taxes and less spending on social programs, does not fundamentally challenge the basic tenets of the social market economy. In addition, the FDP's ever-shifting electoral fortunes show that its recent neoliberal emphasis does not have the same resonance as in other countries.

Part of the explanation for this difference is that as a continental European country, Germans have had centuries of experience with state power. They are much more comfortable with a vigorous, paternalistic state (*Vater Staat*) than the Anglo-American countries with their traditions of more limited state power. Also, contemporary elites believe that divisive class conflict was one of the root causes of Nazism. They are reluctant to rethink the grand postwar class compromise and consensual political style that presumably prevent a return to the bad old days.

In any case, the German marketplace of ideas has provided little room for the type of neoliberal free market ideology that is commonplace in the United States. The following statement, for example, from a prominent German social scientist and former adviser to Chancellor Schröder, expresses views widely held in the United States but rarely expressed in German public discourse:

> As politicians keep talking about health care reform, more and more people will understand that the only health care reform they may benefit from in their lifetime is to eat more vegetables, and stop smoking. Concerning pensions, already today nobody expects the state to deliver anything other than an unending series

of benefit cuts, however dressed up. Those who can afford it have begun to save for their old age. . . . Similarly the number of private schools is growing. . . . In the spirit of true liberalism, more and more people are helping themselves, which will make them even less willing to let the state take the rest of their money to help those who cannot.[8]

Germany has had few "think tanks" systematically challenging the welfare state orthodoxy. The pro–welfare state message has enjoyed a monopoly. Like all monopolies, it is not necessarily supportive of economic growth, without which no sustained improvement can be expected in unemployment or competitiveness.

One of the most common criticisms of the political system today deals with the nature of German democracy. The founders of the Federal Republic were deeply suspicious of average Germans, the vast majority of whom had actively or passively supported the Nazi regime. The Nazis had exploited the more populist features of the Weimar system, especially forms of direct democracy. Thus the Federal Republic was explicitly designed as a more elitist representative democracy with numerous restrictions and safeguards to prevent populist exploitation of the untrustworthy masses. For instance, although the Basic Law does not explicitly prohibit referenda, they are also not mentioned and have never been used at the national level.

Over the years as Germans remade their political values and behaviors, many citizens have expressed dissatisfaction with the constraints of this more limited version of democracy. They looked for reforms that would provide more direct input from citizens. The "extraparliamentary opposition" of the 1960s and 1970s, the new social movements of the 1970s and 1980s, as well as the protests of recent years over the transportation of nuclear waste or over the ambitious Stuttgart 21 train station project are all examples of such dissatisfaction with conventional politics. More generally, the lack of trust in political parties and the growing number of Euroskeptics are consequences of such criticism.

As a result, there have been increasing calls for referenda at the national level, especially over various European initiatives such as bailouts for troubled Eurozone economies. Proponents emphasize the potential for expanding democratic citizenship and note that the German citizenry of today is fully democratized and trustworthy, unlike the populace in 1949. Many also mention that the proliferation of new online technologies has created higher expectations for participation and interactivity. The rapid rise of the Pirate Party since 2009, which threatens the support of the established parties, is another consequence of such trends.

Opponents of direct democracy continue to emphasize Germany's experience with such measures during the Weimar Republic, when referenda were used by the antisystem parties to undermine parliamentary government. Referenda invite the manipulation of the public by demagogues or "populists" who simplify and inject irrelevant emotional arguments into complex issues best dealt with by professional political leaders. The public, it is argued, will not focus on the substance of the referendum but will use it as an opportunity for a plebiscite on the incumbent government. A referendum on the European Stability Mechanism, for example, would likely produce the same electoral response now seen in European parliamentary elections. Most voters would base their EU decision on national, domestic political factors and not on any European-wide considerations. It would become another second- or third-order national election in which voters would use the opportunity to support or punish their incumbent national government and/or vote for extremist parties.

As we have seen, the Federal Republic is a complex political system characterized by the presence of several power centers and veto groups. The national executive with its control over the civil service initiates the broad outlines of policy, but it cannot secure the approval of its policy proposals or their implementation without at least the tacit support of other actors in the political system: the major interest groups, the extraparliamentary organizations of the governing parties, the back-benchers in the legislature, the states, the semipublic institutions, the various institutions of the European Union, and even the opposition party when it has a majority of the delegates in the Bundesrat. Strong opposition by any of these actors will greatly hinder the efforts of the government and chancellor to determine the main guidelines of policy. Successful policy making must be accomplished within the framework of the politico-economic consensus that has emerged since 1949. This means that the system resists any efforts to introduce major innovations within a relatively short time. Change tends to be gradual and incremental, and rarely will it have a transforming effect. The presence of so many "veto players" is increasingly considered a major impediment to reform.

Once again, German federalism is singled out for criticism. The Kohl government's efforts in the late 1990s to change the tax and pension systems, for example, were defeated by the Bundesrat, the second house of parliament, then controlled by the Social Democrats. It was not until 2000 and 2001 that essentially the same tax reform and pension legislation was finally passed. The system has also favored the status quo and upper-income groups, the most organized in the society. As discussed in chapter 9, several federalism reforms over the last decade have attempted to clip the veto power of the states. Unfortunately, the reduction in the amount of legislation that needs Bundesrat approval has not met expectations. Although the second federalism reform has constrained the ability of the states to take on debt, there are still unresolved tensions over the allocation of tax revenues and revenue sharing among the states.

THE FUTURE OF THE WELFARE STATE AND THE NEW POVERTY

The extensive welfare state is the most striking result of this consensus style of governing and the many veto players. Germans have had "cradle-to-grave" security. All of life's core risks are covered in this system: sickness (including long-term nursing care), accident, disability, unemployment, and retirement. Social welfare programs also provide housing subsidies for low-income families and direct cash payments to all parents and guardians to defray some of the costs of raising children. Even a university education in some states is still free, with government grants and loans available to cover living costs. Few countries in the world offer such a comprehensive and generous system of social welfare.

Not surprisingly, the system is also very expensive. In 2008 the total cost for these programs was about 28 percent of GDP, or approximately $880 billion.[9] These programs consume about 55 percent of the total expenditures of local, state, and national governments.[10] To finance the welfare state, Germans pay over 45 percent of their income in taxes, as compared to about 30 percent for Americans. The biggest share of the social welfare budget goes to the pension and health insurance programs, which are financed by employer and employee contributions (see chapter 8). On the employer side, these "fringe benefits" now make up approximately one-third percent of labor costs.[11] Additional fringe benefits, which also usually include additional cash payments for vacations and Christmas holidays, coupled with high wages and salaries, make labor costs in Germany among the highest in the world.[12] High labor costs were responsible for the reluctance of employers to hire new workers and for the high prices for Germany's goods and services in the international marketplace.

Admittedly, much improvement has occurred over the last ten years. Nonwage labor costs have come down from 45 percent to 32 percent, currently below the European Union average. Indeed, unit labor costs in Germany between 2000 and 2012 were essentially unchanged, whereas many other Eurozone countries saw increases of 25 to 30 percent.[13] But one of the results of the years of wage restraint, coupled with the current economic strength, is that by 2012, wages and nonwage costs were rising again. Many wage earners and their union representatives were fed up with years of austerity and flat earnings. It would not be difficult for Germany to once again lose competitiveness through higher wages, increased taxes, and more welfare spending.

Thus, as much as the system has recovered strength in recent years, voters and policy makers alike still must wrestle with systematic questions of whether this system endangers the long-term health and competitiveness of the economy. By 2006, almost 50 percent more was being spent on social welfare programs than on investments in new plants and equipment. Present consumption now exceeds by a wide margin the investments that create the jobs of the future. Market share can still be lost to newly industrialized countries such as China, Korea, and increasingly India that offer low prices and good quality. Eastern neighbors such as Poland, Hungary, and the Czech Republic also offer a well-trained labor force at a fraction of the cost of German labor.

This is not even to mention the ongoing burdens to the social market economy that reunification added. As discussed in chapter 8, the West German pension system, for example, was applied to the new eastern states. By today, eastern pensions are at or exceed the western level, even though eastern contributions fall short of those paid by workers in the west. The difference is made up by tapping the West German pension, health care, and unemployment funds, and when these are depleted, the shortfalls are made up by general revenue. Between 1995 and 2004, the federal subsidy for the once self-supporting pension system grew from 23 percent to 37 percent of the fund's income. Employer-employee contributions accounted for only 63 percent of disbursements.

The welfare system also includes large subsidies to well-organized occupational groups such as farmers and coal miners. Since 1970, national and state governments have spent more than $125 billion to subsidize a declining and inefficient coal-mining industry. Although these subsidies are being phased out, German coal still costs more than the world market price. Agricultural subsidies add hundreds of dollars to the average German's annual food bill. These resources could be better spent in supporting productivity-enhancing policy areas such as education, high-tech research and development, physical infrastructure, or child care facilities.

Above all, there are the challenges of the demographic situation. Lower birth rates and longer life expectancies eventually mean fewer working people supporting more retirees. This is the downside to the "pay as you go" approach to social programs. In 1955 there were five contributing workers for each retiree. By 1990 the rate was four to one; and in 2012 it was three to one. By 2030, according to current predictions, there will be only two contributing employees for each retiree. This is no longer a viable funding model, which is already straining and will eventually bankrupt Germany's finances. One solution, of course, is a longer working life. Already many Germans have eschewed early retirement and thus continue to pay into health care and pension systems. The proportion of Germans aged sixty to sixty-four in the workforce more than doubled between 2000 and 2010. In 2006 the CDU-SPD Grand Coalition government raised the formal retirement age from sixty-five to sixty-seven by 2019.[14] Despite these needed changes, it is still unclear whether this will be enough to maintain the solvency of the system, as well as the still rather generous level of benefits to which Germans have become accustomed.

Yet another solution would be to facilitate higher levels of immigration. Unfortunately, the numbers needed per year, approximately 200,000, to even achieve a modest decline in the overall population over the next decades have rarely been met in recent years. Moreover, the challenges that Germany current faces to properly educate and integrate its residents with a migration background are already daunting. It is difficult to imagine the country achieving the policy and cultural change necessary to become an even more intensive "land of immigration." In addition, it will take a sustained period of growth to repair the damage done during the decade of economic stagnation. After a fifteen-year depression, eastern Germany will need even longer.

Already by the early 1990s the cuts in social welfare programs, slow economic growth, the rising proportion of residents with a migration background, and high unemployment, especially in the former East Germany, combined to produce a poverty problem for the first time in decades. The "new poverty," as Germans term it, refers especially to the condition of the long-term unemployed, single parents with children, low-income pensioners, those with a migration background, and refugees seeking asylum. Slow growth, high unemployment, cuts in social programs, and the emergence of a low-wage sector after the Agenda 2010/Hartz IV reforms also took a toll on the German poverty level. By 2006, it was estimated that roughly 16 percent of the population, or about four million people, lived below the poverty line, as compared to only 2 percent in 1980. In

2011, approximately 15 percent of the population was in poverty or in danger of being in poverty.[15]

The longer a worker is unemployed, the lower his or her level of support. After one year, unemployment compensation, which is based on employer-employee contributions and amounts to about two-thirds of the worker's prior wages, ceases and is replaced by a means-tested "unemployment aid," which since the Agenda 2010 reforms is now part of the welfare system. If a worker qualifies, he or she is entitled to a flat minimum of about $950 per month in addition to payments for children and allowances for housing and heating. However, if the worker's spouse or other family members are employed and earning sufficient income to support the family, he or she would not qualify for any unemployment support. Likewise, unemployed workers with substantial savings could receive reduced benefits or none at all until their savings are drawn down to the maximum savings allowed, about $15,000. During the past twenty-five years, the proportion of unemployed workers in the top tier (wage-based unemployment compensation) has declined from almost 70 percent to slightly above 40 percent, whereas the proportion of unemployed workers dependent on either unemployment aid or welfare has jumped from only 10 percent to almost 40 percent.[16]

Increasingly, social scientists fear the emergence of a permanent underclass of welfare recipients living in urban ghettos with few prospects for upward mobility. This phenomenon, well known in the United States and the UK, poses new challenges for a society generally considered one of the most affluent in the world. Unlike the traditional proletariat, this "*prekariat*," as it is termed in Europe, has few prospects for moving up in economies demanding high levels of skill and education. Low-skilled and often jobless, the "prekariat" have a lifestyle that "increasingly separates them from the mainstream: lots of fast food, alcohol, trash television and large tattoos."[17]

Also similar to France, the UK, and the United States, this emerging "underclass" is increasingly composed of nonwhite individuals or those with a migration background. Many of these individuals are caught in a low-income, poor education, and poverty trap, compounded by language issues and, arguably, cultural dissimilarity. Targeting this alienated segment of the population and unlocking their economic potential has to become an explicit policy priority. Unlike other policy areas discussed in this book, there is very little positive to report in this context. Of course, no western country has found a way to deal effectively with the challenges of a nonnative or nonwhite underclass. At the least, since the early 1990s, Germany has largely avoided xenophobic violence and race riots, which unfortunately have occurred in France and the UK in recent years.

GERMANY AFTER MERKEL

There are also the shorter-term uncertainties that affect all democratic systems. In the fall of 2013, the Federal Republic will experience its eighteenth national election and seventh since unification. As described above, there is more volatility in German voters' party preferences than in previous decades. Polling has, however, consistently shown a big drop in support for Merkel's junior coalition partner, the FDP. This means that a continuation of the current governing coalition is questionable.

Yet the leftist parties will also probably not generate a majority—especially because the Left Party is not yet trusted as an acceptable coalition partner. This makes another Grand Coalition of CDU/CSU and SPD and a third Merkel term a likely prospect. But electoral predictions are especially fraught: the "elephants" might continue their long-term decline; the Pirate Party might surpass the 5 percent threshold; hovering just around the 5 percent electoral threshold, the FDP might not even make it into the next parliament. No one can predict the issues that will come to dominate the campaign—there are always the "unknown unknowns"—and who will be able to capitalize on them.

Since 2005, Angela Merkel has provided solid leadership through some of the most tumultuous economic times since the Great Depression. Indeed, as table 11.1 shows, Merkel's stewardship of the economy through her second term has been impressive, even as warnings of a marked economic slowdown and even another recession in late 2012 increased.

Merkel has a cautious, prudent style that has resonated broadly with German voters looking for a sense of security amid unsettling circumstances. That she has presided over the return of German power in Europe and has steadfastly advocated German interests while simultaneously renewing support for the European project has added to her stature. Few world leaders today command the experience and international connections that she has amassed since 2005. She has consistently been among the most liked and respected politicians of the last decade. Merkel, now often referred to as the "Iron Frau," is also an underestimated and underappreciated politico, successfully outmaneuvering and eliminating almost all intraparty opponents while promoting her supporters. Some critics have even characterized her as a ruthless, autocratic, power-hungry, and unprincipled "godmother."[18] She has also been adept internationally—building strong relationships with leaders like Nicolas Sarkozy in France and Wen Jiabao

Table 11.1.   Germany's Economic Record, 2009–2014

	2009	2010	2011	2012	2013*	2014*
Real GDP growth (percent)	−5.1	4.2	3.0	0.8	0.9	2.2
Employment (millions)	40.4	40.6	41.2	41.6	41.6	41.9
Unemployment (millions)**	3.2	2.9	2.5	2.3	2.4	2.2
Unemployment (percent)**	7.8	7.1	5.9	5.5	5.6	5.2
Inflation (consumer prices, percent)	0.3	1.1	2.3	2.0	1.8	1.8
Federal deficit ($billions)***	−98	−140	−27	3	0.8	18
Federal deficit (percent GDP)	−3.1	−4.1	−0.8	0.1	0.0	0.5
Trade balance (percent GDP)	6.0	6.0	5.7	6.3	6.2	6.2

Source: Deutsches Institut für Wirtschaft, Wochenbericht, nos. 1–2 (2013): 23; for 2012 GDP: Federal Statistical Office.
*Estimate.
**Data from International Labour Organization (United Nations).
***1 euro = $1.35 (January 2013).

in China and outmaneuvering others like Italy's Silvio Berlusconi and a variety of Greek prime ministers.

Whatever her strengths and successes, eventually Germany must move beyond Merkel. Whether that will be as soon as the 2013 Bundestag election or as late as 2017, new leadership will have to rise to the occasion. Unfortunately for the CDU, one of the consequences of Merkel's success in ousting party rivals is that a powerful, competent successor is difficult to discern—although some current minister-presidents may emerge. The Bavarian sister party, the CSU, has been suffering for years with lackluster leaders. It can no longer be counted on to deliver absolute majorities at state and national elections. The FDP is cultivating a new generation, but they are too inexperienced to be effective in the foreseeable future and the party may not even have a parliamentary delegation after 2013. The most promising future leaders in the medium term appear to come from the left—especially the Green Party, but also the SPD as it has worked rather effectively to achieve internal renewal after the 2009 electoral debacle and has substantial talent at the state level.

Whoever follows Merkel will inherit numerous challenges. As the recent economic boom fades, the deeper structural issues with the economy, the demographic situation, eastern Germany, and vested interests and institutions will no longer be obscured and will have to be addressed. The new poverty, rising socioeconomic inequality, and an emergent nonnative underclass are issues to which voters will demand answers. A more volatile electorate, a more fragmented party system, unwieldy coalitions, and demands for more direct forms of democracy will become the new normal in German political life. And all of this will take place in the context of almost permanent austerity. There is little margin to increase revenues from the already highly taxed population. A 2009 constitutional amendment severely restricts deficit spending and new debt. European and global actors will continue to challenge the competitiveness of the economy.

Moreover, as discussed in the previous chapter, the European Union has become stuck in an unstable halfway house between a coordinated group of sovereign states and a true supranational government. A resolution to this tension is pressing, if only to reassure bond and financial markets. The next chancellor will have to continue to manage the increase of German influence and power, as well as the fears and resentment that this generates abroad. Finally, if the more pessimistic predictions about the collapse of the Eurozone come to pass, the next government will have to deal with the fallout from an unprecedented economic catastrophe. Even if the more dire scenarios are avoided, the impact of the Eurozone crisis will be felt for many years.

LOOKING BACK AND LOOKING FORWARD: THE GERMAN EXPERIENCE OF POLITICAL DEVELOPMENT AND THE FUTURE OF GERMAN POWER

Despite the successes of recent years and the positive sense of exceptionalism that currently reigns, there are numerous weaknesses and challenges that contemporary Germany must confront. This is exactly like every other "normal" country today. But, beyond the day-to-day drama, we should not forget the bigger picture. To many Germans, a good part of the nineteenth and twentieth centuries was a traumatic *Irrfahrt*, an error-filled "special path" during which the nation at various times experienced a variety of extremist ideologies—nationalism, fascism, communism—with disastrous consequences for itself and the world. The success of the Federal Republic represented a definitive break from the pattern of political instability, authoritarianism, and aggressive nationalism that had characterized so much of German history. The ongoing challenges that the Federal Republic faces must be considered in the light of this fundamental achievement of creating a genuine and deeply rooted democratic political order.

The success of the reunification process was in part a result of the Federal Republic's performance since 1949. Neither Germany's neighbors in Eastern and Western Europe nor the larger international community would have supported reunification had they not been convinced that Germany and the Germans had truly changed. Within Europe, Germany kept a relatively low profile and indeed acted more like a small state than a major power. Reunification, however, also meant that the question of national identity, which remained unresolved during the forty-year division of Germany and Europe, had been resolved in a manner consistent with the principles and values that have guided the Republic since 1949: political democracy, civil liberties, rule of law, social welfare, and peaceful resolution of conflict. Reunification confirmed the validity of the postwar democratic order.

This postwar experience illustrates that a nation can overcome or change its political culture within a relatively short time. Democratic political stability does not necessarily require the centuries-long evolution characteristic of democracies such as the UK and the United States. Good institutions, a strong constitution, and a system of checks and balances matter immensely.[19] Postwar Germany should alert students of development to the importance of system performance and effectiveness, especially in the early years of a country's development. National ideologies, symbols, power, and prestige are not substitutes for meeting concrete popular demands for social change and economic stability. Postwar Germany also shows how a country can learn from and make amends for a dreadful past in a way that strengthens democracy at home and trust abroad.

Not only has the last decade seen the transformation of Germany from the "sick man of Europe" back to Modell Deutschland, but Germany's power has increased from a variety of perspectives. Germany's economic prowess is perhaps most evident in the Miele vacuums, Birkenstock sandals, and Mercedes sedans populating homes and streets from St. Petersburg to Sao Paulo to Shanghai. Merkel has worked diligently to build ties with emerging economies, especially China: "Germany has not only become a leading exporter to China, but by the end of the year, one German think tank estimated, Berlin might also achieve the holy grail of commerce: a trade surplus with China."[20]

In direct contrast to the Cold War decades, the Federal Republic is now a regular, albeit inconstant, actor in international military and peacekeeping missions. Approximately 10,000 Bundeswehr troops have been deployed around the world since reunification in support of Germany's alliance and international commitments. Since 1990, the country has also increased its deployment of forms of soft power, such as international education and development assistance.

Above all, Germany has become the most influential country in the European Union and especially the Eurozone. Certainly the Federal Republic was always a key advocate of greater European integration, but it always worked in tandem with other member states, especially France, and often deferred to others' leadership. During the ongoing Euro crisis, by contrast, all important decisions were made by or only with Berlin's consent. Unlike previously, other actors such as France, the UK, or Italy have clearly taken a subordinate role. European institutions like the European Commission or the European Central Bank have proven much weaker than expected, only acting with impetus from or approval by Merkel's government. No longer is Germany an economic heavyweight but a political lightweight.

But with increased power come both advantages and drawbacks. On the one hand, Germany's strong position has meant that its national interests have been ably served. For example, the country has been able to issue new public debt at almost 0 percent interest. Its policy preferences, such as low inflation, the European Stability Mechanism, or the lack of joint Euro bonds, have predominated. On the other hand, the exercise of power has provoked much resentment and even hostility in countries such as Greece, Spain, and Italy, which have been the most affected by the crisis. Some of the old fears, the bad sense of exceptionalism, and even the German question have been retrieved from the dustbin of history. People and countries do not like to be scolded or told what to do—a truth Americans long ago have had to accept.

Germans today are in the process of accepting this new, more powerful role. But just as an adolescent has a hard time adjusting to a rapidly growing body, there are hiccups and tensions in the process. Germany did not plan for or scheme to achieve this degree of power in Europe. In fact, Germany constantly sacrificed its short-term self-interest to achieve a greater, European good. But the country is adjusting to its new role. The willingness to take one for the team is declining. A new self-confidence to articulate and implement national interests is evident. Or rather, the country is developing a way to combine its interests with the greater good, but it is also ready to sacrifice the latter for the former.

From outside of the country, many individuals and governments will need to come to terms with the new situation. They will have to accept that Germany will not always be the one that bails out and sacrifices for others. Germany has the right, just like any other normal country, to pursue its self-interest. Others need to understand that as powerful as Germany has become, it is still ultimately limited, with 82 million people and an economy that is not even a quarter the size of the U.S. economy. Even the Eurozone is only two-thirds the size of the U.S. economy (although the European Union's economy is larger). As sound as Germany's economy and public finances have been in recent years, as we mentioned above, there are still quite a few structural weaknesses and vulnerabilities that can very rapidly affect Germany's strength.

But there is little doubt that, however powerful and self-interested Germany has become, its institutions, elites, and citizens are fully and unequivocally committed to democracy, liberalism, and peace. The political system that we have outlined in this book has functioned extraordinarily well for almost seven decades. It will, in all likelihood, continue to do so into the challenging years to come.

NOTES

1. http://www.whitehouse.gov/the-press-office/news-conference-president-obama-4042009.

2. Eric Langenbacher, "Conclusion: The Germans Must Have Done Something Right," in *From the Bonn to the Berlin Republic: Germany at the Twentieth Anniversary of Unification*, ed. Jeffrey J. Anderson and Eric Langenbacher (New York: Berghahn Books, 2010).

3. Alister Miskimmon, William E. Paterson, and James Sloam, eds., *Germany's Gathering Crisis: The 2005 Federal Election and the Grand Coalition* (New York: Palgrave Macmillan, 2008); Hans-Werner Sinn, *Can Germany Be Saved? The Malaise of the World's First Welfare State* (Cambridge, MA: MIT Press, 2009).

4. *Der Spiegel*, July 19, 2010; *Forbes*, March 5, 2012; Michael C. Burda and Jennifer Hunt, "Brookings Papers on Economic Activity," Washington, DC, Spring 2011. For an overview of "Sick Man" to "Economic Miracle" analyses, see Alexander Reisenbichler and Kimberly J. Morgan, "From 'Sick Man' to 'Miracle': Explaining the Robustness of the German Labor Market during and after the Financial Crisis, 2008–2009," paper presented at the American Political Science Association Annual Meeting, Seattle, September 2011.

5. http://www.defense.gov/transcripts/transcript.aspx?transcriptid=2636.

6. Stephen Castle, "O.E.C.D. Warns of Recession in Germany," *New York Times*, September 6, 2012.

7. "Die Verstaubte Verfassung," *Der Spiegel*, May 12, 2003; "Aktion Staub raus," *Der Spiegel*, July 28, 2003. At the time of unification, many East German dissidents, West German Greens, and some Social Democrats wanted unification to take place according to Article 146 of the Basic Law, which would have allowed for an entirely new constitution, requiring approval by the entire electorate in a referendum. The final August 1990 unification treaty included a provision (Article 5) enabling the parliament to examine whether constitutional changes with reference to "strengthening the federal structure and the goals of the state" were necessary. In May 1991, the government and opposition differed on whether and how much the existing constitution should be changed. The governing coalition (Christian Democrats and Free Democrats) supported only a "constitutional committee" to "modernize" the current Basic Law by making changes while stopping short of a new constitution. Largely ignored by the mass media and much of the public, the commission held many meetings and received thousands of proposals, but in the end produced very few changes. The representatives from the governing parties were able to block most of the major proposals of the Social Democrats and Greens. The constitutional changes included two amendments to Article 3 on gender equality and the handicapped, an amendment to Article 20 declaring the state's commitment to environmental protection, and one amendment on local self-government.

8. Wolfgang Streeck, "Endgame? The Fiscal Crisis of the German State" (discussion paper no. 7, Max Planck-Institute for the Study of Societies, Cologne, 2007), 34. The "Endgame" refers to the welfare state. See also his "A State of Exhaustion: A Comment on the German Election of 18 September," *Political Quarterly* 77, no. 1 (January–March 2006), 79–88.

9. http://epp.eurostat.ec.europa.eu/statistics_explained/index.php?title = File:Total_expenditure_on_social_protection_as_%25GDP_in_2008.PNG&filetimestamp = 2011040 3084058.

10. Federal Statistical Office, *Datenreport 2011*, 87.

11. http://www.spiegel.de/international/business/eu-labor-cost-comparison-germany -becoming-more-competitive-a-549003.html.

12. In some fields such as banking, fringe benefits including vacations, vacation bonuses, and other benefits such as subsidized cafeterias now exceed the costs of wages and salaries.

13. http://articles.businessinsider.com/2011-11-28/markets/30449211_1_wage-grow th-unit-labor-big-spike.

14. Labor Ministry and Eurostat figures cited in *Frankfurter Allgemeine Zeitung*, November 18, 2010, 11.

15. http://www.spiegel.de/politik/deutschland/die-armutsgefaehrdung-ist-2011-in-deut schland-gestiegen-a-855560.html.

16. *Der Spiegel*, March 21, 2007, 24. When poverty is defined as 50 percent of the average income, the proportion living in poverty increases to 17 percent. Poverty is associated most closely with a "migration background," large families, and single parents.

17. Adrian Hyde-Price and Charlie Jeffrey, "Germany in the European Union: Constructing Normality," *Journal of Common Market Studies* 39, no. 4 (November 2001): 690.

18. http://www.spiegel.de/international/germany/author-claims-merkel-autocratic-in-new-book-a-851774.html.

19. And not only in Germany. According to a recent much-acclaimed analysis, strong political institutions and the rule of law in support of inclusive economic institutions are critical for sustained economic development and prosperity worldwide. Daron Acemoglu and James A. Robinson, *Why Nations Fail: The Origins of Power, Prosperity, and Poverty* (New York: Crown Publishers, 2012).

20. Anthony Faiola, "As Germany Rises, 'Iron Frau' Unbends a Little," *Washington Post*, September 12, 2012.

Bibliography

The following listing is selected from the English-language literature on postwar German politics. Those students with a command of the German language are directed to the various endnotes in the book. The major German language surveys of the Federal Republic—Wolfgang Rudzio's *Das Politische System der Bundesrepublik Deutschland*, 8th ed. (Wiesbaden: VS Verlag für Sozialwissenschaften, 2011) and Manfred G. Schmidt, *Das politische System Deutschlands: Institutionen, Willensbildung und Politikfelder* (Munich: Beck, 2011)—are important sources. For current developments, the weekly publications *Die Zeit* and *Der Spiegel* are recommended. Parliamentary proceedings are well covered in another weekly, *Das Parlament*.

WEBSITES

As the digital revolution continues, virtually every news organization, think tank, and governmental organization has developed an online presence. Most of these sites are free, and the vast majority of German websites also have English versions. We list a sampling of these websites below. State and local governments, as well as the political parties, also have well-developed websites.

Newsmagazines and Newspapers

Der Spiegel (http://www.spiegel.de/international)
Deutsche Welle (http://www.dw.de)
The Local (http://www.thelocal.de)
The Economist (http://www.economist.com/topics/german-politics)
Bild (http://www.bild.de/news/bild-english/bild-com/home-19858064.bild.html)
Focus (http://www.focus.de)
Die Zeit (http://www.zeit.de/index)
Frankfurter Allgemeine Zeitung (Frankfurt) (http://www.faz.net)
Süddeutsche Zeitung (Munich) (http://www.sueddeutsche.de)
Der Tagesspiegel (Berlin) (http://www.tagesspiegel.de)
Das Parlament/Aus Politik und Zeitgeschichte (http://epaper.das-parlament.de)

Governmental Sources

Bundestag (http://www.bundestag.de/htdocs_e/index.html)
Bundesrat (http://www.bundesrat.de/cln_092/EN/Home/homepage__node.html?__nnn =
    true)
Constitutional Court (http://www.bverfg.de/en/index.html)
Federal Government (http://www.bundesregierung.de/Webs/Breg/EN/Homepage/_node
    .html)
Finance Ministry (http://www.bundesfinanzministerium.de/Web/EN/Home/home.html)
Interior Ministry (http://www.bmi.bund.de/EN/Home)
Federal Center for Political Education/Bundeszentrale für politische Bildung
        (http://www.bpb.de)
Federal Statistical Office/Statistisches Bundesamt (https://www.destatis.de/EN)
German Missions in U.S. (http://www.germany.info/Vertretung/usa/en/Startseite.html)
German Academic Exchange Service/DAAD
        (https://www.daad.org)
Goethe Institute (http://www.goethe.de/enindex.htm)
Facts about Germany (http://www.tatsachen-ueber-deutschland.de/en/head-navi/home
    .html)

Academic Journals

German Politics and Society (http://journals.berghahnbooks.com/gps)
German Politics (http://www.tandfonline.com/toc/fgrp20/current)
German Studies Review (http://www.press.jhu.edu/journals/german_studies_review/
    index.html)
Blätter für deutsche und international Politik (http://www.blaetter.de)

Blogs

https://netzpolitik.org
http://www.nachdenkseiten.de
http://www.spreeblick.com
http://www.stefan-niggemeier.de/blog

Fun Sites

Soccer (http://www.bundesliga.com/en)
Food (http://www.globalgourmet.com/destinations/germany/#axzz26kRetl mV)
Travel (http://www.lonelyplanet.com/germany)
Beer (http://www.bierundwir.de/index.htm)
        (http://www.germanbeerinstitute.com)
Wine (http://www.germanwines.de/Home)
Historical reconstruction (http://www.stadtbild-deutschland.org/forum)
Castles (http://www.germany.travel/en/leisure-and-recreation/palaces-parks-gardens/pal
    aces-parks-gardens.html)

CHAPTER 1: THE HISTORICAL SETTING

Aly, Götz. *Hitler's Beneficiaries: Plunder, Race War, and the Nazi Welfare State*, trans-
    lated by Jefferson Chase (New York: Metropolitan, 2007).

Barraclough, Geoffrey. *The Origins of Modern Germany* (New York: Capricorn Books, 1963, reprint).

Berman, Sheri E. "Civil Society and the Collapse of the Weimar Republic." *World Politics* 49, no. 3 (1997): 401–429.

———. "Modernization in Historical Perspective: The Case of Imperial Germany." *World Politics* 53, no. 3 (2001): 431–462.

Bernhard, Michael. "Democratization in Germany: A Reappraisal." *Comparative Politics* 33, no. 4 (2001): 379–400.

———. *Institutions and the Fate of Democracy: Germany and Poland in the Twentieth Century* (Pittsburgh: University of Pittsburgh Press, 2005).

Blackbourn, David, and Geoff Eley. *The Peculiarities of German History: Bourgeois Society and Politics in Nineteenth-Century Germany* (New York: Oxford University Press, 1984).

Botting, Douglas. *From the Ruins of the Reich, Germany 1945–1949* (New York: Crown, 1985).

Bracher, Karl Dietrich. *The German Dictatorship* (New York: Praeger, 1970).

Broszat, Martin. *The Hitler State* (White Plains, NY: Longman, 1981).

Browning, Christopher R. *Ordinary Men: Reserve Police Battalion 101 and the Final Solution in Poland* (New York: HarperCollins, 1992).

Casey, Stephen. *Cautious Crusade: Franklin D. Roosevelt, American Public Opinion, and the War against Nazi Germany* (New York: Oxford University Press, 2001).

Chickering, Roger. *Imperial Germany and the Great War, 1914–1918* (New York: Cambridge University Press, 1998).

Childers, Thomas. *The Nazi Voter* (Chapel Hill: University of North Carolina Press, 1983).

Clark, Christopher. *Iron Kingdom: The Rise and Downfall of Prussia, 1600–1947* (Cambridge: Belknap Press of Harvard University, 2006).

Craig, Gordon. *The Germans* (New York: Putnam, 1982).

———. *Germany, 1866–1945* (New York: Oxford University Press, 1978).

Epstein, Klaus. *The Genesis of German Conservatism* (Princeton, NJ: Princeton University Press, 1966).

———. "The German Problem, 1945–50." *World Politics* 20, no. 2 (January 1968): 279–300.

Ertman, Thomas. *Birth of the Leviathan: Building States and Regimes in Medieval and Early Modern Europe* (Cambridge: Cambridge University Press, 1997).

Evans, Richard J. *The Third Reich in Power, 1933–1939* (New York: Penguin, 2006).

Falter, Jürgen W., and Reinhard Zintl. "The Economic Crisis of the 1930s and the Nazi Vote." *Journal of Interdisciplinary History* 19, no. 1 (Summer 1988): 55–85.

Fest, Joachim. *Hitler* (New York: Random House, 1975).

Friedländer, Saul. *Nazi Germany and the Jews*, vol. 1 (New York: HarperCollins, 1997).

Friedrich, Carl J. "The Legacies of the Occupation of Germany." In *Public Policy*, ed. John D. Montgomery and Albert O. Hirschman (Cambridge: Harvard University Press, 1968), 1–26.

Fulbrook, Mary. *The Divided Nation: A History of Germany, 1918–1990* (New York: Oxford University Press, 1992).

Gellately, Robert. *Backing Hitler. Consent and Coercion in Nazi Germany* (New York: Oxford University Press, 2001).

Glaessner, Gert Joachim. *German Democracy. From Post–World War II to the Present Day* (London: Berg Publishers, 2005).

Glees, Anthony. *Reinventing Germany: German Political Development since 1945* (Oxford: Berg, 1996).

Goldhagen, Daniel Jonah. *Hitler's Willing Executioners: Ordinary Germans and the Holocaust* (New York: Knopf, 1996).

Goltz, Anna von der. *Hindenburg: Power, Myth and the Rise of the Nazis* (Oxford: Oxford University Press, 2009).

Gray, William Glenn. *Germany's Cold War: The Global Campaign to Isolate East Germany, 1949–1969* (Chapel Hill: University of North Carolina Press, 2003).

Hamann, Brigitte. *Hitler's Vienna: A Dictator's Apprenticeship*, translated from the German by Thomas Thornton (New York: Oxford University Press, 1999).

Hamilton, Richard. *Who Voted for Hitler?* (Princeton, NJ: Princeton University Press, 1982).

Herf, Jeffrey. *Divided Memory: The Nazi Past in the Two Germanys* (Cambridge, MA: Harvard University Press, 1997).

Holborn, Hajo. *A History of Modern Germany, 1840–1945* (New York: Knopf, 1970).

James, Harold. *The German Slump: Politics and Economics, 1924–1936* (New York: Clarendon Press/Oxford University Press, 1986).

Kocka, Jürgen. *Industrial Culture and Bourgeois Society: Business, Labor, and Bureaucracy in Modern Germany* (New York: Berghahn Books, 1999).

Krieger, Leonard. "The Inter-Regnum in Germany: March–August 1945." *Political Science Quarterly* 64, no. 4 (December 1949): 507–532.

———. "The Potential for Democratization in Occupied Germany: A Problem of Historical Projection." In *Public Policy*, ed. John D. Montgomery and Albert O. Hirschman (Cambridge, MA: Harvard University Press, 1968), 27–58.

Laqueur, Walter. *Weimar: A Cultural History* (New York: Putnam, 1974).

Lepsius, M. Rainer. "From Fragmented Party Democracy to Government by Emergency Decree and National Socialist Takeover: Germany." In *The Breakdown of Democratic Regimes: Europe*, ed. Juan J. Linz and Alfred Stephan (Baltimore, MD: Johns Hopkins University Press, 1978), 34–79.

Litchfield, Edward, ed. *Governing Postwar Germany* (Ithaca, NY: Cornell University Press, 1953).

Luebbert, Gregory M. "Social Foundations of Political Order in Interwar Europe." *World Politics* 39, no. 4 (July 1987): 449–478.

Maier, Charles. *The Unmasterable Past: History, Holocaust, and German National Identity* (Cambridge: Harvard University Press, 1988).

Merkl, Peter H. *The Origins of the West German Republic* (New York: Oxford University Press, 1965).

Merritt, Richard L. *Democracy Imposed: U.S. Occupation Policy and the German Public* (New Haven, CT: Yale University Press, 1995).

Moeller, Robert, ed. *West Germany under Construction: Politics, Society and Culture in the Adenauer Era* (Ann Arbor: University of Michigan Press, 1997).

Niven, Bill. *Germans as Victims: Remembering the Past in Contemporary Germany* (Basingstoke: Palgrave Macmillan, 2006).

Patton, David F. *Cold War Politics in Postwar Germany* (New York: St. Martin's, 1999).

Peterson, Edward N. *The American Occupation of Germany: Retreat to Victory* (Detroit, MI: Wayne State University Press, 1977).

Pulzer, Peter. *German Politics, 1945–1995* (New York: Oxford University Press, 1995).

Rittberger, Volker. "Revolution and Pseudo-Democratization: The Formation of the Weimar Republic." In *Crisis, Choice and Change*, ed. Gabriel A. Almond et al. (Boston, MA: Little, Brown, 1973), 285–396.

Sanford, Gregory W. *From Hitler to Ulbricht: The Communist Reconstruction of East Germany 1945–1946* (Princeton, NJ: Princeton University Press, 1983).

Snyder, Timothy. *Bloodlands: Europe between Hitler and Stalin* (New York: Basic Books, 2010).

Speer, Albert. *Inside the Third Reich* (New York: Macmillan, 1968).

Stern, Fritz. *Five Germanys I Have Known* (New York: Farrar, Straus and Giroux, 2006).

Tent, James F. *Mission on the Rhine: Reeducation and Denazification in American-Occupied Germany* (Princeton, NJ: Princeton University Press, 1983).

Van Hook, James C. *Rebuilding Germany: The Creation of the Social Market Economy, 1945–1957* (Cambridge: Cambridge University Press, 2004).

Walser-Smith, Helmut, ed. *The Oxford Handbook of Modern German History* (Oxford: Oxford University Press, 2011).

CHAPTER 2: EASTERN GERMANY BEFORE AND AFTER REUNIFICATION

Adomeit, Hannes. "Gorbachev and German Unification: Revision of Thinking, Realignment of Power." *Problems of Communism*, July–August 1990, 1–24.

Anderson, Christopher, et al., eds. *The Domestic Politics of German Unification* (Boulder, CO: Lynne Rienner, 1993).

Anderson, Jeffrey J., and Eric Langenbacher, eds., *From the Bonn to the Berlin Republic: Germany at the Twentieth Anniversary of Unification* (New York: Berghahn Books, 2010).

Asmus, Ronald D. "A Unified Germany." In *Transition and Turmoil in the Atlantic Alliance*, ed. Robert A. Levine (New York: Crane Russak, 1992), 31–109.

Burgess, John P. "Church-State Relations in East Germany: The Church as a 'Religious' and 'Political' Force." *Journal of Church and State* 32, no. 1 (Winter 1990): 17–36.

Collier, Irwin L., Jr. "The Twin Curse of the Goddess Europa and the Economic Reconstruction of Eastern Germany." *German Studies Review* 20, no. 3 (October 1997): 399–428.

Cooke, Paul. *Representing East Germany since Unification: From Colonization to Nostalgia* (New York: Berg Publishers, 2005).

Czarnowski, Gabriele. "Abortion as Political Conflict in the Unified Germany." *Parliamentary Affairs* 47, no. 2 (April 1994): 252–267.

Deeg, Richard. "Institutional Transfer, Social Learning and Economic Policy in Eastern Germany." *West European Politics* 18, no. 4 (October 1995): 38–63.

Dennis, Mike. *Social and Economic Modernization in Eastern Germany from Honecker to Kohl* (London: Pinter Publishers, 1993).

Drost, Helmar. "The Great Depression in East Germany: The Effects of Unification on East Germany's Economy." *East European Politics and Societies* 7, no. 3 (Fall 1993): 452–481.

Finkel, Steven E., et al. "Socialist Values and the Development of Democratic Support in the Former East Germany." *International Political Science Review* 22, no. 4 (2002): 339–361.

Flockton, Chris, and Eva Kolinsky, eds. *Recasting East Germany* (London: Frank Cass, 1999).

Frowen, Stephen, and Jens Hoelscher, eds. *The German Currency Union: A Critical Assessment* (New York: St. Martin's, 1997).

Fulbrook, Mary. *Anatomy of a Dictatorship* (New York: Oxford University Press, 1995).

———. *The People's State: East German Society from Hitler to Honecker* (New Haven, CT: Yale University Press, 2005).

Garton Ash, Timothy. *The File: A Personal History* (New York: Random House, 1997).

Glaeser, Andreas. *Political Epistemics: The Secret Police, the Opposition, and the End of East German Socialism* (Chicago: University of Chicago Press, 2011).

Goeckel, Robert F. *The Lutheran Church and the East German State* (Ithaca, NY: Cornell University Press, 1990).

Goldberger, Paul. "Reimagining Berlin." *New York Times Magazine*, 5 February 1995, 45ff.

Greenwald, G. Jonathan. *Berlin Witness* (University Park: Pennsylvania State University Press, 1993).

Grix, Jonathan. *The Role of the Masses in the Collapse of the GDR* (New York: Palgrave Macmillan, 2001).

Hamilton, Daniel. "After the Revolution: The New Political Landscape in East Germany." *German Issues*, no. 7. Washington, DC: American Institute for Contemporary German Studies, 1990.

Harrison, Hope M. *Driving the Soviets up the Wall: Soviet–East German Relations, 1953–1961* (Princeton, NJ: Princeton University Press, 2003).

Hefeker, Carsten, and Norbert Wunner. "Promises Made, Promises Broken: A Political Economic Perspective on German Unification." *German Politics* 12, no. 1 (April 2003): 109–134.

Heilemann, Ullrich, and Wolfgang H. Reinicke. *Welcome to Hard Times: The Fiscal Consequences of German Unity* (Washington, DC: Brookings Institution, 1995).

Hirschman, Albert O. "Exit, Voice and the Fate of the German Democratic Republic: An Essay in Conceptual History." *World Politics* 45, no. 2 (January 1993): 173–202.

Howard, Marc Morjé. *The Weakness of Civil Society in Post-Communist Europe* (Cambridge: Cambridge University Press, 2003).

Huelshoff, Michael S., et al., eds. *From Bundesrepublik to Deutschland: German Politics after Unification* (Ann Arbor: University of Michigan Press, 1993).

Jarausch, Konrad H. *The Rush to German Unity* (New York: Oxford University Press, 1994).

Joppke, Christian. *East German Dissidents and the Revolution of 1989: Social Movement in a Leninist Regime* (New York: New York University Press, 1995).

———. "Intellectuals, Nationalism, and the Exit from Communism: The Case of East Germany." *Comparative Studies in Society and History* 37, no. 2 (April 1995): 213–241.

Kelleher, Catherine. "The New Germany: An Overview." In *The New Germany in the New Europe*, ed. Paul B. Stares (Washington, DC: Brookings Institution, 1992), 11–54.

Kinzer, Stephen. "East Germans Face Their Accusers." *New York Times Magazine*, 12 April 1992, 24ff.

Koopmans, Ruud. "The Dynamics of Protest Waves: West Germany, 1965–1989." *American Sociological Review* 58 (October 1993).

Krisch, Henry. *The Political Disintegration of a Communist State: The German Democratic Republic, 1987–1990* (Boulder, CO: Westview Press, 1992).

Kuechler, Manfred. "The Road to German Unity: Mass Sentiment in East and West Germany." *Public Opinion Quarterly* 56, no. 1 (Spring 1992): 53–76.

Lange, Thomas, and Geoffrey Pugh. *The Economics of German Unification* (Northampton: Edward Elgar Publishing, 1998).

Livingston, Robert Gerald. "Relinquishment of East Germany." In *East-Central Europe and the USSR*, ed. Richard F. Starr (New York: St. Martin's, 1991), 83–101.

Lohmann, Susanne. "Dynamics of Informational Cascades: The Monday Demonstrations in Leipzig, East Germany, 1989–1991." *World Politics* 47, no. 1 (October 1994): 42–101.

Maier, Charles S. *Dissolution: The Crisis of Communism and the End of East Germany* (Princeton, NJ: Princeton University Press, 1997).

McAdams, A. James. *Germany Divided: From the Wall to Reunification* (Princeton, NJ: Princeton University Press, 1993).

———. "The Honecker Trial: The East German Past and the German Future." *Review of Politics* 58, no. 1 (1996): 53–80.

———. *Judging the Past in Unified Germany* (Cambridge: Cambridge University Press, 2001).

McFalls, Laurence. *Communism's Collapse, Democracy's Demise?* (New York: New York University Press, 1995).

Merkl, Peter H. *German Unification in the European Context* (University Park: Pennsylvania State University Press, 1993).

Naimark, Norman M. *The Russians in East Germany: A History of the Soviet Zone of Occupation, 1945–1949* (Cambridge, MA: Harvard University Press, 1995).

Patton, David. "Social Coalitions, Political Strategies, and German Unification, 1990–1993." *West European Politics* 16, no. 4 (October 1993): 470–491.

Quint, Peter E. *The Imperfect Union: Constitutional Structure of German Unification* (Princeton, NJ: Princeton University Press, 1997).

Razeen, Sally, and Douglas Webber. "The German Solidarity Pact: A Case Study in the Politics of the Unified Germany." *German Politics* 3, no. 1 (Winter 1994): 18–46.

Rodden, John. *Repainting the Little Red School House: A History of East German Education, 1945–1995* (New York: Oxford University Press, 2002).

Ross, Corey. "East Germans and the Berlin Wall: Popular Opinion and Social Change before and after the Border Closure of August 1961." *Journal of Contemporary History* 39, no. 1 (January 2004): 25–43.

Sarotte, Mary Elise. *1989: The Struggle to Create Post-Cold War Europe* (Princeton, NJ: Princeton University Press, 2009).

———. "Perpetuating U.S. Preeminence: The 1990 Deals to 'Bribe the Soviets Out' and Move NATO In." *International Security* 35, no. 1 (Summer 2010): 110–137.

Segert, Astrid. "Problematic Normalization: Eastern German Workers Eight Years after Unification." *German Politics and Society* 16, no. 3 (Fall 1998): 105–124.

Sinn, Hans Werner. "Germany's Economic Unification: An Assessment after Ten Years." *Review of International Economics* 10, no. 1 (2002): 113–128.

Torpey, John S. *Intellectuals, Socialism and Dissent: The East German Opposition and Its Legacy* (Minneapolis: University of Minnesota Press, 1995).

Whitney, Craig R. *Spy Trader* (New York: Times Books, 1993).

Wiesenthal, Helmut. "German Unification and 'Model Germany': An Adventure in Institutional Conservatism." *West European Politics* 26, no. 4 (October 2003): 37–58.

———. "Post Unification Dissatisfaction, or Why Are So Many East Germans Unhappy with the New Political System?" *German Politics* 7, no. 2 (August 1998): 1–30.

Yoder, Jennifer A. *From East Germans to Germans? The New Postcommunist Elites* (Durham, NC: Duke University Press, 2000).

Zatlin, Jonathan. *The Currency of Socialism: Money and Political Culture in East Germany* (Cambridge: Cambridge University Press, 2007).

———. "Hard Marks and Soft Revolutionaries: The Economics of Entitlement and the Debate on German Monetary Union, November 9, 1989–March 18, 1990." *German Politics and Society* 33 (Fall 1994).

CHAPTER 3: THE SOCIAL AND ECONOMIC SETTING

Adler, Marina A. "Child-Free and Unmarried: Changes in the Life Planning of Young East German Women." *Journal of Marriage and Family* 66, no. 4 (December 2004): 1170–1179.

Annesley, Claire. *Postindustrial Germany: Services, Technological Transformation and Knowledge in Unified Germany* (Manchester: Manchester University Press, 2004).

Berghahn, Volker. *The Americanization of West German Industry, 1945–1973* (New York: Cambridge University Press, 1987).

Bessel, Richard. "Eastern Germany as a Structural Problem in the Weimar Republic." *Social History* 3 (1978): 199–218.

Brettschneider, Frank. "From D-Mark to Euro: The Impact of Mass Media on Public Opinion in Germany." *German Politics* 12, no. 2 (August 2003): 45–64.

Brinkmann, Christian. "Unemployment in the Federal Republic of Germany: Recent Empirical Evidence." In *Unemployment: Theory, Policy and Structure*, ed. Peder J. Pedersen and Reinhard Lund (Berlin: Walter de Gruyter, 1987), 285–304.

Clement, Elizabeth. "The Abortion Debate in Unified Germany." In *Women and the Wende: Social Effects and Cultural Reflections of the German Unification Process*, ed. Elizabeth Tow and Janet Wharton (Amsterdam: Rodopi, 1994).

Conrad, Christopher, et al. "East German Fertility after Unification: Crisis or Adaptation?" *Population and Development Review* 22 (June 1996): 331–358.

Culpepper, Pepper. *The German Skills Machine: Sustaining Comparative Advantage in a Global Economy* (New York: Berghahn Books, 1999).

———. *Quiet Politics and Business Power: Corporate Control in Europe and Japan* (New York: Cambridge University Press, 2011).

Deeg, Richard. *Finance Capitalism Unveiled: Banks and the German Political Economy* (Ann Arbor: University of Michigan Press, 1999).

Ferree, Myra Marx. *Varieties of Feminism: German Gender Politics in Global Perspective* (Stanford, CA: Stanford University Press, 2012).

Franz, Gerhard. "Economic Aspirations, Well-Being and Political Support in Recession and Boom Periods: The Case of West Germany." *European Journal of Political Research* 14, nos. 1 and 2 (1986): 97–112.

Froese, Paul, and Steven Pfaff. "Explaining a Religious Anomaly: A Historical Analysis of Secularization in Eastern Germany." *Journal for the Scientific Study of Religion* 44, no. 4 (2005): 397–422.

Grahl, John, and Paul Teague. "Labour Market Flexibility in West Germany, Britain and France." *West European Politics* 12, no. 2 (April 1989): 91–111.

Grossman, Atina. *Reforming Sex: The German Movement for Birth Control and Abortion Reform, 1920–1950* (New York: Oxford University Press, 1995).

Hall, Peter, and Soskice, David, eds. *Varieties of Capitalism: The Institutional Foundations of Comparative Advantage* (New York: Oxford University Press, 2001).

Heineman, Elizabeth. *What Difference Does a Husband Make? Women and Marital Status in Nazi and Postwar Germany* (Berkeley: University of California Press, 1999).

Herrigel, Gary. *Industrial Constructions: The Source of German Industrial Power* (New York: Cambridge University Press, 1996).

———. *Manufacturing Possibilities: Creative Action and Industrial Recomposition in the United States, Germany, and Japan* (Oxford: Oxford University Press, 2010).

Herzog, Dagmar. *Sex after Fascism: Memory and Morality in Twentieth-Century Germany* (Princeton, NJ: Princeton University Press, 2005).

Huelshoff, Michael G. "Corporatist Bargaining and International Politics." *Comparative Political Studies* 25, no. 1 (April 1992): 3–25.

Hughes, Michael L. *Shouldering the Burdens of Defeat: West Germany and the Reconstruction of Social Justice* (Chapel Hill: University of North Carolina Press, 1999).

Jacoby, Wade. *Imitation and Politics: Redesigning Modern Germany* (Ithaca, NY: Cornell University Press, 2000).

Kolinsky, Eva. *Women in West Germany: Life, Work and Politics* (New York: Berg Publishers, 1989).

Mayer, Karl Ulrich, and Steffen Hillmert. "New Ways of Life or Old Rigidities? Changes in Social Structures and Life Courses and Their Political Impact." *Western European Politics* 26, no. 4 (October 2003): 79–100.

Mintrop, Heinrich. "Teachers and Changing Authority Patterns in Eastern German Schools." *Comparative Education Review* 40, no. 4 (1996).

Mitter, Wolfgang. "Educational Adjustments and Perspectives in a United Germany." *Comparative Education* 28, no. 1 (1992): 45–52.

———. "Educational Reform in West and East Germany in European Perspective." *European Journal of Education* 26, no. 2 (1991): 155–165.

Moeller, Robert. *Protecting Motherhood: Women and the Family in the Politics of Postwar West Germany* (Berkeley: University of California Press, 1993).

Nicholls, A. J. *Freedom with Responsibility: The Social Market Economy in Germany, 1918–1963* (New York: Oxford University Press, 1994).

Peck, Jeffrey. *Being Jewish in the New Germany* (New Brunswick: Rutgers University Press, 2006).

Pollak, Detlef. "The Change in Religion and Church in Eastern Germany after 1989: A Research Note." *Sociology of Religion* 63, no. 3 (2002): 373–387.

Pritchard, Rosalind. "Education Transformed? The East German School System since the Wende." In *Recasting East Germany: Social Transformation after the GDR*, ed. Chris Flockton and Eva Kolinsky (London: Frank Cass, 1999), 126–146.

Puaca, Brian. *Learning Democracy: Education Reform in West Germany, 1945–1965* (New York: Berghahn Books, 2009).

Reich, Simon. *The Fruits of Fascism* (Ithaca, NY: Cornell University Press, 1990).

Schelsky, Helmut. "The Family in Germany." *Marriage and Family Living* 16, no. 4 (November 1954): 330–342.

Schoenbaum, David. *Hitler's Social Revolution* (New York: Doubleday, 1996).

Silvia, Stephen J. *Reinventing the German Economy*, Policy Report No. 8. American Institute for Contemporary German Studies, Washington, DC, 2003.

Smyser, William R. *The German Economy*. (New York: St. Martin's, 1993).

———. *How Germans Negotiate: Logical Goals, Practical Solutions* (Washington, DC: U.S. Institute of Peace Press, 2003).

Streeck, Wolfgang. *Re-forming Capitalism: Institutional Change in the German Political Economy* (Oxford: Oxford University Press, 2009).

Turner, Lowell, ed. *Negotiating the New Germany: Can Social Partnership Survive?* (Ithaca, NY: Cornell University Press, 1998).

Williams, Arthur. "Pluralism in the West German Media: The Press, Broadcasting and Cable." *West European Politics* 8, no. 2 (April 1985): 84–103.

CHAPTER 4: POLITICAL CULTURE, PARTICIPATION, AND CIVIL LIBERTIES

Art, David. *The Politics of the Nazi Past in Germany and Austria* (Cambridge: Cambridge University Press, 2006).

Aust, Stefan. *The Baader-Meinhof Group* (London: Bodley Head, 1986).

Baker, Kendall L., Russell Dalton, and Kai Hildebrandt. *Germany Transformed: Political Culture and the New Politics* (Cambridge, MA: Harvard University Press, 1981).

Banaszak, Lee Ann. "East-West Differences in German Abortion Opinion." *Public Opinion Quarterly* 62, no. 4 (Winter 1998): 545–582.

Bauer-Kaase, Petra, and Max Kaase. "Five Years of Unification: The Germans on the Path to Inner Unity?" *German Politics* 5, no. 1 (April 1996): 1–25.

Becker, Jillian. *Hitler's Children: The Story of the Baader-Meinhof Terrorist Gang* (Philadelphia, PA: Lippincott, 1977).

Berg-Schlosser, Dirk, and Ralf Rytlewski. *Political Culture in Germany* (Oxford: Berg Publishers, 1993).

Braunthal, Gerard. *Political Loyalty and Public Service in West Germany* (Amherst: University of Massachusetts Press, 1990).

Brubaker, Rogers. *Citizenship and Nationhood in France and Germany* (Cambridge, MA: Harvard University Press, 1992).

Bunn, Ronald F. *German Politics and the Spiegel Affair* (Baton Rouge: Louisiana State University Press, 1968).

Campbell, William Ross. "Political Support and Social Capital: A Re-Assessment of the Putnam Thesis in East and West Germany." *German Politics* 20, no. 4 (2011): 568–590.

———. "Social Capital and Democratic Attitudes: Re-Examining the Social Foundations of Democracy in Germany." *Debatte: Journal of Contemporary Central and Eastern Europe* 18, no. 3 (2010): 259–280.

———. "Socialist Values and Political Participation: A Barrier to 'Inner Unity'?" *West European Politics* 34 no. 2 (2011): 362–383.

———. "The Sources of Institutional Trust in East and West Germany: Civic Culture or Economic Performance?" *German Politics* 13, no. 3 (September 2004): 401–418.

Clark, John A., and Jerome S. Legge Jr. "Economics, Racism and Attitudes toward Immigration in the New Germany." *Political Research Quarterly* 50, no. 4 (December 1997): 901–917.

Conradt, David P. "Changing German Political Culture." In *The Civic Culture Revisited*, ed. Gabriel A. Almond and Sidney Verba (Boston: Little, Brown, 1980), 212–272 (1989 Reprint: Sage Publications).

———. "From Output Orientations to Regime Support: Changing German Political Culture." In *Social and Political Structures in West Germany*, ed. Ursula Hoffmann-Lange (Boulder, CO: Westview Press, 1991), 127–142.

———. "Political Culture and Identity: The Post-Unification Search for 'Inner Unity.'" In *Developments in German Politics*, ed. Stephen Padgett et al., vol. 3 (New York: Palgrave Macmillan, 2003), 269–287.

———. "Political Culture in Unified Germany: The First Ten Years." *German Politics and Society* 20, no. 2 (Summer 2002): 43–74.

———. "Political Culture in Unified Germany: Will the Bonn Republic Survive and Thrive in Berlin?" *German Studies Review* 21, no. 1 (February 1998): 83–104.

———. "Political Culture, Legitimacy and Participation." *West European Politics* 4, no. 2 (May 1981): 18–34.

———. "Putting Germany Back Together Again: The Great Social Experiment of Unification." In *Germany in a New Era*, ed. Gary L. Geipel (Indianapolis, IN: Hudson Institute, 1993), 3–17.

———. "West Germany: A Remade Political Culture?" *Comparative Political Studies* 7, no. 2 (July 1974): 222–238.

Cooper, Alice Holmes. *Paradoxes of Peace: German Peace Movements since 1945* (Ann Arbor: University of Michigan Press, 1996).

———. "Public-Good Movements and the Dimensions of Political Process: German Peace Movements since 1945." *Comparative Political Studies* 29, no. 3 (June 1996): 267–289.

Currie, David P. *The Constitution of the Federal Republic of Germany* (Chicago: University of Chicago Press, 1994).

Cusack, Thomas R. "The Shaping of Popular Satisfaction with Government and Regime Performance in Germany." *British Journal of Political Science* 29, no. 4 (October 1999): 641–672.

Dahrendorf, Ralf. *Society and Democracy in Germany* (New York: Doubleday, 1969).

Dalton, Russell J. "Communists and Democrats: Democratic Attitudes in the Two Germanies." *British Journal of Political Science* 24, no. 4 (October 1994): 469–493.

Diskant, James A. "Scarcity, Survival and Local Activism: Miners and Steelworkers, Dortmund 1945–1948." *Journal of Contemporary History* 24, no. 4 (October 1989): 547–574.

Dyson, Kenneth H. F. "Anti-Communism in the Federal Republic of Germany: The Case of the 'Berufsverbot,'" *Parliamentary Affairs* 27, no. 2 (January 1975): 51–67.

Esser, Frank, and Uwe Hartung. "Nazis, Pollution and No Sex: Political Scandals as a Reflection of Political Culture in Germany." *American Behavioral Scientist* 47, no. 8 (April 2004): 1040–1071.

Faist, Thomas. "How to Define a Foreigner? The Symbolic Politics of Immigration in German Partisan Discourse, 1978–1992." *West European Politics* 17, no. 2 (April 1994): 50–71.

Fehrenbach, Heide. *Cinema in Democratizing Germany* (Chapel Hill: University of North Carolina Press, 1996).

Ferree, Myra Marx, et al. *Shaping Abortion Discourse: Democracy and the Public Sphere in Germany and the United States* (New York: Cambridge University Press, 2002).

Fetzer, Joel S. "Religious Minorities and Support for Immigrant Rights in the United States, France and Germany." *Journal for the Scientific Study of Religion* 37 (1998): 41–49.

Franz, Gerhard. "Economic Aspirations, Well-Being and Political Support in Recession and Boom Periods: The Case of West Germany." *European Journal of Political Research* 14, nos. 1 and 2 (1986): 97–112.

Fuchs, Dieter. "The Democratic Culture of Unified Germany." In *Critical Citizens*, ed. Pippa Norris (New York: Oxford University Press, 1999), 123–145.

Fulbrook, Mary. "The State and the Transformation of Political Legitimacy in East and West Germany since 1945." *Comparative Studies in Society and History* 29, no. 2 (April 1987): 211–244.

Glaeser, Andreas. *Divided in Unity: Identity, Germany and the Berlin Police* (Chicago: University of Chicago Press, 2002).

Green, Simon. "Immigration, Asylum and Citizenship in Germany: The Impact of Unification and the Berlin Republic." *West European Politics* 24, no. 4 (October 2001): 82–104.

———. *The Politics of Exclusion: Institutions and Immigration Policy in Contemporary Germany* (Manchester: Manchester University Press, 2004).

Hager, Carol J. *Technological Democracy: Bureaucracy and Citizenry in the German Energy Debate* (Ann Arbor: University of Michigan Press, 1995).

Halfmann, Jost. "Immigration and Citizenship in Germany: Contemporary Dilemmas." *Political Studies* 45, no. 2 (June 1997): 260–274.

Hanshew, Karrin. *Terror and Democracy in West Germany* (Cambridge: Cambridge University Press, 2012).

Hartmann, Heinz. *Authority and Organization in German Management* (Princeton, NJ: Princeton University Press, 1959).

Haug, Frigga. "The Women's Movement in West Germany." *New Left Review*, no. 195 (January/February 1986): 59ff.

Helm, Jutta A. "Citizen Lobbies in West Germany." In *Western European Party Systems*, ed. Peter H. Merkl (New York: Free Press, 1980), 576–596.

Herf, Jeffrey. "War, Peace and Intellectuals: The West German Peace Movement." *International Security* 10, no. 4 (Spring 1986): 172–200.

Hoffmann-Lange, Ursula, ed. *Social and Political Structures in West Germany: From Authoritarianism to Postindustrial Democracy* (Boulder, CO: Westview Press, 1991).

Jarausch, Konrad. *After Hitler: Recivilizing Germans, 1945–1995* (Oxford: Oxford University Press, 2006).

Jennings, M. Kent. "The Variable Nature of Generational Conflict: Some Examples from West Germany." *Comparative Political Studies* 9, no. 2 (July 1976): 171–188.

Karapin, Roger. "Antiminority Riots in Unified Germany." *Comparative Politics* 34, no. 2 (January 2002): 147–167.

———. "Explaining Far-Right Electoral Success in Germany: The Politicization of Immigration-Related Issues." *German Politics and Society* 16, no. 3 (Fall 1998): 24–61.

Katzenstein, Peter J. *West Germany's Internal Security Policy: State and Violence in the 1970s and 1980s* (Ithaca, NY: Cornell University Press, 1990).

Klausen, Jytte. *The Islamic Challenge: Politics and Religion in Western Europe* (New York: Oxford University Press, 2007).

Klingemann, Hans-Dieter, and Richard I. Hofferbert. "Germany: A New 'Wall in the Mind'?" *Journal of Democracy* 5, no. 1 (January 1994): 30–44.

Klopp, Brett. *German Multiculturalism* (Boulder, CO: Praeger Publishers, 2002).

Kolinsky, Eva. "Terrorism in West Germany." In *The Threat of Terrorism*, ed. Juliet Lodge (Boulder, CO: Westview Press, 1988).

Krieger, Leonard. *The German Idea of Freedom* (Chicago: University of Chicago Press, 1957).

Kurthen, Hermann, Werner Bergman, and Rainer Erb. *Antisemitism and Xenophobia in Germany after Unification* (London: Oxford University Press, 1997).

Kvistad, Greg. *The Rise and Demise of German Statism: Loyalty and Political Membership* (Providence, RI: Berghahn Books, 1999).

Langenbacher, Eric. "From an Unmasterable to a Mastered Past: The Impact of History and Memory in the Federal Republic of Germany." *The Federal Republic at 60*, special issue of *German Politics* 19, no. 1 (2010): 24–40.

———. "The Mastered Past? Collective Memory Trends in Germany since Unification." *German Politics and Society* 28, no. 1 (Spring 2010): 42–68.

Langguth, Gerd. "Origins and Aims of Terrorism in Europe." *Aussenpolitik* 37, no. 2 (1986): 163–175.

Lederer, Gerda. "Trends in Authoritarianism: A Study of Adolescents in West Germany and the United States since 1945." *Journal of Cross-Cultural Psychology* 13, no. 3 (September 1982): 299–314.

Lepsius, M. Rainer. "The Nation and Nationalism in Germany." *Social Research* 52, no. 1 (Spring 1985): 43–64.

Lutz, Felix Philipp. "Evolution and Normalization: Historical Consciousness in Germany." *German Politics and Society* 30, no. 3 (Autumn 2012): 35–63.

———. "Historical Consciousness and the Changing of German Political Culture." *German Politics* 11, no. 3 (December 2002): 19–34.

McKay, Joanna. "Women in German Politics: Still Jobs for the Boys?" *German Politics* 13, no. 1 (March 2004): 56–80.

Merritt, Richard L. *Democracy Imposed: U.S. Occupation Policy and the German Public, 1945–1949* (New Haven, CT: Yale University Press, 1995).

———. "The Student Protest Movement in West Berlin." *Comparative Politics* 1, no. 4 (July 1969): 516–533.

Meulemann, Heiner. "Value Change in West Germany, 1950–1980: Integrating the Empirical Evidence." *Social Science Information* 22, nos. 4 and 5 (1983): 777–800.

———. "Value Changes in Germany after Unification: 1990–1995." *German Politics* 6, no. 1 (April 1997): 122–139.

Minkenberg, Michael. "Learning Democracy: Do Democratic Values Adjust to New Institutions?" In *Political Culture in Post-Communist Europe*, ed. Detlef Pollack et al. (Aldershot: Ashgate, 2003), 47–70.

———. "The Radical Right in Public Office: Agenda-Setting and Policy Effects." *West European Politics* 24, no. 4 (October 2001): 1–21.

———. "The Wall after the Wall: On the Continuing Division of Germany and the Remaking of Political Culture." *Comparative Politics* 26, no. 1 (October 1993): 53–68.

Moeller, Robert G. *War Stories: The Search for a Usable Past in the Federal Republic of Germany* (Berkeley: University of California Press, 2001).

Mushaben, Joyce Marie. *The Changing Faces of Citizenship: Social Integration and Political Mobilization among Ethnic Minorities in Germany* (New York: Berghahn Books, 2008).

———. *From Post-War to Post-Wall Generations: Changing Attitudes toward the National Question and NATO in the Federal Republic of Germany* (Boulder, CO: Westview Press, 1998).

Nelkin, Dorothy, and Michael Pollak. *The Atom Besieged: Extraparliamentary Dissent in France and Germany* (Cambridge: MIT Press, 1981).

Neumann, Erich Peter, and Elisabeth Noelle-Neumann. *The Germans, 1947–1966* (Allensbach am Bodensee: Verlag für Demoskopie, 1967).

Noelle-Neumann, Elisabeth. *The Germans: Public Opinion Polls, 1967–1980* (Westport, CT: Greenwood Press, 1981).

———. "Problems with Democracy in Eastern Germany after the Downfall of the GDR." In *Research on Democracy and Society*, ed. Frederick D. Weil, vol. 2 (New York: JAI Press, 1994), 213–231.

O'Brien, Peter. *Beyond the Swastika* (London: Routledge, 1996).

Olick, Jeffrey K., and Daniel Levy. "Collective Memory and the Culture of Constraint: Holocaust Myth and Rationality in German Politics." *American Sociological Review* 62 (December 1997): 921–936.

Oppenheim, A. N. *Civic Education and Participation in Democracy* (Beverly Hills, CA: Sage, 1977).

Pollack, Detlef. "Support for Democracy in Eastern and Western Germany." *Archives of European Sociology* 45, no. 2 (2004): 257–272.

Rabinbach, Anson, and Jack Zipes, eds. *Germans and Jews since the Holocaust* (New York: Holmes and Meier, 1986).

Rist, Ray C. *Guestworkers in Germany: The Prospects for Pluralism* (New York: Praeger, 1978).

Rogowski, Ronald. *Rational Legitimacy: A Theory of Political Support* (Princeton, NJ: Princeton University Press, 1974).

Rohrschneider, Robert. *Learning Democracy: Democratic and Economic Values in Unified Germany* (Oxford: Oxford University Press, 1999).

———. "Report from the Laboratory: The Influence of Institutions on Political Elites' Democratic Values in Germany." *American Political Science Review* 88, no. 4 (December 1994): 927–941.

Rohrschneider, Robert, and Rüdiger Schmitt-Beck. "Trust in Democratic Institutions in Germany: Theory and Evidence Ten Years after Unification." *German Politics* 11, no. 3 (December 2002): 35–58.

Rucht, Dieter, and Jochen Roose. "Neither Decline nor Sclerosis: The Organizational Structure of the German Environmental Movement." *West European Politics* 24, no. 4 (October 2001): 55–81.

Sa'adah, M. Anne. *Germany's Second Chance: Trust, Justice and Democratization* (Cambridge, MA: Harvard University Press, 1998).

Schmid-Drüner, Marion. "Germany's New Immigration Law: A Paradigm Shift?" *European Journal of Migration and Law* 8, no. 2 (July 2006): 191–214.

Schmidt, Rüdiger. "From 'Old Politics' to 'New Politics': Three Decades of Peace Protest in West Germany." In *Contemporary Political Culture: Politics in a Post-modern Age*, ed. John R. Gibbins (Beverly Hills, CA: Sage, 1989), 174–198.

Schönwälder, Karen. "Why Germany's Guestworkers Were Largely Europeans: The Selective Principles of Post-war Labour Recruitment Policy." *Ethnic and Racial Studies* 27, no. 2 (March 2004): 248–265.

Schram, Glenn. "Ideology and Politics: The *Rechtsstaat* Idea in West Germany." *Journal of Politics* 33 (February 1971): 133–157.

Schweigler, Gebhard. "Anti-Americanism in Germany." *Washington Quarterly* 9, no. 1 (Winter 1986): 67–84.

———. *National Consciousness in Divided Germany* (Beverly Hills, CA: Sage, 1975).

Stern, Fritz. *The Failure of Illiberalism: Essays on the Political Culture of Modern Germany* (Chicago: University of Chicago Press, 1975).

Stoess, Richard. "The Problem of Right-Wing Extremism in West Germany." *West European Politics* 11, no. 2 (April 1988): 34–46.

Szabo, Stephen F. *The Successor Generation: International Perspectives of Postwar Europeans* (London: Butterworths, 1983).

Verba, Sidney. "Germany: The Remaking of Political Culture." In *Political Culture and Political Development*, ed. Sidney Verba and Lucien Pye (Princeton, NJ: Princeton University Press, 1965), 130–170.

Wahl, Angelika von. "Gender Equality in Germany: Comparing Policy Change across Domains." *West European Politics* 29, no. 3 (May 2006): 461–488.

Wegener, Bernd. "Solidarity, Justice, and Social Change: Germany's Ten Years of Unification." In *Political Culture in Post-Communist Europe*, ed. Detlef Pollack et al. (Aldershot: Ashgate, 2003), 207–230.

Weil, Frederick D. "Cohorts, Regimes, and the Legitimation of Democracy: West Germany since 1945." *American Sociological Review* 52, no. 3 (June 1987): 308–324.

———. "Tolerance of Free Speech in the United States and West Germany, 1970–1979: An Analysis of Public Opinion Survey Data." *Social Forces* 60, no. 4 (June 1982): 973–992.

Wittlinger, Ruth. *German National Identity in the Twenty-First Century: A Different Republic after All?* (New York: Palgrave Macmillan, 2010).

Young, Brigitte. *Triumph of the Fatherland: German Unification and the Marginalization of Women* (Ann Arbor: University of Michigan Press, 1998).

Zelle, Carsten. "Socialist Heritage or Current Unemployment: Why Do the Evaluations of Democracy and Socialism Differ between East and West Germans?" *German Politics* 8, no. 1 (May 1999): 1–20.

Zimmerman, Ekkart, and Thomas Saalfeld. "The Three Waves of West German Right-Wing Extremism." In *Encounters with the Contemporary Radical Right*, ed. Peter H. Merkl and Leonard Weinberg (Boulder, CO: Westview Press, 1993), 50–74.

CHAPTER 5: THE PARTY SYSTEM AND THE REPRESENTATION OF INTERESTS

Alexis, Marion. "Neo-Corporatism and Industrial Relations: The Case of the German Trade Unions." *West European Politics* 6, no. 1 (January 1983): 75–92.

Betz, Hans-Georg. "Politics of Resentment: Right-Wing Radicalism in West Germany." *Comparative Politics* 23, no. 1 (October 1990): 45–60.

———. "Value Change and Postmaterialist Politics." *Comparative Political Studies* 23, no. 2 (July 1990): 239–256.

Braunthal, Gerard. *The Federation of German Industry in Politics* (Ithaca, NY: Cornell University Press, 1965).

———. Right-Wing Extremism in Contemporary Germany (New York: Palgrave Macmillan, 2009).

———. "Social Democratic–Green Coalitions in West Germany: Prospects for a New Alliance." *German Studies Review* 9, no. 3 (October 1986): 569–597.

———. *The West German Social Democrats, 1969–1982: Profile of Party in Power* (Boulder, CO: Westview Press, 1983).

Breyman, Stephen. *Why Movements Fail: The West German Peace Movement, the SPD, and the INF Negotiations* (Boulder, CO: Westview Press, 1994).

Bürklin, Wilhelm P. "The German Greens: The Post-Industrial, Non-Established and the Party System." *International Political Science Review* 6, no. 4 (October 1985): 463–481.

———. "Governing Left Parties Frustrating the Radical Non-Established Left: The Rise and Inevitable Decline of the Greens." *European Journal of Political Research* 3, no. 2 (September 1987): 109–126.

———. "The Split between the Established and the Non-Established Left in Germany." *European Journal of Political Research* 13 (1985): 283–293.

Chalmers, Douglas A. *The Social Democratic Party of Germany* (New Haven, CT: Yale University Press, 1964).

Chandler, William M., and Alan Siaroff. "Postindustrial Politics in Germany and the Origins of the Greens." *Comparative Politics* 18, no. 3 (April 1986): 303–325.

Clemens, Clay. *Reluctant Realists: The CDU/CSU and West German Ostpolitik* (Durham, NC: Duke University Press, 1989).

Conradt, David P. "The End of an Era in West Germany." *Current History* 81 (1982): 405–408, 438.

———. "The Tipping Point: The 2005 Election and the De-consolidation of the Party System?" *German Politics and Society* 24, no. 1 (Spring 2006): 11–26.

———. *The West German Party System* (Beverly Hills, CA: Sage, 1972).

Cooper, Alice Holmes. "Party-Sponsored Protest and the Movement Society: The CDU/CSU Mobilises against Citizenship Law Reform." *German Politics* 11, no. 2 (August 2002): 88–104.

Davidson-Schmich, Louise. *Becoming Party Politicians: Eastern German State Legislators in the Decade following Democratization* (Notre Dame, IN: University of Notre Dame Press, 2006).

Doering, Herbert, and Gordon Smith, eds. *Party Government and Political Culture in Western Germany* (New York: St. Martin's, 1982).

Doerschler, Peter, and Lee Ann Banaszak. "Voter Support for the PDS over Time: Dissatisfaction, Ideology, Losers and East Identity." *Electoral Studies* 26 (2007): 359–370.

Edinger, Lewis J., and Kurt Schumacher. *A Study in Personality and Political Behavior* (Palo Alto: Stanford University Press, 1965).

Esser, Josef. "State, Business and Trade Unions in West Germany after the 'Political Wende.'" *West European Politics* 9, no. 2 (April 1986): 198–214.

Fichter, Michael. "From Transmission Belt to Social Partnership? The Case of Organized Labor in Eastern Germany." *German Politics and Society* 23 (1991): 1–19.

Fleckenstein, Timo. "The Politics of Labour Market Reforms and Social Citizenship in Germany." *West European Politics* 35, no. 4 (July 2012): 847–868.

Frankland, Gene E. "Green Politics and Alternative Economics." *German Studies Review* 11, no. 1 (February 1988): 111–132.

Frankland, Gene E., and Donald Schoonmaker. *Between Protest and Power: The Green Party in Germany* (Boulder, CO: Westview Press, 1992).

Gapper, Stuart. "The Rise and Fall of Germany's Party of Democratic Socialism." *German Politics* 12, no. 2 (August 2003): 65–85.

Heidenheimer, Arnold J. *Adenauer and the CDU* (The Hague: Martinus Nijhoff, 1960).

Hockenos, Paul. *Joschka Fischer and the Making of the Berlin Republic* (New York: Oxford University Press, 2007).

Hofferbert, Richard I., and Hans-Dieter Klingemann. "The Policy Impact of Party Programmes and Government Declarations in the Federal Republic of Germany." *European Journal of Political Research* 18, no. 3 (May 1990): 277–304.

Hough, Dan, Michael Koß, and Jonathan Olsen. *The Left Party in Contemporary German Politics* (New York: Palgrave Macmillan, 2007).

Joffe, Joseph. "A Peacenik Goes to War." *New York Times Magazine*, 30 May 1999.

Karapin, Roger. *Protest Politics in Germany: Movements on the Left and Right since the 1960s* (University Park: Pennsylvania State University Press, 2007).

Kirchheimer, Otto. "Germany: The Vanishing Opposition." In *Political Opposition in Western Democracies*, ed. Robert A. Dahl (New Haven, CT: Yale University Press, 1966), 237–259.

Kitschelt, Herbert. *The Transformation of European Social Democracy* (Cambridge: Cambridge University Press, 1994).

Koeble, Thomas A. "Trade Unionists, Party Activists, and Politicians: The Struggle for Power over Party Rules in the British Labour Party and the West German Social Democratic Party." *Comparative Politics* 19, no. 3 (April 1987): 253–266.

Linz, Juan. "Cleavage and Consensus in West German Politics: The Early Fifties." In *Party Systems and Voter Alignments: Cross-National Perspectives*, ed. S. M. Lipset and S. Rokkan (New York: Free Press, 1966), 283–316.

Markovits, Andrei S. *The Politics of West German Trade Unions* (New York: Cambridge University Press, 1986).

Markovits, Andrei S., and Philip S. Gorski. *The German Left: Red, Green and Beyond* (New York: Oxford University Press, 1993).

Minkenberg, Michael. "The New Right in Germany." *European Journal of Political Research* 22 (1992): 55–81.

Muller-Rommel, Ferdinand. "Social Movements and the Greens: New Internal Politics in Germany." *European Journal of Political Research* 13, no. 1 (March 1985): 53–67.

Padgett, Stephen. "The German Social Democratic Party: Between Old and New Left." In *Conflict and Cohesion in Western European Social Democratic Parties*, ed. David S. Bell and Eric Shaw (London: Pinter Publishers, 1994), 10–30.

———. *Organizing Democracy in Eastern Germany: Interest Groups in Post-Communist Society* (Cambridge: Cambridge University Press, 2000).

Patton, David. *Out of the East: From PDS to Left Party in Unified Germany* (Albany: State University of New York Press, 2011).

Poguntke, Thomas. *Alternative Politics: The German Green Party* (Edinburgh: Edinburgh University Press, 1993).

———, ed. The Europeanization of National Political Parties: Power and Organizational Adaptation (New York: Routledge, 2007).

Pridham, Geoffrey. *Christian Democracy in Western Germany* (New York: St. Martin's, 1977).

Pulzer, Peter G. J. "Responsible Party Government and Stable Coalition: The Case of the German Federal Republic." *Political Studies* 19 (1971): 1–17.

Rüdig, Wolfgang. "Is Government Good for Greens? Comparing the Electoral Effects of Government Participation in Western and East-Central Europe." *European Journal of Political Research* 45 (2006): 127–154.

Scarrow, Susan E. *Parties and Their Members: Organizing for Victory in Britain and Germany* (New York: Oxford University Press, 1996).

Scharpf, Fritz. *Crisis and Choice in European Social Democracy* (Ithaca, NY: Cornell University Press, 1991).

Silvia, Stephen J. "Left Behind: The Social Democratic Party in Eastern Germany." *West European Politics* 16, no. 2 (April 1993): 24–48.

———. "The West German Labor Law Controversy: A Struggle for the Factory of the Future." *Comparative Politics* 20, no. 2 (January 1988): 155–173.

Silvia, Stephen J., and Wolfgang Schroeder. "Why Are German Employer Associations Declining?" *Comparative Political Studies* 40 (December 2007): 1433–1459.

Sloam, James. *The European Policy of the German Social Democrats* (London: Palgrave Macmillan, 2005).

Spotts, Frederic. *The Churches and Politics in Germany* (Middletown: Wesleyan University Press, 1973).

Thelen, Kathleen A. *How Institutions Evolve: The Political Economy of Skills in Germany, Britain, the United States, and Japan* (Cambridge: Cambridge University Press, 2004).

———. *Union of Parts: Labor Politics in Postwar Germany* (Ithaca, NY: Cornell University Press, 1992).

Thelen, Kathleen, and Christa van Wijnbergen. "The Paradox of Globalization: Labor Relations in Germany and Beyond." *Comparative Political Studies* 36, no. 8 (October 2003): 859–880.

Westle, Bettina, and Oskar Niedermayer. "Contemporary Right-Wing Extremism in West Germany." *European Journal of Political Research* 22 (1992): 83–100.

Wilarty, Sarah. *The CDU and the Politics of Gender in Germany: Bringing Women to the Party* (New York: Cambridge University Press, 2010).

CHAPTER 6: ELECTIONS AND VOTING BEHAVIOR

Alexander, Herbert E., and Rei Shiratori. *Comparative Political Finance among the Democracies* (Boulder, CO: Westview Press, 1994).

Anderson, Christopher J., and Carsten Zelle, eds. *Stability and Change in German Elections* (Westport, CT: Praeger, 1998).

Anderson, Christopher, and Frank Brettschneider. "The Likable Winner versus the Competent Loser." *German Politics and Society* 21, no. 1 (Spring 2003): 95–118.

Barnes, S. H., et al. "The German Party System and the 1961 Federal Election." *American Political Science Review* 56 (1962): 899–914.

Becker, Rolf. "Political Efficacy and Voter Turnout in East and West Germany." *German Politics* 13, no. 2 (June 2004): 317–340.

Cerny, Karl, ed. *The Bundestag Elections of the 1980s* (Durham, NC: Duke University Press, 1990).

———. *West Germany at the Polls* (Washington, DC: American Enterprise Institute, 1978).

Chandler, William M. "Foreign and European Policy Issues in the 2002 Bundestag Elections." *German Politics and Society* 21, no. 1 (Spring 2003): 161–176.

Conradt, David P. "Unified Germany at the Polls." *German Issues*, no. 9. Washington, DC: American Institute for Contemporary German Studies, 1990.

Conradt, David P., and Russell J. Dalton. "The West German Electorate and the Party System: Continuity and Change in the 1980s." *Review of Politics* 50, no. 1 (January 1988): 3–29.

Conradt, David P., and Dwight Lambert. "Party System, Social Structure and Competitive Politics in West Germany." *Comparative Politics* 7, no. 1 (October 1974): 61–86.

Conradt, David P., et al., eds. *Germany's New Politics* (Providence, RI: Berghahn Books, 1995).

———. *Power Shift in Germany: The 1998 Federal Election and the End of the Kohl Era* (New York: Berghahn Books, 2000).

———. *Precarious Victory: The 2002 German National Election and Its Aftermath* (New York: Berghahn Books, 2004).

Culver, Lowell. *The Road to Democracy in Germany: The Role of State and National Elections, 1946–2011* (Lanham, MD: University Press of America, 2012).

Dalton, Russell, ed. *Germans Divided: The 1994 Bundestag Elections and the Evolution of the German Party System* (Oxford: Berg, 1996).

Edinger, Lewis J. "Political Change in Germany: The Federal Republic after the 1969 Election." *Comparative Politics* 2, no. 4 (July 1970): 549–578.

Fuchs, Dieter, and Robert Rohrschneider. "Postmaterialism and Electoral Choice before and after German Unification." *West European Politics* 21, no. 2 (April 1998): 95–116.

Gibson, Rachel K., et al. "German Parties and Internet Campaigning in the 2002 Federal Election." *German Politics* 12, no. 1 (August 2003): 79–108.

Gschwend, Thomas, et al. "Split Ticket Patterns in Mixed Member-Member Proportional Election Systems: Estimates and Analyses of Their Spatial Variations at the German Federal Election, 1998." *British Journal of Political Science* 33, no. 1 (January 2003): 109–128.

Helms, Ludger. "Germany's Crisis and Struggle for Political Self-Reinvention: The 2005 Federal Election in Context." *German Studies Review* 29, no. 2 (2006): 315–330.

Irving, R. E. M., and W. E. Paterson. "The Machtwechsel of 1982–83: A Significant Landmark in the Political and Constitutional History of West Germany." *Parliamentary Affairs* 36, no. 4 (Autumn 1983): 417–435.

———. "Split-Voting in the Federal Republic of Germany: An Analysis of the Federal Elections from 1953 to 1987." *Electoral Studies* 7 (1988): 109–124.

Jesse, Eckhard. "The West German Electoral System: The Case for Reform, 1949–1957." *West European Politics* 10, no. 3 (July 1987): 434–448.

Karp, Jeffrey. "Political Knowledge about Electoral Rules: Comparing Mixed Member Proportional Systems in Germany and New Zealand." *Electoral Studies* 25 (2006): 714–730.

Kitschelt, Herbert. "The 1990 German Federal Election and the National Unification." *West European Politics* 14, no. 1 (January 1991): 121–148.

———. "Political-Economic Context and Partisan Strategies in the German Federal Elections, 1990–2002." *West European Politics* 26, no. 4 (October 2003): 125–152.

Klingemann, Hans-Dieter, and Franz-Urban Pappi. "The 1969 Bundestag Election in the Federal Republic of Germany: An Analysis of Voting Behavior." *Comparative Politics* 2, no. 4 (July 1970): 523–548.

Klingemann, Hans-Dieter, and Bernhard Wessels. "The Political Consequences of Germany's Mixed-Member System: Personalization at the Grass Roots?" In *Mixed-Member Electoral Systems: The Best of Both Worlds?*, ed. Mathew S. Shugart and Martin P. Wattenberg (New York: Oxford University Press, 2001), 279–96.

König, Thomas, et al. "Policy Change without Government Change? German Gridlock after the 2002 Election." *German Politics* 12, no. 2 (August 2003): 86–146.

Kuechler, Manfred. "Maximizing Utility at the Polls?" *European Journal of Political Research* 14, nos. 1 and 2 (1986): 81–95.

Langenbacher, Eric, ed. *Between Left and Right: The 2009 Bundestag Elections and the Transformation of the German Party System* (New York: Berghahn Books, 2010).

———. *Launching the Grand Coalition: The 2005 Bundestag Election and the Future of German Politics* (New York: Berghahn Books, 2006).

Lees, Charles. *Party Politics in Germany: A Comparative Politics Approach* (New York: Palgrave Macmillan, 2005).

———. *The Red-Green Coalition in Germany: Politics, Personalities and Power* (Manchester: Manchester University Press, 2000).

Norpoth, Helmut. "Choosing a Coalition Partner: Mass Preference and Elite Decisions in West Germany." *Comparative Political Studies* 12 (1980): 424–440.

———. "The Making of a More Partisan Electorate in West Germany." *British Journal of Political Science* 14, no. 1 (January 1984): 52–71.

Pappi, Franz Urban, and P. W. Thurner. "Electoral Behaviour in a Two-Vote System: Incentives for Ticket Splitting in German Bundestag Elections." *European Journal of Political Research* 41, no. 2 (March 2002): 207–233.

Proksch, Sven-Oliver, and Jonathan B. Slapin. "Institutions and Coalition Formation: The German Election of 2005." *West European Politics* 29, no. 3 (May 2006): 540–559.

Pulzer, Peter. "The Devil They Know: The German Federal Election of 2002." *West European Politics* 26, no. 2 (April 2003): 153–164.

———. "Germany Votes for Deadlock: The Federal Election of 2005." *West European Politics* 29, no. 3 (May 2006): 560–572.

Rohrschneider, Robert, and Dieter Fuchs. "It Used to Be the Economy: Issues and Party Support in the 2002 Election." *German Politics and Society* 21, no. 1 (Spring 2003): 76–94.

Rüdiger, Schmitt-Beck, et al. "Shaky Attachments: Individual Level Stability and Change of Partisanship among West German Voters, 1984–2001." *European Journal of Political Research* 45 (2006): 581–608.

Rusciano, Frank Louis. "Rethinking the Gender Gap: The Case of West German Elections, 1949–1987." *Comparative Politics* 24, no. 3 (April 1992): 335–357.

Scarrow, Susan E. "Germany: The Mixed-Member System as a Political Compromise." In *Mixed Member Electoral Systems: The Best of Both Worlds?*, ed. Mathew S. Shugart and Martin P. Wattenberg (New York: Oxford University Press, 2001), 55–69.

Schoen, Harald. "Split-Ticket Voting in German Federal Elections, 1953–1990: An Example of Sophisticated Balloting?" *Electoral Studies* 18 (1999): 473–496.

Schrott, Peter R., and David J. Lanoue. "How to Win a Televised Debate: Candidate Strategies and Voter Response in Germany, 1972–87." *British Journal of Political Science* 22, no. 4 (October 1992): 445–467.

Semetko, Holly, and Klaus Schönbach. *Germany's Unity Election, Voters, and the Media* (Cresskill: Hampton Press, 1994).

Wahl, Angelika von. "Gender Equality in Germany: Comparing Policy Change across Domains." *West European Politics* 29, no. 3 (May 2006): 461–488.

Walker, Nancy J. "What We Know about Women Voters in Britain, France, and West Germany." *Public Opinion* 11, no. 1 (May–June 1988): 49ff.

Wüst, Andreas M. "Naturalised Citizens as Voters: Behavior and Impact." *German Politics* 13, no. 2 (June 2004): 341–359.

CHAPTER 7: POLICY-MAKING INSTITUTIONS I: PARLIAMENT AND EXECUTIVE

Abenheim, Donald. *Reforging the Iron Cross: The Search for Tradition in the West German Armed Forces* (Princeton, NJ: Princeton University Press, 1988).

Alter, Alison B. "Minimizing the Risks of Delegation: Multiple Referral in the German Bundesrat." *American Journal of Political Science* 46, no. 2 (April 2002): 299–315.

Blondel, Jean, and Ferdinand Müller-Rommel, eds. *Cabinets in Western Europe* (London: Macmillan, 1988).

Braunthal, Gerard. "The Policy Function of the German Social Democratic Party." *Comparative Politics* 9, no. 2 (January 1977): 127–146.

Clemens, Clay. "The Chancellor as Manager: Helmut Kohl, the CDU and Governance in Germany." *West European Politics* 17, no. 4 (October 1994): 28–51.

Clemens, Clay, and W. E. Patterson, eds. *The Kohl Chancellorship* (London: Frank Cass, 1998).

Conradt, David P. "Chancellor Kohl's Center Coalition." *Current History* 85, no. 514 (November 1986): 357–360, 389–391.

Dyson, Kenneth H. F. "Chancellor Kohl as Strategic Leader: The Case of Economic and Monetary Union." *German Politics* 7, no. 1 (1998): 37–63.

———. *Party, State and Bureaucracy in Western Germany* (Beverly Hills, CA: Sage, 1978).

Green, Simon, and William E. Paterson. *Governance in Contemporary Germany* (New York: Cambridge University Press, 2005).

Helms, Ludger, ed. *Institutions and Institutional Change in the Federal Republic of Germany* (New York: St. Martin's, 2000).

Herspring, Dale R. *Requiem for an Army* (Lanham, MD: Rowman and Littlefield, 1998).

Janes, Jackson, and Stephen Szabo. "Angela Merkel's Germany." *Current History* 106 (March 2007): 106–111.

Jelen, Ted G., and Clyde Wilcox. "Context and Conscience: The Catholic Church as an Agent of Political Socialization in Western Europe." *Journal for the Scientific Study of Religion* 37 (1998): 28–48.

Kim, Dong-Hun, and Gerhard Loewenberg. "The Role of Parliamentary Committees in Coalition Governments." *Comparative Political Studies* 38, no. 9 (November 2005): 1104–1129.

Kitschelt, Herbert, and Wolfgang Streeck. *Germany: Beyond the Welfare State* (London: Frank Cass, 2004).

Kolinsky, Eva. "Political Participation and Parliamentary Careers: Women's Quotas in West Germany." *West European Politics* 14, no. 1 (January 1991): 56–72.

König, Thomas. "Bicameralism and Party Politics in Germany: An Empirical Social Choice Analysis." *Political Studies* 49, no. 3 (August 2001): 411–437.

Korte, Karl-Rudolf. "The Art of Power: The 'Kohl System,' Leadership, and *Deutschlandpolitik*." *German Politics* 7, no. 1 (April 1998): 64–90.

Large, David Clay. *Germans to the Front: West German Rearmament in the Adenauer Era* (Chapel Hill: University of North Carolina Press, 1996).

Livingston, Robert Gerald. "Life after Kohl?" *Foreign Affairs* (November/December 1997): 1–6.

Loewenberg, Gerhard. *Parliament in the German Political System* (Ithaca, NY: Cornell University Press, 1966).

Longhurst, Kerry. "Why Aren't the Germans Debating the Draft? Path Dependency and the Persistence of Conscription." *German Politics* 12, no. 2 (August 2003): 147–165.

Messina, Anthony M. "West Germany's Grand Coalition as a Window on the Dynamics of Noncompetitive Parliamentary Government." *German Politics and Society* 13, no. 2 (Summer 1995): 60–80.

Muller-Rommel, Ferdinand. "The Centre of Government in West Germany: Changing Patterns Under 14 Legislatures (1949–1987)." *European Journal of Political Research* 16, no. 2 (March 1988): 171–190.

Patzelt, Werner J. "Chancellor Schröder's Approach to Political and Legislative Leadership." *German Politics* 13, no. 2 (May 2004): 268–299.

Rohrschneider, Robert. "Pluralism, Conflict, and Legislative Elites in United Germany." *Comparative Politics* 29, no. 1 (October 1996): 43–68.

Saalfeld, Thomas. "The West German Bundestag after 40 Years: The Role of Parliament in a 'Party Democracy,'" In *Parliaments in Western Europe*, ed. Philip Norton (London: Frank Cass, 1991), 68–89.

Schmidt, Manfred G. *Political Institutions in the Federal Republic of Germany* (Oxford: Oxford University Press, 2003).

Schüttemeyer, Suzanne S. "Hierarchy and Efficiency in the Bundestag: The German Answer for Institutionalizing Parliament." In *Parliaments in the Modern World*, ed. Gary W. Copeland and Samuel C. Patterson (Ann Arbor: University of Michigan Press, 1994), 29–58.

Silvia, Stephen J. "Reform Gridlock and the Role of the Bundesrat in German Politics." *West European Politics* 22, no. 2 (April 1999): 167–181.

Smale, Alison. "The Making of Angela Merkel." *International Herald Tribune*, 30 October 2012.

Smith, Gordon. "The Resources of a German Chancellor." *West European Politics* 14, no. 2 (April 1991): 48–61.

Stratman, Thomas, and Martin Baur. "Plurality Rule, Proportional Representation, and the German *Bundestag*: How Incentives to Pork-Barrel Differ across Electoral Systems." *American Journal of Political Science* 46, no. 3 (July 2002): 506–514.

Szabo, Stephen, and Mary N. Hampton. *Reinventing the German Military* (Washington, DC: American Institute for Contemporary German Studies, 2003).

Thaysen, Uwe. *The Bundesrat, the Länder and German Federalism* (Washington, DC: American Institute for Contemporary German Studies, 1994).

Von Beyme, Klaus. *The Legislator: German Parliament as a Centre of Political Decision-Making* (Aldershot: Ashgate, 1998).

Wise, Michael Z. *A Capital Dilemma: Germany's Search for a New Architecture of Democracy* (New York: Princeton Architectural Press, 1998).

CHAPTER 8: POLICY-MAKING INSTITUTIONS II: ADMINISTRATION, SEMIPUBLIC INSTITUTIONS, AND COURTS

Aberbach, Joel, et al. "American and German Federal Executives—Technocratic and Political Attitudes." *International Social Science Journal*, no. 123 (February 1990): 3–18.

——. *Bureaucrats and Politicians in Western Democracies* (Cambridge, MA: Harvard University Press, 1981).

Alber, Jens. "Germany: The Western European Welfare States since World War II." In *Growth to Limits*, ed. Peter Flora, vol. 2 (Berlin: Walter de Gruyter, 1988), 1–154.

Baird, Vanessa A., and Alan Stone. "Why Privatization: The Case of German Telecommunications." *Social Science Quarterly* 79, no. 1 (March 1998): 193–211.

Blankenburg, Erhard. "Changes in Political Regimes and Continuity of the Rule of Law in Germany." In *Courts, Law and Politics in Comparative Perspective*, ed. Herbert Jacob (New Haven, CT: Yale University Press, 1996).

Blum, Ulrich, and Jan Siegmund. "Politics and Economics of Privatizing State Enterprises: The Case of *Treuhandanstalt*." *Governance* 6, no. 3 (July 1993): 397–408.

Busemeyer, Marius R. "Pension Reform in Germany and Austria." *West European Politics* 28, no. 3 (May 2005): 569–591.

Caygill, Howard, and Alan Scott. "Basic Law versus the Basic Norm? The Case of the Bavarian Crucifix Order." *Political Studies* 44 (1996): 505–516.

Clasen, Jochen. *Reforming European Welfare States* (New York: Oxford University Press, 2007).

Clemens, Clay, and William E. Paterson, eds. *German Politics: Special Issue on the Kohl Chancellorship* 7, no. 1 (April 1998): 64–90.

Derlien, Hans-Ulrich. "Repercussions of Government Change on the Career Civil Service in West Germany: The Cases of 1969 and 1982." *Governance* 1, no. 1 (1988): 50–78.

Duckenfield, Mark. "Bundesbank-Government Relations in Germany in the 1990s: From GEMU to EMU." *West European Politics* 22, no. 3 (July 1999): 87–108.

———. "The Goldkrieg: Revaluing the Bundesbank's Reserves and the Politics of EMU." *German Politics* 8, no. 1 (April 1999): 106–130.

Frowen, Stephen F., and Robert Pringle, eds. *Inside the Bundesbank* (New York: St. Martin's, 1998).

Gibson, James L., et al. "On the Legitimacy of National High Courts." *American Political Science Review* 92, no. 2 (June 1998): 343–358.

Goetz, Klaus. "Rebuilding Public Administration in the New German Länder: Transfer and Differentiation." *West European Politics* 16, no. 4 (October 1993): 447–469.

Goodman, John B. *Monetary Sovereignty* (Ithaca, NY: Cornell University Press, 1992).

Hager, Carol J. *Technological Democracy: Bureaucracy and Citizenry in the German Energy Debate* (Ann Arbor: University of Michigan Press, 1995).

Heisenberg, Dorothee. *The Mark of the Bundesbank: Germany's Role in European Monetary Cooperation* (Boulder, CO: Lynne Rienner, 1999).

Herz, John H. "Political Views of the West German Civil Service." In *West German Leadership and Foreign Policy*, ed. Hans Speier and W. Phillips Davison (Evanston, IL: Row, Peterson, 1957), 96–135.

Johnson, Nevil. "The Interdependence of Law and Politics: Judges and the Constitution in West Germany." *West European Politics* 5, no. 3 (July 1982): 236–252.

Kaltenthaler, Karl. "Central Bank Independence and the Commitment to Monetary Stability: The Case of the German Bundesbank." *German Politics* 7, no. 2 (1998): 102–127.

———. *Germany and the Politics of Europe's Money* (Durham, NC: Duke University Press, 1997).

———. "The Restructuring of the German Bundesbank: The Politics of Institutional Change." *German Politics and Society* 14, no. 4 (1996): 23–48.

Katzenstein, Peter J. *Policy and Politics in West Germany: The Growth of a Semi-Sovereign State* (Philadelphia: Temple University Press, 1987).

Kennedy, Ellen. *The Bundesbank* (New York: Council on Foreign Relations Press, 1991).

Kommers, Donald P. *The Constitutional Jurisprudence of the Federal Republic of Germany* (Durham, NC: Duke University Press, 1989).

———. *The Federal Constitutional Court* (Washington, DC: American Institute for Contemporary German Studies, 1994).

———. *Judicial Politics in West Germany: A Study of the Federal Constitutional Court*. (Beverly Hills, CA: Sage, 1976).

König, Klaus. "Bureaucratic Integration by Elite Transfer: The Case of the Former GDR." *Governance* 6, no. 3 (July 1993): 386–396.

Kvistad, Gregg O. "Accommodation or 'Cleansing': Germany's State Employees from the Old Regime." *West European Politics* 17, no. 4 (October 1994): 52–73.

Loedel, Peter Henning. *Deutsche Mark Politics: Germany in the European Monetary System* (Boulder, CO: Lynne Rienner, 1999).

Lohmann, Susanne. "Federalism and Central Bank Independence: The Politics of German Monetary Policy, 1957–92." *World Politics* 50, no. 3 (April 1998): 401–446.

Marsh, David. *The Most Powerful Bank: Inside Germany's Bundesbank* (New York: Times Books, 1992).

Mayntz, Renate. "German Federal Bureaucrats: A Functional Elite between Politics and Administration." In *Higher Civil Servants in the Policymaking Process: A Comparative Exploration*, ed. Ezra Suleiman (New York: Holmes and Meier, 1983), 145–174.

———. "The Higher Civil Service of the Federal Republic of Germany." In *The Higher Civil Service in Europe and Canada*, ed. Bruce L. R. Smith (Washington, DC: Brookings Institution, 1984), 55–68.

Mayntz, Renate, and Hans-Ulrich Derlien. "Party Patronage and Politicization of the West German Administrative Elite, 1970–1987: Toward Hybridization?" *Governance* 2, no. 4 (October 1989): 384–404.

Mayntz, Renate, and Fritz W. Scharpf. *Policymaking in the German Federal Bureaucracy* (New York: Elsevier, 1975).

Putnam, Robert D. "The Political Attitudes of Senior Civil Servants in Western Europe: A Preliminary Report." *British Journal of Political Science* 3, no. 2 (July 1973): 257–290.

Rürup, Bert. "The German Pension System: Status Quo and Reform Options." In *Social Security Pension Reform in Europe*, ed. Martin Feldstein and Horst Siebert (Chicago: University of Chicago Press, 2002), 137–163.

Scharpf, Fritz W. "The Joint Decision Trap: Lessons from German Federalism and European Integration." *Public Administration* 66 (Autumn 1988): 239–278.

Seibel, Wolfgang, G. Grabher, and D. Stark. "Privatization by Means of State Bureaucracy? The Treuhand Phenomenon in Eastern Germany." In *Restructuring Networks in Post-Socialism: Legacies, Linkages, and Localities*, ed. Wolfgang Seibel et al. (Oxford: Oxford University Press, 1997), 284–305.

Sturm, Roland. "The Role of the Bundesbank in German Politics." *West European Politics* 12, no. 2 (April 1989): 1–11.

Whitney, Craig R. "Blaming the Bundesbank." *New York Times Magazine*, 17 October 1993, 19ff.

Woolley, John T. "Linking Political and Monetary Union: The Maastricht Agenda and German Domestic Politics." In *The Political Economy of European Monetary Unification*, ed. Barry Eichengreen and Jeffry Frieden (Boulder, CO: Westview Press, 1994), 67–86.

CHAPTER 9: SUBNATIONAL UNITS: FEDERALISM AND LOCAL GOVERNMENT

Bernt, Matthias. "Partnerships for Demolition: The Governance of Urban Renewal in East Germany's Shrinking Cities." *International Journal of Urban and Regional Research* 33, no. 3 (September 2009): 754–769.

Billerbeck, Rudolf. "Socialists in Urban Politics: The German Case." *Social Research* 47 (1980): 114–140.

Boehling, Rebecca. "U.S. Military Occupation, Grass Roots Democracy, and Local Government." In *American Policy and the Reconstruction of West Germany, 1945–1955*, ed. Harmut Lehmann (Cambridge: Cambridge University Press, 1993), 281–306.

Forgey, Benjamin. "Transforming Berlin." *Washington Post*, 9 January 2000, G1.

Fried, Robert C. "Party and Policy in West German Cities." *American Political Science Review* 70, no. 4 (March 1976): 11–24.

Gunlicks, Arthur B. "Administrative Centralization and Decentralization in the Making and Remaking of Modern Germany." *Review of Politics* 46, no. 3 (July 1984): 323–345.

———. *The Länder and German Federalism* (New York: Palgrave Macmillan, 2003).

————. *Local Government in the German Federal System* (Durham, NC: Duke University Press, 1986).

————. "German Federalism after Unification: The Legal/Constitutional Response." *Publius* 24, no. 2 (Spring 1994): 81–98.

————, ed. *German Public Policy and Federalism: Current Debates on Political, Legal, and Social Issues* (New York: Berghahn Books, 2003).

Häußermann, Hartmut. "Capitalist Futures and Socialist Legacies: Urban Development in East Germany since 1990." *German Politics and Society* 16, no. 4 (Winter 1998): 87–102.

Heidenheimer, Arnold J. "Federalism and the Party System: The Case of West Germany." *American Political Science Review* 52 (1958): 808–828.

Heisler, Barbara Schmitter. "Immigration and German Cities." *German Politics and Society* 16, no. 4 (Winter 1998): 18–41.

Hesse, Joachim J. "The Federal Republic of Germany: From Cooperative Federalism to Joint Policy-Making." *West European Politics* 10, no. 4 (October 1987): 70–87.

Jeffery, Charlie. "Party Politics and Territorial Representation in the Federal Republic of Germany." *West European Politics* 22, no. 2 (April 1999): 130–166.

Jeffery, Charlie, and Peter Savigear, eds. *German Federalism Today* (Leicester: Leicester University Press, 1991).

Karapin, Roger. "Protest and Reform in Asylum Policy: Citizen Initiatives versus Asylum Seekers in German Municipalities, 1989–1994." *German Politics and Society* 21, no. 2 (Summer 2003): 1–45.

Klatt, Hartmut. "Forty Years of German Federalism: Past Trends and New Developments." *Publius* 19, no. 4 (Fall 1989): 185–202.

Lehmbruch, Gerhard. "Party and Federation in Germany: A Developmental Dilemma." *Government and Opposition* 13 (1978): 151–177.

Lohmann, Susanne, et al. "Party Identification, Retrospective Voting, and Moderating Elections in a Federal System: West Germany, 1961–1989." *Comparative Political Studies* 30, no. 4 (August 1997): 420–449.

Pridham, Geoffrey. "A Nationalization Process? Federal Politics and State Elections in West Germany." *Government and Opposition* 8, no. 4 (Fall 1973): 455–473.

Strom, Elizabeth A. *Building the New Berlin: The Politics of Urban Development in Germany's Capital City* (Lanham, MD: Lexington Books, 2001).

Turner, Ed. *Political Parties and Public Policy in the German Länder* (New York: Palgrave Macmillan, 2011).

Umbach, Maiken. *German Federalism: Past, Present, Future* (New York: Palgrave Macmillan, 2002).

Wollmann, Hellmut. "Local Government and Politics in East Germany." *German Politics* 11, no. 3 (December 2002): 153–178.

Ziblatt, Daniel. *Structuring the State: The Formation of Italy and Germany and the Puzzle of Federalism* (Princeton, NJ: Princeton University Press, 2006).

CHAPTER 10: THE RETURN OF GERMAN POWER: THE FEDERAL REPUBLIC'S FOREIGN AND EUROPEAN POLICY

Anderson, Jeffrey J. *German Unification and European Union: The Domestic Politics of Integration Policy* (Cambridge: Cambridge University Press, 1999).

Asmus, Ronald D. *German Strategy and Public Opinion after the Wall, 1990–1993* (Santa Monica, CA: Rand Corporation, 1994).

———. "Is There a Peace Movement in the GDR?" *Orbis* 27, no. 2 (Summer 1983): 301–342.

Banchoff, Thomas. *The German Problem Transformed* (Ann Arbor: University of Michigan Press, 1999).

Barnet, Richard J. *The Alliance: America-Europe-Japan, Makers of the Postwar World* (New York: Simon and Schuster, 1983).

Bulmer, Simon, Charlie Jeffery, William E. Paterson. *Germany's European Diplomacy: Shaping the Regional Milieu* (Manchester: Manchester University Press, 2000).

Bulmer, Simon, and William Paterson. *The Federal Republic of Germany and the European Community* (London: Allen and Unwin, 1987).

Cassell, Mark. *How Governments Privatize: The Politics of Divestment in the United States and Germany* (Washington, DC: Georgetown University Press, 2002).

Cox, Robert Henry. "The Social Construction of an Imperative: Why Welfare Reform Happened in Denmark and the Netherlands but Not in Germany." *World Politics* 53, no. 3 (April 2001): 463–498.

Crawford, Beverly. *Power and German Foreign Policy: Embedded Hegemony in Europe* (New York: Palgrave Macmillan, 2007).

Dettke, Dieter. *Germany Says "No": The Iraq War and the Future of German Foreign and Security Policy* (Washington, DC: Woodrow Wilson Center Press; Baltimore, MD: Johns Hopkins University Press, 2009).

Duch, Raymond M. *Privatizing the Economy: Telecommunications Policy in Comparative Perspective* (Ann Arbor: University of Michigan Press, 1991).

Duffield, John S. *World Power Forsaken: Political Culture, International Institutions, and German Security Policy after Unification* (Palo Alto, CA: Stanford University Press, 1998).

Dyson, Kenneth. "The Franco-German Relationship and Economic and Monetary Union." *West European Politics* 22, no. 1 (January 1999): 25–44.

Gardner Feldman, Lily. *Germany's Foreign Policy of Reconciliation: From Enmity to Amity* (Lanham, MD: Rowman & Littlefield, 2012).

Garton Ash, Timothy. "Germany's Choice." In *Foreign Affairs Agenda 1995* (New York: Council on Foreign Relations, 1995), 68–84.

———. *In Europe's Name: Germany and the Divided Continent* (New York: Random House, 1993).

Gatzke, Hans W. *Germany and the United States* (Cambridge, MA: Harvard University Press, 1980).

Geipel, Gary L. "Germany: Urgent Pressures, Quiet Change." *Current History*, no. 610 (November 1994): 358–363.

Hacke, Christian. "The National Interests of the Federal Republic of Germany on the Threshold of the 21st Century." *Aussenpolitik* 49, no. 2 (1998): 5–25.

Hafner, Katie. "The House We Lived In." *New York Times Magazine*, 10 November 1991, 32ff.

———. "A Nation of Readers Dumps Its Writers." *New York Times Magazine*, 10 January 1993, 22ff.

Haftendorn, Helga. *Coming of Age: German Foreign Policy since 1945* (Lanham, MD: Rowman and Littlefield, 2006).

Harnisch, Sebastian, and Hanns W. Maull, eds. *Germany as a Civilian Power? The Foreign Policy of the Berlin Republic* (Manchester: Manchester University Press, 2001).

Joffe, Josef. "The View from Bonn: The Tacit Alliance." In *Eroding Empire: Western Relations with Eastern Europe*, ed. Lincoln Gordon et al. (Washington, DC: Brookings Institution, 1987), 129–187.

————. "Peace and Populism: Why the European Anti-Nuclear Movement Failed." *International Security* 11, no. 4 (Spring 1987): 3–40.

Joppke, Christian. "Nuclear Power Struggles after Chernobyl: The Case of West Germany." *West European Politics* 13, no. 2 (April 1990): 178–191.

————. "Models of Statehood in the German Nuclear Energy Debate." *Comparative Political Studies* 25, no. 2 (July 1992): 251–280.

Judt, Tony. *Postwar: A History of Europe since 1945* (New York: Penguin, 2005).

Kaltenthaler, Karl. "German Interests in Monetary Integration." *Journal of Common Market Studies* 40, no. 1 (January 2002): 69–87.

Karp, Regina. "The New German Foreign Policy Consensus." *Washington Quarterly* 29, no. 1 (Winter 2005–2006): 61–73.

Katzenstein, Peter. *Tamed Power: Germany in Europe* (Ithaca, NY: Cornell University Press, 1997).

Lees, Charles. "'Dark Matter': Institutional Constraints and the Failure of Party-Based Euroscepticism in Germany." *Political Studies* 50, no. 2 (June 2002): 244–267.

Leibfried, Stephan, and Herbert Obinger. "The State of the Welfare State: German Social Policy between Macroeconomic Retrenchment and Microeconomic Recalibration." *West European Politics* 26, no. 4 (October 2003): 199–218.

Lindberg, Leon. *Politics and the Future of Industrial Society* (New York: David McKay, 1976).

Livingston, Robert Gerald. "United Germany: Bigger and Better." *Foreign Policy*, no. 87 (Summer 1992): 157–174.

Marsh, David. *The Euro: The Battle for the New Global Currency* (New Haven, CT: Yale University Press, 2011).

McAdams, A. James. "Inter-German Detente: A New Balance." *Foreign Affairs* 65, no. 1 (Fall 1986): 136–153.

McNamara, Kathleen. *The Currency of Ideas: Monetary Politics in the European Union* (Ithaca, NY: Cornell University Press, 1998).

Miskimmon, Alister. *Germany and the Common Foreign and Security Policy of the European Union: Between Europeanisation and National Adaptation* (Basingstoke: Palgrave Macmillan, 2007).

Newnham, Randall. "The Price of German Unity: The Role of Economic Aid in the German Soviet Negotiations." *German Studies Review* 22, no. 3 (October 1999): 421–446.

Rattinger, Hans. "The Federal Republic of Germany: Much Ado about (Almost) Nothing." In *The Public and Atlantic Defense*, ed. Gregory Flynn and Hans Rattinger (Totowa: Rowman and Allanheld, 1985), 101–174.

Roller, Edeltraud. "Shrinking the Welfare State: Citizen Attitudes toward Cuts in Social Spending in Germany in the 1990s." *German Politics* 8 (1999): 21–39.

Schweigler, Gebhard. *West German Foreign Policy: The Domestic Setting* (New York: Praeger, 1984).

Seeleib-Kaiser, Martin. "A Dual Transformation of the German Welfare State?" *West European Politics* 25, no. 4 (October 2002): 25–45.

Sinn, Gerlinde, and Hans-Werner Sinn. *Jumpstart: The Economic Unification of Germany* (Cambridge, MA: MIT Press, 1993).

Sloam, James. "'Responsibility for Europe': The EU Policy of the German Social Democrats since Unification." *German Politics* 12, no. 2 (August 2003): 59–78.

Sodaro, Michael J. *Moscow, Germany, and the West from Khrushchev to Gorbachev* (Ithaca, NY: Cornell University Press, 1991).

Sperling, James. "Neither Hegemony nor Dominance: Reconsidering German Power in Post Cold-War Europe." *British Journal of Political Science* 31, no. 2 (April 2001): 389–425.

Stares, Paul B., ed. *The New Germany and the New Europe* (Washington, DC: Brookings Institution, 1992).

Stent, Angela E. *Russia and Germany Reborn: Unification, the Soviet Collapse and the New Europe* (Princeton, NJ: Princeton University Press, 1999).

Streeck, Wolfgang, and Anke Hassell. "The Crumbling Pillars of Social Partnership." *West European Politics* 26, no. 4 (October 2003): 101–124.

Szabo, Stephen F. *Parting Ways: The Crisis in German-American Relations* (Washington, DC: Brookings Institution Press, 2004).

Vail, Martin I. "Rethinking Corporatism and Consensus: The Dilemmas of German Social Protection Reform." *West European Politics* 26, no. 3 (July 2003): 41–68.

Wallander, Celeste A. *Mortal Friends, Best Enemies: German-Russian Cooperation after the Cold War* (Ithaca, NY: Cornell University Press, 1999).

Webber, Douglas. "Franco-German Bilateralism and Agricultural Politics in the European Union." *West European Politics* 22, no. 1 (January 1999): 45–67.

Zelikow, Philip, and Condoleezza Rice. *Germany Unified and Europe Transformed* (Cambridge, MA: Harvard University Press, 1995).

CHAPTER 11: CONCLUSION: GERMANY'S RISE AND FUTURE CHALLENGES

Acemoglu, Daron, and James A. Robinson, *Why Nations Fail: The Origins of Power, Prosperity, and Poverty* (New York: Crown, 2012).

Alesina, Alberto, and Francesco Giavazzi, ed. *Europe and the Euro* (Chicago: University of Chicago Press, 2010).

Buti, Marco, et al., ed. *The Euro: The First Decade* (Cambridge: Cambridge University Press, 2010).

Caldwell, Peter, and Richard Shandley, eds. *German Unification: Expectations and Outcomes* (New York: Palgrave Macmillan, 2011).

Crepaz, Markus, M. L. *Trust beyond Borders: Immigration, the Welfare State, and Identity in Modern Societies* (Ann Arbor: University of Michigan Press, 2008).

Davis, Belinda, et al., eds. *Changing the World, Changing Oneself: Political Protest and Collective Identities in West Germany and the U.S. in the 1960s and 1970s* (New York: Berghahn Books, 2010).

Fleckenstein, Timo. *Institutions, Ideas and Learning in Welfare State Change: Labour Market Reforms in Germany* (Houndmills: Palgrave Macmillan, 2011).

Gehler, Michael. *Three Germanies: West Germany, East Germany and the Berlin Republic* (London: Reaktion Books, 2011).

Häusermann, Siljja. *The Politics of Welfare State Reform in Continental Europe: Modernization in Hard Times* (Cambridge: Cambridge University Press, 2010).

Hodson, Dermot. *Governing the Euro Area in Good Times and Bad* (Oxford: Oxford University Press, 2011).

Hyde-Prince, Adrian, and Charlie Jeffrey. "Germany in the European Union: Constructing Normality." *Journal of Common Market Studies* 39, no. 4 (November 2001): 690.

Miskimmon, Alister, William E. Paterson, and James Sloam. *Germany's Gathering Crisis: The 2005 Federal Election and the Grand Coalition* (New York: Palgrave Macmillan, 2009).

Norris, Pippa. *Democratic Deficit: Critical Citizens Revisited* (New York: Cambridge University Press, 2011).

Picot, Georg. *Politics of Segmentation: Party Competition and Social Protection in Europe* (New York: Routledge, 2012).

Ritter, Gerhard. *The Price of German Unity: Reunification and the Crisis of the Welfare State* (Oxford: Oxford University Press, 2011).

Sinn, Hans-Werner. *Can Germany Be Saved? The Malaise of the World's First Welfare State* (Cambridge, MA: MIT Press, 2007).

Streeck, Wolfgang. "A State of Exhaustion: A Comment on the German Election of 18 September." *Political Quarterly* 77, no. 1 (January–March 2006): 79–88.

Vail, Mark I. *Recasting Welfare Capitalism: Economic Adjustment in Contemporary France and Germany* (Philadelphia: Temple University Press, 2010).

Index

Note: Page numbers in italics refer to figures or tables.

abortion, 37, 38, 52, 72, 121, 122, 141, 177, 232, 257, 258, 290, 201. *See also* unification; women

Adenauer, Konrad, 97, 139, 140, 147, 183, 217, 241–242, 258, 309, 345; chancellor democracy and, 241–242; Christian Democratic Union and, 139; Foundation, 137, 336; influence on state politics, 217, 242; as mayor of Cologne, 320; relations with Bundestag, 219

administration. *See* civil service

administrative courts, 168, 284, 286, 287; nuclear power and, 286

Afghanistan, xii, 3, 94, 161, 235, 256, 258, 340, 341, 343

age, 47, 48, 50, 52, 62, 73, 74, 75, 76, 78–81, 97–100, 101, 105, 114, 117, 122–124, 140, 150, 185, 205, 238, 242, 270, 275, 370. *See also* generational differences

Agenda 2010, xii, 65, 66, 121, 152–154, 163, 169, 171, 200, 201, 207, 250, 251, 256, 279, 354, 364, 370, 371. *See also* Schröder, Gerhard; welfare state

agriculture, 20, 27, 59–61, 67, 161, 173–175, 217, 223, *237*, 254, 273, 301, 308, 346, 350; in German Democratic Republic, 20, 27, 175; European Union and, 174–175, 346, 350. *See also* Common Agricultural Policy; interest groups

Alliance for Germany, 36, 143. *See also* Kohl, Helmut

Alliance for Jobs, 168, 249. *See also* corporatism; Schröder, Gerhard

anti-Semitism, 12–14, 49, 336

Arab Spring, 343

asylum, 17, 118, 119, 370

Augstein, Rudolf, 82

authoritarianism in family, 13, 77–78

Baader-Meinhof gang, 127. *See also* terrorism

Baden-Württemberg, *46, 48, 60*, 83, 112, 146, 157, 162, 165, 213n2, 229, 243, 252, 269, 301, 302, 303, 306, 307, 308, 309–311, *314*, 315, 321, 327n3, 328n8, 328n16

Bad Godesberg program, 147, 149. *See also* Social Democratic Party

Barzel, Rainer, 208, 234, 243

Basic Law (constitution), 22, 96, 106, 107, 109, 118, 124, 136, 139, 176, 177, 185, 218, 219, 229–231, 233, 234, 248, 253, 288, 289, 291, 292, 293, 300, 301, 302, 306, 314, 320, 327, 334, 367, 376n7; attitudes toward, 96, 106; biconfessional schools and, 176–177; Bundesrat and, 230–231; Bundestag and, 136, 218–219; civil liberties in, 107–109, 118, 124; constitutional position of states (Länder) in, 229, 300–301, 306, 314; European Union and, 291–293; Federal Constitutional Court and, 288–289; foreign policy, 334; function of federal chancellor in, 233–234; function of federal president in, 253; local government and, 320; origins of, 22, 302; positive vote of no-confidence in, 226, 234–235; reform of, 367; suffrage and, 185; unification and, 248, 376n7. *See also* Joint Constitutional Commission

Basic Treaty, 29

Bavaria, 5, 10, 14, *46, 48,* 55, 60, 83, 93, 109, 111, 112, 139, 141, 142, 144, 145, 159, 171, 174, 176, 197, 201, 229, 236, 249, 261, 269, 282, 290, 291, 292, 300, 301–304, 306, *307, 308,* 309, 310, 312, 313, *314,* 315, 321, 328n8, 328n16, 358, 373

Berlin, 7, 15, 18–19, 23, 32, 38, 48, 56–57, 72–73, 82, 116, 125, 127, 163, 191, 243, 301–302, 304–306, 315, 324–325, 335; return of capital to, 85, 220–221; *Verfilzung* (entanglement) in, 324; Wall, 3, 25–28, 33, 52n10, 101, 160

Biedenkopf, Kurt, 312

birth rate, 56, 57, 74, 75, 78, 114, 122, 124, 178, 275, 349, 370; eastern Germany and, 56; pension system and, 57, 275, 370

Bismarck, Otto von, 7, 9, 156, 218, 229, 279, 300, 302, 332. *See also* German Empire

Bitburg affair, 95, 247

Blair, Tony, 151, 341

BMW (Bavarian Motor Works), 65

Bonn, 28–30, 33, 36, 39, 57, 95, 97, 128, 147, 160, 177, 219, 220, 237, 293, 261n19, 268, 269, 309, 334, 379

Brandenburg, 6, 38, 46, 48, 56, 57, 60, 83, 163, 178, 221, 229, 230, 245, 291, 302, 304–306, 307, 308, 309, 312, 314, 319, 321, 328n16; Bundesrat vote and, 229–230, 291

Brandt, Willy, 76, 140, 141, 147–150, 184, 208, 225, 234, 235, 242, 243–245, 258, 310, 312, 324, 335; as chancellor, 148–150, 243–245. *See also* Social Democratic Party

Bremen, 7, 46, 48, 57, 60, 83, 108, 155, 191, 213n2, 229, 300, 301, 303, 304, 306, 307–310, 312, 314, 316, 320, 328n16

Britain. *See* United Kingdom

Bundesbank (Federal Bank), viii, 117, 263, 273, 279–282, 352; European Central Bank and, 263, 281–282; European

unification and, 281–282, 352–353; unification and, 244, 281

Bundesrat (Federal Council), vii, 8, 121, 144, 217, 228–233, 253, 258–260, 261n19, 280, 288, 289, 291, 292, 301, 306, 310, 316, 318, 319, 346, 351, 358, 365, 368; changing role of, 292, 316, 319–320, 346, 351, 365, 368; divided parliamentary control of, 232–233; expansion of veto power, 231–232; immigration law and, 291; legislation and, 230, 258–259, 351; structure, membership, organization of, 229, 231, 289

Bundestag (Federal Diet), vii, xi, 100, 103, 104, 120, 121, 154, 155, 157, 160, 181n29, 186, 187, 189, 194, 197, 204, 207, 211, 214n10, 217, 218–222, 224–228, 230, 232, 233, 240, 243, 248, 249, 253, 258–261, 286, 2921, 292, 316, 318, 340, 346, 351, 373, 379; committees, 222, 226, 259, 288, 346; expert commissions and, 228; legislation and, 218, 222, 226–228, 232–233, 257–260; move to Berlin of, 220–221; public attitudes toward, 227–228, 367–368; question period, 225; structure, membership, functions of, 221–225

Bundeswehr. *See* military

bureaucracy. *See* civil service

Bush, George H. W., xii, 39, 94, 145, 199, 249, 341, 342

Bush, George W., 94, 199, 341–342. *See also* Iraq War

cabinet ministers, federal. *See* Federal Cabinet

cable television, 84, 89n76

campaign finance, 138, 158, 171, 194–195; Christian Democrats and, 194–195, 251; Free Democrats and, 158; Social Democrats and, 171

candidate selection, 189–191. *See also* Bundestag

capital resources, distribution of, 62, 68–70

Caritas, 176. *See also* churches

Catholic church and Christian Democratic Union, 111, 139, 156, 204. *See also* churches

census, and civil liberties, 110

centralization, administrative need for, 344

Chancellor. *See* Federal Chancellor
chancellor: role of in Second Reich, 8; role of in Weimar Republic, 10, 12
chancellor candidate debates, 145, 152, 192, 199, 210, 249. *See also* elections, federal
Chernobyl accident and the Greens, 159
China, 58, 86n8, 333, 337, 339, 343, 369, 373, 374
Christian Democratic Union (CDU), 76, 83, 109, 116, 120, 138–146, 188, 192, 195, 196–199, 223, 229–230, 232–235, 242–243, 246–249, 250–253, 303–306, 309–311, 371–373; election of 2005 and, 145, 153, 184, 199–200; election of 2009 and, 146, 158, 186, 200–202; formation of, 138–139; as opposition party, 140–142, 143–144; policies of, 196, 250–253, 343, 371–373; return to power of, 142, 144; unification and, 142–143, 247–248. *See also* elections, federal; Kohl, Helmut; Merkel, Angela; Schäuble, Wolfgang; Stoiber, Edmund
Christian Social Union (CSU), xiii, 83, 111, 112, 116, 120, 137–142, 144–147, 152–157, 164, 167, 171, 174, 176, 180n4, 186, 188, 190–192, 194–197, 200, 201, 204–209, 211, 224, 225, 232, 233, 235–237, 239, 242, 246, 249–251, 259, 292, 302, 303, 306, 308, 310, 313, 343, 358, 372, 373; relationship to CDU, 141–142. *See also* Bavaria; Stoiber, Edmund; Strauss, Franz Josef
churches, 16, 72–74, 112, 115, 127, 139, 147, 150, 176–179, 205, 240, 255, 275; attendance, 73, 201, 204, 207; decline in membership of, 74, 179; in East Germany, 29–30, 31–32, 72–74; finances of, 74, 176–177; political influence of, 177–179. *See also* German Democratic Republic; unification
cities, 5–7, 10, 18, 32, 35, 42, 46, 57, 58, 106, 114–116, 121, 126, 155, 176, 195, 220, 241, 271, 300, 302, 304, 305, 316, 320–327, 329, 359; in eastern Germany, 35, 46, 305, 321–327; financial deficits of, 323–324; housing shortage (squatters) in, 325; party politics in, 322; public services of, 322–323; transportation in, 324–325; zoning and land use regulations in, 324

citizen initiative groups, 34–36, 105–106, 110, 128–129, 159, 179, 322, 325. *See also* Green political party; political participation
citizenship law, 114, 161, 176. *See also* foreign workers
civil liberties, vi, 10, 15, 16, 28, 91, 93, 95, 97, 99, 101, 106–108, 110, 111–113, 155, 161, 178, 256, 289–291, 339, 374; 9/11 and, 112–114; awareness of, 106–108; census and, 110; electronic surveillance (bugging) and, 110–111; Federal Constitutional Court and, 109–111, 289–291; same-sex marriage and, 111–112
civil servants, 68, 109, 136, 176, 223, 224, 229, 231, 237, 239, 253, 257, 260n7, 264–266, 266–270, 272, 273, 284, 287, 289, 293, 294n17, 326; Bundesrat and, 229, 231, 289; Bundestag committees and, 222; as Bundestag deputies, 223–224; compensation of, 268, 272; judiciary and, 284; political attitudes of, 270–271. *See also* radicals
civil service, 108, 109, 136, 223, 238, 260n8, 263–272, 284, 285, 293, 294n10, 326, 368; education and, 269; history of, 263–265; privatization and, 71, 268, 271–272, 275, 323–324, 355; recruitment for, 268–270; reform of, 271–272; stability of, 265; structure of, 265–267; unification and, 271
class structure, 8–9, 13, 61–62, 67–71, 85, 109, 127, 206–207; economic inequality in, 67–71, 102, 370–371, 373; educational system and, 79–80
Clinton, Bill, 151
coalition governments, 36–37, 56, 98, 127, 135, 140, 142–143, 145–146, 148–149, 153, 155–162, 174, 177, 183, 184–185, 188–189, 196–200, 212, 227, 229–230, 232–233, 235–238, 243–244, 246, 251–252, 256, 257, 258; in the states, 301–306, 309. *See also* Grand Coalition
codetermination law, 213. *See also* trade unions
Cold War, 3, 18, 79, 127, 220, 240, 300, 335, 337–338, 359
collective memory, 95–96, 245, 247, 335, 339, 359–360
Common Agricultural Policy (CAP), 174–175, 228, 345–346, 349–350

Communist Party, in Weimar Republic, 10–12, 15. *See also* Party of Democratic Socialism/Left List; Socialist Unity Party

communities (*Gemeinden*), 320–323. *See also* local government

comprehensive school, 79–80. *See also* educational system

concerted action, 167–168

conference committee, 259, 289

confidence vote, 218, 226, 234–235, 246, 255, 261n28, 341. *See also* Afghanistan; Federal Chancellor

conflict, attitudes toward, 98

Constitution. *See* Basic Law

Constitution of German Democratic Republic, 28, 33. *See also* Basic Law

Constitutional Court. *See* Federal Constitutional Court

corporate guilds, 67, 166, 168–170. *See also* interest groups

corporatism, 168

county (*Kreis*) government, 321

courts. *See* judiciary

Czech Republic, 11, 16, 18, 27, 31–32, 45, 55 92, 252, 265, 332, 338–339, 346, 349, 369; East German refugees and, 31–32, 34; German foreign policy and, 338–339; lower wages and, 369; revolution of 1989 and, 31–32

Daimler-Benz, 65

decentralization, historical pattern, 5, 293, 300

defense council, 240

DeGaulle, Charles, 346

democratic values, attitudes toward, 1, 38, 85, 91–93, 97–103, 123, 129, 270–271, 284–285, 334–335, 363, 374. *See also* political culture

denazification, 20, 264–265, 285; civil service and, 264–265

Der Spiegel, 82, 108

Diakonie, 176. *See also* Protestant Church

diffuse support, 98–99

direct democracy, 99, 103, 106, 319, 328n18, 347 367, 373; Basic Law and, 367; citizen initiative groups and, 106. *See also* Green political party

Dresden, 18, 32, 36, 73, 176, 323, 326

Eastern Europe, and unification, 3, 33–34, 40, 124–125

East Germany. *See* German Democratic Republic

Ebert, Friedrich Foundation, 137, 336

economy, 62–71, 279–282; and Euro, 281–282, 348–358; growth, 40, 62–67, 354, 356, 364–365; industrialization, 9, 47, 57–58; Mittelstand, 13, 66; performance of, 3, 44, 64–67, 250, 365; trade balance, 58–59, 371–372

educational system, 78–80; basic structure of, 78–79; in German Democratic Republic, 29, 79, 123–124; proposals for reform of, 19, 79, 137, 165, 178, 232, 244, 271, 313–317, 319; role of states in, 78–80, 313–319

Elbe river, and pollution, 25, 45–46, 54, 144

elections: in German Democratic Republic, 36, 48, 76, 99–104; local, 190–191, 197–298, 213, 230, 310–312; states and, 160–163, 198, 204, 208, 213, 252, 232, 244–249, 292, 303–304, 310–312; turnout, 103, 120, 138, 183, 196, 201, 252, 311, 251

elections, federal: of 1949, 2, 139–142, 147, 155, 184, 195–196, 201, 254; of 1953, 140–141, 147, 180, 195–197, 207, 225; of 1957, 140, 147, 149–150, 155, 184, 195–198, 205, 209; of 1961, 140, 150, 155, 183, 224; of 1965, 140, 194, 195–197, 205, 208, 225, 244; of 1969, 125, 127, 140–141, 149, 155–156, 165, 243–244, 310; of 1972, 140, 196–197, 205, 225, 230, 232, 244, 258; of 1976, 125, 130, 141, 149, 183, 193–194, 197, 205; of 1980, 149, 152, 156–159, 196–197, 246; of 1983, 120, 142, 150–151, 156–159, 183–184, 196–197, 207–211, 246–247; of 1987, 142, 150, 156, 159, 184, 192, 197, 208–209, 214–215, 312; of 1990, 125, 136, 138, 142–143, 150–151, 156, 160, 180–184, 195–200, 209–211, 213, 247–251, 304, 310, 312; of 1994, 143, 184, 198–199, 204–214, 247–249, 254, 303, 312; of 1998, 111, 143, 157, 199, 232, 248; of 2002, 144, 185, 192, 205, 211–213; of 2005, 145, 153, 162, 189, 199–202, 205–209; of 2009, 120, 130, 137, 153,

157–158, 162–163, 184, 186, 192, 199–202, 207, 236
electoral politics, in states, 310–311
electoral system (law), 185–189; reform of, 189, 364–365
Emergency Laws, 106
emergency powers: Federal President and, 253; in Second Reich, 8; in Weimar Republic, 11, 253
environment, 45–47, 159, 162, 237; in former East Germany, 45–47. *See also* Green political party
Erhard, Ludwig, 128, 139–140, 208, 236, 242–244. *See also* Federal chancellor
Euro, 353–355; crisis, 331, 347–348, 355, 357–361, 375. *See also* European Monetary Union; European Stability Mechanism
European Central Bank, 263, 273, 279, 282, 353, 358
European Currency Union, 40, 381, 352–354, 365
European Economic Community (Common Market), 344–346
European Monetary System (EMS), 228, 281, 291, 352
European Union, 344–352; Bundesbank and, 117, 352; federalism and, 319, 331, 350–351, 361, 365, 368; unification and, 337, 339, 344, 348, 352, 354, 359. *See also* Common Agricultural Policy
Evangelical Church in Germany (EKD), 176–178; secret police (Stasi) and, 178; unification and, 178. *See also* churches
expellees, 18, 55, 60, 85, 124, 196, 303, 334–335, 339
exports, importance of, 58–59

family, 74–78; policy, 77, 79; structure, 74–75
Federal Assembly, 253–256
Federal Cabinet, 225, 229, 233, 236–239
Federal Chancellor, 208, 217–219, 222, 225–228, 233–237, 241–253, 368; chancellor democracy and, 233–236; historical evolution, 8, 10, 14; legislation and, 8, 218, 228, 233, 235, 254–255, 274; military and, 218, 235. *See also* positive vote of no-confidence
Federal Chancellor's Office, 228, 237, 239

Federal Constitutional Court, 286–293; Bundesrat and, 230; civil liberties and, 109, 112, 117, 131, 161; decisions of, 109, 131, 188; European Union and, 291–292, 351, 353; independence of, 284; policy making and, 271, 287, 289, 291, 297, 340, 351. *See also* Basic Law
Federal Council. *See* Bundesrat
Federal Diet. *See* Bundestag
Federal Labor Agency, 272–273, 278–279
Federal President, 235–256
Federal Republic of Germany, 5, 13, 18, 21; attitudes toward, 91, 96, 102, 120, 334; formation of, 20–23; provisional character of, 22
federal structure, reform of, 229, 299, 327
Federation of German Employer Associations (BDA), 168. *See also* Interest groups
finance minister, 238
Fischer, Joschka, 160, 162, 199, 265, 340. *See also* Green political party
Flick affair, 82
Focus, 82
foreign policy, 331–360; European unification and, 344–350; Libya, 202, 344; multilateralism, 336; NATO and, 333–334, 338–344, 359; normalization, 343; reconciliation, 335–336, 348; relationship to United States and, 335–336, 342; soft power, 335–336; and Yugoslavia, 340–341. *See also* Arab Spring; Libya; *Ostpolitik*
foreign workers, 72, 75, 114–118, 125, 132, 177, 179; German citizenship and, 114–115, 117
Foster, Sir Norman, 220
Fraktionen (caucuses), 221, 226, 257, 258. *See also* Bundestag
Free Democratic Party (FDP), 142, 145, 154–158, 162–163, 171, 184, 188, 194, 200, 202, 204, 207, 235, 243, 311–312; in coalitions with Christian Democratic Union, 142, 145, 155, 169, 171, 184, 188, 198, 200, 202, 235, 243; election of 2002 and, 145, 157, 162–163, 171, 184, 188, 204, 207, 311–312; electoral system and, 155–156; finances of, 171, 194; in German Democratic Republic, 137, 156, 180, 304; internal divisions of, 149; in party system, 157–58; unification and,

156, 167, 169, 198, 202. *See also* elections, federal

Free German Youth (FDJ), 29

Friedrich Ebert Foundation, 137, 336

Gabriel, Sigmar, 154. *See also* Social Democratic Party

Gauck, Joachim, 38, 154, 254, 256, 312. *See also* Federal President

generational differences in political attitudes, 75–77. *See also* family

Genscher, Hans-Dietrich, 142, 156, 180, 184. *See also* Free Democratic Party; unification

German Democratic Republic (GDR), 25–39, 89, 93 123, 150, 160, 171–172, 178, 290; agriculture in, 27, 175, 223; area of, 25; borders of, 27–30, 32, 35, 52, 93, 118; collapse of, 23, 27, 30–31, 35, 38, 40, 89, 128, 143, 150, 160, 172; churches in, 29–32, 178; courts in, 26, 285; debt of, 30; economy of, 27, 29–31, 36, 40, 47, 49–50; educational system of, 2, 123; environmental problems of, 40, 47, 150; federalism in, 290, 301; Gorbachev and, 30–32, 36–38; history of, 26–33; June 1953 Uprising, 27–28; justice in, 285; labor unions in, 171–172; leadership of, 27, 30–31, 34, 150, 290; local government in, 20, 198; parties in, 26, 31–32, 82, 123, 198; population of, 25–28, 35, 47, 56; social policy of, 29, 178; relations with Federal Republic, 28–30, 37, 178. *See also* Berlin; Honecker, Erich; Krenz, Egon; Modrow, Hans; Party of Democratic Socialism/ Left List; Secret Police; Ulbricht, Walter; unification

German Empire, 8–9; foreign policy of, 9–10; industrialization, 9; Kaiser Wilhelm II, 9–10; *Kulturkampf*, 8–9

German Federation of Labor (DGB), 170. *See also* trade unions

German Industrial and Trade Conference (DIHT), 168. *See also* interest groups

German question, 332–333

globalization, 293

Gorbachev, Mikhail, 3, 30–39, 347, 339

Grand Coalition: 1966–1969, 127, 140, 148–149, 209, 243; 2005–2009, xii, 145, 153, 184, 200, 212, 250–252

Grass, Günter, 336

Greece, 106, 239, 252, 263, 354, 356–358, 375

Green Front, 173, 175. *See also* interest groups

Green political party, 76, 82, 106, 110–111, 120, 123, 137, 144–145, 160–168, 171, 184, 186, 188, 199, 205, 207, 213–214, 232, 249, 309–311, 341; Afghanistan and, 161, 340; census and, 110; elections and, 82, 144–145, 162–163, 171, 184, 188, 199, 205, 207, 213–214, 249, 311; electoral system and, 155, 162–163, 186; finances of, 194; in government, 160–161; no-confidence vote and, 341; same-sex marriage and, 111, 161; state elections and, 76, 137, 144, 162, 309–311; ticket-splitting and, 188; women and, 106, 120, 137, 205, 232; youth and, 123. *See also* civil liberties; peace movement

Gysi, Gregor, 163–164

Habermas, Jürgen, 95

Hamburg, 7, 17–18, 42, 46, 57, 72–73, 112, 176, 178, 304, 306–308, 320, 323

Hartz IV reforms, 65, 86, 165, 202, 250, 279, 364

Havel, Vaclav, 34

health care system, 251, 276–278; changes in, 251, 276–277; health funds, 277–278

hearings of Bundestag committees, 226, 228. *See also* Bundestag

Heinemann, Gustav, 254, 256. *See also* Federal President

Herrhausen, Alfred, 128

Herzog, Roman, 254–255. *See also* Federal President

Hesse, 46, 48, 60, 83, 144, 152, 229, 301–308, 311–315, 321, 328

Heuss, Theodor, 253–254. *See also* Federal President

Hindenburg, Paul von, 10–12, 218. *See also* Weimar Republic

Historikerstreit (Historians Dispute), 95

Hitler, Adolf, 11–17, 92–94, 96, 101; attitudes toward, 92–94, 96, 101. *See also* National Socialism

Holocaust, 17, 23, 31, 95, 101, 113–114; Berlin, Memorial to the Murdered Jews of Europe, 221, 335; and foreign policy, 114, 247; popular knowledge of, 254–255

Honecker, Erich, 29–31, 33; collapse of GDR and, 30–31, 33; policies of, 30, 33; resignation of, 32. *See also* German Democratic Republic

Hungary, 17, 18, 20, 27, 31–34, 39, 52, 332, 338, 345, 350, 369

ideology of electorate, 202–203

immigration, 117–118, 225, 291, 370; reform, 225, 370. *See also* citizenship law

income inequality, 68, 70, 102; sex differentials in, 78, 121, 132

industrial interests and political parties, 155, 168–169. *See also* Flick affair

inflation, 11, 16, 43, 63–64, 138, 244, 280–281, 353, 356, 364, 375. *See also* Bundesbank

interest groups, 166–179; agriculture, 173–176; Bundestag and, 189, 259, 346; business, 104, 167–169, 173, 179, 194, 274–275; candidate recruitment and, 189–192; churches, 176–179; governmental bureaucracy and, 167, 179, 257, 259; labor, 104, 167–169, 173, 274–275

interest in politics, general pattern, 98, 104, 120, 132

Iraq war, 152, 210–211, 250, 311, 341–342; 2002 election and, 152, 210–211, 311, 341–342; Schröder, Gerhard, and, 152, 210–211, 250, 311, 341; U.S. relations and, 250, 342, 360

Italy, 125–126, 132, 174, 281, 299, 340, 342, 345, 348, 353, 355

Jewish congregations, 72, 176, 182

Joint Constitutional Commission, 232. *See also* Basic Law

judicial review, 283, 287–289, 292, 296, 365. *See also* Federal Constitutional Court

judiciary, 284–293; attitudes and values, 282–284; court structure and, 285–287; in eastern Germany, 285; reform of, 265; socialization and recruitment of, 284–285; Third Reich and, 14, 263–265, 283

Junkers, 8, 59

Kaderakte, 51. *See also* Stasi

Kapp Putsch, 11

Kiesinger, Kurt-Georg, 140, 208, 242–244, 260, 312. *See also* Grand Coalition

Kirch, Leo, 84. *See also* television and radio

Kirchhof, Paul, 210, 215

Kohl, Helmut, 30, 33, 36, 46, 116, 142–143, 151, 161, 184, 197–199, 208–209, 232, 235, 242–243, 246–249, 312, 349, 359; Basic Law and, 111, 272, 319; Bitburg Affair and, 95; chancellor, performance as, 30, 95, 141–143, 156, 171, 197–199, 232, 235–236, 246–249, 281, 368; Christian Democratic Union and, 141–143; finance scandal and, 144, 195, 251; minister-president, 141; population and, 39, 81, 325; private television and, 81–84, 192; unification and, 33, 36, 82, 150, 160–161, 205, 302–303; U.S.-Soviet relations and, 36–39, 143, 247–248. *See also* Christian Democratic Union; elections, federal; Federal Chancellor; unification

Köhler, Horst, 146, 157, 254–256. *See also* Federal President

Kosovo, 161, 258, 340, 343

Krenz, Egon, 32–33, 36

Krieger, Leonard, 107

Künast, Renate, 175

labor market, 45, 65–67, 154, 250, 278, 279, 354, 364

labor unions, 104, 115, 168–173, 240, 276. *See also* trade unions

Lafontaine, Oskar, 150–153, 162–164, 198, 236, 248–250, 304. *See also* Left Party; Social Democratic Party

Länder. *See* states

land use, zoning regulations and, 106, 230, 271, 324

Left Party, 4, 48, 70, 82, 99, 137–139, 153–155, 171, 186–188, 194–197, 204–207, 213, 250, 256, 305, 310, 322, 372, 394; formation of, 162–163

legal codes, 28, 107, 244. *See also* judiciary

legal process, role of social class in, 103, 111–112, 118

legislation, 257–260; Bundesrat and, 8, 230–233; Bundestag and, 218, 220–224, 226; initiation process of, 222, 257–260; role of executive in, 11, 228, 235, 248 liberalism, 6–7, 76, 127, 156, 363, 367, 375. *See also* Federal Republic of Germany; Free Democratic Party

Libya, 202, 311, 344, 359

Life Partnership Law, 111–112, 161. *See also* same-sex marriage

local government, 106, 268, 278, 320–327; eastern Germany and, 299, 321, 323, 326; scandals and, 323–324

Lower Saxony, 46, 48, 60, 71, 151–152, 229, 249, 256, 301–303, 306–312, 314, 321

Lübke, Heinrich, 254. *See also* Federal President

Ludendorff, Erich, 14

Lufthansa, 272

Luxemburg, Rosa Foundation, 137

mad cow disease, 161, 175

Maizière, Lothar de, 50, 237

Mecklenburg–West Pomerania, 46, 48, 56, 60, 83, 229, 296, 305–308, 314, 319, 321, 328

media, 83–85, 192–193; and campaigns, 120, 169, 193, 226, 249–250; Internet, 81, 83, 110, 164–165, 193, 256; print/news-papers, 26, 60, 72, 80–85, 95, 120, 132, 147, 192, 256, 279; television, 60, 80–84, 92, 102, 177, 192–193, 226, 249–250, 285, 290, 313, 319, 336

Merkel, Angela, 4, 56, 66, 113, 120, 144–146, 153–154, 169, 184, 200–202, 209–212, 250–252, 256, 319, 343, 355–358, 364–365, 372–373; economy and, 66, 144, 153, 169, 202, 209, 211–212, 251–252, 256, 319, 343, 355–358, 364–365, 372–373; election of 2005 and, 66, 120, 145, 153–154, 157, 162, 184, 192, 201, 209–211, 236, 250, 260, 311; election of 2009 and, 120, 153–154, 184, 192, 200, 209, 211, 236, 252, 256, 292, 373; Euro crisis and, 154, 201–202, 233, 252, 348–349, 355–360, 364–365; European Union and, 113, 144, 146, 228, 233, 252, 292, 319, 339, 348, 357–359, 364–365, 373; foreign policy and, 4, 146, 212, 250–251, 336, 339, 342, 358–360; Free Democratic Party and, 145, 157–158, 184, 200–202, 236, 256, 259, 311–312; Grand Coalition and, 56, 66, 113, 145, 153, 157, 169, 184, 200, 209, 212, 233, 250–251, 256, 319, 356,

372; Social Democratic Party and, 120, 144–146, 153–154, 162, 184, 200–202, 209–210, 212, 236, 250. *See also* Christian Democratic Union; Euro Crisis; Federal Chancellor

Metal Workers Union, 170, 172–173

Mielke, Erich, 51. *See also* Stasi

migration, migration background, 56, 107, 114–116, 129, 190–191, 293, 323, 370

military, 2, 6–7, 23, 35, 101, 146, 161, 220, 235, 240–241, 332, 339–341; Afghan-istan and, 161, 235, 256, 340–341, 343; attitudes toward, 339, 342; conscription, 146, 343; financial support for, 339–341, 348; reform, 343–344; role of, 9, 211, 239–241, 246, 338, 340; unification and, 2, 6–7, 23, 35, 101, 220, 240–241, 332, 339–341

Ministerpräsident (ministerpresident), 22, 109, 229, 312–313. *See also* states

Mittelstand, 13, 66. *See also* economy

Mitterrand, François, 39, 353

Modell Deutschland, 4, 374

Modrow, Hans, 36

monarchy, attitudes toward, 91–92, 96

Muslims (Islam), 72–73, 112–113, 117, 126, 176, 225. *See also* citizenship law

National Democratic Party (NPD), 109, 125, 310. *See also* radicals

national identity, 2, 51, 92–96, 101, 159–160, 334–335, 360, 374; relations with United States and, 334–335; sense of, 2, 51, 92–96, 101, 159–160, 335, 360, 374

National People's Army (NVA), 240–241)

national politics and state elections, 310–312

national pride, sense of, 16, 93–94, 99–100, 247, 335

National Socialism, 11–13, 15, 17, 77, 95, 101–103, 125, 221; attitudes of Germans toward, 101; capitalism and, 13, 15, 101; East Germans and, 101–103; family and, 13, 77; origins of, 11–12; SS, 15, 17, 95, 125, 221. *See also Historikerstreit*; Hitler, Adolf

NATO, 94, 147, 150, 159, 247, 258, 334, 336, 338–342, 359; and Afghanistan, 94, 258, 340–341, 343; attitudes of Germans toward, 209, 339, 342, 391; and German

foreign policy, 147, 159, 247, 258, 334, 336, 338–342, 359
NATO missile decision, 94, 150; Green political party and, 158–159, 197; Kohl, Helmut, and, 209; peace movement and, 159, 197, 246–247; Schmidt, Helmut, and, 209, 246–247
New Forum, 32–33
new poverty, 368–373
new social movements, 106, 179
North Rhine–Westphalia, 46, 48, 60, 67, 72, 83, 144, 146, 150, 153–154, 158, 164–165, 213, 219, 229, 230, 250, 255, 256, 302, 306–307, 309–315, 321
nuclear power, 27–28, 45, 106, 111, 137, 146, 150, 158, 161–162, 202, 228, 246, 252–253, 258–259, 286, 338–339, 345. See also Green political party

Obama, Barack, 193, 342–343, 358, 361, 363
occupation: government, 2–3, 11, 18–23, 68, 70, 72, 7, 97, 203, 217, 241, 265, 268, 282, 288, 290, 300, 302, 333, 357; structure, 70, 77, 217, 265, 300, 302. See also Basic Law
Oder-Neisse line, 18, 25, 269, 303
Office for the Protection of the Constitution, 318
opposition in East Germany, 26, 30–36, 39. See also New Forum
opposition party, attitudes toward, 99, 198
Ostpolitik (Eastern policy), 148, 244, 335. See also Brandt, Willy; Social Democratic Party

parliament: attitudes toward, 4, 98, 102, 120, 198, 291; in Second Reich, 7–10, 92; in Weimar Republic, 10–12, 125. See also Bundesrat; Bundestag; legislation; Reichstag
parliamentary investigations, 52, 126, 175
particularism, 300, 327. See also states
parties, political: attitudes toward, 91, 96, 98–99, 119–120, 179, 322; in Basic Law, 22, 96, 106, 109, 136, 139, 185, 226, 230, 233–234; in East Germany, 29–39, 51, 72, 82, 99, 223–225; influence on media of, 83, 129, 164, 169, 261; origins of, 241, 264, 366. See also Christian Democratic Union; Free Democratic Party; Green

political party; National Democratic Party; Party of Democratic Socialism; Pirate Party; Social Democratic Party
party discipline in parliament, 220–221, 226, 228, 232
party finance, 194–195
Party of Democratic Socialism/Left List, 38, 52, 137, 165, 186–187, 198, 305. See also Left Party; Radical Left; Socialist Unity Party
party preference, 203–206
party state, 135–138, 290
party systems in states, 309–312
peace movement, 106, 159, 240; Green political party and, 106, 159, 197, 247; military and, 240, 246–247; Schmidt, Helmut, and, 246
pension system, 76, 152, 244, 251, 274–276, 369; aging and, 76; Bundesrat and, 368; reform of, 152, 274–275; unification and, 251, 369
Pirate Party, 76, 113, 137–138, 164–166, 184, 193–194, 205, 214, 310, 367, 372; liquid feedback, 193
Platzeck, Mathias, 312
Pöhl, Karl Otto, 281
Poland, 3, 16, 18, 20, 27, 32, 34, 45, 55, 60, 85, 244, 252, 290, 333, 336, 339, 349, 369; and East German refugees, 32, 55, 114–117, 124
police, 96, 102–103, 110–113, 116, 126, 128, 230, 256, 301, 313, 318, 321, 325, 338; in East Germany, 25–27, 30, 32, 38, 102–103, 178, 223
political asylum, 17, 118–119
political culture: antisystem sentiment and, 91, 96, 129; changes in, 96–98, 113, 125, 127, 263, 374; conflict and, 98, 113, 129; definition of, 91–92; democratic values and, 95–99, 101–103, 129; in eastern Germany, 4, 93–94, 98–105, 123, 125; elites and, 103, 125; founding of Federal Republic and, 91, 241, 274; leadership and, 93, 97, 109, 121, 191; national division and, 4, 99, 101, 374; national identity and, 91, 93–95, 101, 374; occupation and, 97, 115, 127, 223, 260; party competition and, 98–99; performance of system and, 97–99, 103, 191, 374; political education and, 97, 102, 115, 117, 123, 129, 191, 260, 351;

privatization and, 93; representation and parliament, 98, 125, 223; unification and, 99, 101–105, 121, 123, 125, 223, 374; Weimar Republic and, 91, 103, 125, 127, 131, 284

political development, 373–376; past political systems and, 2, 12–13

political participation, 105–106, 183, 193; new forms of, 105–106, 193; voter involvement in campaigns, 193. *See also* citizen initiative groups; interest in politics; political culture; voting behavior

political prisoners, 17, 27, 51

population of Federal Republic, 55–56, 182, 306; aging and, 40, 57, 75, 124, 349, 364; migration and, 1, 15, 40–41, 55–57, 73, 75, 115, 141, 191, 293, 306, 349, 370; unification and, 1, 35, 40–41, 55–56, 223, 225, 278

positive vote of no-confidence, 226, 234. *See also* Bundestag; Federal Chancellor

poverty, 37, 68, 116, 121, 199, 368, 370–373; "prekariat," 371

Powell, Colin, 342

President. *See* Federal President

press, 81–85. *See also* media; television and radio

private employment agencies, 279

privatization, 71, 93, 155, 268, 271–275, 324, 355

proportional electoral system, 185. *See also* electoral law; Free Democratic Party

protest voting, 48

Prussia, rise of, 6–8. *See also* Bismarck, Otto von

question hour in Bundestag, 225

radical left, 126–127, 309. *See also* Grand Coalition; Party of Democratic Socialism; political culture; terrorism

radical right, 125–126, 163, 165; National Socialist Underground, 48–49. *See also* National Democratic Party; political culture

radicals, civil liberties and, 125, 127, 166, 202, 209, 313. *See also* civil service

Rau, Johannes, 150, 254, 255, 312–313. *See also* Federal President

Reagan, Ronald, 95, 247

Rechtsstaat, 50, 107, 366. *See also* civil liberties; political culture

reconciliation, 241, 245, 335–336, 348

Red Army Faction (RAF), 127–128, 318; Stasi and, 26–30, 37–39, 51–52, 128, 178, 223, 251, 256, 260, 296, 326

redistribution, socioeconomic, 61, 70–71

Reformstau, 255, 312, 328n16

refugees, 18, 32, 73, 97, 114, 118, 124, 325, 340, 370. *See also* population of Federal Republic

regional economic development, 301, 316–317, 322

Reichstag, 8, 12, 15, 135, 180, 218, 220. *See also* Bundestag; Parliament

religion: beliefs in, 73–74, 107; in eastern Germany, 86, 88, 227; Jewish communities, 72, 176, 335; Muslims, 72–73, 176; party preference and, 217–220. *See also* churches

reunification, 25–53, 59, 74, 76, 92, 96, 100, 147, 156, 175, 197, 205, 211, 242, 245, 321, 335, 352, 354, 359, 363, 369, 374. *See also* unification

revenue sharing, 314–316, 319, 368

Revolution of 1989, summary of events, 33, 35, 37–40

Rhineland-Palatinate, 46, 60, 83, 109, 141, 151, 213, 229, 301, 303–309, 313–314, 321, 328

Riester-Rente, 275. *See also* pension system

Round Table, 36

Russia, 9–10, 22, 45, 56, 251, 332–336, 339, 341–343

Saarland, 46, 48, 60, 164, 229, 303–304, 307–308, 314, 316, 328

same-sex marriage, 111–112, 161; election of 2002 and, 112, 161; Green political party and, 111

Sarkozy, Nicolas, 372

Sarrazin, Thilo, 117

Saxony, 11, 26, 42, 45–48, 56, 60, 71, 83, 126, 146, 151–152, 165, 204, 256, 296, 302, 304, 307–309, 311–314, 321, 328

Saxony-Anhalt, 46, 48, 56, 60, 83, 165, 229, 296, 302, 304, 312, 314, 316, 328

Scharping, Rudolf, 151, 248, 312. *See also* elections, federal, 1994; Social Democratic Party

Schäuble, Wolfgang, 143–145, 237, 248, 251, 357. *See also* Christian Democratic Union

Scheel, Walter, 156, 244, 254. *See also* Free Democratic Party; *Ostpolitik*

Schiller, Karl, 148

Schleswig-Holstein, 46, 48, 60, 164, 213, 229, 301, 303, 306–311, 316, 319, 321, 328

Schmidt, Helmut, 89, 94, 141–142, 149–150, 183, 208, 235, 242, 245–246, 281, 352; Bundesbank and, 281, 352; as federal chancellor, 89, 94, 141–142, 149–150, 183, 208, 235, 242, 245–246, 281, 352; NATO missiles and, 94 150, 246; in Social Democratic party, 141–142, 149–150, 235, 242, 246

schools. *See* educational system

Schröder, Gerhard, 65–66, 72, 111, 132, 144, 168–169, 175, 233, 236, 249–251, 275–279, 311–312, 348, 354, 360, 366; confidence vote and, 228, 235–236; election of 1998 and, 151–153; election of 2002 and, 81–82, 84, 172–172, 192, 199, 208, 211; election of 2005 and, 84, 153, 200–201, 209–211, 226; policies of, 65–66, 72, 111, 132, 144, 168–169, 175, 233, 236, 249–251, 275–279, 311–312, 348, 354, 360, 366; relations with United States, 145, 256, 338–344; Social Democratic Party and, 161, 303–304. *See also* Agenda 2010; elections; Federal Chancellor; Social Democratic Party

Schumacher, Kurt, 147. *See also* Social Democratic Party

Schweigler, Gebhard, 350, 361

semipublic institutions, 4, 168, 263–264, 272–273, 368

September 11, 2001 (9/11), 112, 126, 152, 249. *See also* civil liberties; terrorism

Serbia, 340

Siemens, 170

Slovenia, 18, 338, 345, 350, 354

social capital, 104–105. *See also* interest groups

social class, 102, 203–204, 209, 213; capital resources and, 13–14, 62, 71, 85, 101; education and, 62, 78–79, 102, 115–116, 147, 165, 213, 237; income structure and, 61–62, 68, 78, 102, 116, 165, 273–274; new middle class, 203, 206–207; voting behavior and, 201–209, 213

Social Democratic Party (SPD), 30, 34–35, 38–39, 85, 103, 110, 123, 137, 138, 141, 145–146, 153, 162–163, 171, 184, 186–188, 201–204, 224, 305, 312; election of 1998 and, 248–249; election of 2002 and, 249, 141, 145, 162–163, 171, 184, 187–188, 312; election of 2005 and, 85, 123, 145, 153, 162, 171, 184, 188, 200–204, 224, 235, 249; election of 2009 and, 103, 123, 137, 138, 141, 145–146, 153, 162–163, 171, 184, 186–188, 201–204, 224, 305, 312; new Left and, 108, 109, 127, 171, 201; program of, 146–148; public image of, 110, 202; unification and, 30, 34–35, 38–39, 99–103. *See also* elections, federal

socialism, decline of in postwar period, 100–102

Socialist Unity Party (SED), 26, 33. *See also* German Democratic Republic; Party of Democratic Socialism/Left List; Radical Left; unification

social market economy, 3, 35, 62–63, 139, 147, 331, 334, 364–366, 369. *See also* welfare state

social security system, 42, 268; changes in, 77, 171, 272, 368, 385

sociodemographic structure and voting, 203–206. *See also* voting behavior

soft power, 335–337, 359, 375

Solidarity Pact, 43, 232, 314, 316, 385. *See also* unification

Sontheimer, Kurt, 135, 180, 262

Soviet Union, 3, 6, 20, 28, 36–39, 40, 45, 51, 55, 60, 86, 114, 124–125, 301, 318, 327, 339; Perestroika, 30–32

Spain, 63, 113, 132, 137, 252, 345, 348–350, 355–357, 375

Spartakus League, 10

specialized court system, 286

Spiegel affair, 108. *See also* Flick affair

Springer, Axel, 81–82, 84

Stasi (Ministry for State Security): activities of, 27, 38, 52; churches and, 30, 178; files of, 27, 37–38, 260; origins of, 26–27; terrorism and, 26–27, 128. *See also* German Democratic Republic; Honecker, Erich states (Länder): constitutional structure of, 287; economic equalization between, 60–61, 314–318; education and, 230, 301, 313, 315–319, 351; influence of, 217, 229, 231, 259, 261, 289, 300–301, 310, 321; leaders of, 312–314; origins of, 299–301. *See also* Bundesrat; educational system; police

statism, 13

Steinbrück, Peer, 154. *See also* Social Democratic Party

Steinmeiner, Frank Walter, 153–154, 192, 209–210. *See also* Social Democratic Party

Stoiber, Edmund, 144–145, 157, 192, 208, 210–211, 249, 251, 312–313. *See also* Christian Democratic Union; Christian Social Union

Stolpe, Manfred, 178, 312

Strauss, Franz-Josef, 108, 141–144, 183, 197, 209, 303, 312. *See also* Christian Democratic Union; Christian Social Union; *Spiegel* affair

strikes, 10, 171, 172, 287

Stuttgart 21 train station project, 162, 253, 310

tax collection, 176, 246, 301, 322–323. *See also* revenue sharing; states

television and radio, 83–85; unification and, 83, 89, 92, 136

terrorism, 111, 113, 126, 211, 235, 256, 318, 341; Islamic groups and, 126; National Socialist Underground, 49, 126, 318, 344. *See also* police; radical left; radical right; radicals; Stasi

Thatcher, Margaret, 39

Thuringia, 45–48, 56, 60, 83, 204, 229, 302, 304, 307–308, 312

ticket splitting, 157, 188. *See also* voting behavior

trade, 58–59, 168, 173, 228, 281, 339, 347, 350, 3722, 374, 392–393. *See also* economy

trade unions, 67, 161, 170–172, 201, 207, 250; Social Democratic Party and, 127, 146–147. *See also* interest groups

Treuhand (Trusteeship Authority), 128, 264. *See also* unification

Turks, 55, 114, 117

Ulbricht, Walter, 29, 51. *See also* German Democratic Republic

unemployment: 1998 election and, 42–43, 143–144, 179, 199, 209, 211, 248–249; 2002 election and, 65, 144, 152, 171, 199, 209–211, 249, 279; 2005 election and, 43, 62, 64–66, 123, 171, 199, 210–211, 249–250, 372; 2009 election and, 202, 211–212; East German economy and, 39–40, 63, 100, 123, 124, 247, 274, 281, 305, 370; insurance, 40, 42–43, 62, 153, 274, 276, 278, 356, 369; voting behavior and, 105, 123, 199, 209, 211

unification, of East and West Germany: agriculture and, 27, 59, 175, 181, 217, 223, 301; costs of, 41–43, 46, 51, 85, 220; East German opposition and, 30–35, 39, 99; economy and, 30, 35–40, 47, 49, 63–64, 70, 102, 121, 169, 172, 175, 247–251, 279–280, 332; education and, 49, 102, 123–124, 159; environment and, 159–160; European Union and, 175, 217, 291, 299, 344. 348–350; Final Treaty of, 37, 305; France and, 7, 13, 23, 86, 92, 121, 125, 217, 241, 280–281, 299, 300, 305, 328, 332, 337, 344, 348, 352, 371, 386; labor unions and, 169, 172, 240; local government and, 4, 102–103, 198; political culture and, 99, 101–103, 121, 123, 125, 131; political parties and, 99, 123, 136, 142–143; psychological problems of, 47; Soviet Union and, 3, 25, 33, 37–40, 85–86, 124–125, 241, 290, 301, 337; Stasi and, 37–39; states (Länder) and, 300–301; United Kingdom and, 2, 6, 13, 92, 217, 305, 332, 337; United States and, 25, 34–36, 39, 63–64, 73, 86, 247, 251, 305; wall in the head, 47, 50; West Germans and, 30, 35, 38, 99, 100, 124, 136, 198, 202, 248, 392; women and, 37–40, 43, 121, 122, 179, 232. *See also* Genscher, Hans-Dietrich; German Democratic Republic; Kohl, Helmut

United Kingdom, 333–334, 345, 353–354, 349–350, 363–364

United Nations, 29, 122, 338–339, 343; Security Council, 311, 338, 344

United States, 10–13, 20, 25, 34, 36, 39, 62, 63, 67, 76, 80, 86–87, 94, 98, 106–107, 247–251, 268, 280, 286–287, 305, 310–311, 322, 333–344, 353, 355, 357,

366, 371, 374, 386; relations with
Germany, 357–359
universities, 45, 78, 80, 82, 118, 123, 127,
159, 169, 232, 255, 269, 313, 319. *See
also* educational system
urbanization, 9, 57–58. *See also* cities

ver.di (United Service Sector Union),
170–172. *See also* trade unions
Versailles, Treaty of, 11, 14, 333
vocational education, 78, 80, 88, 115–116,
123, 278
Vogel, Bernhard, 312
Volkswagen, 15, 65, 71, 170, 303
voting behavior: candidates, 185, 187, 189,
191, 193, 199, 209, 211; issues, 193, 206,
209, 211, 213; party policies and, 199,
206, 209, 211, 213; registration rules,
185; social change and, 206. *See also*
elections, federal; elections, states and

Walesa, Lech, 34
Wanka, Johanna, 237
Wehner, Herbert, 148. *See also* Social
Democratic Party
Weimar Republic (1919–1933): constitution
of, 10, 12, 22, 91–92, 96, 125, 131, 137,
218, 225, 229, 233, 234, 320; failure of,
10–12; leadership of, 10–12, 147, 156;
political culture of, 91, 103, 125, 127,

131, 284; political parties of, 10, 22, 135,
137, 170. *See also* National Socialism;
political culture
Weizsäcker, Richard von, 254–256, 262,
313. *See also* Federal President
welfare state, 43, 62, 118, 151, 161–162,
201, 247, 256, 273, 331, 366–369, 376,
380
Westerwelle, Guido, 146, 157–158, 237,
239, 311, 344. *See also* Free Democratic
Party
West Germany. *See* Federal Republic of
Germany
women: discrimination against, 120, 133;
election of 2009 and, 120, 122, 137, 158,
191, 205, 206, 236; party preference of,
206, 212; in public office, 269, 278;
recruitment of, 269; social and legal
status of, 4, 119, 121, 177, 191, 269, 364;
unification and, 37, 43, 56, 121–122, 232.
See also abortion; population of Federal
Republic
Wulff, Christian, 81, 146, 251, 254, 256,
313. *See also* Federal President

youth, 122–124; attitudes toward, 122, 124;
in political organizations, 16, 74, 82,
105, 123, 177, 191; unemployment and,
105, 123–124; unification and, 29, 74, 76,
105, 122–124; voting turnout and, 76,
105, 123

About the Authors

David P. Conradt has been a professor of political science at East Carolina University since 1993. From 1968 to 1993 he was at the University of Florida (Gainesville). He has also held joint appointments at universities in Konstanz, Mannheim, Cologne, and Dresden. Among his recent publications are *Politics in Europe*, coauthor (2012); *A Precarious Victory: Schröder and the German Elections of 2002* (2005); and *Power Shift in Germany: The 1998 Election and the End of the Kohl Era* (2000). He has also published a variety of articles and monographs on German political culture, parties, and elections, including "The Shrinking Elephants: The 2009 Election and the Changing Party System" (*German Politics and Society*, 2010). In 2005 the president of the Federal Republic awarded him the Merit Cross of the Federal Republic of Germany for his body of work.

Eric Langenbacher is a visiting assistant professor and director of honors and special programs in the Department of Government, Georgetown University, where he received his PhD in 2002. He was awarded a Fulbright grant in 1999–2000 and held the Ernst Reuter Fellowship at the Free University of Berlin in 1999–2000, and he was voted faculty member of the year by the graduating seniors of Georgetown's School of Foreign Service in 2009. His book projects include *Power and the Past: Collective Memory and International Relations* (2010), *From the Bonn to the Berlin Republic: Germany at the Twentieth Anniversary of Unification* (2010); and *Between Left and Right: The 2009 Bundestag Election and the Transformation of the German Party System* (2010). He is also the managing editor of *German Politics and Society*.